T0178126

Lecture Notes in Computer Science 14675

Founding Editors

Gerhard Goos

Juris Hartmanis

Editorial Board Members

The series Lecture Notes in Computer Science (LNCS), including its subseries Lecture Notes in Artificial Intelligence (LNAI) and Lecture Notes in Bioinformatics (LNBI), has established itself as a medium for the publication of new developments in computer science and information technology research, teaching, and education.

LNCS enjoys close cooperation with the computer science R & D community, the series counts many renowned academics among its volume editors and paper authors, and collaborates with prestigious societies. Its mission is to serve this international community by providing an invaluable service, mainly focused on the publication of conference and workshop proceedings and postproceedings. LNCS commenced publication in 1973.

José Manuel Ferrández Vicente ·
Mikel Val Calvo · Hojjat Adeli
Editors

Bioinspired Systems for Translational Applications

From Robotics to Social Engineering

10th International Work-Conference on the Interplay
Between Natural and Artificial Computation, IWINAC 2024
Olhâo, Portugal, June 4–7, 2024
Proceedings, Part II

Springer

Editors
José Manuel Ferrández Vicente
Universidad Politécnica de Cartagena
Cartagena, Spain

Mikel Val Calvo
Polytechnic University of Valencia
Valencia, Spain

Hojjat Adeli ⓘ
Ohio State University
Columbus, OH, USA

ISSN 0302-9743 ISSN 1611-3349 (electronic)
Lecture Notes in Computer Science
ISBN 978-3-031-61136-0 ISBN 978-3-031-61137-7 (eBook)
https://doi.org/10.1007/978-3-031-61137-7

This Springer imprint is published by the registered company Springer Nature Switzerland AG
The registered company address is: Gewerbestrasse 11, 6330 Cham, Switzerland

If disposing of this product, please recycle the paper.

Preface

The main topic of these IWINAC/ICINAC 2024 volumes is to study intelligent systems inspired by the natural world, in particular biology. Several algorithms and methods and their applications are discussed, including evolutionary algorithms. Bio-inspired intelligent systems have thousands of useful applications in fields as diverse as machine learning, biomedicine, control theory, telecommunications, and why not music and art. These volumes cover both the theory and practice of bio-inspired artificial intelligence, along with providing a bit of the basis and inspiration for the different approaches. This is a discipline that strives to develop new computing techniques through observing how naturally occurring phenomena behave to solve complex problems in various environmental situations. Brain-inspired computation is one of these techniques that covers multiple applications in very different fields. Through IWINAC/ICINAC we provide a forum in which research in different fields can converge to create new computational paradigms that are on the frontier between neural and biomedical sciences and information technologies.

As a multidisciplinary forum, IWINAC is open to any established institutions and research laboratories actively working in the field of natural or neural technologies. But beyond achieving co-operation between different research realms, we wish to actively encourage co-operation with the private sector, particularly SMEs, as a way of bridging the gap between frontier science and societal impact.

In this edition, four main themes outline the conference topics: Neuroscience, Affective Computing, Robotics, and Translational Systems.

1) Machine learning holds great promise in the development of new models and theories in the field of Neuroscience, in conjunction with classical statistical hypothesis testing. Machine learning algorithms have the potential to reveal interactions, hidden patterns of abnormal activity, brain structure and connectivity and physiological mechanisms of brain and behavior. In addition, several approaches for testing the significance of the machine learning outcomes have been successfully proposed to avoid "the dangers of spurious findings or explanations void of mechanism" by means of proper replication, validation, and hypothesis-driven confirmation. Therefore, machine learning can effectively provide relevant information to take great strides toward understanding how the brain works. The main goal of this field is to build a bridge between two scientific communities, the machine learning community, including lead scientists in deep learning and related areas within pattern recognition and artificial intelligence, and the neuroscience community. Artificial Intelligence has become the ultimate scale to test the limits of technological advances in dealing with Life Science challenges and needs. In this sense, the interplay between Natural and Artificial Computation is expected to play a most relevant role on the diagnosis, monitoring and treatment of Neurodegenerative Diseases, using the advanced computational solutions provided by Machine Learning and Data Science. This requires us to interchange new ideas, launch projects and contests, and eventually create an

inclusive knowledge-oriented network with the aim of empowering researchers, practitioners and users of technological solutions for daily life experience in the domains of Neuromotor and Linguistic competence functional evaluation, clinical explainability, and rehabilitation by interaction with humans, robots, and gaming avatars, not being strictly limited to only these, but inclusively open to others related. The use of Machine Learning-based Precision Medicine in monitoring daily life activity and providing well-being conditions to especially sensitive social sectors is one of the most relevant objectives. Case study descriptions involving neurodegenerative diseases (Alzheimer's disease, fronto-temporal dementia, cerebrovascular damage and stroke, autism, Parkinson's disease, amyotrophic lateral sclerosis, multiple sclerosis, Huntington's chorea, etc.) are included. Mild cognitive impairment (MCI) is considered the stage between the mental changes that are seen between normal ageing and early-stages of dementia. Indeed, MCI is one of the main indicators of incipient Alzheimer's disease (AD) among other neuropsychological diseases. The growth of these diseases is generating a great interest in the development of new effective methods for the early detection of MCI because, although no treatments are known to cure MCI, this early diagnosis would allow early intervention to delay the effects of the disease and accelerate progress towards effective treatment in its early stages. Although there have been many years of research, the early identification of cognitive impairment, as well as the differential diagnosis (to distinguish significant causes or typologies for its treatment), are problems that have been addressed from different angles, but are still far from being solved. Diverse types of tests have already been developed, such as biological markers, magnetic resonance imaging, and neuropsychological tests. While effective, biological markers and magnetic resonance imaging are economically expensive, invasive, and require time to get a result, making them unsuitable as a population screening method. On the other hand, neuropsychological tests have a reliability comparable to biomarker tests, and are cheaper and quicker to interpret.

2) Emotions are essential in human-human communication, cognition, learning and rational decision-making processes. However, human-machine interfaces (HMIs) are still not able to understand human sentiments and react accordingly. With the aim of endowing HMIs with the emotional intelligence they lack, Affective Computing focuses on the development of artificial intelligence by means of the analysis of affects and emotions, such that systems and devices could be able to recognize, interpret, process and simulate human sentiments.

Nowadays, the evaluation of electrophysiological signals plays a key role in the advancement towards that purpose since they are an objective representation of the emotional state of an individual. Hence, the interest in physiological variables like electroencephalogram, electrocardiogram, or electrodermal activity, among many others, has notably grown in the field of affective states detection. Furthermore, emotions have also been widely identified by means of the assessment of speech characteristics and facial gestures of people under different sentimental conditions. It is also worth noting that the development of algorithms for the classification of affective states in social media has experienced a notable increase in recent years. In this sense, the language of posts included in social networks, such as Facebook or Twitter, is evaluated with the aim of detecting sentiments of the users of those media tools.

Affective Computing and Sentiment Analysis is intended to be a meeting point for researchers who are interested in any of those areas of expertise related to sentiment analysis, and want to initiate their studies or are currently working on these topics. Hence, manuscripts introducing new proposals based on the analysis of physiological measures, facial recognition, speech recognition, or natural language processing in social media are examples of affective computing and sentiment analysis.

3) Over recent decades there has been an increasing interest in using machine learning, and in the last few years, deep learning methods, combined with other vision techniques, to create autonomous systems that solve vision problems in different fields. This special session is designed to serve researchers and developers to publish original, innovative and state-of-the art algorithms and architectures for real time applications in the areas of computer vision, image processing, biometrics, virtual and augmented reality, neural networks, intelligent interfaces and biomimetic object-vision recognition.

This study provides a platform for academics, developers, and industry-related researchers belonging to the vast communities of Neural Networks, Computational Intelligence, Machine Learning, Deep Learning, Biometrics, Vision Systems, and Robotics, to discuss, share experience and explore traditional and new areas of computer vision, machine and deep learning combined to solve a range of problems. The objective of the workshop is to integrate the growing international community of researchers working on the application of Machine Learning and Deep Learning Methods in Vision and Robotics in a fruitful discussion on the evolution and the benefits of this technology to society.

4) Finally, Artificial Intelligence (AI) has become a catalyst for innovation in a wide variety of disciplines, playing a pivotal role in solving contemporary challenges. This session focuses on the translational applications of AI in multiple fields, highlighting how the technology is transforming key sectors in response to the needs of today's society. Grid and power infrastructure management is one of the domains where AI is revolutionizing efficiency and reliability. Through predictive analytics, optimization and proactive maintenance, AI enables a smarter and more resilient power grid, crucial in a world seeking decarbonization and the use of renewable energy. In agriculture, AI drives precision farming, improving agricultural production, water resource management and crop quality. In civil engineering, AI-assisted planning and design streamline construction projects and optimize infrastructure. Smart cities and urban planning benefit from AI to optimize transportation, waste management and the quality of life of inhabitants. In education, AI personalizes teaching and assessment, tailoring learning to the individual needs of students. In nutrition and food science, AI algorithms are used for creating healthy diets and detecting contaminants in food. This topic will explore how AI fosters innovation and transformation in these diverse areas, highlighting the solutions this technology offers to address current challenges and improve the quality of life in modern society. From smarter power grids to safer food, AI is paving the way to a more efficient and sustainable future in a variety of multidisciplinary fields.

The wider view of the computational paradigm gives us more elbow room to accommodate the results of the interplay between nature and computation. The

IWINAC/ICINAC forum thus becomes a methodological approximation (set of intentions, questions, experiments, models, algorithms, mechanisms, explanation procedures, and engineering and computational methods) to the natural and artificial perspectives of the mind embodiment problem, both in humans and in artifacts. This is the philosophy that continues in IWINAC meetings, the "interplay" movement between the natural and the artificial, facing this same problem every two years. This synergistic approach will permit us not only to build new computational systems based on the natural measurable phenomena, but also to understand many of the observable behaviors inherent to natural systems.

The difficulty of building bridges between natural and artificial computation was one of the main motivations for the organization of IWINAC 2024. The IWINAC/ICINAC 2024 proceedings contain the 99 works selected by the Scientific Committee from more than 193 submissions, after the refereeing process. The type of peer review used was single blind with an average number of reviews received per submission of 2.5, and an average number of papers per reviewer of 3 with external reviewers involved, outside the PC. The first volume, entitled Artificial Intelligence for Neuroscience and Emotional Systems and Health Applications, includes all the contributions mainly related to the new tools for analyzing neural data, or detecting emotional states, or interfacing with physical systems. The second volume, entitled Bioinspired Systems for Translational Applications: from Robotics to Social Engineering, contains the papers related to bioinspired programming strategies and all the contributions oriented to the computational solutions to engineering problems in different application domains, such as biomedical systems or big data solutions.

An event of the nature of IWINAC/ICINAC 2024 cannot be organized without the collaboration of a group of institutions and people who we would like to thank now, starting with Universidad de Granada and Universidad Politécnica de Cartagena. The collaboration of the Universidade do Algarve (UAlg), Nova University of Lisbon (NOVA) and Universidad Politécnica de Madrid (UPM), was crucial, as was the efficient work of the Local Organizing Committee, with Hugo Gamboa (NOVA), Joao de Sousa (UAlg), Pedro Gómez Vilda (UPM), Simao Souza (UAlg), Margarida Madeira (UAlg), Jaime Martins (UAlg), Carla Quintao (NOVA) and Luis Silva (NOVA). In addition to our universities, we received financial support from Red Nacional en Inteligencia Artificial para Neurociencia y Salud Mental (IA4NSM) and Apliquem Microones 21 s.l.

We want to express our gratitude to our invited speakers Hojjat Adeli, from Ohio State University (USA), Zidong Wang from Brunel University, London (UK), Nuno M. Garcia from Universidad de Lisboa (Portugal), and Asoke Nandi, from Brunel University, London (UK) for accepting our invitation and for their magnificent plenary talks.

We would also like to thank the authors for their interest in our call and the effort in preparing the papers, condition sine qua non for these proceedings. We thank the Scientific and Organizing Committees, in particular the members of these committees who acted as effective and efficient referees and as promoters and managers of pre-organized sessions on autonomous and relevant topics under the IWINAC/ICINAC global scope.

Our sincere gratitude goes also to Springer for their help and collaboration in all our joint editorial ventures.

Finally, we want to express our special thanks to BCD eventos, our technical secretariat, and to Ana María García, for making this meeting possible, and for arranging all the details that comprise the organization of this kind of event.

We want to dedicate these volumes of the IWINAC proceedings to Profs. Rodellar, Sánchez-Andrés and Mira.

June 2024

José Manuel Ferrández Vicente
Mikel Val Calvo
Hojjat Adeli

Organization

General Chair

José Manuel Ferrández Vicente   Universidad Politécnica de Cartagena, Spain

Organizing Committee

Mikel Val Calvo   Univ. Politécnica de Valencia, Spain

Honorary Chairs

Hojjat Adeli   Ohio State University, USA
Rodolfo Llinás   New York University, USA
Zhou Changjiu   Singapore Polytechnic, Singapore

Local Organizing Committee

Hugo Gamboa   Universidade NOVA de Lisboa, Portugal
Pedro Gómez-Vilda   Universidad Politécnica de Madrid, Spain
Joao de Sousa   Universidade de Algarve, Portugal
Simao Souza   Universidade de Algarve, Portugal
Margarida Madeira   Universidade de Algarve, Portugal
Jaime Martins   Universidade de Algarve, Portugal
Carla Quintao   Universidade NOVA de Lisboa, Portugal
Luis Silva   Universidade NOVA de Lisboa, Portugal

Invited Speakers

Hojjat Adeli   Ohio State University, USA
Zidong Wang   Brunel University, UK
Nuno M. Garcia   Universidade de Lisboa, Portugal
Asoke Nandi   Brunel University, UK

Field Editors

Sung-Bae Cho	Yonsei University, South Korea
Emilia Barakova	Eindhoven Univ. of Technology, Netherlands
Gema Benedicto	Universidad Politécnica de Cartagena, Spain
Diego Castillo-Barnes	Universidad de Granada, Spain
Enrique Dominguez	Universidad de Málaga, Spain
Félix de la Paz	Univ. Nacional de Educación a Distancia, Spain
Antonio Fernández-Caballero	Universidad Castilla-La Mancha, Spain
Jose García-Rodríguez	Universitat d'Alacant, Spain
Andrés Gómez-Rodellar	University of Edinburgh, UK
Pedro Gómez-Vilda	Universidad Politécnica de Madrid, Spain
Juan Manuel Górriz	Universidad de Granada, Spain
David Guijo-Rubio	Universidad de Córdoba, Spain
Marina Jodra	Universidad Complutense de Madrid, Spain
Vicente Julián-Inglada	Universitat Politècnica de València, Spain
Krzysztof Kutt	Jagiellonian University, Poland
Fco. Jesús Martínez Murcia	Universidad de Málaga, Spain
Rafael Martínez Tomás	Univ. Nacional de Educación a Distancia, Spain
Jiri Mekyska	Brno University of Technology, Czechia
Ramón Moreno	Grupo Antolin, Spain
Grzegorz J. Nalepa	Jagiellonian University, Poland
Andrés Ortiz	Universidad de Málaga, Spain
Daniel Palacios-Alonso	Universidad Rey Juan Carlos, Spain
José T. Palma	Universidad de Murcia, Spain
Jorge Pérez-Aracil	Universidad de Alcalá, Spain
Javier Ramírez	Universidad de Granada, Spain
Mariano Rincón Zamorano	Univ. Nacional de Educación a Distancia, Spain
Sancho Salcedo	Universidad de Alcalá, Spain
Jose Santos Reyes	Universidade da Coruña, Spain
Fermín Segovia	Universidad de Granada, Spain
Antonio Tallón	Universidad de Huelva, Spain
Ramiro Varela	Universidad de Oviedo, Spain

International Scientific Committee

Amparo Alonso Betanzos, Spain
Jose Ramon Álvarez-Sánchez, Spain
Margarita Bachiller Mayoral, Spain
Francisco Bellas, Spain
Emilia I. Barakova, Netherlands

Guido Bologna, Switzerland
Paula Bonomini, Argentina
Enrique J. Carmona Suárez, Spain
José Carlos Castillo, Spain
Germán Castellanos-Dominguez, Colombia

Contents – Part II

Social and Civil Engineering Through Human AI Translations

Smart Renewable Energies: Advancing AI Algorithms in the Renewable Energy Industry

Bioinspired Applications

Contents – Part I

Artificial Intelligence in Neurophysiology

Neuromotor and Cognitive Disorders

**Intelligent Systems for Assessment, Treatment, and Assistance in
Early Stages of Alzheimer's Disease and Other Dementias**

Socio-Cognitive, Affective and Physiological Computing

Affective Computing and Context Awareness in Ambient Intelligence

Learning Tools to Lecture

Machine Learning in Computer Vision and Robotics

Unsupervised Detection of Incoming and Outgoing Traffic Flows in Video Sequences

Jose D. Fernández-Rodríguez[1,2]([✉]) [iD], Pablo Carmona-Martínez[1],
Rafaela Benítez-Rochel[1,2] [iD], Miguel A. Molina-Cabello[1,2] [iD],
and Ezequiel López-Rubio[1,2] [iD]

[1] Department of Computer Languages and Computer Science, University of Málaga,
Málaga, Spain
{josedavid,pcm6tq1}@uma.es
{benitez,miguelangel,ezeqlr}@lcc.uma.es
[2] Instituto de Investigación Biomédica de Málaga - IBIMA, Málaga, Spain

Abstract. As traffic cameras become prevalent, and a considerable amount of traffic videos are stored for various purposes, new possibilities and challenges open in the automatic analysis of traffic scenes. Advances in deep learning also enable new ways to characterize traffic in such videos automatically. This work is motivated by the need to understand traffic flow without human supervision, especially the localization of road intersections in scenes from traffic cameras. For this purpose, a method is proposed that uses a deep learning neural network for vehicle detection, an object tracker to recover vehicle trajectories from the detections, and unsupervised machine learning techniques to detect potential incoming and outgoing traffic flows from the vehicle trajectories in the video sequences. A wide range of real and synthetic videos have been used to test the goodness of the proposal with satisfactory results, from traffic cameras at different heights and angles, different traffic patterns, and various weather conditions.

Keywords: Unsupervised learning · Object tracking · Object detection · Video surveillance · Deep learning

1 Introduction

In recent years, video surveillance has been widely used for traffic data collection, monitoring, or surveillance for all types of traffic scenarios, such as highways, intersections, and roundabouts [6,8,10]. The main objective of the video surveillance system in traffic is to monitor driving behaviors. It can play a vital role in detecting/predicting congestion, accidents, and other anomalies apart from collecting statistical information about the status of road traffic. In this field, many studies have been conducted focusing on different aspects such as scene analysis [2,5], vehicle detection and tracking [1,9,14], anomalous trajectory detection

J. M. Ferrández Vicente et al. (Eds.): IWINAC 2024, LNCS 14675, pp. 3–12, 2024.
https://doi.org/10.1007/978-3-031-61137-7_1

[17,24], traffic monitoring [3,11], emergency management [12,22], event detection [13,16], etc.

With the applications of deep convolutional neural networks and the vast amount of traffic camera video available to anyone, it is only a matter of time before intelligent systems that monitor traffic through video-based traffic surveillance become increasingly common.

Most of the works published so far can be considered a first step in using deep learning in traffic applications because most of them find several difficulties in urban traffic scenarios such as intersections. The recognition and tracking process complexity is higher in these environments because vehicles typically involve more acceleration/deceleration, waiting, and turning from different entry points than typical highway traffic. Also, vehicles tend to occlude each other or be occluded by roadside infrastructures [6].

Recently, some researchers have applied deep learning to overcome those specific traffic analysis difficulties at intersections. For example, in [15], a CNN-based tool was developed for the automatic extraction of vehicle trajectories at crossroads, but the applicability of the proposed method can be improved, and [19] uses deep-learning (Yolov4) for vehicle detection with a camera installed at an intersection but it presents severe limitations.

This paper is aimed at facilitating comprehension of traffic flow in intersections watched by static cameras without human supervision using deep neural networks. It proposes a method that detects the points along the border of the scene. In this way, points where vehicles enter and exit from the scene are automatically detected. This enables the automation of the analysis of road intersection videos without the need to determine the position of the roads manually. Autonomous recovery of this information allows further analysis of the videos, such as detecting anomalous trajectories relative to others. Still, this work is not concerned with this additional analysis.

The remainder of this paper is organized as follows. Section 2 provides a detailed description of the methodology used for detecting potential incoming and outgoing traffic flows in traffic videos at intersections. Section 3 describes the settings items and the data set used for the experiments and the assessment of the performance of the proposed method. Finally, conclusions are drawn in Sect. 4.

2   Methodology

The proposed method to detect vehicle entry and exit locations in traffic videos depicting an intersection is given next. First of all, an object detection deep neural network $\mathcal{F}$ is employed to extract a set of object detections S_t in the current video frame $\mathbf{X}_t$ for each time instant t:

$$S_t = \mathcal{F}(\mathbf{X}_t) = \{(a_{t,i}, b_{t,i}, c_{t,i}, d_{t,i}) \mid i \in \{1, ..., N_t\}\} \tag{1}$$

where N_t is the number of object detections at time instant t. The upper left corner of the bounding box for the i-th object detection at time t is noted $(a_{t,i}, b_{t,i})$ while the lower right corner is noted $(c_{t,i}, d_{t,i})$.

Secondly, the output of the object detection network is supplied to a tracking method $\mathcal{G}$ that receives the current set of object detections S_t and the previous set of tracked objects Q_{t-1} and outputs the current set of tracked objects Q_t:

$$Q_t = \mathcal{G}\left(S_t, Q_{t-1}\right) = \{(\alpha_{t,j}, \beta_{t,j}, \gamma_{t,j}) \mid j \in \{1, ..., M_t\}\} \tag{2}$$

where M_t is the number of object tracks at time instant t. The centroid of the j-th tracked object at time t is noted $(\alpha_{t,j}, \beta_{t,j})$, and $\gamma_{t,j}$ is an integer that uniquely identifies the tracked object.

At the beginning of the video, the set of tracked objects is empty:

$$M_0 = 0, \ Q_0 = \emptyset \tag{3}$$

The tracked objects corresponding to all time instants up to the current time t are comprised in the set R_t:

$$R_t = \bigcup_{\tau=1}^{t} Q_\tau \tag{4}$$

Next, the set V_t of the first and last occurrences of all tracked objects up to the current time t is computed:

$$V_t = \{(\alpha_{\tau,j}, \beta_{\tau,j}, \gamma_{\tau,j}) \in R_t \mid \\ (\forall\, (\alpha_{\tau',j}, \beta_{\tau',j}, \gamma_{\tau,j}) \in R_t : \tau' \leq \tau) \vee (\forall\, (\alpha_{\tau',j}, \beta_{\tau',j}, \gamma_{\tau,j}) \in R_t : \tau' \geq \tau)\} \tag{5}$$

Then the elbow method for the k-means unsupervised clustering algorithm is run in order to obtain an optimal number of clusters k to cluster the set V_t. The elbow method selects the value of k that is associated with the maximum curvature of the curve of the Mean Quantization Error (MQE) as a function of k:

$$MQE_{k,t} = \frac{1}{|V_t|} \sum_{(\alpha_j, \beta_j, \gamma_j) \in V_t} \min_{h \in \{1, ..., k\}} \left\| (\alpha_j, \beta_j) - (\bar{\alpha}_{h,k}, \bar{\beta}_{h,k}) \right\|^2 \tag{6}$$

where $|\cdot|$ stands for the cardinal of a set, $\|\cdot\|$ stands for the Euclidean norm of a vector, and $(\bar{\alpha}_{h,k}, \bar{\beta}_{h,k})$ is the h-th cluster center obtained by the k-means algorithm for k clusters.

Let us note $\hat{k}$ the value selected by the elbow method. Then the associated set of cluster centers is:

$$C_t = \left\{ \left(\hat{\alpha}_h, \hat{\beta}_h \right) \mid h \in \left\{ 1, ..., \hat{k} \right\} \right\} \tag{7}$$

The set C_t is regarded as a concise representation of the set of observed centroids R_t. If vehicle detection and tracking have reasonably low error rates, the cluster centroids in C_t mark the places where vehicles enter and exit the scene in the camera viewport.

Fig. 1. The initial image frame for the first video synthesized with CARLA (left) and for the video *Highway* from the 2014 CDNET dataset (right). Initial/final points from each detected vehicle trajectory are drawn over the frame. Points that are grouped within the same cluster (after applying K-means) are drawn in the same color. Cluster centroids are in black. Each centroid represents an area near the border where either a whole road or an individual lane gets out of frame.

3   Experimental Results

This section presents the results obtained by applying the previously described methodology in a series of experiments with various videos of road intersections from the perspective of a traffic camera.

3.1   Methods

The system is implemented using OpenCV to read image frames from recorded videos or retrieve a live stream from a traffic camera, if available. For vehicle detection, the deep learning network Yolov5 is used. Specifically, of the range of publicly available sub-models, yolov5x6 is used. This sub-model is trained on the COCO dataset, and has a mAP@0.5 score of 72.7 [21]. Objects of COCO classes *car*, *motorcycle*, and *truck* are considered to be vehicle detections. Any other detections are discarded. Vehicle detections are fed to Norfair, a publicly available state-of-the-art object tracker with standard assignment heuristics and Kalman filters [20]. Default parameters are used for these components.

For each vehicle trajectory, starting and ending points are retrieved, and clustered using the K-means algorithm. The number of clusters is estimated with the elbow method. This method consists of repeatedly computing clustering with different cluster numbers, measuring the clustering performance (see Sect. 2 for details), and taking the point of maximum curvature for the clustering metric. The objective is to get cluster centroids to mark the positions of the roads and/or road lanes in a road intersection.

3.2   Datasets

To test the proposed method, a wide range of videos selected from several well-known datasets has been used. Three videos have been synthesized using CARLA

Fig. 2. The initial image frame for videos Hasserisvej-1 (left) and Hadsundvej-1 (right) from the AAU RainSnow Dataset. Left: the road end to the right of the image is obscured by a large tree, resulting in the detections corresponding to that road end being inside the intersection. Right: detected vehicles in a parking lot lead to an incorrectly placed cluster centroid (over the parking lot instead of over the road to its side). See the caption of the Fig. 1 for details.

[7], and depict three different views of the same three-way intersection. These videos were scripted to include cars speeding, tailgating other vehicles, and unnecessarily switching lanes among dense traffic flow, to test the robustness of the proposed method when applied to videos with cars engaged in dangerous, nonconventional behaviors.

Apart from these synthetic videos, a total of 14 videos have been chosen from three state-of-the-art datasets. Seven videos are from the AAU Rain-Snow Traffic Surveillance Dataset[1] [4]. From this dataset, we take the following videos: Hadsundvej-1, Hadsundvej-2, Hasserisvej-1, Hasserisvej-2, Hasserisvej-3, Hjorringvej-2, and Ostre-3. These are videos recorded while raining and snowing, to validate the proposed method in bad weather conditions. For each intersection, all videos are from the same camera, but from different times and weather conditions.

Another six videos are taken from the Ko-PER Intersection dataset [18]. These are named Seq1_SK_1, Seq1_SK_4, Seq2_SK_1, Seq2_SK_4, Seq3_SK_1, and Seq3_SK_4, respectively. Of these, videos whose name is the same except for the ending number were recorded at the same time in the same intersection, but from cameras in different places and orientations. This is useful to test the proposed method with different viewing angles of the same vehicles. All videos depict four-way intersections, but some recordings do not include incoming/outgoing vehicles in one of the four ways.

While the proposed method has been conceived to be applied to videos from road intersections, we also test it in one video showing a non-branching road segment: the video titled *Highway* from the 2014 CDNET datasetDataset [23] (http://changedetection.net/).

---

[1] https://www.kaggle.com/datasets/aalborguniversity/aau-rainsnow.

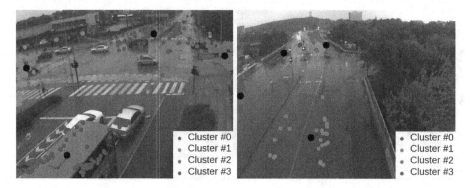

Fig. 3. The initial image frames for videos Hjorringvej-2 and Ostre-3, from the AAU RainSnow Dataset, with results obtained using yolov5x6 for detections. See the caption of Fig. 1 for details.

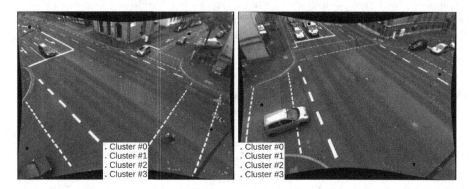

Fig. 4. The initial image frames for videos Seq1_SK_1 and Seq1_SK_4. See the caption of Fig. 1 for details.

3.3 Results

The same three-way intersection is used with several camera views in the case of the three videos synthesized using CARLA. Only the first video is shown in the left side of Fig. 1 (for a summary of results in the other two videos, see Table 1). For the first video (Fig. 1) there are several false starting/ending points of trajectories in the middle of the image. This happens because at that point cars pass below a semaphore pole, and sometimes the method loses track of vehicle trajectories in these circumstances. The right side of Fig. 1 shows the result of applying the proposed method to a traffic camera video of a straight road segment. One cluster marks the far end of the road, while two clusters are placed at the nearest road ending, corresponding to the two lanes of the road.

Regarding the videos from the AUU RainSnow Dataset, Hadsundvej-1 and Hadsundvej-2 (Fig. 2 shows the first one) show a four-way intersection with a parking lot in one of the intersection's corners, full of cars. These cars are also

Table 1. Summary of results. Each row corresponds to the performance of the proposed method for a video. Performance is measured by counting the number of cluster centroids placed over a road end. A false negative means that a road end in the video had no cluster centroid over it. Percentages are expressed over the ground truth (i.e., the number of road ends with vehicle traffic in the scene). A false positive means that a cluster centroid is placed inside or around the road intersection instead of over a road end. The last row shows aggregate figures for all videos.

video	number of road ends with vehicles entering/exiting the scene				
	ground truth	detected with 1 cluster	detected with > 1 cluster	false negatives	false positives
CARLA #1	3	3 (100%)	0 (0%)	0 (0%)	0
CARLA #2	3	2 (67%)	1 (33%)	0 (0%)	0
CARLA #3	3	3 (100%)	0 (0%)	0 (0%)	0
Hadsundvej-1	4	3 (75%)	0 (0%)	1 (25%)	1
Hadsundvej-2	4	3 (75%)	0 (0%)	1 (25%)	1
Hasserisvej-1	4	3 (75%)	1 (25%)	0 (0%)	0
Hasserisvej-2	4	3 (75%)	1 (25%)	0 (0%)	0
Hasserisvej-3	4	3 (75%)	1 (25%)	0 (0%)	0
Hjorringvej-2	4	4 (100%)	0 (0%)	0 (0%)	0
Ostre-3	3	0 (0%)	2 (67%)	1 (33%)	0
Seq1_SK_1	4	4 (100%)	0 (0%)	0 (0%)	0
Seq1_SK_4	4	4 (100%)	0 (0%)	0 (0%)	0
Seq2_SK_1	3	2 (67%)	1 (33%)	0 (0%)	0
Seq2_SK_4	3	2 (67%)	1 (33%)	0 (0%)	0
Seq3_SK_1	4	4 (100%)	0 (0%)	0 (0%)	0
Seq3_SK_4	4	3 (75%)	0 (0%)	1 (25%)	0
Highway	2	1 (50%)	1 (50%)	0 (0%)	0
TOTAL	60	47 (78%)	9 (15%)	4 (7%)	2

detected by the proposed method, and their presence distorts the clustering enough to displace one of the cluster centroids to the point that it is over the parking lot rather than over one of the roads, so it does not detect the position of the road in any of these two videos. Furthermore, the off-road cluster centroid must be considered a false positive. It should also be noted that both videos are shot from the same camera but at different times. Relatively worse weather in Hadsundvej-2 leads to vehicles in the farthest road ending remaining undetected, shifting the cluster centroid corresponding to that road ending toward the center of the intersection.

Videos Hasserisvej-1 to Hasserisvej-3 (Fig. 2 shows the first one) show another four-way intersection, this one with one of the roads obstructed by a big tree. Even in this case, the proposed method correctly places a cluster centroid in the position where the vehicles enter/exit the intersection, next to the tree blocking the view of the corresponding road ending. In all three videos, two cluster centroids (one per lane) are detected at the road ending closest to the camera. Finally, Hjorringvej-2 shows a four-way intersection and Ostre-3 a three-way one (Fig. 3). In the first case, one cluster centroid is placed over each road ending, while in the second case, the main road has two cluster centroids at each road ending (marking the lanes), and the detections for the other road ending are erroneously merged into one of these clusters, leaving that road ending unmarked.

With respect to the videos from the Ko-PER dataset, for Seq1_SK_1 and Seq1_SK_4 (Fig. 4), the 4 clusters roughly correspond to the road endings. As can be seen, there are some initial/final trajectory points inside the road intersection, because of tracking errors, but these do not significantly influence the placement of the cluster centroids in most cases. On the other hand, for Seq1_SK_4 (right image), the orange cluster contains both points from two road endings, but the resulting cluster centroid is still placed over one of them (the one to the upper right). From the same dataset, clusters were also detected for videos Seq2_SK_1, Seq2_SK_4, Seq3_SK_1 and Seq3_SK_4 (not shown in any Figure, but results summarized in Table 1).

Results are summarized in Table 1. Each row show results for a video:

- The number of road endings in the video with vehicles entering or exiting through that end. This can be considered the ground truth.
- The number of road endings with exactly one cluster centroid placed over it.
- The number of road endings with more than one cluster centroid placed over it.
- The number of road endings that remain undetected (i.e. with no cluster centroid placed over it). This can be considered the number of false negatives.
- The number of cluster centroids that are placed inside or around the road intersection and cannot be considered to correspond to any of the road endings. This can be considered the number of false positives.

While the first of these items is the ground truth, the rest are results from the proposed method. Globally, 60 road endings with vehicle traffic are present in the 17 videos. Of these, the method places a single cluster centroid in around three-quarters of them, two cluster centroids in around one in ten, and no cluster centroids (false negatives) in around one in twenty.

4   Conclusions

Traffic surveillance videos from road intersections show traffic patterns that can be used to extract information about the scene. In particular, in this work, a method has been proposed that can automatically recover those potential incoming and outgoing traffic flows. This method works by detecting the position of the vehicles in each image frame. Then, from these frame-by-frame detections, vehicle trajectories are reconstructed by using a tracker method. By applying unsupervised clustering to these trajectories, the resulting cluster centroids enable an automatic understanding of the incoming and outgoing flows.

The proposed method has been tested with a set of videos, both from publicly available datasets and synthetically generated. Experimental results demonstrate that using better object detection models reduces the number of false negatives and false positives in the placement of cluster centroids in the road ends. Since the method is robust to false starting/ending points of the vehicle trajectories, it also works when vehicles follow nonconventional trajectories (speeding, tailgating, repeatedly switching lanes) and in bad weather conditions (raining and snowing).

Acknowledgements. This work was partially supported by the Ministry of Science and Innovation of Spain, grant number PID2022-136764OA-I00, the Autonomous Government of Andalusia (Spain) under project UMA20-FEDERJA-108, and the University of Malaga (Spain) under grants B1-2021_20 (project name Detection of coronary stenosis using deep learning applied to coronary angiography), B1-2022_14 (project name Deteccion de trayectorias anomalas de vehiculos en camaras de trafico) and B1-2023_18 (project name Sistema de videovigilancia basado en camaras itinerantes robotizadas). The authors acknowledge the grant of the Universidad de Mlaga and the Instituto de Investigacion Biomedica de Malaga y Plataforma en Nanomedicina-IBIMA Plataforma BIONAND.

References

1. Abbas, A., Sheikh, U., Al-Dhief, F., Haji Mohd, M.N.: A comprehensive review of vehicle detection using computer vision. Telecommun. Comput. Electron. Control (TELKOMNIKA) **19**, 838–850 (2021). https://doi.org/10.12928/TELKOMNIKA.v19i3.12880

2. Abbas, Q., Ibrahim, M.E.A., Jaffar, M.: Video scene analysis: an overview and challenges on deep learning algorithms. Multimedia Tools Appl. **77**(16), 20415–20453 (2018). https://doi.org/10.1007/s11042-017-5438-7

3. Abbasi, M., Shahraki, A., Taherkordi, A.: Deep learning for network traffic monitoring and analysis (NTMA): a survey. Comput. Commun. **170**, 19–41 (2021)

4. Bahnsen, C.H., Moeslund, T.B.: Rain removal in traffic surveillance: does it matter? IEEE Trans. Intell. Transp. Syst. **20**, 2802–2819 (2018). https://doi.org/10.1109/TITS.2018.2872502

5. Chong, Y.S., Tay, Y.H.: Modeling representation of videos for anomaly detection using deep learning: a review. arXiv arXiv:1505.00523 (2015)

6. Datondji, S.R.E., Dupuis, Y., Subirats, P., Vasseur, P.: A survey of vision-based traffic monitoring of road intersections. IEEE Trans. Intell. Transp. Syst. **17**, 2681–2698 (2016)

7. Dosovitskiy, A., Ros, G., Codevilla, F., Lopez, A., Koltun, V.: CARLA: an open urban driving simulator. In: Proceedings of the 1st Annual Conference on Robot Learning, pp. 1–16 (2017)

8. Ercan Avsar, Y.O.: Moving vehicle detection and tracking at roundabouts using deep learning with trajectory union. Multimedia Tools Appl. **17**, 6653–6680 (2021)

9. Fernández, J.D., García-González, J., Benítez-Rochel, R., Molina-Cabello, M.A., López-Rubio, E.: Anomalous trajectory detection for automated traffic video surveillance. In: Ferrández Vicente, J.M., Álvarez-Sánchez, J.R., de la Paz López, F., Adeli, H. (eds.) Bio-inspired Systems and Applications: from Robotics to Ambient Intelligence, IWINAC 2022. LNCS, vol. 13259, pp. 173–182. Springer, Cham (2022). https://doi.org/10.1007/978-3-031-06527-9_17

10. Jahongir Azimjonov, A.O.: A real-time vehicle detection and a novel vehicle tracking systems for estimating and monitoring traffic flow on highways. Adv. Eng. Inf. **50**, 101393 (2021)

11. Jain, N.K., Saini, R.K., Mittal, P.: A review on traffic monitoring system techniques. In: Ray, K., Sharma, T.K., Rawat, S., Saini, R.K., Bandyopadhyay, A. (eds.) Soft Computing: Theories and Applications. AISC, vol. 742, pp. 569–577. Springer, Singapore (2019). https://doi.org/10.1007/978-981-13-0589-4_53

12. Lopez-Fuentes, L., van de Weijer, J., González-Hidalgo, M., Skinnemoen, H., Bagdanov, A.: Review on computer vision techniques in emergency situations. Multimedia Tools Appl. **77**(13), 17069–17107 (2018). https://doi.org/10.1007/s11042-017-5276-7

13. Mo, X., Sun, C., Zhang, C., Tian, J., Shao, Z.: Research on expressway traffic event detection at night based on Mask-SpyNet. IEEE Access **10**, 69053–69062 (2022)

14. Molina-Cabello, M.A., Luque-Baena, R.M., Lopez-Rubio, E., Thurnhofer-Hemsi, K.: Vehicle type detection by ensembles of convolutional neural networks operating on super resolved images. Integr. Comput. Aided Eng. **25**(4), 321–333 (2018)

15. Abdeljaber, O., Adel Younis, W.A.: Extraction of vehicle turning trajectories at signalized intersections using convolutional neural networks. Arab. J. Sci. Eng. **45**, 8011–8025 (2020)

16. Pramanik, A., Sarkar, S., Maiti, J.: A real-time video surveillance system for traffic pre-events detection. Accid. Anal. Prev. **154**, 106019 (2021)

17. Raja, R., Sharma, P.C., Mahmood, M.R., Saini, D.K.: Analysis of anomaly detection in surveillance video: recent trends and future vision. Multimed. Tools Appl. **82**, 12635–12651 (2022)

18. Strigel, E., Meissner, D., Seeliger, F., Wilking, B., Dietmayer, K.: The Ko-PER intersection laserscanner and video dataset. In: 17th International IEEE Conference on Intelligent Transportation Systems (ITSC), pp. 1900–1901. IEEE (2014)

19. Tak, S., Lee, J.D., Song, J., Kim, S.: Development of AI-based vehicle detection and tracking system for C-ITS application. J. Adv. Transp. **2021**, 1–15 (2021). https://doi.org/10.1155/2021/4438861

20. Tryolabs: Reference repository for Norfair. https://github.com/tryolabs/norfair/

21. Ultralytics: Reference repository for YoloV5. https://github.com/ultralytics/yolov5

22. Tavares, J.F., Borges, M.R.S., Vivacqua, A.S.: Preparing a smart environment to decision-making in emergency traffic control management. In: Murayama, Y., Velev, D., Zlateva, P. (eds.) ITDRR 2018. IAICT, vol. 550, pp. 12–21. Springer, Cham (2019). https://doi.org/10.1007/978-3-030-32169-7_2

23. Wang, Y., Jodoin, P.M., Porikli, F., Konrad, J., Benezeth, Y., Ishwar, P.: CDnet 2014: an expanded change detection benchmark dataset. In: Proceedings of the IEEE Conference on Computer Vision and Pattern Recognition Workshops, pp. 387–394 (2014)

24. Zhao, X., Su, J.R., Cai, J., Yang, H., Xi, T.: Vehicle anomalous trajectory detection algorithm based on road network partition. Appl. Intell. **52**, 8820–8838 (2022). https://doi.org/10.1007/s10489-021-02867-5

A Decentralized Collision Avoidance Algorithm for Individual and Collaborative UAVs

Julian Estevez[1]([✉]), Daniel Caballero-Martin[2], Jose Manuel Lopez-Guede[2], and Manuel Graña[3]

[1] Group of Computational Intelligence, Faculty of Engineering of Gipuzkoa, University of the Basque Country UPV/EHU, San Sebastian, Spain
`julian.estevez@ehu.eus`
[2] Group of Computational Intelligence, Faculty of Engineering of Vitoria, University of the Basque Country, UPV/EHU, Vitoria, Spain
[3] Group of Computational Intelligence, Faculty of Computer Science, University of the Basque Country, UPV/EHU, San Sebastian, Spain

Abstract. This paper presents an innovative approach to enhance collision avoidance in a group of Unmanned Aerial Vehicles (UAVs) connected by a cable. The proposed algorithm leverages Artificial Potential Fields (APFs) to navigate UAVs through complex environments while taking into account the constraints imposed by the interconnecting cable. The article outlines the algorithm's theoretical foundation, implementation details, and provides comprehensive simulation results to demonstrate its efficacy in an experiment. The findings contribute to advancing the field of UAV swarm coordination and collision avoidance.

1 Introduction

Urban UAVs are experiencing a huge advance in the last years. Moreover, recent research on cooperative UAV systems offers the possibility to perform more complex tasks including the cooperative transportation of different objects, something that single multirotor drones cannot cope with. In these collaborative systems, when transporting objects, dynamic and kinematic conditions that are external to the drones affect the UAVs control and performance. These technological solutions will have different capabilities based on their characteristics of affordability, speed and cost.

Our research group has long been researching about the cooperative transportation of cables by a team of quadrotors [1–3] (Fig. 1). The cable, which is a deformable linear object, acts as a elastic passive object that links otherwise isolated and independent quadrotors, introducing dynamic interactions among the robots in the form of non-linear constraints and requiring a carefully designed control strategy.

UAVs will have to coexist with other general aviation vehicles, such as helicopters, so they must be safely accommodated at lower altitudes. However, the

J. M. Ferrández Vicente et al. (Eds.): IWINAC 2024, LNCS 14675, pp. 13–22, 2024.
https://doi.org/10.1007/978-3-031-61137-7_2

framework and infrastructure to safely manage the low-altitude airspace and UAS operations therein does not exist yet [4], although it has been a research objective in last years [5].

Hence, a strategy for collision avoidance is essential for the correct working of the network of UAVs of different sizes and purposes, but the problem is far from being totally resolved yet [4]. UAVs must be able to avoid buildings, electric infrastructure and aerial cables, natural elements such as trees and birds, and other UAVs.

In self-organizing cluster flights and cooperative systems, orders can be transmitted between the robots; however, the optimal solution for the full automation of these systems implies that the UAV can operate in absence of external orders. Therefore, a distributed collision avoidance method is required to prevent collisions assuming self-organized flight conditions [6], which gets harder with linked cooperative drone systems.

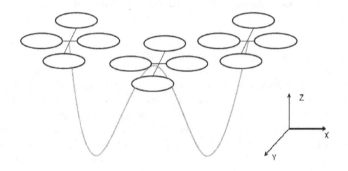

Fig. 1. Cooperative transportation of a cable with quadrotors

In this article, we present a distributed collision avoidance algorithm for autonomous UAVs realizing cooperative transportation tasks, based on potential field models. Due to the extra restrictions in distance and speed between drones carrying a cable, a spatial formation strategy is also proposed. Finally, we test the approach in different stress scenarios, including cooperative and individual drones.

The article is organized as follows: in Sect. 2, a state of art of the current obstacle avoidance methods is covered. Next, the details for the proposed solution are described in Sect. 3. The validation of this methodology is presented in Sect. 4, through an experiment and its results. Finally, the article ends in Sect. 5 with conclusions and future work in this area.

2   State of Art

Obstacle avoidance techniques do not refer strictly to the navigation of aerial robots, but many algorithms were proposed for other robotic tasks, i.e.: manipulators control, soccer playing robots, or autonomous driving in highways [7].

Some specific methods have been employed for self-organizing UAV flights. Reynolds first presented a distributed flock behavior model in 1987 [8], which is inspired in the natural behaviour of birds. This technique is based on a delicate equilibrium of speed alignment of different members of the flock, a cohesion to maintain the average position of the mates surrounding each member, and the strict safe distance keeping. Next, ant colony algorithm was also proposed, which is also based on the natural behavior of real ants which enables them to find the shortest paths between nest and food sources, and can be expanded to multi-UAV systems for robots to find the optimum route from any position in the swarm, including the route to avoid obstacles [9]. Genetic and particle swarm optimization algorithms were also applied [10], which are based on the offline computation of trajectories through stochastic search requiring thousands of tests and mutations carried out by algorithms. Thus, these systems lacked online performance. Most of algorithms presented till now are useful for the collaborative path-planning of the swarm of UAVs to reach a goal and avoid a fixed obstacle. However, other algorithms focus on *collision avoidance*, meaning that robots avoid each other, which is a requirement for surveillance tasks, or for independent drones coexisting in the same scenario pursuing different purposes.

Originally, the most simple and direct way for creating paths free of collisions among robots, was to adjust the speed without an automatization of the control process [11], typically requiring the intervention of a human-operated control. Approaches based on speed adjustment by mixed integer linear programming have been successfully applied in aircrafts and UAVs for collision avoidance [12], although this technique suffers from a huge computational complexity.

Another technique is sequential convex programming (SCP), which has been to approximate collision-free regions by incrementally drawing hyperplanes in UAVs operating space [13]. However, this method may lead to infeasible trajectories. Typically several SCP iterations are required to find a feasible solution [14].

A technique that is receiving great attention in research is the use of artificial potential fields [15], which has been widely used for the obstacle avoidance of other robotic systems.

A recent review article [6] compares which of these algorithm proposals have been tested in real environments and which simulated. Each method was found to have inherent practical difficulties. Thus, a compromise solution is required for the online calculus of self-organizing UAV flights in practical applications.

However, extra difficulties emerge when RPAS fly collaboratively for the transport of any payload. Most of bibliography in this field is focused on the obstacle avoidance [16,17]. However, the optimization of the collision avoidance between other UAVs or mobile obstacles is far from being resolved [16,18].

In order to achieve that goal, this paper proposes an algorithm based on artificial potential field, with some enhancements involving the formation of the cooperative system of transportation of cables, so that they can safely avoid another UAV.

3   Methodology

We propose a methodology for the collision avoidance of cooperative systems of RPAS linked through a passive dynamic link such a cable. This configuration aims to be able to avoid both individual and team systems of UAVs, as well as static obstacles.

Due to the restrictions of the task, careful modeling is required in order to perform the cable transportation smoothly. Our collision avoiding approach is based on an enhancement of potential field algorithm. As an extra requirement, in order to maintain the proper distance among drones for the transportation task, a flight spatial formation strategy is proposed.

The algorithm proposed in Subsect. 3.1 will act as the desired values of the quadrotors to fly when affected by the proximity of other aerial robots or the attractive field of the final goal. In our methodology, we consider that the attractive field just affects the leader drone of the cooperative system carrying the cable [19]. Thus, we modelled a *follow-the-leader* formation described in Subsect. 3.2 for the quadrotors to fly together and keeping the right distance to convey the cable, in the absence of sudden repulsive force that slightly alter the formation.

3.1   Collision Avoidance

The artificial potential field algorithm is widely used in robot trajectory planning and collision avoidance because of its simplicity, low computation cost, smooth trajectory generation capability and the ability to perform on real time. Though it does not obtain the shortest path, it does get the safest one [20]. The algorithm is ruled by two types of forces: attractive and repulsive forces. Total artificial potential field force results in the sum of these two terms:

$$F_{APF} = F_{att} + F_{rep} \tag{1}$$

Following the mathematical demonstration in [21] and the equation of the Khatib's potential attractive, the attractive potential $U_{att}(x, y)$ is as follows:

$$U_{att} = \frac{1}{2}k_a((x_{pos} - x_{ref})^2 + (y_{pos} - y_{ref})^2) \tag{2}$$

where x_{pos} and y_{pos} are the (x, y) position of the robot in each moment, x_{ref} and y_{ref} are the goal coordinates and k_a is the attractive force coefficient. If we calculate the partial derivative of the attractive potential over x and y coordinates, we obtain the first components of the robot speed.

$$v_x^{att} = -k_a(x_{pos} - x_{ref}) \tag{3}$$

$$v_y^{att} = -k_a(y_{pos} - y_{ref}) \tag{4}$$

Similarly, we can obtain the velocity for the repulsive components of speed:

$$U_{rep} = \begin{cases} \frac{1}{2}k_r(\frac{1}{\rho_{dist}} - \frac{1}{r_{dist}}) & if(\rho_{dist} \leq r_{dist}) \\ 0 & if(\rho_{dist} > r_{dist}) \end{cases} \tag{5}$$

where r_{dist} is the maximum distance of potential repulsive influence, ρ_{dist} is the closest distance between the quadrotor and the obstacle: $\rho_{dist} = \sqrt{x_{dist}^2 + y_{dist}^2}$, and x_{dist} and y_{dist} refer to those distances in $x - y$ plane.

$$v_x^{rep} = \begin{cases} -k_r(1 - \frac{\rho_{dist}}{r_{dist}})\frac{(x_{pos}-x_{ref})}{\rho_{dist}^3} & if(\rho_{dist} \leq r_{dist}) \\ 0 & if(\rho_{dist} > r_{dist}) \end{cases} \tag{6}$$

$$v_y^{rep} = \begin{cases} -k_r(1 - \frac{\rho_{dist}}{r_{dist}})\frac{(y_{pos}-y_{ref})}{\rho_{dist}^3} & if(\rho_{dist} \leq r_{dist}) \\ 0 & if(\rho_{dist} > r_{dist}) \end{cases} \tag{7}$$

where k_r is the repulsive force constant. Hence, the total speed of the quadrotors due to the APF results in:

$$\begin{aligned} v_x^{APF} &= v_x^{att} + v_x^{rep} \\ v_y^{APF} &= v_y^{att} + v_y^{rep} \end{aligned} \tag{8}$$

All the terms are illustrated in Fig. 2.

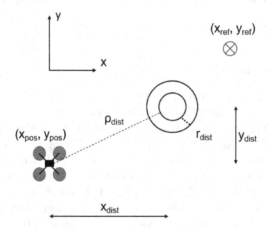

Fig. 2. Illustration of the terms in artificial potential field

The details of the dynamics modeling and control for the UAVs to follow the desired position in each moment are provided in Estevez et al. [22], not repeated here to avoid plagiarism issues.

Potential field requires different implementation for individual and cooperative UAVs. Single UAVs create a circular respulsive field centered in their degree of freedom. In the case of cooperative systems transporting the cable, also a potential repulsive field around each robot will be created. This design permits scalability of the system and be able of include as many quadrotors as desired in the team. The radius of the potential field of the team quadrotors must be proportionate to the Euclidean distance between them, so that they do not overlap. A representation of this model is shown in Fig. 3. Thus, the total horizontal velocities in x-y axes of the desired position of each RPAS will be a sum of all the attractive and repulsive components that may affect them along the trajectory.

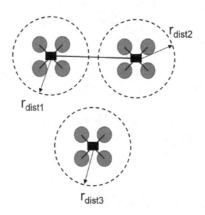

Fig. 3. Potential field creation for single and cooperative UAS

3.2 System Formation

Our approach is based on a column platoon formation of UAVs transporting the deformable linear object due to its advantages in obstacle avoidance and the need to just develop a leader, technologically advanced, UAV in the system. Our case is inspired in ground robotics, based on a leader-following platoon formation [23] with an extra constraint of maintaining a horizontal Euclidean distance between robots. Orientation and position of each robot are calculated in every moment. The graphic configuration can be seen in Fig. 4. L and F represent the leader's and follower's variables respectively. In our case, as a simplification of the model and due to the maneuverability of UAVs, setting ψ angle to 0, while θ and φ are positive, produces a motion in the X, Y axes, respectively. λ corresponds to the desired distance between robots.

Finally, equations of the desired position of the follower UAV with respect to the leader, are shown in Eq. 9.

$$
\begin{cases}
x_F = x_L + \lambda_x \cos(\psi_L) - \lambda_y \sin(\psi_L) \\
y_F = y_L + \lambda_x \sin(\psi_L) + \lambda_y \cos(\psi_L)
\end{cases}.
\tag{9}
$$

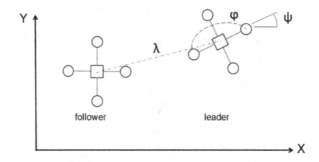

Fig. 4. Leader-following platoon model

4   Experiments and Results

We implemented an experiment for testing our algorithm, consisting in the collision avoidance between a single UAV and a team of UAVs.

The main aim of these exercises is to test the robustness and scalability of our solution. Apart from the non-collision statement, our problem presents extra difficulties in the case of the team of quadrotors to convey the cable smooth and precisely, so that they keep the formation and avoid the collapse of the deformable linear object.

Considering real conditions drones for goods delivery, we chose the parameters of the drones and potential field terms as shown in Table 1:

Table 1. Potential field parameters

Parameter	Value
attractive constant, k_a	0.02
repulsive constant, k_r	0.6
repulsive radius, r_{dist}	5 m
time increment, dt	0.1 s

On the other hand, we equipped all the drones with a cascaded closed-loop of PD controllers, and we set following dynamic parameters for the simulations: mass, $m_q = 1.2$ kg, rotational inertia moments; $J_{xx} = J_{yy} = 1.5 \cdot 10^{-2}$ kgm^2, $J_{zz} = 3 \cdot 10^{-2}$ kgm^2; propeller thrust coefficient, $b = 3 \cdot 10^{-6}$ Ns^2, drag coefficient, $d = 1 \cdot 10^{-7}$ Nms^2. The PD controller parameters are set as follows: $k_{p\varphi} = 0.65$, $k_{d\varphi} = 0.18$, $k_{p\theta} = 0.65$, $k_{d\theta} = 0.18$, $k_{p\psi} = 0.4$, $k_{d\psi} = 0.5$, for the inner loop, and $k_p = 0.3$, $k_d = 1$ for the outer loop. Simulations were implemented in Python. The starting point of three multirotors is shown in Fig. 5. The starting coordinates of each robot is $(10, 2)$, $(10, 6)$ and $(10, 18)$ respectively. Distances are measured in metres. Drones at the bottom of the image are linked by a 8 m long cable. We consider that all the drones have the collision avoidance capacity.

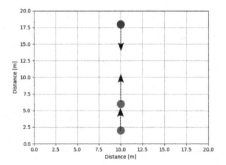

Fig. 5. Experiment starting spatial configuration. Blue dot represents the leader drone.

Finally, the results of the experiment and the trajectory of the UAVs in the collision avoidance maneuver is shown in Fig. 6.seria bueno poner algun tipo de flecha indicando la direccion de movimiento, sino es dificil de interppretar la imagen.

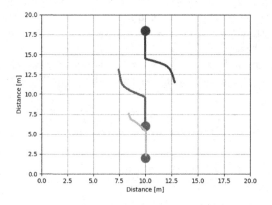

Fig. 6. Collision avoidance trajectories computed from the initial spatial configuration.

5   Conclusions

As we can see, the UAVs got not to collide and started their collision avoiding maneuver when they reached to a threshold of a 5m distance approximately. Due to the article lengths limitations, authors only show in Results the end of the maneuver, and it is out of the scope of the current article the way back of the drones to the original path. We consider that artificial potential field is a strategy that is still useful for moving quadrotors situations, and in addition to this, it remains a simple, efficient, and computationally cheap strategy. As future work, implementation of this technique in physical drone experimentation is planned.

Acknowledgments. The work in this paper has been partially supported by FEDER funds for the MICIN project PID2020-116346GBI00, research funds from the Basque Government as the Grupo de Inteligencia Computacional, Universidad del Pais Vasco, UPV/EHU with code IT1689-22. Additionally, the authors participate in Elkartek projects KK-2022/00051 and KK-2021/00070. Authors have also received support by Fundacion Vitoria-Gasteiz Araba Mobility Lab.

References

1. Estevez, J., Lopez-Guede, J.M., Graña, M.: Quasi-stationary state transportation of a hose with quadrotors. Robot. Auton. Syst. **63**(Part 2(0)), 187–194 (2015). Cognition-oriented Advanced Robotic Systems
2. Estevez, J., Lopez-Guede, J.M., Graña, M.: Particle swarm optimization quadrotor control for cooperative aerial transportation of deformable linear objects. Cybern. Syst. **47**(1–2), 4–16 (2016)
3. Estevez, J., Garate, G., Lopez-Guede, J.M., Larrea, M.: Review of aerial transportation of suspended-cable payloads with quadrotors. Drones **8**(2), 35 (2024)
4. Bahabry, A., Wan, X., Ghazzai, H., Menouar, H., Vesonder, G., Massoud, Y.: Low-altitude navigation for multi-rotor drones in urban areas. IEEE Access **7**, 87716–87731 (2019)
5. Cicala, M., D'Amato, E., Notaro, I., Mattei, M.: Distributed UAV state estimation in UTM context. In: 2019 6th International Conference on Control, Decision and Information Technologies (CoDIT), pp. 557–562. IEEE (2019)
6. Huang, Y., Tang, J., Lao, S.: Collision avoidance method for self-organizing unmanned aerial vehicle flights. IEEE Access **7**, 85536–85547 (2019)
7. Górriz, J.M., et al.: Computational approaches to explainable artificial intelligence: advances in theory, applications and trends. Inf. Fus. **100**, 101945 (2023)
8. Reynolds, C.W.: Flocks, herds and schools: a distributed behavioral model. In: Proceedings of the 14th Annual Conference on Computer Graphics and Interactive Techniques, pp. 25–34 (1987)
9. Duan, H., Zhang, X., Wu, J., Ma, G.: Max-min adaptive ant colony optimization approach to multi-UAVs coordinated trajectory replanning in dynamic and uncertain environments. J. Bionic Eng. **6**(2), 161–173 (2009)
10. Sahingoz, O.K.: Generation of Bezier curve-based flyable trajectories for multi-UAV systems with parallel genetic algorithm. J. Intell. Robot. Syst. **74**, 499–511 (2014). https://doi.org/10.1007/s10846-013-9968-6
11. Mehdi, S.B., Cichella, V., Marinho, T., Hovakimyan, N.: Collision avoidance in multi-vehicle cooperative missions using speed adjustment. In: 2017 IEEE 56th Annual Conference on Decision and Control (CDC), pp. 2152–2157. IEEE (2017)
12. Ioan, D., Prodan, I., Olaru, S., Stoican, F., Niculescu, S.-I.: Mixed-integer programming in motion planning. Annu. Rev. Control. **51**, 65–87 (2021)
13. Morgan, D., Chung, S.-J., Hadaegh, F.Y.: Model predictive control of swarms of spacecraft using sequential convex programming. J. Guidance Control Dyn. **37**(6), 1725–1740 (2014)
14. Schoels, T., Palmieri, L., Arras, K.O., Diehl, M.: An NMPC approach using convex inner approximations for online motion planning with guaranteed collision avoidance. arXiv arXiv:1909.08267 (2019)
15. Heidari, H., Saska, M.: Collision-free trajectory planning of multi-rotor UAVs in a wind condition based on modified potential field. Mech. Mach. Theor. **156**, 104140 (2021)

16. Pizetta, I.H.B., Brandão, A.S., Sarcinelli-Filho, M.: Avoiding obstacles in cooperative load transportation. ISA Trans. **91**, 253–261 (2019)
17. Jackson, B.E., Howell, T.A., Shah, K., Schwager, M., Manchester, Z.: Scalable cooperative transport of cable-suspended loads with UAVs using distributed trajectory optimization. IEEE Robot. Autom. Lett. **5**(2), 3368–3374 (2020)
18. Gimenez, J., Gandolfo, D.C., Salinas, L.R., Rosales, C., Carelli, R.: Multi-objective control for cooperative payload transport with rotorcraft UAVs. ISA Trans. **80**, 491–502 (2018)
19. Garriga-Casanovas, A., Rodriguez y Baena, F.: Complete follow-the-leader kinematics using concentric tube robots. Int. J. Robot. Res. **37**(1), 197–222 (2018)
20. Sun, J., Tang, J., Lao, S.: Collision avoidance for cooperative UAVs with optimized artificial potential field algorithm. IEEE Access **5**, 18382–18390 (2017)
21. Iswanto, M.A., Wahyunggoro, O., Cahyadi, A.I.: Artificial potential field algorithm implementation for quadrotor path planning. Int. J. Adv. Comput. Sci. Appl. **10**(8), 575–585 (2019)
22. Estevez, J., Graña, M., Lopez-Guede, J.M.: Online fuzzy modulated adaptive PD control for cooperative aerial transportation of deformable linear objects. Integr. Comput. Aided Eng. **24**(1), 41–55 (2017)
23. Pruner, E., Necsulescu, D., Sasiadek, J., Kim, B.: Control of decentralized geometric formations of mobile robots. In: 2012 17th International Conference on Methods & Models in Automation & Robotics (MMAR), pp. 627–632. IEEE (2012)

Improved Surface Defect Classification from a Simple Convolutional Neural Network by Image Preprocessing and Data Augmentation

Francisco López de la Rosa[1,2], Lucía Moreno-Salvador[1],
José L. Gómez-Sirvent[1,3], Rafael Morales[1,2], Roberto Sánchez-Reolid[1,3],
and Antonio Fernández-Caballero[1,3(✉)]

[1] Instituto de Investigación en Informática de Albacete, Universidad de Castilla-La Mancha, Calle de la Investigación 2, Albacete, Spain
[2] Departamento de Ingeniería Eléctrica, Electrónica, Automática y Comunicaciones, Universidad de Castilla-La Mancha, Avenida de España s/n, Albacete, Spain
[3] Departamento de Sistemas Informáticos, Universidad de Castilla-La Mancha, Avenida de España s/n, Albacete, Spain
antonio.fdez@uclm.es

Abstract. Convolutional neural networks (CNNs) play an important role in an increasing number of image processing tasks. There is an obvious demand to improve their classification performance and efficiency. Current research in this area tends to focus on developing increasingly complex models and algorithms to achieve this end. However, research into computer vision techniques and data augmentation tends to be neglected. This paper demonstrates that even a very simple CNN model achieves high performance in surface defect classification on the NEU dataset thanks to image preprocessing and data augmentation. The initial F1-score of 0.9646 without image preprocessing increases to 0.9727 when preprocessing is carried out. The simple CNN then achieves an F1-score of 0.9854 after data augmentation.

Keywords: Surface defect classification · image preprocessing · data augmentation · convolutional neural network

1 Introduction

Industry 4.0 is now a reality as its principles are being adopted by various industries, including manufacturing [3,4,18]. Now, the majority of manufacturing processes are monitored and much data is collected for post-analysis to diagnose the efficiency of processes and take improvement measures. One such process is visual inspection [8]. Traditionally, visual inspection has been carried out by human experts who have devoted their efforts to locating and classifying defects. However, this classification is subjective and can lead to classification errors. To

J. M. Ferrández Vicente et al. (Eds.): IWINAC 2024, LNCS 14675, pp. 23–32, 2024.
https://doi.org/10.1007/978-3-031-61137-7_3

solve this problem, machine learning and deep learning algorithms are being used to assist human experts in these inspection tasks [2,6,11,15], taking advantage of the large amount of data collected.

The data used for visual inspection is usually in the form of images. The device used to take these images depends mainly on the minimum resolution that allows classification. For example, there are tasks where the resolution limit of the human eye (0.1 mm) is sufficient, while other tasks require resolution limits of a few nanometres, leading to the use of powerful microscopy tools such as scanning electron microscopes [12]. Images taken in industrial environments are sometimes difficult to classify. These environments are in a constant state of flux, which can cause images to be affected by changes in brightness, the appearance of noise and other factors. Fortunately, these challenges can be overcome, at least in part, by using image preprocessing techniques [5]. These techniques, usually based on computer vision algorithms, improve the quality of the image with the aim of making it easier to classify. However, the use of these techniques is time and resource consuming, which can limit their usability in certain applications (e.g. some on-the-fly classification tasks).

Although the amount of data collected is huge, it is difficult to build defect datasets because, fortunately, the majority of inspected samples are not defective. Moreover, sometimes a dataset alone is not enough to train deep learning algorithms such as CNNs, which now play an important role in defect detection and classification [10]. It is therefore necessary to generate synthetic data to increase the number of instances of each defect class and to improve the performance of the different classifiers. This synthetic data can be generated by using data augmentation techniques [13], which can be based on image transformations [14], or more complex generative models such as synthetic training data [19] and generative adversarial networks (GANs) [7].

This study aims to analyse the impact of image preprocessing and data augmentation on the classification performance of a simple CNN designed from scratch. This is done using the NEU surface defect database (https://www.kaggle.com/datasets/kaustubhdikshit/neu-surface-defect-database). It contains up to six different defect classes that occur during the hot rolling process of steel plates [1,9,16,20]. In a first experiment, raw images from the database are fed to the CNN. In the second experiment, the images fed to the CNN are preprocessed to improve their quality. In the third experiment, the number of images used to train the CNN is multiplied using data augmentation techniques. Finally, the CNN classification performance is evaluated for each experiment using a set of performance metrics, and the results are discussed.

2   Materials

2.1   The NEU Dataset

The NEU dataset consists of six classes of defects commonly encountered in the hot rolling of steel: *crazing, inclusion, patches, pitted surface, rolled-in scale* and *scratches*). The dataset contains 1800 grey scale images, 300 per class. The size of each image is 200 × 200 pixels. The description of the main characteristics of the six defect classes is summarised in Table 1. In addition, Fig. 1 shows some examples of defects for each class. Note that defects within the same class can look very different due to lighting, noise, material changes, etc. This, together with the fact that defects in different classes can be very similar, makes the classification task much more difficult.

Table 1. Description of the defect classes

Defect class	Description
Crazing	Defects in this class appear as cracks along the surface of the steel.
Inclusion	Remnants of impurities pressed into the steel during the rolling process.
Patches	Spots of various shapes that appear all over the steel surface.
Pitted surface	A particular type of corrosion that forms circular patterns that penetrate into the metal.
Rolled-in scale	This type of defect is caused by the introduction of the mill scale into the steel during rolling.
Scratches	Signs of wear and tear caused by the rollers during the process

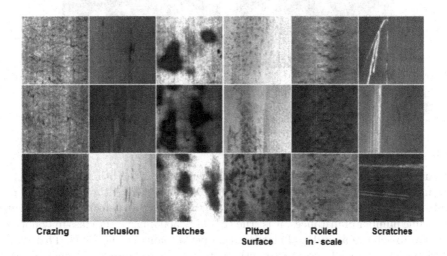

Crazing   Inclusion   Patches   Pitted Surface   Rolled in - scale   Scratches

Fig. 1. NEU dataset defect classes

2.2 Image Preprocessing

Most work using images as the main data source requires an image preprocessing. Image preprocessing is used to improve image quality, increase contrast, remove noise and generally facilitate the correct classification of images. In addition, all data used as input to a CNN model must be of the same size and format. Image preprocessing is therefore also used to homogenise the input data.

One of the aims of this study is to analyse the impact of image preprocessing In this case, the preprocessing strategy adopted involves the use of the Contrast Limited Adaptive Histogram Equalisation (CLAHE) algorithm to normalise the value of the pixels of the image [17]. The main advantage of this algorithm is its ability to locally improve the contrast in the image. This is achieved by dividing the image into small sections, called mosaics, and then applying the histogram equalisation technique to each of these mosaics.

Figure 2 shows the application of the CLAHE algorithm to an *inclusion* type defect. As can be seen, in the original image the minimum and maximum pixel values were 39 and 79 respectively. On the other hand, after running CLAHE, the minimum and maximum values are 35 and 137. Thus, the contrast in the image has increased, leading to a better visual identification of the defect.

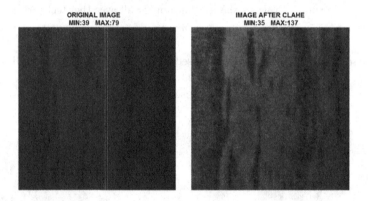

Fig. 2. Example of CLAHE preprocessing algorithm

2.3   Data Augmentation

Apart from image preprocessing, data augmentation is the other main strategy to improve the performance of the simple CNN classifier. Although there is no imbalance problem in the case of the NEU dataset, since all defect classes contain the same number of instances, it is true that only 300 images per class may not be enough to achieve an optimal classification performance of the CNN. Therefore, the experiment aims to generate synthetic images to evaluate the impact of data augmentation on the classification performance of a simple CNN.

With this in mind, data augmentation techniques are used to generate three additional datasets: *DS2*, which contains twice the number of images of the original train dataset, *DS4*, which contains four times the number of images of the original train dataset, and *DS8*, which contains eight times the number of images of the original train dataset. Although there are complex models such as GANs (generative adversarial networks) that give good results in similar tasks, the authors decided to use classical data augmentation techniques such as geometric transformations and adding blur. These techniques are described below.

Geometric Transformation Techniques. As the name suggests, geometric transformation techniques involve applying geometric transformations to an image. In this work, up to four different geometric transformations have been used. And these are:

- **Random scaling** applies a random scaling factor in the range 0.5 to 1.5, changing the dimensions of the image proportionally. To maintain the original dimensions of the image, the synthetic image will be filled with the average pixel value of the original image if necessary.
- **Horizontal translation** introduces horizontal variations in the position of pixels by randomly shifting them, simulating changes in the perspective or shot of the image. In this case, the maximum displacement allowed is set to 20% of the image width. Again, the image is filled with the average pixel value of the original image when necessary.
- **Flipping** flips the image horizontally or vertically.
- **Rotation** transformation is the process of rotating an image about a given point. In the context of image processing, this means changing the orientation of the image by a given angle. Rotation can be clockwise or counter-clockwise.

Blur Addition Techniques. Blur addition techniques basically rely on the use of filters or masks to introduce noise, to simulate that the image was captured in non-ideal conditions. In this work, the authors have introduced **Gaussian noise**, which reduces the contrast between adjacent pixels, gradually smoothing the image. Figure 3 collects an example of each data augmentation image used in this work.

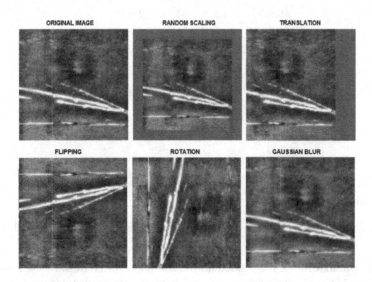

Fig. 3. Data augmentation techniques used in this study

3   Methodology

3.1   Simple Convolutional Neural Network

As mentioned in the previous sections, the CNN model used in this paper is a simple architecture designed from scratch. As can be seen in Table 2, the proposed architecture consists of a total of five convolutional blocks, which are composed of a convolutional layer, a max-pooling layer, and ReLU activation. Finally, after the last convolutional block, a flattening layer flattens the output, which passes through three dense layers. Note that the size of the output of the last layer corresponds to the number of classes to be classified. This last layer is activated by SoftMax activation.

Table 2. Specification of the proposed CNN architecture

Layer	Output size	Filter size
Input	$200 \times 200 \times 1$	
Conv 1	$196 \times 196 \times 32$	5×5
MaxPool 1	$98 \times 98 \times 32$	2×2
Conv 2	$94 \times 94 \times 32$	5×5
MaxPool 2	$47 \times 47 \times 32$	2×2
Conv 3	$44 \times 44 \times 64$	4×4
MaxPool 3	$22 \times 22 \times 64$	2×2
Conv 4	$19 \times 19 \times 64$	4×4
MaxPool 4	$9 \times 9 \times 64$	2×2
Conv 5	$8 \times 8 \times 128$	2×2
MaxPool 5	$4 \times 4 \times 128$	2×2
Flatten 1	2048	
Dense 1	512	
Dense 2	256	
Dense 3	6	

3.2   Training Strategy

The training strategy that has been adopted in this work is explained below.

Data Preparation. As mentioned above, up to five different datasets have been handled in this work. The first corresponds to the original dataset (*DS1*). The second contains the preprocessed images of the original dataset (*DS1+PP*). The third dataset is the first with synthetic images (*DS2*). Its training set contains twice as many images as the previous ones. Finally, the fourth ($DS4$) and fifth ($DS8$) datasets have training sets with four and eight times the number of images of the original training set.

The data splitting approach adopted for the experiments consists of randomly selecting, for each iteration, a stratified sample of 15% of the images for the test set, another 15% for the validation, and the remaining 70% for the training set. The data augmentation techniques are also randomly selected to generate one, three or seven synthetic images from each image of the training set to build the different augmented datasets ($DS2$, $DS4$ and $DS8$).

Hyperparameter Tuning. A grid search algorithm is implemented to fine tune the hyperparameters of the model. The hyperparameters to be tuned are the learning rate and the optimiser. The values that these hyperparameters can take are collected in Table 3.

Table 3. Grid search hyperparameters considered for tuning of the CNN

Hyperparameters	Values
Optimiser	ADAM, SGD
Learning rate	10^{-3}, 10^{-4}

Model Evaluation. Finally, the test set is used to evaluate the performance of the models generated by the grid search algorithm. The metric chosen to perform this evaluation is the F1-score. The model with the highest F1-score and the lowest validation loss is selected as the optimal model for each experiment.

4   Results and Discussion

Each model was trained for 100 consecutive epochs, selecting categorical cross-entropy as the loss function. However, early stopping conditions were introduced to avoid excessive overfitting. Thus, if the validation loss did not improve for 10 consecutive epochs, the training of the model was automatically stopped. Under these training conditions, each of the grid search hyperparameter combinations is used to train the model 100 times. For each of these 100 times, the training, validation and test sets are randomly selected according to the rules explained in the previous sections. This process is repeated for all five datasets. Table 4 shows the optimal hyperparameter configuration for each of the datasets, along with its average F1-score and validation loss. The results for the other configurations are available on request.

Looking at the results, it is apparent that the ADAM optimiser performs better than the SGD in every experiment. Although both learning rates work

Table 4. Best hyperparameter configuration for each experiment

ID.	Optimiser	LR	F1	Val. loss
DS1	ADAM	10^{-4}	0.9646	0.0858
DS1+PP	ADAM	10^{-4}	0.9727	0.0558
DS2	ADAM	10^{-4}	0.9660	0.0995
DS4	ADAM	10^{-4}	0.9804	0.0513
DS8	ADAM	10^{-4}	0.9854	0.0628

well, 10^{-4} slightly outperforms 10^{-3} in all cases. Finally, there is a clear tendency for the F1-score to improve with both preprocessing and data augmentation (see Fig. 4). The F1-score starting point corresponds to *DS1* or, which is the same, to the original dataset without any image preprocessing or data augmentation.

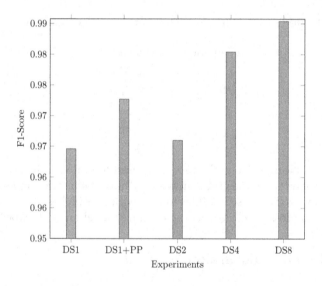

Fig. 4. F1-score evolution

Figure 4 shows that the F1-score increases from 0.9646 to 0.9727 when image preprocessing is applied (*DS1+PP*), which is an increase of 0.84%. The next step consisted in applying data augmentation to the original dataset after pre-processing. First, the number of images in the original training set was doubled, creating *DS2*. Surprisingly, there is a drop in the F1-score, from 0.9727 to 0.9660. However, this drop is corrected when more images were generated in *DS4* and *DS8*, which achieve scores of 0.9804 and 0.9854 respectively. Therefore, by apply-ing data augmentation together with image preprocessing techniques, the simple CNN is able to correctly classify the totality of the defects, increasing the F1-score from an initial 0.9646 to a final 0.9854, an increase of 2.16%. Although this is a small percentage, it can make the difference between a good classifier and a worse one.

5   Conclusions

This research paper has investigated the influence of image preprocessing and data augmentation on the performance of a simple CNN model. First, the dataset and the image preprocessing and data augmentation strategies were presented. Then, the architecture of the proposed simple CNN model was described. Next, the training strategy and its steps were detailed. Finally, the results of the different experiments were presented and discussed.

There is one main conclusion that can be drawn from this work. Most efforts are devoted to the development of new efficient models with better and better classification performance. However, the authors of this work have shown that a very simple CNN model, with correct image preprocessing and high quality data augmentation, can achieve great classification results. Therefore, progress in model development cannot ignore solid tools such as image preprocessing and data augmentation when it comes to going one step further in classification tasks.

Acknowledgements. Grant 2023-PRED-21291 funded by Universidad de Castilla-La Mancha and by "ESF Investing in your future". Grant BES-2021-097834 funded by MCIN/AEI/ 10.13039/501100011033 and by "ESF Investing in your future". Grant 2022-GRIN-34436 funded by Universidad de Castilla-La Mancha and by "ERDF A way of making Europe".

References

1. Chazhoor, A., Ho, E., Gao, B., Woo, W.: A review and benchmark on state-of-the-art steel defects detection. SN Comput. Sci. **5**, 114 (2024)
2. Cumbajin, E., et al.: A systematic review on deep learning with CNNs applied to surface defect detection. J. Imaging **9**(10), 193 (2023)
3. Cumbajin, E., et al.: A real-time automated defect detection system for ceramic pieces manufacturing process based on computer vision with deep learning. Sensors **24**(1), 232 (2024)
4. Garrido-Hidalgo, C., Roda-Sanchez, L., Fernández-Caballero, A., Olivares, T., Ramírez, F.J.: Internet-of-Things framework for scalable end-of-life condition monitoring in remanufacturing. Integr. Comput. Aided Eng. **31**(1), 1–17 (2024)
5. Gómez-Sirvent, J.L., de la Rosa, F.L., Sánchez-Reolid, R., Morales, R., Fernández-Caballero, A.: Defect classification on semiconductor wafers using Fisher vector and visual vocabularies coding. Measurement **202**, 111872 (2022)
6. Górriz, J.M., et al.: Computational approaches to explainable artificial intelligence: advances in theory, applications and trends. Inf. Fus. **100**, 101945 (2023)
7. He, X., Chang, Z., Zhang, L., Xu, H., Chen, H., Luo, Z.: A survey of defect detection applications based on generative adversarial networks. IEEE Access **10**, 113493–113512 (2022)
8. Huang, S.H., Pan, Y.C.: Automated visual inspection in the semiconductor industry: a survey. Comput. Ind. **66**, 1–10 (2015)

9. Iannino, V., et al.: A hybrid approach for improving the flexibility of production scheduling in flat steel industry. Integr. Comput. Aided Eng. **29**(4), 367–387 (2022)

10. Jha, S.B., Babiceanu, R.F.: Deep CNN-based visual defect detection: survey of current literature. Comput. Ind. **148**, 103911 (2023)

11. Lin, J., Ma, L., Yao, Y.: A spectrum-domain instance segmentation model for casting defects. Integr. Comput. Aided Eng. **29**(1), 63–82 (2022)

12. de la Rosa, F.L., Gómez-Sirvent, J.L., Morales, R., Sánchez-Reolid, R., Fernández-Caballero, A.: A deep residual neural network for semiconductor defect classification in imbalanced scanning electron microscope datasets. Appl. Soft Comput. **131**, 109743 (2022)

13. de la Rosa, F.L., Gómez-Sirvent, J.L., Morales, R., Sánchez-Reolid, R., Fernández-Caballero, A.: Defect detection and classification on semiconductor wafers using two-stage geometric transformation-based data augmentation and SqueezeNet lightweight convolutional neural network. Comput. Ind. Eng. **183**, 109549 (2023)

14. de la Rosa, F.L., Gómez-Sirvent, J.L., Sánchez-Reolid, R., Morales, R., Fernández-Caballero, A.: Geometric transformation-based data augmentation on defect classification of segmented images of semiconductor materials using a ResNet50 convolutional neural network. Exp. Syst. Appl. **206**, 117731 (2022)

15. de la Rosa, F.L., Sánchez-Reolid, R., Gómez-Sirvent, J.L., Morales, R., Fernández-Caballero, A.: A review on machine and deep learning for semiconductor defect classification in scanning electron microscope images. Appl. Sci. **11**(20), 9508 (2021)

16. Pang, W., Tan, Z.: A steel surface defect detection model based on graph neural networks. Meas. Sci. Technol. **35**(4), 046201 (2024)

17. Pizer, S.M., et al.: Adaptive histogram equalization and its variations. Comput. Vis. Graph. Image Process. **39**(3), 355–368 (1987)

18. Roda-Sanchez, L., Olivares, T., Garrido-Hidalgo, C., de la Vara, J.L., Fernández-Caballero, A.: Human-robot interaction in Industry 4.0 based on an Internet of Things real-time gesture control system. Integr. Comput. Aided Eng. **28**(2), 159–175 (2021)

19. Schmedemann, O., Baass, M., Schoepflin, D., Schüppstuhl, T.: Procedural synthetic training data generation for AI-based defect detection in industrial surface inspection. Procedia CIRP **107**, 1101–1106 (2022)

20. Zhang, Y., Shen, S., Xu, S.: Strip steel surface defect detection based on lightweight YOLOv5. Front. Neurorobotics **17**, 1263739 (2023). https://doi.org/10.3389/fnbot.2023.1263739

Prediction of Optimal Locations for 5G Base Stations in Urban Environments Using Neural Networks and Satellite Image Analysis

Iván García-Aguilar[1,2]([⊠]), Jesús Galeano-Brajones[3], Francisco Luna-Valero[1], Javier Carmona-Murillo[3], Jose David Fernández-Rodríguez[1,2], and Rafael M. Luque-Baena[1,2]

[1] ITIS Software, University of Málaga, C/ Arquitecto Francisco Peñalosa, 18, 29010 Málaga, Spain
ivangarcia@uma.es
[2] Biomedical Research Institute of Málaga (IBIMA), C/ Doctor Miguel Díaz Recio, 28, 29010 Málaga, Spain
[3] Department of Computing and Telematics Engineering, University of Extremadura, C/ Sta. Teresa Jornet, 38, 06800 Mérida, Spain

Abstract. Deploying 5G networks in urban areas is crucial for meeting the increasing demand for high-speed, low-latency wireless communications. However, the complex topography and diverse building structures in urban environments have challenges in identifying suitable locations for base stations. This research explores leveraging deep learning neural networks to analyze satellite imagery, creating a predictive tool for identifying potential rooftop locations. Integrating these predictions into a user-friendly desktop application simplifies the site selection process, reducing the need for costly and labor-intensive site visits in 5G network deployment. This approach democratizes the deployment process, making it accessible to a broader audience. The combination of advanced technology and satellite imagery offers a promising solution to efficiently deploy 5G base stations in urban landscapes, contributing to the widespread adoption of this technology in densely populated areas and advancing 5G connectivity globally.

Keywords: Convolutional Neural Network (CNN) · Deep Learning (DL) · 5G Deployment

1 Introduction

The demand for high-speed communications has led to the implementation of 5G networks, offering fast data speeds, low latency, and reliable communication. Despite its potential, the success of the 5G revolution relies heavily on the effective deployment of 5G base stations in densely populated urban environments.

J. M. Ferrández Vicente et al. (Eds.): IWINAC 2024, LNCS 14675, pp. 33–43, 2024.
https://doi.org/10.1007/978-3-031-61137-7_4

Growing urban areas and the increasing demand for wireless connectivity necessitate addressing challenges in identifying suitable locations, particularly on building rooftops. Urban environments, with their intricate topography and diverse building structures, present significant obstacles. Identifying suitable locations for 5G base stations involves geospatial assessments and meticulous planning, which consume considerable resources and time. Inefficiencies in this process can impede 5G expansion in urban areas and substantially raise deployment costs.

Optimizing base station deployment is crucial for efficiency and cost reduction. Articles like [1] focus on the transition to 5G wireless networks, while others such as [2,3] emphasize energy consumption and deployment optimization. In [4], energy efficiency in 5G networks, especially in rural areas, is highlighted. Qi Wang et al. [5] address challenges in urban 5G network deployment, emphasizing issues with millimeter wave signals. The main challenge is deploying an ultra-high density of base stations (BSs) for satisfactory communication coverage. [6] focuses on implementing 5G base stations for optimal signal coverage and cost management. Deep learning, particularly convolutional neural networks, has revolutionized image analysis and object segmentation approaches [7–9]. Notably, models like U-Net [10], FPN [11], PSPNet [12], and Mask R-CNN [13] focus on segmentation. These models, exemplified in [14], directly identify specific elements in satellite images, representing a significant advancement in computer vision. They are essential for simplifying and optimizing the implementation of 5G networks in urban environments.

This work presents a solution that leverages the capabilities of Convolutional Neural Networks (CNN) in deep learning to address the challenge of identifying suitable locations for 5G base stations in urban environments. This approach aims to simplify selecting installation locations, thereby reducing the dependence on costs related to site visits or time-consuming tasks, ultimately democratizing the implementation process. This accelerates the deployment of 5G base stations and makes it accessible to a broader audience, paving the way for widespread 5G connectivity in densely populated urban areas.

The remainder of the article is organized as follows. In Sect. 2, the proposed methodology is presented. Subsequently, in Sect. 3, the conducted experiments are detailed, including the selected models, the applied dataset, and the evaluated metrics. Finally, in Sect. 4, the conclusions are elaborated.

2   Methodology

The suggested method for predicting optimal 5B base station locations in urban settings comprises two subsystems. Initially, a satellite image is segmented with a preprocessing phase to align it with the chosen model (see Subsect. 2.1). The resulting segmented image is then input into the base station deployment simulator, guiding the deployment strategy (outlined in Subsect. 2.2).

2.1 Segmentation of Satellite Images

This subsection describes the procedure to obtain the segmentation of a satellite image using convolutional neural networks. Our proposal begins with a dataset composed of several annotated images, which were processed individually to train the model in the next step.

$$\mathbf{D} = \{(\mathbf{F}_l) \mid l \in \{1, ..., N\}\} \tag{1}$$

D represents the labeled dataset, while $\mathbf{F}_l$ denotes each individual frame. N corresponds to the total number of images that compose the entire dataset. The starting point is to train a deep convolutional neural network, designated as $\mathcal{G}$ for object segmentation. A strategy based on K-fold is considered, where we have K subsets of data divided into training, validation, and testing.

In the second step, image transformations enhance training using the Data Augmentation technique. To address this challenge, the Albumentations library[1] has been employed, allowing a series of transformations to be applied to the original images. These transformations have been applied to the dataset to generate an expanded set of transformed data without incurring model overfitting. Formally, the process can be expressed as follows:

$$D' = \{X'_1, X'_2, \ldots, X'_m\}, where X'_j = T(X_i) \tag{2}$$

D' represents the extended dataset of transformed images, and X'_j are the transformed images obtained by applying the transformation T to the original image X_i. This results in a larger dataset without increasing the labeling workload. Additionally, normalization of training images is conducted to enhance model training. This normalization aims to eliminate differences in magnitude among the various image features. This is achieved through the standardization technique, expressed as:

$$X_{normalized} = \frac{X - \mu}{\sigma} \tag{3}$$

where X represents an image in the training set, μ is the mean of the image features and σ is the standard deviation of the image features. Z-score normalization is applied to each pixel in the image, making the mean zero and the standard deviation one. This ensures that all image features have a consistent scale, reducing noise during model training and improving result accuracy.

At this point, the third step is based on training the G model to segment satellite images to identify buildings. For this purpose, a series of parameters related to this task were determined previously. The loss function is defined as follows:

$$L(\theta_M) = \frac{1}{N_{training}} \sum_{i=1}^{N_{training}} IoU(\mathbf{Y}_i, f_M(\mathbf{X}_i; \theta_G)) \tag{4}$$

where $N_{training}$ is the number of examples that compose the training subset. Y_i are the Ground truth annotations for the example i, $f_M(\mathbf{X}_i; \theta_G)$ the prediction

---

[1] https://albumentations.ai.

determined by the model G for the example i. θ_G represents the parameters of the model G. After defining the loss function, the model is optimized. In this case, the ADAM optimizer is selected. The formula for the optimization of the model parameters is as follows:

$$\theta_M^* = \arg \min_{\theta_M} L(\theta_M) \qquad G' = Fine\_Tuned\{G\} \tag{5}$$

The set of parameters is searched for θ_M, which minimizes the loss function L. Once this is defined, the segmentation model G is trained. To enhance the result of processing a non-square image resized to 288×288 pixels, a sliding window technique is employed to divide the image into small regions and make predictions. The requirement to transform the input image was due to the restrictions imposed by the configuration and the data set used during the model training. In this context, the model has been designed to process images with only specific dimensions, 288×288 pixels. This limitation imposed by the model architecture implies that any input image not complying with this dimension must transform to fit the model requirements. Subsequently, the information from all predictions is combined to obtain the final segmentation results.

Firstly, the image is divided into small windows of 288×288 pixels with a displacement S of 20 pixels. This can be mathematically represented as:

$$W_{i,j} = F(I_{val}, i, j) \qquad S_{i,j} = G'(W_{i,j}) \tag{6}$$

where $W_{i,j}$ is a sub-image extracted from the validation image I_{val} at position (i, j), and F is the function that extracts a region from the image. Next, for each sub-image $W_{i,j}$, a prediction is made using the trained model G', resulting in a segmentation for that region, $S_{i,j}$. Subsequently, the information from all segmentations $S_{i,j}$ are combined to obtain the final segmentation S_{final}. A unified mask is generated by summing the pixel values of masks associated with detections. Pixels in the consolidated mask are marked as true when the corresponding sums exceed zero.

2.2   Base Station Deployment

In this phase, an Ultra-Dense Networks (UDNs) simulator based on the model is employed [15]. The objective is to simulate the deployment of base stations in an ultra-dense network. The deployment process is carried out randomly using Poisson Point Processes, which considers social attractors in the network [16]. Poisson Point Processes are a mathematical tool for modeling the distribution of random events in space. In the context of base station deployment, they are used to model the random locations of base stations within a geographic region. This can be expressed through the intensity of the Poisson point process formula:

$$\lambda(x, y) = \frac{Expected\ number\ of\ base\ stations}{dA} \tag{7}$$

where $\lambda(x, y)$ is the intensity of the point process at coordinates (x, y) and dA represents an elemental area in the geographic plane.

Social attractors are also considered in the base station deployment simulation. These social attractors may represent areas with a higher density of users or activities, influencing the placement of base stations. The influence of social attractors on deployment intensity can be expressed as:

$$\lambda_s(x, y) = \lambda(x, y) \times \alpha_s \tag{8}$$

where $\lambda_s(x, y)$ is the intensity of the point process adjusted for social attractors at coordinates (x, y) and α_s is a factor representing the influence of social attractors on base station density. This approach allows for modeling different severity levels in the heterogeneity of the traffic demands within the network.

3   Experiments

This study aims to evaluate the proposed methodology's effectiveness based on the segmentation done by the convolutional neural networks and the solution obtained. The study involves a comparison of several models applying one specific dataset. Below is a detailed description of each of the architectures used to evaluate their performance, as well as information on the dataset, the metrics used, and the results obtained.

3.1   Convolutional Neural Networks

The presented approach is adaptable to any neural DCNN-based object segmentation model. For conducting the experiments, three architectures were selected:

– U-Net [10]: Widely used CNN for image segmentation, known for its U-shaped structure that captures intricate details and high-level patterns.
– FPN (Feature Pyramid Network) [11]: Applied in object detection and image segmentation, FPN enhances detection across scales by combining features from different pyramid levels, facilitating precise segmentation of objects of varying sizes.
– PSPNet (Pyramid Scene Parsing Network) [12]: An image scene segmentation model utilizing a feature pyramid to analyze images at various scales, contributing to comprehensive scene understanding and context extraction.

The pre-trained models were selected from the *SMP* (Segmentation Models Pytorch) library[2], and were previously trained on the COCO dataset (Common Objects in Context) [17]. The COCO dataset offers diverse, challenging images with various object scales and compositions, making it valuable for training real-world object detection models widely used in deep learning applications.

---

[2] https://github.com/qubvel/segmentation_models.pytorch.

3.2 Dataset

The dataset used consists of images that are labeled for the segmentation task. The choice of this dataset is based on its size, which is sufficiently large to achieve optimal results in the project. This dataset was obtained from the crowdAI platform. The dataset is linked to the following challenge[3]. In this challenge, a dataset of RGB satellite images and annotations indicating the location of buildings in each image are provided. The goal of this challenge is to train a model capable of detecting all buildings in a new image. To work with this dataset, it is divided into three essential parts: training, testing, and validation. Since this project employs the K-Fold technique, the data is distributed as follows in each experiment: 75% for training and 25% for testing. Additionally, 20% of the training dataset is set aside for validation purposes.

The training dataset for the neural network consists of 280,741 satellite images, each with dimensions of 300×300 pixels in RGB format. These training images are provided with annotations in MS-COCO format and presented in a JSON file. Figure 1 shows the annotations based on the segmentation provided by each image.

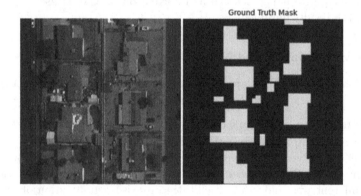

Fig. 1. Image extracted from the dataset along with its segmentation.

3.3 Evaluation

The principal metric for evaluation is Intersection over Union (IoU), a widely accepted measure for assessing segmentation model accuracy. IoU calculation involves matching model detections with Ground Truth (GT) annotations using established criteria, comparing overlap between detected and actual building areas. This process identifies true positives, false positives, and false negatives. An accuracy-recall curve is generated based on these values, illustrating how accuracy varies with adjustments to confidence thresholds in model detections.

---

[3] https://www.crowdai.org/challenges/mapping-challenge.

Lastly, the average IoU for the building class is calculated, representing an overall measure of the model's accuracy in segmenting buildings across various confidence thresholds.

3.4   Results

The results section is split into two main parts. The first part covers the quantitative and qualitative outcomes of training the segmentation model, including objective metrics and visual examples demonstrating its effectiveness. The second part examines how precise building segmentation has impacted the planning and success of antenna deployment in urban environments, providing a qualitative analysis to assess its real-world applicability.

Training Segmentation Models

The U-Net model outperforms the FPN and PSPNet models across all evaluation stages, as shown in Table 1. During training, U-Net achieved a low loss function of 0.0935, indicating effective adjustment to the data, and an IoU value of 0.8307, indicating strong segmentation capability. In validation, U-Net maintained high performance with a loss function of 0.0983 and an IoU value of 0.8228. In the test stage, U-Net displayed a loss function of 0.1214 and an IoU value of 0.8002, confirming its accuracy and consistency. Conversely, FPN and PSPNet models performed similarly, with comparable loss function and IoU values. However, in the test stage, both experienced a decline in performance. FPN recorded a loss function of 0.1214 and an IoU value of 0.8002, while PSPNet had a slightly higher loss function of 0.1383 and an IoU value of 0.7758, indicating slightly inferior performance compared to U-Net. Figure 2 illustrates the evolution of the loss function and IoU values for each stage, highlighting U-Net's suitability for image segmentation.

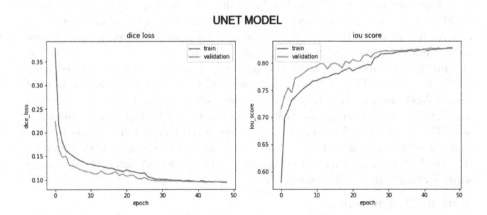

Fig. 2. Evolution of loss function and IoU values for each evaluated stage and model.

Table 1. Results obtained based on training the selected models in the different stages.

Model	Stage	Loss Function	IoU
U-Net	Training	0.0935	0.8307
	Validation	0.0983	0.8228
	Test	0.1214	0.8002
FPN	Training	0.09351	0.8306
	Validation	0.0983	0.8228
	Test	0.1214	0.8002
PSP	Training	0.1205	0.7880
	Validation	0.1156	0.7950
	Test	0.1383	0.7758

Table 2. Results of U-Net model training and evaluation with cross-validation.

Stage	Loss Function	IoU
Training	0.0940	0.8287
Validation	0.0818	0.8490
Test	0.1103	0.8171

Since the U-Net model demonstrated superior performance in the various stages of training, validation, and testing compared to the other models, cross-validation training was conducted to assess its robustness and generalization further. These results are presented in Table 2. In the case of cross-validation training, a slightly higher loss function is obtained, 0.0940, compared to the non-cross-validated result of 0.0935. The IoU value decreased slightly to 0.8287 from 0.8307, suggesting that the cross-validated model may incur a minor penalty in terms of accuracy. In the validation stage, the cross-validated model demonstrated improved performance compared to the non-cross-validated model. The loss function reduced from 0.0983 to 0.0818, and the IoU value increased from 0.8228 to 0.8490. This indicates that the model can generalize and achieve a more robust accuracy. In the test stage, the U-Net model with cross-validation maintains a strong performance with a loss function of 0.1103 and an IoU value of 0.8171. While a slight penalty is observed in the training stage, this is more than compensated for in terms of accuracy on unseen data, thus determining that the U-Net model with cross-validation is the preferred choice for the image segmentation task in this context.

Stations Deployment

The primary motivation lies in the need to develop a specialized neural network for detecting terraces and rooftops to accurately simulate the deployment of 5G base stations. The UDN simulator used is based on an ultra-dense network model, where the deployment of base stations is randomly carried out through Poisson Point Processes (PPP). This model considers social attractors in the network, such as offices and shopping centers, to model a realistic traffic demand distribution. The rooftop and terrace detection neural network plays a crucial role by providing detailed information about urban topology and the presence of relevant structures, such as buildings and rooftops. This information is integrated with the UDN simulator, allowing for more realistic planning of 5G base station deployment based on the location of these structures. Precisely detecting rooftops and terraces with the neural network ensures that 5G base stations are placed in viable locations to simulate real-world deployments, avoiding placing a base station in the middle of a street. The collaboration between the detection technology and the UDN simulator enables evaluating and optimizing next-generation network deployments in urban environments, considering social attractor factors and specific geographic features. Figure 3, presented below, visually exemplifies the autonomous deployment conducted as a result of this work. A red mask identifies the segmentation of the buildings. Each of the dots in the image indicates the position where the base stations will be installed for deployment.

Fig. 3. Base Stations Previsualization. (Color figure online)

4   Conclusions

According to the work presented, a significant improvement has been achieved in planning and deploying 5G base stations in urban and suburban environments by implementing a specialized neural network for detecting rooftops and terraces. Based on the various segmentation models evaluated, U-Net has demonstrated its ability to achieve precise segmentation of structures, with an Intersection over Union (IoU) value consistently high during the training stages, validation, and testing stages. Furthermore, the application of cross-validation has improved performance during the validation stage, with an average loss function of 0.0818 and an average IoU value of 0.8490, confirming the model's generalization capability. Integrating the neural network with the Unified Data Networks (UDN) simulator has resulted in an autonomous deployment solution, providing an efficient and precise tool for planning and deploying base stations in urban areas. As for future lines of research, expansion of the neural network for the detection of other urban elements or research into the optimization of real-time data-based 5G base station deployment algorithms are identified as areas for continued improvement and optimization of the proposed solution.

Acknowledgements. This work is partially supported by the Ministry of Science and Innovation of Spain under grants PID2022-136764OA-I00, TED2021-131699B-I00 funded by MICIU/AEI/10.13039/501100011033 and by the "European Union NextGenerationEU/PRTR" and PID2020-112545RB-C54, and by the University of Málaga (Spain) under grants B1-2021 20, B4-2023 13, B1-2022 14 and by the Fundación Unicaja under project PUNI-003 2023.

References

1. Cheng, X., Hu, Y., Varga, L.: 5G network deployment and the associated energy consumption in the UK: a complex systems' exploration. Technol. Forecast. Soc. Chang. **180**, 121672 (2022)
2. Zeng, Q.: Optimization of millimeter-wave base station deployment in 5G networks. In: 2022 Thirteenth International Conference on Ubiquitous and Future Networks (ICUFN), pp. 117–121 (2022)
3. Mohammadnejad, Z., Al-Khafaji, H.M.R., Mohammed, A.S., Alatba, S.R.: Energy optimization for optimal location in 5G networks using improved barnacles mating optimizer. Phys. Commun. **59**, 102068 (2023)
4. Karlsson, A., Al-Saadeh, O., Gusarov, A., Challa, R.V.R., Tombaz, S., Sung, K.W.: Energy-efficient 5G deployment in rural areas. In: 2016 IEEE 12th International Conference on Wireless and Mobile Computing, Networking and Communications (WiMob), pp. 1–7 (2016)
5. Wang, Q., Zhao, X., Lv, Z., Ma, X., Zhang, R., Lin, Y.: Optimizing the ultra-dense 5G base stations in urban outdoor areas: coupling GIS and heuristic optimization. Sustain. Urban Areas **63**, 102445 (2020)
6. Wang, C.-H., Lee, C.-J., Wu, X.: A coverage-based location approach and performance evaluation for the deployment of 5G base stations. IEEE Access **8**, 123320–123333 (2020)
7. García-Aguilar, I., García-González, J., Luque-Baena, R.M., López-Rubio, E.: Automated labeling of training data for improved object detection in traffic videos by fine-tuned deep convolutional neural networks. Pattern Recogn. Lett. **167**, 45–52 (2023)
8. Kaur, R., Singh, S.: A comprehensive review of object detection with deep learning. Digit. Sig. Process. **132**, 103812 (2023)
9. García-Aguilar, I., García-González, J., Luque-Baena, R.M., López-Rubio, E., Domínguez, E.: Optimized instance segmentation by super-resolution and maximal clique generation. Integr. Comput. Aided Eng. **30**(3), 243–256 (2023)
10. Ronneberger, O., Fischer, P., Brox, T.: U-Net: convolutional networks for biomedical image segmentation. In: Navab, N., Hornegger, J., Wells, W.M., Frangi, A.F. (eds.) MICCAI 2015. LNCS, vol. 9351, pp. 234–241. Springer, Cham (2015). https://doi.org/10.1007/978-3-319-24574-4_28
11. Lin, T.-Y., Dollár, P., Girshick, R., He, K., Hariharan, B., Belongie, S.: Feature pyramid networks for object detection (2017)
12. Zhao, H., Shi, J., Qi, X., Wang, X., Jia, J.: Pyramid scene parsing network (2017)

13. He, K., Gkioxari, G., Dollár, P., Girshick, R.: Mask R-CNN. In: 2017 IEEE International Conference on Computer Vision (ICCV), pp. 2980–2988 (2017)
14. Ichim, L., Popescu, D.: Road detection and segmentation from aerial images using a CNN based system. In: 2018 41st International Conference on Telecommunications and Signal Processing (TSP), pp. 1–5 (2018)
15. Luna, F., Zapata-Cano, P.H., González-Macías, J.C., Valenzuela-Valdés, J.F.: Approaching the cell switch-off problem in 5G ultra-dense networks with dynamic multi-objective optimization. Futur. Gener. Comput. Syst. **110**, 876–891 (2020)
16. Mirahsan, M., Schoenen, R., Yanikomeroglu, H.: HetHetNets: heterogeneous traffic distribution in heterogeneous wireless cellular networks. IEEE J. Sel. Areas Commun. **33**(10), 2252–2265 (2015)
17. Lin, T.-Y., et al.: Microsoft COCO: common objects in context. In: Fleet, D., Pajdla, T., Schiele, B., Tuytelaars, T. (eds.) ECCV 2014. LNCS, vol. 8693, pp. 740–755. Springer, Cham (2014). https://doi.org/10.1007/978-3-319-10602-1_48

Enhanced Cellular Detection Using Convolutional Neural Networks and Sliding Window Super-Resolution Inference

Iván García-Aguilar[1,2(✉)], Rostyslav Zavoiko[3],
Jose David Fernández-Rodríguez[1,2], Rafael Marcos Luque-Baena[1,2],
and Ezequiel López-Rubio[1,2]

[1] ITIS Software, University of Málaga, C/ Arquitecto Francisco Peñalosa, 18, 29010 Málaga, Spain
ivangarcia@uma.es
[2] Biomedical Research Institute of Málaga (IBIMA), C/ Doctor Miguel Díaz Recio, 28, 29010 Málaga, Spain
[3] Málaga, Spain

Abstract. Histopathology currently serves as the standard for breast cancer diagnosis, but its manual execution demands time and expertise from pathologists. Artificial intelligence, particularly in digital pathology, has made significant strides, offering new opportunities for precision and efficiency in disease diagnosis. This study presents a methodology to enhance cell nuclei detection in breast cancer histopathological images using convolutional neural network models to apply super-resolution and object detection. Several model architectures are explored, and their performance is evaluated regarding accuracy and sensitivity. The results affirm the potential of the proposed approach for automated cell nuclei identification. These AI advancements in digital pathology open avenues for early and precise cancer detection, influencing clinical practices and patient well-being and improving diagnostic efficiency.

Keywords: Convolutional Neural Networks · Super-resolution · Object Detection · Nuclei · Cancer Diagnosis

1 Introduction

Histopathology examines disease presence, extent, and progression through microscopic tissue analysis. Thin sections are obtained using a microtome after fixing the sample in formaldehyde and embedding it in paraffin or resin. These cells are then stained to highlight cellular components before microscopic observation. In clinical medicine, a pathologist analyzes histological sections to formulate a pathology report, which is crucial for cancer diagnosis and treatment decisions. However, the reliance on visual analysis, particularly in specific areas of interest, can lead to errors in nucleus counting and classification. This may

J. M. Ferrández Vicente et al. (Eds.): IWINAC 2024, LNCS 14675, pp. 44–54, 2024.
https://doi.org/10.1007/978-3-031-61137-7_5

result in a false diagnosis or misjudgment, which presents a risk to patients by potentially overlooking harmful cells and compromising treatment efficacy. Nowadays, the increase in data generation and collection and the improvement in computational capacity have led to the application of Deep Learning in many fields such as video surveillance [1–4] or autonomous drive [5,6], improving computer vision compared to classical techniques.

In cancer cell detection, the application of neural networks has emerged as an essential tool to improve accuracy and efficiency in the early diagnosis and monitoring of cancer progression. The collection and use of medical images, such as those obtained by microscopy, have enabled applying techniques based on deep learning to get an early and effective diagnosis. Although conventional methods such as microscopy and biochemical tests have been instrumental in detecting cancer cells, they have significant limitations in accuracy and efficiency, especially for those with biological variability. Recent research has demonstrated significant advances. Hou et al. propose a sparse Convolutional Autoencoder [7], which efficiently detects and encodes nuclei in histopathology tissue images. Other works, such as NucDETR [8], introduce a transformer-based approach for automated nucleus detection in histopathology images, addressing the challenges of manual detection. This leverages the success of transformer models in object detection tasks and offers simplicity and reduced post-processing requirements. Tian et al. [9] present a novel semi-supervised learning framework addressing the challenge of acquiring extensive labeled data. This approach utilizes unlabeled images for reconstruction, enhancing the detection network by promoting spatial consistency between original and reconstructed images. Additionally, [10] proposes an end-to-end graph-based nuclei feature alignment (GNFA) method to enhance cross-domain nuclei detection in histopathology images. This method addresses challenges such as limited nuclei features and the presence of background pixels by leveraging a nuclei graph convolutional network (NGCN) to generate sufficient discriminative features for successful alignment. Despite the advances, this field still has outstanding challenges, such as needing more annotated data or identifying small elements.

Compared to other emerging methods, our approach proposes a solution based on the re-inference of super-resolved areas to improve detection without re-training or modifying the model. The term super-resolved areas refers to regions of the image that undergo super-resolution techniques, resulting in greater clarity and detail than the original resolution. In the framework of our proposal, these enhanced areas play a crucial role in object detection by providing richer and more detailed information. Importantly, super-resolution improves the visual quality of the relevant areas and contributes significantly to the accuracy of the detection process. Allowing the model to benefit from more detailed information without re-training avoids this procedure's computational and time costs. Furthermore, by not modifying the original model architecture, the integrity and consistency of its performance are maintained, which is particularly valuable in environments where stability and efficiency are paramount.

The following sections are structured as follows: Sect. 2 shows the proposed methodology, Sect. 3 on page 4 explains the experiments supporting our proposal, and Sect. 4 on page 9 explains our conclusions.

2   Methodology

The proposed methodology for enhancing image detection is shown in Fig. 1. The approach involves a Deep Learning neural network designed for object detection, denoted as $\mathcal{M}$ to process an input image $\mathbf{X}_{LR}$ to produce a set of detections $\mathcal{S}$.

$$S = \mathcal{M}(\mathbf{X}_{LR}) \tag{1}$$

$$S = \{(\alpha_i, \beta_i, \gamma_i, \delta_i, \epsilon_i, \omega_i) \mid i \in \{1, ..., N\}\} \tag{2}$$

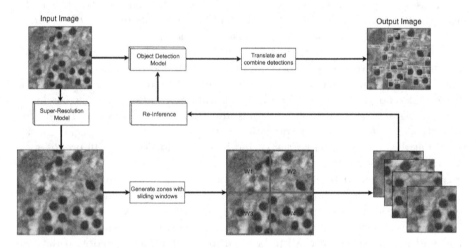

Fig. 1. Workflow of the proposed technique.

Here, N represents the number of detections, $(\alpha_i, \beta_i) \in \mathbb{R}^2$ denotes the coordinates of the upper left corner of the ith detection within the input $\mathbf{X}$, $(\gamma_i, \delta_i) \in \mathbb{R}^2$ represents the coordinates of the lower right corner of the ith detection within $\mathbf{X}$, ϵ_i is the class label of the detection, and $\omega_i \in \mathbb{R}$ signifies the class score of the detection. For this proposal, consideration of the *epsilon*$_i$ class label of the detection will be omitted. The main goal is to increase the total number of detections, regardless of their specific class. This strategic decision is driven by the objective of increasing the exhaustiveness of the detection model. In this context, specific focus is placed on detections characterized by a class score $\omega_i \in \mathbb{R}$ that exceeds a predefined threshold set at 50%. This threshold serves as a confidence criterion, ensuring that only detections with a class score above 50% are valid.

The second step is to process the input image $\mathbf{X}_{LR}$, which has a low resolution, with a convolutional neural network $\mathcal{F}$ to enhance the resolution. The model generates a high-resolution image, denoted as $\mathbf{X}_{HR}$, through a specific upscaling factor (e.g., upscaling factor = 2).

$$\mathbf{X}_{HR} = \mathcal{F}(\mathbf{X}_{LR}) \tag{3}$$

Then, a sliding windows approach is applied to the super-resolved image X_{HR}, incorporating user-defined displacement parameters d:

$$x_{\text{windows}} = i \times d \qquad y_{\text{windows}} = j \times d \tag{4}$$

Where the coordinates of the sliding window are represented by $(x_{\text{windows}}, y_{\text{windows}})$. The indices representing the window's position are i and j. For each window $\mathcal{I}_{\text{window}}$, perform re-inference using the object detection model to obtain an additional set of bounding boxes denoted as S'.

$$S' = \left\{ \left(\tilde{\alpha}_i, \tilde{\beta}_i, \tilde{\gamma}_i, \tilde{\delta}_i, \epsilon_i, \omega_i \right) \mid i \in \{1, ..., I\} \right\} \tag{5}$$

Where I represents every super-resolved window extracted from X_{HR}. After the re-inference process, coordinates $(\tilde{\alpha}_i, \tilde{\beta}_i, \tilde{\gamma}_i, \tilde{\delta}_i)$ are obtained in the super-resolved image. It is necessary to undo the up-scaling and the displacement to translate these coordinates to the original image.

$$x_{\text{original}} = \frac{x'}{f} + x_{\text{window}}, \quad y_{\text{original}} = \frac{y'}{f} + y_{\text{window}} \tag{6}$$

Detections belonging to the same entity are grouped using the Intersection over Union (IOU). The formula for IOU between two bounding boxes is:

$$IOU(A, B) = \frac{\text{Area of Intersection}}{\text{Area of Union}} \tag{7}$$

Bounding boxes with an Intersection over Union (IOU) greater than a pre-defined threshold are grouped. After grouping coincident detections of the same element, selecting the most accurate detection becomes necessary. A weighting is applied to the detections obtained within the generated sliding windows to facilitate this. The decision to assign five times more importance to bounding boxes obtained in the initial inference stage on the normal-resolution image without super-resolution is motivated by the need to handle scenarios where, despite accurate detection of a cell in the first stage, re-inference through sliding windows may only yield partial detections of the same cell.

$$w_{\text{initial}} = \text{selected weigth} \times w_{\text{initial reinference}} \tag{8}$$

$$w_{\text{window}} = 1 \times w_{\text{initial reinference}} \tag{9}$$

The reason for this weighting stems from recognizing that the initial inference, conducted on the original low-resolution image, holds paramount significance. It should exert a more substantial influence in determining the precise position and shape of the cell. Re-inference, occurring after super-resolution and sliding window scanning, may face limitations due to potential partial cell detections.

After clustering bounding boxes for the same element, the average of all established bounding boxes is determined. Subsequently, the Euclidean distance between the calculated average and each bounding box is computed:

$$D(\text{bbox}_{\text{average}}, \text{bbox}_i) = \sqrt{\sum_{j=1}^{n}(\text{bbox}_{\text{average}}^{(j)} - \text{bbox}_i^{(j)})^2} \tag{10}$$

Where n represents the dimensionality of the bounding boxes. Following this, the index of the bounding box with the smallest distance to the average is identified:

$$\text{index}_{\text{min}} = \arg\min_i \left(\sum_{j=1}^{n}(\text{bbox}_{\text{average}}^{(j)} - \text{bbox}_i^{(j)})^2 \right) \tag{11}$$

Finally, the closest bounding box to the calculated average is obtained as:

$$\text{closest}_{\text{bbox}} = \text{bbox}_{\text{index}_{\text{min}}} \tag{12}$$

A unified class label is obtained by majority voting among the class labels in the clustering operation for each element, and a unified class score is computed as the maximum of the class scores.

3   Experiments

This section is composed of a series of subsections. First, the dataset used is described to provide a context for the type of elements to be identified and to discuss the attributes of the data. Subsequently, several models focused on object detection are stated, which have been subsequently evaluated with well-defined metrics. Finally, the results are provided, comprising a comparative analysis between the raw object detection models and the results obtained after applying the described methodology.

3.1   Dataset

In the field of breast pathology, a series of datasets have been published that open the possibility of applying algorithms and deep learning models. In this case, a group of datasets called NuCLS [11] has been chosen. Non-pathological individuals (NPs) were employed to generate these datasets, following two strategies to acquire nuclei labels.

The first strategy (single-rater) aimed for broad data collection across numerous fields of view, with NPs receiving feedback and coordinators standardizing annotations. The second strategy (multi-rater) measured reliability using annotations from multiple NPs on a smaller set of shared fields alongside pathologist annotations for comparison. The project seeks to obtain a considerable amount

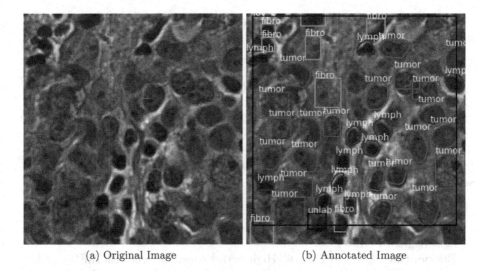

(a) Original Image   (b) Annotated Image

Fig. 2. Example of the annotated images that compose the NuCLS Dataset.

of high-quality data, which is why the reviewed single-rater dataset was used to fine-tune object detection models in this project. The NuCLS dataset contains breast cancer slides from 125 patients obtained from TCGA, a US National Cancer Institute project. The NuCLS dataset creators concentrated on triple-negative breast cancer images, marked by the absence of estrogen, progesterone receptors, and HER2 protein. This aggressive cancer type exhibits poorer survival rates. The complete dataset consists of 1744 images. An advantageous characteristic of this dataset is the substantial variability in cell types and patterns, enabling the training and evaluation of pathology-based object detection models using Convolutional Neural Networks. The objective of this study is to detect the maximum number of cells possible, making the specific cell types (classes) irrelevant to this proposal. Figure 2 shows an example of a labeled frame.

3.2 Super-Resolution Model

The use of super-resolution involves the application of advanced models and techniques to increase the number of pixels that compose the input. A series of models are available for super-resolution applications such as [12,13]. One of the most effective models is FastSRCNN (Fast Super-Resolution Convolutional Neural Network) [14]. This convolutional neural network was designed to address the super-resolution task efficiently and quickly. It has many advantages, such as preserving fine details during the resolution enhancement process. Compared to other models, it is particularly fast, making it suitable for applications that require results in a short time. It is important to note that the proposed methodology allows flexibility in switching to other super-resolution techniques according to the specific needs of the problem to be solved, thus ensuring the method's adaptability.

3.3   Object Detection Models

Object detection models capable of identifying cell nuclei are required to apply the presented methodology. The dataset was divided into training, validation, and test subsets with proportions of 70%, 20%, and 10%, respectively. Following data splitting, fine-tuning was performed on various object detection models from the Tensorflow Object Detection Model Zoo[1]. The following models were selected:

- **SSD MobileNetV2 FPNLite** [15]: SSD (Single Shot Detector) is a single-shot object detection model using MobileNetV2 for feature extraction and lightweight FPNLite.
- **EfficientDet D0 and D2** [16]: High-performance models with BiFPN architecture, utilizing EfficientNet for scalability. D0 has a 3-layer, 64-filter BiFPN, and D2 features a scaled EfficientNet and a 5-layer, 112-filter BiFPN.
- **CenterNet Hourglass 104 512 × 512** [17]: CenterNet adopts a unique keypoint network to detect central points, leveraging an Hourglass backbone for deep feature extraction from stacked convolutional and max-pooling modules.

The choice of these models is based on the diversity of architectures to determine the improvement after applying the proposed methodology. The evaluation of SSD addresses the need for efficient single-stage models, while EfficientDet D0 and D2 represent variants of an efficient and scalable family. On the other hand, CenterNet provides a unique perspective. The generic design allows versatile adaptation to explore and evaluate new architectures.

3.4   Results

Metrics like Mean Average Precision (MAP) were utilized to assess the proposed approach. The COCO evaluator[2] was employed for mAP, considering multiple confidence thresholds across IoU values from 0.5 to 0.95. This range enables a detailed evaluation of model performance regarding overlap with ground truth bounding boxes. The results are shown from the exhaustive evaluation of several object detection models, both in their original state (RAW) and after applying the proposed methodology (OURS). The main metric used to quantify the performance of the models was the Mean Average Precision (mAP), considering different Intersection over Union (IoU) configurations.

---

[1] https://github.com/tensorflow/models/blob/master/research/object_detection/g3doc/tf2_detection_zoo.md.

[2] https://github.com/cocodataset/cocoapi/blob/master/PythonAPI/pycocotools/cocoeval.py.

Table 1. Results obtained after using different object detection models comparing the Raw model and the presented methodology. The best results are marked in **bold**.

Model	Method	Area All IoU 0.50:0.95	Area All IoU 0.50	Area All IoU 0.75	Area Small IoU 0.50:0.95	Area Medium IoU 0.50:0.95
EfficientDet D0	RAW	0.244	0.462	**0.226**	0.207	0.280
	OURS	**0.253**	**0.502**	0.216	**0.213**	**0.291**
EfficientDet D2	RAW	0.195	0.356	0.196	0.175	0.212
	OURS	**0.239**	**0.459**	**0.221**	**0.235**	**0.242**
SSD MobileNetV2	RAW	0.262	0.502	0.241	0.258	0.271
	OURS	**0.296**	**0.593**	**0.261**	**0.266**	**0.319**
CenterNet Hourglass 104	RAW	0.097	0.161	**0.103**	0.078	0.114
	OURS	**0.098**	**0.171**	0.102	**0.078**	**0.117**

The obtained analysis reveals overall improvements using the presented methodology. A sustained elevation in Mean Average Precision (mAP) is discernible across various Intersection over Union (IoU) configurations, underscoring the effectiveness of this approach in different object detection scenarios. Notably, deploying the methodology generates overall performance improvements and demonstrates a uniformly positive impact regardless of the base model chosen. This finding underscores the overall robustness and applicability of the proposed method, suggesting that its implementation can consistently produce positive results across a spectrum of object detection environments. Table 1 compares the mean average precision (mAP). The results obtained by each proposal are shown.

Beyond the overall performance improvement, the performance optimization of our methodology is particularly striking in the total area under different IoU values, where a more pronounced increase in mAP is observed. This specific result underlines the methodology's effectiveness in scenarios requiring a high degree of overlap between predictions and actual annotations.

While the RAW model occasionally exhibits a marginally higher Mean Average Precision (MAP), providing quantitative insights into the improvement is crucial. Our methodology, labeled as OURS, consistently outperforms the RAW model across various evaluation metrics. For example, considering the Area All with IoU 0.50:0.95, OURS achieves a notable improvement, with an increase of approximately 3.5% compared to RAW. This emphasizes the effectiveness of our methodology in enhancing object detection accuracy in scenarios requiring a high degree of overlap. Examining specific areas, such as Area Small and Medium with IoU 0.50:0.95, OURS demonstrates significant advancements. Area Small has an improvement of around 3.1%, while Area Medium shows an enhancement of approximately 4.9%. These results underscore the ability of OURS to address challenges associated with object detection in contexts with varying dimensions, especially in smaller and medium-sized regions. Table 1 presents a comprehensive overview of the quantitative results obtained from different object detection models, comparing the RAW model with OURS. The values in **bold** highlight the superior performance of OURS across diverse model configurations and evaluation criteria.

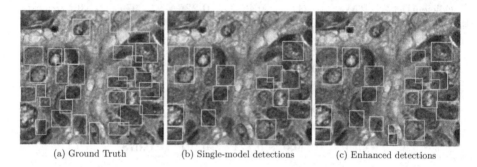

(a) Ground Truth   (b) Single-model detections   (c) Enhanced detections

Fig. 3. Comparison of the detections obtained. The left-hand side is the Ground Truth, followed by the Raw model, and on the right-hand side is the presented methodology using the EfficientDet D2 model.

Figures 3 and 4 provide a visual comparison of the detections obtained by applying the model in its original state (RAW) and the proposed methodology (OURS). These figures highlight how our methodology's application has significantly influenced the cell detection process.

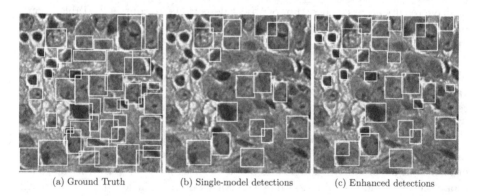

(a) Ground Truth   (b) Single-model detections   (c) Enhanced detections

Fig. 4. Comparison of the detections obtained. The left-hand side is the Ground Truth, followed by the Raw model, and on the right-hand side is the presented methodology using the SSD model.

As seen in the images, the number of detections increases when applying the OURS methodology compared to the RAW model. This observation underlines our approach's effectiveness in improving the system's ability to accurately identify and delimit the cells present in the analyzed images.

4 Conclusions and Future Lines

In conclusion, the results obtained in this study support the effectiveness of the presented methodology in improving the performance of object detection models compared to their original versions. The consistency in the observed improvements, regardless of the base model and variations in IoU configurations, highlights our approach's overall relevance and applicability in computer vision. In a quantitative analysis, the positive impact of the methodology is especially highlighted by observing the significant increase in Mean Average Precision (mAP), being most notably evident in the case of SSD MobileNet V2, where the best result was achieved with a mAP of 0.296 in the total area with IoU of 0.50:0.95. As illustrated in Figs. 1 and 2, visual comparisons further support the quantitative improvement, showing a substantial increase in the number of detections.

Considering the achievements obtained, several lines of research are open for future development. One promising direction is integrating more advanced deep learning techniques and considering emerging model architectures, which could contribute to the evolution and continuous improvement of the proposed methodology. In addition, incorporating specialized data augmentation techniques could enhance the methodology's ability to address specific challenges in complex environments.

Acknowledgement. This work is partially supported by the Ministry of Science and Innovation of Spain, grant number PID2022-136764OA-I00, project name Automated Detection of Non Lesional Focal Epilepsy by Probabilistic Diffusion Deep Neural Models. It is also partially supported by the University of Málaga (Spain) under grants B1-2021_20, project name Detection of coronary stenosis using deep learning applied to coronary angiography; B4-2022, project name Intelligent Clinical Decision Support System for Non-Obstructive Coronary Artery Disease in Coronarographies; B1-2022_14, project name Detección de trayectorias anómalas de vehículos en cámaras de tráfico; and, by the Fundación Unicaja under project PUNI-003_2023, project name Intelligent System to Help the Clinical Diagnosis of Non-Obstructive Coronary Artery Disease in Coronary Angiography. The authors thankfully acknowledge the computer resources, technical expertise and assistance provided by the SCBI (Supercomputing and Bioinformatics) center of the University of Málaga. They also gratefully acknowledge the support of NVIDIA Corporation with the donation of a RTX A6000 GPU with 48Gb. The authors also thankfully acknowledge the grant of the Universidad de Málaga and the Instituto de Investigación Biomédica de Málaga y Plataforma en Nanomedicina-IBIMA Plataforma BIONAND.

References

1. García-Aguilar, I., García-González, J., Luque-Baena, R.M., López-Rubio, E.: Object detection in traffic videos: an optimized approach using super-resolution and maximal clique algorithm. Neural Comput. Appl. **35**(26), 18999–19013 (2023)
2. Ushasukhanya, S., Naga Malleswari, T.Y.J., Karthikeyan, M., Jayavarthini, C.: An intelligent deep learning based capsule network model for human detection in indoor surveillance videos. Soft. Comput. **28**(1), 737–747 (2023)

3. García-Aguilar, I., García-González, J., Luque-Baena, R.M., López-Rubio, E.: Automated labeling of training data for improved object detection in traffic videos by fine-tuned deep convolutional neural networks. Pattern Recogn. Lett. **167**, 45–52 (2023)

4. García-Aguilar, I., Luque-Baena, R.M., López-Rubio, E.: Improved detection of small objects in road network sequences using CNN and super resolution. Exp. Syst. **39**(2), e12930 (2022)

5. García-Aguilar, I., García-González, J., Medina, D., Luque-Baena, R.M., Domínguez, E., López-Rubio, E.: Detection of dangerously approaching vehicles over onboard cameras by speed estimation from apparent size. Neurocomputing **567**, 127057 (2024)

6. Khan, S.A., Lee, H.J., Lim, H.: Enhancing object detection in self-driving cars using a hybrid approach. Electronics **12**(13), 2768 (2023)

7. Le Hou, V., et al.: Sparse autoencoder for unsupervised nucleus detection and representation in histopathology images. Pattern Recogn. **86**, 188–200 (2019)

8. Obeid, A., Mahbub, T., Javed, S., Dias, J., Werghi, N.: NucDETR: end-to-end transformer for nucleus detection in histopathology images. In: Qin, W., Zaki, N., Zhang, F., Wu, J., Yang, F. (eds.) Computational Mathematics Modeling in Cancer Analysis, CMMCA 2022. LNCS, vol. 13574, pp. 47–57. Springer, Cham (2022). https://doi.org/10.1007/978-3-031-17266-3_5

9. Tian, C., Lei, S., Wang, Z., Li, A., Wang, M.: Semi-supervised nuclei detection in histopathology images via location-aware adversarial image reconstruction. IEEE Access **10**, 42739–42749 (2022)

10. Wang, Z., et al.: Cross-domain nuclei detection in histopathology images using graph-based nuclei feature alignment. IEEE J. Biomed. Health Inform. **28**(1), 78–88 (2024)

11. Amgad, M., et al.: NuCLS: a scalable crowdsourcing approach and dataset for nucleus classification and segmentation in breast cancer. GigaScience **11**, giac037 (2022)

12. Lai, W.-S., Huang, J.-B., Ahuja, N., Yang, M.-H.: Deep Laplacian pyramid networks for fast and accurate super-resolution. In: 2017 IEEE Conference on Computer Vision and Pattern Recognition (CVPR), pp. 5835–5843 (2017)

13. Kim, J., Lee, J.K., Lee, K.M.: Accurate image super-resolution using very deep convolutional networks (2016)

14. Dong, C., Loy, C.C., Tang, X.: Accelerating the super-resolution convolutional neural network. In: Leibe, B., Matas, J., Sebe, N., Welling, M. (eds.) ECCV 2016. LNCS, vol. 9906, pp. 391–407. Springer, Cham (2016). https://doi.org/10.1007/978-3-319-46475-6_25

15. Liu, W., et al.: SSD: single shot multibox detector. In: Leibe, B., Matas, J., Sebe, N., Welling, M. (eds.) ECCV 2016. LNCS, vol. 9905, pp. 21–37. Springer, Cham (2016). https://doi.org/10.1007/978-3-319-46448-0_2

16. Tan, M., Pang, R., Le, Q.V.: EfficientDet: scalable and efficient object detection (2020)

17. Duan, K., Bai, S., Xie, L., Qi, H., Huang, Q., Tian, Q.: CenterNet: keypoint triplets for object detection (2019)

Exploring Text-Driven Approaches
for Online Action Detection

Manuel Benavent-Lledo[1]📇, David Mulero-Pérez[1]📇, David Ortiz-Perez[1]📇,
Jose Garcia-Rodriguez[1(✉)]📇, and Sergio Orts-Escolano[2]📇

[1] Department of Computer Technology, University of Alicante, Raspeig, Spain
{mbenavent,dmulero,dortiz,jgarcia}@dtic.ua.es
[2] Department of Computer Science and Artificial Intelligence, University of Alicante,
Raspeig, Spain
sorts@ua.es

Abstract. The use of task-agnostic, pre-trained models for knowledge transfer has become more prevalent due to the availability of extensive open-source vision-language models (VLMs), and increased computational power. However, despite their widespread application across various domains, their potential for online action detection has not been fully explored. Current approaches rely on pre-extracted features from convolutional neural networks. In this paper we explore the potential of using VLMs for online action detection, emphasizing their effectiveness and capabilities for zero-shot and few-shot learning scenarios. Our research highlights the potential of VLMs in this field through empirical demonstrations of their robust performance, positioning them as a powerful tool for further enhancing the state of the art in online action detection.

Keywords: Online action detection · transformer · VLM · zero-shot · few-shot

1 Introduction

The goal of online action detection is to detect the occurrence of an action as soon as it happens, in other words classifying each frame of a video stream without any access to the future. This task has acquired much attention in recent years due to its wide range of applications including video surveillance [16,26], autonomous driving [23,30] or human-robot interaction [17,31].

Unlike action recognition or action segmentation, where videos are already trimmed for classification or they are trimmed and then classified, respectively. The online setting presents notable challenges closer to real world applications, such as the lack of information, the observation of partial actions or the large variability of negative data comprising background frames.

J. M. Ferrández Vicente et al. (Eds.): IWINAC 2024, LNCS 14675, pp. 55–64, 2024.
https://doi.org/10.1007/978-3-031-61137-7_6

Modeling the long-range temporal dependencies is essential to tackle this problem. Recurrent Neural Networks (RNN) have dominated this area for several years [1,12,14,37] and in spite of their theoretical ability to retain information of the past, results show they tend to struggle with long-range temporal dependencies and they have been surpassed by transformer based architectures.

Transformers have set up as a standard in the state-of-the-art because of the excellent performance shown in natural language processing [40], image analysis [11] and video analysis [2,28] thanks to the power of the self-attention mechanism for long-range temporal modeling. Several works have previously applied transformers to the online action detection problem [24,34,38,41], achieving outstanding performance. However, they rely on pre-extracted features and a high computation cost due to the attention mechanism. In contrast, vision-language models have demonstrated outstanding results for action recognition and video understanding.

In this paper we explore text-driven approaches for action recognition, focusing on the challenging task of online action detection. The aim is to demonstrate the zero-shot and few-shot capabilities of these approaches and provide insights into their potential for online action detection. We conduct extensive experiments on various input sizes besides addressing the limitations of this type of architectures using popular datasets, THUMOS14 and TVSeries. To the best of our knowledge, this is the first approach for zero-shot and few-shot online action detection.

The remaining of the paper is structured as follows. Section 2 summarizes relevant literature including action recognition, VLMs and online action detection. Section 3 delves into the methodology used for the experimentation. In Sect. 4 we present the experimental setup, results and ablation study. Finally, conclusions from this work are drawn in Sect. 5.

2   Related Works

2.1   Online Action Detection

In the last years, transformer architectures have achieved a breakthrough success in action recognition and video understanding [2,5,6,28], surpassing previous works based on different types of architectures [3,4,32] such as recurrent neural networks [12,14,37] and convolutional neural networks [7,8,13]. Video-transformer architectures exploit image-based transformers and use a transformer encoder for temporal aggregation.

On this basis, OadTR [34] was the first transformer introduced for online action detection, although it uses pre-extracted features using ResNet-200 [19] for RGB data and BN-Inception [20] for extracting features from optical flow. A transformer encoder captures the relationships between historical observations, while a decoder extracts auxiliary information by aggregating anticipated future clip representations. Similarly, the authors of LightTR [24] introduced a encoder-decoder transformer architecture with a simplified self-attention layers for more efficient online action detection.

In Colar [39], the problem is tackled considering that given a category, its representative frames exhibit various characteristics but category-level modeling can provide complimentary guidance to the temporal dependencies modeling. Authors propose an effective exemplar-consultation mechanism that first measures the similarity between a frame and exemplary frames, and then aggregates exemplary features based on the similarity weights.

A different approach was presented in LSTR [38]. A temporal modeling algorithm based on transformers employs long and short-term memory mechanism to model long-range dependencies, following a FIFO logic for storing the representations that are used during the encoding and decoding stages.

TesTRa [41] also addressed the problem using long and short-term memory mechanisms besides focusing on the issue of the computational complexity growing quadratically with the length of the considered dynamics. In this way the apply two different kinds of temporal smoothing kernels reusing much of the computation from frame to frame, and running faster than equivalent sliding-windows based transformers.

Alternatively, in an effort to improve the performance of recurrent neural networks the authors of MiniROAD [1] propose applying non-uniform weights to the loss computed at each time step after investigating the underlying reasons of RNNs not capturing long-range dependencies adequately. This allows the model to learn from the predictions made in an environment that better resembles the inference stage with an increased efficiency and yielding equal or better results. On the other side, WOAD [15] presents a weakly supervised framework for online action detection, being able to train using only video-level labels. To do so, two-jointly trained modules are used: a temporal proposal generator and an online action recognizer. LSTMs are used for aggregation of information.

2.2 Vision-Language Models

Vision-Language models (VLMs) have become a hot research topic in various fields due to their numerous applications and capabilities. Extending the basis of CLIP [29] to the video domain has resulted in many notable works as Video-CLIP [36]. Nevertheless, the computational requirements of video processing have resulted in a shift towards more efficient architectures such as [9,22,25,27].

Despite the fact that VLMs provide remarkable results, as stated in [33] pre-training requires an enormous computational cost and therefore using pre-trained models is essential in most cases. Moreover, the contrastive loss used for contrastive learning is dependent on the batch size as remarked in [35]. In this work, authors propose the use of text embeddings as initialization of a frozen classifier for action recognition. Experimental results demonstrate the efficacy of their proposal is lower for the same vision transformer, ViT-B/16 [11] as ActionCLIP [33], but it is compensated by using a larger one, ViT-L/14.

3   Methodology

Our work relies on the *"pretrain-prompt-finetune"* framework presented in [33]. This multimodal framework was introduced to face the problems of traditional action recognition methods, which address the task as a classic and standard 1-of-N majority vote problem, in which labels are mapped into numbers. Leveraging this framework instead allows to model the task as a vision-text multimodal learning problem, enhancing the representation through the use of natural language and enabling zero-shot and few-shot transfer. The overview of the presented architecture is depicted in Fig. 1. The framework consists of 3 parts:

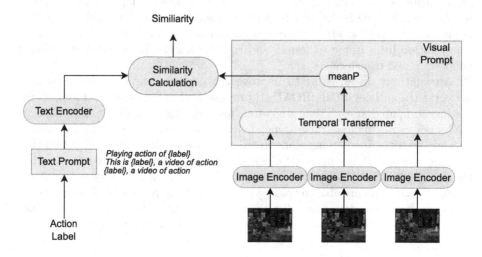

Fig. 1. Overview of the architecture. The image and text encoder extract unimodal features from video frames and action label. A 6-layer transformer temporally aggregates the frames (visual prompt). The action label is transformed into a extended text prompt in 3 different ways: prefix, suffix or cloze prompt. Finally, a similarity score is computed from text and visual embeddings.

Pre-train. Pre-training has a large impact on vision-language models. Given the requirements of this architecture we are interested in multimodal contrastive learning which aims to draw pairwise unimodal representations close to each other. This first step uses large scale datasets and has a huge computational cost. For this reason, in this work we use existing pre-trained models.

Prompt. Following [33], "prompt" is defined as reformulating the downstream task to act more like the upstream pre-training task. For this problem, matching the text and visual features extracted from the text and video encoders, respectively.

Fine-tune. It is well-known that fine-tuning on specific datasets will enhance the results significantly. Moreover, since the prompt step introduced additional parameters it is necessary to train the whole framework end-to-end.

Formally, this problem is model as $P(f(x,y)|\theta)$ instead of the classical $P(x,y|\theta)$, where x is the input video, y the original label belonging to $|\mathcal{Y}|$ and f a similarity function. The highest similarity score is the classification result during testing, in other words it is like a matching process:

$$\hat{y} = \underset{y \in \mathcal{Y}}{argmax} P(f(x,y)|\theta) \tag{1}$$

We use separate unimodal encoders for video frames and text. We use CLIP [29] pre-trained weights for this purpose with patch size 16, balancing the accuracy and computational requirements. Then, we aggregate the frames using 6 transformer encoder layers to encode temporal features. We train the model end-to-end using the Kullback-Leibler (KL) divergence to compute the loss as the amount of videos is much larger than the fixed labels. This is calculated as:

$$\mathcal{L} = \frac{1}{2}\mathbb{E}_{(x,y)\ \mathcal{D}} = [KL(p^{x2y}(x), q^{x2y}(x)) + KL(p^{y2x}(y), q^{y2x}(y))] \tag{2}$$

where p_i^{x2y} and p_i^{y2x} are the softmax-normalized video-to-text and text-to-video similarity scores calculated as:

$$p_i^{x2y}(x) = \frac{exp(s(x,y_i)/\tau)}{\sum_{j=1}^{N} exp(s(x,y_j)/\tau)}, p_i^{y2x}(y) = \frac{exp(s(y,x_i)/\tau)}{\sum_{j=1}^{N} exp(s(y,x_j)/\tau)} \tag{3}$$

where τ is a learnable temperature parameter and $s(\cdot)$ is the cosine distance between the two modalities:

$$s(x,y) = \frac{v \cdot w^{\mathsf{T}}}{\|v\| \cdot \|w\|}, s(y,x) = \frac{w \cdot v^{\mathsf{T}}}{\|w\| \cdot \|v\|} \tag{4}$$

4 Experiments

In this section, we evaluate the proposed method on widely used benchmarks, comparing the results to the state-of-the-art and showcasing the ability for zero-shot and few-shot transfer. Finally, we conduct ablation studies to evaluate the effectiveness of the different components.

4.1 Experimental Setup

Datasets. We conduct experiments on two widely used benchmarks, THU-MOS14 [21] and TVSeries [10]. The former includes sports videos from 20 action categories containing 200 videos for validation and 213 for testing. THUMOS14 challenges for online action detection contain drastic intra-category varieties, motion blur, short action instances, etc. Following previous work, we train the model on the validation set and evaluate performance on the test set. On the other side, TVSeries gathers about 16 h of video from 6 popular TV series. In total there are 6231 instances belonging to 30 different classes comprising daily actions. This benchmark exhibits challenges such as the temporal overlapping of actions, unconstrained perspectives and a large number of background frames.

Metrics. We follow previous methods [34,38,41] to evaluate the performance of our model, reporting per-frame mean Average Precision (mAP) to evaluate on the THUMOS14 dataset, and per-frame mean calibrated Average Precision (mcAP) to evaluate on TVSeries. The mAP is a widely used metric that needs the Average Precision (AP) of each class. The calibrated Average Precision was introduced in [10] to compensate the ratio of positive versus negative frames, in other words, to reduce the probability of falsely detecting background frames with higher confidence than true positives. It is calculated as follows:

$$ cPrec = \frac{TP}{TP + \frac{FP}{w}} = \frac{w \cdot TP}{w \cdot TP + FP} \tag{5} $$

where w is the ratio between negative and positive frames.

Implementation Details. We leverage the work from [33,35] for the implementation of the architecture. We use pre-trained CLIP [29] ViT-B/16 for feature extraction. Frame features are aggregated using a 6-layer transformer encoder.

Training Details. AdamW is used as optimizer alongside a learning rate of 5×10^{-5} with a cosine learning schedule. We train the models for 50 epochs with 0.2 weight decay and a resolution of 224×224. We experiment with different segments lengths (4, 8, 16 and 32 frames) with a downsampling rate of 6. Experiments have been conducted using 2 NVIDIA RTX 4090.

4.2   Zero-Shot/Few-Shot Action Detection

Due to the capabilities of VLMs for zero-shot and few-shot detection, we experiment with 7 different setups for the architecture varying the frame aggregation and segment length, the number of seen frames for prediction. We test segments lengths containing 4, 8, 16 and 32 frames. For each length we evaluate the effect of the Transformer encoder initialized to kinetics [33] and only CLIP initialization, since the transformer is not trained we apply directly mean pooling over the encoded features. For each setting, we evaluate the zero-shot capabilities and few-shot capabilities with 1, 2, 4 and 8 training samples. Figure 2 shows the results on THUMOS14 and TVSeries dataset for zero-shot and few-shot online action detection.

Results show that, in general, there is a tendency towards improved results with a higher number of frames obtaining a mAP of 31.52% for THUMOS14 dataset using a 16-frame window and the Kinetics initialization from [33]. The best results for TVSeries are obtained by the kinetics initialization with a 32-frame window with a mcAP of 76%. Although it is also worth mentioning that without transformer layers (only mean pooling) and 4 input frames 75.97% is obtained and with the same settings as THUMOS14 best result, the mcAP is 75.95%.

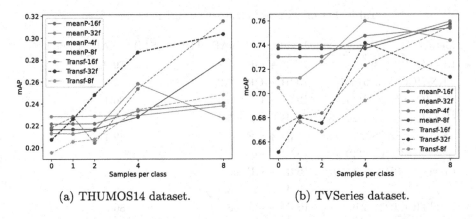

(a) THUMOS14 dataset.   (b) TVSeries dataset.

Fig. 2. Zero-shot and few-shot results.

4.3   Comparison with State-of-the-Art Methods

Given the best results for zero-shot and few-shot segment length and initialization, we train different models and compare them to state-of-the-art results (see Table 1). We use Kinetics initialization with a 16-frame segment length as it provided the best results for zero-shot and few-shot. Despite performing worse than existing methods, most previous work make use of pre-extracted features using RGB and optical flow data while our approach presents an end-to-end RGB model which is only comparable to Colar [39], however this model does not offer zero-shot and few-shot capabilities, as we do. Furthermore, we evaluate the performance of the model freezing CLIP, *i.e.* the image and text encoders, demonstrating that the features of this model can be used directly, reducing the computational cost during training. Finally, we have experimented with the approach presented in [35] where the text encoder embedding is used as weights of a multi-layer perceptron (MLP), despite significantly reducing the training cost, freezing CLIP encoder provides better results.

These results also highlight the capabilities of zero-shot and few-shot learning. We can see a minor reduction of 0.05% in mcAP for TVSeries but a more relevant decrease in THUMOS14 mAP with a difference of 15.17%, demonstrating the ability of text-driven approaches for online action detection.

Table 1. Comparison to state-of-the-art methods.

Method	Inputs	mAP (THUMOS14)	mcAP (TVSeries)
RED (2017) [14]	RGB + OF	45.3	79.2
TRN (ICCV 2019) [37]	RGB + OF	47.2	83.7
IDN (CVPR 2020) [12]	RGB + OF	60.3	86.1
OadTR (CVPR 2020) [34]	RGB + OF	65.2	87.2
LSTR (NeurIPS 2021) [38]	RGB + OF	69.5	89.1
TesTra (ECCV 2022) [41]	RGB + OF	71.2	-
Colar (CVPR 2022) [39]	RGB + OF	66.9	88.1
	RGB	58.6	86.8
LightTR (2023) [24]	RGB + OF	68.5	86.6
Ours (end-to-end)	RGB	46.69	75.45
Ours (frozen CLIP)	RGB	43.74	75.95
Ours (classifier as [35])	RGB	38.0	72.3

5   Conclusion

In this paper we have explored text-driven approaches for the online action detection task. Taking advantage of the "pre-train, prompt, fine-tune" framework, we have propose a novel approach for text-driven online action detection with zero-shot and few-shot capabilities experimenting on the main datasets for this task, THUMOS14 and TVSeries.

Despite not surpassing the state-of-the-art results, we have introduced a baseline for end-to-end RGB models exploiting pre-trained VLMs. Our extensive experiments have determined the most adequate segment length and temporal aggregators. Furthermore, we evaluate the performance of the models on different approaches with a reduced computational cost, an essential aspect when using transformers for video understanding.

Future work may delve deeper into the feature aggregation to improve the current results. As experimental results show, pre-extracted features only imply a small reduction in accuracy compared to training an end-to-end model, a more advanced temporal aggregation mechanism may be used with a bigger batch size to better exploit the contrastive loss. Finally, future research could also focus on enhancing the explainability [18] of the model's decisions, thereby ensuring transparency and interpretability in its functioning.

Acknowledgments. We would like to thank "A way of making Europe" European Regional Development Fund (ERDF) and MCIN/AEI/10.13039/501100011033 for supporting this work under the "CHAN-TWIN" project (grant TED2021-130890B-C21). HORIZON-MSCA-2021-SE-0 action number: 101086387, REMARKABLE, Rural Environmental Monitoring via ultra wide-ARea networKs And distriButed federated Learning and CIAICO/2022/132 Consolidated group project "AI4Health" funded by Valencian government. This work has also been supported by a Spanish national and two regional grants for PhD studies, FPU21/00414, CIACIF/2021/430 and CIACIF/2022/175. Finally, we would like to thank the support of the University Institute for Computer Research at the UA.

References

1. An, J., Kang, H., Han, S.H., Yang, M.H., Kim, S.J.: Miniroad: minimal RNN framework for online action detection. In: ICCV, pp. 10341–10350, October 2023
2. Arnab, A., Dehghani, M., Heigold, G., Sun, C., Lučić, M., Schmid, C.: Vivit: a video vision transformer (2021)
3. Azorin-Lopez, J., Saval-Calvo, M., Fuster-Guillo, A., Garcia-Rodriguez, J.: A novel prediction method for early recognition of global human behaviour in image sequences. Neural Process. Lett. **43**(2), 363–387 (2015)
4. Azorín-López, J., Saval-Calvo, M., Fuster-Guilló, A., García-Rodríguez, J.: Human behaviour recognition based on trajectory analysis using neural networks. In: IJCNN, pp. 1–7 (2013)
5. Bao, H., Dong, L., Piao, S., Wei, F.: Beit: Bert pre-training of image transformers. arXiv preprint arXiv:2106.08254 (2021)
6. Benavent-Lledo, M., Mulero-Pérez, D., Ortiz-Perez, D., Rodriguez-Juan, J., Berenguer-Agullo, A., Psarrou, A., Garcia-Rodriguez, J.: A comprehensive study on pain assessment from multimodal sensor data. Sensors **23**(24) (2023)
7. Benavent-Lledó, M., Oprea, S., Castro-Vargas, J.A., Martinez-Gonzalez, P., Garcia-Rodriguez, J.: Interaction estimation in egocentric videos via simultaneous hand-object recognition. In: SOCO, pp. 439–448 (2022)
8. Benavent-Lledo, M., Oprea, S., Castro-Vargas, J.A., Mulero-Perez, D., Garcia-Rodriguez, J.: Predicting human-object interactions in egocentric videos. In: IJCNN, pp. 1–7 (2022)
9. Cheng, F., Wang, X., Lei, J., Crandall, D., Bansal, M., Bertasius, G.: Vindlu: a recipe for effective video-and-language pretraining (2023)
10. De Geest, R., Gavves, E., Ghodrati, A., Li, Z., Snoek, C., Tuytelaars, T.: Online action detection. In: Leibe, B., Matas, J., Sebe, N., Welling, M. (eds.) ECCV 2016. LNCS, vol. 9909, pp. 269–284. Springer, Cham (2016). https://doi.org/10.1007/978-3-319-46454-1_17
11. Dosovitskiy, A., et al.: An image is worth 16x16 words: transformers for image recognition at scale (2021)
12. Eun, H., Moon, J., Park, J., Jung, C., Kim, C.: Learning to discriminate information for online action detection. In: CVPR, June 2020
13. Flórez-Revuelta, F., García-Chamizo, J.M., Garcia-Rodriguez, J., Hernández Sáez, A., et al.: Representation of 2d objects with a topology preserving network (2002)
14. Gao, J., Yang, Z., Nevatia, R.: Red: Reinforced encoder-decoder networks for action anticipation (2017)
15. Gao, M., Zhou, Y., Xu, R., Socher, R., Xiong, C.: Woad: weakly supervised online action detection in untrimmed videos. In: CVPR, pp. 1915–1923, June 2021
16. García-Rodríguez, J., García-Chamizo, J.M.: Surveillance and human-computer interaction applications of self-growing models. Appl. Soft Comput. **11**(7), 4413–4431 (2011)
17. Gomez-Donoso, F., Orts-Escolano, S., Garcia-Garcia, A., Garcia-Rodriguez, J., Castro-Vargas, J.A., Ovidiu-Oprea, S., Cazorla, M.: A robotic platform for customized and interactive rehabilitation of persons with disabilities. Pattern Recogn. Lett. **99**, 105–113 (2017)

18. Górriz, J., Álvarez Illán, I., Álvarez Marquina, A., Arco, J., Atzmueller, M., et al.: Computational approaches to explainable artificial intelligence: advances in theory, applications and trends. Inf. Fusion **100**, 101945 (2023)
19. He, K., Zhang, X., Ren, S., Sun, J.: Deep residual learning for image recognition. In: CVPR, pp. 770–778 (2016)
20. Ioffe, S., Szegedy, C.: Batch normalization: accelerating deep network training by reducing internal covariate shift. In: ICML, pp. 448–456 (2015)
21. Jiang, Y.G., Liu, J., et al.: Thumos challenge: Action recognition with a large number of classes (2014)
22. Ju, C., Han, T., Zheng, K., Zhang, Y., Xie, W.: Prompting visual-language models for efficient video understanding (2022)
23. Kim, J., Misu, T., Chen, Y.T., Tawari, A., Canny, J.: Grounding human-to-vehicle advice for self-driving vehicles. In: CVPR, June 2019
24. Li, R., Yan, L., Peng, Y., Qing, L.: Lighter transformer for online action detection, ICIGP 2023, pp. 161–167. Association for Computing Machinery (2023)
25. Li, Z., et al.: A strong baseline for temporal video-text alignment (2023)
26. Ni, P., Lv, S., Zhu, X., Cao, Q., Zhang, W.: A light-weight on-line action detection with hand trajectories for industrial surveillance. Digital Commun. Networks **7**(1), 157–166 (2021)
27. Papalampidi, P., et al.: A simple recipe for contrastively pre-training video-first encoders beyond 16 frames (2023)
28. Piergiovanni, A., Kuo, W., Angelova, A.: Rethinking video vits: sparse video tubes for joint image and video learning (2022)
29. Radford, A., et al.: Learning transferable visual models from natural language supervision (2021)
30. Ramanishka, V., Chen, Y.T., et al.: Toward driving scene understanding: a dataset for learning driver behavior and causal reasoning. In: CVPR (2018)
31. Tong, L., Ma, H., Lin, Q., He, J., Peng, L.: A novel deep learning bi-gru-i model for real-time human activity recognition using inertial sensors. IEEE Sens. J. **22**(6), 6164–6174 (2022)
32. Viejo, D., Garcia, J., Cazorla, M., Gil, D., Johnsson, M.: Using GNG to improve 3D feature extraction-application to 6DoF egomotion. Neural Netw. **32**, 138–146 (2012)
33. Wang, M., Xing, J., Liu, Y.: Actionclip: a new paradigm for video action recognition (2021)
34. Wang, X., et al.: Oadtr: online action detection with transformers. In: ICCV, pp. 7565–7575, October 2021
35. Wu, W., Sun, Z., Ouyang, W.: Revisiting classifier: transferring vision-language models for video recognition. In: AAAI Conference, vol. 37, pp. 2847–2855 (2023)
36. Xu, H., et al.: Videoclip: contrastive pre-training for zero-shot video-text understanding (2021)
37. Xu, M., Gao, M., Chen, Y.T., Davis, L.S., Crandall, D.J.: Temporal recurrent networks for online action detection. In: ICCV, October 2019
38. Xu, M., et al.: Long short-term transformer for online action detection. In: NeurIPS (2021)
39. Yang, L., Han, J., Zhang, D.: Colar: effective and efficient online action detection by consulting exemplars. In: CVPR (2022)
40. Zhao, W.X., et al.: A survey of large language models (2023)
41. Zhao, Y., Krähenbühl, P.: Real-time online video detection with temporal smoothing transformers. In: European Conference on Computer Vision (ECCV) (2022)

Deep Learning for Assistive Decision-Making in Robot-Aided Rehabilitation Therapy

David Martínez-Pascual(✉) , José. M. Catalán , Luis D. Lledó ,
Andrea Blanco-Ivorra , and Nicolás García-Aracil

Robotics and Artificial Intelligence Group of the Bioengineering Institute, Miguel
Hernández University, Avenida de la Universidad, s/n. 03202 Elche, Alicante, Spain
{david.martinezp,jcatalan,llledo,ablanco,nicolas.garcia}@umh.es

Abstract. The use of robotic rehabilitation devices has emerged as a
promising approach to enhance motor recovery during rehabilitation.
One of the significant challenges while using these devices is the ability
to decide when to provide assistance to the patient. In this regard, we
propose a Deep Learning-based solution that can learn from a therapist's
criteria when a patient requires assistance during robot-aided rehabilitation therapy. We have trained and evaluated the proposed model with
data from different patients during a point-to-point game modality. To
make the model more universal, we have applied a series of transformations to the trajectory data before using them as inputs. The proposed
model has been evaluated using different metrics and has shown an accuracy of 93.21% and an F1-Score of 85.05% with the validation dataset.
Furthermore, the model has achieved an accuracy of 69.32% and an F1-
Score of 63.31% with users who were not involved in the model learning
process.

Keywords: Rehabilitation Robotics · Neurorehabilitation · Deep
Learning · Exergames

1 Introduction

Around 15 million people worldwide suffer from cerebrovascular accident (CVA)
every year [21]. The number of CVAs is also expected to increase by 34% between
2015 and 2035 in the European Union (EU). In most cases, CVAs survivors experience hemiparesis, which causes a significant deterioration in their health-related
quality of life (HRQoL) [15,17]. In most cases, an appropriate rehabilitation program can help people suffering from hemiparesis to at least partially recover limb

This research was funded by the Spanish Ministry of Universities through the Research
and Doctorate Supporting Program FPU20/05137, through the project PID2019-
108310RB-I00, and through the project PID2022-139957OB-I00; by the Spanish
Agency of Innovation through the project PLEC2022-009424, and through the project
TED2021-130431B-I00.

J. M. Ferrández Vicente et al. (Eds.): IWINAC 2024, LNCS 14675, pp. 65–74, 2024.
https://doi.org/10.1007/978-3-031-61137-7_7

movement [2]. In this context, robotic rehabilitation devices have proven to be a promising approach to support the rehabilitation process for motor recovery after stroke. These robotic devices provide highly standardized and intensive therapy while providing tools to monitor the patient's recovery progress. The main purpose of robotic rehabilitation devices is to assist the patient in performing exercises that are designed to make therapy attractive and fun, with the aim of motivating the patient.

Some studies suggest that the use of robots in therapy to provide therapist-robot-patient interactions has potential advantages over conventional therapist-patient interactions in occupational rehabilitation [7]. However, there is currently a lack of understanding regarding the benefits of therapist-robot-patient interactions, as in most robot-assisted therapies the patient only interacts with the robot.

Several assistance methods based on different robotic rehabilitation devices can be found in the literature, which differs mainly in the strategy used to provide assistance to the user [3,4,14]. However, none of these methods involve the interaction of the therapist. In a previous study, it was observed that a therapist is better equipped to determine the appropriate way and time to assist the patient during exercises than a typical fixed assistance method implemented in a robotic rehabilitation device [5]. In other words, real-time assistance provided by a therapist is better adapted to the needs of the patients, maximizing their effort and potentially improving patient recovery, which professionals have identified as a critical factor in rehabilitation outcomes [8,13].

This study aims to investigate a new intelligent assistance approach for rehabilitation robotics that can better adapt to the needs of patients. Our strategy is to develop an assistance-as-needed method based on the therapists' decision-making, to provide better adaptation of the assistance provided to the patients. With this purpose, a Deep Learning model has been trained and evaluated using data collected in a previous study by our research group [5]. In that study, different patients played a point-to-point serious game and a therapist provided assistance when considered necessary. Based on the movements performed by a patient, our model classifies whether assistance is needed during a robot-aided exercise according to the therapist's criteria.

2   Materials and Methods

2.1   Subjects

The study has been performed in La Pedrera Hospital (Denia, Spain) with patients suffering from neurological conditions (shown in Table 1). The rehabilitation therapists were responsible for establishing the inclusion criteria, which included: adults with hemiparesis/hemiplegia, oriented to the three spheres (social, temporal, and spatial), with the capacity of collaboration and understanding the tasks instruction and all relevant information from the study. The STREAM test was employed to evaluate the patient's coordination, functional voluntary movement, and range of motion [1]. Only the score obtained from the upper limb was taken into account.

The experimental protocol was approved by the Ethical Committee of La Pedrera Hospital. All patients were informed properly by the rehabilitation team and the researchers in charge of doing the experimentation and they gave written consent before starting pointing out they understood the purpose and requirements of the study.

Table 1. Information about the patients.

Patients	Sex	Age (years)	Diagnostic	Laterality	STREAM
1	Male	72	Abdominal Dystension	Right	10/16
2	Male	51	Basal Ganglia hematoma	Right	11/16
3	Male	70	Bilateral SARS-CoV2 pneumonia	Left	N/A
4	Male	78	Ischemic stroke atherothrombotic	Right	11/16
5	Female	84	Ischemic stroke	Right	7/16
6	Male	69	Protuberance ischemic stroke	Left	7/16
7	Male	69	Thalamic capsule-lacunar stroke	Right	0/16
8	Male	62	Chronic ischemic heart disease	Right	8/16

Note. **N/A**, not available value; **ACM**, Artery Cerebral Middle; **STREAM**, Stroke Rehabilitation Assessment of Movement, the value indicate the score obtained for the upper limb movement.

2.2 Experimental Setup and Data Collection

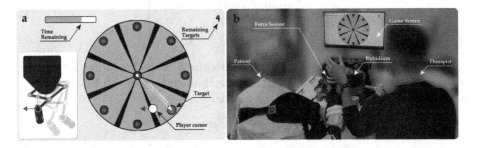

Fig. 1. Overview of the different elements of the experimental setup. **(a)** Overview of the point-to-point game used during the rehabilitation sessions. On the left, the Rubidium robot, an upper-limb rehabilitation device is shown. The Rubidium robot is commercialized and distributed by the spin-off iDRhA [11]. **(b)** Image of the experimental setup.

The setup used for data collection is shown in Fig. 1. As described in [5], an upper-limb rehabilitation robotic device called Rubidium (Fig. 1) was employed in the study. This rehabilitation robotic platform is an articulated parallelogram mechanism driven by two electric motors that perform movements in a horizontal plane. It supports the weight of the patient's forearm as they rest their arm on an orthosis anchored to the end effector.

The virtual task performed in the study consists of a point-to-point modality where patients must reach a point on the periphery of the roulette shown in Fig. 1 from its center.

In this study, a master-slave assistance strategy was used in which the robotic rehabilitation device does not provide assistance to the patient, but rather the assistance is provided by the therapist interacting directly with the patient. The therapist applied force on the end effector of the Rubidium, for which an onRobot HEX force sensor attached to the end-effector was added to the robot to register the assistance (Fig. 1). In this way, we are able to measure the force exerted by the therapist, and the time at which the assistance is given.

2.3   Data Processing

It is intended that the method proposed in this work can be used during different serious games or exercises based on the dynamics of achieving goals. Therefore, it is necessary to apply a series of transformations to the data acquired from the Rubidium rehabilitation robot before their introduction as inputs to the Deep Learning model. The applied processing has been represented in Fig. 2.

First, each of the trajectory points P_r between the starting point S_r and the target point G_r has been taken. To each P_r the transformation $_rT^u$ has been applied. By applying $_rT^u$ we transform $S_r \rightarrow S_u = (0,0)$ and P_r is aligned with the X-axis. The transformation $_rT^u$ is expressed as:

$$_rT^u = \begin{bmatrix} cos(\theta_x) & -sin(\theta_x) & 0 & -S_{r,x} \\ sin(\theta_x) & cos(\theta_x) & 0 & -S_{r,y} \\ 0 & 0 & 1 & 0 \\ 0 & 0 & 0 & 1 \end{bmatrix} \tag{1}$$

where θ_x is the angle of the vector $\boldsymbol{PG}$ with the X-axis. Applying $_rT^u$ we can obtain the trajectory performed by the user P_a aligned with the X-axis, as well as the target point G_a located on the X-axis.

$$P_a =_r T^u \cdot P_r \tag{2}$$

$$G_a =_r T^u \cdot G_r \tag{3}$$

Finally, a scale factor has been applied to P_a in the X-axis to transform $G_a \rightarrow G_u = (1,0)$:

$$P_u = \begin{bmatrix} \frac{1}{G_{a,x}} & 0 & 0 & 0 \\ 0 & 1 & 0 & 0 \\ 0 & 0 & 1 & 0 \\ 0 & 0 & 0 & 1 \end{bmatrix} \cdot P_a \tag{4}$$

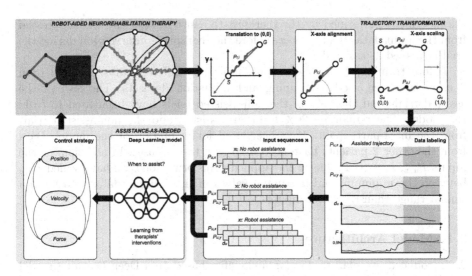

Fig. 2. Assistance-as-needed proposed strategy during robot-aided therapy. The patient performs a movement and the end-effector of the robot Cartesian coordinates are acquired. According to the starting point S_r and the goal position G_r the trajectory is aligned with the X-axis and scaled. In order to train the model and learn from the therapist's assistance criteria according to the measurements of the force sensor placed on the end-effector of the robot. The trajectories are split into sequences of two seconds. The sequences are introduced to the Deep Learning model as inputs, which learns from the therapist's interventions and classifies if the patient needs assistance according to the performed movements.

Once the transformations are applied, the distance to the target d_u has been calculated for each instance:

$$d_u = \|\overrightarrow{P_u G_u}\| \tag{5}$$

To detect the assistance provided by the therapist, the force F was measured with the force sensor placed on the end effector of the robot. For each P_u, if F is greater than 0.5N, the trajectory is labeled as assisted. On the contrary, is labeled as not assisted. In this sense:

$$Y = \begin{cases} 0 & \text{if } F \leq 0.5 \\ 1 & \text{if } F > 0.5 \end{cases} \tag{6}$$

In order to learn if the patient needs assistance, the dataset $\mathcal{D} : (x, y)$ has been used for model training, where $x \in X = \{P_{u,x}, P_{u,y}, d_u\}$ is the input and $y \in Y$ is the output. As the problem is addressed as a multivariate time-series classification, we use as input a vector x_t which contains the last two second measurements to predict y_t. The data is acquired from the Rubidium robot at 33 Hz, so x_t is composed of the last 66 samples, $(x_{t-65}, x_{t-64}, ..., x_{t-1}, x_t) \in X$.

We must note that only the data obtained from the patient's performed movements are introduced as inputs of the model. Once the assistance was detected, the movement performed by the therapist to assist the patient was suppressed from the input data. Hence, the x_t before the therapist's intervention during the trial is labeled as assisted.

Before training, $\mathcal{D}$ has been split into three different subsets. Data from 6 users has been used as training and validation datasets. The 80% of the assisted trials and the 80% of the non-assisted trials have been used to train the model. The remaining 20% from the assisted and the non-assisted trials from the intra-participants have been used for validation of the model. Data from the other 2 patients have been used as a test dataset. In addition, as the inputs $P_{u,x}, d_u \in (0, 1)$ due to the applied transformations, we have scaled $P_{u,y}$ between the minimum and maximum values of the training dataset to be in a similar range than the other inputs.

2.4   Model Architecture

As introduced, we plan to develop a classifier based on a Deep Learning model in order to learn from the therapist when to assist. The problem can be defined as learning a classification function $\hat{y} = f(x_t)$, such that $\hat{y}_t \approx y_t, \forall x_t \in X$.

We propose to train a Deep Learning model based on the Encoder proposed by Serrà et al., whose architecture is specially designed for time series classification [20]. The model is composed of one-dimensional convolutional layers, with a convolutional attention mechanism to summarize the time axis, and a final fully-connected layer.

The first convolution is composed of 128 filters of length 5; the second convolution is composed of 256 filters of length 11; the third convolution is composed of 512 filters of length 21. Each convolution is followed by an instance normalization operation [22] whose output is fed to the Parametric Rectified Linear Unit (PReLU) activation function [10]. The output of PReLU is followed by a dropout operation (with a rate equal to 0.2) and a final max-pooling of length 2. After these layers, half of the filters are input to a time-wise softmax activation, which acts as an attention mechanism [16] for the other half of the filters. The result of the attention mechanism for all filters is finally passed through a fully-connected layer of 256 neurons and an instance normalization layer. Finally, a layer with one neuron is used as the output of the model. In the fully-connected layers, the Sigmoid activation function [18] was used for our binary classification problem. The total number of trainable parameters of the model is 3188865.

The model has been implemented and trained using Keras and Tensorflow [9], using the Binary Cross-Entropy loss function [19] and a batch size of 256. To avoid overfitting, the validation dataset loss has been monitored, stopping the training if the measured loss did not improve for 5 epochs. After the early stopping occurred, the parameters of the model that obtained the minimum loss were restored.

Table 2. Model evaluation results. The accuracy, the recall, the specificity, the false positive rate, the false negative rate, and the F1-Score are used to evaluate the performance of the proposed model to classify when the assistance during robot-aided exercises.

Metric	Training	Validation	Test
Accuracy (%)	95.00	93.21	69.32
Recall (%)	88.93	76.81	58.65
Specificity (%)	96.60	98.72	78.10
False positive rate (%)	3.39	1.28	21.90
False negative rate (%)	11.07	23.19	41.35
F1-Score (%)	88.12	85.05	63.31

3 Results and Discussion

Table 2 collects the accuracy, the recall, the specificity, the false positive rate, and the F1-Score when evaluating the proposed model with the training, validation, and test datasets [12]. In Fig. 3 the Receiver Operating Characteristic (ROC) curve has been represented for the validation and test datasets, and the area under the curves (AUC) values have been included [6]. In addition, the confusion matrices for the validation and test datasets are represented in Fig. 4.

The evaluation metrics show a high model performance with patients involved in the learning process. With the validation dataset, the model achieves 93.21% accuracy, a false positive rate of 1.28%, a false negative rate of 11.07%, and an F1-Score of 85.05%. In Fig. 3 it can also be observed how the proposed model achieves high performance with the validation dataset, with a ROC curve close to

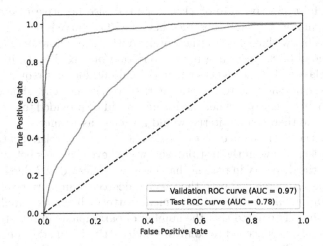

Fig. 3. Receiver Operating Characteristic (ROC) curves obtained with the proposed classifier for the validation and test datasets.

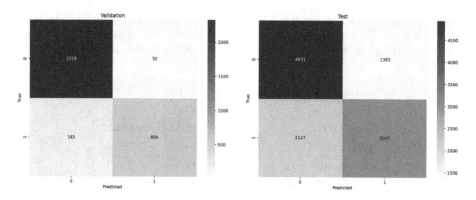

Fig. 4. Confusion matrices obtained with the proposed classifier for the validation and test datasets.

the ideal classifier, with an AUC value of 0.97. According to Fig. 4, the proposed model can classify 2319 non-assisted trajectory sequences and 606 assisted trajectory sequences correctly. It is worth noting that only 183 assisted trajectory sequences were incorrectly classified as non-assisted. These results are considered positive since some sequences during assisted trajectories are distant from the therapist's intervention. This means that certain sequences may be classified as non-assisted, but if the patient fails to reach their goal, it may be detected that they require assistance at a later time. Additionally, the model has identified that the patient would require assistance in only 30 sequences during non-assisted trajectories.

Regarding the results obtained with the test dataset, it can be observed that the performance of the proposed model decreases with patients who are not involved in the model training. The accuracy obtained with these patients is 69%, with a false positive rate of 21.90% and a false negative rate of 41.35%. Furthermore, in Fig. 3 it can be observed how the ROC curve is further away from the ideal classifier with respect to that obtained with the validation dataset, with an AUC value of 0.78. According to the confusion matrix (Fig. 4), it is possible to correctly classify 4931 sequences where the patient does not require assistance and 3045 where he/she requires assistance. However, special care should be taken with the 1383 false positives, where assistance would be provided to patients who, according to the therapist's criteria, would not need assistance.

Although the performance of the assistance-as-needed classification model has shown a decrease with the test dataset, we believe that this behavior can be attributed to the disparity in patient diagnoses, as indicated in Table 1. The variation in diagnoses, combined with the varying degrees of impairment among the patients, would result in different movement patterns being executed by them. Moreover, it should be noted that the number of participants in this study is low, and further analysis is needed to confirm this hypothesis. In addition, according to [2] the personalization of the rehabilitation therapy is a key to the motor and cognitive impairment recovery. Hence, we will study how to personalize the proposed model for each patient, based on a global assistance-as-needed model.

4 Conclusion

In this work, we propose a Deep Learning-based solution to learn from a therapist's criteria when a patient needs assistance during robot-aided rehabilitation therapy. The proposed model has been trained and evaluated with data from different patients during a point-to-point game modality. A series of transformations have been applied to the trajectory data before their introduction as inputs of the model in order to universalize the method.

The proposed model has been evaluated using different metrics, indicating an accuracy of 93.21% and an F1-Score of 85.05% with the validation dataset, while achieving a 69.32% accuracy and a 63.31% F1-Score with users not involved in the model learning process.

We believe that the results achieved are promising, and we pretend to include a larger number of patients in the model training and evaluation to develop an assistance-as-needed method for robot-aided therapies. In addition, we will study how to personalize the model for each patient starting from a global model, using techniques such as transfer learning.

References

1. Ahmed, S., Mayo, N.E., Higgins, J., Salbach, N.M., Finch, L., Wood-Dauphinee, S.L.: The stroke rehabilitation assessment of movement (stream): a comparison with other measures used to evaluate effects of stroke and rehabilitation. Phys. Therapy **83**(7), 617–630 (2003). https://doi.org/10.1093/ptj/83.7.617
2. Alessandro, L., et al.: Multidisciplinary rehabilitation for adult patients with stroke. Medicina **80**(1), 54–68 (2020)
3. Blank, A.A., French, J.A., Pehlivan, A.U., O'Malley, M.K.: Current trends in robot-assisted upper-limb stroke rehabilitation: promoting patient engagement in therapy. Curr. Phys. Med. Rehabil. Rep. **2**(3), 184–195 (2014). https://doi.org/10.1007/s40141-014-0056-z
4. Catalán, J.M., et al.: Patients' physiological reactions to competitive rehabilitation therapies assisted by robotic devices. J. NeuroEng. Rehabil. **20**(41) (2023)
5. Catalán, J.M., et al.: Tele-rehabilitation versus local rehabilitation therapies assisted by robotic devices: a pilot study with patients. Appl. Sci. **11**(14), 6259 (2021)
6. Flach, P.A.: Roc analysis. In: Encyclopedia of Machine Learning and Data Mining, pp. 1–8. Springer (2016)
7. Fong, J., Ocampo, R., Gross, D.P., Tavakoli, M.: Intelligent robotics incorporating machine learning algorithms for improving functional capacity evaluation and occupational rehabilitation. J. Occup. Rehabil. **30**, 362–370 (2020)
8. Friedrich, M., Gittler, G., Halberstadt, Y., Cermak, T., Heiller, I.: Combined exercise and motivation program: effect on the compliance and level of disability of patients with chronic low back pain: a randomized controlled trial. Arch. Phys. Med. Rehabil. **79**(5), 475–487 (1998). https://doi.org/10.1016/S0003-9993(98)90059-4

9. Gulli, A., Pal, S.: Deep learning with Keras. Packt Publishing Ltd. (2017)
10. He, K., Zhang, X., Ren, S., Sun, J.: Delving deep into rectifiers: surpassing human-level performance on imagenet classification. In: Proceedings of the IEEE International Conference on Computer Vision, pp. 1026–1034 (2015)
11. iDRhA: https://idrha.es/
12. Koyejo, O.O., Natarajan, N., Ravikumar, P.K., Dhillon, I.S.: Consistent binary classification with generalized performance metrics. Advances in neural information processing systems **27** (2014)
13. Maclean, N., Pound, P., Wolfe, C., Rudd, A.: A critical review of the concept of patient motivation in the literature on physical rehabilitation. Soc. Sci. Med. **50**(4), 495–506 (2000). https://doi.org/10.1016/s0277-9536(99)00334-2
14. Marchal-Crespo, L., Reinkensmeyer, D.: Review of control strategies for robotic movement training after neurologic injury. J. Neuro Eng. Rehabil. **6**, 20. https://doi.org/10.1186/1743-0003-6-20
15. Nichols-Larsen, D.S., Clark, P., Zeringue, A., Greenspan, A., Blanton, S.: Factors influencing stroke survivors' quality of life during subacute recovery. Stroke **36**(7), 1480–1484 (2005)
16. Niu, Z., Zhong, G., Yu, H.: A review on the attention mechanism of deep learning. Neurocomputing **452**, 48–62 (2021)
17. van Peppen, R., et al.: Kngf clinical practice guideline for physical therapy in patients with stroke. review of the evidence. Nederlands Tijdschrift voor Fysiotherapie **114**(5) (2004)
18. Pratiwi, H., et al.: Sigmoid activation function in selecting the best model of artificial neural networks. J. Phys. Conf. Ser. **1471**, 012010. IOP Publishing (2020)
19. Ruby, U., Yendapalli, V.: Binary cross entropy with deep learning technique for image classification. Int. J. Adv. Trends Comput. Sci. Eng. **9**(10) (2020)
20. Serra, J., Pascual, S., Karatzoglou, A.: Towards a universal neural network encoder for time series. In: CCIA, pp. 120–129 (2018)
21. Stevens, E., Emmett, E., Wang, Y., C., M., C, W.: The Burden of Stroke in Europe: The challenge for policy makers. Stroke Alliance for Europe (2017)
22. Ulyanov, D., Vedaldi, A., Lempitsky, V.: Instance normalization: The missing ingredient for fast stylization. arXiv preprint arXiv:1607.08022 (2016)

Text-Driven Data Augmentation Tool for Synthetic Bird Behavioural Generation

David Mulero-Pérez$^{(\boxtimes)}$ [ID], David Ortiz-Perez [ID], Manuel Benavent-Lledo [ID], Jose Garcia-Rodriguez [ID], and Jorge Azorin-Lopez [ID]

Department of Computer Technology, University of Alicante, Alicante, Spain
{dmulero,dortiz,mbenavent,jgarcia,jazorin}@dtic.ua.es

Abstract. Environmental conservation and biodiversity monitoring efforts have been greatly enhanced by the use of deep learning and computer vision technologies, particularly in protected areas such as parks and wildlife reserves. However, the development of accurate species recognition and behaviour understanding models is limited by the lack of detailed action annotations and reliance on static images, despite the availability of several animal datasets. This paper explores the use of generative models to tackle the challenge of creating comprehensive and diverse synthetic video data for identifying bird species and their behaviour. By utilising and fine-tuning different generative models, this study assesses the feasibility of synthetic video data generation to overcome these limitations. Our work focuses on generating realistic and varied video sequences that can improve machine learning algorithms for bird action detection and species recognition, thereby contributing to the protection and management of natural habitats. Throughout this investigation, we aim to provide new methodologies and tools for wildlife conservation technology, enhancing the monitoring and safeguarding of bird populations in their natural environments.

Keywords: Synthetic data · Data augmentation · Video generation · Bird behaviour

1 Introduction

The development of deep learning and computer vision technologies has ushered in a new era of environmental conservation and biodiversity monitoring, particularly in protected natural habitats such as parks and wildlife reserves [14,16]. An essential aspect of these efforts is the precise identification of animal species and the comprehension of their behaviours through video analysis [20]. Birds present a unique challenge and opportunity due to their diverse species and behaviours. Developing sophisticated models to predict bird species and their actions from video data holds immense potential for enhancing the management and protection of natural environments. However, this development is heavily

J. M. Ferrández Vicente et al. (Eds.): IWINAC 2024, LNCS 14675, pp. 75–84, 2024.
https://doi.org/10.1007/978-3-031-61137-7_8

contingent upon the availability of comprehensive and diverse video datasets. In this context, explainability becomes important as it ensures that the decisions made by these models are transparent and understandable [7], which is crucial for building trust among conservationists, researchers, and the general public.

Although there are numerous datasets available that catalogue animals, such as AnimalKingdom [13] and VB100 [5], many of these datasets are limited in their focus on static images. Additionally, they often lack annotations for the specific actions performed by the animals, which is a fundamental aspect for understanding their behaviour and interactions within their ecosystems. The lack of specificity and uniformity in the data format limits the ability to create models that can accurately recognise actions and identify species from video footage.

Generative models have emerged as a promising solution to augment existing datasets in response to these challenges. In particular, the use of generative models to create synthetic video data of animals, especially birds, performing various actions offers a novel approach to overcome the limitations of current datasets. The models have the potential to generate realistic and varied video sequences that can significantly enhance the training and performance of machine learning algorithms for action detection and species recognition in birds.

In this paper, we have focused on using and fine-tuning different generative models to assess the viability of these techniques for data augmentation purposes, as shown in Fig. 1. The aim of this study is to bridge the gap in available datasets by generating synthetic video data that closely mimics real-world observations. Our exploration into the use of generative models for data augmentation is detailed in this paper, evaluating their effectiveness in creating useful datasets for applications such as bird action detection. This investigation aims to contribute to the wider field of wildlife conservation technology by providing new tools and methodologies for safeguarding and monitoring bird populations in their natural habitats.

In summary, our contributions are the following:

- We have developed a comprehensive pipeline for fine-tuning and utilising generative video models specifically tailored for the field of bird action recognition.
- Additionally, we have conducted a thorough evaluation and comparison of various generative techniques' performance in the context of bird action recognition.

The remainder of the paper is structured as follows: Sect. 2 discusses related works and relevant datasets. Section 3 proposes a pipeline that utilises generative video models. The results are presented in Sect. 4. Finally, in Sect. 5, we present the conclusions of our work.

2 Related Works

The proliferation of deep learning and computer vision applications requires an expansive and detailed dataset for training purposes. The development of robust

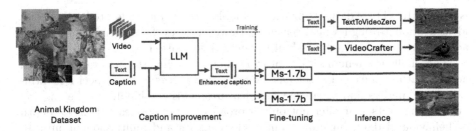

Fig. 1. End-to-End Pipeline for Synthetic Video Generation. The Text 2VideoZero and VideoCrafter models are used in conjunction with the Video2Video models to produce higher quality videos. The text-to-video-ms-1.7b model has been retrained using the AnimalKingdom dataset and improved captions.

classification models [21] for bird species detection and action recognition is particularly challenging due to the scarcity of labelled data [17]. However, the lack of data variability limits the models' ability to accurately understand the nuanced behaviours and appearances of diverse bird species. To address this issue, it is necessary to increase the amount of labelled data available for training. Synthetic video generation is a promising way to fill this gap and overcome the limitations imposed by the inadequacies of current datasets [4,12]. By simulating a broad spectrum of scenarios and conditions, synthetic data offers the vital variability and scope often absent in traditional datasets.

2.1 Birds Datasets

In the broader scope of animal datasets, the primary focus has been on cataloguing various animal species, encompassing details such as kind, species, and the actions they are performing, often annotated with bounding boxes [2,23]. A standout in this category is the Animal Kingdom dataset [13], a comprehensive collection designed to deepen our understanding of animal behaviours across a spectrum of environmental conditions and viewpoints. This dataset is notable due to its breadth and depth, comprising 50 h of annotated videos for video grounding tasks, 30,000 video sequences for fine-grained multi-label action recognition. Covering 850 species across 6 major animal classes, Animal Kingdom offers an unparalleled resource for the study of animal behaviour, including a significant subset dedicated to birds. With data on thousands of bird species performing hundreds of distinct actions, this dataset presents a goldmine for fine-tuning generative models aimed at bird video generation, thereby enhancing model performance in this specialised domain.

VB100 dataset [5] also offers multimodal data, including both video and audio recordings of birds engaging in various actions. It focuses on 100 bird species native to North America. This geographical specificity might limit its applicability for detecting species in Europe, where local species diversity and behaviours could differ significantly. In addition to video datasets, there are also several image-based datasets such as Birds525 [6], CUB-200-2011 [18], and

NABirds [19]. These datasets provide valuable insights for models to learn species identification through visual features. However, they fall short in supporting action detection due to the lack of temporal information.

The challenge remains in capturing and analysing the full range of bird actions, although each dataset has its strengths, particularly in species identification and understanding static visual features. This gap highlights the ongoing need for datasets that offer not only a broad range of species but also a depth of behavioural data, including temporal dynamics and multimodal inputs, to advance the field of bird action recognition significantly (Table 1).

Table 1. Datasets used for bird species recognition.

Name	Modalities	Labeled data	Samples	Bird species	Actions
VB100 [5]	Video, Audio	Species, actions	1416	100	–
Animal Kingdom [13]	Video, Audio	Species, actions	50h	1000	140
Birds525 [6]	Image	Species	84635	525	–
CUB-200-2011 [18]	Image	Species	5,994	200	–
NABirds [19]	Image	Species	48000	400	–

2.2 Generative Models

The advent of generative models for synthetic videos has led to significant advances but faces challenges in temporal coherence and realism. The exploration of generative image models based on textual descriptions has opened new avenues for generating photo-realistic images of animals, enriching the field with detailed and diverse visual data. This approach has seen remarkable applications in creating images that capture the essence and diversity of animal species with unprecedented fidelity.

In the realm of leveraging commonsense knowledge for image generation, the work of CD-GAN [22] presents a pioneering approach. It proposes a novel methodology to generate photo-realistic images grounded in entity-related commonsense knowledge. It incorporates generates high-resolution images guided by various commonsense knowledge in multiple stages to maintain text-image consistency. It has been demonstrated on the widely used CUB-birds dataset and achieves competitive results, showcasing its efficacy in generating realistic images consistent with textual descriptions.

However, the use of text-to-image models, while groundbreaking for static image generation, falls short when the goal extends to simulating behaviours or actions, necessitating a shift towards video generation models. For example, Text2Video-Zero [9] adapts text-to-image methods for video generation, and despite its enhanced scene consistency, it struggles with temporal stability. On the other hand, VideoFusion [11] employs a decomposed diffusion process for improved video quality but grapples with realism in dynamic scenes. Similarly,

Gen-2 Video [3] and VideoCrafter [1] offer detailed control over video editing through textual and visual descriptions, yet faces challenges in balancing structure and content for realistic portrayal. Collectively, these methods demonstrate progress but also highlight the ongoing need for refinement in realistic and temporally coherent video generation.

3 Synthetic Video Generation

In the pursuit of enriching the dataset for bird species detection and action recognition, our efforts have been directed towards the utilisation and fine-tuning of generative video models. This approach significantly augments the diversity and volume of bird video data available, facilitating the creation of synthetic videos depicting birds engaging in a variety of actions. The cornerstone of this endeavour is the AnimalKingdom dataset [13], renowned for its extensive collection of videos and accompanying textual descriptions of each video, including the actions performed.

3.1 Enhancing Captions

Due to the fact that the textual descriptions provided by the AnimalKingdom dataset were found to be somewhat lacking in detail, we devised a pipeline to enhance these descriptions using Vision Language Models (VLMs) and Large Language Models (LLMs). The initial phase involved employing the *Blip2* model [10] for video captioning, guided by prompts designed to elicit detailed descriptions of the bird's surroundings and its behaviour. Specifically, we asked, "Is the bird at any particular location like a river or forest? Describe the landscape." and "Is the bird sitting, standing, or engaging in any other observable behaviour? Describe it." The responses generated from these prompts were then amalgamated with the original dataset descriptions. A subsequent inference was performed on the LLM model *Mistral-7B-v0.1* [8] using a templated prompt that aimed to condense the information into cohesive sentences. This process yield more detailed video descriptions, capturing nuances such as background elements and the bird's actions more effectively.

3.2 Generative Video Models

These enhanced descriptions are used to fine-tune the *text-to-video-ms-1.7b* model based on the VideoFusion architecture. The model was trained using both the original and the newly generated descriptions, resulting in two fine-tunined versions for comparative evaluation against the original model. In addition to refining the descriptions, we explored the potential of two new generative models, VideoCrafter [1] and TextToVideoZero [9]. These models, building upon the StableDiffusion2 architecture [15], have demonstrated the capability to produce high-quality videos. However, a notable limitation was their treatment of temporal dynamics, often resulting in videos with static backgrounds. To address this issue, we incorporated a video2video model, *zeroscope_v2_576w*, designed to enhance video realism by introducing motion and dynamism into the scenes. The integration of this model has markedly improved the realism and dynamic quality of the generated videos, making them more closely resemble real-life footage.

The development of these synthetic processing and generation pipelines has been instrumental in producing highly realistic videos. This has enabled us to generate a small dataset to validate our proposal for different bird species, such as: Shoebill, Great Reed Warbler, Cardinal, Tawny Owl or Sparrowhawk bird. Figure 2 shows some of the frames generated for various species. The qualitative evaluation of these videos will further attest to the efficacy of our approach in generating synthetic data that closely mimics real-world scenarios, thereby enriching the available dataset for bird species detection and action recognition research.

| Cuckoo | Red cardinal | Tawny Owl | Sparrow | Reed Warbler |

Fig. 2. Examples of synthetic videos generated for various bird species.

4   Results

This section presents the results obtained from generating synthetic bird videos using various text prompts across different video generation models. The experimentation involve the use of pre-trained models such as Text2VideoZero and VideoCrafter, followed by the application of a video-to-video (V2V) model to enhance the overall quality of the generated content. The aim of the subsequent V2V processing is to introduce more temporally coherent details, significantly improving the fluidity of the animations and minimising common artefacts such as flickering. The initial results show that the bird movements and actions are convincingly realistic, with commendable temporal coherence. However, the variability in the generated videos is limited, and the backgrounds tend to be overly simplistic and lacked intricacy.

To overcome these limitations, we fine-tune the *text-to-video-Ms-1.7b* model, using both the original video captions from the AnimalKingdom dataset and the extended captions derived from the responses previously generated. The aim of this approach is to enhance the video content by adding more detailed and dynamic backgrounds, which could potentially increase the realism and diversity of the generated videos. The videos produced by these fine-tuned models show a significant improvement in terms of environmental richness and detail, featuring more dynamic and varied backgrounds as well as movements from the birds.

However, this enhancement come at a cost. The fidelity of the videos noticeably decreased compared to those generated by the pre-trained models. The fine-tuned models successfully introduced a greater depth of scene complexity, but slightly compromised on the visual clarity and sharpness that characterised the original generative models' outputs. Figure 3 shows an example of an original video from the Animal Kingdom and VB100 dataset, as well as synthetic videos generated by the models. To generate the synthetic example videos, the following text prompt was used "A cardinal bird eats from the ground".

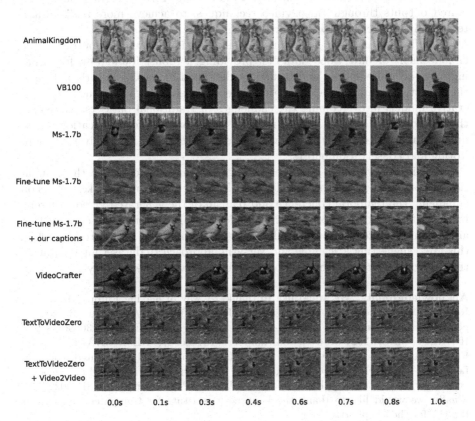

Fig. 3. Comparative analysis of video sequences of Cardinal bird (*Cardinalis cardinalis*) from different datasets, including AnimalKingdom and VB100, alongside sequences generated by AI generative models such as Text2Video-Zero with Stable Diffusion 2, VideoCrafter, and text-to-video-ms-1.7b.

5   Conclusions

In this study, we have explored the capabilities of generative models in augmenting video datasets, specifically focusing on the identification and behaviour analysis of bird species. Our research leverage and fine-tune various generative video models to create synthetic data that address the significant limitations posed by existing animal datasets, mainly their focus on static images and lack of detailed behavioural annotations.

The core of our work involved developing a sophisticated pipeline for generating synthetic videos that not only depict birds in various actions but also incorporate enhanced descriptions and backgrounds. This process involved improving video descriptions with the aid of LLMs and fine-tuning models using both original and enhanced descriptions. Additionally, we explored the use of cutting-edge models such as VideoCrafter and TextToVideoZero, further refining their generated outputs through video2video techniques, to achieve more realistic and temporally coherent video sequences.

Our findings suggest that this pipeline significantly contributes to the enhancement of bird video datasets, providing a robust foundation for training more accurate species and behaviour detection models. The variability and the realistic nature of the generated videos underscore the potential of generative models in overcoming the challenges of traditional datasets. Moreover, the methodology adopted in this research holds promise for application across different animal categories, opening avenues for comprehensive biodiversity monitoring and conservation efforts.

As a future work, we propose refining this pipeline to enable the generation of domain-specific synthetic datasets. This improvement will likely focus on enhancing the temporal coherence and realism of the generated videos, thereby broadening the scope of deep learning applications in environmental conservation and wildlife monitoring. Our work lays a foundational stone for future research in this area, suggesting a scalable and versatile approach to dataset augmentation that could revolutionise the field of wildlife conservation technology.

Acknowledgments. We would like to thank "A way of making Europe" European Regional Development Fund (ERDF) and MCIN/AEI/10.13039/501100011033 for supporting this work under the "CHAN-TWIN" project (grant TED2021-130890B-C21). HORIZON-MSCA-2021-SE-0 action number: 101086387, REMARKABLE, Rural Environmental Monitoring via ultra wide-ARea networKs And distriButed federated Learning. This work has also been supported by a Spanish national and two regional grants for PhD studies, FPU21/00414, CIACIF/2021/430 and CIACIF/2022/175. Finally, we would like to thank the University Institute for Computer Research at the UA for their support.

References

1. Chen, H., et al.: Videocrafter2: Overcoming data limitations for high-quality video diffusion models. arXiv preprint arXiv:2401.09047 (2024)
2. Chen, K., Song, H., Change Loy, C., Lin, D.: Discover and learn new objects from documentaries. In: Proceedings of the IEEE Conference on Computer Vision and Pattern Recognition, pp. 3087–3096 (2017)
3. Esser, P., Chiu, J., Atighehchian, P., Granskog, J., Germanidis, A.: Structure and content-guided video synthesis with diffusion models. arXiv e-prints pp. arXiv–2302 (2023)

4. Garcia-Garcia, A., et al.: The robotrix: an extremely photorealistic and very-large-scale indoor dataset of sequences with robot trajectories and interactions. In: 2018 IEEE/RSJ International Conference on Intelligent Robots and Systems (IROS), pp. 6790–6797 (2018). https://doi.org/10.1109/IROS.2018.8594495
5. Ge, Z., et al.: Exploiting temporal information for dcnn-based fine-grained object classification. In: 2016 International Conference on Digital Image Computing: Techniques and Applications (DICTA), pp. 1–6. IEEE (2016)
6. Gerry: Birds 525 Species- image classification (2023). https://www.kaggle.com/datasets/gpiosenka/100-bird-species. Accessed 26 Feb 2024
7. Górriz, J., Álvarez Illan, I., et al.: Computational approaches to explainable artificial intelligence: advances in theory, applications and trends. Inf. Fusion **100**, 101945 (2023). https://doi.org/10.1016/j.inffus.2023.101945. https://www.sciencedirect.com/science/article/pii/S1566253523002610
8. Jiang, A.Q., et al.: Mistral 7b. arXiv preprint arXiv:2310.06825 (2023)
9. Khachatryan, L., et al.: Text2video-zero: text-to-image diffusion models are zero-shot video generators. arXiv:2303.13439 (2023)
10. Li, J., Li, D., Savarese, S., Hoi, S.: Blip-2: bootstrapping language-image pre-training with frozen image encoders and large language models (2023)
11. Luo, Z., et al.: Videofusion: decomposed diffusion models for high-quality video generation. In: IEEE/CVF CVPR (2023)
12. Martinez-Gonzalez, P., Oprea, S., Garcia-Garcia, A., Jover-Alvarez, A., Orts-Escolano, S., Garcia-Rodriguez, J.: Unrealrox: an extremely photorealistic virtual reality environment for robotics simulations and synthetic data generation. Virt. Real. **24**, 271–288 (2020)
13. Ng, X.L., Ong, K.E., Zheng, Q., Ni, Y., Yeo, S.Y., Liu, J.: Animal kingdom: a large and diverse dataset for animal behavior understanding. In: Proceedings of the IEEE/CVF Conference on Computer Vision and Pattern Recognition (CVPR), pp. 19023–19034 (2022)
14. Pino, J., Rodà, F., Ribas, J., Pons, X.: Landscape structure and bird species richness: implications for conservation in rural areas between natural parks. Landsc. Urban Plan. **49**(1–2), 35–48 (2000)
15. Rombach, R., Blattmann, A., Lorenz, D., Esser, P., Ommer, B.: High-resolution image synthesis with latent diffusion models. In: Proceedings of the IEEE/CVF Conference on Computer Vision and Pattern Recognition, pp. 10684–10695 (2022)
16. Ruiz-Ponce, P., Ortiz-Perez, D., Garcia-Rodriguez, J., Kiefer, B.: Poseidon: a data augmentation tool for small object detection datasets in maritime environments. Sensors **23**(7) (2023). https://www.mdpi.com/1424-8220/23/7/3691
17. Song, Q., et al.: Benchmarking wild bird detection in complex forest scenes. Eco. Inf. **80**, 102466 (2024)
18. Van Horn, G., et al.: Building a bird recognition app and large scale dataset with citizen scientists: the fine print in fine-grained dataset collection. In: 2015 IEEE Conference on Computer Vision and Pattern Recognition (CVPR), pp. 595–604 (2015). https://doi.org/10.1109/CVPR.2015.7298658
19. Van Horn, G., et al.: Building a bird recognition app and large scale dataset with citizen scientists: the fine print in fine-grained dataset collection. In: Proceedings of the IEEE Conference on Computer Vision and Pattern Recognition, pp. 595–604 (2015)
20. Vélez, J., et al.: An evaluation of platforms for processing camera-trap data using artificial intelligence. Methods Ecol. Evol. **14**(2), 459–477 (2023)
21. Yang, W., et al.: A forest wildlife detection algorithm based on improved yolov5s. Animals **13**(19), 3134 (2023)

22. Zhang, G., et al.: CD-GAN: commonsense-driven generative adversarial network with hierarchical refinement for text-to-image synthesis. Intell. Comput. **2**, 0017 (2023)
23. Zhang, L., Gao, J., Xiao, Z., Fan, H.: Animaltrack: a benchmark for multi-animal tracking in the wild. Int. J. Comput. Vision **131**(2), 496–513 (2023)

Deep Learning for Enhanced Risk Assessment in Home Environments

Javier Rodriguez-Juan, David Ortiz-Perez, Jose Garcia-Rodriguez[✉],
and David Tomás

Universidad de Alicante, Alicante, Spain
{jrodriguez,dortiz,jgarcia}@dtic.ua.es, dtomas@dlsi.ua.es

Abstract. This work is focused on advancing automatic scene analysis and ambient assisted living systems to support individuals requiring special care, such as the elderly or those visually impaired. The study explores the most effective techniques in Video Captioning and Object Detection, proposing a Deep Learning pipeline for Risks Assessment in home environments. Key elements include the integration of SwinBERT for Video Captioning and YOLOv7 for Object Recognition. Additionally, the effectiveness and limitations of the Risks Assessment pipeline are evaluated through various architectures, utilizing the Charades dataset, known for its natural and spontaneous depiction of household activities. The experimentation demonstrates how the integration of both models increases the results up to 7% in the Object Detection task, which is fundamental for the correct identification of potential risks. This comprehensive approach aims to develop more human-aligned and accurate systems for aiding vulnerable populations in their daily lives.

Keywords: ambient assisted living · risks assessment · object detection

1 Introduction

In the current era, the evolution of automated systems along with advancements in Deep Learning (DL) is leading to remarkable breakthroughs across various fields. Ambient Assisted Living (AAL) is one of these areas where artificial intelligence systems have the potential to significantly advance and enhance the quality of life for many individuals suffering from diseases and impairments.

AAL is a field of research that focuses on developing technologies and systems to support elderly or disabled individuals in their daily lives, enabling them to live independently and safely in their own homes or assisted living facilities. AAL research typically involves the integration of various technologies such as sensors, actuators, smart devices, and artificial intelligence algorithms to create intelligent environments that can monitor the activities of individuals, detect emergencies or changes in behavior, and provide assistance or alerts when necessary. Within this field outstands researches aimed at the risk assessment, health monitoring or social interaction. Regarding social interaction, Social Assistive Robots (SAR) [7,12] have been effective in monitoring and assisting older adults at home. SAR's are designed to monitor, assist, and provide social, cognitive, and physical stimulation for elderly individuals living alone and at risk of frailty.

Although various works on risk detection for dependent individuals exist, most focus on creating systems that detect only one specific risk, with many emphasizing future fall prediction based on balance impairments or gait history. In contrast, this work introduces an integrated system capable of predicting a broad spectrum of potential and imminent risks for dependant individuals. Utilizing the latest advancements in Computer Vision and Video-To-Text models, this system analyzes the scene's context to perform risk prediction. The main contributions of this study include:

- Introducing a novel risk assessment framework capable of detecting various types of risks within home environments.
- Proposing an innovative taxonomy for correlating a set of objects with potential risks that may arise in homes.
- Enhancing the safety of dependent individuals in their daily activities by creating a system that can potentially be installed in their homes.

The developed system has been evaluated based on its ability to recognize objects, which is the primary factor considered for computing risks in this study. Despite the restrictions imposed by the experimentation, the system yielded promising results that demonstrate its effectiveness for application in homes to prevent risks to individuals such as those with cognitive impairments, disabilities, or special needs children.

This article is structured into four additional sections. Section 2 reviews studies pertinent to the key themes of our research. Section 3 details the methodology employed to acquire evaluation data. Following this, Sect. 4 outlines the various experiments conducted. The article concludes with Sect. 5, where findings are synthesized and conclusion derived from the study are presented.

2   Related Work

In this section, a review of the literature covering the state-of-the-art in Risk Assessment, as well as the methods used as the basis for developing this study, is carried out. These fields serve as the foundation for the proposed experimentation.

2.1   Risks Assessment

Risk assessment [23] is the task of predicting potential risks for individuals based on the provided input data, which within the target scope of this study are typically images or videos. This task is prevalent in various fields such as healthcare or construction. In construction [11], Computer Vision techniques are employed to prevent risks among builders. These risks may include the development of unsafe behaviors [2,3], entering hazardous areas, or not wearing protective equipment.

Regarding AAL, Yared and Abdulrazak [23] extensively explored indoor risks for the elderly, identifying major risks such as falls, fires, burns, gas intoxication, and inactivity. Additionally, they discuss various risk detection algorithms and assistive technologies designed to improve elder safety. Research typically concentrates on developing systems that address one of the mentioned risks. For instance, Agrawal et al. [1] use machine learning and wireless sensors to predict fall risk in the elderly. While their method shows acceptable results, the integration of DL could further enhance performance, as demonstrated by Savadkoohi et al. [18]. Their study employs DL architectures like Long-Short Term Memory and Convolutional Neural Networks to develop the One-One-One Deep Neural Network, achieving nearly 100% precision in fall-risk prediction.

2.2 Object Detection

When conducting a Risk Assessment of a specific scene, identifying the objects [24] within the scene's context is vital for determining potential risks to dependent individuals. Accordingly, a review has been conducted of this extensively researched area within the Computer Vision community.

Currently, the predominant architectures for action detection tasks are categorized into two types. Firstly, two-stage models are recognized for their high precision, albeit at the expense of increased complexity and slower performance, with the architecture proposed in the work of Ren et al. [16] serving as an example. Conversely, single-stage models perform all computations in one step, offering faster inference times but at a reduced accuracy, exemplified by the YOLO architecture [21]. This architecture is particularly suitable for real-time object recognition and localization due to its speed and forms the basis for some of the experiments in this study. The application of YOLO architectures have been already used in AAL, as seen in Siyuan Chen's study [4], where a virtual assistant recognizes the environment to assist the elderly or prevent injuries. A significant challenge in AAL object detection is multi-scale recognition, especially for detecting small objects like sockets or obstacles in home settings, a known issue with the YOLO model. To overcome this, various multi-scale detection techniques have been developed, including multi-reference detection [15], which establishes image references to predict bounding boxes.

2.3 Video Captioning

Video Captioning [8] is the task aimed at generating captions (*i.e.* descriptions) from input videos which describes what is happening in the video. Video Captioning tasks can be classified differently depending on the description granularity, with Standard Video Captioning aiming to produce single-sentence summaries of videos, whereas Dense Video Captioning seeks to provide more extensive descriptions that capture fine-grained spatial and temporal details.

Traditional approaches to Video Captioning rely on the encoder-decoder architecture [13], where convolutional neural networks [5,6,20] extract visual features, and recurrent neural networks are employed for generating text based on these features. The growing interest in identifying detailed video events has led to an increase in the popularity of Dense Video Captioning among researchers. A notable example is the work by Yang et al. [22], which uses a Transformer-based encoder-decoder architecture with time tokens to seamlessly understand and generate sequences of tokens containing both textual semantic information and temporal localization information. The advent of Large Language Models (LLMs) has also influenced this field. A standout model that utilizes LLM for generating video captions is LaViLa [25], which provides comprehensive coverage of lengthy videos, enhances the temporal synchronization between visual information and text, and significantly increases the diversity of the generated text. However, despite their capacity for generating detailed descriptions, LLMs incur high computational costs, making them less suitable for real-time applications. Within these DL models, it is also important to apply explainability [26] techniques to understand the predictions of the model.

3   Methodology

In this section, it is exposed the methodology employed to achieve the proposed objective, starting with the framework for scene analysis to extract relevant information, followed by the method for associating this information with potential risks. Figure 1 shows the complete system pipeline.

3.1   Objects Extraction

To extract objects from videos, a combination of the Video Captioning Swin-BERT model [9] and the Object Detection YOLOv7 [21] is employed. Swin-BERT, a transformer-based model for video captioning, processes video frame patches to adapt flexibly to variable-length inputs. It leverages densely sampled video frames and optimizes sparse attention masks for improved long-range sequence modeling, demonstrating high description accuracy. On the other hand, YOLOv7 includes improvements such as Extended-ELAN, or enhanced learning without disrupting the gradient path, and innovative model scaling for concatenation-based models to maintain optimal structure during scaling. It also introduces a planned re-parameterized convolution to improve compatibility with various network architectures and a dual-label assigner approach for deeper supervision.

During object extraction, both models serve as complementary mechanisms, increasing the reliability of detected objects and enhancing the object recognition rate. Since these models perform different tasks, they focus on different aspects of the video, thus broadening the range of detectable objects. SwinBERT's proven capability in scene description is leveraged to extract critical information from videos, focusing on key objects. To identify objects from SwinBERT captions,

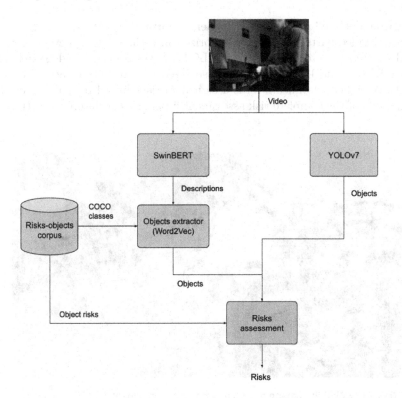

Fig. 1. End-to-end pipeline used for the risks assessment task.

element-wise operations compare each caption token against possible classes in our object set, detailed further in the experimentation section. Considering the semantics of tokens is crucial, as different tokens may represent the same concept. For this, word embedding are leveraged for semantic analysis. In addition, YOLOv7 identifies not only primary, but also secondary objects that may pose a threat, as it is able to perform a comprehensive analysis to extract almost all objects present in the scene.

3.2   Risks Identification

Once objects are extracted from SwinBERT and YOLOv7, a unified set was created by eliminating duplicates. Subsequently, risks associated with these objects were identified using a risk-objects corpus[1], developed specifically for this study. This corpus employs a three-level taxonomy linking objects, their properties, and associated risks, inspired by the properties-oriented taxonomy in [14]. It innovatively relates 56 objects from the COCO2017 [10] dataset with potential home environment risks. Risks are then prioritized based on detection source, with

---

[1] https://github.com/javirodrigueez/indoor-risks-assessment/tree/main/risks_data.

SwinBERT-detected objects given higher importance due to the model's focus on crucial video parts. Risks are categorized into three levels: Level 1 for risks linked to objects detected only by YOLOv7, Level 2 for those detected solely by SwinBERT, and Level 3 for risks associated with objects identified by both models. A higher relevance level is assigned to risks linked to multiple objects. An example of the complete risk assessment pipeline's execution is illustrated in Fig. 2.

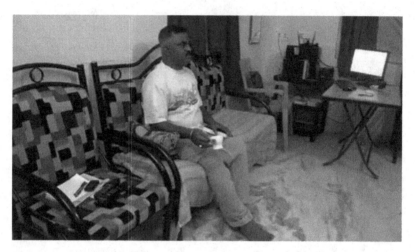

Risk 1 [Lv.2]: If the person makes an imprecise movement, he/she may fall out of the chair. Associated with "Couch" [Lv. 2] and "Chair" [Lv.1]
Risk 2 [Lv.2]: If the object is positioned in an unexpected location within the room, it can potentially cause individuals to trip over it, leading to accidental falls. Associated with "Book" [Lv.2] and "Chair" [Lv.1]
Risk 3 [Lv.1]: If the object collides with something or is not used properly, its content can be spilt. Associated with "Cup" [Lv.1]

Fig. 2. Subset of risks generated from a sample video of the selected dataset used.

4   Experiments

In this section, insights about the conducted experimentation is provided. The primary focus of this experimentation is on the Object Detection task, as it serves as the foundation for the system to accurately perform the risks identification, which is the main goal of the study.

4.1   Setup and Data

The proposed experimentation is done using Charades [19] as evaluation dataset. Charades is a comprehensive dataset consisting of 9,848 videos, each approximately 30 s long, showcasing daily home activities. It was generated through crowdsourcing, where 267 individuals across three countries via Amazon Mechanical Turk were involved. Charades aimed to capture the casual and realistic essence of everyday tasks. This approach was chosen to retain the individual biases of the contributors, ensuring the authenticity of the depicted daily activities.

During this experimentation the numbers of objects that can be detected are limited to 56 objects commonly found in houses. This is because during experimentation YOLOv7 pre-trained on COCO2017 dataset is used, which is limited to the detection of 80 objects, where only 56 of them are related with house environments. As stated in the methodology section, the object extraction from SwinBERT descriptions are done using word embeddings. This word embeddings are extracted using a Word2Vec[2] model available through the Gensim library API and the comparison of embeddings to identify objects are done using cosine similarity, where the threshold to detect matches between pairs of tokens was obtained empirically. Similarly, confidence threshold used for YOLOv7 model was derived experimentally.

In the experiments, three different pre-training approaches for SwinBERT are utilized. A comparison is made between the absence and presence of the Swin-BERT model in the system to analyze whether adding this model to the object detection pipeline enhances detection accuracy. Three pretrained checkpoints for SwinBERT are employed to assess the model's capabilities with varying training data. Each of these checkpoints contains a SwinBERT model pretrained on one of the following datasets: MSVD, MSR-VTT, and VATEX. These three pre-training methods have been chosen due to the differences in their training data. MSVD and MSR-VTT train the model with short captions, while VATEX provides richer captions that describe the videos in more detail. MSVD provides three captions for each video, while MSR-VTT provides five, enriching the model's understanding of the content. Moreover, MSR-VTT captions tend to be slightly longer than those of MSVD. Results are obtained in terms of Recall metric, which specifies the amount of correctly recognised objects from the list of annotated objects for each Charades dataset's videos.

4.2   Results

To conduct the experimentation, a subset of 1,430 videos from the Charades train set is used. These videos have an annotated set of objects with at least one of the objects belonging to one of the 56 COCO2017 classes previously mentioned. For this purpose we randomly selected 3,000 videos from the Charades train set and then we filtered the videos from this subset to only include those with at least one object from the 56 of the COCO2017. Additionally, the annotations within these videos were filtered to exclusively feature objects belonging to the COCO2017 classes subset mentioned in methodology section. Table 1 shows the results of the experimentation.

---

[2] Pre-trained model word2vec-google-news-300 are used.

Table 1. Recall evaluation of the Object Detection pipeline over 1,430 subset of videos from Charades dataset. Last row represents Recall when only using YOLO detection.

Model	Recall
MSVD	0.1046
MSR-VTT	0.0915
VATEX	0.2047
YOLO	0.5082
MSVD+YOLO	0.5351
MSR-VTT+YOLO	0.5359
VATEX+YOLO	**0.5719**

As is shown in the results, the best Recall score is obtained when using YOLOv7 with VATEX pre-training of SwinBERT model. Results reflect the efficiency of YOLOv7 to detect a high quantity of objects, as the consequence of removing this model from the pipeline decreases the results in more than a 0.3, which is more than a 50% reduction. Also it must be noted the pipeline's improvement when SwinBERT is added, as the results when a pre-trained Swin-BERT is used exceeded in all cases the 0.5 obtained when using YOLOv7 alone. Comparing the results obtained from the usage of the different SwinBERT pre-trainings it can be observed that highest score is achieved by VATEX. This is the consequence of the type of data which this dataset provides to the model during the training process. In comparison to MSVD and MSR-VTT, VATEX dataset is composed by larger and more detailed descriptions. This implies that training SwinBERT in this data produces that SwinBERT generates denser descriptions in comparison to the other pre-trainings. Denser descriptions increases the possibilities of the appearance of objects, so higher scores can be achieved. More details about pre-training SwinBERT in the previously mentioned datasets can be seen in [17].

Although the demonstrated improvement achieved by the addition of Swin-BERT the system remains with a maximum Recall of 0.57 for the Object Detection task. This outcome is influenced by multiple factors that restricted the effectiveness of the experiment. Firstly, the varying quality of videos in the Charades dataset, a consequence of its crowdsourced nature, posed a challenge. The lower quality of certain videos in our subset hindered accurate object recognition in some scenes. Secondly, the scope of annotations for objects in Charades is limited. While it provides details for the most relevant objects in each video, it does not encompass all objects present in the scenes. As a result, many detected objects were not factored into the final score computation due to their absence in the provided annotation set.

5 Conclusion

This study introduced a novel framework for conducting risk assessments in home environments, leveraging descriptions generated by a Video Captioning model. The methodology employed a YOLOv7 model for Object Detection tasks, complemented by an experimental application of the SwinBERT Video Captioning model to evaluate its potential to enhance object detection accuracy beyond that of YOLOv7 alone. Additionally, this research presented a new corpus taxonomy linking detected objects with associated risks, offering a foundational resource for the research community to further explore this area.

The experimentation highlighted the efficacy of Video Captioning in identifying a greater number of relevant objects, suggesting a promising new direction for investigating how video-to-text generative models can contribute to advancements in Object Detection tasks, particularly within the Charades dataset.

Future research directions include exploring Large Language Models for more detailed video analysis and studying human behavior recognition to better understand interactions within their environments. Such systems hold promise for significantly improving the quality of life for dependent individuals.

Acknowledgment. We would like to thank "A way of making Europe" European Regional Development Fund (ERDF) and MCIN/AEI/10.13039/501100011033 for supporting this work under the "CHAN-TWIN" project (grant TED2021-130890B-C21. HORIZON-MSCA-2021-SE-0 action number: 101086387, REMARKABLE, Rural Environmental Monitoring via ultra wide-ARea networKs And distriButed federated Learning. CIAICO/2022/132 Consolidated group project "AI4Health" funded by Valencian government and International Center for Aging Research ICAR funded project "IASISTEM". This work has also been supported by a Spanish regional grant for PhD studies, CIACIF/2022/175 and a research initiation grant from the University of Alicante, AII23-12. Finally we would like to thanks the support of the University Institute for Computer Research at the UA.

References

1. Agrawal, D.K., et al.: Fall risk prediction using wireless sensor insoles with machine learning. IEEE Access **11**, 23119–23126 (2023)
2. Azorin-Lopez, J., et al.: A novel prediction method for early recognition of global human behaviour in image sequences. Neural Process. Lett. **43**(2), 363–387 (2016)
3. Azorín-López, J., et al.: Human behaviour recognition based on trajectory analysis using neural networks. In: IJCNN, pp. 1–7 (2013)
4. Chen, S.: Toward ambient assistance: a spatially-aware virtual assistant enabled by object detection. In: ICCEA, pp. 494–501 (2020)
5. Flórez-Revuelta, F., et al.: Representation of 2d objects with a topology preserving network, April 2002
6. José García-Rodríguez and Juan Manuel García-Chamizo: Surveillance and human-computer interaction applications of self-growing models. Appl. Soft Comput. **11**(7), 4413–4431 (2011)
7. Gomez-Donoso, F., et al.: A robotic platform for customized and interactive rehabilitation of persons with disabilities. Pattern Recogn. Lett. **99**, 105–113 (2017)

8. Islam, S., Dash, A., Seum, A., Raj, A.H., Hossain, T., Shah, F.M.: Exploring video captioning techniques: a comprehensive survey on deep learning methods. SN Comput. Sci. **2**(2), 120 (2021)
9. Lin, K., Li, L., Lin, C.-C., Ahmed, F., Gan, Z., Liu, Z., Yumao, L., Wang, L.: End-to-end transformers with sparse attention for video captioning, Swinbert (2022)
10. Lin, T.-Y., et al.: Microsoft coco: Common objects in context (2015)
11. Liu, J., Luo, H., Liu, H.: Deep learning-based data analytics for safety in construction. Autom. Constr. **140**, 104302 (2022)
12. Luperto, M., Monroy, J., Jennifer, R., et al.: Integrating social assistive robots, iot, virtual communities and smart objects to assist at-home independently living elders: the movecare project. Int. J. Soc. Robot. **15**(3), 517–545 (2023)
13. Naik, D., Jaidhar, C.D.: Video captioning using sentence vector-enabled convolutional framework with short-connected lstm. Multimed. Tools Appl. **83**(4), 11187–11213 (2024)
14. Puig, X., Ra, K., Boben, M., Li, J., Wang, T., Fidler, S.: and Antonio Torralba. Simulating household activities via programs, Virtualhome (2018)
15. Redmon, J., Farhadi, A.: Yolo9000: Better, faster, stronger (2016)
16. Ren, S., He, K., Girshick, R., Sun, J.: Towards real-time object detection with region proposal networks, Faster r-cnn (2016)
17. Rodríguez-Juan, J., Ortiz-Perez, D., Garcia-Rodriguez, J., et al.: Indoor scenes video captioning. In: SOCO, pp. 153–162. Springer, Cham (2023). https://doi.org/10.1007/978-3-031-42536-3_15
18. Savadkoohi, M., Oladunni, T., Thompson, L.A.: Deep neural networks for human's fall-risk prediction using force-plate time series signal. Expert Syst. Appl. **182**, November 2021
19. Sigurdsson, G.A., et al.: Hollywood in homes: Crowdsourcing data collection for activity understanding (2016). https://arxiv.org/abs/1604.01753
20. Viejo, D., Garcia, J., Cazorla, M., Gil, D., Johnsson, M.: Using gng to improve 3d feature extraction-application to 6dof egomotion. Neural Networks **32**, 138–146 (2012). Selected Papers from IJCNN 2011
21. Wang, C.-Y., Bochkovskiy, A., Liao, H.-Y.M.: Yolov7: trainable bag-of-freebies sets new state-of-the-art for real-time object detectors (2022)
22. Yang, A., et al.: Vid2seq: large-scale pretraining of a visual language model for dense video captioning (2023)
23. Yared, R., Abdulrazak, B.: Ambient technology to assist elderly people in indoor risks. Computers, 5(4) (2016)
24. Zaidi, S.S.A., et al.: A survey of modern deep learning based object detection models. Digital Signal Process. **126**, 103514 (2022)
25. Zhao, Y., Misra, I., Krähenbühl, P., Girdhar, R.: Learning video representations from large language models. In: CVPR, pp. 6586–6597, June 2023
26. Górriz, J.M., et al.: Computational approaches to explainable artificial intelligence: advances in theory, applications and trends. Inf. Fusion **100**, 101945 (2023)

Lightweight CNNs for Advanced Bird Species Recognition on the Edge

Adrian Berenguer-Agullo, Javier Rodriguez-Juan, David Ortiz-Perez, and Jose Garcia-Rodriguez[(⊠)]

Department of Computer Technology, University of Alicante, Alicante, Spain
{aberenguer,jrodriguez,dortiz,jgarcia}@dtic.ua.es

Abstract. This study embarked on a comprehensive exploration of deploying lightweight CNN models for the real-time classification of bird species, particularly focusing on their application within edge computing environments. Given the critical importance of rapid species identification in conservation efforts and ecological monitoring, this research aimed to evaluate the balance between model accuracy and computational efficiency. By meticulously selecting metrics such as Raspberry Pi inference time, accuracy on the Birds525 and CUB-200-2011 test sets or model size, we assessed the performance of various pre-trained models. Additionally, we fine-tuned the models to our specific task. Our findings reveal significant insights into the trade-offs between speed and accuracy, highlighting models like EfficientNetV2 (92% accuracy) and MobileNetV3 (0.082 inference time on Raspberry pi) variants as promising candidates for edge-based wildlife monitoring applications. These discoveries underscore the feasibility of employing deep learning techniques in real-time, resource-constrained settings, offering a quality paradigm for ecological research and conservation strategies.

Keywords: ligthweight models · convolutional networks · edge computing

1 Introduction

The International Union for Conservation of Nature (IUCN) has identified approximately 27,000 species from their evaluations as facing the threat of extinction. Furthermore, a 2019 report from the United Nations on biodiversity suggests that the total number of species at risk could surpass a million when considering all species [26]. This data reflects the threats that wild animals suffer because of the current environmental challenges. Derived from this events researchers, scientists and ecologists are making efforts on improving the comprehension of the animal biodiversity in order to be able to put measures to alleviate these problems.

As data collection is crucial for acquiring knowledge about animal biodiversity, researchers use camera traps to classify and monitor the behavior of wild

J. M. Ferrández Vicente et al. (Eds.): IWINAC 2024, LNCS 14675, pp. 95–104, 2024.
https://doi.org/10.1007/978-3-031-61137-7_10

animals [20]. Once the data is collected, a study must be conducted to draw conclusions and take action, but manually analyzing all the data can be very time-consuming and difficult for organizations. To improve the efficiency and reduce the costs associated with this study, Deep Learning (DL) is being used to automate this process. In papers such as [18], it is shown that DL can not only increase efficiency in terms of time and cost, but can also perform a better analysis compared to manual analysis.

This research is also particularly concerned with Protected Natural Areas (PNA) [5], which are under global threat despite their critical ecological importance, as highlighted by earlier discussed challenges. Given their sensitivity to alterations in their habitats and significant ecological functions, birds serve as crucial indicators of the health of these environments. Consequently, accurate identification and understanding of bird species and their behavior is essential for assessing ecosystem health and developing appropriate conservation strategies.

In this study, DL techniques are utilized to conduct a comparative analysis of various convolutional-based models for the analysis and automatic recognition of bird species. A key goal of the study is to develop a system capable of performing real-time species identification using lightweight devices such as the Raspberry Pi, which can be easily deployed in PNAs for bird monitoring. Due to these requirements, models that are efficient in terms of inference time and size are prioritized to fulfill the constraints of time and space. The main contributions of this research are summarized as follows:

- Evaluation of lightweight CNN models for real-time bird identification on edge devices, showcasing the balance between accuracy and efficiency.
- Performance assessment of the models on a macro-dataset, synthesized by the authors from the Birds525 and CUB-200-2011 datasets, aimed to explore their generalization abilities and implications for ecological monitoring.
- Highlight the potential of deploying deep learning in conservation efforts, with a focus on tailored model selection for ecological applications.

This article is structured into four additional sections. Section 2 delves into relevant studies on DL in bird species recognition and edge computing's role in ecological research. Section 3 outlines our methodology, covering dataset handling, model selection, and training. Experimental setups, evaluation metrics, and results are presented in Sect. 4, providing insights into each model's performance. The paper concludes in Sect. 5, summarizing our key findings and suggesting future research directions, aimed at enhancing biodiversity conservation through technology.

2   Related Works

In this section the most relevant literature concerning the study is reviewed. As the goal is to create a real-time classification system for bird species this section covers the bird species recognition using DL and the application of edge computing to these problem.

2.1   Bird Species Recognition

As mentioned in the previous section, the growing concern among ecologists and professionals has led researchers to apply Machine Learning (ML) techniques to the wildlife ecosystem. While this study focuses on the application of these technologies to bird species, these techniques have also been widely applied to other animals, such as snakes [2]. In the mentioned study, 22 different snake species were classified using 5 well-known ML techniques, achieving a maximum accuracy of 89.22%.

The evolution of ML techniques has also spurred advancements in bird species recognition methods. This progression is evident in the variety of methods used in this field, ranging from classical ML algorithms (e.g., SVM classifiers) to advanced DL methods. In [19], the authors employed a combination of SVM classifiers and Decision Trees to classify bird species from images, achieving a maximum accuracy of 83.87%. Although ML techniques yield good results, their performance diminishes when faced with classifying a large number of species. In such cases, the use of DL techniques is more advantageous, despite the need for a large dataset to train these complex networks effectively. In [1], the authors conducted a comparison of ML and DL Computer Vision techniques for classifying 20 different species. This study not only highlights the superiority of DL models over ML models for handling bird images but also showcases the high capabilities of these architectures, with the highest accuracies exceeding 98% when using convolutional models like DenseNet or GoogleNet. Within DL, it is also important to apply explainability [10] techniques to understand the predictions of the model.

Although this study focuses on image analysis, it is not the most common method of bird species classification, as bird species are usually recognized by their vocalizations (i.e., audio data) [29]. Species recognition through vocalizations also benefits from DL, as the same convolutional architectures used for image analysis can be applied to feature extraction and classification of bird species using audio inputs. A well-known vocalization analysis system is Bird-NET [14], capable of distinguishing between almost 1000 European and North American bird species by sound.

2.2   Edge Computing

In the realm of computational advancements, edge computing has emerged as a transformative approach for real-time data processing, particularly relevant to deploying ML and DL models in immediate applications [6, 8]. By processing data close to where it's generated-on devices at the network's edge-edge computing significantly reduces latency and enhances the efficiency of data handling. This paradigm shift is crucial for applications requiring rapid decision-making and immediate feedback, such as environmental monitoring and wildlife observation, where the speed of data processing can be as critical as the accuracy of the models themselves.

The fusion of edge computing with DL technologies has unlocked new possibilities for real-time analysis and recognition tasks [31]. In the context of animals species identification, leveraging edge computing allows for the deployment of sophisticated DL models directly onto field devices. These models are specially optimized for edge deployment, focusing on efficiency and compactness without sacrificing performance [15,16]. This approach ensures that species recognition can be performed instantaneously, directly on the device, thereby minimizing the need for continuous data transmission to centralized servers. Such advancements are particularly beneficial in remote locations where network connectivity is limited, enabling robust species monitoring and data collection in near real-time [30].

Furthermore, the integration of edge computing with DL models for species recognition holds significant implications for wildlife conservation efforts [32]. It enables more effective monitoring of ecosystems, allowing for immediate detection and response to environmental changes or the presence of specific species. By facilitating the rapid processing and analysis of environmental data at the source, edge computing stands as a cornerstone technology that enhances our ability to understand and preserve the natural world. Applications like eBird[1] or Merlin Bird ID[2] are clear examples of this integration with tools like bird observations from any location, recognition with sound and images and bird lists exploring [21].

3   Methodology

In this section, we focus on the comprehensive approach to evaluate the performance of various lightweight Convolutional Neural Network (CNN) [3,4,27] models in the task of bird species identification. The methodology encompasses several key phases: dataset selection and preparation, model selection and training, performance evaluation, and comparison analysis.

3.1   Datasets

We utilized two primary datasets: the Birds525 [9] Species dataset and the Caltech-UCSD Birds-200-2011 (CUB-200-2011) [28] dataset. The Birds525 dataset, features images of 525 bird species, serving as a diverse source for training and testing the models. The CUB-200-2011 dataset, a widely recognized benchmark in bird species recognition, comprises images of 200 bird species with detailed annotations.

Birds525 Species Dataset. The Birds525 dataset represents a comprehensive collection of bird species imagery, featuring 525 distinct bird species. It is comprised of 84,635 training images, 2,625 test images, and 2,625 validation images,

---

[1] https://ebird.org/home.

[2] https://merlin.allaboutbirds.org/.

equating to 5 images per species for both testing and validation purposes. Each image within the dataset is a 224 × 224 RGB image, capturing a single bird that occupies at least 50% of the image frame. This careful selection and preparation process is expected to guarantee that even moderately complex models can achieve training and test accuracies in the mid-90% range. The dataset predominantly features male species images, comprising about 80% of the total, which may introduce a bias towards more colorfully depicted males over the typically less vibrant females.

Caltech-UCSD Birds-200-2011 (CUB-200-2011) Dataset. The CUB-200-2011 dataset serves as an extensive resource for bird species recognition, building upon its predecessor, the CUB-200 dataset, by doubling the number of images per class and introducing new part location annotations. This dataset encompasses 200 bird species categories with a total of 11,788 images of different sizes. Each image is annotated with 15 part locations, 312 binary attributes, and a bounding box, providing a rich set of data points for detailed species analysis and recognition.

The CUB-200-2011 dataset's comprehensive annotations and increased image count per class make it a widely acknowledged benchmark in the field of bird species identification. This dataset comprises a set of different perspectives for each species, underlining its significance for training models that require a deep understanding of avian biodiversity and specific species characteristics.

3.2 Training

To explore the generalization capabilities of the models, we combine these datasets into a macro-dataset, aiming to obtain more diverse training foundation which can significantly enhance the generalization capabilities of the model. This integration process involves standardizing image dimensions and normalizing pixel values to enhance model robustness against overfitting. Then, the macro-dataset is split into training, validation, and test sets, ensuring an equal representation of each species across these partitions. This macro-dataset was used to train the CNN models considered in this study.

Prior to our main analysis, we individually trained the models on each dataset to assess if the increased diversity and complexity of the training data leads to enhanced accuracy and better generalization in different testing situations. A notable outcome could be the demonstration of enhanced model performance on individual datasets, evidencing the ability of the model to not only learn generalized features applicable across a broad spectrum of bird species, but also to maintain high levels of specificity and accuracy when evaluated in more constrained contexts. This dual assessment provides insights into the trade-offs between model generalization and specialization.

Finally, model performance is evaluated based on inference time on the Raspberry Pi 4 Model B[3]. Accuracy metrics are calculated separately for each dataset

---

[3] https://www.raspberrypi.com/products/raspberry-pi-4-model-b/.

and the combined test set to assess the specificity of the model and generalization ability. Inference time, measured in milliseconds per image, provides insight into each model's suitability for real-time identification tasks.

4 Experiments

The experimentation is focused on the use of a macro-dataset which comprises both datasets mentioned above with the objective of enhancing the generalization capabilities of the models, for them to be able to identify birds species under different perspectives and environmental conditions on the edge.

4.1 Setup

In our experimentation, we rigorously evaluate the performance of various lightweight CNN models. For this purpose, we select a range of pre-trained [17] models, including GoogleNet [22], ResNet152 [11], DenseNet161 [13], EfficientNetV2_s [24], MnasNet1_0 [23], MobileNetV3_small [12], and MobileNetV3_large [12], all of which were initially trained on the ImageNet dataset [7]. These models are chosen for their diversity in architecture and efficiency in handling image classification tasks, making them suitable candidates for deployment on the edge, on resource-constrained devices such as the Raspberry Pi.

To ensure a fair and consistent comparison [25] across all models, standard training procedures are employed, with each model being fine-tuned on our assembled macro-dataset. This approach allows us to directly assess the impact of dataset diversity and model architecture on the generalization capabilities of each CNN model. Training of the models is conducted on a computing setup featuring a NVIDIA GeForce RTX 3090.

4.2 Results

Our analysis is guided by a set of meticulously chosen metrics, designed to holistically evaluate each model's capabilities and efficiency. These metrics include Raspberry Pi inference time, accuracy on both the Birds525 and CUB-200-2011 test sets, model size in megabytes (MB), and training time over 100 epochs. These parameters are selected not only for their relevance in assessing the technical performance of the models, but also for their practical implications in applications on the edge where computational resources and response times are critical.

Our training and testing procedures incorporate simple yet effective transformation techniques to enhance model robustness and generalization. The dataset transformations include resizing images to 256 pixels and center cropping to 224 pixels. These preprocessing steps are crucial for aligning the input data with the expectations of the models and for introducing variability that helps prevent overfitting.

We have derived insightful conclusions from the comparison across three tables. Table 1 presents a holistic view, juxtaposing inference time on Raspberry Pi, accuracy across both datasets, individual dataset accuracies, model size, and training duration. Notably, EfficientNetV2 stands out for its highest combined dataset accuracy of 0.9217, demonstrating superior generalization capabilities. Conversely, MobileNetV3 Small, with the lowest inference time (0.082 s), exemplifies the critical balance between speed and accuracy, essential for real-time applications. The variance in model sizes and inference times underscores the computational constraints consideration when deploying models on edge devices.

Table 1. Metrics comparison for the different models. From left to right, columns refer to: the CNN model used, the time of inference on the Raspberry Pi in seconds, the accuracy of the model on both datasets, the accuracy of the model on the Birds525 dataset, the accuracy of the model on the CUB dataset, the size of the model in Mega Bytes and the time spent for training in hours.

Model	RPI(s)	Both	Birds525	CUB	Size(MB)	Training(h)
GoogleNet [22]	0.470	0.8975	0.8033	0.9821	24	4.8
ResNet152 [11]	3.018	0.9057	0.8211	0.9817	227	14.4
DenseNet161 [13]	2.127	0.8770	0.7715	0.9728	116	15.2
EfficientNetV2 [24]	1.041	**0.9217**	**0.8474**	0.9886	82.7	9.90
MNASNet [23]	0.261	0.9191	0.8410	**0.9893**	16.9	3.87
MobileNetV3 Small [12]	**0.082**	0.8949	0.7974	0.9825	**9.8**	**3.84**
MobileNetV3 Large [12]	0.190	0.9097	0.8215	0.9890	21.1	4.32

Delving into dataset-specific performances, Table 2 and Table 3 offer a more nuanced understanding. Table 2, focusing on the Birds525 dataset, reveals EfficientNetV2's remarkable top accuracy of 0.9943, paired with a moderate model size and training time, highlighting its efficiency and robustness in handling diverse bird species imagery. On the other hand, MobileNetV3 Small and Large models, despite their lower accuracies, present an intriguing option due to their minimal model sizes and reduced training hours, suggesting a viable pathway for applications with stringent storage and computational resource limitations.

Table 3's examination of the CUB-200-2011 dataset outcomes further accentuates the distinctions in model performances. Here, EfficientNetV2 again leads in accuracy (0.8504), solidifying its position as a highly effective model for bird species recognition tasks. Interestingly, the disparities in training times between models become narrower within this dataset context, indicating a potential dataset-specific optimization convergence among the models.

EfficientNetV2's standout performance across metrics suggests it as a formidable choice for balancing accuracy with computational efficiency. However, the appeal of MobileNetV3 variants for their ultra-fast inference times and minimal footprint cannot be overlooked, especially in scenarios where real-time data processing is paramount, and computational resources are limited.

Table 2. Metrics comparison of the models on the Birds525 dataset.

Model	RPI(s)	Accuracy	Size(MB)	Training(h)
GoogleNet [22]	0.471	0.9783	24	6.30
ResNet152 [11]	2.983	0.9714	227	15.10
DenseNet161 [13]	2.056	0.9714	116	14.80
EfficientNetV2 [24]	1.036	**0.9943**	82.7	9.39
MNASNet [23]	0.233	0.9878	16.9	6.63
MobileNetV3 Small [12]	**0.081**	0.9832	**9.8**	**3.91**
MobileNetV3 Large [12]	0.188	0.9859	21.1	4.43

Table 3. Metrics comparison of the models on the CUB-200-2011 dataset.

Model	RPI(s)	Accuracy	Size(MB)	Training(h)
GoogleNet [22]	0.464	0.8008	24	4.60
ResNet152 [11]	2.912	0.8008	227	4.80
DenseNet161 [13]	2.113	0.8203	116	4.90
EfficientNetV2 [24]	1.033	**0.8504**	82.7	4.00
MNASNet [23]	0.232	0.8364	16.9	2.50
MobileNetV3 Small [12]	**0.078**	0.7927	**9.8**	**2.16**
MobileNetV3 Large [12]	0.188	0.8101	21.1	2.32

This comparative analysis not only underscores the advancements in lightweight CNN architectures but also guides future research and deployment strategies for real-time bird species recognition, emphasizing the critical need to tailor model selection to the specific requirements and constraints of the application environment.

5   Conclusion

Our investigation into lightweight CNN models for real-time bird species identification underscores the pivotal role of edge computing in ecological conservation. Through comprehensive metrics evaluation, EfficientNetV2 showcased an optimal blend of accuracy and efficiency. Meanwhile, MobileNetV3 models offered rapid processing capabilities. The research underlines the feasibility and critical considerations of deploying deep learning models in resource-limited settings for environmental studies. Future directions include enhancing model efficiency and integrating these technologies into broader conservation practices. This work enriches the dialogue on leveraging edge computing and deep learning for biodiversity preservation, marking a step forward in technological applications for environmental sustainability.

Acknowledgment. We would like to thank "A way of making Europe" European Regional Development Fund (ERDF) and MCIN/AEI/10.13039/501100011033 for supporting this work under the "CHAN-TWIN" project (grant TED2021-130890B-C21. HORIZON-MSCA-2021-SE-0 action number: 101086387, REMARKABLE, Rural Environmental Monitoring via ultra wide-ARea networKs And distriButed federated Learning. This work has also been supported by a Spanish regional grant for PhD studies, CIACIF/2022/175, a research initiation grant from the University of Alicante, AII23-12, and ValgrAI grant for MSc studies. Finally we would like to thanks the support of the University Institute for Computer Research at the UA.

References

1. Alswaitti, M., et al.: Effective classification of birds' species based on transfer learning. JECE **12**, 15 (2022)
2. Amir, A., Zahri, N.A.H., Yaakob, N., Ahmad, R.B.: Image classification for snake species using machine learning techniques. In: Phon-Amnuaisuk, S., Au, T.-W., Omar, S. (eds.) CIIS 2016. AISC, vol. 532, pp. 52–59. Springer, Cham (2017). https://doi.org/10.1007/978-3-319-48517-1_5
3. Azorin-Lopez, J., et al.: A novel prediction method for early recognition of global human behaviour in image sequences. Neural Process. Lett. **43**(2), 363–387 (2016)
4. Azorín-López, J., et al.: Human behaviour recognition based on trajectory analysis using neural networks. In: IJCNN, pp. 1–7 (2013)
5. Cazalis, V., et al.: Effectiveness of protected areas in conserving tropical forest birds. Nat. Commun. **11**(1), 4461 (2020)
6. Chen, J., Ran, X.: Deep learning with edge computing: a review. Proc. IEEE **107**(8), 1655–1674 (2019)
7. Deng, J., et al.: Imagenet: a large-scale hierarchical image database. In: 2009 IEEE Conference on Computer Vision and Pattern Recognition, pp. 248–255 (2009)
8. Fanariotis, A., et al.: Power efficient machine learning models deployment on edge IoT devices. Sensors **23**(3) (2023)
9. Gerry. Birds 525 species- image classification, April 2023
10. Górriz, J.M., et al.: Computational approaches to explainable artificial intelligence: advances in theory, applications and trends. Inf. Fusion **100**, 101945 (2023)
11. He, K., Zhang, X., Ren, S., Sun, J.: Deep residual learning for image recognition. In: Proceedings of the IEEE Conference on Computer Vision and Pattern Recognition (CVPR), June 2016
12. Howard, A., et al.: Searching for mobilenetv3. In: Proceedings of the IEEE/CVF International Conference on Computer Vision (ICCV), October 2019
13. Huang, G., Liu, Z., van der Maaten, L., Weinberger, K.Q.: Densely connected convolutional networks. In: Proceedings of the IEEE Conference on Computer Vision and Pattern Recognition (CVPR), July 2017
14. Kahl, S., et al.: Birdnet: a deep learning solution for avian diversity monitoring. Eco. Inform. **61**, 101236 (2021)
15. Kim, R., et al.: A method for optimizing deep learning object detection in edge computing. In: ICTC, pp. 1164–1167 (2020)
16. Kristiani, E., et al.: ISEC: an optimized deep learning model for image classification on edge computing. IEEE Access **8**, 27267–27276 (2020)
17. Lucas, L., et al.: Detecting and locating trending places using multimodal social network data. Multimed. Tools Appl. **82**(24), 38097–38116 (2023)

18. Norouzzadeh, M.S., et al.: Automatically identifying, counting, and describing wild animals in camera-trap images with deep learning. Proc. Natl. Acad. Sci. **115**(25), E5716–E5725 (2018)
19. Qiao, B., Zhou, Z., Yang, H., Cao, J.: Bird species recognition based on SVM classifier and decision tree. In: EIIS, pp. 1–4 (2017)
20. Schindler, F., Steinhage, V.: Identification of animals and recognition of their actions in wildlife videos using deep learning techniques. Eco. Inform. **61**, 101215 (2021)
21. Sullivan, B.L., et al.: The ebird enterprise: an integrated approach to development and application of citizen science. Biol. Cons. **169**, 31–40 (2014)
22. Szegedy, C., et al.: Going deeper with convolutions. In: Proceedings of the IEEE Conference on Computer Vision and Pattern Recognition (CVPR), June 2015
23. Tan, M., et al.: Mnasnet: platform-aware neural architecture search for mobile (2019). arXiv:1807.11626
24. Tan, M., Le, Q.: Efficientnetv2: smaller models and faster training. In: Meila, M., Zhang, T. (eds.) In: Proceedings of the 38th International Conference on Machine Learning. Proceedings of Machine Learning Research, vol. 139, pp. 10096–10106. PMLR, 18–24 Jul 2021
25. Teterja, D., et al.: A performance evaluation of lightweight deep learning approaches for bird recognition. In: Advances in Computational Intelligence, pp. 328–339 (2023)
26. Prem, H.T.: What are the biggest threats to wildlife and why? February 2020
27. Viejo, D., Garcia, J., Cazorla, M., Gil, D., Johnsson, M.: Using GNG to improve 3d feature extraction-application to 6DoF egomotion. Neural Netw. **32**, 138–146 (2012)
28. Wah, C., et al.: Caltech-ucsd birds-200-2011. Technical report CNS-TR-2011-001, California Institute of Technology (2011)
29. Xie, J., et al.: A review of automatic recognition technology for bird vocalizations in the deep learning era. Eco. Inform. **73**, 101927 (2023)
30. Xie, Y., et al.: Recognition of big mammal species in airborne thermal imaging based on yolo v5 algorithm. Remote Sensing Ecol. Conservation **18**(2) (2022)
31. Zaidi, S.S.A., et al.: A survey of modern deep learning based object detection models. Digital Signal Process. **126**, 103514 (2022)
32. Zhong, Y., et al.: A lightweight automatic wildlife recognition model design method mitigating shortcut learning. Animals **13**(5) (2023)

Learning Adaptable Utility Models
for Morphological Diversity

Francella Campos-Alfaro[1], Carlos Jara[1], Alejandro Romero[2(✉)],
Martín Naya-Varela[2], and Richard J. Duro[2]

[1] Tecnológico de Costa Rica, Cartago, Costa Rica
{cfrancella29,carlosjaravas}@estudiantec.cr
[2] Integrated Group for Engineering Research, Universidade da Coruña,
A Coruña, Spain
{alejandro.romero.montero,martin.naya,richard}@udc.es

Abstract. This paper introduces an approach to the integration of
open-ended learning in modular robotics. We aim to provide these
robots, equipped with morphological adaptability, with the capability
to autonomously learn utility models specific to each morphology, discovering objectives on their own through a motivational system designed
for open-ended learning. This system incorporates intrinsic motivations
based on novelty and introduces a unique intrinsic motivation based
on frustration to prevent learning stagnation. Furthermore, the paper
addresses the autonomous learning of world models, enabling the robot
to identify its morphology, all within the framework of a cognitive architecture. Experimental results showcase the effectiveness of this approach
in both real and simulated environments.

Keywords: Modular robots · Open-ended learning · Cognitive
architecture · Morphology Recognition

1 Introduction

The quest for autonomous learning in robotics has led to a convergence of interdisciplinary research spanning robotics, artificial intelligence, and cognitive science. Central to the concept of autonomous learning is the notion of open-ended
learning [23], characterized by the fact that robots are continuously faced with
new domains and goals that they must learn. Recent studies have shed light on
how this approach fosters resilience in robots, enabling them to adapt to unfore-
seen challenges and acquire novel skills over time [21]. In particular, the work of
different researchers [7,20,24] has demonstrated how providing for open-ended
learning empowers robots to discover and set their own goals.

This work was funded by the European Union's Horizon 2020, research and innovation
programme under GA 101070381 ('PILLAR-Robots'), by MCIN (PID2021-126220OB-
I00), by Xunta de Galicia (EDC431C-2021/39), and by the Xunta de Galicia (ED481B).
Special thanks to the CESGA.

J. M. Ferrández Vicente et al. (Eds.): IWINAC 2024, LNCS 14675, pp. 105–115, 2024.
https://doi.org/10.1007/978-3-031-61137-7_11

One key component to enable autonomous open-ended learning in robots are motivational systems rooted on the concept of intrinsic motivations. The work of [14,17,22], among others, sheds light on the integration of intrinsic motivations, particularly those driven by novelty and competence as a means to encourage exploration and goal discovery in robots. By harnessing the power of intrinsic motivations, robots can become not merely reactive agents but proactive learners, driven by a desire for novelty and a quest for mastery.

The relevance of the morphology of the robot for its learning processes is the focus of the field of Artificial Embodied Intelligence (AEI) [4,15], which emphasizes the emergence of intelligence as an interaction between brain, morphology and the different environments the robot must operate in. In fact, it has been suggested that not only is the static morphology of the robot relevant for learning, but that its morphological history can be harnessed to improve the learning results [3]. In this line, [5,9,13], among others, have proposed different approaches to the implementation of morphological development processes and studied their effect on the learning capabilities of robots. In general, these studies have considered standard robots that were modified to introduce morphological developmental capabilities such as the capability of extending some extremities to simulate growth.

In the last decade, modular robots have emerged as a promising platform [11], offering the potential for adaptive morphologies and versatile capabilities. Within this field, the emphasis has usually been placed on building modular structures that could be easily reconfigured, but for which most behaviors were directly programmed. When learning was considered, it was carried out by traditional means, that is, without taking into account the fact that a potentially changing morphology was available.

Now, if one takes hints from the morphological development advances, one could hypothesize that, as modular design empowers robots to dynamically reconfigure their physical structure, it can open up a path to enhance their ability to learn and respond to varying environmental challenges. To achieve this objective, a need arises for cognitive architectures that can provide some stability to the learning processes involved and some structure to the components learnt and used. The deployment of cognitive architectures has emerged as a promising approach to facilitate autonomous learning in robots [10]. By endowing robots with cognitive capabilities, these architectures enable them to synthesize sensory information, reason about their environment, and adapt their behavior in real-time. These comprehensive frameworks orchestrate the integration of different knowledge components, providing a holistic approach to lifelong open-ended learning autonomy (LOLA) [18]. Consequently, modular morphological design together with an open-ended learning cognitive architecture can serve as the cornerstone for advancing autonomous learning in robots. These elements can synergistically interact, forming the building blocks for developing adaptive and self-improving robotic systems.

In this context, our work contributes to these developments by studying the integration of open-ended learning approaches within the field of modular robots.

Leveraging the motivational system of a cognitive architecture, this work studies the effect of incorporating intrinsic motivations such as novelty and frustration, as well as providing autonomous morphology identification strategies to modular robotic systems with the aim empowering robots to continually enhance themselves and adaptively solve problems. By embracing the principles of modular design, open-ended learning, and intrinsic motivation, we provide a path towards new possibilities for improving performance in dynamic environments.

2   Motivational System for Open-Ended Learning

The framework underpinning this work is the e-MDB cognitive architecture [2]. Designed to facilitate lifelong open-ended learning within real robotic systems. This architecture enables artificial agents to learn from their experiences in order to accomplish their objectives in dynamic and unfamiliar environments. It comprises three principal components:

- A real time Learning System that facilitates the creation and acquisition of the different knowledge components required for the operation of the architecture. In particular, utility models [1,19], as evaluators of states in different domains and for different tasks, and world models to represent the robot's operating domains.
- A Memory System that stores and associates goals, models, and acquired knowledge. Utilizing a contextual representation [6], it facilitates knowledge reuse and association, ensuring proper linkage between utility models and their corresponding world models. This aspect enables the robot to determine which utility model to employ with each morphology.
- A Motivational System that establishes the robot's motivations, identifies new goals, and selects active ones. Its operation is based on needs and drives [8] that are domain-independent, which allows it to assign purpose to the robot regardless of its operating domain. A detailed explanation of its operation can be found in [17]. In this work, the motivational system comprises two primary motivations based on novelty and frustration, which enable the continual enhancement and adaptive problem-solving capabilities of the robot. Both motivations are implemented as drives and are described below.

2.1   Novelty-Based Intrinsic Motivation. Enhancing Exploration

One key aspect of motivational systems, as proposed by [14] or [17], is the incorporation of a novelty-based intrinsic motivation. This component drives the robot towards exploring its environment, encouraging curiosity and the discovery of new goals. By prioritizing visiting novel/unexplored regions within the state space, this motivation prompts the robot to sample the state space, facilitating the creation of models and/or the pursuit of goal points.

In this paper, this novelty-search behavior, is implemented by means of a deliberative skill that manipulates the robot's actuators. This skill enables the robot to anticipate the perceptual states resulting from its actions and to select actions based on the novelty of the ensuing state. Novelty can be quantified as the distance between the new state, post-action, and a series of recent perceptual states stored in a memory. Therefore, the novelty value for the k-th candidate state, denoted as $s_{c,k}$, is calculated as follows:

$$Nov = 1 - \frac{1}{M} \sum_{i=1}^{M} dist(s_{c,k}, s_i)^n, k \in [1, N]$$

Here, n represents a coefficient regulating the balance between the significance of distant and nearby states, s_i denotes the i-th state in the memory, N denotes the number of randomly considered candidates, and M is the number of perceptual states stored in memory.

2.2 Frustration-Based Intrinsic Motivation. Preventing Learning Stagnation

The novelty-based motivation by itself may lead to learning stagnation under some specific circumstances. Thus, here we propose its integration with a frustration-based motivation within the Motivational System. This component serves as a mechanism to prevent learning stagnation and encourage perseverance in the face of challenges. When the robot encounters obstacles or setbacks, the frustration-based motivation kicks in, stimulating the exploration of alternative strategies and pathways to achieve its goals.

Frustration is implemented as a short-term memory system, in which the robot stores the most recent perceptual states it has encountered. This enables the robot to detect if it has been revisiting nearby perceptual states for a significant period without making progress towards its goals. To determine the frustration level, the following equation is used:

$$F = 1 - \sqrt{\sigma_m} = 1 - \sqrt{\frac{1}{M} \sum_{i=1}^{M} (s_i - \mu)^2}$$

where σ_m represents the standard deviation of the normalized data stored in memory, s_i denotes the i-th perceptual state stored in memory, and μ is the mean of the M perceptual states stored in memory. Thus, this equation quantifies the frustration level based on the variability of the stored perceptual states.

3 Deliberative Decision-Making with World and Utility Models

The availability of world models and utility models in robotics plays a fundamental role in deliberative decision-making. World models represent the robot's understanding of the physical environment as well as the robot's own morphology. On the other hand, utility models encapsulate the robot's preferences and objectives, assigning utility values to different actions and their potential outcomes. Through these models, the robot can assess the anticipated consequences of its actions and select the best strategy to achieve its goals. Therefore, by combining world and utility models, the robot can engage in deliberative planning, considering various options and choosing the most promising action based on its understanding of the environment, its own morphology, and its goals. This approach enables the robot to make informed and adaptable decisions, even in complex and changing scenarios.

In the following subsections we will describe our approaches for the learning process of world models and utility models.

3.1   World Model Learning

World models are functions that describe a robot's behavior in a specific domain. They can be viewed as predictors that take the current state of the robot, represented by a set of perceptions, along with the action the robot applies, and predict the next state. However, perceptions are closely tied to the domain (and morphology) in which the model was trained, meaning that predictions made using a world model may not be valid for a different morphology. This underscores the importance of autonomously learning world models, as in open-ended learning scenarios domains can change without prior notice.

In this work, world models are represented as Artificial Neural Networks (ANN). Therefore, to train and learn the world models we need to autonomously generate the data necessary for training the ANN. This can be achieved by having the robot randomly interacting with the environment, since any action in the environment provides valid information for the world model learning process. In the experiments presented, we set up a simulation using CoppeliaSim, and executed sets of actions grouped into sequences. Several sequences were created and run until the predictive accuracy of the model improved to the desired level.

3.2   Utility Model Learning

Expected Utility Models, or value functions in Reinforcement Learning (RL) terminology, provide an estimation of the utility of each point in the state space and can be used to evaluate the utility of state space points with respect to reaching a goal. As before, we represent these models as ANNs. Again, to learn them, we have to autonomously generate the data to train the ANN. In this case, the robot's knowledge of the goal, or the pathways (traces) it took to get there in the state space, must serve as the foundation for the training of these models. Thus, the robot needs to explore its domain in order to be able to find goal points. To this end, the exploration method motivated by novelty was employed. During the exploration stage, the robot stores traces to the goal, meaning every point in the state space it has visited in chronological order before reaching the goal. Once the robot reaches the goal, a real utility value of 1 is assigned to this state, and points in this trace are assigned decreasing values as a function of their distance to the goal. This process is depicted in Fig. 1.

Episodic memory	
P_{10}	1.0
P_9	0.8
P_8	0.6
P_7	0.4
P_6	0.2

Fig. 1. Utility model learning process.

To be able to minimize the ambiguities or biases in the learning process it is important to produce a significant amount of traces with a variety of starting points to be employed as the database to correctly train the ANN.

4   Experimental Setup: EMERGE Robot

In order to run some experiments contemplating all of the aspects commented, the robotic platform used is the EMERGE modular robot [12]. It is an open-source robot, designed to allow a fast assembly of the different robotic configurations. It avoids complex self-reconfiguration mechanisms requiring an external manipulator for modifying the morphology. The current version of the robot is based on an actuated module with only one rotational degree of freedom, controlled by a servomotor, and four connection faces. The connection faces have 4 magnetic connectors to establish the mechanical connection between modules. EMERGE has its own simulation model in CoppeliaSim [16] for performing fast experimentation, which was used to carry out preliminary tests before moving to the real robot and where the world models were learned.

To provide for a methodological study of the problem of combining modular robotics with cognitive architectures, we have made use of the two morphologies shown in Fig. 2: a robot with two actuated EMERGE modules, and a robot with three actuated EMERGE modules.

The ANN used for learning the world model has 9 inputs: 6 for perceptions, representing the spatial position of the robot's end module in the X, Y, and Z axes, as well as the angular position of each of the 3 motors in the modules used. Additionally, there are 3 inputs for the actions applied to the module's motors. The ANN has 3 densely connected hidden layers with 27 neurons each, that use *tanh* activation functions, and a linear activation function in the output layer. The optimizer used for the weight adjustment was the Adam optimizer together with a Huber loss function. There are 6 outputs of the world model, one for each of the predicted perceptions.

Fig. 2. Both simulated and real representations of 2-module (left) and 3-module robot (right).

The output of this world model is re-described before being used in the UM. It is used to determine the distance between the robot's end-point position and the position of a colored ball introduced in the scenario. Consequently, the UM has only one input, consisting of the relative distance between the ball and the robot's end-point position Meanwhile the output corresponds to the expected utility, and its values are in the range [0,1]. The UM is also an ANN, that is also updated using an Adam optimizer with a Huber loss function.

In the simulator, the inputs were obtained directly from CoppeliaSim, both before and after execution. However, for the real robot, the current position of the actuators was obtained from their memory, and the position of the robot's end point was acquired using an OptiTrack tracking system. Actions were randomly generated within the working range of the EMERGE modules ($-7°$ to $7°$) in both simulation and real-world experiments.

5   Experimental Results

This section outlines a series of experimental results obtained to evaluate the effectiveness of the proposed motivational system in discovering and learning how to reach different objectives with different morphologies in open-ended learning scenarios. Several independent experiments were run with the morphologies depicted in Fig. 2 in a scenario with a colored ball. The objective is for the robot, whatever its morphology, to discover the location of the goal (colored ball) and learn to reach it regardless of its position in the environment. To do so, it will have to learn the specific world model associated to each morphology and also learn the utility model to be able to reach the goal in a deliberative way. The experiments were conducted both in simulation and with the real robot.

Figure 3 illustrates the impact of intrinsic motivations, novelty and frustration, on the robot's behavior and decision-making. It shows the number of time steps needed for the robot to achieve the goal with the two different morphologies and with three different methods to guide its behavior: using just random actions as a baseline method, using a motivational system based on novelty to choose actions, and using the motivational system with novelty and frustration proposed here.

In Fig. 3 left, when the 3 module morphology is being used, it can be seen that during exploration through random movements, the robot's movement patterns are highly variable, involving up to 350 steps in a single trace. However, when the robot is guided by the motivational system where only novelty-driven exploration is implemented, the average number of steps is significantly reduced to around 30, indicating more efficient exploration and that the corresponding utility model was learned faster. Despite this improvement, it is possible to see that in some moments the robot may still encounter stagnation points where it remains stuck, causing it to need many more steps to discover the goal, sometimes up to 150 steps. At this point, the introduction of a frustration mechanism proves beneficial. As shown by the turquoise lines, it detects the robot's repetitive behavior and injects this motivation for a dynamic response, enabling the robot to overcome such impasses, and reducing the step count to an average of 30 steps. It is also important to note that in the last case, the variability in the results of 5 runs for each experiment is also much lower than in the other cases, supporting the efficiency of the implementation.

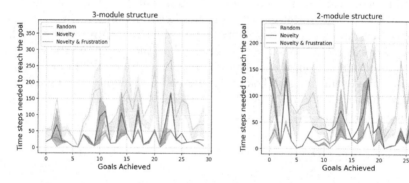

Fig. 3. Performance results for 5 independent runs of the experiment with the 2 tested morphologies. Left: 3-module morphology. Right: 2-module morphology.

A similar behavior can be observed in Fig. 3 right, where the results for the morphology with two modules are presented. These results also serve to highlight the efficiency of the proposed system for each of the different morphologies tested.

On the other hand, Fig. 4 shows how the use of a cognitive architecture facilitates learning processes and knowledge reuse. It depicts the difference between using a cognitive architecture framework to continue past learning processes or do it from scratch. It can be seen that when changing morphology (marked in the figures by vertical lines), once the models for reaching the goal have been learned, it is not necessary to relearn them again (see the pink line), unlike what happens when not using a cognitive architecture (see the green dotted line). The architecture links the learned utility models with the corresponding world models, so that it is possible to identify which morphology is current and reuse the already acquired knowledge.

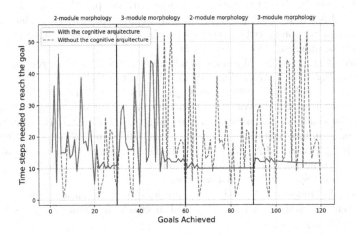

Fig. 4. Robustness to domain and morphological changes.

Additionally, to illustrate the behavior of the robot with the different morphologies, some videos of the real robot can be found in: https://github.com/alejandro-romero/IWINAC_2024.

6   Conclusion

In conclusion, this paper has presented a new approach into the realm of autonomous learning in modular robotics, emphasizing the synergy between morphological adaptability, open-ended learning, and intrinsic motivations. The development of utility models tailored to specific morphologies, coupled with the ability of robots to autonomously recognize their configurations, demonstrates the capability of this approach to enhance adaptability and autonomy.

We also showed that a cognitive architecture can provide a structured framework for robots to seamlessly integrate morphology recognition into the learning and decision-making processes. By leveraging intrinsic motivations rooted in both novelty and frustration, our approach not only encourages exploratory behavior but also serves as a dynamic safeguard against learning stagnation, fostering continual improvement.

Now, as future research there is a need for addressing issues related to further refining the interplay between morphology recognition and utility model adaptation and extending this framework to more complex robotic systems.

References

1. Romero, A., Bellas, F., Prieto, A., Duro, R.J.: Utility model re-description within a motivational system for cognitive robotics. In: 2018 IEEE/RSJ International Conference on Intelligent Robots and Systems (IROS), pp. 2324–2329. IEEE (2018)
2. Becerra, J.A., Romero, A., Bellas, F., Duro, R.J.: Motivational engine and long-term memory coupling within a cognitive architecture for lifelong open-ended learning. Neurocomputing **452**, 341–354 (2021)
3. Bongard, J.: Morphological change in machines accelerates the evolution of robust behavior. Proc. Natl. Acad. Sci. **108**(4), 1234–1239 (2011)
4. Chrisley, R.: Embodied artificial intelligence. Artif. Intell. **149**(1), 131–150 (2003)
5. Deimel, R., Irmisch, P., Wall, V., Brock, O.: Automated co-design of soft hand morphology and control strategy for grasping. In: 2017 IEEE/RSJ International Conference on Intelligent Robots and Systems (IROS), pp. 1213–1218. IEEE (2017)
6. Duro, R.J., Becerra, J.A., Monroy, J., Bellas, F.: Perceptual generalization and context in a network memory inspired long-term memory for artificial cognition. Int. J. Neural Syst. **29**(06), 1850053 (2019)
7. Gottlieb, J., Oudeyer, P.Y., Lopes, M., Baranes, A.: Information-seeking, curiosity, and attention: computational and neural mechanisms. Trends Cogn. Sci. **17**(11), 585–593 (2013)
8. Hawes, N.: A survey of motivation frameworks for intelligent systems. Artif. Intell. **175**(5–6), 1020–1036 (2011)
9. Ivanchenko, V., Jacobs, R.A.: A developmental approach aids motor learning. Neural Comput. **15**(9), 2051–2065 (2003)
10. Kotseruba, I., Tsotsos, J.K.: 40 years of cognitive architectures: core cognitive abilities and practical applications. Artif. Intell. Rev. **53**(1), 17–94 (2020)
11. Liu, J., Zhang, X., Hao, G.: Survey on research and development of reconfigurable modular robots. Adv. Mech. Eng. **8**(8), 1687814016659597 (2016)
12. Moreno, R., Faiña, A.: Emerge modular robot: a tool for fast deployment of evolved robots. Front. Robot. AI **8**, 699814 (2021)
13. Naya-Varela, M., Faina, A., Duro, R.J.: Morphological development in robotic learning: a survey. IEEE Trans. Cognit. Dev. Syst. **13**(4), 750–768 (2021)
14. Oudeyer, P.Y., Kaplan, F., Hafner, V.V.: Intrinsic motivation systems for autonomous mental development. IEEE Trans. Evol. Comput. **11**(2), 265–286 (2007)
15. Pfeifer, R., Iida, F.: Embodied artificial intelligence: Trends and challenges. Lecture notes in computer science, pp. 1–26 (2004)
16. Rohmer, E., Singh, S.P.N., Freese, M.: Coppeliasim (formerly v-rep): a versatile and scalable robot simulation framework. In: Proceedings of the International Conference on Intelligent Robots and Systems (IROS) (2013)
17. Romero, A., Bellas, F., Becerra, J.A., Duro, R.J.: Motivation as a tool for designing lifelong learning robots. Int. Comput.-Aided Eng. **27**(4), 353–372 (2020)
18. Romero, A., Bellas, F., Duro, R.J.: A perspective on lifelong open-ended learning autonomy for robotics through cognitive architectures. Sensors **23**(3), 1611 (2023)
19. Romero, A., Prieto, A., Bellas, F., Duro, R.J.: Simplifying the creation and management of utility models in continuous domains for cognitive robotics. Neurocomputing **353**, 106–118 (2019)
20. Santucci, V.G., Baldassarre, G., Mirolli, M.: Which is the best intrinsic motivation signal for learning multiple skills? Front. Neurorobot. **7**, 22 (2013)

21. Santucci, V.G., Oudeyer, P.Y., Barto, A., Baldassarre, G.: Intrinsically motivated open-ended learning in autonomous robots (2020)
22. Schmidhuber, J.: Formal theory of creativity, fun, and intrinsic motivation (1990–2010). IEEE Trans. Auton. Ment. Dev. 2(3), 230–247 (2010)
23. Sigaud, O., et al.: A definition of open-ended learning problems for goal-conditioned agents. arXiv preprint arXiv:2311.00344 (2023)
24. Volpi, N.C., Polani, D.: Goal-directed empowerment: combining intrinsic motivation and task-oriented behaviour. IEEE Trans. Cognitive Dev. Syst. (2020)

Deep Learning-Based Classification of Invasive Coronary Angiographies with Different Patch-Generation Techniques

Ariadna Jiménez-Partinen[1,3]($\boxtimes$) , Esteban J. Palomo[1,3] ,
Karl Thurnhofer-Hemsi[1,3,4] , Jorge Rodríguez-Capitán[2,3,4] ,
and Ana I. Molina-Ramos[2,3,4]

[1] Department of Computer Languages and Computer Science, University of Málaga,
Bulevar Louis Pasteur, 35, 29071 Malaga, Spain
{ariadna,ejpalomo}@uma.es, karlkhader@lcc.uma.es
[2] Cardiology Deparment, Hospital Universitario Virgen de la Victoria, 29010 Malaga,
Spain
[3] Instituto de Investigación Biomédica de Málaga y Plataforma en
Nanomedicina-IBIMA Plataforma BIONAND, C/ Severo Ochoa, 35, Málaga
TechPark, 29590 Malaga, Spain
[4] Centro de Investigación Biomédica en Red de Enfermedades Cardiovasculares
(CIBERCV), Instituto de Salud Carlos III (ISCIII), Avenida Monforte de Lemos, 3-5.
Pabellón 11. Planta 0, 28029 Madrid, Spain

Abstract. Medical imaging is one of the areas where computer-aided
diagnosis could improve the efficiency of diagnosis in clinical settings.
Cardiovascular artery disease (CAD) is diagnosed by invasive coronary angiography (ICA). This paper reports on performance analysis
for binary classification of ICA images by grouping severity ranges and
evaluates how performance is affected by the degree of lesions and the
patch generation technique considered. An annotated dataset of ICA
images was used, categorizing lesions into seven possible ranges: ¡20%,
[20%, 50%), [50%, 70%), [70%, 90%), [90%, 98%], 99% and 100%. In this
study, three pre-trained CNN architectures were trained using different
categories of lesion severity as input, and their F-measures and accuracy
were computed, achieving a performance above 90%.

Keywords: Invasive Coronary Angiography · Sliding window
technique · Classification · Convolutional Neural Network · Deep
Learning

1 Introduction

Invasive coronary angiography (ICA) imaging is considered the gold standard
method for diagnosing coronary artery disease (CAD) and percutaneous coronary intervention (PCI) guidance because of the high definition of the vessels
[23]. The ICA procedure consists of X-ray videos taken from different projections
of both left and right coronary arteries, LCA and RCA, respectively. Anatomy

© The Author(s), under exclusive license to Springer Nature Switzerland AG 2024
J. M. Ferrández Vicente et al. (Eds.): IWINAC 2024, LNCS 14675, pp. 116–125, 2024.
https://doi.org/10.1007/978-3-031-61137-7_12

and blood flow of coronary arteries can be visualized because of the injection of a radiocontrast agent into coronary arteries [20]. ICA videos allow the evaluation of luminal stenosis. However, visual estimation assesses the severity percentage, which could be affected by subjectivity and has high interobserver variability [11,24].

Computer-aided diagnosis based on deep learning could yield a more efficient diagnosis with more robust assessments, resulting in decision support and workload reductions. The application of deep learning in cardiac imaging is generally focused on detection, segmentation, and classification tasks. Although there has been increased attention in this field, only a few methods have been ascertained because of the lack of high-quality open-access available datasets, being the main drawback [13]. Developing a labeled dataset is a complex and time-consuming task. For instance, studies have explored methods to generate synthetic patches with lesions, increasing the sample data as a data augmentation technique [17].

The most common architectures used are convolutional neural networks (CNNs) and CNN-derived architectures, which are used in classification, segmentation, and detection tasks [2,19,22]. Segmentation problems imply dividing images into objects, mainly distinguishing the background of regions of interest. Rank-based ensemble methods have been studied for ICA segmentation. Masks were used as input of five models whose outputs were ranked, obtaining a framework that achieved <90% of Dice Similarity Coefficient (DSC) [18]. Segmentation and estimation of the percentage diameter stenosis of lesions could be performed using encoder-decoder fully CNN based on U-Net [15]. In an image, the detection task is based on drawing bounding boxes that cover regions of interest and indicate a class label. In medical imaging, the regions of interest are commonly lesion regions. Different approaches have been proposed in the cardiac area, for instance, comparisons between eight detector architectures to detect single severe lesions, standing out Faster-RCNN Inception ResNet-V2 as the most accurate method [5]. The classification output is the assignation of a probability class to an image. The task can be focused on classifying the whole image into a class or patch-based classification, where the frame is divided into sub-images as input of the model [16]. A first approach could be to classify ICA images into LCA and RCA images, where without lesion images were used as input of pre-trained CNN-based model, attaining a 0.99 F-measure [6]. Inception-v3 was implemented to classify ICA images into LCA or RCA; then a keyframe selection was carried out with LSTM (long-short-term memory) and, finally, these keyframes were classified into stenosis or non-stenosis by an Inception-v3 classifier [4].

Most of the state-of-the-art work in cardiac imaging is raw image-based, exploiting complex CNN-based frameworks, but an essential prior phase of pre-processing and studying how to optimize these few raw data available had yet to be reported. The proposed framework is focused on patch generation by sliding windows to use as input for different CNN architectures. This way, proposed pre-processings, and models were analyzed. Sliding window techniques had been utilized as part of the workflow in detection [12], segmentation [14] and classification [1,3,8,10,21] problems.

This work aims to propose sliding window-based pre-processing methods to optimize the classification performance of CNNs to approach deep learning solutions to diagnosis tasks in clinician settings.

The rest of the paper is organized as follows. Section 2 describes in detail the methodology used to solve our problem. Several experimental setups and results are reported in Sect. 3. Finally, Sect. 4 outlines the conclusions of the paper.

2 Methodology

2.1 Dataset

The CADICA dataset [9] used includes videos of ICA images from 42 patients acquired at Hospital Universitario Virgen de la Victoria, Málaga, Spain. They have been included within the regulation set by the local ethical committee of the hospital, and patient consent was waived because this is a retrospective study with anonymized data. Different projections of both coronary arteries, right (RCA) and left (LCA), are included. The dataset is divided into patients and then into several video records stored as sequential frames in PNG format. These frames are labeled according to their clinical Cardiovascular Artery Disease (CAD) diagnosis. The CAD diagnosis is assessed according to the degree of narrowing of the coronary artery concerning the regular width of a healthy artery. Usually, this assessment is done visually by comparing the narrowed segment with adjacent healthy areas. The lesion degrees can be ranged between ¿0% and 100% of narrowing, i.e., total occlusion, which implies the blockage of the blood through the artery. Lesions are located by bounding boxes and labeled into seven possible ranges: <20%, [20%, 50%), [50%, 70%), [70%, 90%), [90%, 98%], 99%, and 100%. If a frame is unlabeled, it is considered as a healthy instance. Figure 1 shows a sample of each category. A total of 6,112 frames were used, with 6,130 labels. Notice that a frame may have no label, one, or more than one.

2.2 Data Preprocessing

The raw data consists of 512×512 pixels PNG files and ground truth TXT files where the location and size of bounding boxes are reported. Every image was cropped to 472×472 pixels to remove black edges. Next, frames were divided into patches, i.e., sub-images. For this purpose, to obtain 118×118 pixels size, two patch generation techniques were used: a grid of 4×4 and sliding window technique, which glides a window over ICA images, generating overlapped patches. The sliding window configuration is based on two parameters: the window size of $m \times n$ pixels and the stride, which is the step size and measures the degree of overlap between consecutive patches. The selected size must be suitable to the size of the image to cover it without requiring zero-padding.

The following conditions were considered when ascribed a category to a patch. If any bounding box falls into the generated patch, it is considered a "non-lesion" class. A patch is assigned to the bounding box category if the intersection

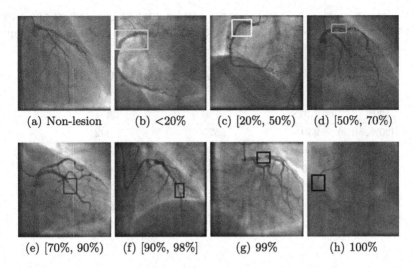

(a) Non-lesion   (b) <20%   (c) [20%, 50%)   (d) [50%, 70%)

(e) [70%, 90%)   (f) [90%, 98%]   (g) 99%   (h) 100%

Fig. 1. Samples of the seven ranges in which patches are categorized.

between the window and the bounding box, expressed as a percentage, is higher than the Lesion Patch Inclusion Threshold (LPIT) settled; otherwise, the patch is discarded. The highest degree is chosen if there is more than one bounding box. The combination of window size, stride, and LPIT configures the different strategies for processing studies. This work evaluated grid-based splitting with 50% and 90% of LPIT, and the sliding window technique with 90% of LPIT and 59 pixels as stride was evaluated. A grid division with 50% of LPIT was inapplicable because of the vast number of patches potentially generated.

The number of "non-lesion" patches increased vastly because they came from complete "non-lesion" frames and also from surrounding areas of frames with lesions. In order to reduce the number of "non-lesion" patches, background patches have been removed. Patches have been considered as background when vessel pixels are not present or they represent few pixels. The Table 1 summarizes the number of patches this procedure generates.

Studying how the performance is affected by the LPIT used is interesting because the necessary lesion context is evaluated. A lower LPIT implies a lower percentage of bounding boxes required to assess a category, so the model uses samples with less information about the lesion. However, different patch generation techniques let us estimate the effect on the performance of the different number of samples used to train the model.

3   Experimental Results

In order to evaluate the goodness of the proposed methodology, several experiments have been carried out. The following subsections describe the methods used and the results obtained.

Table 1. Number of patches generated for each established strategy. "Grid", "SW", and "LPIT" refer to a 4×4 grid and sliding window as patch generation techniques; and lesion patch inclusion threshold, respectively.

Category	Grid - LPIT 50%	Grid - LPIT 90%	SW - LPIT 90%
"Non-lesion"	72,187	71,607	221,097
<20%	1,678	796	3,351
[20%, 50%)	930	525	1,992
[50%, 70%)	866	386	1,489
[70%, 90%)	780	443	1,695
[90%, 98%]	835	412	1,822
99%	61	38	134
100%	204	149	436

3.1 Training and Experiments Description

This work aims to analyze the impact on the performance of the binary "lesion" / "non-lesion" classification when different pre-processings are applied. In this case, three combinations, depicted previously in Sect. 2.2, of patch generation techniques and LPIT are considered. Additionally, different binary problems were settled, where the positive class results were obtained by grouping different categories of the interval selected. For example, < 50% "lesion" class consider as positive class the assemblage of < 20% and [20%,50%) categories. Figure 2 illustrates positive class considered. The negative class for each binary problem was created extracting randomly the same number of samples from the "non-lesion" category. Both classes were divided into training (80%) and test (20%) sets by videos, i.e., frames of the same video in the train set are unavailable for the test set because frames of the same sequence are very similar. This way allows for estimating a fairer performance evaluation.

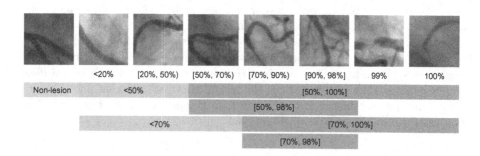

Fig. 2. Category grouping diagram.

Regarding the training process, some hyperparameters were settled: validation frequency 50 iterations, validation patience 5, and 50 as maximum epochs, while the batch size was set according to the number of training patches to keep the rate of iterations in all training processes. The optimizer and the initial learning rate were RMSProp (Root Mean Square Propagation) and 0.001, respectively. A factor of 0.1 in the learning rate was applied every 10 epochs to ensure convergence. Additionally, 5-fold stratified cross-validation was implemented to compare all these possibilities reliably.

Three pre-trained deep network architectures widely used were chosen: MobileNet-V2, ResNet-18, and DenseNet-201.

To evaluate and compare the performance of the methods to classify ICA images, based on the number of test samples count as True Positive (TP), True Negative (TN), False Positive (FP) and False Negative (FN), the following metrics were computed: Precision, Recall, and Specificity, that are involved in the performance metrics used. F-measure, which is one of the related metrics that provides good overall performance because it integrates Precision and Recall measures under the concept of harmonic mean [7], and the Area Under the ROC Curve (AUC), which corresponds to the integral of the ROC curve where the Recall versus the Specificity is reported for different thresholds of classification scores. The mentioned measures range in $[0, 1]$ (the higher is better), and are defined as follows:

$$Precision = \frac{TP}{TP + FP} \qquad Recall = \frac{TP}{TP + FN} \qquad (1)$$

$$Specificity = \frac{TN}{FP + TN} \qquad F\text{-}measure = 2 \cdot \frac{Pre \cdot Rec}{Pre + Rec} \qquad (2)$$

The proposed models were implemented in MATLAB R2023a on a computer system with an Intel Core i7-4790 processor, 32 GB of RAM, and an NVIDIA GeForce RTX 4090 GPU card. Furthermore, no layer of chosen pre-trained methods was frozen, so all weights were updated during the training process according to the input class information.

3.2   Results

In Tables 2 and 3, the average and standard deviation of F-measure and Accuracy, respectively, obtained in test sets with 5-fold stratified cross-validation are reported. The highest values by rows are remarked in bold. DenseNet-201 is the architecture that most often gets the best results, followed by ResNet-18. F-measure and Accuracy metrics attained outstanding results between 70% and 91% of performance. The highest value achieved is 0.91 of F-measure and Accuracy with [70%, 100%] as positive class and sliding window technique. In most cases, the sliding window technique returns higher outcomes, which could be explained by the larger number of training samples.

Comparing the two selected LPIT values with the same patch generation technique, an LPIT of 90% achieves more excellent results than 50%. It could be interpreted as, although a softer threshold gets more samples, a higher one obtains better outcomes because the samples generated for the positive class must cover a more extensive area of the bounding box. Hence, the positive class is more accurate and most easily differentiable from the negative class.

Finally, referring to the categories used as a positive class, severe lesions are better classified than mild-moderate ones. This fact is reasonable because the more significant the lesion, the easier it is to distinguish it from a healthy vessel. For example, DenseNet-201, sliding window and 90% of LPIT, attained 0.91 of F-measure with [70%, 100%] and [70%,98%] positive class, but it decreases to 0.88 with [50%, 100%] and [50%,98%].

Table 2. F-measure and standard deviation obtained on the test set with 5-fold stratified cross-validation. "Grid", "SW", and "LPIT" refer to a 4×4 grid and sliding window as patch generation techniques; and lesion patch inclusion threshold, respectively.

Positive class	Strategy		CNN		
	Patch generation	LPIT	MobileNet-V2	ResNet-18	DenseNet-201
< 50%	Grid	50%	0.710 ± 0.076	**0.782 ± 0.010**	0.782 ± 0.050
	Grid	90%	0.812 ± 0.033	**0.816 ± 0.026**	0.815 ± 0.024
	SW	90%	0.785 ± 0.025	0.804 ± 0.005	**0.810 ± 0.013**
< 70%	Grid	50%	**0.815 ± 0.022**	0.783 ± 0.040	0.796 ± 0.013
	Grid	90%	**0.801 ± 0.030**	0.797 ± 0.047	0.800 ± 0.025
	SW	90%	0.736 ± 0.044	**0.779 ± 0.023**	0.768 ± 0.010
[50%, 98%]	Grid	50%	0.810 ± 0.026	0.804 ± 0.019	**0.814 ± 0.030**
	Grid	90%	0.805 ± 0.025	**0.824 ± 0.022**	0.806 ± 0.024
	SW	90%	0.841 ± 0.013	0.855 ± 0.020	**0.877 ± 0.014**
[70%, 98%]	Grid	50%	**0.776 ± 0.021**	0.771 ± 0.050	0.766 ± 0.030
	Grid	90%	0.764 ± 0.029	**0.813 ± 0.064**	0.757 ± 0.031
	SW	90%	0.874 ± 0.021	0.894 ± 0.017	**0.915 ± 0.030**
[50%, 100%]	Grid	50%	0.794 ± 0.015	**0.799 ± 0.038**	0.780 ± 0.015
	Grid	90%	0.790 ± 0.040	0.814 ± 0.032	**0.817 ± 0.032**
	SW	90%	0.848 ± 0.019	0.875 ± 0.011	**0.881 ± 0.022**
[70%, 100%]	Grid	50%	0.742 ± 0.049	0.787 ± 0.049	**0.796 ± 0.023**
	Grid	90%	0.735 ± 0.067	**0.761 ± 0.097**	0.738 ± 0.029
	SW	90%	0.835 ± 0.037	0.864 ± 0.015	**0.909 ± 0.019**

Table 3. Accuracy and standard deviation obtained on the test set with 5-fold stratified cross-validation. "Grid", "SW", and "LPIT" refer to a 4×4 grid and sliding window as patch generation techniques; and lesion patch inclusion threshold, respectively.

Positive class	Strategy		CNN		
	Patch generation	LPIT	MobileNet-V2	ResNet-18	DenseNet-201
< 50%	Grid	50%	0.746 ± 0.044	**0.799 ± 0.005**	0.797 ± 0.038
	Grid	90%	**0.825 ± 0.021**	0.822 ± 0.020	0.824 ± 0.020
	SW	90%	0.808 ± 0.019	0.821 ± 0.004	**0.825 ± 0.010**
< 70%	Grid	50%	**0.823 ± 0.015**	0.795 ± 0.027	0.810 ± 0.009
	Grid	90%	**0.815 ± 0.020**	0.810 ± 0.036	0.808 ± 0.020
	SW	90%	0.770 ± 0.029	**0.798 ± 0.017**	0.794 ± 0.007
[50%, 98%]	Grid	50%	0.824 ± 0.020	0.819 ± 0.015	**0.825 ± 0.024**
	Grid	90%	0.823 ± 0.017	**0.834 ± 0.019**	0.818 ± 0.021
	SW	90%	0.854 ± 0.011	0.866 ± 0.017	**0.886 ± 0.011**
[70%, 98%]	Grid	50%	0.793 ± 0.015	**0.795 ± 0.034**	0.790 ± 0.024
	Grid	90%	0.778 ± 0.023	**0.825 ± 0.051**	0.777 ± 0.028
	SW	90%	0.883 ± 0.016	0.825 ± 0.015	**0.919 ± 0.027**
[50%, 100%]	Grid	50%	0.805 ± 0.017	**0.810 ± 0.030**	0.788 ± 0.014
	Grid	90%	0.809 ± 0.031	0.823 ± 0.026	**0.827 ± 0.028**
	SW	90%	0.862 ± 0.015	0.883 ± 0.008	**0.889 ± 0.017**
[70%, 100%]	Grid	50%	0.773 ± 0.031	0.807 ± 0.037	**0.810 ± 0.016**
	Grid	90%	0.770 ± 0.050	**0.784 ± 0.071**	0.763 ± 0.025
	SW	90%	0.853 ± 0.029	0.875 ± 0.013	**0.913 ± 0.016**

4   Conclusions

This study reports the evaluation of how the performance of the binary classification is affected depending on the severity degree of ICA images considered into the positive class, i.e., the "lesion" class, and the patch-processing followed. Three CNN architectures were chosen for the binary classification task. The "lesion" class was established by grouping the seven possible ranges of lesion degree. Results reported that severe lesions higher than 50% (¿80% F-measure) are better classified than mild-to-moderate lesions. Additionally, DensetNet-201 is a good-to-go model whose outcomes stand out over other models. Finally, a patch-generation sliding window-based improved results, achieving ¿90% of F-measure.

Acknowledgments. This work is partially supported by the Autonomous Government of Andalusia (Spain) under project UMA20-FEDERJA-108, and also by the Ministry of Science and Innovation of Spain, grant number PID2022-136764OA-I00. It includes funds from the European Regional Development Fund (ERDF). It is also partially supported by the University of Málaga (Spain) under grants B1-2019_01, B1-2019_02, B1-2021_20, B4-2022, B1-2022_14, and by the Fundación Unicaja under project PUNI-003_2023. The authors thankfully acknowledge the computer resources, technical expertise and assistance provided by the SCBI (Supercomputing and Bioinformatics) center of the University of Málaga. They also gratefully acknowledge the support of NVIDIA Corporation with the donation of a RTX A6000 GPU with 48Gb. The authors also thankfully acknowledge the grant of the Universidad de Málaga and the Instituto de Investigación Biomédica de Málaga y Plataforma en Nanomedicina-IBIMA Plataforma BIONAND.

References

1. Alqudah, A., Alqudah, A.M.: Sliding window based deep ensemble system for breast cancer classification. J. Med. Eng. Technol. **45**(4), 313–323 (2021)
2. Cai, L., Gao, J., Zhao, D.: A review of the application of deep learning in medical image classification and segmentation. Annals Trans. Med. **8**(11) (2020)
3. Ciga, O., Xu, T., Nofech-Mozes, S., Noy, S., Lu, F.I., Martel, A.L.: Overcoming the limitations of patch-based learning to detect cancer in whole slide images. Sci. Rep. **11**(1), 8894 (2021)
4. Cong, C., Kato, Y., Vasconcellos, H.D., Lima, J., Venkatesh, B.: Automated stenosis detection and classification in x-ray angiography using deep neural network. In: 2019 IEEE International Conference on Bioinformatics and Biomedicine (BIBM), pp. 1301–1308. IEEE (2019)
5. This is to inform you that corresponding author has been identified as per the information available in the Copyright form. This is to inform you that corresponding author has been identified as per the information available in the Copyright form. Danilov, V.V., et al.: Real-time coronary artery stenosis detection based on modern neural networks. Sci. Rep. **11**(1), 1–13 (2021)
6. Eschen, C.K., et al.: Classification of left and right coronary arteries in coronary angiographies using deep learning. Electronics **11**(13), 2087 (2022)
7. Grandini, M., Bagli, E., Visani, G.: Metrics for multi-class classification: an overview. arXiv preprint arXiv:2008.05756 (2020)
8. Haryanto, T., Suhartanto, H., Arymurthy, A.M., Kusmardi, K.: Conditional sliding windows: an approach for handling data limitation in colorectal histopathology image classification. Inform. Med. Unlocked **23**, 100565 (2021)
9. Jiménez-Partinen, A., et al.: CADICA: a new dataset for coronary artery disease (2024)
10. Lam, C., Yu, C., Huang, L., Rubin, D.: Retinal lesion detection with deep learning using image patches. Investigative Ophthal. Vis. Sci. **59**(1), 590–596 (2018)
11. Leape, L.L., Park, R.E., Bashore, T.M., Harrison, J.K., Davidson, C.J., Brook, R.H.: Effect of variability in the interpretation of coronary angiograms on the appropriateness of use of coronary revascularization procedures. Am. Heart J. **139**(1), 106–113 (2000)
12. Lee, J., Bang, J., Yang, S.I.: Object detection with sliding window in images including multiple similar objects. In: 2017 International Conference on Information and Communication Technology Convergence (ICTC), pp. 803–806. IEEE (2017)
13. Litjens, G., Ciompi, F., Wolterink, J.M., de Vos, B.D., Leiner, T., Teuwen, J., Išgum, I.: State-of-the-art deep learning in cardiovascular image analysis. JACC: Cardiovascular Imaging **12**(8 Part 1), 1549–1565 (2019)
14. Ma, J., He, Y., Li, F., Han, L., You, C., Wang, B.: Segment anything in medical images. Nat. Commun. **15**(1), 654 (2024)

15. Menezes, M.N., et al.: Development of deep learning segmentation models for coronary x-ray angiography: quality assessment by a new global segmentation score and comparison with human performance. Rev. Port. Cardiol. **41**(12), 1011–1021 (2022)
16. Ovalle-Magallanes, E., Alvarado-Carrillo, D.E., Avina-Cervantes, J.G., Cruz-Aceves, I., Ruiz-Pinales, J., Correa, R.: Deep learning-based coronary stenosis detection in x-ray angiography images: Overview and future trends. In: Artificial Intelligence and Machine Learning for Healthcare: Vol. 2: Emerging Methodologies and Trends, pp. 197–223 (2022)
17. Ovalle-Magallanes, E., Avina-Cervantes, J.G., Cruz-Aceves, I., Ruiz-Pinales, J.: Improving convolutional neural network learning based on a hierarchical bezier generative model for stenosis detection in x-ray images. Comput. Methods Programs Biomed. **219**, 106767 (2022)
18. Park, J., et al.: Selective ensemble methods for deep learning segmentation of major vessels in invasive coronary angiography. Med. Phys. (2023)
19. Rawat, W., Wang, Z.: Deep convolutional neural networks for image classification: a comprehensive review. Neural Comput. **29**(9), 2352–2449 (2017)
20. Rigatelli, G., Gianese, F., Zuin, M.: Modern atlas of invasive coronary angiography views: a practical approach for fellows and young interventionalists. Int. J. Cardiovasc. Imaging **38**(5), 919–926 (2022)
21. Yang, Y., et al.: Robust collaborative learning of patch-level and image-level annotations for diabetic retinopathy grading from fundus image. IEEE Trans. Cybernet. **52**(11), 11407–11417 (2021)
22. Zhou, S.K., et al.: A review of deep learning in medical imaging: imaging traits, technology trends, case studies with progress highlights, and future promises. Proc. IEEE **109**(5), 820–838 (2021)
23. Zhou, Y., Guo, H., Song, J., Chen, Y., Wang, J.: Review of vessel segmentation and stenosis classification in x-ray coronary angiography. In: 2021 13th International Conference on Wireless Communications and Signal Processing (WCSP), pp. 1–5. IEEE (2021)
24. Zir, L.M., Miller, S.W., Dinsmore, R.E., Gilbert, J., Harthorne, J.: Interobserver variability in coronary angiography. Circulation **53**(4), 627–632 (1976)

Bio-inspired Computing Approaches

Refinement of Protein Structures with a Memetic Algorithm. Examples with SARS-CoV-2 Proteins

Juan Luis Filgueiras and José Santos[✉]

CITIC (Centre for Information and Communications Technology Research),
Department of Computer Science and Information Technologies, University of A
Coruña (Spain), Coruna, Spain
{juan.filgueiras.rilo,jose.santos}@udc.es

Abstract. Considerable progress has recently been made in protein structure prediction with deep learning methods. However, the structures predicted with these methods often require a subsequent refinement process to correct imperfections in the prediction. This paper uses and compares different possibilities for this refinement, including our memetic algorithm, which combines differential evolution with a state-of-the-art refinement method from the Rosetta environment. The comparison and analysis are performed with selected proteins from the SARS-CoV-2 virus.

Keywords: Protein structure prediction · Protein structure refinement · Differential evolution · Memetic algorithms

1 Introduction

In Protein Structure Prediction (PSP), given the amino acid sequence of the protein, traditional methods look for a homologous sequence of an already solved protein, i.e., whose structure is known by time-consuming and expensive laboratory methods, such as X-ray crystallography or nuclear magnetic resonance. With high sequence homology ($\geq 50\%$ sequence identity), the protein structures are the same. Other PSP "threading" methods attempt to fit a protein sequence into a library of protein folds corresponding also to solved proteins.

The most difficult alternative in PSP is "ab initio", when no information about already solved proteins is used, only the primary structure (amino acid sequence of the protein) is employed. This ab initio alternative is based on two considerations of Anfinsen's dogma [3]: (i) the amino acid sequence information determines the final 3D native conformation and (ii) the thermodynamic hypothesis, which states that the native structure has the lowest Gibbs free energy.

Thus, once an energy model associated with the possible protein conformations has been defined, ab initio prediction becomes a problem of finding the conformation with the minimum energy. Therefore, the use of ab initio PSP search methods has been intensively explored, particularly with the use of Evolutionary Algorithms (EAs) and other metaheuristics, with simplified lattice models

J. M. Ferrández Vicente et al. (Eds.): IWINAC 2024, LNCS 14675, pp. 129–139, 2024.
https://doi.org/10.1007/978-3-031-61137-7_13

(protein components are located at the sites of a lattice) of protein representation [10, 16, 17], as well as with off-lattice atomic models of proteins (without the localization constraint) [8, 19].

In this line of research, our previous work in PSP has focused on the use of atomic models using the Rosetta system [14] (one of the most successful protein design software environments). We have used EAs in the search and optimization of protein structures that correspond to the native structure, with the advantage of the global search of EAs, in this case in the huge space of possible protein conformations. We defined memetic combinations when the EA incorporates the traditional PSP technique of fragment insertions (short protein fragments of solved proteins, iteratively inserted into the target protein with a simulated annealing procedure) [7, 18]. Niching methods were also integrated into the memetic algorithm in order to obtain a variety of structurally different optimized protein conformations [18, 19].

In contrast to the use of search techniques to discover the structure with the minimum energy, another possibility in PSP is the prediction of the contact map, which represents the distance between all possible amino acid pairs in the folded structure of the protein by means of a two-dimensional binary matrix. This is the basic and underlying idea of recent methods based on deep learning architectures to predict protein structure.

These methods such as *AlphaFold2* [9] (in the DeepMind company) and *RoseTTAFold* [5] (in the same Rosetta group at the University of Washington) are successful methods in this line. These recent methods based on deep learning have provided greatly improved prediction results on a large set of proteins, as discussed in [7]. However, the protein structures provided by these methods often have imperfections such as collisions between different atoms, especially the atoms of the amino acid side chains. Consequently, a refinement process is required to correct these imperfections, an optimization process that must relocate the atoms to minimize the energy of the protein conformation [1].

In this refinement step, two optimization approaches are applied in our work: the one used in the Rosetta system [14], with its "Relax" protocol, and our memetic combination between Differential Evolution [13] and the methods used by that Rosetta Relax protocol. A refinement analysis is performed, comparing both alternatives and using different protein components of the SARS-CoV-2 virus, components selected to exemplify the need for protein refinement. Conformations predicted by PSP methods will be used for the analysis of this refinement process.

The remainder of the article is structured as follows. The methods employed are explained in Sect. 2, with a brief introduction to the Rosetta protein representation and energy model, as well as its refinement protocol. Our memetic solution for the refinement (*Relax-DE*) is also schematized. The results of the experiments are presented in Sect. 3, using different approaches to refine the structures of selected SARS-CoV-2 protein components. Finally, a discussion and the main conclusions obtained from the results are presented in Sect. 4.

2   Methods

2.1   Rosetta Relax Process

Rosetta Relax is the refinement protocol used by the Rosetta software suite [14]. It uses the all-atom representation of proteins and their associated energy model. Protein conformations are represented by the dihedral angles of the protein backbone and the rotation angles of the side chains. Figure 1 illustrates these angles.

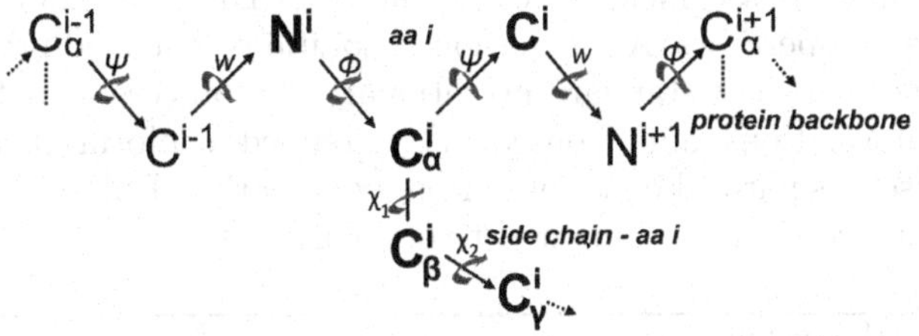

Fig. 1. All-atom protein representation with the dihedral angles ω (bond angle between consecutive amino acids), ϕ and ψ, together with the rotation angles χ of the side chains of amino acids (aa).

The energy model is referred to as *Ref2015* [2] and is defined as the weighted sum of 19 individual energy terms, such as Van der Waals (short-range attractive and repulsive forces) and electrostatic related interactions, solvation modeling, and hydrogen and disulfide bonds (energy terms described in [2]).

From an initial conformation of the protein, the Rosetta Relax process primarily refines the side chains by optimizing the positions of their atoms for the *Ref2015* energy minimization. Rosetta Relax uses two processes in this refinement: i) a *Repacker*, which changes the rotation angles of the side chains (working with a library of a discrete set of possible side chain configurations) and using a simulated annealing procedure to search for structures of minimum energy. ii) a *Minimizer*, which refines the torsion angles of the side chains as well as the dihedral angles of the protein backbone, but with a greedy minimization.

The Rosetta Relax process is schematized in the following script ("FastRelax" modern version of Rosetta):

```
repeat 5
    Repacker − repulsive weight  0.02   Minimizer − tolerance  0.01
    Repacker − repulsive weight  0.25   Minimizer − tolerance  0.01
    Repacker − repulsive weight  0.55   Minimizer − tolerance  0.01
    Repacker − repulsive weight  1.00   Minimizer − tolerance  0.00001
    update_best

endrepeat
```

Thus, there are five cycles in which the *Repacker* and *Minimizer* are applied sequentially in four rounds, changing some parameters in each round. The first value (in each row of each round), associated with the *Repacker*, sets a factor used to scale the repulsive term in the *Ref2015* energy model (repulsive force between atoms in different residues), which is increased in each round. The second value is associated with the *Minimizer* and defines a convergence tolerance parameter used in the greedy minimization. Consequently, greedy iterations can be lower than a default value (2,000), depending on the greedy convergence. The final structure returned in each cycle is the initial structure of the next cycle. Given the stochasticity of the *Repacker*, the Relax process returns the conformation with the lowest energy of the 5 cycles (*update_best* test).

2.2   Relax-DE

Relax-DE is our proposed memetic combination of DE [6,13] and the Rosetta Relax local search operators. A population of solutions (encoded protein conformations) evolves with the standard evolutionary DE process to obtain energy-optimized conformations and, consequently, refined conformations. DE was selected because it is natural to adapt our previous work in PSP with DE [18,19], in addition to its robustness compared to other EAs. [6].

Algorithm 1. Relax-DE.

1: Initial population: perturbed structures from a starting structure
2: **repeat**
3:     **for all** solution x_p in the population **do**
4:         Let $x_1, x_2, x_3 \in$ population, randomly obtained $\{x_1, x_2, x_3, x_p$ different from each other$\}$
5:         Let $R \in \{1, ..., n\}$, randomly obtained $\{$n is the search space dimensionality (dihedral angles plus torsion angles of the side chains$\}$
6:         **for** $i = 1$ *to* n **do**
7:             Pick $r_i \in U(0, 1)$ uniformly from the open range (0,1).
8:             **if** $(i = R) \vee (r_i < CR)$ **then**
9:                 $y_{pi} \leftarrow x_{1i} + F(x_{2i} - x_{3i})$
10:            **else**
11:                $y_{pi} = x_{pi}$
12:            **end if**$\{$CR - crossover probability, F - weight factor$\}$
13:        **end for**$\{y_p = [y_{p1}, y_{p2}...y_{pn}]$ is a new generated candidate solution for $x_p\}$
14:        y'_p = Repacker-Minimizer(y_p) $\{$Refined candidate y'_p applying Rosetta's *Repacker* and *Minimizer* on solution $y_p\}$
15:        **if** $Ref2015(y'_p) \leq Ref2015(x_p)$ **then**
16:            Replace solution x_p by y'_p $\{$Replaces solution x_p by y'_p if y'_p has a better (lower) or equal value of $Ref2015\}$
17:        **end if**
18:    **end for**
19: **until** termination criterion is met
20: **return** $z \in$ population$\backslash \forall t \in$ population, $Ref2015(z) <= Ref2015(t)$

Protein conformations are encoded by the dihedral angles (ϕ and ψ) of the protein backbone and the torsion angles (χ) of the amino acid side chains (dihedral angles w are not encoded because they are fixed and cannot rotate, being equal to the w angles of the starting structure). The angles are encoded in the range [-1,1] in the genotypic solutions, whereas they are decoded to the range $[-180°, 180°]$ when calculating the conformational energy (*Ref2015*). The initial population starts from an initial structure subject to refinement. This initial structure is slightly perturbed at the dihedral angles of the backbone (ϕ and ψ) and at the torsion angles of the side chains (perturbations of $-0.5°, 0.5°]$) to define the initial set of solutions in the initial population.

These solutions are now optimized with a standard DE process, as schematized in the pseudocode of Algorithm 1. DE uses two basic operators in the evolutionary process: a perturbation/mutation process and a crossover operation to define alternative or candidate solutions (lines 6–13 in the pseudo-code). Following the usual nomenclature in DE, for each "target" solution x_p in the population, a "candidate" solution y_p is considered. To define the candidate solution, a "donor" vector $x_1 + F * (x_2 - x_3)$ is firstly calculated, considering a perturbation defined by the weighted difference (weight factor F) between two randomly selected vectors (x_2 and x_3) and applied on a "base" vector (x_1).

To define the base vector (x_1), we combine two standard DE schemes: the one that selects the base vector (x_1) randomly (95% of the cases), a scheme that provides low selective pressure, with the DE scheme that selects x_1 as the best vector from the current population (5% of the cases). Then, the genetic material of the donor vector is crossed with the target vector x_p (with a crossover probability CR) to define its candidate solution y_p. The index R in the pseudocode guarantees that at least one parameter of the candidate vector comes from the donor vector (line 8). The mutation/crossover operators are applied only to the side chain angles (maintaining the backbone structure of the base vector x_1 for defining candidate y_p).

The memetic combination is defined by including the fine-tuning or refinement of these candidate solutions (line 14). Each candidate (y_p) is locally refined by applying the operators *Repacker* and *Minimizer* (with less depth in the search with respect to Rosetta Relax, as detailed later in the setup of the refinement approaches). The sequential application of these two operators locally improves the candidate solutions by refining the angles of the candidate conformation (now including the backbone angles), a process that can also resolve conflicts/collisions (atoms in the same position) in the candidate conformation due to the genetic operators, defining the refined candidate solutions y'_p.

Finally, a selection process determines which solution remains in the next generation by comparing the fitness (*Ref2015* energy) of the target vector x_p and its refined candidate solution y'_p, passing to the next generation the one with better (lower) energy (lines 15-16 in the pseudocode).

3   Results

3.1   Setup of the Refinement Approaches

Different proteins were considered for refinement. Their initial structures can be the deposited structures in PDB [12] or structures predicted with deep learning-based approaches (*AlphaFold2* and *RoseTTAFold*). The default settings provided by their servers were used: the Multiple Sequence Alignment (MSA) of the protein target sequence is used as input and the five best candidate models (in terms of prediction confidence) are provided by the *AlphaFold2* server [4] and the best model by the *RoseTTAFold2* server [15]. Moreover, structures deposited in PDB can also be considered as initial structures, as these may have irregularities in their experimentally solved structures.

Three SARS-CoV-2 protein components were used: the "structural" *Nucleo-capsid (N)* protein (PDB code *6WZQ*), the "non-structural protein" *nsp9* (PDB code *6W4B*) and the "accessory" protein *orf8* (PDB code *7JTL*). These proteins were selected as the predictions have different levels of confidence, making them good targets to exemplify and analyze the refinement required.

Regarding the refinement alternatives, Rosetta Relax was run with the process discussed above (Sect. 2.1), i.e., with 5 cycles of 4 consecutive rounds of the *Repacker* and *Minimizer* operators. In Relax-DE, the DE defining parameters were experimentally adjusted to generate candidate solutions (protein conformations) with few collisions, implying a weight factor with a low value ($F = 0.05$) and a crossover probability with a high value ($CR = 0.95$) (which guarantees that most of the genetic material comes from the donor vector, minimizing collisions).

The comparison between Rosetta Relax and Relax-DE was performed with the same computational time. The time required for 1,000 independent runs of Rosetta Relax was taken as a reference. For each protein, Relax-DE was run with that time as a limit. A population of 100 solutions was considered, which allows the evolutionary process to be maintained for several generations with this time limit. Note that, with the same computational time, Rosetta Relax generates 1,000 solutions, while Relax-DE provides 100 optimized solutions. Rosetta Relax bases its success on the stochasticity of independent runs (usually a large number) with independent paths to optimized solutions. In contrast, Relax-DE concentrates the search on promising areas found in successive generations of the evolutionary process, providing fewer optimized solutions than Rosetta Relax.

Finally, in the Relax-DE memetic combination with the *Repacker* and *Minimizer* operators (Algorithm 1), only one cycle of the *Repacker-Minimizer* combination was applied (script of Sect. 2.1), also with a low value of the maximum number of iterations (200) in the *Minimizer* operator. This was done with the aim of not applying the local search provided by these operators with a high depth in the search, in order to locally refine the DE candidate solutions and without a rapid decrease of the genetic variability in the memetic combination.

Two basic metrics are used in the analysis of the refined structures: i) the RMSD (Root Mean Squared Deviation, considering the C_α atoms of the protein backbone) between the native structure deposited in PDB and the refined structure, after an optimal superposition of both structures, which provides a distance measure to evaluate the displacement with respect to the deposited structure. ii) the *Ref2015* energy of the refined and starting structures. In addition, other structural quality metrics, provided by the Molprobity suite [11], are considered.

3.2 Refinement of Predicted Structures

Figure 2 shows representative examples of refinement with the selected proteins. The first example corresponds to protein *6WZQ* (upper row). Three initial structures are considered, corresponding to the structure deposited in PDB (left column) and the structures predicted with the highest prediction confidence by *AlphaFold2* (middle column) and *RoseTTAFold* (right column).

The graphs of Fig. 2 are common representations in structure prediction and refinement, as they show the level of optimization (in *Ref2015* energy terms) versus the distance to a reference structure. Note that the proteins considered have an entry in the PDB database [12], as their structures were solved with X-ray diffraction (in the three proteins used). Therefore, their native folded structure is known a priori (structures deposited in PDB), so these proteins can be considered as benchmarks. Consequently, for each protein, its PDB-deposited structure can act as a reference to measure the distance (RMSD) between each candidate refined structure and itself. The ideal solution would have a minimized energy and would be as close as possible to the reference.

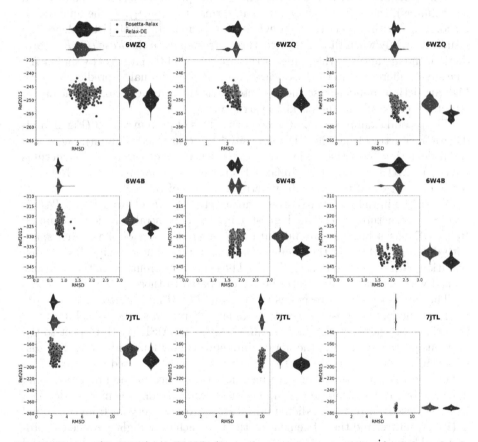

Fig. 2. Energy (*Ref2015*) vs. RMSD (from the native structure, in Å) of the refined structures of three proteins (*6WZQ* - upper row, *6W4B* - middle row, *7JTL* - bottom row), when an initial structure is refined with Rosetta Relax (gray) and Relax-DE (blue). The initial structures to be refined correspond to the PDB-deposited structure of the protein (left column) and the structures predicted, with the highest confidence, by *AlphaFold2* (central column) and *RoseTTAFold* (right column). The violin plots show the quartiles (inner white lines) and the median (light blue mark) of the refined structure distributions in terms of their RMSD and energy. (Color figure online)

The first case (Fig. 2, left column) starts from the same structure deposited in PDB as the initial structure to be refined. This is interesting since this structure may have inaccuracies in the positions of the atoms, so it is possible to check how refinement methods improve its structural quality. The first consideration is that the distribution of the final solutions refined with the memetic algorithm (Relax-DE) has a better energy (in terms of median and best value) with respect to the distribution of solutions obtained with Rosetta Relax, and using in both cases the same computational time. In both refinement methods, the solutions do not deviate too far from the original structure, with final conformations around 2-3 angstroms (Å) (RMSD) with respect to the PDB-deposited structure.

When the initial structure corresponds to the predictions (Fig. 2, central and left columns), the differences are minor in terms of the energy of the final distributions, and with respect to the previous case (starting from the PDB-deposited structure). Only when the initial structure corresponds to the *RoseTTAFold* prediction, the distances of the refined structures are slightly large (between 3-4 Å). The small differences, in the three cases, are due to high-quality predictions with high prediction confidence, so the predicted structures are very close to the native structure, especially in the backbone structure.

The second example uses initial conformations of protein *6W4B* (Fig. 2, middle row). Starting from the PDB-deposited structure (left column), there is a small deviation from the initial structure, with most of the refined structures having RMSD less than 1 Å. Relax-DE clearly outperforms Rosetta Relax in terms of energy and is also slightly better in terms of RMSD.

When the initial structure corresponds to the *AlphaFold2* and *RoseTTAFold* predicted structures with the highest confidence (central and left columns), Relax-DE has solutions that fall into two different areas of the search space with different RMSDs to the reference structure, providing a similar RMSD distribution with respect to Rosetta Relax. The energy distributions of the solutions refined with Relax-DE are clearly better compared to those of Rosetta Relax.

The third example corresponds to protein *7JTL* (Fig. 2, bottom row). Starting from the PDB-deposited structure, Relax-DE presents a better solution distribution in terms of energy, with similar results in RMSD. With respect to the previous protein examples, the major difference is now found in the RMSD distributions when the initial structure corresponds to a predicted structure. This is because the predicted structures have low confidence in the predictions and due to poor MSA information as input to the deep learning schemes (as detailed in [7]). Consequently, the predicted initial structures are very far from the actual native structure, and the refinement methods (which only slightly refine the protein backbone structure) only search in conformational space around the initial structure, providing refined structures distant by about 10 Å (with the initial structure of *AlphaFold2*) and 8 Å (with the initial structure of *RoseTTAFold*). Note that the energies (especially with proteins *6W4B* and *7JTL*) are better with respect to the first case (left column) since the predictions provide initial structures that, even with possible collisions in the side chain atoms, have better quality with respect to the structures deposited in PDB.

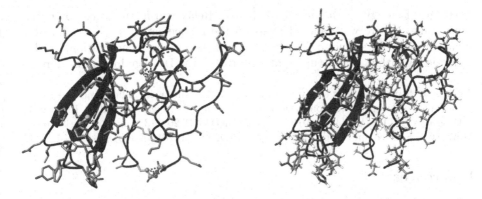

Fig. 3. Snapshots of protein *7JTL*. Left: Initial structure, predicted with *AlphaFold2*, showing clashes in some atoms (pink). Right: Best refined structure with Relax-DE. The protein backbone is in blue and depicted with the standard cartoon visualization. (Color figure online)

Figure 3 shows an example of refinement. The example corresponds to protein *7JTL* when the best structure predicted by *AlphaFold2* is used as the initial structure. Molprobity software [11] provides structural quality metrics such as "Clashscore". This Clashscore value specifies the number of overlaps per 1,000 atoms (smaller numbers are better). For example, the Clashscore value of the initial solution predicted with *AlphaFold2* is 35.87 while the value of the best refined solution (best energy) with Relax-DE is 3.64. The ChimeraX software, used for visualization of the protein structures in Fig. 3, detects 21 clashes between nearby atoms (shown in pink in Fig. 3, left part, with the default options for clash detection), while no clashes are present in the refined structure. Similarly, Molprobity provides an overall measure of structural quality, "Molprobity score" (which combines several geometric scores, lower values are better), with a value of 3.18 for the initial structure and a value of 1.67 for the best refined structure with Relax-DE. These comments regarding the improvement in structural quality are general to the different examples, with the initial structures predicted with the deep learning approaches having the highest number of clashes.

4   Conclusions

In this work, a memetic algorithm for protein refinement was proposed and compared with respect to the widely used Rosetta Relax refinement protocol. The memetic algorithm combines differential evolution with the local search procedures of the Rosetta Relax process. Thus, the memetic solution integrates the advantage of the global search of the evolutionary algorithm, in the huge protein conformational space, with the local search procedures of Rosetta Relax that locally refine the protein conformations, providing better refined conformations (in terms of energy) with respect to Rosetta Relax and in the same computational time. Future work should focus on the refinement of local areas of the structure with low structural quality, as well as on the incorporation, in the memetic algorithm, of self-tuning alternatives of the DE-defining parameters.

Acknowledgments. This study was funded by the Xunta de Galicia and the European Union (European Regional Development Fund - Galicia 2014-2020 Program), with grants CITIC (ED431G 2019/01), GPC ED431B 2022/33, and by the Spanish Ministry of Science and Innovation (project PID2020-116201GB-I00)).

References

1. Adiyaman, R., McGuffin, L.J.: Methods for the refinement of protein structure 3D models. Int. J. Mol. Sci. **20**(9), 2301 (2019)
2. Alford, R.F., et al.: The Rosetta all-atom energy function for macromolecular modeling and design. J. Chem. Theory Comput. (2017)
3. Anfinsen, C.: Principles that govern the folding of proteins. Science **181**(96), 223–230 (1973)
4. AlphaFold2 server. https://colab.research.google.com/github/sokrypton/ColabFold/blob/main/AlphaFold2.ipynb
5. Baek, M., et al.: Accurate prediction of protein structures and interactions using a three-track neural network. Science **373**(6557), 871–876 (2021)
6. Das, S., Mullick, S., Suganthan, P.: Recent advances in differential evolution - an updated survey. Swarm Evol. Comput. **27**, 1–30 (2016)
7. Filgueiras, J., Varela, D., Santos, J.: Protein structure prediction with energy minimization and deep learning approaches. Nat. Comput. **22**, 659–670 (2023)
8. Garza-Fabre, M., Kandathil, S., Handl, J., Knowles, J., Lovell, S.: Generating, maintaining, and exploiting diversity in a memetic algorithm for protein structure prediction. Evol. Comput. **24**(4), 577–607 (2016)
9. Jumper, J., Evans, R., Pritzel, A., et al.: Highly accurate protein structure prediction with AlphaFold. Nature **596**, 583–589 (2021)
10. Márquez-Chamorro, A., Asencio-Cortés, G., Santiesteban-Toca, C., Aguilar-Ruiz, J.: Soft computing methods for the prediction of protein tertiary structures: A survey. Appl. Soft Comput. **35**, 398–410 (2015)
11. Molprobity. http://molprobity.biochem.duke.edu/
12. Protein Data Bank. http://www.wwpdb.org
13. Price, K., Storn, R., Lampinen, J.: Differential evolution. a practical approach to global optimization (2005)
14. Rosetta system. http://www.rosettacommons.org
15. RoseTTAFold2 server. https://colab.research.google.com/github/sokrypton/ColabFold/blob/main/RoseTTAFold2.ipynb
16. Santos, J., Diéguez, M.: Differential evolution for protein structure prediction using the HP model. In: Ferrández, J.M., Álvarez Sánchez, J.R., de la Paz, F., Toledo, F.J. (eds.) IWINAC 2011. LNCS, vol. 6686, pp. 323–333. Springer, Heidelberg (2011). https://doi.org/10.1007/978-3-642-21344-1_34
17. Varela, D., Santos, J.: A hybrid evolutionary algorithm for protein structure prediction using the Face Centered Cubic lattice model. In: Proceedings of ICONIP 2017. LNCS, vol. 10634, pp. 628–638 (2017). https://doi.org/10.1007/978-3-319-70087-8_65

18. Varela, D., Santos, J.: Niching methods integrated with a differential evolution memetic algorithm for protein structure prediction. Swarm Evol. Comput. **71**, 101062 (2022)
19. Varela, D., Santos, J.: Protein structure prediction in an atomic model with differential evolution integrated with the crowding niching method. Nat. Comput. **21**, 537–551 (2022)

Evolutionary Algorithms for Bin Packing Problem with Maximum Lateness and Waste Minimization

Jesús Quesada[1], Francisco J. Gil-Gala[1]([✉]), Marko Đurasević[2],
María R. Sierra[1], and Ramiro Varela[1]

[1] Department of Computer Science, University of Oviedo, Oviedo, Spain
giljavier@uniovi.es
[2] Faculty of Electrical Engineering and Computing, University of Zagreb, Zagreb, Croatia

Abstract. The Bin Packing Problem (BPP) is a well-known NP-hard problem with numerous real-world applications. This study aims to minimize waste and maximum lateness in a one-dimensional BPP. To solve the problem, we exploit a classical greedy algorithm in two different settings: it is firstly adapted as decoder in a standard Genetic Algorithm (GA), and it is also exploited to build a solution from scratch, in this case, guided by heuristic rules that are evolved automatically by Genetic Programming (GP). We conducted an experimental study to assess the performance of the proposed algorithms and to compare them against a Price-and-Branch (P&B) algorithm taken from the literature. The results show that the greedy algorithm guided by heuristics evolved by GP performs better than GA and that it produces solutions very close to the lower bounds provided by P&B, even in some cases improving the best-known upper bounds.

Keywords: Bin Packing Problem · Maximum lateness minimisation · Heuristics · Hyper-heuristics

1 Introduction

The Bin Packing Problem (BPP) is a classical NP-hard problem with diverse applications in real-world scenarios, for example in plastic roll manufacturing [14]. Consequently, considerable research effort has been dedicated over the last years to develop exact methods [1,13], metaheuristics [11], and hyper-heuristics [12] for effectively addressing a variety of packing and cutting problems.

The most classic formulation of the BPP involves a set of items, each having a given weight, and a set of identical bins with fixed capacities. Normally, the main goal is to determine the minimum number of bins required to accommodate all items or to reduce the waste produced in the bins, ensuring that no bin surpasses its capacity. This paper focuses on the one-dimensional variant introduced in [1], in which each item has a due date, and the goal is to minimize the waste produced and the maximum lateness simultaneously.

This study introduces evolutionary algorithms as solution methods for the one-dimensional bin packing problem with lateness minimization. Specifically, we propose the application of Genetic Programming (GP) to generate heuristics automatically that are then exploited by a greedy algorithm; the resulting search algorithm is termed GP-XX herein, where XX identifies the *training set* used by GP to evolve the heuristics. The same base greedy algorithm is adapted as decoder in a standard Genetic Algorithm (GA), which is taken as baseline for the purpose of comparison. Additionally, we compare our solutions with the Price-and-Branch (P&B) algorithm proposed in [1], which produces tight lower and upper bounds. It is clear that the three considered algorithms, namely GA, GP-XX and P&B, have quite different characteristics. While P&B is an exact algorithm that provides lower and upper bounds working in any-time fashion, it generally takes a very long time until either an exact solution or some tight lower and upper bounds are reached. GA is a stochastic algorithm that may produce improved upper bounds over time, but it can commonly get stuck in local optima unless it is combined with powerful local search algorithms. The issue with the previous two approaches is that they usually require a substantial amount of time to obtain good solutions. On the other hand, GP, which differs from GAs by the representation it uses, offers an alternative way of solving optimisation problems. Instead of solving a concrete problem instance, it generates a heuristic procedure that can be used to solve numerous problems quite efficiently. Although the generation process of such heuristics takes quite some time, once generated, they can be reused for solving new problems in significantly less time than both P&B and GA. Overall, the contributions of this paper are:

1. Adaptation of a greedy algorithm for constructing solutions for BPP to minimise both waste and maximum lateness simultaneously;
2. Adaptation of GP and GA to solve the BPP exploiting the proposed greedy algorithm;
3. Extensive experimental analysis of the proposed methods and comparison to the state-of-the-art, as far as we know, the P&B method proposed in [1].

The rest of the paper is organised as follows. In the next section, the specific BPP variant is defined. Section 3 details the solution builder method considered, namely the greedy algorithm. Next, in Sect. 4, we describe the GP and the GA proposed in this work. Finally, Sects. 5 and 6 report the experimental analysis and the main conclusions of our study.

2   Problem Definition

In the problem at hand, we must pack a set of n items into a set of n bins of capacity C, the item j ($1 \leq j \leq n$) has a weight w_j ($0 < w_j \leq C$) and due date d_j ($0 \leq d_j$). Each bin is available at a time slot over a planning horizon $1, 2, \ldots, n$. Each item will be packed into a specific bin, i.e., into a specific time slot; this will determine the completion time i of an item j. The goal is to minimize both the number of bins used and the maximum lateness incurred, subject to the following constraints:

$$\sum_{j=1}^{n} w_j x_{ij} \leq C, \qquad 1 \leq i \leq n,$$

$$\sum_{i=1}^{n} x_{ij} = 1, \qquad 1 \leq j \leq n, \tag{1}$$

$$y_i \in \{0,1\}, \qquad 1 \leq i \leq n,$$

$$x_{ij} \in \{0,1\}, \qquad 1 \leq i,j \leq n.$$

where the binary decision variables y_i and x_{ij} denote whether or not bin i has been used and if item j is packed on bin i respectively. If $x_{ij} = 1$, the lateness of item j is defined as $L_j = i - d_j$. Following [1], we consider the objective function

$$0.5 \cdot \sum_{i=1}^{n} y_i + 0.5 \cdot \max_{1 \leq j \leq n} L_j \tag{2}$$

to optimize both criteria simultaneously.

3   The Solution Method

Algorithm 1 shows the greedy algorithm proposed in [12], which is adapted in this study to be exploited in combination with GP and GA to minimise both waste and maximum lateness. In each iteration, the unpacked item with the highest priority, in accordance with a given priority rule (PR), which fits into the *active* bin, is packed until all items are packed. Upon completion of the current bin, it is incorporated into the partial plan, and a new empty bin is taken. One of the most popular heuristics (or priority functions) for BPP is *Best Fit* (BF). In the context of Algorithm 1, it assigns a priority of $1/w_j$ to bin j and so it selects the largest bin that fits in the active bin. BF may be appropriate for waste minimisation; however, it would probably be ineffective for maximum lateness minimisation. As pointed, in this study we exploit the above greedy algorithm in combination with both GA and GP. In the first case, the greedy algorithm is used as decoder, where a chromosome is a permutation of the bins. Besides, we exploit GP to evolve new priority rules suitable for the considered objectives, which may depend on more problem attributes than the weights of the bins, which is the only attribute considered by BF.

4   Evolutionary Algorithms

The proposed evolutionary algorithms follow a generational scheme similar to other methodologies found in existing literature [6]. Initially, individuals are randomly grouped into pairs of parents. Subsequently, each parent pair undergoes the crossover operation, generating two children, which are then subjected to mutation with a given probability. In this scheme, the best child always passes to the next population, whereas the second individual selected is determined as the best one among the two parents and the remaining child. Consequently, this evolutionary scheme mitigates premature convergence and has an implicit form of elitism. This evolutionary approach is used by GP and GA, with some modifications elaborated upon in the following subsections.

4.1 Genetic Programming

GP is frequently employed in evolving heuristics [3,6,16]. This popularity emanates from the natural encoding of heuristics as expression trees, offering interpretability and efficiency generally surpassing linear representations or neural networks [10]. As usual, we chose classical genetic operators, namely subtree crossover and mutation. In this context, evaluating each individual involves using the encoded heuristic to guide the schedule builder (Algorithm 1). In the cases where two heuristics achieve identical fitness, tie-breaking favours the smallest expression.

One of the key points in GP is to establish a proper set of symbols, which must include terminals that encode domain-specific information and functions that combine these terminals into expressions. Building upon previous research [12], where only waste was minimized, we have introduced new terminals related to lateness. These additions are highlighted in Tables 1 and 2. One noteworthy addition to the terminals is TT, which represents the sum of the tardiness generated by all items packed so far, with $Tardiness_j = \max(i - d_j, 0)$, if $x_{ij} = 1$, being the tardiness of item j. Similarly, we have defined the terminal TL for total lateness. We have also introduced the concept of slack, defined as $Sl_j = d_j - T_j$.

Algorithm 1: Greedy algorithm

Input: The set of items to be packed L , a Priority Function PF
Output: A packing plan S
  1: $S = \emptyset$;
  2: Take the bin at time slot 0 as active bin;
  3: **while** $L \neq \emptyset$ **do**
  4:    $L' =$ items in L that fit in the active bin;
  5:    **if** $L' \neq \emptyset$ **then**
  6:      Select the item j with highest priority in L', using PF;
  7:      Pack the item j in the active bin;
  8:      Remove the item j from L;
  9:    **else**
10:      Add the current bin to S;
11:      Take the bin at the next time slot as active bin;
12: **Return** S;

Table 1. Terminal set used to build expression trees. The *active* bin is the one that is being built at the decision point.

Symbol	Description
C	The capacity of bins
w_j	Width of the candidate item j
F	Current load in the active bin
DW	Number of different widths in the instance
$DWNP$	Number of different widths in the unpacked items
W_j	Free space in the active bin after adding the item j
R_j	Number of times the active built bin could be repeated if the item j is added
I	Number of bins equal to the active bin in the cutting plan
N_j	Number of items with width w_j already in the active bin
N	Number of items in the active bin
T	Current time of the system
TT	Total Tardiness generated by packed items
TL	Total Lateness generated by packed items
d_j	Due Date of the candidate item j
Sl_j	Slack of the candidate item j

Table 2. Function set used to build expression trees.

Binary functions	$-$	$+$	$/$	$\times$	max	min	
Unary functions	$-$	pow_2	$sqrt$	exp	ln	max_0	min_0

4.2 Genetic Algorithm

As mentioned previously, in this study we apply a GA with permutation encoding where the order of the bins in a chromosome expresses their priorities, i.e. the order in which they will be packed into bins. This encoding allows GA to exploit the greedy algorithm (Algorithm 1) as a solution decoder by simply choosing the item in L' that is the leftmost one in the chromosome sequence. Besides, GA exploits conventional mating and mutation operators designed for permutation encoding (see Table 3).

Table 3. Parameters used to execute GP and GA.

Parameter name	GP	GA
Initialisation	Ramped half-and-half	Random
Population size	200	200
Crossover operator	Subtree	OX, CX, PMX
ratio	1.00	1.00
Mutation operator	Subtree	Swap, Substring
ratio	0.02	0.2
Chromosome length	2^8-1	Number of items

5   Experimental Analysis

The purpose of the experimental study is to assess the effectiveness of GA and GP, and to establish a comparison with the P&B algorithm described in [1]. As far as we know, P&B is the only solution method currently considered state-of-the-art for the BPP variant considered here. Additionally, we analyze the heuristics obtained by GP by assessing their ability to generalize on new problem instances.

5.1   Set up

The algorithms were coded in Java 8, without external libraries, and run on a Dell PowerEdge R740: 2 x Intel Xeon Gold 6132 (2.6GHz, 28 cores) with 128GB RAM. We used the parameters provided in Table 3 for GP and GA. Each crossover operator had an equal chance of being selected at with a probability of $1/3$, whereas each mutation operator had a probability of $1/2$ of being selected. Given the stochastic nature of evolutionary algorithms, we executed GP and GA 30 times per configuration to ensure statistically significant results. GP was set to stop at 50 generations, and GA was executed for the equivalent runtime required by GP to complete those generations for comparable results.

We experimented on the set of instances for the BPP proposed by Arbib and Marinelli in [1]. This set comprises 53 non-IRUP instances[1], where the number of items n ranges from 20 to 200, and the due dates for each item are randomly generated. We randomly divided this set into a training set of 27 instances and a test set of 26. From the instances in the training set, we created several subsets named T27, T10, T5, and T3, which contain 27, 10, 5, and 3 instances, respectively. Additionally, we created three training sets, each containing only one instance. These sets were named T1S, T1M, and T1L, where the instances are either small-sized, medium-sized, or large-sized. We will use these instances as training set in GP to evolve heuristics. On the other hand, the test set will be used to evaluate the performance of the obtained heuristics on a set of unseen instances in training.

5.2   Results

Table 4 shows the results obtained by GP and GA, as well as the results from P&B reported in [1]. In all three cases, the results correspond to the 26 instances in the test set. GP was exploited in two variants: GP-S and GP-TN. The second one works in the conventional way, i.e., a training set of N instances (N=27 in this case) is used to obtain 30 heuristics (one in each run of GP), and then these 30 heuristics were used to solve each one of 26 the instances of the test set. The last two columns in Table 4 show the best and average values of the objective function (see Eq. 2) for each one of the 26 instances of the test set. Regarding

---

[1] The integer round-up property (IRUP) means that its optimal value is given by the smallest integer greater than or equal to the optimal value of its LP relaxation.

Table 4. Results from GP-S, GP-27, GA and P&B (upper and lower bounds, LB and UB).

Instance	P&B		GA		GP − S		GP − T27	
	LB	UB	Best	Avg.	Best	Avg.	Best	Avg
040_06970	11.50	12.00	12.50	13.00	12.00	12.00	12.00	12.47
040_03610	14.50	15.00	15.50	16.00	15.00	15.10	15.50	15.65
060_01950	19.50	20.00	22.00	22.60	20.00	20.50	20.00	20.98
060_03820	16.00	16.50	18.00	18.60	16.50	16.50	16.50	16.93
060_06390	17.00	17.50	20.00	20.70	18.00	18.20	18.00	18.85
080_08620	19.50	19.50	21.50	22.40	19.50	19.50	19.50	20.00
100_05080	27.00	27.50	31.00	31.80	27.50	27.90	27.50	28.73
100_07330	25.50	26.00	29.00	30.10	26.00	26.00	26.00	26.45
120_08940	32.00	32.50	37.50	38.80	32.50	32.80	32.50	33.18
120_06550	43.00	43.50	49.50	51.30	43.50	43.70	43.50	43.95
120_04500	38.50	39.50	45.50	46.50	39.00	39.80	40.00	40.98
120_07400	44.00	45.00	52.00	52.90	45.00	45.10	45.00	46.10
140_04470	54.50	55.00	64.00	65.70	55.00	55.00	55.00	55.93
140_03730	46.00	46.50	56.00	57.30	47.50	47.80	47.50	48.85
160_00140	44.00	44.50	53.00	54.70	44.50	45.00	45.00	45.70
160_02790	60.00	60.50	72.50	74.00	61.00	61.80	61.00	62.13
160_02060	51.00	51.50	61.00	63.70	52.00	52.50	52.50	53.30
180_03590	53.50	54.00	65.00	66.40	54.00	55.00	54.50	55.83
180_07160	53.50	54.00	65.50	67.20	54.00	54.70	55.00	55.37
180_04390	62.00	63.50	73.50	76.80	63.00	63.80	63.50	64.48
180_08210	62.00	63.00	76.00	78.00	63.50	63.90	64.00	65.22
200_01750	59.50	60.50	71.50	73.50	60.50	61.10	61.00	62.17
200_01240	60.50	62.50	72.50	74.80	62.00	62.80	62.50	63.65
200_02000	66.00	68.00	81.00	82.40	67.00	67.90	67.50	68.68
200_06370	59.50	61.00	73.50	75.60	60.50	61.10	61.50	62.15
200_02720	81.00	82.00	97.00	99.40	81.50	81.90	82.00	82.93

GP-S, it works in rather different way. GP-S evolved 30 heuristics focused in just one of the instances of the test set. To do that, it used only one of these instances for training, so that one may expect that the evolved heuristics are overfitted for that instance. The values in columns 6 and 7 in the table show the best and average values of the objective function for the same instance used in training. In this way, one may not expect that the heuristic generalizes well for unseen instances, but the procedure may be considered as a suitable method to solve a particular instance. As expected, these results are better than those from GP-T27.

GP-TN with the other values of N (10, 5, 2, 1) achieved worse results than GP-T27. These results are summarized in Table 5, which reports the sum of the fitness values (best and average) attained by resolving all the instances in the test set using all tested configurations.

Table 5. Aggregation of the results obtained in Table 4, together with results from other variants of GP-XX

Algorithm	Best	Average
P&B	–	1141.00
GA	1336.00	1374.23
GP-S	1140.50	1150.92
GP-T27	1148.50	1170.68
GP-T10	1152.00	1174.18
GP-T5	1151.50	1177.12
GP-T3	1152.00	1177.12
GP-T1L	1153.00	1195.42
GP-T1M	1154.50	1186.55
GP-T1S	1164.50	1238.28

The results above show that GP performs better than GA and that it was able to improve some upper bounds calculated by P&B. ans that none of the solutions obtained can be confirmed as optimal.

It is also worth mentioning that while GP-TN may take several minutes for training (depending on the size of the training set), the resulting heuristics can be efficiently applied to solve the entire test set as well as any similar instance in just a few milliseconds. This differs from GA or P&B, which may take anywhere from a few seconds to several minutes, depending on the size of the problem instance.

To better outline the differences in GP between training with one or several instances, Fig. 1 shows the convergence of GP[2] under a time constraint of 220 min as a stopping criterion. This is the average time required to perform 50 generations with the training set of 27 instances. GP was executed 30 times from each training set; in each run the best heuristic after every 2.2 min was saved so that we collected a total of 100 heuristics in each run. Then, the obtained heuristics are evaluated on the test set. These values are showed in Fig. 1 averaged for each time point and training set. From these experiments, we can see that training with a single instance yields the worst results (in particular if the instance is very small), followed by training with three instances, as it was be expected. Conversely, training with 5, 10, or 27 instances provides similar results. Here, we have to be aware of the difference in the number of generations reached in each single run (50 with T27, 111 with T10, 442 with T5, 1071 with T3, 709957 with TS, 10485 with TM and 5169 with TL). Considering this, we can assume that GP-T27 would have still some room to improve if it were given more time, while the other variants seem to show premature convergence.

---

[2] By "convergence of GP" we mean the convergence of the results obtained by the best rule obtained by GP at each time point.

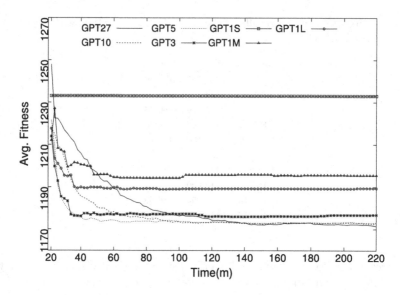

Fig. 1. Evolution of solutions produced by heuristics (average from 30 runs) trained via GP with different sizes (1, 3, 5, 10 and 27) solving the test set over 220 min.

6   Conclusions and Future Work

In this study, Genetic Programming (GP) and Genetic Algorithms (GA) were employed to solve the one-dimensional Bin Packing Problem, simultaneously focusing on optimising waste and maximum lateness. Our experimental analysis compares GP and GA against a Price-and-Branch (P&B) algorithm, which, as far as we know, is the unique method proposed in the literature for solving the considered problem. The results show that GP outperforms GA, achieving significantly better results, and that it achieves a similar performance than P&B. Furthermore, we demonstrated that heuristics obtained through GP can be efficiently applied to solve similar instances, producing high-quality solutions in just a few milliseconds. This contrasts GA and P&B, which may require several seconds or even minutes for the largest problem instances.

For future work, we are interested in evolving heuristics for multi-objective minimisation involving more than one objective function to be optimised simultaneously [4,15], as well as the use of sets of heuristics (ensembles) as an alternative, which could improve the results obtained by single heuristics [8,9]. In addition, some improvements can be introduced in the genetic operators used by GP and GA, such as local search [5,7].

Acknowledgements. This work has been partly supported by the Croatian Science Foundation under project IP-2022-10-5398 and the Spanish Government under project MCINN-23-PID2022.

References

1. Arbib, C., Marinelli, F.: Maximum lateness minimization in one-dimensional bin packing. Omega **68**, 76–84 (2017)
2. Coffman, E.G., Galambos, G., Martello, S., Vigo, D.: Bin Packing Approximation Algorithms: Combinatorial Analysis, pp. 151–207. Springer US, Boston, MA (1999)
3. Durasević, M., Jakobović, D., Knežević, K.: Adaptive scheduling on unrelated machines with genetic programming. Appl. Soft Comput. **48**, 419–430 (2016)
4. Durasević, M., Gil-Gala, F.J., Jakobović, D.: Constructing ensembles of dispatching rules for multi-objective tasks in the unrelated machines environment. Integrated Comput.-Aided Eng. **30**, 275–292 (2023)
5. Falkenauer, E.: A hybrid grouping genetic algorithm for bin packing. J. Heurist. **2**(1), 5–30 (1996)
6. Gil-Gala, F.J., Mencía, C., Sierra, M.R., Varela, R.: Evolving priority rules for on-line scheduling of jobs on a single machine with variable capacity over time. Appl. Soft Comput. **85**, 105782 (2019)
7. Gil-Gala, F.J., Sierra, M.R., Mencía, C., Varela, R.: Genetic programming with local search to evolve priority rules for scheduling jobs on a machine with time-varying capacity. Swarm Evol. Comput. **66**, 100944 (2021)
8. Gil-Gala, F.J., Durasević, M., Varela, R., Jakobović, D.: Ensembles of priority rules to solve one machine scheduling problem in real-time. Inform. Sci. **634**, 340–358 (2023),
9. Gil-Gala, F.J., Durasević, M., Sierra, M.R., Varela, R: Evolving ensembles of heuristics for the travelling salesman problem. Nat. Comput. **22**, 671–684 (2023)
10. Jia, Y.H., Mei, Y., Zhang, M.: Learning heuristics with different representations for stochastic routing. IEEE Trans. Cybernet. **53**(5), 3205–3219 (2023)
11. Munien, C., Ezugwu, A.E.: Metaheuristic algorithms for one-dimensional bin-packing problems: a survey of recent advances and applications. J. Intell. Syst. **30**(1), 636–663 (2021)
12. Quesada, J., Gil-Gala, F.J., Durasevic, M., Sierra, M., Varela, R.: An analysis of heuristic templates in genetic programming for one-dimensional cutting and packing problems. In: Proceedings of the Companion Conference on Genetic and Evolutionary Computation, pp. 623–626 (2023)
13. Sweeney, P.E., Paternoster, E.R.: Cutting and packing problems: a categorized, application-orientated research bibliography. J. Operat. Res. Soc. **43**(7), 691–706 (1992)
14. Varela, R., R. Vela, C., Puente, J., Sierra, M., Gonzalez-Rodriguez, I.: An effective solution for a real cutting stock problem in manufacturing plastic rolls. Annals Operat. Res. **166**, 125–146 (02 2009)
15. Zhang, F., Mei, Y., Nguyen, S., Zhang, M.: Multitask multiobjective genetic programming for automated scheduling heuristic learning in dynamic flexible job-shop scheduling. IEEE Trans. Cybernet., 1–14 (2022)
16. Zhang, F., Mei, Y., Nguyen, S., Tan, K.C., Zhang, M.: Instance-rotation-based surrogate in genetic programming with brood recombination for dynamic job-shop scheduling. IEEE Trans. Evol. Comput. **27**, 1192–1206 (2023)

Stationary Wavelet Entropy and Cat Swarm Optimization to Detect COVID-19

Meng Wu[1] , Shuwen Chen[1,2(✉)] , Jiaji Wang[1,3] , Shuihua Wang[4] ,
Juan Manuel Gorriz[5] , and Yudong Zhang[3,6(✉)]

[1] School of Computer Engineering, Jiangsu Second Normal University, Nanjing,
Jiangsu 211200, China
chenshuwen@126.com
[2] State Key Laboratory of Millimeter Waves, Southeast University, Nanjing,
Jiangsu 210096, China
[3] School of Computing and Mathematical Sciences, University of Leicester,
Leicester LE1 7RH, UK
yudongzhang@ieee.org
[4] Department of Biological Sciences, Xi'an Jiaotong-Liverpool University, Suzhou,
Jiangsu 215123, China
[5] Department of Signal Theory, Networking and Communications,
University of Granada, Granada 52005, Spain
[6] Department of Information Technology, Faculty of Computing and Information
Technology, King Abdulaziz University, Jeddah 21589, Saudi Arabia

Abstract. Accurate and efficient approaches are urgently needed to cope with the rapid spread of COVID-19 worldwide. A novel approach is presented in this paper, which combines Stationary Wavelet Entropy (SWE) and Cat Swarm Optimization (CSO) to enhance the precision and effectiveness of COVID-19 detection. SWE, a signal processing technique, extracts informative features from medical data. At the same time, CSO, a bio-inspired optimization algorithm, is used to fine-tune the parameters of a feed-forward neural network. Integrating these two techniques within our methodology addresses the complex and evolving nature of COVID-19 detection tasks. SWE efficiently captures irregularities and patterns in medical data, providing valuable inputs to the neural network, while CSO automates parameter tuning, optimizing the network's performance. Experimental results demonstrate the efficacy of our approach, showcasing its ability to accurately identify COVID-19 cases in diverse medical datasets. The synergy between SWE and CSO offers a promising avenue for enhancing COVID-19 detection, contributing to the global effort to combat the pandemic.

Keywords: stationary wavelet entropy · cat swarm optimization · Covid-19 · machine learning · optimization

Supported by the open project of State Key Laboratory of Millimeter Waves (Grant No. K202218), the "Qinglan Project" of Jiangsu University and it is part of the PID2022-137451OB-I00 project funded by the CIN/AEI/10.13039/501100011033 and by FSE+.

J. M. Ferrández Vicente et al. (Eds.): IWINAC 2024, LNCS 14675, pp. 150–162, 2024.
https://doi.org/10.1007/978-3-031-61137-7_15

1   Introduction

Late in 2019, a new coronavirus with the official name SARS-CoV-2 emerged in the world, sparking the COVID-19 worldwide pandemic [1]. This infectious respiratory disease rapidly spreads across borders, affecting millions of individuals and causing unprecedented challenges for public health systems, economies, and societies worldwide [2]. Understanding, detecting, and managing COVID-19 has become a paramount concern for researchers, healthcare professionals, and governments [3].

The significance of COVID-19 lies in its high transmission rate and potential to cause severe illness and, in some cases, lead to fatal outcomes [4]. The virus has posed substantial hurdles in the form of overwhelmed healthcare systems, unprecedented lockdowns, and social distancing measures. Accurate and efficient detection methods are essential for prompt medical intervention and curbing the spread of the virus.

Amidst these challenges, artificial intelligence and machine learning have risen to the occasion, offering innovative solutions for detecting and managing [5]. One such approach is using feed-forward neural networks, a class of deep learning models that have demonstrated remarkable capabilities in various domains, including image and signal processing, natural language understanding, and, importantly, medical diagnosis [6,7].

A feed-forward neural network, also known as a multi-layer perceptron, is an artificial neural network designed to process input forward. This structure consists of an input layer, one or more layers that are hidden, and a layer for output. Each layer has linked nodes, or neurons, which use weighted connections to process and transfer information [8]. Feed-forward neural networks may learn complicated patterns from data using this design, and they can then predict or categorize data based on the input.

This paper presents our contributions to the ongoing efforts to detect COVID-19 using advanced computational techniques. Specifically, we introduce a novel approach that combines Stationary Wavelet Entropy (SWE) and Cat Swarm Optimization (CSO) for COVID-19 detection. While Cat Swarm Optimization, a signal processing approach influenced by nature, is used to optimize the parameters of neural networks, Stationary Wavelet Entropy has demonstrated potential in extracting useful features from medical data [9]. To improve the precision and effectiveness of COVID-19 detection, our suggested strategy uses the complementary strengths of these two elements.

The structure of this paper is organized to provide a comprehensive understanding of our approach. In the following sections, we will delve into the background and related work, explain the methodology in detail, present experimental results, and discuss the implications of our findings. By the end of this paper, readers will gain insights into a promising avenue for improving COVID-19 detection through the fusion of Stationary Wavelet Entropy and Cat Swarm Optimization within the framework of feed-forward neural networks.

2   Background

The paper [10] introduced a COVID-19 diagnosis method that combines wavelet entropy and particle swarm optimization. In consideration that the data set was small, the evaluation method adopted K-fold cross-validation to make the results fairer and more accurate. The sensitivity, specificity, precision, accuracy, F1 score, MCC and FMI were 76.89±1.18, 77.64±2.10, 77.50±1.62, 77.26±1.13, 77.18±1.01, 54.54±2.26 and 77.19±1.01 respectively. The experiment results showed this approach was better than other advanced methods.

The study suggests a method for automatically diagnosing COVID-19 using chest CT imaging data. The algorithm combined WE and ELM. While ELM was used for training, WE was utilized to extract picture characteristics. The K-fold cross-validation was used as the final step. Using 296 chest CT scans as input, the MCC and FMI were 53.35 ± 2.26

The paper [11] combined the gray-level cooccurrence matrix and particle swarm optimization algorithm. The authors utilized the former to extract features and the latter to identify the best course of action. Finally, the K-old cross-validation was used to validate the method. In this way, higher performance has been gained.

A new method for diagnosing COVID-19 has been proposed in the article [8]. This research applied a multiple-distance gray-level co-occurrence matrix to extract features from chest CT images. Then, the system is optimized using the GA algorithm. Besides, the feed-forward neural network processed and classified input data and ran ten times to produce results, which shows that this method was exceptional. The mean value of sensitivity was 83.38, and the mean square error was 1.40, while the mean value of accuracy was 82.26, and the mean square error was 0.96.

The simulations in the paper [12] were performed on a dataset in which there were 320 healthy controls and 320 infected with COVID-19. This simulation extracted features of images using the gray-level co-occurrence matrix and classified images using a random vector function link. The authors then used K-fold cross-validation to verify the GR model's output. The indicators were above 77 for sensitivity, accuracy, F1-score, and FMI.

3   Dataset

Our dataset has two types of images, including 296 images in total. Half of the images are COVID-19, and the rest are healthy control (HC). Figure 1 shows the chest CT scans of a patient with COVID-19 and one healthy individual, respectively.

GGO, consolidation, and other rare effusions within the pleura or pericardium are the prevalent characteristics of CT imaging of individuals with COVID-19. For COVID-19 to be identified more precisely, it is critical to recognize these similar characteristics.

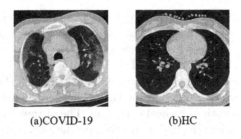

(a)COVID-19   (b)HC

Fig. 1. Sample of COVID-19 and HC

4   Methodology

4.1   Feed-Forward Neural Network

A feed-forward neural network-often referred to as an MLP-plays a crucial part in many machine learning applications [13], including COVID-19 detection. The different layers that make up its architecture include an input layer, one or more hidden layers, and an output layer [14,15]. Figure 2 can serve as a representation of the model.

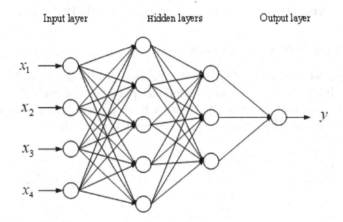

Fig. 2. Feed-forward Neural Network Model

The input layer serves as the entry point for data into the neural network [16]. In the context of COVID-19 detection, this layer receives initial data, including features extracted from medical images or patient records [17]. Since each neuron corresponds to a different feature, the input layer is crucial for representing the characteristics of the input data.

One or more hidden layers process the data after the input layer. Neurons within these hidden layers perform complex calculations involving learned weights and biases [15]. As a result, the network is able to identify intricate patterns and correlations in the data. The complexity of the issue will determine the depth and width of these hidden layers.

The last layer is the output layer of the neural network. It generates predictions or classifications based on the processed data. For COVID-19 detection, the output layer provides an output that indicates whether the input corresponds to a COVID-19 case or another medical condition. The output can be a probability score or a binary decision, depending on the specific task.

An activation function is connected to each neuron in the network. Due to activation functions, which provide non-linearity in the model and enable complex interactions within the data, the network may mimic these interactions [18]. The sigmoid function, ReLU (Rectified Linear Unit), and tanh (Hyperbolic Tangent) are often used activation functions.

The weights and biases of a feed-forward neural network's neurons are adjusted during training to reduce the discrepancy between expected results and actual goal values. This process enables the network to learn from data and improve performance. Common optimization techniques include gradient descent and backpropagation, which iteratively refine the network's parameters.

In our proposed approach for COVID-19 detection, the feed-forward neural network serves as the core element for processing and classifying input data. We leverage its ability to learn complex patterns and extract meaningful features, thereby enhancing the accuracy and efficiency of COVID-19 detection.

4.2   Stationary Wavelet Entropy

In our suggested method for COVID-19 detection, Stationary Wavelet Entropy (SWE), a critical signal processing technique, plays a vital role. SWE offers a unique way to extract valuable information from data, making it an essential component of our methodology [19]. Its flowchart is shown in Fig. 3.

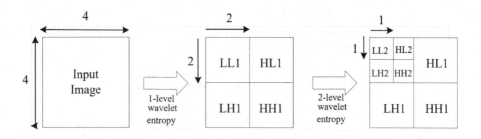

Fig. 3. Flowchart of Calculating SWE

At its core, SWE is based on wavelet transforms, mathematical operations used to decompose a signal into multiple frequency components. Unlike traditional Fourier transforms, wavelet transforms provide both time and frequency localization, making them particularly useful for analyzing non-stationary signals, such as those encountered in medical data [20].

The concept of entropy, borrowed from information theory, is applied to the wavelet coefficients obtained from the decomposition. Entropy measures the degree of randomness or unpredictability in a signal. In the context of SWE, it quantifies the complexity or irregularity of the different frequency components of a signal.

In the context of COVID-19 detection, SWE can be applied to various types of medical data, such as chest X-ray images or electrocardiogram (ECG) signals. By decomposing these data into wavelet coefficients and calculating entropy values for each component, SWE can help highlight distinctive patterns or irregularities associated with COVID-19 infection [21].

For example, in chest X-ray images, SWE may reveal unique textural patterns or structural irregularities specific to COVID-19-related lung abnormalities. These patterns can serve as discriminative features for classification tasks.

One of the strengths of SWE lies in its ability to extract informative features from complex medical data. In our proposed approach for COVID-19 detection, we integrate SWE with a feed-forward neural network to enhance the network's ability to discriminate between COVID-19 cases and other conditions.

The SWE-generated features act as valuable inputs to the neural network, enriching the dataset with information that may not be readily apparent from raw data. This integration allows the neural network to learn and utilize these enhanced features, ultimately improving the accuracy of COVID-19 detection.

4.3   Cat Swarm Optimization

A bio-inspired optimization technique called Cat Swarm Optimization (CSO) imitates the group behavior of cats during their foraging and hunting activities [22]. Like real cats collaborate and compete to find prey, CSO employs a swarm of artificial "cats" to collectively search for optimal solutions to complex optimization problems.

CSO's key features and principles make it an essential element of our COVID-19 detection methodology [23]. These include exploration and exploitation, adapt-ability, and diversity.

CSO takes exploration and exploitation into account. Some "cats" in the swarm explore the solution space to discover new promising solutions, while others exploit known good solutions to refine them further [24]. This dual strategy ensures that CSO can avoid getting stuck in local optima and continue its search for the global optimum.

Furthermore, CSO is highly adaptable, allowing the swarm to dynamically ad-just its behavior based on the progress in finding the optimal solution [25] [26]. This adaptability proves advantageous in optimization tasks where the characteristics of the solution space may change over time.

Moreover, the diversity maintained within the swarm of artificial cats in CSO enables the exploration of a wide range of potential solutions, which is crucial for tackling complex and multifaceted optimization problems.

In our COVID-19 detection approach, CSO is essential in adjusting the feed-forward neural network's parameters (discussed in Sect. 2). This optimization entails adjusting various neural network parameters, such as learning rates, weights, and biases, to maximize the network's performance [27] [28].

Integrating CSO with the neural network offers several advantages, including automated parameter tuning, enhanced model performance, and adaptation to changing data [21]. CSO automates the labor-intensive parameter tuning process, allowing the neural network to adapt and optimize itself continuously. This CSO-guided parameter adjustment markedly improves the neural network's capacity to correctly categorize COVID-19 instances, leading to a more robust and effec-tive COVID-19 detection system. Additionally, CSO's adaptability proves valu-able in medical applications like COVID-19 detection, where data characteristics may evolve, enabling the swarm to adjust its optimization strategy to accom-modate changing conditions.

4.4 K-Fold Cross-Validation

K-fold cross-validation is a crucial machine-learning approach for assessing and verifying prediction models [29]. Its primary purpose is to assess how well a model can predict new, unseen data while utilizing the available dataset. With this method, one data split is not overly relied upon, and a reliable indicator of a model's generalization ability is provided [30].

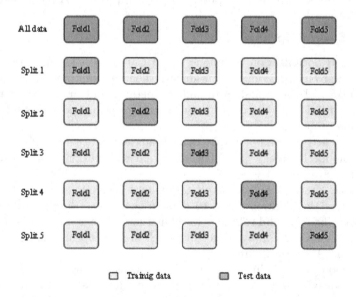

Fig. 4. Diagram of K-fold cross-validation (K=5)

When doing K-fold cross-validation, the dataset is divided into K approxi-mately equal-sized subgroups, or "folds." After that, the model is developed and assessed K times, with each assessment using the rest of the K-1 folds as the training group and a fresh fold as the validation set [31]. K different performance estimations for the model are the end outcome, typically measured using accuracy, precision, recall, or F1 score metrics. These K estimates are aggregated to obtain the final performance metric, often by calculating the average. Figure 4 displays the diagram of K-fold cross-validation.

K-fold cross-validation brings several advantages to model evaluation. Firstly, it ensures that the model's performance assessment is not overly dependent on a specific random data split. This reduces the risk of drawing misleading conclusions based on a single data partition and provides a more reliable measure of how well the model generalizes to diverse data points.

Moreover, this technique maximizes the utilization of available data for training and validation, mitigating issues related to overfitting or underfitting. It is particularly crucial when dealing with limited datasets, where every data point's contribution to model training and evaluation is valuable.

Additionally, K-fold cross-validation aids in understanding the balance between bias and variance in the model. A significant bias issue may be indicated by consistently poor performance across several folds, indicating that the model is too oversimplified to represent the underlying patterns in the data accurately. On the other hand, a large variance in performance may point to a high variance problem, meaning the model is very sensitive to changes in the training data.

Furthermore, K-fold cross-validation is vital in hyperparameter tuning, where the model's configuration parameters are optimized for better performance. Assessing the model under different parameter settings across multiple folds assists in selecting the optimal setup.

However, it's essential to consider the computational cost associated with K-fold cross-validation. This approach can be computationally costly, especially for large datasets, as the model is trained and tested K times. Thus, selecting a suitable value for K relies on several variables, such as the size of the dataset and the available processing resources. One typical option for K is 10.

4.5   Evaluation

Metrics that are frequently employed in the areas of statistics and machine learning include sensitivity, specificity, precision, accuracy, F1 score, MCC (Matthews Correlation Coefficient), and FMI (Fowlkes-Mallows Index) [32], particularly in the context of binary classification tasks [33].

Sensitivity (True Positive Rate or Recall): Sensitivity quantifies the share of accurate positive predictions among all instances of positive behavior. It is deter-mined as:
Displayed equations are centered and set on a separate line.

$$Sensitivity = TP/(TP + FN) \tag{1}$$

where FN (False Negatives) is the number of real positive occurrences that were mistakenly categorized as negative and TP (True Positives) is the number of positively observed cases that were properly predicted to be positive.

Specificity: The percentage of accurate negative predictions compared to all actual negative cases is known as specificity. It is determined as: Displayed equations are centered and set on a separate line.

$$Specificity = TN/(TN + FP) \tag{2}$$

where FP (False Positives) is the number of real negative cases that were mistakenly categorized as positive and TN (True Negatives) is the number of negative instances that were properly predicted to be negative.

Precision (Positive Predictive Value): Precision is the percentage of correctly anticipated positive events among all positive cases. It has been set as: Displayed equations are centered and set on a separate line.

$$Precision = TP/(TP + FP) \tag{3}$$

Accuracy: The percentage of accurate forecasts (including true positives and true negatives) among all predictions serves as a gauge of overall model performance. It has been established as: Displayed equations are centered and set on a separate line.

$$Accuracy = (TP + TN)/(TP + TN + FP + FN) \tag{4}$$

F1 Score: The harmonic mean of sensitivity and accuracy is the F1 score. Being able to manage the trade-off between accuracy and sensitivity makes it a helpful statistic when there is an imbalance between the two groups. The F1 score can be calculated by using: Displayed equations are centered and set on a separate line.

$$F1Score = 2 * (Precision * Sensitivity)/(Precision + Sensitivity) \tag{5}$$

Matthews Correlation Coefficient (MCC): The MCC measure is particularly helpful when working with unbalanced datasets since it considers all four values of the confusion matrix (TP, TN, FP, and FN). The calculation is Displayed equations are centered and set on a separate line.

$$MCC = (TP*TN - FP*FN)/\sqrt{(TP + FP)(TP + FN)(TN + FP)(TN + FN)} \tag{6}$$

Fowlkes-Mallows Index (FMI): The geometric mean of accuracy and sensitivity is measured by the FMI. It is established by: Displayed equations are centered and set on a separate line.

$$FMI = \sqrt{Precision * Sensitivity} \tag{7}$$

These metrics help evaluate the performance of binary classification models and assess how well a model can discriminate between two classes (e.g., positive and negative) based on its predictions. The metric choice depends on the problem's specific characteristics and the application's relative importance of false positives and negatives.

5   Experiment and Discussion

5.1   Statistical Evaluation

Table 1 reports the outcomes of ten 10-fold cross-validation runs. The dataset is split into ten folds of the same size. Each run utilizes one of the remaining nine folds as the training set and a different fold as the validation set. Sensitivity (83.18±2.78), specificity (85.14±1.72), precision (84.87±1.25), accuracy (84.16±1.05), F1 (83.98±1.28), MCC (68.38±2.09), and FMI (84.00±1.27) are the seven indicators' MSD values.

Table 1. Results of 10 runs of 10-fold cross-validation

Run	Sen	Spc	Prc	Acc	F1	MCC	FMI
1	85.81	83.78	84.11	84.80	84.95	69.61	84.95
2	83.78	85.81	85.52	84.80	84.64	69.61	84.65
3	78.38	85.81	84.67	82.09	81.40	64.37	81.46
4	81.76	87.84	87.05	84.80	84.32	69.72	84.36
5	83.78	85.14	84.93	84.46	84.35	68.93	84.36
6	83.78	84.46	84.35	84.12	84.07	68.24	84.07
7	80.41	85.81	85.00	83.11	82.64	66.31	82.67
8	82.43	87.16	86.52	84.80	84.43	69.67	84.45
9	83.11	83.11	83.11	83.11	83.11	66.22	83.11
10	88.51	82.43	83.44	85.47	85.90	71.08	85.94
MSD	83.18±2.78	85.14±1.72	84.87±1.25	84.16±1.05	83.98±1.28	68.38±2.09	84.00±1.27

5.2   Comparison to State-of-the-Art Methods

Five cutting-edge COVID-19 recognition methods are compared with the proposed SWE-CSO model: WEPSO [10], WE-ELM [34], GLCM-PSO [11], MDGLCM-GA [8], and GLCM-RVFL [12]. Table 2 lists the outcomes, with the top outcomes being bolded. The best results are obtained with our suggested SWE-CSO model for six metrics. Our suggested model comes in second in sensitivity, only behind MDGLCM-GA (83.38

Table 2. Comparison with State-of-the-art Approaches

Run	Sen	Spc	Prc	Acc	F1	MCC	FMI
WEPSO [10]	76.89±1.18	77.64±2.10	77.50±1.62	77.26±1.13	77.18±1.01	54.54±2.26	77.19±1.01
WE-ELM [34]	75.54±2.54	77.77±1.51	77.27±1.04	76.66±1.14	76.38±1.42	53.35±2.26	76.39±1.41
GLCM-PSO [11]	77.36±2.47	78.99±2.31	78.69±1.55	78.18±0.86	77.99±1.06	56.41±1.73	78.01±1.05
MDGLCM-GA [8]	**83.38±1.40**	81.15±2.08	81.59±1.57	82.26±0.96	82.46±0.88	64.57±1.90	82.47±0.88
GLCM-RVFL [35]	78.81±1.75	75.34±1.92	76.20±1.12	77.08±0.68	77.46±0.73	54.22±1.35	77.48±0.74
SWE-CSO (Ours)	83.18±2.78	**85.14±1.72**	**84.87±1.25**	**84.16±1.05**	**83.98±1.28**	**68.38 ±2.09**	**84.00±1.27**

(Bold means the best)

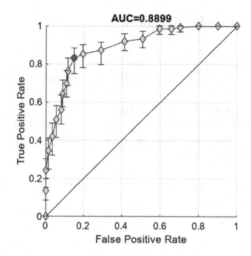

Fig. 5. ROC Curve of our method

5.3   ROC Curve

The basic purpose of the ROC curve (Receiver operating characteristic curve) is to assess how an index affects the categorization or diagnosis of two different types of tests (such as patients and normal people) and to find the best index cut-off value. The ordinate shows the true-positive rates, representing sensitivity, and the higher the index, the higher the diagnostic accuracy. The horizontal coordinate shows false-positive rates, representing 1- specificity, and the lower the index, the lower the false error rate.

The curve splits the entire graph in half. AUC (Area Under Curve) denotes the prediction accuracy and is the region beneath the curve. The region beneath the curve and prediction accuracy increase with increasing AUC values [35]. The closer the slope is to the highest left corner (smaller X, larger Y), the more accurate the forecast becomes.

The value of the AUC of our method is 0.8899, as shown in Figure 5, which has strong performance in COVID-19 detection.

6   Conclusion and Future Research

This study suggests a fresh strategy for detecting COVID-19 that combines Stationary Wavelet Entropy (SWE) and Cat Swarm Optimization (CSO). We use the feed-forward neural network as the core element for processing and classifying input data. Features generated by SWE are served as valuable inputs to the neural networks to enrich datasets. CSO is essential for adjusting the settings of the feed-forward neural network. Seven factors are used to estimate the model: sensitivity, specificity, accuracy, precision, F1-score, MCC, and FMI. Ten 10-fold cross-validation runs produced the following results: 83.18±2.78

Three areas can be improved: (a) Other infectious illnesses of the chest are not taken into consideration. (b) Only one dataset is used to assess the model. (c) The model has room for improvement in sensitivity.

In the future, we plan to include the identification of other diseases, such as pneumonia and tuberculosis. To improve our model, a larger open-source data collection will be sought after by us for training, and we'll employ a range of datasets to evaluate the model.

References

1. Kovács, K.D.: Determination of the human impact on the drop in NO2 air pollution due to total COVID-19 lockdown using Human-Influenced Air Pollution Decrease Index (HIAPDI). Environ. Pollut. **306**, 119441 (2022)
2. Díaz, A., Esparcia, C., López, R.: The diversifying role of socially responsible investments during the COVID-19 crisis: A risk management and portfolio performance analysis. Econ. Anal. Policy **75**, 39–60 (2022)
3. Watson, O.J., et al.: Global impact of the first year of COVID-19 vaccination: a mathematical modelling study. Lancet. Infect. Dis **22**(9), 1293–1302 (2022)
4. Yuan, Y., et al.: The development of COVID-19 treatment. Front. Immunol. **14**, 1125246 (2023)
5. Robinson, P.C., et al.: COVID-19 therapeutics: challenges and directions for the future. Proc. Natl. Acad. Sci. **119**(15), e2119893119 (2022)
6. Han, X., et al.: A survey on deep learning in COVID-19 diagnosis. J. Imaging **9**(1), 1 (2022)
7. Górriz, J.M., et al.: Artificial intelligence within the interplay between natural and artificial computation: advances in data science, trends and applications. Neurocomputing **410**, 237–270 (2020)
8. Jiang, X., et al.: COVID-19 diagnosis by multiple-distance gray-level cooccurrence matrix and genetic algorithm. Inter. J. Patient-Centered Healthcare **12**(1), 309951 (2022)
9. Jovanovic, D., et al.: Feature selection by improved sand cat swarm optimizer for intrusion detection. in 2022 International Conference on Artificial Intelligence in Everything (AIE). IEEE (2022)
10. Wang, J.-J.: COVID-19 diagnosis by wavelet entropy and particle swarm optimization. Intell. Comput. Theories Appli. **13394**, 600–611 (2022)
11. Wang, J., Graham, L.: COVID-19 diagnosis by gray-level cooccurrence matrix and PSO. Inter. J. Patient-Centered Healthcare **12**(1), 309118 (2022)
12. Tang, W.: Gray level co-occurrence matrix and RVFL for Covid-19 Diagnosis. EAI Endorsed Trans. e-Learning **8**(2) (2023)
13. Fernandez-Garcia, M.E., et al.: Double-layer stacked denoising autoencoders for regression. in 9th International Work-Conference on the Interplay Between Natural and Artificial Computation (IWINAC), Puerto de la Cruz, Spain (2022)
14. Hu, M., et al.: Automated layer-wise solution for ensemble deep randomized feed-forward neural network. Neurocomputing **514**, 137–147 (2022)
15. Xue, Y., Tong, Y., Neri, F.: An ensemble of differential evolution and Adam for training feed-forward neural networks. Inf. Sci. **608**, 453–471 (2022)
16. García-Aguilar, I., et al.: enhanced image segmentation by a novel test time augmentation and super-resolution. In: 9th International Work-Conference on the Interplay Between Natural and Artificial Computation (IWINAC), Puerto de la Cruz, Spain (2022)

17. Voutsinas, S., et al.: Development of a multi-output feed-forward neural network for fault detection in Photovoltaic Systems. Energy Rep. **8**, 33–42 (2022)
18. Brotons, M.J.E., Cabello, M.A.S., García-Rodríguez, J.: Live TV streaming latency measurement using YOLO. in 9th International Work-Conference on the Interplay Between Natural and Artificial Computation (IWINAC), Puerto de la Cruz, Spain (2022)
19. Das, S., Dandapat, S.: Automated detection of heart murmurs from the PCG signal using stationary wavelet transform. In: 2022 IEEE 19th India Council International Conference (INDICON). IEEE (2022)
20. Li, X., Sun, J.: Facial emotion recognition via stationary wavelet entropy and particle swarm optimization. In: Cognitive Systems and Signal Processing in Image Processing, pp. 145–162. Elsevier (2022)
21. Yao, C.: Hearing loss classification via stationary wavelet entropy and cat swarm optimization. In: Cognitive Systems and Signal Processing in Image Processing, pp. 203–221. Elsevier (2022)
22. Li, Y., Wang, G.: Sand cat swarm optimization based on stochastic variation with elite collaboration. IEEE Access **10**, 89989–90003 (2022)
23. Mangalampalli, S., Swain, S.K., Mangalampalli, V.K.: Multi objective task scheduling in cloud computing using cat swarm optimization algorithm. Arab. J. Sci. Eng. **47**(2), 1821–1830 (2022)
24. Seyyedabbasi, A.: Binary sand cat swarm optimization algorithm for wrapper feature selection on biological data. Biomimetics **8**(3), 310 (2023)
25. Seyyedabbasi, A., Kiani, F.: Sand cat swarm optimization: a nature-inspired algorithm to solve global optimization problems. Eng. Comput. **39**(4), 2627–2651 (2023)
26. Bahrami, M., Bozorg-Haddad, O., Chu, X.: Cat swarm optimization (CSO) algorithm. Adv. Optimiz. Nature-inspired Algorithms, 9-18 (2018)
27. Wu, D., et al.: Modified sand cat swarm optimization algorithm for solving constrained engineering optimization problems. Mathematics **10**(22), 4350 (2022)
28. Chu, S.-C., Tsai, P., Pan, J.-S.: Cat swarm optimization. In: Yang, Q., Webb, G. (eds.) PRICAI 2006. LNCS (LNAI), vol. 4099, pp. 854–858. Springer, Heidelberg (2006). https://doi.org/10.1007/978-3-540-36668-3_94
29. Vu, H.L., et al.: Analysis of input set characteristics and variances on k-fold cross validation for a recurrent neural network model on waste disposal rate estimation. J. Environ. Manage. **311**, 114869 (2022)
30. Zhang, X., Liu, C.-A.: Model averaging prediction by K-fold cross-validation. J. Econ. **235**(1), 280–301 (2023)
31. De Bruin, S., et al.: Dealing with clustered samples for assessing map accuracy by cross-validation. Eco. Inform. **69**, 101665 (2022)
32. Gaye, A., et al.: Extraction and physicomechanical characterisation of Typha Australis fibres: sensitivity to a location in the plant. J. Nat. Fibers **20**(1), 2164106 (2023)
33. Villanueva-Castellote, Á., et al.: Ex vivo evaluation of antibiotic sensitivity in samples from endodontic infections. J. Oral Microbiol. **15**(1), 2160536 (2023)
34. Han, X.: Covid-19 diagnosis by wavelet entropy and extreme learning machine. EAI Endorsed Trans. e-Learning **8**(1), 1–7 (2022)
35. Tang, W.: Gray level co-occurrence matrix and RVFL for Covid-19 diagnosis. EAI Endorsed Trans. e-Learning **8**(2), 1–14 (2023)

Private Inference on Layered Spiking Neural P Systems

Mihail-Iulian Pleşsa[✉], Marian Gheoghe, and Florentin Ipate

Department of Computer Science, University of Bucharest, Bucharest, Romania
`plesamihailiulian@gmail.com`

Abstract. Layered Spiking Neural P systems (LSN P systems) are a special class of Spiking Neural Networks (SNNs) used to solve classification problems. These types of networks are inspired directly by the biological brains, and their main advantage is low energy consumption when run on neuromorphic hardware. Since this special type of hardware is not yet available on conventional computers, the most convenient method for using an LSN P system to perform data classification is through a cloud platform. This raises privacy concerns for the users since they expose their data to the cloud provider. This paper presents a new privacy-preserving inference protocol for LSN P systems. The protocol allows one party, called the client, to use a pre-trained LSN P system hosted by another party, called the server, without compromising the privacy of the input or the result. The paper also discusses two brute-force attacks on the protocol and shows that the probability that the server compromises the client's confidentiality is negligible.

Keywords: Privacy-preserving · Spiking Neural P systems · Machine learning as a service

1 Introduction

Spiking Neural Networks (SNNs) are a new type of neural network inspired directly by the biological brain [10]. Unlike current deep learning networks that are trained through gradient descent, SNNs are more efficient in terms of energy consumption when run on neuromorphic hardware [8,12,13,32]. There are several mathematical models of the spiking neuron, the most well-known being leaky integrate-and-fire, Hodgkin-Huxley and Spiking Neural P systems [14,18,31]. Layered Spiking Neural P systems (LSN P systems) are a subclass of SN P systems designed to solve classification problems [33]. Although the accuracy of this type of system outperforms other SNN approaches, the main advantage in terms of energy consumption is obtained only if they are run on neuromorphic hardware. A feasible way to use such a platform is through a cloud platform. Among the advantages of this strategy, the most important are reduced costs, flexibility, and scalability [30]. Nevertheless, the major drawback is the privacy compromise on behalf of the user [6]. Consider the following scenario: a pre-trained LSN P system is deployed on a remote server to solve classification problems. A client wants to classify some confidential data using the remote LSN P system. Since privacy is important for the client, it cannot simply upload the data to the server.

© The Author(s), under exclusive license to Springer Nature Switzerland AG 2024
J. M. Ferrández Vicente et al. (Eds.): IWINAC 2024, LNCS 14675, pp. 163–172, 2024.
https://doi.org/10.1007/978-3-031-61137-7_16

We solve this problem by proposing a new privacy-preserving inference protocol for LSN P systems. Our construction allows the client to use a pre-trained LSN P system hosted on a remote server without compromising the privacy of the data it wants to classify. With the proposed construction, the server cannot learn any information about the client's data or the classification result with a non-negligible probability. The security of the protocol is based on additive secret sharing, thus being efficient from a computational point of view [4]. The paper is structured as follows: in Sect. 2, we present related work on SNN, SN P systems and various privacy-preserving machine learning algorithms; in Sect. 3, we give a brief overview of the LSN P system, in Sect. 4 we show our approach on private inference for LSN P system and discuss the complexity of two brute-force attacks, Sect. 5 is left for the conclusions and further directions of research.

2   Related Work

SNNs and SN P systems have many practical applications, which justifies the effort to build methods by which they can be used safely and privately. In [9], the authors used SNNs for EEG classification. In [28], SNN applications for image classifications are discussed. A new approach of series forecasting using SN P systems is presented in [19] while [34] shows how to construct a convolutional neural network using such systems.

Regarding privacy-preserving machine learning, most approaches are based on homomorphic encryption (HE) [1]. The idea of these cryptographic schemes is to allow data processing in encrypted format. In [20], the authors used HE for secure aggregation in swarm learning. In [24] is presented a new privacy-preserving image classification algorithm based on HE. In [11], the authors propose a general method of using an pre-trained neural network to make predictions over encrypted data and [2] presented a protocol that allows multiple parties to train a neural network hosted on a remote server using their local data without revealing it to the server.

In addition to the works stated above, in [7], the authors proposed a guide on how to use homomorphic encryption for bioinformatics applications, and [3] presents one of the first extensive solutions for privacy-preserving machine learning. Also, in [27], the authors did an extensive survey on privacy-preserving methods for machine learning as a service, e.g., machine learning models deployed on a remote server.

There are also papers discussing the privacy aspects of SNNs. In [16], the authors discuss the privacy-preserving weights transfer from a trained artificial neural network to an SNN. In [29], the authors proposed a decentralized learning method for SNNs using federated learning.

We note that classical HE methods are not suitable for constructing privacy-preserving inference for LSN P systems for two reasons [5]. First of all, the HE schemes are defined over a finite field. This is in contradiction to how the potential values of spiking neurons are modeled over a dense set. Secondly, HE schemes do not preserve the operations from the plaintext space in the ciphertext space. Consider, for example, the Paillier cryptosystem [22]. Given a ciphertext and a constant, to compute a ciphertext that encrypts the product between the initial plaintext and the constant, the ciphertext must be raised to the power of the constant. Simply multiplying the ciphertext with the constant will not result in a valid ciphertext, i.e., a ciphertext that encrypts the product between the corresponding plaintext and the constant. The energy efficiency of spiking neural networks relies on the neuromorphic hardware. Changing the configuration of such hardware from performing the operations over the clear data to operations over the ciphertext space implied increased costs [25].

3   Layered Spiking Neural P Systems

LSN P systems were proposed in [33] as a new model for spiking neural networks designed to solve classification problems. There are two types of neurons in the system: proposition neurons and rule neurons. The system is composed of four layers:

1. The input layer has k proposition neurons denoted as σ_{pi}^1, $1 \leq i \leq k$, where k represents the number of features of the input. The spiking rules of these neurons are in the form $r_i^1 : E^1/a^{\alpha_i} \to a^{\alpha^i}$ where α_i is the potential value of neuron σ_{pi}^1 and $E^1 = \{\alpha_i \geq 0\}$.
2. The hidden layer has n rule neurons denoted as σ_{rj}^2, $1 \leq j \leq n$, where n represents the number of possible classes in which the input can be classified. The spiking rules for these neurons are in the form $r_j^2 : E^2/a^{\theta_j} \to a^{\theta^i}$ where θ_j is the potential value of the neuron σ_{rj}^2 and $E^2 = \{\theta \geq 0\}$.
3. The comparison layer has one proposition neuron denoted as σ_{p1}^3. This neuron spikes according to the rule $r_1^3 : E^3/a^o \to a^o$ where o is the potential value of the neuron and $E^3 = \{o \geq 0\}$.
4. The output layer has n rule neurons denoted as σ_{rj}^4. The spiking rules for these neurons are in the form $r_1^4 : E_j^4/a^{\theta_j} \to a$; d_j where $E_j^4 = \{\theta_j \geq o\}$ and d_j represents a time delay equal to j.

The input of the LSN P system is a vector of real numbers from the interval $[0, 1]$. The potential value of each input neuron σ_{pi}^1 is initialized with the corresponding value from the input vector. The output of the system, i.e., the classification results, is the index of the neurons that fire in the output layer. Each layer from the system is fully connected with the next layer through synapses. The weight of the synapse that connects the proposition neuron σ_{pi}^1 with the rule neuron σ_{rj}^2 is denoted by w_{ij}^1. It is initialized with a value chosen uniformly at random from the interval $[0, 1]$. Apart from the synapses that connect the input layer with the hidden layer, all the other weights are 1. The learning process of an LSN P system involves updating the weights for each sample in the training dataset according to the Widrow-Hoff rule:

$$\boldsymbol{W} \leftarrow \boldsymbol{W} + \eta \left(t - \tilde{t}\right) \boldsymbol{\alpha} \tag{1}$$

where W is the weight matrix between the input and the hidden layer, t represents the output of the system, $\tilde{t}$ denotes the true classification label, and α is the vector of potential values of the input neurons. An overview of the LSN P system is depicted in Fig. 1.

4   Private Inference

In this section, we first present our protocol that allows a client to classify data using a pre-trained LSN P system hosted on a server without compromising the privacy of the data. We then introduce a security analysis from the perspective of a brute-force attack.

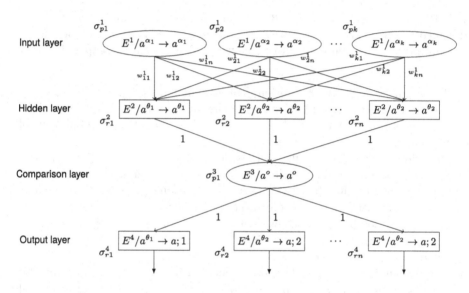

Fig. 1. LSN P system

4.1   The Protocol

The protocol involves two parties, denoted as the client and the server. The server exposes a pre-trained LSN P system thorough a service. The client wants to use the service to classify data without revealing it to the server. Formally, the main security requirement of the protocol is that the probability of the server learning information about the client's data is negligible [15]. Let α be the client's input. α represents a vector of k potential values modeled as real numbers from the interval $[0, 1]$. We denote the security parameter by r. The protocol goes like follows:

The client side - Phase 1

1. The client use Algorithm 1 to split the input vector $\boldsymbol{\alpha}$ into r shares such as $\boldsymbol{\alpha} \leftarrow \sum_{i=1}^{r} \boldsymbol{\alpha}^{(i)}$.

2. The client randomly generates r vectors of k real numbers from the set $[0,1]$ denoted as $\boldsymbol{\alpha}^{(r+1)}, \ldots, \boldsymbol{\alpha}^{(2r)}$.

3. The client randomly generates a secret permutation π over the set $\{1, 2, \ldots, 2r\}$.

4. The client sends to server the ordered set $S = \left(\boldsymbol{\alpha}^{(\pi(1))}, \boldsymbol{\alpha}^{(\pi(2))}, \ldots, \boldsymbol{\alpha}^{(\pi(2r))} \right)$.

The server side

1. For each input vector, $\boldsymbol{\alpha}^{(i)}$, $1 \leq i \leq 2r$, the server runs the LSN P system and records the potential values of the neurons $\sigma_{r1}^4, \sigma_{r2}^4, \ldots, \sigma_{rn}^4$ into the vector $\boldsymbol{\theta}^{(i)}$.

2. The server sends the client the ordered set $\left(\boldsymbol{\theta}^{(1)}, \boldsymbol{\theta}^{(2)}, \ldots, \boldsymbol{\theta}^{(2r)} \right)$.

The client side - Phase 2

1. Using the secret permutation π the client computes $\boldsymbol{\theta} \leftarrow \sum_{i=1}^{r} \boldsymbol{\theta}^{(\pi^{-1}(i))}$.

2. The client determines the classification result, i.e., the label, for the input vector $\boldsymbol{\alpha}$ as the index of the maximum element from the vector $\boldsymbol{\theta}$.

Algorithm 1. Shares generation

    Input: $\boldsymbol{\alpha}$
    Output: $\boldsymbol{\alpha}^{(1)}, \boldsymbol{\alpha}^{(2)}, \ldots, \boldsymbol{\alpha}^{(r)}$

1: **for** i = 1 to r-1 **do**
2:     $\boldsymbol{\alpha}^{(i)} \xleftarrow{\$} [0,1]^k$ ▷ Choose $r-1$ random vectors from the set $[0,1]$
3: **end for**
4: $\boldsymbol{\alpha}^{(r)} \leftarrow \boldsymbol{\alpha} - \sum_{i=1}^{r-1} \boldsymbol{\alpha}^{(i)}$ ▷ Set the last vector such as the sum of the r shares is $\boldsymbol{\alpha}$

The protocol is depicted in Fig. 2. The following theorem captures the correctness of the protocol:

Theorem 1. *The result of the classification returned by the protocol is the same as the result of the classification returned by the LSN P system on the input $\boldsymbol{\alpha}$.*

Proof. We analyze the running of an LSN P system at each step of its execution on the input $\boldsymbol{\alpha}$.

1. On a input vector $\boldsymbol{\alpha} \in S$, the potential value of the proposition neuron σ_{pi}^1 is initialed with α_i, $1 \leq i \leq k$.

2. The firing rule $r_i^1 : E^1/a^{\alpha_i} \to a^{\alpha_i}$, $E^1 = \{\alpha_i \geq 0\}$ is applied and the proposition neuron σ_{pi}^1 sends its potential value to each rule neuron σ_{rj}^2, $1 \leq j \leq n$.

3. Given the set of weights between the input layer and the hidden layer, the potential value of the rule neuron σ_{rj}^2 becomes $\theta_j = \sum_{i=1}^{k} w_{ij}^1 \alpha_i$.

4. The firing rule $r_2^j : E^2/a^{\theta_j} \to a^{\theta_j}$, $E^2 = \{\theta_j \geq 0\}$ is applied and the rule neuron σ_{rj}^2 seds its potential value to the proposition neuron σ_{p1}^3.

5. The firing rule $r_1^3 : E^1/a^o \to a^o$, $E^3 = \{o \geq 0\}$ where $o = \max(\theta_1, \theta_2, \ldots, \theta_n)$ is applied and the neuron sends its potential value to each rule neuron σ_{rj}^4.

6. The firing rule $r_1^4 : E_j^4/a^{\theta_j} \to a$; j, $E_j^4 = \{\theta_j \geq o\}$ is applied and the rule neuron σ_{rj}^4 sends a spike at the moment j to the environment if its action potential θ_j is greater or equal o, i.e., only the rule neuron with the maximal potential value will fire.

7. The result of the classification is the time moment at which one of the output neurons fires, i.e., the index of the rule neuron with the maximal potential value.

Similarly, when the LSN P system is run with the input $\alpha^{(t)}$, the potential value of the rule neuron σ_{rj}^4 will be $\theta_j^{(t)} = \sum_{i=1}^{k} w_{ij}^1 \alpha_i^{(t)}$.

After the LSN P system is run over the all the inputs $\left(\alpha^{(1)}, \alpha^{(2)}, \ldots, \alpha^{(2r)}\right)$ the client will receive the order set of potential values $\left(\theta^{(1)}, \theta^{(2)}, \ldots, \theta^{(2r)}\right)$ and compute θ as:

$$\theta_j = \sum_{t=1}^{r} \theta_j^{(t)} = \sum_{t=1}^{r} \sum_{i=1}^{k} w_{ij}^1 \alpha_i^{(t)} = \sum_{i=1}^{k} w_{ij}^1 \sum_{t=1}^{r} \alpha_i^{(t)} \tag{2}$$

Since $\sum_{t=1}^{r} \alpha^{(t)} = \alpha$, we get:

$$\theta_j = \sum_{i=1}^{k} w_{ij}^1 \alpha_i \tag{3}$$

The value θ_j obtained in (3) by the client represents the potential value of the rule neuron σ_{rj}^4 when the LSN P system is run with the input α so the label computed by the client as the index of the maximum value between $\theta_1, \theta_2, \ldots, \theta_n$ corresponds to the time moment at which the LSN P system spikes with the input α. Therefore, the results computed using the protocol correspond to the results obtained directly over the input. □

4.2 Security Discussion

The main idea behind the security of the protocol is based on the fact that the server does not know which of the vectors received from the client are shares of the inputs. This is due to the random shuffling based on the secret permutation π in step 4 of the first phase of the client side.

There are two ways to attack the protocol from a brute-force perspective. We denote by P_{attack} the probability that the server determines the input of

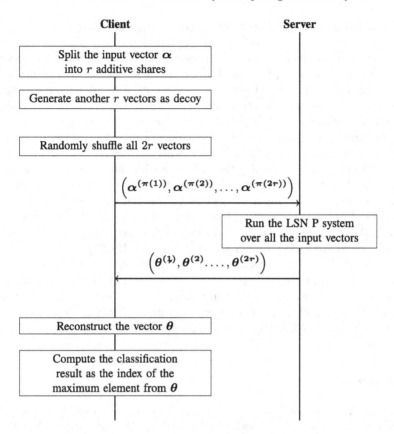

Fig. 2. Privacy-preserving inference protocol

the client. The first way is for the server to try to find out the permutation π, thus determining the positions of the input shares. Since the permutation is considered over a set of $2r$ elements, the probability that the server finds the one generated by the client is:

$$P_{attack} = \frac{1}{(2r!)} \qquad (4)$$

The second way is for the server to try every possible combination of r elements from the ordered set received from the client. The number of such combinations is given by $\binom{2r}{r}$; thus, the probability that the server finds the combination that sums the input is:

$$P_{attack} = \frac{1}{\binom{2r}{r}} \qquad (5)$$

In both cases, the probability that the server finds the input of the client has a negligible upper bound for $r \geq 1$:

$$P_{attack} \leq \frac{1}{2^r} \qquad (6)$$

5   Conclusions and Further Directions of Research

In this paper, we introduced a new privacy-preserving inference protocol for LSN P systems [33]. The protocol allows a client to classify data using a pre-trained LSN P system hosted on a remote server without compromising the confidentiality of the input or the result. The idea of the protocol is to split the input into r additive shares, which are then mixed with other r decoy shares chosen uniformly at random. All the $2r$ shares are then sent to the server to be classified. Since the client is the only one who can distinguish between a real share and a decoy one, he is also the only one who can reconstruct the result. We also discussed two brute-force attacks and showed that the probability that the server determines the input of the client decreases exponentially in r.

The first direction of research is to construct a formal proof of security for the protocol following a cryptographic approach [17]. One approach is to consider a proof by reduction to the problem of the subset sum [21,26]

The second direction of research is to perform experiments to analyze the running time of the protocol. This is an important consideration when deploying a privacy-preserving protocol for machine learning tasks since most such systems have a large number of users. Therefore, the aspect of scalability is essential. A first version of an LSN P simulator for experiments is provided in [23] as a work in progress.

References

1. Acar, A., Aksu, H., Uluagac, A.S., Conti, M.: A survey on homomorphic encryption schemes: theory and implementation. ACM Comput. Surv. (Csur) **51**(4), 1–35 (2018)
2. Aono, Y., Hayashi, T., Wang, L., Moriai, S., et al.: Privacy-preserving deep learning via additively homomorphic encryption. IEEE Trans. Inform. Forensics Sec. **13**(5), 1333–1345 (2017)
3. Bost, R., Popa, R.A., Tu, S., Goldwasser, S.: Machine learning classification over encrypted data. Cryptology ePrint Archive (2014)
4. Chattopadhyay, A.K., Saha, S., Nag, A., Nandi, S.: Secret sharing: a comprehensive survey, taxonomy and applications. Comput. Sci. Rev. **51**, 100608 (2024)
5. Doan, T.V.T., Messai, M.L., Gavin, G., Darmont, J.: A survey on implementations of homomorphic encryption schemes. J. Supercomput., 1–42 (2023)
6. Domingo-Ferrer, J., Farras, O., Ribes-González, J., Sánchez, D.: Privacy-preserving cloud computing on sensitive data: a survey of methods, products and challenges. Comput. Commun. **140**, 38–60 (2019)
7. Dowlin, N., Gilad-Bachrach, R., Laine, K., Lauter, K., Naehrig, M., Wernsing, J.: Manual for using homomorphic encryption for bioinformatics. Proc. IEEE **105**(3), 552–567 (2017)
8. Galán-Prado, F., Morán, A., Font, J., Roca, M., Rosselló, J.L.: Compact hardware synthesis of stochastic spiking neural networks. Int. J. Neural Syst. **29**(08), 1950004 (2019)
9. Ghosh-Dastidar, S., Adeli, H.: Improved spiking neural networks for eeg classification and epilepsy and seizure detection. Integrated Comput.-Aided Eng. **14**(3), 187–212 (2007)

10. Ghosh-Dastidar, S., Adeli, H.: Spiking neural networks. Int. J. Neural Syst. **19**(04), 295–308 (2009)
11. Gilad-Bachrach, R., Dowlin, N., Laine, K., Lauter, K., Naehrig, M., Wernsing, J.: Cryptonets: applying neural networks to encrypted data with high throughput and accuracy. In: International Conference on Machine Learning, pp. 201–210. PMLR (2016)
12. Grassmann, C., Anlauf, J.K.: Fast digital simulation of spiking neural networks and neuromorphic integration with spikelab. Int. J. Neural Syst. **9**(05), 473–478 (1999)
13. Han, B., Roy, K.: Deep spiking neural network: energy efficiency through time based coding. In: Vedaldi, A., Bischof, H., Brox, T., Frahm, J.-M. (eds.) ECCV 2020. LNCS, vol. 12355, pp. 388–404. Springer, Cham (2020). https://doi.org/10.1007/978-3-030-58607-2_23
14. Ionescu, M., Păun, G., Yokomori, T.: Spiking neural P systems. Fundamenta informaticae **71**(2-3), 279–308 (2006)
15. Katz, J., Lindell, Y.: Introduction to modern cryptography: principles and protocols. Chapman and hall/CRC (2007)
16. Kim, Y., Venkatesha, Y., Panda, P.: Privatesnn: privacy-preserving spiking neural networks. In: Proceedings of the AAAI Conference on Artificial Intelligence, vol. 36, pp. 1192–1200 (2022)
17. Kobeissi, N., Nicolas, G., Tiwari, M.: Verifpal: cryptographic protocol analysis for the real world. In: Bhargavan, K., Oswald, E., Prabhakaran, M. (eds.) INDOCRYPT 2020. LNCS, vol. 12578, pp. 151–202. Springer, Cham (2020). https://doi.org/10.1007/978-3-030-65277-7_8
18. Lobo, J.L., Del Ser, J., Bifet, A., Kasabov, N.: Spiking neural networks and online learning. An Overview Perspect. Neural Netw. **121**, 88–100 (2020)
19. Long, L., et al.: A time series forecasting approach based on nonlinear spiking neural systems. Int. J. Neural Syst. **32**(08), 2250020 (2022)
20. Madni, H.A., Umer, R.M., Foresti, G.L.: Swarm-fhe: fully homomorphic encryption-based swarm learning for malicious clients. Inter. J. Neural Syst., 2350033 (2023)
21. Nguyen, P., Stern, J.: The hardness of the hidden subset sum problem and its cryptographic implications. In: Wiener, M. (ed.) CRYPTO 1999. LNCS, vol. 1666, pp. 31–46. Springer, Heidelberg (1999). https://doi.org/10.1007/3-540-48405-1_3
22. Paillier, P.: Public-key cryptosystems based on composite degree residuosity classes. In: International Conference on the Theory and Applications of Cryptographic Techniques, pp. 223–238. Springer (1999)
23. Plesa, M.I.: LSNP-Simulator. https://github.com/miiip/LSNP-Simulator (2024), (Accessed 28 February 2024)
24. Rovida, L., Leporati, A.: Encrypted image classification with low memory footprint using fully homomorphic encryption. Inter. J. Neural Syst. (2024)
25. Schuman, C.D., et al.: A survey of neuromorphic computing and neural networks in hardware. arXiv preprint arXiv:1705.06963 (2017)
26. Siqueira, H., Santana, C., Macedo, M., Figueiredo, E., Gokhale, A., Bastos-Filho, C.: Simplified binary cat swarm optimization. Integra. Comput.-Aided Eng. **28**(1), 35–50 (2021)
27. Tanuwidjaja, H.C., Choi, R., Baek, S., Kim, K.: Privacy-preserving deep learning on machine learning as a service-a comprehensive survey. IEEE Access **8**, 167425–167447 (2020)
28. Vaila, R., Chiasson, J., Saxena, V.: Deep convolutional spiking neural networks for image classification. arXiv preprint arXiv:1903.12272 (2019)

29. Venkatesha, Y., Kim, Y., Tassiulas, L., Panda, P.: Federated learning with spiking neural networks. IEEE Trans. Signal Process. **69**, 6183–6194 (2021)
30. Wang, X., Wang, Y., Cui, Y.: Energy and locality aware load balancing in cloud computing. Integrat. Comput.-Aided Eng. **20**(4), 361–374 (2013)
31. Wang, Z., Guo, L., Adjouadi, M.: A generalized leaky integrate-and-fire neuron model with fast implementation method. Int. J. Neural Syst. **24**(05), 1440004 (2014)
32. Young, A.R., Dean, M.E., Plank, J.S., Rose, G.S.: A review of spiking neuromorphic hardware communication systems. IEEE Access **7**, 135606–135620 (2019)
33. Zhang, G., Zhang, X., Rong, H., Paul, P., Zhu, M., Neri, F., Ong, Y.-S.: A layered spiking neural system for classification problems. Int. J. Neural Syst. **32**(08), 2250023 (2022)
34. Zhou, C., Ye, L., Peng, H., Liu, Z., Wang, J., Ramirez-de Arellano, A.: A parallel convolutional network based on spiking neural systems. Inter. J. Neural Syst. (2024)

Cooperative Multi-fitness Evolutionary Algorithm for Scientific Workflows Scheduling

Pablo Barredo[ID] and Jorge Puente[(✉)][ID]

University of Oviedo, Gijón, Spain
{uo237136,puente}@uniovi.es
http://www.di.uniovi.es/iscop

Abstract. Scheduling problems require evolutionary methods, but they often struggle with complexity. To enhance solutions, heuristic knowledge can be integrated into fitness functions, although this may introduce bias towards local minima. This paper proposes a cooperative multi-fitness approach that combines genetic diversity with heuristic solutions to support a standard fitness function. Lamarckism can assist in the reconstruction of chromosomes, for direct evaluation by the standard fitness decoder. This combination of genetic diversity and heuristic knowledge aims to achieve superior solutions. This evaluation approach is applied to a genetic algorithm for scientific workflow scheduling, minimizing total execution time in cloud computing.

Keywords: cooperative multi-fitness · evolutionary algorithms · scientific workflow · cloud computing

1 Introduction

Cloud computing is a model of distributed computing that offers virtual, scalable, and dynamic resources based on a pay-as-you-use approach. Infrastructure as a Service (IaaS) stands out as a key offering within cloud computing, boasting benefits such as improved efficiency, rapid deployment, accessibility, and extensive virtualization capabilities. These attributes have positioned cloud computing as an attractive option for researchers conducting compute-intensive experiments via scientific workflows (sWF).

For researchers, obtaining computational results promptly while minimizing the operational costs of leased processing infrastructure is crucial. Therefore, the makespan, which is the completion time of the final task in a workflow, is a critical Quality of Service (QoS) metric. The duration required to process scientific workflows can vary significantly, ranging from minutes to days, influenced by the workflow's complexity (spanning from tens to thousands of tasks and handling data from kilobytes to terabytes) and the performance characteristics of the cloud infrastructure, which comprises hosts of different capacities and features.

J. M. Ferrández Vicente et al. (Eds.): IWINAC 2024, LNCS 14675, pp. 173–182, 2024.
https://doi.org/10.1007/978-3-031-61137-7_17

Furthermore, in order to manage and execute these workflows efficiently, it is essential to optimise the allocation of tasks across the diverse virtual machines available in the cloud environment. Given the complexity of this scheduling challenge, which is recognised as NP-complete [5], to find feasible solutions, there is a compelling case for the use of approximate strategies, including evolutionary algorithms.

In the literature we can find different evolutionary algorithm proposals that introduce a multi-fitness approach to achieve better solutions than a single fitness function algorithm. They either use a different fitness function at different stages of the algorithm [8], or try to analyse different perspectives of the same solution, as in the case of multi-fitness learning [9]. However, to the best of our knowledge, there are no approaches that simultaneously apply multiple decoding functions to achieve the same fitness objective.

This paper proposes a new evolutionary strategy based on a previously presented mono-objective genetic algorithm (GA) [1] but using the novel idea of cooperative multi-fitness (CMF) to obtain low makespan schedules. To accomplish this, we introduce a polymorphic decoding system that supports a main standard fitness function alongside several heuristic fitness functions. These functions generate alternative schedules from the same chromosome, which are then ranked in a competitive manner.

The chromosome is reconstructed using Lamarckism from the best obtained schedule, as if it had been generated by the standard fitness function. This approach aims to find a synergy between the different fitness functions, which would improve the global performance of the evolutionary algorithm.

The remaining of the paper is organized as follows. In the next section, we define the workflow scheduling problem. Section 3 introduces the genetic algorithm structure, followed by the definition of the novel concept of Cooperative Multi-Fitness in Sect. 4. Section 5 reports the experimental study, and finally, Sect. 6 presents the paper's conclusions.

2   The Scientific Workflow Scheduling Model

In distributed computing environments, scientific workflows are often represented as a series of interconnected tasks bound by order-dependent relationships. A task is queued for execution only after receiving data from tasks that precede it. Each completed task produces a set of data that is then required to start the next tasks in the sequence. Such workflows, widely used in various scientific disciplines such as bioinformatics (e.g. 1000genome, SoyKB), agroecosystem studies (e.g. Cycles) or astronomy (e.g. Montage) [4], typically adopt the structure of a Directed Acyclic Graph (DAG). In this graph-based representation, tasks are denoted as nodes, while the dependencies between them are represented as edges, effectively mapping the execution paths of the workflow.

In the study of scientific workflows, they are conceptualised as a Directed Acyclic Graph (DAG) denoted by $G = (T, A)$. Here, $T = t_1, t_2, ..., t_n$ corresponds to the set of n nodes, each symbolising a different task within the workflow, while

$A = (t_i, t_j)|1 \leq i \leq n, 1 \leq j \leq n, i \neq j$ encapsulates the arcs or the dependency links that exist between these tasks. Each node in this graph is labelled with a value representing the computational workload of its task in $MFLOPs$ (Million Floating Point Operations), and each arc is designated as $data(i,j)$, indicating the size of the data in MB (Megabytes) that needs to be transferred from task t_i to task t_j. In addition, the graph includes t_{entry} and t_{end} as dummy tasks that have no computational or communication requirements, serving as the entry and exit points of the workflow, respectively.

In this context, cloud resources are provided by an IaaS (Infrastructure as a Service) cloud service provider, offering a variety of heterogeneous VMs or hosts. The collection of VMs is denoted as $M = vm_1, vm_2, ..., vm_m$, with each VM characterized by a tuple $< pc, nb, ds >$, representing its capabilities. Here, pc stands for the processing capacity measured in $GFLOPS$ (Giga Floating Point Operations per Second), nb is the available network bandwidth available in MB/sec (Megabytes per Second), and ds is the disk read/write speed, also in MB/sec.

2.1   Workflow Scheduling Problem Overview

The challenge of scheduling a workflow represented by $G = (T, A)$ on an IaaS platform consisting of a set of VMs M is encapsulated in the problem tuple (G, M). The objective is twofold: first, to identify a feasible scheduling solution $S = (Hosts, Order)$, where $Hosts$ describes the assignment of tasks to specific VMs and $Order$ maintains a topological order of the tasks within G. The goal is then to refine this solution to ensure that the maximum task completion time, or *makespan*, of the workflow is as short as possible, thereby achieving an optimal schedule.

Specifically, the goal is:

$$minimize\ EFT(t_{exit}) \tag{1}$$

where $EFT(t_{exit})$ is the estimated finish time of the task t_{exit}.

In scheduling tasks and determining the projected *makespan* value, we follow the DNC model as outlined by [1]. In the following subsections, the DNC model will be formally introduced and detailed, providing a comprehensive framework for understanding its application and importance in optimising workflow scheduling in cloud computing environments.

Definition 1. *Let ct_i^k represent the computation time for executing task t_i on virtual machine vm_k. This computation time is calculated as follows:*

$$ct_i^k = \frac{size(i)}{pc_k} \tag{2}$$

here, $size(i)$ denotes the computational load of task t_i, quantified in GFLOPs, and pc_k refers to the processing capability of the virtual machine vm_k, measured in GFLOPs per second (GFLOPS).

Definition 2. *The time required for transferring data between tasks t_i and t_j, assigned to virtual machines vm_k and vm_l respectively, is given by:*

$$dt_{i,j}^{k,l} = \begin{cases} \frac{data(i,j)}{ds_k} & if\ k = l \\ \frac{data(i,j)}{min(ds_k, nb_k, nb_l)} & if\ k \neq l \end{cases} \tag{3}$$

where $data(i,j)$ represents the size of the data to be transferred from t_i to t_j, with vm_k and vm_l being the virtual machines on which these tasks are executed. According to the DNC model, if tasks t_i and t_j are hosted on the same VM, the data transfer involves local disk reads, otherwise nb_k and nb_l, the network bandwidths of vm_k and vm_l respectively, must also be considered.

Definition 3. *The Estimated Finish Time (EFT) of task t_i on virtual machine vm_k is determined by adding its Estimated Start Time (EST), the time for input data acquisition, computation time, and the time for output data handling, represented as:*

$$EFT(i,k) = EST(i,k) + input(i,k) + ct_i^k + output(i,k) \tag{4}$$

The $input_{i,k}$ denotes the time to receive all input data for task t_i on vm_k from its predecessors, calculated as:

$$input(i,k) = \sum_{t_j \in pred(t_i)} dt_{j,i}^{l,k} \tag{5}$$

with each predecessor task t_j executed on its designated machine vm_l. The $output_{i,k}$ refers to the time to write all output data of i to k's local disk, defined by:

$$output(i,k) = \frac{\sum_{t_j \in succ(t_i)} data(i,j)}{ds_k} \tag{6}$$

In the DNC model, scheduling employs an insertion strategy that seeks the earliest available slot on a VM that can accommodate the task's compute and data transfer durations, while meeting precedence constraints.

Definition 4. *The Estimated Start Time (EST) for task t_i on vm_k refers to the availability of vm_k post-processing of all its preceding tasks, expressed as:*

$$EST(i,k) = avail(i,k, \max_{t_j \in pred(t_i)}(EFT(j,l))) \tag{7}$$

Here, $avail(i,k,m)$ indicates the earliest time slot on vm_k following time m that can accommodate the execution of t_i, considering the finish times of all predecessor tasks t_j on their respective machines m_l.

3   Overview of the Genetic Algorithm Approach

This section introduces the GA framework developed to address the Workflow Scheduling Problem. It describes the core elements of the GA from [1], and the new decoding scheme that evaluates the effectiveness of each solution through multiple fitness metrics. This algorithm operates on a generational basis, incorporating mechanisms such as random selection and tournament-based replacement among parents and offspring. This strategy inherently introduces a level of elitism within the algorithm. The GA is designed to work with a variable number of supporting fitness functions ($l_{fitness}$), which requires the specification of several key parameters: the size of the population (pop_{size}), the maximum number of generations (max_{gens}), the probabilities for crossover and mutation (p_c and p_m respectively).

The encoding framework is constructed upon task permutations with designated VM allocations [10,11]. A gene is defined as a tuple (i,k), where $1 \leq i \leq |T|$ denotes task index and $1 \leq k \leq |M|$ signifies the VM index, crafting a chromosome that encapsulates such a gene for each task. Task sequences must adhere to a topological order, positioning each task in a gene post its preceding task and pre its subsequent task within the chromosome. Thus, all initial and genetically operated individuals must align with the dependency constraints of tasks.

The crossover process deals with both task sequencing and VM allocations for offspring. The CrossoverOrder methodology, as described in Zhu (2016), is designed to ensure that there are no violations of task dependencies, as each task pair's order is preserved from at least one parent.

The mutation mechanism carefully alters the task sequence without disrupting dependency orders. Initially, a task T_i is randomly chosen, and it is relocated within the sequence segment of feasible positions. Subsequently, T_i's VM assignment is randomly changed among available VMs, ensuring the mutated chromosome remains valid within the task dependency framework.

The initial population, consisting of pop_{size} members, is created by randomly selecting tasks in adherence to a topological ordering, coupled with random, yet valid, VM assignments for each task.

New Decoding Schema. The schedule deduced from a chromosome using the standard fitness function ($StdFit$) follows the DNC evaluation model for decoding. Genes within a chromosome are sequentially processed from left to right. For each gene (i,k), task t_i is scheduled at the earliest feasible insertion starting time of vm_k that fulfils its predecessors' completion time and task processing requirements. The makespan of the overall schedule is determined by the latest completion time of all tasks. This standard decoding function ($StdFit$) is assisted by the other supporting fitness functions ($l_{fitness}$) in the cooperative multi-fitness evaluation which is described in the next subsection.

4   Cooperative Multi-fitness Functions Evaluation

The main advantage of the $StdFit$ fitness function is its ability to directly decode chromosome information. It takes full advantage of the genetic diversity of the standard solution encoding. Additional fitness functions will play a supporting role by providing heuristic knowledge about the problem being solved, while still being able to combine this knowledge with chromosome information to produce

---

Algorithm 1. Cooperative-Multi-Fitness function

Require: A solution to evaluate, and a list $l_{fitness}$ of supporting fitness functions
Ensure: Selects the best schedule and makespan
    Evaluates the solution with three algorithms
    Initialize $minValue \leftarrow$ Decode solution using $StdFit$
    Initialize $bestEvaluator \leftarrow StdFit$
    for each $evaluator$ in $l_{fitness}$ **do**
        $result \leftarrow$ Decode solution using $evaluator$
        if $result < minValue$ **then**
            $minValue \leftarrow result$
            $bestEvaluator \leftarrow evaluator$
        end if
    end for
    Lamarckism: recode solution using $bestEvaluator$ schedule
    Return the schedule and makespan of $bestEvaluator$

---

alternative possibly better schedules. In addition to the $StdFit$ function. In this work we have considered two fitness functions proposed in [1] from the decomposition of the HEFT heuristic [7] in its two stages:

RankFit: *Task order based in ranking*
In this first function, only the assignment of the chromosome machines is used. The ordering of tasks is defined by the initial ranking stage of the HEFT heuristic, where the task with the maximum pending computation and communication work is scheduled first. The priority is defined as follows:

$$prioDNC(t_i) = \overline{input_i} + \overline{ct_i} + \overline{output_i} + max_{t_j \in succ(t_i)}(prioDNC(t_j)) \quad (8)$$

where $\overline{ct_i}$ is the average execution time of task t_i, and $\overline{input_i}$ and $\overline{output_i}$ are the average communication times between task t_i and all its predecessors and successors respectively.
HeftFit: *task to VMs mapping based on earliest finish time*
The second function only considers the task order of the chromosome. The VM assignment is determined by the second stage of the HEFT heuristic. Tasks are assigned to the VM with the shortest finish time, based on the Eq. 4, which considers computation time and data transfer for input and output.

The Algorithm 1 describes the cooperative multi-fitness. In addition to the solution to be evaluated, it is necessary to provide a list ($l_{fitness}$) of all supporting fitness functions to be executed. Both $StdFit$ and every supporting fitness function generate a schedule and its corresponding makespan. The algorithm selects the minimum of these. To promote a truly cooperative multi-fitness, the Lamarckian learning method [3] is used in the final stage of the evaluation phase to facilitate convergence towards possible better solutions. As a result, the chromosome's gene order and the machine-task mapping are recoded based on the resulting topological order of the best generated schedule. Cooperation should be revealed because in case the heuristic schedules are the best, their good features are transferred into the chromosomes, so that the basic fitness function *StdFit* can extract them by direct decoding the chromosome.

5   Experimental Study

This section presents the methodology used to evaluate the performance of the proposed multi-fitness method when executed on different types of problems and under various hardware scenarios. The study aims to determine whether the use of a multi-fitness approach with the pair of heuristic supporting fitness functions considered can achieve better results than the previously developed mono-objective genetic algorithm HEFT-GA [1]. To conduct this test, we first define the families of problems that we will use from a standard repository. These problems, which are well known and cover different areas of science, should serve to test performance under a wide range of conditions, including compute-intensive and data-intensive scenarios.

5.1   Benchmark Instances

For our analysis, we selected a repository of real workflow executions called WFCommons [2], which contains numerous instances of varying sizes, from dozens to thousands of tasks. We selected three applications and four instances per application, ranging from small to large.

Firstly, **1000genome** a data-intensive application with a high ratio of communication to computation with instances of 82, 164, 492, and 738 tasks. Next, **Cycles** a compute-intensive application with instances of 67, 133, 437, and 1091 tasks. Finally, **SRASearch** a data-intensive application, with 22, 42, 84 and 104 tasks instances.

5.2   Benchmark Platform

We have developed a Java application using the well-established JMetal framework [6], which follows the implementation of [1]. Their solutions are already validated to be precise, so we will focus on working only with the a priori makespan obtained directly from the schedule solution of the evolutionary algorithm.

Designed to simulate a diverse computing environment, the considered infrastructure scenario splits the hosts into two groups. One group operates with a disk speed of 200 MB/s, while the other is limited to a disk speed of 20 MB/s. The hosts are equipped with a CPU capacity of 441 GFLOPS, and network bandwidth of 125 MB/s.

The experimentation scales the number of servers from 1 to 16, doubling at each step (i.e., 1, 2, 4, 8, 16). This approach allows for a comprehensive analysis of the effectiveness of the CMF model over a range of infrastructure sizes and configurations.

To conduct this experimentation, we have a Linux computer with an 12th Gen Intel(R) Core(TM) i9-12900 2.40 GHz and 32 GB of RAM. All the experiments runs are configured with an initial population of 100 individuals and 1000 generations. The crossover has a probability of 1.0 and the mutation is 0.1. Each experiment is run 10 times per workflow instance and number of hosts.

5.3   Efficiency of the Cooperative Multi-fitness Approach

In this section, we explore the effectiveness of the new CMF approach depending on the different list of supporting fitness functions, focusing on optimizing the workflow completion time. Given that makespan values can significantly differ based on the specific characteristics of each workflow, we employ the *makespan percentage error* (*MPE*) as a metric to gauge performance:

$$MPE = \frac{makespan_{GA-HEFT} - makespan}{makespan_{GA-HEFT}} \tag{9}$$

Here, *makespan* denotes the completion time of the solution under evaluation, while $makespan_{GA-HEFT}$ represents the baseline makespan achieved by the genetic algorithm using GA-HEFT genetic algorithm which has been identified as the most effective and precise approach in a prior research [1]. The *MPE* value serves as a comparative measure, where positive values indicate solutions that surpass the quality of GA-HEFT's outcomes, and negative values signify inferior performance relative to the GA-HEFT benchmark. Table 1 shows average *MPE* results across all infrastructure scenarios for every instance of each problem. Overall, CMF produces better results with respect to GA-HEFT [1] in both 1000genome and Cycles instances, and very similar results in SRASearch instances (quality drops only below 1%). Statistical analysis using the non-parametric Friedman test for paired samples (using standard 0.05 significance level) indicates significant differences between the methods. A Bonferroni post-hoc analysis reveals CMF is statistical significantly better than GA-HEFT. We also study the contribution of every support fitness functions by alternatively excluding either *RankFit* or *HeftFit* from $l_{fitness}$ list. The results correspond to CMF-NR and CMF-NH columns in Table 1. It is evident that CMF does not always produce superior results. In fact, in 1000genome, CMF without *RankFit* performs better in one instance and is equals in the remaining instances. Similarly, in the more complex instance of the Cycles problem, CMF without *HeftFit* yields significantly better results. A statistical analysis was conducted to compare the multi-fitness algorithms. The results indicate that CMF is significantly better than the other versions, while there are no significant differences between CMF-NR and CMF-NH.

By examining the contribution of each function in every generation, we can determine the percentage of individuals that evaluate each function. The percentage varies throughout the algorithm's evolution, as shown in Fig. 1 for an instance of the SRASearch problem. It is worth noting that the contribution of heuristic functions, particularly *HeftFit*, is most significant in the first quarter of the generations since the algorithm starts with random solutions. However, this distribution may differ significantly depending on the characteristics of the instance and the bias introduced by each heuristic function.

Table 1. Average MPE over the different host configurations and instances with CMF (standard + HeftFit + RankFit), CMF-NR (standard + HeftFit) and CMF-NH (standard + RankFit) (in bold the best value for each problem instance).

Problem	Tasks	CMF	CMF-NR	CMF-NH
1000genome	82	**0.15**	**0.15**	−1.61
	164	0.08	**0.13**	−2.80
	492	**0.19**	**0.19**	−2.17
	738	**0.30**	**0.30**	−1.86
Cycles	67	**5.60**	3.46	5.22
	133	**5.78**	2.50	3.83
	437	**5.69**	0.83	4.65
	1091	1.49	0.87	**6.12**
SRASearch	22	**−0.56**	−0.62	−1.33
	42	**−0.01**	−0.47	−0.89
	84	**−0.68**	−1.39	−2.38
	104	**-0.50**	−1.01	−2.02

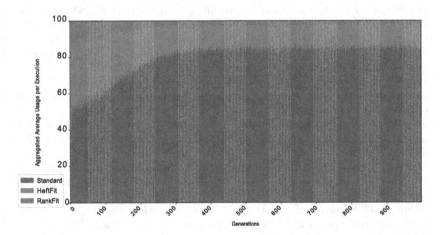

Fig. 1. Diagram of the contributions, by colors, of the different fitness functions across the evolution of CMF algorithm in a 42 task SRASearch instance using 16 hosts.

6   Conclusion

This study examines a new method for solving the workflow scheduling problem to minimise the makespan. It introduces a novel decoding schema for evolutionary algorithms that aims to utilize multiple support fitness functions in conjunction with a primary base fitness function. The focus is on the use of hybrid fitness evaluators, which combine heuristic knowledge with only a part of the solution to build its schedule. The decoding process chooses the schedule from the fitness function that minimises the makespan for a solution. Afterwards, the solution is recoded for direct evaluation by the basic fitness decoder, using Lamarckism.

A GA has been developed that utilises a standard fitness decoder ($StdFit$) together with two hybrid fitness functions ($RankFit$ and $HeftFit$). The performance of the GA was assessed using three well-known scientific workflows in a heterogeneous infrastructure. The results show that this novel approach can improve the performance of the original mono-objective genetic algorithm in these problems or generate solutions of similar quality at least.

The following steps involve extending this approach to multi-objective versions of the problem, such as optimizing makespan and energy consumption, so that it can be directly applied on standard algorithms such as NSGA-II. In addition, new supporting fitness functions will be investigated to create synergies and improve each objective.

Acknowledgements. This research has been supported by the Spanish Government under research grants PID2022-141746OB-I00 and TED2021-131938B-I00.

References

1. Barredo, P., Puente, J.: Precise makespan optimization via hybrid genetic algorithm for scientific workflow scheduling problem. Nat. Comput. **22**, 615–630 (2023)
2. Coleman, T., Casanova, H., Pottier, L., Kaushik, M., Deelman, E., Ferreira da Silva, R.: WfCommons: a framework for enabling scientific workflow research and development. Future Gener. Comput. Syst. **128**, 16–27 (2022)
3. Houck, C.R., Joines, J.A., Kay, M.G.: Utilizing Lamarckian evolution and the Baldwin effect in hybrid genetic algorithms. North Carolina State Univ., Department of Industrial Engineering (1996)
4. Juve, G., Chervenak, A., Deelman, E., Bharathi, S., Mehta, G., Vahi, K.: Characterizing and profiling scientific workflows. Futur. Gener. Comput. Syst. **29**(3), 682–692 (2013)
5. Madni, S.H.H., Abd Latiff, M.S., Abdullahi, M., Abdulhamid, S.M., Usman, M.J.: Performance comparison of heuristic algorithms for task scheduling in IaaS cloud computing environment. PLoS ONE **12**(5), 1–26 (2017)
6. Nebro, A.J., Pérez-Abad, J., Aldana-Martin, J.F., García-Nieto, J.: Evolving a multi-objective optimization framework. Appl. Optim. Swarm Intell., 175–198 (2021)
7. Topcuoglu, H., Hariri, S., Wu, M.Y.: Performance-effective and low-complexity task scheduling for heterogeneous computing. IEEE Trans. Parallel Distrib. Syst. **13**(3), 260–274 (2002)
8. Wu, C., et al.: Genetic Algorithm with Multiple Fitness Functions for Generating Adversarial Examples.: IEEE Congress on Evolutionary Computation, CEC 2021 - Proceedings, 1792–1799, p. 2021. Kraków, Poland (2021)
9. Yates, C., Christopher, R., Tumer, K.: Multi-fitness learning for behavior-driven cooperation. In: GECCO 2020 - Proceedings of the 2020 Genetic and Evolutionary Computation Conference, pp. 453–461. Cancun. (2020)
10. Ye, X., Li, J., Liu, S., et al.: A hybrid instance-intensive workflow scheduling method in private cloud environment. Nat. Comput. **18**, 735–746 (2019)
11. Zhu, Z., Zhang, G., Li, M., Liu, X.: Evolutionary multi-objective workflow scheduling in cloud. Trans. Parallel Distributed Syst. **27**(5), 1344–1357 (2016)

A Genetic Approach to Green Flexible Job Shop Problem Under Uncertainty

Sezin Afsar[1], Jorge Puente[1], Juan José Palacios[1(✉)],
Inés González-Rodríguez[2], and Camino R. Vela[1]

[1] Department of Computing, University of Oviedo, Campus of Gijón, Spain
{afsarsezin,puente,palaciosjuan,crvela}@uniovi.es
[2] Department of Mathematics, Statistics and Computation, University of Cantabria,
Santander, Spain
gonzalezri@unican.es

Abstract. Flexible job shop scheduling problem with energy and makespan minimization objectives, and uncertain processing times that are modeled with intervals is addressed in this work. The problem is solved by a genetic algorithm using a lexicographic goal programming approach and the results evaluated with respect to the lower and upper bounds that come from various sources and methods.

Keywords: flexible job shop · green scheduling · interval · genetic algorithm

1 Introduction

Scheduling problems aim to allocate limited resources to complete a number of tasks under various constraints. One of the main objectives of scheduling problems has been minimizing the makespan which is defined as the completion time of all tasks. As climate change and energy issues related to it continue to escalate, there has been a growing emphasis on improving the energy efficiency of processes. Although minimizing total completion time remains to be important, we believe that alternative ways of task scheduling should be explored to minimize the environmental impact.

The classical *job shop scheduling problem* (JSP) considers a setting where each task can be performed by only one machine whereas the *flexible* variant (FJSP) arises in a context where certain tasks, or all of them, have the flexibility to be executed by different machines. Performing the same task using different resources may result in different processing times as well as different power consumption profiles. As stated in [13], even the most basic versions of JSP are classified as NP-hard. It is reasonable to expect that the flexible variant renders even less suitable to be solved by exact algorithms given that it has an even larger solution space due to flexibility. Therefore, in this work we propose a genetic algorithm to obtain good solutions in a reasonable amount of time. We also use a commercial exact solver to assess the quality of our results.

J. M. Ferrández Vicente et al. (Eds.): IWINAC 2024, LNCS 14675, pp. 183–192, 2024.
https://doi.org/10.1007/978-3-031-61137-7_18

Although in the deterministic variant all parameters of the problem are assumed to be known in advance, many of them are subject to change in real life events such as processing times due to machine or human factors. Uncertain task durations in scheduling problems are commonly approached with stochastic modelling where they are assumed to follow a probability distribution [17]. However, it is often not possible to have enough data at hand to accurately estimate a probability distribution. Another modelling approach is to use fuzzy numbers to represent uncertain processing times in FJSP [16]. It requires much less information about the durations and hence has a computational advantage. In the most uncertain cases, where the amount of prior knowledge is minimal, intervals tend to be the only available information, requiring only a lower and an upper bound to model the task durations. They can be also understood as a uniform probability distribution given the lack of more information.

The literature on interval JSP and FJSP is relatively limited. The authors of [10] address a JSP that minimizes tardiness with respect to interval due dates and processing times and propose a genetic algorithm to solve it. In [14], a hybrid approach combining Particle Swarm Optimization (PSO) and a genetic algorithm is employed to address a flexible JSP with interval processing times. Multi-objective interval JSPs are investigated in [11,12]. In the former, a multi-objective artificial bee colony algorithm is suggested, while the latter proposes a dynamical neighbourhood search for lexicographic minimization of carbon footprint and makespan. In [2], a JSP with interval task durations minimizing makespan is considered and a genetic approach is proposed whereas in [3], an artificial bee colony algorithm is used to solve the same problem.

To the best of our knowledge this is the first time a flexible JSP with interval processing times that minimizes makespan and total energy consumption is tackled. The contributions of this work can be summarized as follows:

- A new formulation is presented for total energy consumption which is the sum of active and passive use inspired by the pay-per-use cost model in data centres. To cut cost, factory workers switch on each machine when the first task scheduled on it needs to be executed, and off when the last one has finished.
- Uncertainty in task execution times is modelled as an interval covering all observed values.
- A heuristic model is introduced to define new lower bounds for total energy consumption.
- A Constraint Programming (CP) model is formalized and solved by a commercial solver to generate lower and upper bounds in both objectives.
- An evolutionary algorithmic approach is applied to find pseudo-optimal schedules in single and lexicographic multi-objective versions.

The rest of the paper is organized as follows: the problem definition is introduced in Sect. 2, the metaheuristic algorithm is explained in Sect. 3, the experimental results are given in Sect. 4 and finally the conclusion and future research directions are presented in Sect. 5.

2 Problem Definition

In the classical JSP, there is a set of jobs $\{J_1, \ldots, J_n\}$ and each job J_i consists of a set of tasks $\{o_{i1}, \ldots, o_{iN_i}\}$ to be sequentially completed. Each task has to be performed on a particular machine from the set $M = \{M_1, \ldots, M_m\}$. In the flexible variant of the problem some (or all) tasks can be carried out on a subset of machines. The set of machines that can perform a given task o_{ij} is denoted as $M(o_{ij}) \subseteq M$. Both JSP and FJSP have *job precedence constraints*, that is, the tasks of a job should be completed in a fixed order. Moreover, a machine can work on at most one task at a given moment and cannot be interrupted until the completion of the task. Due to the flexible nature of the problem, the processing time of a task o_{ij} depends on the machine $M_k \in M(o_{ij})$ and hence denoted as d_{ijk}.

A solution to our problem is comprised of two parts: an assignment of all tasks to machines τ and a feasible schedule s, i.e., an allocation of starting times st_{ij} for all tasks o_{ij} on the appointed machines τ_{ij} while respecting aforementioned constraints. In this work, we focus on two objectives: minimizing makespan (completion time of the last task) and minimizing total energy consumption.

In practical scenarios, it is common to have uncertainty on the time required to complete a task, rather than having them precisely determined beforehand. In such cases, only approximate knowledge regarding the time needed is available. When only the maximum and minimum time it takes for each task are known, the uncertain processing time can be modeled as a closed interval denoted as $\mathbf{a} = [\underline{a}, \bar{a}] = \{x \in \mathbb{R} : \underline{a} \le x \le \bar{a}\}$. We refer to the FJSP with interval uncertainty as *Interval Flexible Job Shop* (IFJSP).

In order to compute our objective functions on a schedule with interval processing times, we need the arithmetic operations of *addition* and *maximum* between intervals, but also the *addition* and *product* of a scalar value and an interval. Assuming that $\mathbf{a} = [\underline{a}, \bar{a}]$, $\mathbf{b} = [\underline{b}, \bar{b}]$ are two intervals, the addition is defined as $\mathbf{a} + \mathbf{b} = [\underline{a} + \underline{b}, \bar{a} + \bar{b}]$ and the maximum calculated as $\max(\mathbf{a}, \mathbf{b}) = [\max(\underline{a}, \underline{b}), \max(\bar{a}, \bar{b})]$. Given an interval $\mathbf{a}$ and a value $r \in \mathbb{R}$, the addition and product are defined as $\mathbf{a} + r = [\underline{a} + r, \bar{a} + r]$ and $r\mathbf{a} = [r\underline{a}, r\bar{a}]$ respectively. When in need of comparing values, there is no natural order in the set of closed intervals. Instead, several ranking methods coexist in the literature [8]. In recent interval scheduling literature (i.e. [3]), the midpoint ranking (MP) appears to be the most used comparison method, according to which $\mathbf{a} \le_{MP} \mathbf{b}$ *iff* $m(\mathbf{a}) \le m(\mathbf{b})$ where $m(\mathbf{a}) = (\underline{a} + \bar{a})/2$.

In the literature of energy-aware scheduling problems, different approaches are proposed to incorporate energy impact to the schedule optimization. In [7] the authors only consider the energy consumed while the machines are idle. On the other hand, in [6] all machines are assumed to be *on* from the initial moment until the completion of the last task. In this work, we assume that each machine $M_k \in M$ is initially turned *off* and does not consume energy until it is turned *on* by an operator. It is safe to assume that workers are conservative when making this decision. They would turn *on* the machine when there is a possibility of it being used, which corresponds to the earliest moment when the first task scheduled on it, f_k, may start: $\underline{st}_{f_k}$, where $\mathbf{st}_{f_k} = [\underline{st}_{f_k}, \overline{st}_{f_k}]$. The machine M_k stays *on* until it is certain that is not needed anymore, at the completion time of its last task, l_k, that is, $\overline{ct}_{l_k}$, where $\mathbf{ct}_{l_k} = [\underline{ct}_{l_k}, \overline{ct}_{l_k}]$, both of them with respect to schedule s. During this period of time, the machine consumes a certain amount of *passive power* PP_k per unit of time. We denote the passive energy consumption as $PE_k = PP_k(\overline{ct}_{l_k} - \underline{st}_{f_k})$. When machine M_k is *active* executing a task o_{ij}, it consumes a certain amount of power AP_{ijk} per unit of time. Active energy consumption of M_k is computed as $\mathbf{AE}_k = \sum_{i,j,\tau_{ij}=k}(AP_{ijk}\,\mathbf{d}_{ijk})$, with $i \in \{1,\ldots,n\}$, $j \in \{1,\ldots,N_i\}$. Notice that the active energy consumption depends on the machine and the task duration, which is uncertain in our problem, whereas the passive energy is a deterministic value given by the worker's decision on when to turn on/off each machine. Total energy consumption is then defined as $\mathbf{TE} = \sum_{k \in M}(PE_k + \mathbf{AE}_k)$. We may also consider that passive energy PE_k has two different parts: the passive energy consumed while potentially executing a task, and the one that is consumed while the machine is idle *for sure* (which we will refer to as *idle energy*).

3   Solving Methodology

In this work we minimize two objectives: total energy consumption, $\mathbf{TE}$, and makespan, $\mathbf{C}_{max}$. Since our main target is still minimizing makespan, we apply a lexicographic multi-objective approach with goal programming. $\mathbf{C}_{max}$ acts as the primary objective until a pre-set goal is reached, after which the minimization of $\mathbf{TE}$ becomes the driving force of the optimization. In terms of comparison, it means that if there are two schedules having equal makespan values or below the goal, then the one with less $\mathbf{TE}$ value is considered to be better.

When solving both single and multi-objective scheduling problems, genetic algorithms (GA) are one of the most used methods. In general terms, a GA starts from an initial population P_0 consisting of a set of solutions. These solutions are then evaluated with respect to an objective function and an iterative process starts. At every iteration i a pair of individuals is selected from P_i. Crossover and mutation operators are applied to each pair with respective probabilities p_c and p_m to produce a new population of off-springs O_i. Next, O_i is evaluated and a replacement operator is used to join P_i and O_i and obtain P_{i+1}. The iterative process continues until the stopping criterion is met.

In this work, we adopt an encoding based on a double sequence (chromosome). The first one is a list consisting of a permutation of all tasks whilst respecting the precedence constraints. The second sequence is a list of machines corresponding to the tasks following the same order as the first sequence. Given a chromosome with this encoding, the represented schedule is decoded as follows: each task listed in the initial sequence is scheduled on the machine given by the second sequence at the earliest feasible insertion starting time [4].

In the initial population, individuals are generated by encoding a randomly generated topological order of tasks as a permutation with repetition. A machine sequence that is consistent with it is created afterwards. During the selection phase, individuals from the population are randomly selected and paired. After that, crossover is applied to each pair (parents) to create two new solutions (offsprings) with certain crossover probability. Here we consider Job Order Crossover (JOX) which randomly selects a subset of jobs from a parent and carries the relative gene order over to the offspring ensuring that the precedence constraints are respected. Each offspring undergoes a mutation with a certain probability. The mutation operation plays a crucial role in maintaining diversity among the individuals, thereby preventing the population from becoming stuck at any local optima. In this work, we use the mixed mutation operator that randomly applies (50%) one of these two operators:

- Randomly updates machine assignments of all tasks of the chromosome.
- In the chromosome, a task is randomly selected and reinserted within the subsequence of tasks that maintains the topological order: (i.e. between its predecessor and its successor in its job order)

Finally, a 4:2 tournament is applied where both parents and their offsprings are sorted with respect to their fitness values and the best two individuals are kept. In case of a tie between the top two, the third individual is selected to replace one of them and to be preserved in the population. The combination of these selection and replacement operators ensure the elitism of the best individual of the population in successive generations. The algorithm stops when a certain number of generations is reached.

4   Experimental Results

This experimental study is aimed at testing the quality of solutions that are obtained with the proposed Genetic Algorithm. To that end, 12 flexible JSP instances with uncertain processing times and active and passive power uses are taken from [5] (which are uncertain versions of DPdata benchmark instances [1]). In their work the authors utilize triangular fuzzy numbers to model uncertainty in task durations, that is, a task duration is represented with three components, $\widehat{a} = (a_1, a_2, a_3)$. In our work, the middle component is discarded and the other two are used as min and max values of an interval task duration, as $a = [a_1, a_3]$.

The difficulty of an instance is known to increase alongside the size of its solution space. Consequently, it is of interest to categorize the instances based on their properties to provide a more insightful analysis of the results later on. The instances $\{07a, \dots, 12a\}$ have 15 jobs and 8 resources whereas the instances $\{13a, \dots, 18a\}$ are larger having 20 jobs and 15 resources. Besides size, flexibility also plays an important role in instance difficulty which is measured as average number of alternative machines per task denoted as μ. We can separate the instances in three groups having low (l), medium (m) and high (h) flexibility. Low flexibility instances are $\{07a, 10a, 13a, 16a\}$ with $\mu \leq 1.3$, medium flexibility instances are $\{08a, 11a, 14a, 17a\}$ with $2.4 \leq \mu \leq 3$ and the ones with high flexibility are $\{09a, 12a, 15a, 18a\}$ with $\mu \geq 4.0$.

A series of preliminary experiments have been run for the parameter setting of the algorithm. The final setup is a population size of 100, max number of generations is 10000 and crossover and mutation probabilities are both set to 1.0. The GA has been implemented in C++ and all the experiments have been run on a PC with Intel Xeon Gold 6132 processor at 2.6 Ghz and 128 Gb RAM with Linux (CentOS v6.10). It is executed 10 times per instance to obtain representative results. Genetic algorithm execution times are all under 86 s for this configuration. Given the novelty of the problem definition and the energy objective, there are no existing results to directly compare our results to. Therefore, various methods and results are used to obtain good quality lower and upper bounds for this problem. We denote LB_{obj} and UB_{obj} the respective $m(\mathbf{LB}_{obj})$, $m(\mathbf{UB}_{obj})$ values, where $\mathbf{LB}_{obj}$ and $\mathbf{UB}_{obj}$ are lower/upper bounds to objective function $obj \in \{\mathbf{C}_{max}, \mathbf{TE}\}$. Since the MP ranking method has been chosen for comparison, we report this value for the objective values for the sake of clarity.

Constraint programming (CP) is widely recognized as an effective method for addressing scheduling problems in the literature. Two single-objective CP models under the same constraints are built, minimizing $\mathbf{C_{max}}$ and $\mathbf{TE}$ respectively. They are referred to as CP_{ms} and CP_{en} respectively in Table 1 and solved with the commercial solver IBM ILOG CP Optimizer 12.9 using an implementation on C++ with a time limit of 6 h and single thread [9]. The time limit is reached in all instances yielding in a lower and an upper bound. The average gap between the LB and the best solution (UB) that the solver finds after 6 h is approximately 32.5% for both objectives which indicates that the instances are not trivial to solve.

Next, a heuristic method is developed which assumes that all tasks are processed on the most *energy-efficient* machines (the ones with lowest energy consumption for the task) among the alternatives without pausing between tasks. Its results are given in column 4 of Table 1. It is important to note that the heuristic provides LB_{TE} values 33% better than CP's on average despite not taking the precedence constraints into account and consequently, these tighter LBs allow us to evaluate the experimental results more accurately.

Lastly, the best-known LBs for the deterministic version of FJSP that minimizes makespan from [15] are considered for our problem and given in the last column of Table 1, since the LBs for the crisp version of the instances are valid $LB_{C_{max}}$ values as well. Table 1 reports the summary of all bounds for makespan and total energy. The best LB and UBs, hence the ones utilized in this work, are marked bold.

Two objective functions are optimized with a lexicographic goal programming approach in this study. Makespan has the highest priority, and according to Table 1, $Crisp_{ms}$ provides the best LBs for this objective. To test the capabilities of our method, for each instance we set the makespan goal as $Goal = (1 + \alpha)\,Crisp_{ms}$ where $0 < \alpha < 1$. Due to the lexicographical nature of the problem, when α is large the goal is easier to reach and we can focus more on minimizing $\mathbf{TE}$, being more difficult the smaller α is. We use 4 different α values: 0.25, 0.50, 0.75 and 0.99.

Table 1. LBs and UBs obtained via CP, the heuristic method and crisp instances

Instances	CP_{en}		Heu_{en}	CP_{ms}		$Crisp_{ms}$
	LB_{TE}	UB_{TE}	LB_{TE}	$LB_{C_{max}}$	$UB_{C_{max}}$	$LB_{C_{max}}$
07a	4,420,870	5,445,250	5,074,850	1,905.0	2,412.0	2,187.0
08a	3,439,320	4,751,820	4,280,450	1,409.0	2,142.0	2,061.0
09a	2,922,610	5,109,080	4,361,320	1,380.0	2,126.0	2,061.0
10a	4,241,860	5,333,430	4,862,820	1,889.5	2,391.5	2,178.0
11a	3,711,870	5,159,880	4,636,950	1,379.0	2,138.5	2,017.0
12a	2,707,110	4,836,900	4,083,080	1,323.0	2,100.5	1,969.0
13a	5,842,050	7,371,560	6,797,380	1,836.0	2,333.0	2,161.0
14a	4,654,750	7,255,800	6,382,990	1,350.5	2,234.0	2,161.0
15a	3,388,250	6,497,010	5,267,490	1,334.0	2,230.0	2,161.0
16a	5,514,720	6,911,420	6,408,300	1,843.0	2,333.5	2,148.0
17a	4,170,250	6,492,430	5,686,210	1,325.5	2,220.0	2,088.0
18a	3,474,250	6,650,000	5,379,080	1,294.5	2,204.0	2,057.0

For fairer comparisons, we use the *relative error* (RE) between the middle point of each objective value $m(\mathbf{f}_{obj})$, $obj \in \{\mathbf{C}_{max}, \mathbf{TE}\}$ and its best reported lower bound LB_{obj}. Given a solution, for each objective value:

$$RE(f_{obj}) = \frac{m(\mathbf{f}_{obj}) - LB_{obj}}{LB_{obj}}$$

The $RE(f_{C_{max}})$ values are presented in Table 2. The second column contains the best values obtained by CP_{ms}. The results of single-objective versions of GA minimizing only C_{max} (GA_{ms}) or TE (GA_{en}) are given in the third and last column respectively. The remaining columns show the results of the lexicographic approach using different α values. As the α value increases, $RE(f_{C_{max}})$ also increases as one would expect. The results of $\alpha = 0.99$ are very similar to those obtained with the single-objective GA_{en}, which shows us that increasing the α would not necessarily lead to different results.

The $RE(f_{TE})$ values are given in Table 3. Enabling the metaheuristic to explore solutions with larger makespan allows us to get close to the TE values found by the solver minimizing only this objective function. Furthermore, the similarity between the results of the last two columns indicates that testing an α value higher than 0.99 is not of great interest for this problem.

We should point out the fact that the flexibility group l instances (lowest flexibility) have the smallest $RE(f_{TE})$ values whereas group h instances have the largest ones. The proportionality between flexibility and relative error shows that the flexibility of an instance has a direct impact on the solution quality.

In Fig. 1 the $RE(f_{C_{max}})$ and $RE(f_{TE})$ values given in Tables 2 and 3 are plotted for three instances with different flexibility levels. Note that all solu-

Table 2. $RE(f_{C_{max}})$ obtained with CP and GA with different α values

Instances	Flex.	CP_{ms}	GA_{ms}	$GA_{lex}(0.25)$	$GA_{lex}(0.50)$	$GA_{lex}(0.75)$	$GA_{lex}(0.99)$	GA_{en}
07a	l	10.3%	14.4%	17.0%	25.4%	25.3%	25.3%	25.3%
08a	m	4.1%	12.9%	14.2%	23.4%	23.9%	24.9%	24.9%
09a	h	3.2%	16.4%	18.2%	22.9%	24.3%	24.3%	24.3%
10a	l	9.8%	14.3%	16.5%	20.4%	22.6%	22.6%	22.6%
11a	m	6.1%	15.6%	17.4%	21.7%	25.9%	25.5%	25.5%
12a	h	6.9%	19.2%	21.1%	25.4%	28.2%	27.9%	27.9%
13a	l	8.2%	16.5%	17.3%	22.5%	22.0%	22.0%	22.0%
14a	m	3.5%	14.7%	16.1%	21.5%	21.3%	20.0%	20.0%
15a	h	3.2%	15.8%	18.4%	24.3%	28.3%	30.1%	30.1%
16a	l	8.7%	15.5%	17.6%	22.1%	22.9%	22.9%	22.9%
17a	m	6.5%	17.6%	19.5%	22.0%	25.1%	24.7%	24.7%
18a	h	7.4%	21.6%	21.4%	25.8%	32.4%	30.6%	30.6%

Table 3. $RE(f_{TE})$ obtained with CP and GA with different α values

Instances	Flex.	CP_{en}	GA_{ms}	$GA_{lex}(0.25)$	$GA_{lex}(0.50)$	$GA_{lex}(0.75)$	$GA_{lex}(0.99)$	GA_{en}
07a	l	7.3%	10.9%	9.3%	8.2%	8.1%	8.1%	8.1%
08a	m	11.0%	15.7%	15.1%	12.5%	12.5%	12.5%	12.5%
09a	h	17.1%	27.8%	27.1%	22.4%	21.7%	21.7%	21.7%
10a	l	9.7%	11.2%	9.8%	9.0%	9.1%	9.1%	9.1%
11a	m	11.3%	16.5%	16.1%	12.7%	12.0%	12.0%	12.0%
12a	h	18.5%	25.9%	25.7%	22.2%	20.7%	20.3%	20.3%
13a	l	8.4%	10.4%	9.1%	8.4%	8.1%	8.1%	8.1%
14a	m	13.7%	19.4%	18.5%	15.2%	15.0%	15.3%	15.3%
15a	h	23.3%	33.8%	32.8%	28.1%	26.6%	26.9%	26.9%
16a	l	7.9%	10.1%	9.2%	8.0%	8.1%	8.1%	8.1%
17a	m	14.2%	20.8%	20.4%	16.7%	16.2%	16.1%	16.1%
18a	h	23.6%	32.8%	31.6%	28.0%	26.0%	26.3%	26.3%

tions obtained by different methods have both a makespan and a total energy value and therefore their REs can be plotted on the same graph where x and y-axes are $RE(f_{C_{max}})$ and $RE(f_{TE})$ respectively. It can be observed that the CP_{ms} and CP_{en} constitute the two extremes whereas GA_{ms} and GA_{en} frame the grey points which are the results of the lexicographic approach with different α values. In other words, the metaheuristic algorithm using both single and multi-objective approaches allows us to explore the solution space between the two single-objective CP solutions and depicts the trade-off between these two objectives. Although the flexibility of an instance affects the solution quality that can be achieved within a certain number of generations, the algorithm keeps finding solutions that balances max completion time and total consumed energy.

Lastly, to evaluate the impact of the new energy model with respect to the one proposed in [5], we have adapted their energy objective to intervals and tested both approaches using the GA_{ms} and GA_{en}. The main difference between the two energy models lies in how they treat *idle energy*, and the empirical results show that the new energy model leads to a significant improvement in this aspect. The *idle energy* decreases 16% under GA_{ms} and 42% under GA_{en} with respect to the

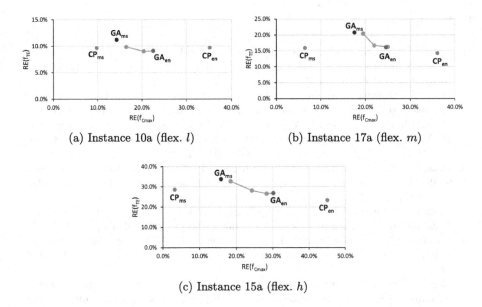

(a) Instance 10a (flex. l)   (b) Instance 17a (flex. m)

(c) Instance 15a (flex. h)

Fig. 1. RE values of three instances from different flexibility groups

existing energy model in average across the instances, being this improvement similar for all of them (0.06 standard deviation).

5   Conclusion

This work addresses a green flexible job shop scheduling problem with interval processing times, aiming to minimize both makespan and total energy consumption. To better reflect reality, we propose a new energy model in which each machine turns *on* with it is first needed and *off* after the last task is completed. The problem's flexible nature allows us to consider alternative machines with different task durations and energy consumption profiles, and find a trade-off between the two conflicting objectives. We implement a genetic algorithm coupled with lexicographic goal programming to solve this multi-objective problem. We evaluate its performance in comparison to lower and upper bounds obtained from the crisp version of the problem, besides a heuristic method and a CP model that we develop. The results indicate that it is possible to find good solutions efficiently that consume less energy and do not significantly delay task completion.

One potential future research direction could be to use memetic algorithms to improve solution quality. Additionally, it would be valuable to thoroughly evaluate the robustness of the solutions found under uncertain conditions.

Acknowledgements. This research has been supported by the Spanish Government under research grants TED2021-131938B-I00 and PID2022-141746OB-I00.

References

1. Dauzère-Pérès, S., Paulli, J.: An integrated approach for modeling and solving the general multiprocessor job-shop scheduling problem using tabu search. Ann. Oper. Res. **70**, 281–306 (1997)
2. Díaz, H., González-Rodríguez, I., Palacios, J.J., Díaz, I., Vela, C.R.: A genetic approach to the job shop scheduling problem with interval uncertainty. In: Lesot, M.-J., Vieira, S., Reformat, M.Z., Carvalho, J.P., Wilbik, A., Bouchon-Meunier, B., Yager, R.R. (eds.) IPMU 2020. CCIS, vol. 1238, pp. 663–676. Springer, Cham (2020). https://doi.org/10.1007/978-3-030-50143-3_52
3. Díaz, H., Palacios, J.J., González-Rodríguez, I., Vela, C.R.: An elitist seasonal artificial bee colony algorithm for the interval job shop. Integrated Comput.-Aided Eng. **30**(3), 223–242 (2023)
4. Díaz, H., Palacios, J.J., González-Rodríguez, I., Vela, C.R.: Fast elitist ABC for makespan optimisation in interval JSP. Nat. Comput. **22**(4), 645–657 (2023)
5. García Gómez, P., González-Rodríguez, I., Vela, C.R.: Reducing energy consumption in fuzzy flexible job shops using memetic search. LNCS, vol. 13259, pp. 140–150 (2022)
6. García Gómez, P., González-Rodríguez, I., Vela, C.R.: Enhanced memetic search for reducing energy consumption in fuzzy flexible job shops. Integr. Comput.-Aided Eng. **30**(2), 151–167 (2023)
7. González, M.A., Oddi, A., Rasconi, R.: Multi-objective optimization in a job shop with energy costs through hybrid evolutionary techniques. In: Proceedings of ICAPS 2017, pp. 140–148 (2017)
8. Karmakar, S., Bhunia, A.K.: A comparative study of different order relations of intervals. Reliable Comput. **16**, 38–72 (2012)
9. Laborie, P., Rogerie, J., Shaw, P., Vilím, P.: IBM ILOG CP optimizer for scheduling: 20+ years of scheduling with constraints at IBM/ILOG. Constraints **23**(2), 210–250 (2018)
10. Lei, D.: Interval job shop scheduling problems. Int. J. Adv. Manuf. Technol. **60**, 291–301 (2012)
11. Lei, D.: Multi-objective artificial bee colony for interval job shop scheduling with flexible maintenance. Int. J. Adv. Manuf. Technol. **66**, 1835–1843 (2013)
12. Lei, D., Guo, X.: An effective neighborhood search for scheduling in dual-resource constrained interval job shop with environmental objective. Int. J. Prod. Econ. **159**, 296–303 (2015)
13. Lenstra, J., Rinnooy Kan, A., Brucker, P.: Complexity of machine scheduling problems. In: Hammer, P., Johnson, E., Korte, B., Nemhauser, G. (eds.) Studies in Integer Programming, Annals of Discrete Mathematics, vol. 1, pp. 343–362. Elsevier (1977). https://doi.org/10.1016/S0167-5060(08)70743-X
14. Li, X., Gao, L., Wang, W., Wang, C., Wen, L.: Particle swarm optimization hybridized with genetic algorithm for uncertain integrated process planning and scheduling with interval processing time. Comput. Ind. Eng. **135**, 1036–1046 (2019)
15. Mastrolilli, M., Gambardella, L.M.: Effective neighbourhood functions for the flexible job shop problem. J. Sched. **3**(1), 3–20 (2000)
16. Palacios, J.J., González, M.A., Vela, C.R., González-Rodríguez, I., Puente, J.: Genetic tabu search for the fuzzy flexible job shop problem. Comput. Oper. Res. **54**, 74–89 (2015)
17. Pinedo, M.L.: Scheduling: Theory, Algorithms, and Systems, vol. 29. Springer (2012)

Social and Civil Engineering Through Human AI Translations

AI Emmbedded in Drone Control

Daniel Caballero-Martin[1,4], Jose Manuel Lopez-Guede[1,4(✉)],
Julian Estevez[2,4], and Manuel Graña[3,4]

[1] Faculty of Engineering of Vitoria-Gasteiz, University of the Basque Country,
UPV/EHU, Vitoria-Gasteiz, Spain
jm.lopez@ehu.es
[2] Faculty of Engineering of Gipuzkoa, University of the Basque Country,
UPV/EHU, San Sebastian, Spain
[3] Faculty of Computer Science, University of the Basque Country,
UPV/EHU, San Sebastian, Spain
[4] Group of Computational Intelligence, University of the Basque Country,
UPV/EHU, San Sebastian, Spain

Abstract. The significant improvement of drones has supported research in advanced technologies, highlighting the integration of Artificial Intelligence (AI). This study examines the impact of AI on drones, addressing several areas from automation to complex real time decision making. In fields unrelated to logistics and cargo transportation, the synergy between drones and AI has led to notable progress in areas such as agriculture, construction, security and exploration. This combination the generation of new applications, although on the other hand, it poses ethical and regulatory challenges. In summary, AI not only transforms logistics but also drives innovation in several industries, offering a safer and more efficient future.

Keywords: Artificial Intelligence Algorithms · Drones · Cargo
Transport · Autonomous Decisions

1 Introduction

Due to the precision of AI algorithms, revolutionary advances are being made, giving rise to techniques such as Machine Learning (ML) that provide autonomy in decision making. There are many ML systems and it is of special interest to make a classification based on some basic criteria. One of the most widespread and significant classification criteria is the way in which the training of these systems or algorithms is carried out. In this type of classification, four significant methodologies can be distinguished: supervised learning, unsupervised learning, semi-supervised learning and reinforcement learning.

The main characteristic of supervised learning is the use of labeled data for training algorithms whose objective is to perform a classification with the greatest possible precision. One significant application of this type of algorithms is the identification of SPAM emails. Some of the main algorithms of this paradigm

J. M. Ferrández Vicente et al. (Eds.): IWINAC 2024, LNCS 14675, pp. 195–204, 2024.
https://doi.org/10.1007/978-3-031-61137-7_19

are Random Forest (RF) [1], K-Nearest Neighbors (KNN) [2], Support Vector Machine (SVM) [3], etc. In the opposite sense, unsupervised learning is presented.

The main characteristic of this type of procedures is the ability to group previously unlabeled data sets. The application of these algorithms is especially interesting in data exploration, customer segmentation or image recognition techniques. One of the most important and significant technique of this type of paradigm is the K-Means algorithm [4]. Because labeling data sometimes is difficult, some algorithms are trained using labeled and unlabeled data. This approach is called semi-supervised learning. Most techniques in this paradigm are a combination of supervised and unsupervised algorithms.

Another of the most significant techniques is Reinforcement Learning (RL) [5], based on interaction with the environment, applying solutions sequentially, establishing a penalty and reward system based on the feedback received from the environment. Many robots are based on RL to learn various tasks such as learning to walk or overcome obstacles.

The continuous technological development of drones marks an important milestone in various industrial sectors by increasing their performance and capacity. This advancement not only revolutionizes traditional fields such as agriculture, infrastructure inspection and environmental monitoring, but also optimizes flight trajectories and facilitates cargo transportation. This phenomenon is related to the integration of AI in the field of drones. Technology has evolved from automation to the ability to make complex decisions autonomously and in real time. The impact of Deep Learning (DL) algorithms and massive data processing technologies becomes crucial. The advances made in this field give rise to the creation of autonomous navigation systems, offering greater flexibility when optimizing flight trajectories, especially in constantly changing environments. In addition, AI has demonstrated a crucial role in identifying possible failures, improving the reliability and intrinsic safety of Unmanned Aerial Vehicles (UAVs).

On the other hand, in both the civilian and military domains, there are ethical and regulatory challenges that AI poses in relation to autonomous decision making with drones. The balance between human supervision and system autonomy becomes a crucial point of discussion. The field of cargo transportation has been completely transformed by AI, particularly in the field of logistics operations, allowing the creation of flexible routes, revolutionizing the planning process.

The current literature focuses on specific tasks or algorithms, such as logistics [6–8], trajectory optimization [9], object detection [10], agricultural operations [11, 12] and inventory [13]. A wide range of notable contributions in this field are explored, from the application of DL algorithms for real time object detection and recognition to the use of massive data processing techniques for dynamic trajectory optimization.

The rest of the paper is organised as follows. Section 2 presents the applications and types of AI algorithms in drones. Finally, the article ends in Sect. 3 with conclusions and future work in this area.

2   Drone Operations Supported by AI Algorithms

2.1   Delivery Systems

One of the most promising applications of AI in this field is adaptive mathematical modelling, achieving a substantial improvement in the understanding of the structure of freight transport, reducing costs, delivery times and increasing the efficiency and profitability of this type of operations [14]. These models are particularly useful in circumstances where external factors (distance, weight, load size, adverse weather conditions, etc.) affect the transport of cargo.

The coordination of multiple drones to transport a cargo is another of the important challenges [15]. Because on some occasions, the characteristics of the cargo do not allow to be transported with a single drone, algorithms must be implemented capable of compensating for the mobility of the network of drones involved in the operation. Not only must the control of the drones be taken into account, but there are also external agents (moving inertia, wind,coordination, etc.) that must be counteracted by the control algorithms. An error in the computation of this type of algorithm could mean losing both the drone network and the cargo being transported [16]. Manufacturers are working on developing advanced drones using ML models to improve coordination and safety. It is also necessary to monitor and control the operation of several drones in real time [17]. To carry out this control, telemetry systems and sensors in drones can be used, capable of sending information to a control center in real time, guaranteeing stable connectivity and an efficient identification and location capacity [18,19]. One of the most used paradigms consists of transporting a fleet of drones in trucks to the urban areas of cities (last mile delivery). From this point, drones are launched with the corresponding packages for delivery [6]. Once the delivery is complete, each drone returns to the truck to pick up the next package [20]. To optimize parcel collection and distribution points on roads, the development of AI algorithms is proposed in charge of choosing these optimal points [21]. In the case of package delivery with drones from a single truck, the problem arises of determining the optimal route of the truck and the sequence of travel of the drones in order to satisfy customer demands in the most efficient way possible, due to that late delivery is a critical problem [20,22]. This methodology includes a graph based formulation and a Benders decomposition method [20].

Other research addresses same day delivery problem with vehicles and drones [8]. A Deep Q-Learning (DQN) approach is proposed to assign clients to vehicles or drones dynamically. The method learns the value of assigning a new client to vehicles or drones by demonstrating superiority compared to the reference policies. This approach uses different fleets of vehicles based on capacity and speed, optimizing same-day delivery. These studies reflect the diversity of approaches to address the challenges in generating itineraries for the delivery of packages with drones and other vehicles applied to the last mile delivery paradigm, highlighting the importance of considering diverse fleets, energy efficiency and DL to optimize the package distribution.

2.2 Optimization and Complexity Associated with Cargo and Resources

Despite the notable advances in AI that allow the implementation of complex algorithms for autonomous decision making and route planning by drones, there are various additional challenges that need to be addressed, such as battery management, adverse weather conditions, airspace regulations, weight restrictions and optimizing recipient waiting time [23].

For collaborative drone delivery systems, GA is used for route planning [14]. This approach aims to minimize route length, delivery time and energy consumption, thus addressing key challenges in drone delivery system efficiency. On the other hand, another approach based on RL and Deep Neural Networks (DNN) is used to optimize route planning and task assignment in collaborative delivery systems, taking into account factors such as workload, location and capacity of drones [24]. By implementing a Deep Reinforcement Learning (DRL) approach, a comprehensive decision making framework is established, where the drone develops its local policy by directly observing the state of the environment in its vicinity and receiving messages from the drones neighbors. This method aims to encourage cooperation between drones in the generation of highly optimized multiple trajectories. This collaborative approach implicitly leads to the minimization of resources needed to carry out operations [25]. The uniqueness of this approach lies in its ability to adapt in real time to changes in the environment, such as modifications in topology or adjustments in resource availability. Furthermore, by promoting the cooperative generation of optimal trajectories, this distributed RL framework effectively acts in the overall minimization of the resources required to carry out drone logistics operations. The application of this innovative approach provides an advanced solution for the collaborative management of drones in dynamic and complex environments.

When addressing the challenges of cargo transportation with drones, both the specific conditions of the products to be transported and the characteristics of the cargo must be taken into account. One of the most important aspects is the need to carry out rapid delivery of perishable products, involving research into bi-objective mathematical models. These models aim to reduce distribution costs and avoid value losses that may occur during the process [14]. Cargo characteristics, such as weight, size, fragility and handling needs, also play a key role in choosing the right drone. A drone with a heavy load may require greater lifting capacity, while a drone with fragile cargo may require a protection system to prevent damage during transport.

2.3 Emergency Situations

In emergency situations and disaster zones, quick access to medical services and supplies can mean the difference between life and death. In this context, drones emerge as a tool capable of providing vital support in areas affected by disasters. Another of the fundamental characteristics is the possibility of transmitting information in real time to medical and emergency teams, being able to provide a much more clarifying vision of the situation, giving clairvoyance in strategic decision making. Optimal trajectory planning is one of the main applications of AI algorithms in these types of circumstances, maximizing the speed and safety of life support deliveries, avoiding obstacles and ensuring efficient and fair delivery of supplies [26,27].

To address this challenge, numerous studies use algorithms such as Q-Learning (QL), K-Means or Genetic Algorithms (GA) to carry out the feasibility analysis [8], achieving the most efficient distribution possible [14]. Due to the high demand for the use of drones for this type of operation, an analysis of transport networks should be performed by applying AI algorithms to predict demand in specific geographical areas [28].

2.4 Drone Identification and Detection

The proliferation of drones has generated great expectations due to their ability to be applied in various areas. However, they have also generated concern due to their misuse and the potential threat they represent due to their invasive nature [29]. In this sense, an increase is observed in the field of detection and monitoring, where comparisons are made between methods based on Linear Kalman Filters (LKF) and Nonlinear Polynomial Regression (NPR) [29]. One of the most innovative features in drone detection involves the use of skinny patterns and Iterative Neighborhood Component Analysis (INCA) [30]. This classification model uses techniques such as Decision Trees (DT), SVM, KNN and Ensemble Classifiers (EC), achieving a classification accuracy of 99.72% with a KNN algorithm [30].

It is essential to be able to identify and detect drones in real time to ensure safety. For this reason, drone detection and tracking systems are designed that combine multiple DL [31,32] and computer vision techniques using the Yolo-v4 model to detect drones and generate video patterns to track them [33]. On the other hand, an end to end model is developed for the detection and classification of different drones using YOLOv2 as a detection model [34].

One of the most novel and promising approaches, surpassing existing methods in the detection and identification of drones, is the use of multiscale time/frequency convolutional neural networks based on radio frequency signals [35] using DNN [35]. Additionally, the use of Deep Reinforcement Learning (DRL) to counter drones in 3D space using another drone is explored [36]. This method uses the DQN algorithm that combines imitation learning and RL to hunt down target drones [36].

As an innovative technique, the acoustic characteristics of drones are used, complemented by advanced DL techniques for their identification [37]. The introduction of a hybrid drone acoustic dataset, which includes audio recordings from real drones and artificially generated audio samples, has been instrumental in improving the detection of these types of aircraft [37]. Additionally, applying Generative Antagonistic Networks (GANs) to generate drone audio snippets has proven beneficial in detecting new and unknown drones, thereby improving physical infrastructure security and privacy [37].

2.5 Flight Control and Safety

In the field of drones, one of the fundamental aspects is to achieve control of the aircraft by carrying out research that provides important advances in the fields of visual navigation, flight control, safety and route planning. Visual navigation combines optical flow algorithms and supervised learning techniques (KNN, SVM) to calculate flight speed and improve identification of its motion state [38]. Additionally, a method is investigated to combine DQN with artificial potential field algorithms to avoid obstacles during flight and enable safer and more efficient drone navigation [39].

In the field of security, countermeasure systems that use RL are developed to Counter Unmanned Aerial Systems (C-UAS) [40]. These systems use spoofing and meaconing algorithms to neutralize an intruder drone's GNSS receiver and direct it to a sure kill zone (SZ). This technology has proven effective in identifying and reducing unauthorized drone flights, thereby improving safety in a variety of scenarios. On the other hand and as a complementary aspect to security, there is a need to implement systems that guarantee the detection of intrusions through algorithms that provide this capacity. Intrusion detection algorithms based on QL (Q-TCID) are presented, improving the accuracy in the detection of malicious attacks in Internet of Drones (IoD) systems [41].

2.6 Agricultural Operations

Drone equipped with Convolutional Neural Networks (CNNs) are proving effective in detecting plant diseases. By performing detailed image analysis, specific patterns can be observed, allowing farmers to take the necessary preventive measures to improve overall crop health. By combining RL algorithms and neural networks, efficient spray planning can be realised [42,43]. This combination (monitoring and spraying) leads to an increase in crop quality and quantity.

Pollination, essential for the production of some foods, is supported by drones equipped with AI algorithms that are capable of identifying unpollinated flowers and, if necessary, carrying out artificial pollination [11]. Another of the most significant techniques in this area is the detection and control of floods caused by weeds [12]. Using algorithms like SVM [44], RF [45] and KNN [46], drones can identify flood prone areas and precisely eradicate weeds, obtaining a guarantee of agricultural production [47].

3   Conclusions and Future Work

The convergence between AI and drones reveals a large number of promising advances for the application of this type of paradigm in a multitude of applications. This analysis has not only provided an in depth overview of the algorithms, but also highlights innovative applications, thus offering a comprehensive view of the technological cutting edge in this dynamic field. Among the novel applications identified, advanced solutions stand out for the optimization of trajectories, detection and recognition of objects in real time, as well as the development of autonomous navigation systems. In addition, the progressive integration of drones in agriculture is observed.

In the field of transportation, the emerging application of drones in collaborative transportation stands out, allowing the efficient delivery of products and services. This collaborative approach extends to last mile delivery, where drones play a crucial role in the logistics chain, shortening distances and optimizing the delivery of goods to final destinations. Furthermore, these pioneering applications not only enrich our current understanding of the capabilities of AI in drones, but also outline essential directions for future research.

The future outlook for this technology is highly promising, although it faces some significant obstacles. The design of efficient and sustainable batteries stands as a fundamental challenge, since it constitutes a pillar for the advancement of operations related to AI algorithms and drones. On the other hand, but no less important, ethical, regulatory and privacy aspects are crucial to establish defined standards in this technical field.

If these essential aspects can be successfully addressed, the future of this technology looks extremely interesting in the logistics field, agriculture, surveillance and in the transformation of employment. Resolving the challenges raised will not only open new possibilities in terms of efficiency and applications, but will also contribute to forging a solid ethical and regulatory framework. Consequently, an exciting and transformative future is foreseen for the integration of AI and drones in both society and industry.

Acknowledgements. The authors were supported by the Vitoria-Gasteiz Mobility Lab Foundation, a governmental organization of the Provincial Council of Araba and the local council of Vitoria-Gasteiz under the following project grant: "Generación de mapas mediante drones e Inteligencia Computacional".

References

1. Hatwell, J., Gaber, M., Azad, R.: CHIRPS: explaining random forest classification. Artif. Intell. Rev. **53**, 5747–5788 (2020)
2. Zhang, Z.: Introduction to machine learning: K-nearest neighbors. Annals Trans. Med. **4**(11), 218 (2016)
3. Nieto, D.M.C., Quiroz, E A.P., Lengua, M.A.C.: A systematic literature review on Support Vector Machines applied to regression. In: 2021 IEEE Sciences and Humanities International Research Conference (SHIRCON), vol. 4 p. 4 (2021)

4. Ahmed, M., Seraj, R., Islam, S.M.S.: The K-Means algorithm: a comprehensive survey and performance evaluation. Electronics **9**(8), 1295 (2020)
5. Padakandla, S.: A survey of reinforcement learning algorithms for dynamically varying environments. ACM Comput. Surv. (CSUR) **54**(6), 1–25 (2021)
6. Borghetti, F., Caballini, C., Carboni, A., Grossato, G., Maja, R., Barabino, B.: The use of drones for last-mile delivery: a numerical case study in Milan, Italy. Sustainability **14**(3), 1766 (2022)
7. Raivi, A., Huda, S.M.A., Alam, M., Moh, S.: Drone routing for drone-based delivery systems: a review of trajectory planning, charging, and security. Sensors **23** (2023)
8. Chen, X., Ulmer, M.W., Thomas, B.W.: Deep Q-Learning for same-day delivery with vehicles and drones. Euro. J. Operat. R. **298**(3), 939–952 (2022)
9. Saeed, R.A., Omri, M., Abdel-Khalek, S., Ali, E.S., Alotaibi, M.F.: Optimal path planning for drones based on swarm intelligence algorithm. Neural Comput. Appli. **34**(12), 10133–10155 (2022)
10. Dabbiru, L., Goodin, C., Carruth, D., Boone, J.: Object detection in synthetic aerial imagery using Deep Learning. Proceedings of SPIE, 1254002 (5 pp.); 1254002(5.)-1254002 (5 pp.) (2023)
11. Hiraguri, T., et al.: Autonomous drone-based pollination system using AI classifier to replace bees for greenhouse tomato cultivation. IEEE Access **11**, 99352–99364 (2023)
12. Murad, N.Y., Mahmood, T., Forkan, A.R.M., Morshed, A., Jayaraman, P.P., Siddiqui, M.S.: Weed detection using deep learning: a systematic literature review. Sensors **23**(7), 3670 (2023)
13. Naranjo, M., et al.: Object detection-based system for traffic signs on drone-captured images. Drones **7**(2), 112 (2023)
14. Zhang, J., Li, Y.: Collaborative vehicle-drone distribution network optimization for perishable products in the epidemic situation. Comput. Operat. Res. **149**, 106039 (2023)
15. Estevez, J., Garate, G., Lopez-Guede, J.M., Larrea, M.: Review of aerial transportation of suspended-cable payloads with quadrotors. Drones **8**(2), 35 (2024)
16. Ito, S.: Load and wind aware routing of delivery drones. Drones **6**(2), 50 (2022)
17. Alex, C., Vijaychandra, A.: Autonomous cloud based drone system for disaster response and mitigation. In: 2016 International Conference on Robotics and Automation for Humanitarian Applications (RAHA), pp. 183-186 (2016)
18. Tan, Y., Wang, J., Liu, J., Kato, N.: Blockchain-assisted distributed and lightweight authentication service for industrial unmanned aerial vehicles. IEEE Internet of Things J. **9**(18), 16928–16940 (2022)
19. Doole, M., Ellerbroek, J., Hoekstra, J.M.: Investigation of merge assist policies to improve safety of drone traffic in a constrained urban airspace. Aerospace **9**(3), 120 (2022)
20. Bruni, M.E., Khodaparasti, S., Moshref-Javadi, M.: A logic-based Benders decomposition method for the multi-trip traveling repairman problem with drones". Comput. Operat. Res. **145**, 105845 (2022)
21. Saleu, R.G.M., Deroussi, L., Feillet, D., Grangeon, N., Quilliot, A.: The parallel drone scheduling problem with multiple drones and vehicles. Euro. J. Operat. Res. **300**(2), 571–589 (2022)
22. Chen, M.-H., Lan, Y.-Q., Hu, J., Xu, Z.: An improved edge recombination algorithm for scheduling problems of drone package delivery. J. Dis. Math. Sci. Cryptography **21**(2), 423–426 (2018)

23. Lieret, M., Kogan, V., Doell, S., Franke, J.: Automated in-house transportation of small load carriers with autonomous unmanned aerial vehicles. In: 2019 IEEE 15th International Conference on Automation Science and Engineering (Case), pp. 1010-1015 (2019)

24. Luo, Q., Luan, T.H., Shi, W., Fan, P.: Deep reinforcement learning based computation offloading and trajectory planning for Multi-UAV cooperative target search. IEEE J. Selected Areas Commun. 41(2), 504–520 (2022)

25. Rahim, S., Razaq, M.M., Chang, S.Y., Peng, L.: A Reinforcement learning-based path planning for collaborative UAVs. In: 37th Annual Acm Symposium on Applied Computing, pp. 1938-1943 (2022)

26. Zhang, J., Li, Y.: Collaborative vehicle-drone distribution network optimization for perishable products in the epidemic situation. Comput. Operat. Res. 149, 106039 (2023)

27. Ghelichi, Z., Gentili, M., Mirchandani, P.B.: Drone logistics for uncertain demand of disaster-impacted populations. Trans. Res. Part C-Emerging Technol. 141, 103735 (2022)

28. Wu, S., Yang, Q., Yang, Z.: Integrating express package delivery service with offline mobile sales: a new potential solution to sustainable last-mile logistics in rural China. Inter. J. Logistics-Res. Appli. (2022)

29. Abu Zitar, R., Mohsen, A., Seghrouchni, A.E., Barbaresco, F., Al-Dmour, N.A.: Intensive review of drones detection and tracking: linear kalman filter versus nonlinear regression, an analysis case. Arch. Comput. Methods Eng. 30(5), 2811–2830 (2023)

30. Akbal, E., Akbal, A., Dogan, S., Tuncer, T.: An automated accurate sound-based amateur drone detection method based on skinny pattern. Digital Signal Process. 136, 104012 (2023)

31. Rongqi, J., Yang, Z., Yueping, P.A.: Review on intrusion drone target detection based on deep learning. In: 2021 IEEE 4th Advanced Information Management, Communicates, Electronic and Automation Control Conference (IMCEC), pp. 1032-1039 (2021)

32. Chen, Y., Aggarwal, P., Choi, J., Kuo, C.-.J.: A Deep Learning Approach to Drone Monitoring. In: 2017 Asia-Pacific Signal and Information Processing Association Annual Summit and Conference (APSIPA ASC 2017), pp. 686-691 (2017)

33. Kim-Phuong, P., Thai-Hoc, L., Trung-Thanh, N., Ngoc-Long, L., Huu-Hung, N., Van-Phuc, H.: Multi-model deep learning drone detection and tracking in complex background conditions. In: 2021 International Conference on Advanced Technologies for Communications (ATC), pp. 189-194 (2021)

34. Yi, K.Y., Kyeong, D., Seo, K.: Deep learning based drone detection and classification. Trans. Korean Instit. Elect. Eng. 68(2), 359–363 (2019)

35. Mandal, S., Satija, U.: Time-frequency multiscale convolutional neural network for rf-based drone detection and identification. IEEE Sensors Lett. 7(7), 7003304 (2023)

36. Cetin, E., Barrado, C., Pastor, E.: Countering a drone in a 3D space: analyzing deep reinforcement learning methods. Sensors 22(22), 8863 (2022)

37. Al-Emadi, S., Al-Ali, A., Al-Ali, A.: Audio-based drone detection and identification using deep learning techniques with dataset enhancement through generative adversarial networks. Sensors 21(15), 4953 (2021)

38. Gong, Y., Liu, X.: Flight state recognition for UAV optical flow velocity measurement. J. Phys: Conf. Ser. 012025, 9 (2023)

39. Li, J., Shen, D., Yu, F., Zhang, R.: Air channel planning based on improved deep Q-learning and artificial potential fields. Aerospace 10(9), 758 (2023)

40. Da Silva, D.L., Machado, R., Coutinho, O.L., Antreich, F.: A soft-kill reinforcement learning counter unmanned aerial system (c-uas) with accelerated training. IEEE Access **11**, 31496–31507 (2023)
41. Wu, M., Zhu, Z., Xia, Y., Yan, Z., Zhu, X., Ye, N.: A Q-learning-based two-layer cooperative intrusion detection for internet of drones system. Drones **7**(8), 502 (2023)
42. Hafeez, A., et al.: Implementation of drone technology for farm monitoring and pesticide spraying: a review. Inform. Proc. Agricult., 192-203 (2023)
43. Huang, Y.Y., Li, Z.-W., Yang, C.-H., Huang, Y.-M.: Automatic path planning for spraying drones based on deep Q-Learn. J. Internet Technol. **24**(3), 565–575 (2023)
44. Kok, Z.H., Shariff, A.R.M., Alfatni, M.S.M., Khairunniza-Bejo, S.: Support vector machine in precision agriculture: a review. Comput. Electr. Agricul. **191**, 106546 (2021)
45. Wei, P., et al.: early crop mapping based on sentinel-2 time-series data and the random forest algorithm. Rem. Sensing **15**(13), 3212 (2023)
46. Li, Y., Ercisli, S.: Data-efficient crop pest recognition based on KNN distance entropy. Sustainable Comput.-Inform. Syst. **38**, 100860 (2023)
47. Iqbal, U., Riaz, M.Z.B., Zhao, J., Barthelemy, J., Perez, P.: Drones for flood monitoring, mapping and detection: a bibliometric review. Drones **7**(1), 32 (2023)

Dual-System Recommendation Architecture for Adaptive Reading Intervention Platform for Dyslexic Learners

J. Ignacio Mateo-Trujillo[1,2], Diego Castillo-Barnés[1,2],
Ignacio Rodríguez-Rodríguez[1,2(✉)], Andrés Ortiz[1,2], Alberto Peinado[1,2],
Juan L. Luque[3], and Auxiliadora Sánchez-Gómez[3]

[1] Communications Engineering Department, University of Málaga,
29004 Málaga, Spain
jimateo@ic.uma.es, ignacio.rodriguez@uma.es
[2] Andalusian Data Science and Computational Intelligence Institute (DaSCI),
Granada, Spain
[3] Department of Developmental and Educational Psychology, University of Málaga,
29004 Málaga, Spain

Abstract. Dyslexia poses substantial literacy challenges with profound academic and psychosocial impacts for affected children. Though evidence affirms that early reading interventions can significantly improve outcomes, traditional one-size-fits-all approaches often fail to address readers' unique skill gaps. This study details an adaptive reading platform that customizes word recognition tasks to each learner's evolving abilities using embedded recommender engines. Initial standardized assessments categorize words by difficulty and cluster readers by competency level. An integrated word generator then expands the benchmark lexicon by algorithmically manipulating phonetic properties to modulate complexity. Dual intra-user and inter-user systems track learner performance to tailor content to individuals' pacing. Heuristic bootstrapping and simulated user data facilitate cold start recommendations and evaluate model robustness. Analysis of five virtual readers response patterns demonstrates platform reliability against volatility. Successive interventions display narrowing score dispersion alongside upwards literacy trajectories. Logarithmic score progressions signify responsive tuning to emerging mastery, accelerating advancement, and tapering gains as maximal outcomes reached. Results validate system effectiveness in optimizing challenge levels to unlock growth for neurological diversity. Rapid stabilization around optimal zones signifies an efficiently learned model while improved achievement confirms scaffolding precision. Learning curves substantiate tailored recommendation efficacy and signal user transitions from constructing new knowledge to demonstrative skill gains. Overall, the approach shows immense promise in administering personalized, engagement-focused reading support.

© The Author(s), under exclusive license to Springer Nature Switzerland AG 2024
J. M. Ferrández Vicente et al. (Eds.): IWINAC 2024, LNCS 14675, pp. 205–214, 2024.
https://doi.org/10.1007/978-3-031-61137-7_20

Keywords: Dyslexia · Reading Intervention · Adaptive
Recommendation Systems · Word Generator · Simulated Learner
Modeling

1 Introduction

Reading is a cornerstone of learning, yet for children with dyslexia, developing
competent reading skills poses immense challenges that profoundly impact their
academic trajectories and emotional wellbeing. Dyslexia is a specific learning disability affecting the learning of accurate and fluent word recognition despite adequate intelligence and educational opportunities. Core difficulties include phonological processing deficits, slow reading speed, and poor spelling [12].

It is imperative not to delay intervention until manifest reading failure
becomes evident [12]. Substantial research shows that evidence-based, intensive
reading interventions during early elementary years can significantly improve
the trajectory of children with dyslexia [15]. Targeted instruction in fundamental reading competencies such as phonological awareness, decoding, and word
recognition allows struggling readers to gain momentum instead of falling irre-
vocably behind grade-level expectations.

Current best practices endorse tiered reading interventions featuring iterative
assessment and incremental, skills-based instruction for readers with dyslexia [4].
Standard protocols specify baseline universal screenings to identify children at
risk for reading disorders, followed by increasing layers of small-group intervention for those requiring supplementary support. Adaptive intervention models
build on this frame-work but underscore the need to calibrate instruction directly
to each learner's strengths and skill gaps identified through progress monitoring [1]. This can be achieved with the most advanced techniques [7,8].

The personalized reading intervention trials are enabled by an automated
recommendation system that selects each word presented to readers based on
their individual performance profiles. The system leverages baseline universal
screenings and ongoing progress monitoring to tailor content difficulty to every
child's skills and challenges.

Initially, a comprehensive battery of reading assessments offers critical benchmarking insights. All participants complete standardized measures evaluating
word recognition accuracy, decoding skill, oral reading fluency, reading comprehension, phonological awareness, and rapid automatized naming [3,5]. By
comparing results across the cohort using exploratory analysis, researchers can
categorize words according to difficulty levels that generally align with children's
capabilities at each developmental stage.

The intervention trials themselves feature a word generator that transforms
the benchmark seed words into new vocabulary by applying systematic phonetic changes that introduce varying complexity [17]. Rules governing permissi-
ble alterations ensure all output retains coherence per the phonological patterns
of Spanish.

Crucially, the recommendation engine modulates word difficulty dynamically
for each readers over a series of brief reading tests using both intra-user and inter-

user recommendation systems [10]. Words are scored along two parameters: the baseline ranking inherited from seed words via the generator, and a correctness factor that increases/decreases difficulty respectively when reader succeed/fail on a given word.

By tracking user-specific scores in persistent matrices, the system personalizes content to each reader's pace of mastery. Matrix factorization techniques impute missing scores to address sparsity, thereby predicting optimal recommendations despite limited user histories.

2   Materials and Methods

2.1   Data and Exploratory Analysis

The dataset underpinning this research originates from a robust longitudinal study by the Leeduca Research Group investigating reading disabilities in children. Over the past decade, researchers have conducted recurring universal screenings of early elementary readers to trace development of linguistic competencies related to dyslexia [4]. The initiative adapts a response-to-intervention framework successful in the United States and Finland for systematic evaluation and tiered support provision [16].

Participants comprise several thousand children aged 4 to 10 years old attending public schools in Spain. Readers complete triannual standardized assessments evaluating phonological awareness, verbal short-term memory, rapid automatized naming, visual word recognition, phonological decoding skill, reading fluency, and reading comprehension [3].

For this study's reading intervention trials, researchers utilize data from a particular subset of reading inventory subtests using consistent stimuli. These fixed-form screenings pose the same series of words for each administration, allowing comparison of results across all readers tested. The expert-selected words covers beginner through advanced difficulty levels. Analysis of responses on these measures provides baseline difficulty rankings for the word generator's seed lexicon feeding the personalized intervention system.

Readers are clustered by their average response time percentile, with the bottom 30% categorized as delayed readers. Observing the two-dimensional distribution after applying principal component analysis, struggling readers concentrate in a distinct region, significantly lagging their peers in both accuracy and eficiency [14].

Beyond descriptive insights, the reading performance data enables customization of the intervention trials' difficulty levels aligned to readers' capabilities. Seed words are scored based on children's accuracy in recognizing words during the screenings. Words frequently missed earn higher difficulty ratings, while those easily identified receive lower scores.

Finally, this research implementation adheres to rigorous ethical standards regarding human subject research. The University of Malaga's medical ethical committee reviewed and approved the protocol for universal dyslexia screening and personalized reading intervention trials. Moreover, partnership with the

Andalusian regional Department of Education ensured cooperative participation from directors and teachers in the public schools surveyed. All collected data complies with European Union general data protection regulations regarding privacy and consent in research contexts.

2.2   Description of the Intervention Trial

Each iterative intervention task links to one of the baseline universal screening assessments by drawing its seed word pool from those vocabulary lists. As described previously, the screenings feature a set order of 100 words curated by dyslexia specialists to range from easy to advanced difficulty. The sequencing aims to build reader confidence by presenting simpler words initially, followed by more challenging content in the middle, and ending with some previously mastered words to avoid frustration [2].

At the start of an intervention trial, the system selects an opening word with a difficulty score calculated from the specific seeds that learner failed in his/her most recent screening. For readers who correctly identified all their screening words, the engine computes average metrics across all exposures within that activity. This customized starting calibration adjusts baseline word difficulty to every child's current capability.

Thereafter, the recommendation engine dynamically modulates word complexity contingent on performance within the intervention itself. Readers types the word presented on screen and the system codes responses as right or wrong, updating the difficulty score accordingly. This responsive process repeats until 80 new words are tested. At that point, the system transitions to present previously mastered words from the screening for the remainder of the 100 word activity.

2.3   Word Generator

A key enabler of the personalized reading intervention system is an integrated word generator module that algorithmically transforms seed words into new related words [17]. This expansion mechanism plays a vital role in bolstering the breadth and adaptability of word recommendations to meet each learner's needs.

The generator takes an input word and systematically applies modifications modeled on alterations known to impact reading difficulty for individuals with dyslexia. Examples include vowel replacement, consonant substitution, syllable insertion/removal, and stress position changes. Crucially, permitted manipulations adhere to Spanish language phonetic principles to ensure all output retains coherence and pronounceability [11].

The system applies user-defined constraints on the phonemic distance between input and output words based on a metric calculated from phonetic attribute positions. This aims to balance difficulty tuning with semantic consistency. Users can specify modification types to focus on consonant versus vowel alterations, inflecting complexity factors accordingly.

By overlaying these phonetic changes onto baseline word difficulty rankings, the generator expands recommendations along an enriched spectrum of challenges related to impaired phonological processing abilities underlying dyslexia [12]. Output mixes real words present in lexical databases with pseudowords. Expanding interventions beyond existing language extends personalization and bolsters skill building.

2.4   Embedded Intra/Inter-user Recommender Engines

Central to the adaptive reading intervention platform is a two-tiered recommendation engine that customizes word difficulty to each learner's evolving performance and challenges. The intra-user system leverages data accrued within a child's own trial sequence to modulate words selection responsively. This intra-user system consists of three matrices: M2, W2 and S2, all of the same dimensions (n x m, where n is the number of seed words and m is the number of permitted phonetic changes). M2 stores the evolving difficulty scores for words tested, W2 records the specific words mapped to each score, and S2 contains predicted scores for each unseen level of difficulty. Figure 1 explains the structure of the matrices.

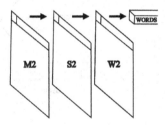

Fig. 1. Intra-user recommendation system. Data structure in parallel arrays

As readers complete intervention trials, their responses populate persistent matrices tracking word difficulty rankings along two parameters: the intrinsic complexity inherited from seed words and a dynamic correctness factor that increases or decreases difficulty when a given word is answered correctly or incorrectly [6]. Initially, M2 is empty since readers have not yet responded to generated words, and with the word generator, W2 is filled with all possible combinations that can be generated from the seed words. Thus, the system preemptively predicts scores for words not yet shown using a heuristic process to partially populate the matrix. Thereafter, the factorization method stochastic gradient descent (SGD) fills missing values to complete matrix S2 for personalized recommendations. This matrix enables lookup of appropriate difficulty levels. Mapping evolving performance to words items in this manner allows the system to home in on the optimal challenge point for each reader. However, with limited entries, these matrices become sparse. Matrix factorization via stochastic gradient descent imputes missing values to predict suitable recommendations despite cold-start limitations.

Recommendations are generated by searching a specified score representing the desired difficulty level to the matrix W2, which supplies phonetically related output words matching that target complexity. Adjusting this score point according to user responses and supplemental inter-user data provides the closed-loop adaptivity that personalizes interventions to every reader's zone of proximal development.

Additionally, an inter-user approach propagates insights across the broader user base to enhance personalization for readers with limited interaction histories. This collaborative filtering system features analogous M1, W1, and S1 matrices that leverage difficulty data from peer learners' experiences through the same SGD factorization technique. By accounting for crowd knowledge, the inter-user model compensates for cold start limitations when beginning trials with new participants. Figure 2 summarizes all the process.

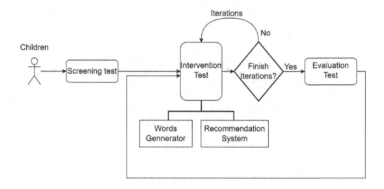

Fig. 2. General operating diagram of the recommender system

2.5   Surmounting Cold Start and Limited Data Hurdles

Two key challenges arose in developing the personalized reading intervention system: overcoming cold start limitations and augmenting limited real-world reader data. Thoughtful approaches to address these constraints enabled robust model training and evaluation.

Cold start refers to difficulties making recommendations due to insufficient user histories in the initial stages [9]. As readers undertake just a few trials, the intra-user performance matrices tracking per-word difficulty rankings remain sparse. To seed these matrices, the system incorporates a heuristic bootstrapping method that assigns pseudo-random difficulty scores to unevaluated word-change combinations. A correctness modulation factor then adjusts these placeholders based on learner responses. Once adequate samples accumulate, matrix factorization derives a complete score matrix for refined difficulty lookup.

The second obstacle involved expanding the dataset breadth needed to train and evaluate the dual recommender engines. To circumvent limited real-world reader coverage, the team adopted generative modeling techniques popularized for artificial data synthesis [13]. Specifically, we formulated parametric equations mirroring the aggregate performance distribution patterns uncovered in existing trial sequences, using logistic curves. By tuning equation parameters, researchers could simulate realistic virtual readers manifesting the spectrum of attested learning trajectories.

Crucially, introducing controlled variability into the generative formulas avoids simply replicating the same response sequences. This yields sufficiently distinct virtual learners following plausible achievement growth trends [13].

3   Results

A pivotal metric assessing model robustness tracks variability in aggregated user performance over successive interventions. Figure 4 illustrates the entropy or dispersion of total correct responses decreasing as trials advance. Narrowing variability between virtual learners signifies the platform's reliability against volatile user inputs (Fig. 3).

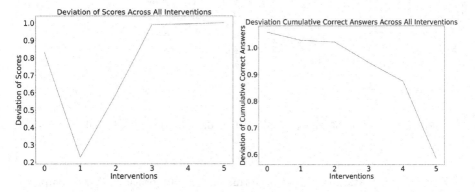

Fig. 3. Standard deviation of scores   **Fig. 4.** Standard deviation accumulated successes

Specifically, the system demonstrates responsiveness stability by distinguishing genuine capability growth from stochastic performance fluctuations. Tight reattunement to evolving comprehension acts as a check against overfitting to spurious input spikes.

In effect, narrowing dispersion reaffirms dual effectiveness: reliable tuning maintains learner-appropriate challenge levels to enhance outcomes, while avoidance of over-correction signifies noise-tolerance crucial for practical deployment.

A pivotal objective within the adaptive intervention trials is expediting learner convergence to optimal recommendation stability. As readers undertake successive words challenges, the system progressively homes in on difficulty levels targeting each individual's zone of proximal development. Rapid attunement marks a key performance indicator, affirming responsive model recalibration based on incremental mastery.

Prompt stabilization holds manifold significance for system efficacy and readers outcomes alike. On the computational side, accelerated tuning via steepest-gradient matrix factorization signifies an efficiently learned learner model. Behaviorally, narrowing the gap between a child's current capabilities and the tool's estimations enables properly scaffolded content to stimulate skill advancement.

So, by rapidly converging stability around optimal challenge levels, the intervention both fulfills its adaptivity premises and creates conditions conducive to literacy advancement in neurodiverse learners. Preliminary usage trends underscore promising outcomes from this learner-centered, growth-oriented approach. This process can be seen in Fig. 5 and Fig. 6.

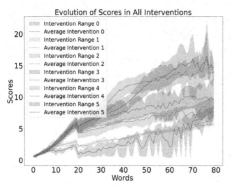

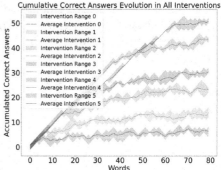

Fig. 5. Evolution of scores

Fig. 6. Evolution of accumulated successes

Rigorous evaluation of model performance and adaptation efficacy employs data from five simulated readers per trial iteration. As illustrated, deviation bands establish that recommended difficulty levels fluctuate within consistent boundaries over successive interventions for these reliable virtual profiles. Narrow oscillations signify the platform's robustness against erratic responses in maintaining calibrated content difficulty tuned to evolving learner development.

Additionally, (Table 1 and Table 2) aggregated metrics document marked improvements in multiple engagement and learning indicators as interventions progress. For example, words recognition rates across the cohort climbed nearly 20% over six simulated trial sequences.

Critically, these trends dispel fears that overly responsive difficulty tuning might foster user dependency on the system. Rather, manufactured volatility in

Table 1. Deviation Successes and Scores max mean by intervention (1–3).

Intervention	Deviation	Scores Max Mean
1	1.057	7.612
2	1.027	5.701
3	1.021	8.762

Table 2. Deviation Successes and Scores max mean by intervention (4–6).

Intervention	Deviation	Scores Max Mean
4	0.944	10.259
5	0.874	16.021
6	0.585	16.507

the synthetic response patterns confirms the engine's facility in distinguishing genuine achievement advances from stochastic perturbations.

Analysis of scored longitudinal data reveals performance improvements following a logarithmic progression over successive interventions. Initially, gains accumulate gradually as the recommendation engine incrementally recalibrates to reader proficiency level. After sufficient trials for system attunement and skill solidification alike, advancement accelerates notably.

As proficiency stabilizes, enhancement rates taper, suggesting users approach maximal achievable outcomes for their profile. Such growth deceleration signals user transition from active construction of new knowledge scaffolds to demonstrative fluency gains through reinforced practice.

4   Conclusions

This study details a personalized reading intervention platform that tailors presented words to the distinctive needs and evolving skills of struggling beginner readers. The dual recommendation architecture, integrating intra-user and inter-user engines, enables responsive tuning of word recognition exercise difficulty based on individual performance. Supplemental simulated learner modeling facilitates cold start recommendations and evaluates system robustness. Multiple experiments resoundingly validate effectiveness on key indicators. Narrowing accumulated successes dispersion across virtual profiles over successive trials signifies reliability against volatile responses while upholding stability in difficulty calibration to match users' proximal development. Logarithmic achievement trajectories characterize incremental tuning to emergent competencies, driving demonstrable accuracy gains until maximal literacy potential reached. Broadly, results endorse the feasibility of automated, adaptive platforms for unlocking literacy in neurodiverse populations.

Ongoing efforts emphasize honing recommendation velocity to prolong periods of steep advancement. Enhanced customization through supplementary dataset integration also holds immense potential to boost outcomes. On the computational side, optimized matrix factorization algorithms promise more elegant balancing of exploration and exploitation tradeoffs endemic to personalized learning systems.

This research marks a pivotal moment for assistive technologies, promising transformative impacts for millions of dyslexic children globally through its innovative approach and potential for widespread application.

Acknowledgments. This research is part of the TED2021-132261B-I00 funded by MICIU/AEI/10.13039/501100011033 and by European Union NextGenerationEU/PRTR as well as UMA20-FEDERJA-086 (Consejería de Economía y Conocimiento, Junta de Andalucía) and by European Regional Development Funds (ERDF). Work by D.C.-B. is supported by the MICIU/AEI/FJC2021-048082-I 'Juan de la Cierva Formacion' grant. Work by I.R.-R. is funded by Plan Andaluz de Investigación, Desarrollo e Innovación (PAIDI), Junta de Andalucía.

References

1. Al Otaiba, S., et al.: To wait in tier 1 or intervene immediately: a randomized experiment examining first-grade response to intervention in reading. Except. Child. **81**(1), 11–27 (2014)
2. Allington, R.L.: What really matters when working with struggling readers. Read. Teach. **66**(7), 520–530 (2013)
3. Babiloni, C., et al.: Cortical sources of resting state EEG rhythms are abnormal in dyslexic children. Clin. Neurophysiol. **123**(12), 2384–2391 (2012)
4. Compton, D.L., Fuchs, D., Fuchs, L.S., Bryant, J.D.: Selecting at-risk readers in first grade for early intervention: a two-year longitudinal study of decision rules and procedures. J. Educ. Psychol. **98**(2), 394 (2006)
5. De Vos, A., Vanvooren, S., Vanderauwera, J., Ghesquiere, P., Wouters, J.: A longitudinal study investigating neural processing of speech envelope modulation rates in children with (a family risk for) dyslexia. Cortex **93**, 206–219 (2017)
6. Eckert, T.L., Hier, B.O., Hamsho, N.F., Malandrino, R.D.: Assessing children's perceptions of academic interventions: the kids intervention profile. Sch. Psychol. Q. **32**(2), 268 (2017)
7. Górriz, J.M., et al.: Computational approaches to explainable artificial intelligence: advances in theory, applications and trends. Inform. Fusion **100**, 101945 (2023)
8. Górriz, J.M., et al.: Artificial intelligence within the interplay between natural and artificial computation: advances in data science, trends and applications. Neurocomputing **410**, 237–270 (2020). https://doi.org/10.1016/j.neucom.2020.05.078
9. Lika, B., Kolomvatsos, K., Hadjiefthymiades, S.: Facing the cold start problem in recommender systems. Expert Syst. Appl. **41**(4), 2065–2073 (2014)
10. Lops, P., De Gemmis, M., Semeraro, G.: Content-based recommender systems: state of the art and trends. Recommender Systems Handbook, pp. 73–105 (2011)
11. Muñoz-Basols, J., Lacorte, M.: Lingüística hispánica actual: guía didáctica y materiales de apoyo. Routledge (2017)
12. Peterson, R.L., Pennington, B.F.: Developmental dyslexia. The lancet **379**(9830), 1997–2007 (2012)
13. Prottasha, N.J., et al.: Transfer learning for sentiment analysis using BERT based supervised fine-tuning. Sensors **22**(11), 4157 (2022)
14. Scarborough, H.S.: Predicting the future achievement of second graders with reading disabilities: contributions of phonemic awareness, verbal memory, rapid naming, and iq. Ann. Dyslexia **48**, 115–136 (1998)
15. Simmons, D.C., Coyne, M.D., Kwok, O.m., McDonagh, S., Harn, B.A., Kame'enui, E.J.: Indexing response to intervention: a longitudinal study of reading risk from kindergarten through third grade. J. Learn. Disabil. **41**(2), 158–173 (2008)
16. Vaughn, S., Fletcher, J.M.: Response to intervention with secondary school students with reading difficulties. J. Learn. Disabil. **45**(3), 244–256 (2012)
17. Whitney, C., Cornelissen, P.: Letter-position encoding and dyslexia. J. Res. Read. **28**(3), 274–301 (2005)

Accurate LiDAR-Based Semantic Classification for Powerline Inspection

J. Luna-Santamaria$^{(\boxtimes)}$, I.G. Rodríguez, J.R. Martínez-de Dios, and A. Ollero

University of Seville, Seville 41004, Spain
{javierluna,igrodriguez,jdedios,aollero}@us.es

Abstract. Mandatory power grid inspection includes the periodic measurement of the distances between vegetation and electrical assets. This paper presents an efficient and accurate method for segmenting LiDAR-based maps leveraging both LiDAR reflectivity and point cloud geometric information to classify points into *Powerline, Tower, Vegetation*, and *Soil*. It is based on two steps: 1) initial online segmentation using the LiDAR reflectivity and local point cloud spatial distribution and 2) offline segmentation refinement using the cloud global spatial distribution. The method obtains a very accurate classification and enables accurate measurement of distances from vegetation to the electrical assets. Its performance was evaluated in sets of powerline inspection experiments in two power grid scenarios with different conditions and vegetation.

Keywords: LiDAR segmentation · Unmanned Aerial Systems

1 Introduction

There is a strong demand to develop automated cost-effective solutions to automatize powerline inspection tasks. Power grid inspection has been traditionally performed by teams of workers climbing or using cranes or man-fits to access the electric lines and assets, involving extensive manpower in highly dangerous environments. One mandatory inspection task is to measure the distances between vegetation and the electrical lines and towers. Different aerial vehicles including manned and unmanned helicopters [1], Vertical Take-Off and Landing (VTOL) vehicles [2], and quadrotors [3] have been used. Quadrotors have been endowed with capacity of perching on powerlines to recharge their batteries [4] to extend flight endurance. These vehicles first collect 3D LiDAR (Light Detection And Ranging) point clouds and images of the surroundings of the powerline. Later, days or weeks after the recording, the registered data is processed to build vegetation maps and measure vegetation-power assets distances. This procedure is very inefficient, and requires repeating data gathering if in the analysis the collected data is found to be of insufficient quality for the inspection.

Some mapping techniques capable of online obtaining 3D maps for powerline inspection have been developed, see e.g. [5]. This paper proposes an efficient LiDAR-only processing method for segmenting 3D powerline maps and extracting accurate measurements of the distances between vegetation and powerlines

J. M. Ferrández Vicente et al. (Eds.): IWINAC 2024, LNCS 14675, pp. 215–224, 2024.
https://doi.org/10.1007/978-3-031-61137-7_21

and electrical towers. The method segments *Powerlines*, *Towers*, *Vegetation*, and *Soil* by leveraging the LiDAR's point cloud reflectivity and spatial distribution in two steps. First, the LiDAR scans are online processed classifying points into the four possible classes. Second, a global refinement step enhances the online segmentation to ensure accurate distance measurements. Finally, the proposed method measures the distance between each vegetation point and the nearest point of a powerline or tower. Potential risks are assessed according to different distance ranges, which can be customized depending on the requirements. The proposed scheme is very accurate, robust for everyday operation, and efficient. It has been implemented in C++ using PCL and ROS Noetic, and validated in powerline inspection experiments conducted in different environments and type of vegetation.

This paper is organized as follows. Section 2 briefly summarizes the main works related to the paper. Section 3 describes the proposed method and its components. The experimental validation is presented in Sect. 4. Finally, Sect. 5 closes the paper and highlights the main future research.

2   Related Work

Significant R&D effort has been devoted to automatic object segmentation for powerline inspection. LiDARs and cameras are the most widely applied sensors. Most segmentation methods for powerline inspection are based on the geometry of the point clouds. Work [6] proposes a learning method based on Markov Random Fields to assign semantic labels to point cloud segments. Work [7] segments powerlines using skeleton structure extraction and construction of 3D voxels. Other methods use heuristic information leveraging geometric fitting. For instance, [8] proposed an unified energy function over objectiveness and geometry fitting in indoor and office environments.

In recent years Deep Learning (DL) has been applied to powerline segmentation. Work [9] segments LiDAR point clouds into categories ground, vegetation, electrical tower, and building using Convolutional Neural Networks (CNNs). Work [10] proposes the use of a global-local Graph Attention CNN to segment towers, powerlines, low vegetation, and others. Although these methods have solid performance, they have high computational cost that constraints online onboard execution. In addition, DL requires labour-intensive training stages and large annotated datasets, which involve additional operational difficulties.

Some few methods complement the LiDAR point cloud geometrical information with reflectivity information. Work [11] leverages the LiDAR point reflectivity to detect and classify traffic signs using an optimized intensity threshold and contour recognition. Work [12] models the LiDAR reflection return to determine the properties of the scanned surface. Other methods perform the segmentation using mainly visual information. Work [13] uses a multilayer perceptron for tower detection and classification using two multi-layer perceptron neural networks. Work [14] applies DL-based segmentation to RGB images used to create the point cloud and back-projects the pixel class in segmented images onto the LiDAR 3D points. Work [15] uses DL scheme based on featured pyramid networks and YOLACT to detect electrical elements. Work [16] proposed a deep neural Fully Convolutional Network (FCN). There are also methods that combine point cloud geometry and visual information. Work [17] fuses features extracted from the RGB image together with LiDAR data and feed them to a CNN for object segmentation. Work [18] shows that fusing LiDAR data and visual images improves the detection performance especially at long ranges.

Despite the significant effort, the high computational cost of existing LiDAR-based segmentation methods prevents their use for onboard online inspection.

3 Method

The proposed approach adapts the method described in [19] to separate the map points in four different classes: *Powerline*, *Tower*, *Vegetation*, and *Soil*. Similarly to [19], to distinguish among each category, we consider point cloud spatial distribution and take advantage of the fact that metallic and no metallic points tend to present different reflectivity values (r). Despite the remarkable results achieved by [19], its geometrical analysis of the metallic points is based solely on their local neighborhood. Object segmentation is used to measure the distances between objects classified as *Vegetation*, and *Powerline* and *Tower*. A single misclassified *Tower* or *Powerline* point can cause unacceptable errors in those distances. In general, it is not possible to ensure accurate classification of every point using solely local geometry, and online segmentation does not take advantage of the global geometry of the environment, that is required to refine the segmentation. Hence, to avoid these problems, our method includes a post processing step that considers global geometrical information to refine point classification. The proposed method consists of two steps. First, *Online Segmentation* processes in real-time consecutive scans to obtain a coarse classification the points among the four classes. Second, *Full Map Refinement* step refines the initial classifications by identifying the different elements of the map and checking the fulfillment of different properties related to their geometry and distribution.

3.1 Online Segmentation

Figure 1 shows the processing pipeline of this stage. First, N consecutive LiDAR scans are accumulated to obtain a denser representation of the environment. Online segmentation starts with the extraction of soil points, given their predominant presence in the scans. To achieve this, the accumulated points are fitted to a plane using RANSAC algorithm and those contained in the surface are classified as *Soil*.

Once the soil is segmented, the remaining points are first analysed by their reflectivity. Points with reflectivity below T_r are considered as metallic points, otherwise they are classified as *Vegetation*. Next, taking advantage of spatial geometrical information, the points belonging to class *Powerline* should be those

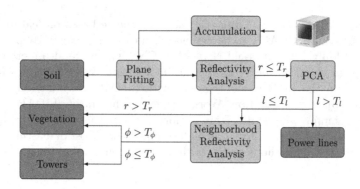

Fig. 1. Processing pipeline of *Online Segmentation*.

that are distributed most distinctly along a single direction within the set of metallic points. Thus, by conducting a Principal Component Analysis (PCA), a linearity metric l can be computed with the resulting eigenvalues, see Eq. 1. For each potential metallic point p_i, PCA is applied to the set of potential metallic points, whose distance to p_i is below a value R_l, see Eq. 2. Points p_i with high linearity, $l > T_l$, are classified as *Powerline*.

$$l = \frac{\lambda_1}{\lambda_2 + \lambda_3} \tag{1}$$

$$\text{PCA}\{\{n : \|p_i - n\| \leq R_l\}\}, \forall i \tag{2}$$

Finally, the remaining points are a combination of tower and vegetation points. We rely on the predominance of high reflectivity points around true vegetation points to perform an initial segmentation of towers. For each point p, we obtain the sets n_h and n_l with the points whose distance to p is below a value R_t and have respectively high and low reflectivity values. Then, we calculate the metric $\phi = \frac{|n_h|}{|n_l|}$. If point p has $\phi > T_\phi$, it is classified as *Tower*. Otherwise, p is classified as *Vegetation*. *Online Segmentation* provides an initial classification of every point from every LiDAR scan, which is then refined in *Full Map Refinement* to achieve an accurate final segmented map.

3.2   Full Map Refinement

Given the large number of points produced by the soil and the consistency of the planar soil hypothesis, the soil segmentation performed in *Online Segmentation* is significantly accurate and robust. *Full Map Refinement* does not perform refinements on the soil cloud; it only downsamples it to reduce the computational cost and enhance visualization. Conversely, the input vegetation, powerline, and tower clouds (obtained by *Online Segmentation*) present a large number of misclassifications since the local information used in *Online Segmentation* is not enough to ensure accurate segmentation. The processing scheme of *Full Map Refinement* is shown in Fig. 2. First, it processes the input powerline and tower clouds (resulting from *Online Segmentation*) to reject the points that are not caused by powerlines or towers. This results in the ensured powerlines cloud and the ensured towers cloud. Second, these two ensured clouds are used to accurately classify all the points in all the input clouds.

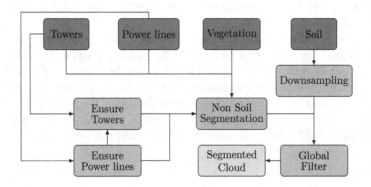

Fig. 2. Processing pipeline of *Full Map Refinement*.

The input powerline cloud created by *Online Segmentation* includes misclassified vegetation and tower points. All the vegetation points in this cloud are rejected by obtaining clusters and studying their geometry with PCA. A clustering method based on Euclidean distance is applied to obtain clusters of nearby points. Next, the class of each cluster is assigned. Powerline clusters can be easily distinguished from vegetation clusters using PCA given their very high linearity. Hence, all the clusters which meet the linearity condition $l > T_{el}$ are merged and classified as *Powerline*. The rest of the points are removed. The resulting cloud (ensured powerlines) has no vegetation but can include some few points originated by towers. Although most of them are discarded in this step, some tower points might have been included in the cloud. These misclassifications are rejected after processing of the tower cloud, which is described as follows.

Most misclassifications in the input tower cloud correspond to vegetation. Since towers have linear geometry, they can be distinguished from vegetation by also using clustering and PCA. The clustering is also based on the Euclidean distance. However, it is not possible to reject all vegetation clusters using only PCA-based criteria since tower clusters do not exhibit the same level of linearity as powerline clusters. To distinguish them, we exploit the fact that towers are in contact with powerlines, and add an additional condition regarding the connectivity with powerlines. Joining both conditions, a cluster is ensured as *Tower* if it satisfies: 1) a linearity higher than T_{et}, and 2) a distance to a powerline point below d_{et}. The resulting cloud is the ensured towers cloud.

Once we have obtained the ensured powerlines and towers clouds, they are used to classify every point in all the input clouds (resulting from *Online Segmentation*). The processing of the input powerline cloud is as follows. For each point we compute the distance to the nearest point in the ensured towers cloud.

If that distance is lower than a refinement distance d_r, the point is definitely classified as *Tower*. Otherwise, it is considered as caused by a powerline and, classified as *Powerline*. The processing of the input vegetation cloud is similar. If the distance from a point in the input vegetation cloud to its closest point in the towers cloud is lower than d_r, it is classified as *Tower*. Otherwise, it is classified as *Vegetation*. The processing of the input tower cloud is similar –and not repeated for brevity.

Lastly, we perform a global filtering to correct minor misclassifications. The vegetation cloud can include points caused by grass that appear surrounded by soil points and disturb visualization. They are simply removed. The vegetation cloud also includes some spurious points at the locations of powerlines and towers caused by the effect of surface roughness on reflectivity. We perform a statistical fashion filter to re-assign the class of these points with the most frequent class among its local neighbourhood (points within a distance lower than d_r).

4   Validation

The proposed segmentation method was implemented in C++ using PCL and ROS Noetic, and validated in different environments with the *LR-M* aerial robot developed by the GRVC Robotics Lab from the University of Seville, see Fig. 3. Based on the DJI Matrice 600 platform, *LR-M* is equipped with a Livox Horizon 3D LiDAR pointing at a pitch angle of 40°. The input of the proposed method is the registered LiDAR clouds of the mapping algorithm FAST-LIO2 [20], which showed the best performance in [5]. The parameters mentioned in Sect. 3 were set

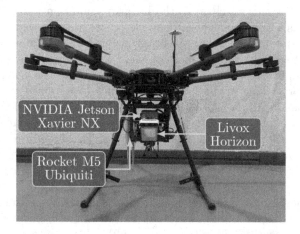

Fig. 3. *LR-M* aerial robot used in the experiments.

Table 1. Values of the method parameters used in the experimental results.

Online		Refinement	
Parameter	Value	Parameter	Value
N	5	T_{el}	0.99
T_r	13	T_{et}	0.68
T_l	0.90	d_{et}	0.05 m
T_ϕ	4	d_r	1.5 m
R_l	0.4 m		
R_t	1.5 m		

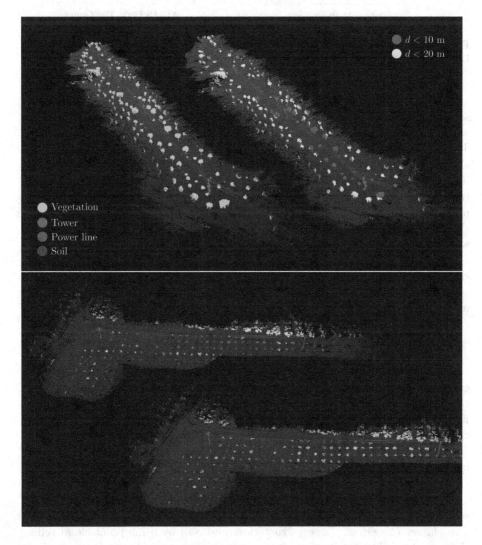

Fig. 4. Segmented maps and automatic distance measurement results in two scenarios: top) Doñana National Park, and bottom) ATLAS Flight Test Center.

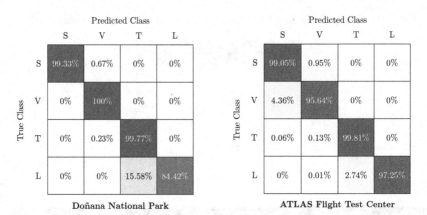

Fig. 5. Resulting confusion matrices from full map segmentation in two scenarios: left) Doñana National Park, and right) ATLAS Flight Test Center.

as shown in Table 1. Several experiments were conducted in different challenging scenarios: Doñana National Park (Andalusia, Spain), in which there is a tower with some sensors and solar panels, and ATLAS Flight Test Center (Villacarrillo, Jaen, Spain), which includes a plastic hanging from a powerline to emulate a foreign object in contact with the powerline. Figure 4 shows the resulting semantic map in one experiment in each site. After segmentation, we measured the distances between vegetation points and tower and powerline points. The vegetation points whose distance to powerline points or tower points is lower than 10 m are shown in red colour, reflecting high risk. And those with distance between 10 and 20 m are shown in yellow, medium risk.

Accurate distance measurement necessarily requires very robust point classification. We compared the results of our method with a ground truth obtained by manually labelling the point clouds. Figure 5 shows the resulting confusion matrices in both experiments. The diagonal of these matrices has values very close to 100% evidencing the very high *True Positive* rates achieved. Remarkably for our application, the very few misclassified points only occur between soil and vegetation, or between powerlines and towers. No points caused by soil or vegetation are erroneously classified as powerlines or towers. Conversely, for powerline and towers classification, there are only some scarce points representing in the worst case 0.23% of misclassifications between these and soil or vegetation. Errors in distinguishing within powerlines and towers occur only at points very close to their intersection.

5   Conclusions

This paper presented a processing method for efficient LiDAR-only point cloud segmentation in powerline inspection. The method classifies each LiDAR point into classes *Powerline*, *Tower*, *Vegetation*, and *Soil* by using point cloud reflectivity and spatial distribution. It consists of two steps. First, the points are online classified using LiDAR reflectivity and local spatial distribution information. Second, the method leverages the point cloud global spatial distribution to refine the initial segmentation ensuring accurate classification. The method has been experimentally evaluated in two powerline environments with different types of objects and vegetation. It achieved an exceptional classification accuracy in which no points caused by soil or vegetation are misclassified as powerlines or towers, hence enabling accurate automatic measurement of distances from vegetation to the electrical assets. Extending the validation to a wider range of power grids environments is object of current development.

Acknowledgments. This work was supported by the R+D+i project TED2021-131716B-C22, funded by MCIN/AEI/10.13039/501100011033 and by the European Union NextGenerationEU/PRTR. This work was also supported by Spanish project RESISTO (2021/C005/00144188) funded by FEDER (Fondo Europeo de Desarrollo Regional) from Ministerio de Asuntos Económicos y Transformación Digital.

References

1. Li, H., Wang, B., Liu, L., Tian, G., Zheng, T., Zhang, J.: The design and application of smartcopter: an unmanned helicopter based robot for transmission line inspection. Chin. Automat. Congress, 697–702 (2013)
2. de Britto Vidal Filho, W., de Almeida Pinto, A.M.: Vtol aerial robot for inspection of transmission line. In: Proceedings of International Conference on Applied Robotics for the Power Industry, pp. 1–4 (2014)
3. Takaya, K., Ohta, H., Kroumov, V., Shibayama, K., Nakamura, M.: Development of uav system for autonomous power line inspection. In: Int, Control and Computing, Conference on System Theory (2019)
4. Paneque, J., Martínez-de Dios, J., Ollero, A., Hanover, D., Sun, S., Romero, A., Scaramuzza, D.: Perception-aware perching on powerlines with multirotors. IEEE Robot. Autom. Lett. **7**(2), 3077–3084 (2022)
5. Paneque, J., Valseca, V., Martínez-de Dios, J. R., Ollero, A.: Autonomous reactive lidar-based mapping for powerline inspection. In: International Conference on Unmanned Aircraft Systems (2022)
6. Perez-Perez, Y., Golparvar-Fard, M., El-Rayes, K.: Segmentation of point clouds via joint semantic and geometric features for 3d modeling of the built environment. Autom. Constr. **125**, 103584 (2021)
7. Yang, J., Kang, Z.: Voxel-based extraction of transmission lines from airborne lidar point cloud data. IEEE J. Selected Topics Appli. Earth Observat. Rem. Sens. **11**(10), 3892–3904 (2018)
8. Pham, T.T., Do, T.-T., Sünderhauf, N., Reid, I.: Scenecut: joint geometric and object segmentation for indoor scenes. In: IEEE International Conference on Robotics and Automation, pp. 3213–3220. IEEE (2018)
9. Pu, S.: Real-time powerline corridor inspection by edge computing of uav lidar data. The Int. Archives of Photogr., Remote Sensing & Spatial Inform. Sci. **42**, 547–551 (2019)
10. Wen, C., Li, X., Yao, X., Peng, L., Chi, T.: Airborne lidar point cloud classification with global-local graph attention convolution neural network. ISPRS J. Photog. Remote Sens. **173**, 181–194 (2021)

11. Riveiro, B., Díaz-Vilariño, L., Conde-Carnero, B., Soilán, M., Arias, P.: Automatic segmentation and shape-based classification of retro-reflective traffic signs from mobile lidar data. IEEE J. Selected Topics Appli. Earth Observat. Remote Sens. 9(1), 295–303 (2015)

12. Tatoglu, A., Pochiraju, K.: Point cloud segmentation with lidar reflection intensity behavior. In: IEEE International Conference on Robotics and Automation, pp. 786–790 (2012)

13. Sampedro, C., Martinez, C., Chauhan, A., Campoy, P.: A supervised approach to electric tower detection and classification for power line inspection. In: International Joint Conference on Neural Networks, pp. 1970–1977 (2014)

14. WuDunn, M., Dunn, J., Zakhor, A.: Point cloud segmentation using rgb drone imagery. In: International Conference on Image Processing, pp. 2750–2754 (2020)

15. Vemula, S., Frye, M.: Real-time powerline detection system for an unmanned aircraft system. In: International Conference on Systems, Man, and Cybernetics, pp. 4493–4497 (2020)

16. Li, B., Chen, C., Dong, S., Qiao, J.: Transmission line detection in aerial images: an instance segmentation approach based on multitask neural networks. Signal Processing: Image Commun. 96, 116278 (2021)

17. Krispel, G., Opitz, M., Waltner, G., Possegger, H., Bischof, H.: Fuseseg: lidar point cloud segmentation fusing multi-modal data. In: IEEE/CVF Winter Conference on Applications of Computer Vision, pp. 1874–1883 (2020)

18. Meyer, G.P., Charland, J., Hegde, D., Laddha, A., Vallespi-Gonzalez, C.: Sensor fusion for joint 3d object detection and semantic segmentation. In: Proceedings IEEE/CVF Conference on Computer Vision and Pattern Recognition (2019)

19. Valseca, V., Paneque, J., Martínez-de Dios, J., Ollero, A.: Real-time lidar-based semantic classification for powerline inspection. In: International Conference on Unmanned Aircraft Systems, pp. 478–486 (2022)

20. Xu, W., Cai, Y., He, D., Lin, J., Zhang, F.: Fast-lio2: fast direct lidar-inertial odometry. IEEE Trans. Rob. 38(4), 2053–2073 (2022)

RESISTO Project: Automatic Detection of Operation Temperature Anomalies for Power Electric Transformers Using Thermal Imaging

David López-García[1]([✉]), Fermín Segovia[1], Jacob Rodríguez-Rivero[3],
Javier Ramírez[1], David Pérez[2], Raúl Serrano[2], and Juan Manuel Górriz[1]

[1] Department of Signal Theory, Networking and Communications,
University of Granada, Granada, Spain
dlopez@ugr.es
[2] ATIS Soluciones & Seguridad, Granada, Spain
[3] e-Distribución Redes Digitales, Madrid, Spain

Abstract. The RESISTO project represents a pioneering initiative in Europe aimed at enhancing the resilience of the power grid through the integration of advanced technologies. This includes artificial intelligence and thermal surveillance systems to mitigate the impact of extreme meteorological phenomena. RESISTO endeavors to predict, prevent, detect, and recover from weather-related incidents, ultimately enhancing the quality of service provided and ensuring grid stability and efficiency in the face of evolving climate challenges. In this study, we introduce one of the fundamental pillars of the project: a monitoring system for the operating temperature of different regions within power transformers, aiming to detect and alert early on potential thermal anomalies. To achieve this, a distributed system of thermal cameras for real-time temperature monitoring has been deployed in The Doñana National Park, alongside servers responsible for the storing, analyzing, and alerting of any potential thermal anomalies. An adaptive prediction model was developed for temperature forecasting, which learns online from the newly available data. In order to test the long-term performance of the proposed solution, we generated a synthetic temperature database for the whole of the year 2022. Overall, the proposed system exhibits promising capabilities in predicting and detecting thermal anomalies in power electric transformers, showcasing potential applications in enhancing grid reliability and preventing equipment failures.

Keywords: RESISTO project · Anomaly detection · Smart grids · Machine learning · Thermal imaging · Electric Power Transformers

1 Introduction

1.1 Introduction to the RESISTO Project

The sixth report [1] prepared by the Intergovernmental Panel on Climate Change of the United Nations (IPCC) highlights that meteorological phenomena are

J. M. Ferrández Vicente et al. (Eds.): IWINAC 2024, LNCS 14675, pp. 225–245, 2024.
https://doi.org/10.1007/978-3-031-61137-7_22

becoming increasingly extreme and frequent due to global warming. According to the report, these changes in weather patterns are posing significant challenges to communities worldwide. This trend has been the catalyst for the development of the RESISTO project[1] which aims to ensure that electrical grids are prepared to mitigate and reduce the impact of these extreme meteorological phenomena.

Under the leadership of Endesa's Grids subsidiary, e-distribución, the RESISTO project stands as a groundbreaking technological innovation and research transfer initiative in Europe. Its primary objective is to enhance the power grid of the Doñana National Park, located in Andalusia, in the south of Spain, through the innovative integration of artificial intelligence and a comprehensive array of cutting-edge technologies. These include thermal surveillance cameras, weather stations, fire sensors, and an autonomous drone fleet. By leveraging these advancements, the RESISTO project aims to mitigate the adverse effects of weather-related phenomena, such as extreme heat, wind, water, and other potential risks on the power grid, which elevates the quality of service provided to the region. To achieve this goal, RESISTO has proposed a pioneering solution focusing on four crucial areas:

1. Planning: Utilizing AI and Big Data for prediction and prevention, identifying high-risk areas prone to incidents during specific weather conditions.
2. Detection: Monitoring the grid using sensors, thermal cameras, and surveillance equipment to control vegetation growth.
3. Recovery: Employing AI and a fleet of drones for real-time incident location and providing crucial support for operational and maintenance tasks, especially in remote or hard-to-access areas.
4. Adaptation through continuous learning of the machine-learning algorithm implemented, which will be fed with the acquired data to enhance the grid's resilience and efficiency over time.

As the largest electricity company in Spain and one of the largest in the world (serving millions of customers in Spain and several other countries), Endesa and all the public and private institutions involved in the project, bring unparalleled expertise to the endeavor.

1.2 Mitigating Transformer Risks in Electricity Networks

The oversight of electricity networks demands meticulous consideration towards potential overloads [2,3], given their prominence as a significant source of issues impacting power transformers, responsible for approximately 12% of total failures [4]. Specially, transformer malfunctions pose a considerable hazard, capable of igniting fires that, given the urban positioning of transformers, can lead to severe economic and personal ramifications [5]. In recent years, different reports examining the likelihood of failure in power transformer components have been

---

[1] Official website: https://www.endesa.com/en/press/press-room/news/energy-sector/endesa-presents-pioneering-project-europe-reduce-negative-effects-weather-power-grid.

published by various authors and international organizations [6–9]. Among these organizations, the International Council on Large Electric Systems (CIGRE) has categorized failure types into six distinct categories based on the component responsible for the failure [10]: winding (38%), tap changer (31%), bushing (17%), auxiliary (11%) core (1%) and tank (1%). In order to mitigate these failures, beyond routine maintenance of installations, a series of measurement should be conducted regularly. These, among others [11] encompass monitoring operational temperatures [12]. Consequently, the measurement of both transformer and ambient temperature constitutes a fundamental component of standard protocols for power transformer monitoring [13,14]. These parameters are pivotal variables that necessitate accurate and uninterrupted measurement and can further serve as predictors for other variables, such as reactive power or current intensity [15].

Early failure prevention techniques in the electrical grid, as well as a significant reduction in associated risks, are closely linked to artificial intelligence techniques that allow us to identify and notify of these failures. Artificial intelligence, and more specifically, big data and machine learning, have made a strong impact in various sectors of society in recent years [16,17] This includes several and diverse areas such as autonomous transportation [18], neuroscience [19–21], healthcare [22,23] or automatic text translation [24]. The management of the electrical grid has also been heavily influenced by the emergence of artificial intelligence. For example, these techniques provide the electrical grid with the capability to make intelligent decisions in response to sudden changes in customer energy demand, abrupt increases or decreases in renewable energy production, or extreme weather phenomena. With the increase in data volume, it is also possible to employ machine learning for the detection and prevention of anomalous behaviour [25,26].

In this article, we describe and discuss the development of one of the core modules of the RESISTO project: the monitoring of the thermal performance of power electric transformers. The proposed solution integrates a distributed network of thermal cameras strategically positioned to capture real-time thermal data across various installations. To achieve this, we employ adaptive machine learning algorithms commonly used in time series forecasting, enabling us to predict the expected thermal behavior of the transformer. Consequently, this facilitates the real-time detection and reporting of potential thermal anomalies.

2   Materials and Methods

2.1   Thermographic Data Acquisition

Temperature measurement of power transformers typically involves the use of sensors that are integrated into the transformer equipment, serving, to some extent, as components of the transformer system. While this method may be the most uncomplicated and direct, it carries the drawback of being susceptible to potential transformer issues, resulting in a loss of its predictive capability for identifying transformer malfunctions [27]. Contrary, thermal imaging, which is a well-established technology that enables the detection of the heat emitted by objects with temperatures above absolute zero [28], presents several benefits. The most crucial is the system's complete independence from the power transformer, operating without direct physical contact, thereby avoiding susceptibility to potential transformer failures (such as high temperature peaks or excessively frequent temperature fluctuations that may harm the sensors). Moreover, it proves to be a more scalable system, capable of monitoring not only the overall temperature of the transformer but also distinct components independently or adjacent equipment. This technology has proven effective in various applications, such as monitoring civil structures [29,30], inspecting machinery [31], and addressing temperature issues in the nuclear industry [32]. Additionally, it has recently been suggested for the correction and monitoring of temperature-related issues in electrical substations and power transformers [33–35].

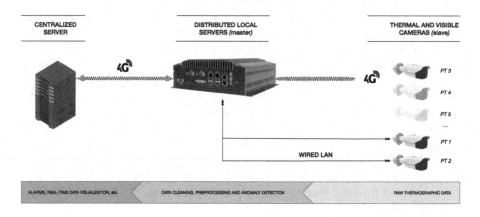

Fig. 1. Simplified diagram of the thermographic data acquisition system.

System Architecture. The thermography data acquisition and processing system comprises 20 thermal cameras and 9 industrial PCs controlling them (Fig. 1) The technical specifications of the diverse camera models and industrial PCs are detailed in the subsequent sections. Industrial PCs establish connections with the cameras in two distinct manners. In cases where the camera coexists in the same power control center as the industrial PC, both are physically linked through an Ethernet cable. Alternatively, when the camera is situated at a different location than the controlling industrial PC, they establish communication through a 4G communication. The radio-link connections are secured using a VPN to adhere to and ensure project security requirements. While contemplating connectivity options, the notion of utilizing radio-links was considered. However, this idea was dismissed due to inadequate coverage in several deployment sites.

The capture of thermal images is initiated upon request from the industrial PC. The acquisition frequency is contingent upon the type of connection established between the industrial PC and the camera (one image per minute for physical links and one image every 5 min for radio links). To achieve this, the industrial PC connects to the camera using TCP network protocol (Transmission Control Protocol) and requests the image. Once received, the industrial PC is responsible for its storage and processing, as described further in subsequent sections. To maintain meticulous control over the acquisition time and ensure a simple and scalable data management approach, the images are stored in individual files with filenames based on the acquisition timestamp, following the format yyyy-MM-dd HH:MM:SS.

Ultimately, in order to perform different tasks such as monitoring, control, or data extraction, the industrial PCs are equipped with 4G connectivity, enabling external access using the SSH protocol. Similar to the aforementioned radio-links, these communications are also safeguarded by VPN for enhanced security.

Thermographic Cameras. At the moment, three different models of thermographic cameras were employed for monitoring the temperature of twenty power transformers, two power lines and their surroundings (Fig. 2). The specifications of the different models are described below:

Hikvision Thermographic Network Bullet Camera: This particular model (DS-2TD2137T-4/P) operates at a frame rate of 50 Hz and provides thermal images with a resolution of 384×288 pixels. It has a field of view (FOV) of $90° \times 65.3°$ and a focal length of 4.4 mm, effectively covering the transformer's body and its surroundings. The Noise Equivalent Temperature Difference (NETD) is ≤ 35 mK and the temperature interval of detection ranges from $-20°$ to $550°$ with an accuracy of $\pm 2°$. It supports several network protocols including IPv4/IPv6, TCP, UDP, etc. and different security protocols such as user authentication (ID and PW), MAC address binding, HTTPS encryption, among others.

Hikvision Bi-spectrum Thermography Network Bullet Camera: This model (DS-2TD2628T-3/QA) presents two acquisition modules, one thermal and one optical. The thermal module operates at a frame rate of 50 Hz and provides thermal images with a resolution of 256×192 pixels. It has a FOV of $50° \times 37.3°$, a focal length of 3.6 mm, the NETD is ≤ 40 mK and the temperature interval of detection ranges from $-20°$ to $550°$ with an accuracy of $\pm 2°$. The optical module provides images with a resolution of 2688×1520 pixels. It has a FOV of $84° \times 43.1°$ and a focal length of 4.3 mm and supports the same network and security protocolos as the previous models. This camera model was used to monitoring both power transformers, power lines and their surroundings.

Sunell Temperature Alarm Bullet Network Camera: This model (SN-TPC6401KT-F II) operates at a frame rate of 50 Hz providing thermal images with a resolution of 640×512 pixels and different focal lengths (15, 25, 35 and 50 mm). The FOV depends on the selected focal length. The (NETD) is ≤ 40 mK and the temperature interval of detection ranges from $-20°$ to $150°$ with an accuracy of $\pm 2°$. It also supports several network and security protocols.

Hikvision Network IR Speed Dome: Finally, we installed a PTZ (Pan, Tilt and Zoom) camera model (DS-2DF8425IX-AELW(T5)) in a specific power line not for monitoring temperatures but to meet other requirements of the project such as the control of the avifauna. These type of cameras are usually employed for monitoring wide areas in high-definition, such as rivers, forests, roads, etc.

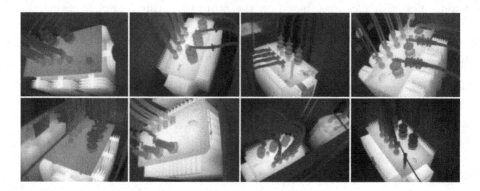

Fig. 2. Raw thermographic images obtained by DS-2TD2137T-4/P cameras in eight randomly selected power transformation centers.

Industrial PCs. Four industrial PCs (TBOX-2825) are collecting, storing and analyzing the thermographic data recorded by the cameras. The equipment has been chosen to ensure the proper functioning of the system under adverse weather conditions, given that the locations where they will be deployed may experience extreme temperatures in both summer and winter. This model can operate within a temperature range of $-20°$ to $70°$, with humidity levels between 10% and 95%, and ensures storage integrity within a range of $-40°$ to $80°$. It features an Intel Whiskey Lake 8th Gen Core i5-8265U CPU (Quad-core 1.6 GHz, burst to 3.9 GHz, TDP 15 W), single DDR4 memory (16 GB), and 2.5" SATA storage (4 TB).

2.2   Thermal Anomalies Detection System

This section outlines the general operation of the proposed thermal anomaly detection solution. This program runs continuously on each of the distributed servers and is independent of the thermal image acquisition system defined earlier. When a thermal image is captured by the camera and received on the server, the latter processes this image to verify if the resgistered temperature of each monitored region of the transformer falls within optimal margins estimated by an adaptive prediction model. If not, a thermal anomaly alarm is generated. The flowchart of the proposed solution is depicted in Fig. 3. Below, we provide a more detailed description of each module within the system.

Thermographic Data Processing. The thermal image processing is managed by the segmentation and temperature extraction submodules. Image segmentation is carried out in two different ways. Firstly, through an automated segmentation process, and secondly, by manually-defined masks established a priori. Both the manual and the automatic segmentation processes are described below.

Table 1. Nine selected regions of interest and their labels

Region of interest (ROI)	ROI label
Primary terminal (1) and high voltage bushing	in_1
Primary terminal (2) and high voltage bushing	in_2
Primary terminal (3) and high voltage bushing	in_3
Secondary terminal (1) and low voltage bushing	out_1
Secondary terminal (2) and low voltage bushing	out_2
Secondary terminal (3) and low voltage bushing	out_3
Secondary terminal (4) and low voltage bushing	out_4
Transformer body	body
Background (building walls, fences, etc.)	background

Manually-Defined Segmentation Masks. Nine regions of interest (ROI) have been defined from which to extract and monitor their operating temperature. These regions are listed in Table 1 and include the three primary windings terminals and their high voltage bushings, the four secondary windings terminals and their low voltage bushings, the body of the transformer, and the background temperature (e.g., building walls, excluding cables or other elements that may be a source of heat and could generate false alarms). The thermal cameras have been strategically installed and oriented to capture, as much as possible, the operating temperature of these regions of interest. To extract the temperature of each region, individual masks have been manually-defined for the scene captured by each camera (Fig. 4). In this way, the operating temperature of a specific region is extracted by computing the arithmetic mean of the top 5% of pixels with the highest temperature within that region. This process is repeated for the remaining regions in each scene, extracting and appending the operation temperature to the temperature time series.

Automatic Segmentation. The primary aim of the automatic segmentation process is not to extract the operation temperature of each region, but rather to compute and longitudinally store the sizes of various areas generated by the segmentation algorithms. This data will be utilized to identify anomalies in the scene that extend beyond purely thermal characteristics, such as excessive vegetation growth, the presence of intruders, or fires. Given the fixed positions of the cameras, they capture similar scenes over time. Consequently, the number

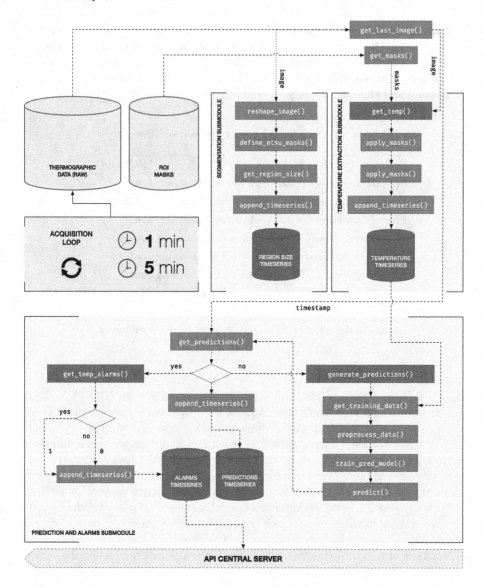

Fig. 3. Flowchart of the proposed thermal anomaly detection system.

of pixels belonging to each region automatically generated by the segmentation algorithms should remain relatively consistent across images. Any deviation from this consistency may suggest unusual occurrences warranting further analysis. The automatic segmentation process primarily relies on two segmentation algorithms: the Otsu segmentation algorithm [36] and the Maximally Stable Extremal Regions Algorithm (MSER) [37].

The Otsu's method is a non-parametric algorithm widely employed for threshold selection in image segmentation tasks and is characterized by its effectiveness in maximizing the separability of resulting classes in gray levels. This approach hinges on utilizing the zeroth- and first-order cumulative moments of the gray-level histogram, reducing the threshold selection task to an optimization problem aimed at maximizing class separability. Formally, in a scenario with two classes, the threshold k^* is determined as showed in Eq. 1, where σ_B^2 represents the class separability and can be computed as $\omega_0\omega_1(\mu_1 - \mu_0)^2$, being ω_i and μ_i the probability and mean of class i.

$$\sigma_B^2(k^*) = \max_{1 < k < L} \sigma_B^2(k) \tag{1}$$

Otsu's method offers a means to categorize pixels within an image based on their intensity levels, yet it does not consider the spatial relationships between pixels. In contrast, the Maximally Stable Extremal Regions Algorithm incorporates this spatial information into the segmentation process. Consequently, regions within the image characterized by similar intensity levels but disjointed spatially (i.e., separated by pixels with differing intensity levels) are identified as distinct regions. This algorithm was originally devised to tackle stereo problems in image analysis (specifically, establishing correspondence between multiple images of the same scene captured from different viewpoints). MSER has found application in various other image analysis tasks, such as tracking colored objects [38] or detecting color-based regions [39]. A recent work employed this exact methodology to automatically segment parts of an electric power transformer [34]. The fundamental concept underlying MSER can be easily described as follows: Imagine a grayscale image represented as a 3D structure, with each point corresponding to a pixel with a height proportional to its intensity level. When a fluid is released onto a point, it spreads outward, encompassing a progressively wider area and incorporating points with lower heights (intensity levels). If this process unfolds simultaneously across multiple points, distinct regions emerge, gradually interconnecting as the fluid level rises. The process terminates when a stability criterion is met, which is continuously checked as the fluid falls.

The proposed solution employed a combination of both algorithms. First, the Otsu's method quantized the registered thermographic image, previously configured to extract nine different regions (multiclass version of the Otsu's algorithm, see Fig. 4B). Then, the MSER algorithm is applied iteratively to each Otsu's region, thus spatially separated subregions of equal intensity are considered independently (Fig. 4C). Finally, the number of pixels contained in each region is extracted and stored as time series of region sizes that can be analyzed.

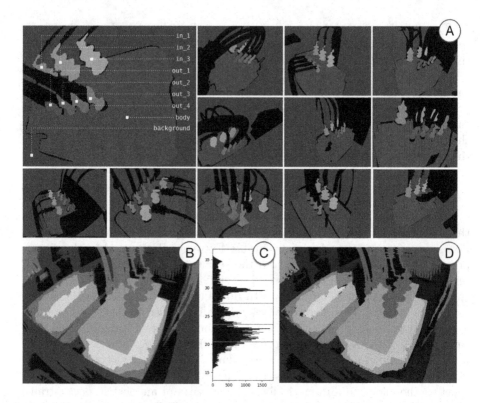

Fig. 4. Manually-defined masks and automatic segmentation results. (A) Twelve examples of manually-defined segmentation masks are displayed. (B) Five distinct regions automatically detected by Otsu's algorithm. (C) The temperature histogram is depicted alongside the four thresholds used to delineate these five regions. Finally, (D) depicts the application of the MSER algorithm to each previously identified region, facilitating the identification of spatially separated subregions of equal intensity and resulting in a total of 12 final regions.

Prediction Model and Alarms. Once an image is captured and processed by the segmentation and temperature extraction submodules, the predictions and alarms submodule determines whether the extracted temperatures for each region fall within the expected margins. If not, an anomalous temperature alarm is generated for the specific region and sent to the central server for the operator to evaluate the situation and take appropriate action. These margins are not fixed and depend on various factors such as the time of day, ambient temperature, season, current weather conditions, and the transformer's current workload. It is indeed true that the temperature recorded by the cameras exhibits stationary behavior over time, resulting in daily "duck" curves 5. These curves, as will be seen in detail later, depict the transformer's load profile over 24 h. Due to this observed stationarity, future predictions are calculated adaptively based on past observations, prior to the temperature signal recording. The functioning of the proposed predictive model and the configuration parameters used are explained in detail below.

Auto-regressive Prediction Model. Autoregressive models are a class of simple machine learning models that automatically predict the next element in a sequence of data based on previous elements in that sequence. Autoregression is thus a statistical technique used in time series forecasting that assumes the current value of a time series is a function of its previous values. The number of previous values considered to generate the prediction at the current time is known as the model order (or lag) and is typically denoted by the letter p. Thus, an autoregressive model of order p is denoted as $AR(p)$, and the value of the current sample is calculated based on the previous p samples, as indicated in the following equation:

$$y_t = c + \sum_{p}^{i=1} \phi_i y_{t-i} + \epsilon_t = c + \phi_1 y_{t-1} + \phi_2 y_{t-2} + \ldots + \phi_p y_{t-p} + \epsilon_t \qquad (2)$$

where c is a constant, ϵ_t is white noise, and ϕ_i are the coefficients of the model to be estimated during training. These coefficients represent the importance of each predictor in the final predicted value. The choice of the model order p depends on the amount of information we want to capture to predict future samples. Thus, a higher-order model p will capture more information from the time series than a lower-order one. This might lead us to believe that predictions could be more accurate when we increase the value of p. However, this is not always the case; moreover, more complex autoregressive models require higher computational costs. The choice of the model order depends on the nature of the time series data being worked with and must represent a trade-off between capturing enough information to make accurate predictions and the associated computational cost. The proposed model order is individually adjusted for each camera, ensuring that it is always trained with information from the previous 24 h leading up to the current time point.

Training Procedure. The proposed prediction model is adaptive, meaning its parameters are recurrently updated based on newly available temperature data. This is known as online learning. Such algorithms are suitable for environments where the training data changes rapidly. The choice of retraining frequency is crucial, as the predictive model needs to adapt to the transformer's new daily temperature conditions to make accurate predictions. However, overly frequent retraining should be avoided, as it would incur high computational costs and, more importantly, risk overfitting the model. If a thermal anomalies is occurring and the model is being retrained very frequently (e.g., every time a new temperature value is recorded), it could learn from this anomalous behavior and make predictions accordingly, resulting in a false negative (predicted temperature and recorded anomalous temperature being similar, thus not triggering an alarm).

In the proposed solution, the adaptive prediction model is retrained every 720 min (12 h). As mentioned earlier, the model order will depend on the frequency of thermal image acquisition but will always be configured to use the latest 24 h for retraining. Thus, the model is trained with the latest 24 h of available data to predict the temperature for the next 12-h time window. These predictions, along with the recorded temperature and the size of regions detected by automatic segmentation algorithms, are permanently stored on the server as a time series of data. After the next 12 h, the system will not have temperature predictions, so they need to be regenerated. To do this, we retrain the predictive model, incorporating the new temperature values recorded in the last 12 h into the training data, and predict the next time window. This way, as mentioned earlier, the model adapts to the transformer's new temperature conditions and makes predictions accordingly.

Anomaly Detection System. The proposed alarm generation system is straightforward. As long as temperature predictions are available for the time of capturing the current thermal image, the prediction and alarm generation submodule simply needs to check that the difference between the recorded temperature and the estimate does not exceed a predefined threshold (a margin of 15°) for each region of interest. Adjusting this threshold allows for tuning the sensitivity of the anomaly detection system. Thus, after acquiring a thermal image, a temporary table is generated containing the recorded temperature data, the expected values for each ROI, and a control bit associated with each ROI indicating the presence or absence of a thermal anomaly alarm (Table 2). This table information is extracted and sent to the central server through an available API. Upon receipt, the operator can take appropriate action, such as requesting a live video stream to visually inspect the monitored equipment's status. Due to storage space constraints on the server, these temporary tables are periodically deleted as new tables are generated, as they contain redundant information.

Table 2. Information table containing the registered temperature, the predicted temperature and a the generated alarm for each region of interest.

	in-1	in-2	in-3	out-1	out-2	out-3	out-4	body	back
temperature	25.78	25.77	25.47	28.03	28.57	28.77	27.21	30.97	21.28
prediction	27.39	27.33	27.02	29.66	30.2	30.41	28.83	32.76	23.04
alarm	0	0	0	0	0	0	0	0	0

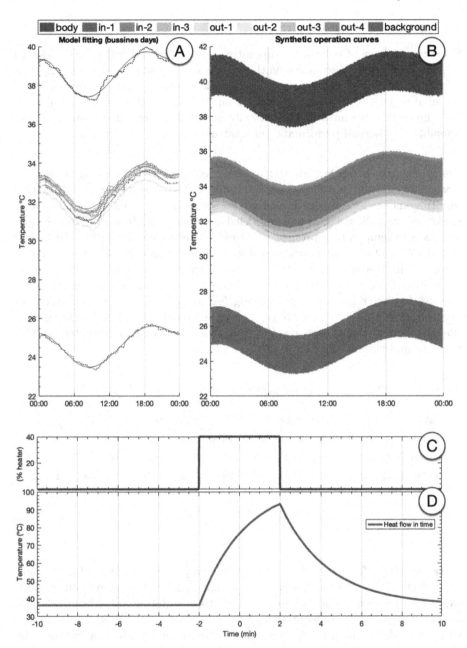

Fig. 5. Synthetic data generation. (A) This figure displays the fifth-order polynomial curves associated with each region that have been fitted to the actual temperature data model. These curves are subsequently used to extrapolate the transformer's operational curves throughout the entire year. (B) Standard Error of the Mean (SEM) of the 365 synthetic daily curves generated. (C and D) Thermal anomalies generated according to the mathematical model of the thermal system designed for the transformer.

2.3   Synthetic Data Generation

Since the amount of recorded temperature data is limited, we have decided to generate a sufficiently extensive synthetic database to test the system's long-term performance. This database comprises the daily temperature curves of each of the nine regions of interest selected for analysis (see Table 1) over a full year. To achieve this, we have mathematically modeled a thermal system to closely resemble the thermal performance of the transformer.

Temperature Models. Firstly, we must consider that the energy demand from both industry and network users differs between weekdays and weekends, resulting in distinct temperature curves observed in the data records. Therefore, weekdays and holidays need to be modeled independently. To accomplish this, we selected the temperature profiles T_{reg} from two complete days (2023-10-18 and 2023-10-29) of the real records, which we will use as models to fit the synthetic data we will generate later. The next step is to fit a polynomial curve T_{pol} (of order 5 in this case) to the previously selected real temperature model, repeating this step for each region of interest. In Fig. 5A, we display the 9 polynomial curves of each region of interest fitted to the real recorded data. Additionally, we assume that the approximation error $e = T_{reg} - T_{pol}$ follows a Gaussian distribution with mean μ_e and variance σ_e.

Table 3. Daily temperatures extracted from AEMET.

date	T_{max}	T_{min}	date	T_{max}	T_{min}	date	T_{max}	T_{min}
1-Jan-2022	20.9	0.5	3-May-2022	19.0	9.4	2-Sep-2022	33.1	18.4
2-Jan-2022	20.6	-0.4	4-May-2022	17.2	8.5	3-Sep-2022	32.5	16.9
3-Jan-2022	20.4	-1.3	5-May-2022	24.0	7.8	4-Sep-2022	33.2	11.8
...	...	...	...	...	...	...	...	...

Extrapolation for One Full Year. The temperature recorded by the camera reflects the amount of radiated heat captured by the camera sensor. This captured radiation originates from the emitted radiation of each transformer region as well as the ambient temperature at that time. Thus, in accordance with Stefan-Boltzmann's law, the radiation from the transformer captured by the camera sensor for a specific day could be modeled as:

$$\gamma_{day} = \alpha\epsilon\sigma[(T_{reg} + 273.15)^4 - (T_{day} + 273.15)^4] \tag{3}$$

where α is the camera's reception coefficient, ϵ is the emissivity of the transformer material, σ is the Stefan-Boltzmann constant ($5.67 \cdot 10^{-8}$ W/m^{2}K^4), T_{reg} is the average operating temperature of the model calculated as $(\max(T_{reg}) + \min(T_{reg}))/2$ y T_{day} is the average ambient temperature of the day to be modeled, also calculated as $(\max(T_{day}) + \min(T_{day}))/2$.

Therefore, the synthetic temperature curve for a specific day is modeled as indicated in the following equation, where we introduce the error e_{day}, calculated as a sequence of random numbers generated from a Gaussian distribution with mean μ_{day} and variance σ_{day}, adjusted to the temperature of the day to be modeled:

$$T_{op} = e_{day} + [(T_{pol} + 273.15) + \gamma_{day}] - 273.15 \qquad (4)$$

To model the entire year, we have utilized historical temperature records from the area, stored by the Spanish State Meteorological Agency (AEMET)[2] These records include daily maximum and minimum temperatures for the entire year 2022, as depicted in the Table 3.

Generación sintética de anomalías térmicas. Finally, to the previously generated synthetic temperature records, we added thermal anomalies caused by overheating on random days throughout the year. To simulate such thermal anomalies, we designed a heating function that mimics the heating and cooling of a random region of the transformer over a short period of time. Thus, the temperature increments or decrements over time follow the following nonlinear balance equation:

$$mc_p \frac{dT}{dt} = UA(T_a - T) + \epsilon\sigma A(T_a^4 - T^4) + \beta Q \qquad (5)$$

where m is the mass in kg, c_p is the specific heat in J/kgK, U is the heat transfer coefficient in W/m^2K, A is the surface area in m^2, ϵ is the emissivity, σ is the Stefan-Bolztman constant in $W/(m^2K^4)$, β is the heater factor, Q is the heater output, and y T_a y T are the current temperature and heater temperature respectively in degrees Kelvin. The thermal anomaly generated after apply this heating function over short period of time is depicted in Fig. 5D.

Once we have the temperature time series for the entire year 2022, we need to generate the sequence of corresponding thermal images. That is, for each time point in the series corresponding to the analyzed transformer regions, we generate an image where the pixels belonging to each region have the temperature value at that time point.

---

[2] Link to the source: https://opendata.aemet.es/.

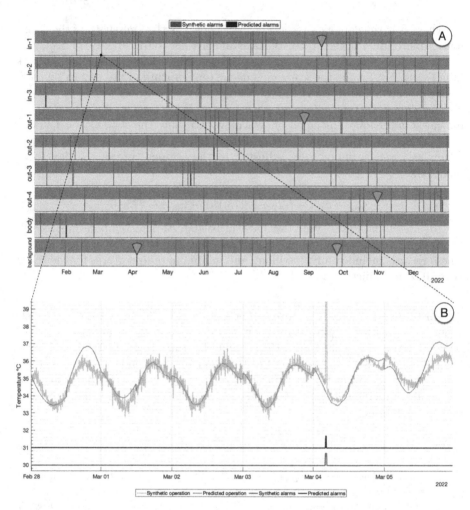

Fig. 6. Simulation results. (A) This figure juxtaposes the synthetically generated alarms and those predicted by the proposed model after running the simulation script for the synthetic database of the year 2022. False positives are marked with red triangles. (B) Expansion of the previous graph, showing the synthetic temperature values and those predicted by the proposed model. As we can observe, the system correctly detects the thermal anomaly depicted in the image on May 4th in the in_1 region.

3   Results and Discussion

3.1   Simulation Results

After generating the synthetic database for the entire year 2022, a script was launched to simulate the system's operation throughout that period. To accomplish this, the main program was iteratively and continuously fed with the previously generated synthetic images. This approach enabled the main program to interpret these synthetic images as those collected by the cameras. Accordingly, based on the configuration parameters, it analyzed them, generated historical temperature records, trained the predictive model adaptively, made future temperature predictions, and generated alarms upon detecting a thermal anomaly. The results of this simulation are depicted in Fig. 6A, which juxtaposes synthetically introduced thermal anomalies and alarms generated by the prediction model. These results are highly promising, indicating correct detection of the vast majority of anomalies by the system. In specific transformer regions, false positives were observed rarely throughout the year (in_1 in September, out_1 in August, out_4 in October, and *background* in April and September). These false positives (marked with a red triangle in the figure) can be corrected by adjusting the alarm threshold without compromising anomaly prediction capability. Figure 6B provides a more detailed view of both the temperature time series and predictions made by the proposed model. In this example, the introduced thermal anomaly is accurately detected by the model. Table 4 displays the temperature deviation calculated as the absolute difference between the temperature predicted by the model and the temperature recorded by the camera throughout the year for each analyzed region. It can be observed that, in the worst-case scenario, the deviation does not exceed $0.6 \pm 4.0\,°C$.

3.2   Registered Temperature Time Series

In Fig. 7, we present the actual temperature series recorded from December 16, 2023, to January 7, 2024, for the 9 regions of interest analyzed, alongside the predictions made by the proposed model. As indicated in Table 4, the deviation between the actual and predicted temperature values does not exceed $0.81 \pm 1.1\,°C$ in the worst-case scenario. Throughout the displayed period, as depicted in the figure, no alarms were triggered in any region. The results obtained from analyzing the remaining thermal cameras are similar to those depicted in this figure.

Table 4. Temperature deviations between both real and synthetic records and the predictions made by the proposed model in both cases.

	in-1	in-2	in-3	out-1	out-2	out-3	out-4	body	back
ΔT_{syn}	$.62 \pm 1.6$	$.49 \pm 1.3$	$.66 \pm 2.7$	$.55 \pm 1.3$	$.59 \pm 4$	$.56 \pm 2.8$	$.63 \pm 1.5$	$.67 \pm 2.5$	$.59 \pm 4$
ΔT_{reg}	$.63 \pm .87$	$.64 \pm .89$	$.76 \pm 1.1$	$.58 \pm .87$	$.61 \pm .99$	$.6 \pm .99$	$.66 \pm .93$	$.65 \pm .94$	$.81 \pm 1.1$

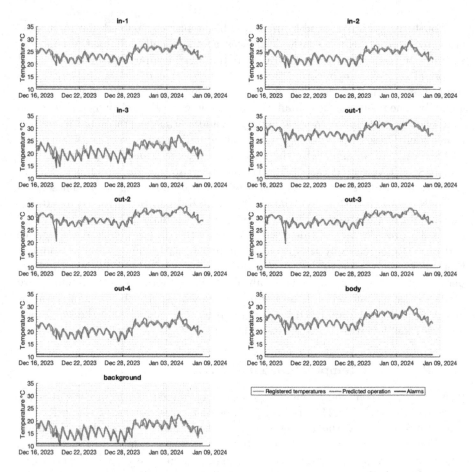

Fig. 7. Registered temperature records. In this figure, we present the real temperature records obtained from December 16, 2023, to January 7, 2024, in transformer CT49024-master-CATR2. Alongside, the predictions made by the proposed model for all analyzed regions of the transformer are depicted, as well as the record of alarms generated during this period.

4   Conclusions

In this paper, we introduce one of the core modules of RESISTO, a pioneering technological innovation and research transfer project in Europe. Its primary objective is to enhance the resilience of the electrical grid against meteorological phenomena, thereby improving the quality of service provided to customers in the region. Specifically, we focus on describing the development of a key pillar of the project: the detection of anomalies in the operating temperature of power transformers. To achieve this, a distributed system of servers and strategically positioned thermal cameras has been deployed in the Doñana Natural Park, enabling real-time monitoring of the operating temperature of different regions of interest in the power transformers. The anomaly detection process is divided into three distinct submodules. The segmentation submodule is responsible for automatically segmenting the thermal images captured by the cameras, as well as applying manually defined masks. The temperature extraction submodule extracts and stores the operating temperature of each region of interest. Finally, the anomaly detection and alarm generation system analyzes the recorded operating temperature, predicts the expected operating temperature, and generates alarms if there is a significant deviation between the two. For this latter module, we have developed an adaptive and autoregressive machine learning model capable of predicting the expected operating temperature in real-time for the upcoming hours. To assess the long-term performance of the model, and given the limited availability of real data at present (due to the project's youth), we have generated a synthetic database by mathematically modeling a thermal system similar to that of the transformer. Simulations over a year of synthetic data demonstrate the system's functioning in detecting anomalies in response to sudden changes in the operating temperature in different regions of the transformers. Furthermore, we demonstrate how this system not only operates effectively for synthetic data but also for real data collected by the distributed network of 20 thermal cameras.

Acknowledgments. This work is part of the PID2022-137451OB-I00 and PID2022-137629OA-I00 projects, funded by the CIN/AEI/10.13039/501100011033 and by FSE+. Additionally, this work was also supported by the University of Granada and Endesa Distribución under the RESISTO (ref. 2021/C005/00144188) contracts.

References

1. Intergovernmental Panel on Climate Change (IPCC): Climate Change 2021 – The Physical Science Basis: Working Group I Contribution to the Sixth Assessment Report of the Intergovernmental Panel on Climate Change. Cambridge University Press, Cambridge (2021)
2. Vitolina, S.: Development of lifetime data management algorithm for power transformers. In: Proceedings of the International Conference on Intelligent Systems, Modelling and Simulation (ISMS), September 2015, pp. 452–457 (2015)
3. Müllerová, E., Hrůza, J., Velek, J., Ullman, I., Stříska, F.: Life cycle management of power transformers: results and discussion of case studies. IEEE Trans. Dielectr. Electr. Insul. **22**(4), 2379–2389 (2015)
4. Yazdani-Asrami, M., Taghipour-Gorjikolaie, M., Razavi, S.M., Gholamian, S.A.: A novel intelligent protection system for power transformers considering possible electrical faults, inrush current, CT saturation and over-excitation. Int. J. Electr. Power Energy Syst. **64**, 1129–1140 (2015)
5. Dolata, B., Coenen, S.: Online condition monitoring becomes standard configuration of transformers-practical application for optimized operation, maintenance and to avoid failures. In: E-ARWtr2016 Transformers, Advanced Research Workshop on Transformers, La Toja Island, Spain, vol. 2 (2016)
6. Barkas, D.A., Chronis, I., Psomopoulos, C.: Failure mapping and critical measurements for the operating condition assessment of power transformers. Energy Rep. **8**, 527–547 (2022)

7. Christina, A.J., Salam, M.A., Rahman, Q.M., Wen, F., Ang, S.P., Voon, W.: Causes of transformer failures and diagnostic methods - a review. Renew. Sustain. Energy Rev. **82**(Part I), 1442–1456 (2018)
8. Haghjoo, F., Mostafaei, M.: Flux-based method to diagnose and identify the location of turn-to-turn faults in transformers. IET Gener. Transm. Distrib. **10**(4), 1083–1091 (2016)
9. Setayeshmehr, A., Akbari, A., Borsi, H., Gockenbach, E.: A procedure for diagnosis and condition based maintenance for power transformers. In: Conference Record of IEEE International Symposium on Electrical Insulation, September 2004, pp. 504–507 (2004)
10. Ali Reza Abbasi: Fault detection and diagnosis in power transformers: a comprehensive review and classification of publications and methods. Electr. Power Syst. Res. **209**, 107990 (2022)
11. Bakar, N., Abu-Siada, A., Islam, S.: A review of dissolved gas analysis measurement and interpretation techniques. IEEE Electr. Insul. Mag. **30**(3), 39–49 (2014)
12. Kunicki, M., Borucki, S., Zmarzły, D., Frymus, J.: Data acquisition system for on-line temperature monitoring in power transformers. Meas. J. Int. Meas. Confed. **161**, 107909 (2020)
13. Peimankar, A., Weddell, S.J., Jalal, T., Lapthorn, A.C.: Evolutionary multi-objective fault diagnosis of power transformers. Swarm Evol. Comput. **36**, 62–75 (2017)
14. Velasquez-Contreras, J.L., Sanz-Bobi, M.A., Arellano, S.G.: General asset management model in the context of an electric utility: application to power transformers. Electr. Power Syst. Res. **81**(11), 2015–2037 (2011)
15. Ramírez, J., et al.: Power transformer forecasting in smart grids using NARX neural networks. In: Valenzuela, O., Rojas, F., Herrera, L.J., Pomares, H., Rojas, I. (eds.) ITISE 2019. CS, pp. 401–414. Springer, Cham (2020). https://doi.org/10.1007/978-3-030-56219-9_26
16. Górriz, J.M., et al.: Artificial intelligence within the interplay between natural and artificial computation: advances in data science, trends and applications. Neurocomputing **410**, 237–270 (2020)
17. Górriz, J.M., et al.: Computational approaches to explainable artificial intelligence: advances in theory, applications and trends. Inf. Fus. **100**, 101945 (2023)
18. Ma, Y., Wang, Z., Yang, H., Yang, L.: Artificial intelligence applications in the development of autonomous vehicles: a survey. IEEE/CAA J. Automatica Sinica **7**(2), 315–329 (2020)
19. López-García, D., Peñalver, J.M.G., Górriz, J.M., Ruz, M.: MVPAlab: a machine learning decoding toolbox for multidimensional electroencephalography data. Comput. Meth. Programs Biomed. **214**, 106549 (2022)
20. López-García, D., Sobrado, A., Peñalver, J.M.G., Górriz, J.M., Ruz, M.: Multivariate pattern analysis techniques for electroencephalography data to study flanker interference effects. Int. J. Neural Syst. **30**(7), 2050024 (2020)
21. Peñalver, J.M.G., López-García, D., González-García, C., Aguado-López, B., Górriz, J.M., Ruz, M.: Top-down specific preparatory activations for selective attention and perceptual expectations. Neuroimage **271**, 119960 (2023)
22. López-García, D., Ruz, M., Ramírez, J., Górriz, J.M.: Automatic detection of sleep disorders: multi-class automatic classification algorithms based on support vector machines. In: International Conference on Time Series and Forecasting, ITISE 2018, vol. 3, pp. 1270–1280 (2018)
23. Chen, P.H.C., Liu, Y., Peng, L.: How to develop machine learning models for healthcare. Nat. Mater. **18**(5), 410–414 (2019)

24. Mohamed, Y.A., Kannan, A., Bashir, M., Mohamed, A.H., Adiel, M.A.E., Elsadig, M.A.: The impact of artificial intelligence on language translation: a review. IEEE Access **12**, 25553–25579 (2024)

25. Azad, S., Sabrina, F., Wasimi, S.: Transformation of smart grid using machine learning. In: 2019 29th Australasian Universities Power Engineering Conference, AUPEC 2019, pp. 1–6 (2019)

26. Hossain, E., Khan, I., Un-Noor, F., Sikander, S.S., Sunny, M.S.H.: Application of Big Data and machine learning in smart grid, and associated security concerns: a review. IEEE Access **7**, 13960–13988 (2019)

27. de Melo, A.S., Calil, W.V., Salazar, P.D.P., Liboni, L.H.B., Costa, E.C.M., Flauzino, R.A.: Applied methodology for temperature numerical evaluation on high current leads in power transformers. Int. J. Electr. Power Energy Syst. **131**, 107014 (2021)

28. Mariprasath, T., Kirubakaran, V.: A real time study on condition monitoring of distribution transformer using thermal imager. Infrared Phys. Technol. **90**, 78–86 (2018)

29. Sirca, G.F., Adeli, H.: Infrared thermography for detecting defects in concrete structures. J. Civ. Eng. Manag. **24**(7), 508–515 (2018)

30. Linjun, L., Dai, F., Zaniewski, J.P.: Automatic roller path tracking and mapping for pavement compaction using infrared thermography. Comput. Aided Civ. Infrastruct. Eng. **36**(11), 1416–1434 (2021)

31. Bagavathiappan, S., Saravanan, T., George, N.P., Philip, J., Jayakumar, T., Raj, B.: Condition monitoring of exhaust system blowers using infrared thermography. Insight-Non-Destr. Test. Cond. Monit. **50**(9), 512–515 (2008)

32. Itami, K., Sugie, T., Vayakis, G., Walker, C.: Multiplexing thermography for international thermonuclear experimental reactor divertor targets. Rev. Sci. Instrum. **75**(10 II), 4124–4128 (2004)

33. Zarco-Periñán, P.J., Martínez-Ramos, J.L., Zarco-Soto, F.J.: A novel method to correct temperature problems revealed by infrared thermography in electrical substations. Infrared Phys. Technol. **113**, 103623 (2021)

34. Segovia, F., et al.: Connected system for monitoring electrical power transformers using thermal imaging. Integr. Comput. Aided Eng. **30**(4), 353–368 (2023)

35. Ramirez, J., et al.: Prediction of transformer temperature for energy distribution smart grids using recursive neural networks. In: ITISE 2019. Proceedings of Papers, Volume 1, September 2019, pp. 167–177 (2019)

36. Otsu, N.: A threshold selection method from gray-level histograms. IEEE Trans. Syst. Man Cybern. **9**(1), 62–66 (1996)

37. Matas, J., Chum, O., Urban, M., Pajdla, T.: Robust wide-baseline stereo from maximally stable extremal regions. Image Vis. Comput. **22**(10 SPEC. ISS.), 761–767 (2004)

38. Donoser, M., Bischof, H.: Efficient maximally stable extremal region (MSER) tracking. In: Proceedings of the IEEE Computer Society Conference on Computer Vision and Pattern Recognition, vol. 1, pp. 553–560 (2006)

39. Chavez, A., Gustafson, D.: Color-based extensions to MSERs. In: Bebis, G. (ed.) ISVC 2011. LNCS, vol. 6939, pp. 358–366. Springer, Heidelberg (2011). https://doi.org/10.1007/978-3-642-24031-7_36

RESISTO Project: Safeguarding the Power Grid from Meteorological Phenomena

Jacob Rodríguez-Rivero[1]([✉]), David López-García[2], Fermín Segovia[2],
Javier Ramírez[2], Juan Manuel Górriz[2], R. Serrano[3], D. Pérez[3], Ivan Maza[4],
Anibal Ollero[4], Pol Paradell Solà[5], Albert Gili Selga[5],
Jose Luis Domínguez-García[5], A. Romero[1], A. Berro[1], Rocío Domínguez[1],
and Inmaculada Prieto[1]

[1] e-Distribución Redes Digitales, Madrid, Spain
jacob@ugr.es
[2] Department of Signal Theory, Networking and Communications,
University of Granada, Granada, Spain
[3] ATIS Solutions, Peligros, Spain
[4] GRVC Robotics Lab, University of Seville, Seville, Spain
[5] Power Electronics Department, Catalonia Institute for Energy Research—IREC,
Jardins de les Dones de Negre 1, 2ª pl., Sant Adrià del Besòs, 08930 Barcelona, Spain

Abstract. The RESISTO project, a pioneer innovation initiative in Europe, endeavors to enhance the resilience of electrical networks against extreme weather events and associated risks. Emphasizing intelligence and flexibility within distribution networks, RESISTO aims to address climatic and physical incidents comprehensively, fostering resilience across planning, response, recovery, and adaptation phases. Leveraging advanced technologies including AI, IoT sensors, and aerial robots, RESISTO integrates prediction, detection, and mitigation strategies to optimize network operation. This article summarizes the main technical aspects of the proposed solutions to meet the aforementioned objectives, including the development of a climate risk detection platform, an IoT-based monitoring and anomaly detection network, and a fleet of intelligent aerial robots. Each contributing to the project's overarching objectives of enhancing network resilience and operational efficiency.

Keywords: RESISTO project · Smart grids · Artificial intelligence · Thermal imaging · Aerial robots · Internet of Things

1 Introduction

The RESISTO project aims to enhance the resilience of electrical networks, minimizing the impact of extreme climate events and related risks on service provision. In response to the increasing frequency of such events, as highlighted in the latest IPCC report [1], RESISTO emphasizes intelligence and flexibility within distribution networks to effectively mitigate these challenges. The project adopts a comprehensive approach to resilience, addressing climatic events (water, wind, fire) as well as physical incidents (human, animal, others). Innovations and developments across all resilience conceptual phases (Planning, Response, Recovery, and Adaptation) are central to RESISTO's objectives.

– In the planning phase, RESISTO focuses on prediction and prevention by leveraging existing tools to identify high-risk areas under specific climatic conditions and utilizing climate prediction tools. Moreover, the project assesses potential risks from physical actions, including those from animals and humans, with the consideration of aerial robots to gather data and images for integration into planned models.
– During the response phase, RESISTO emphasizes detection, proposing options for coarse sensing through real-time grid monitoring and nearby IoT-based sensors. Aerial robots play a crucial role in minimizing detection time for overhead line failures, verifying warnings, and assessing environmental conditions. Advanced 3D systems aid in creating virtual decision tables for response and mitigation actions.
– In the recovery/mitigation phase, RESISTO explores several strategies, including the use of Dynamic Thermal Line Rating (DTLR) to optimize power flows and integrate with grid reconfiguration algorithms. Additionally, RESISTO explores the role of renewables in enhancing network stability and security, offering functionalities such as "Black-Start" and "Grid-Forming".
– In the adaptation phase, RESISTO focuses on learning to improve resilience, incorporating aerial robots to generate data for integration into machine learning methods. This phase also involves equipment planning and adaptation through the use of 3D digital twins of electrical networks, facilitating visualization and understanding of decisions and actions' impacts.

1.1 Objectives

The primary technical objectives of the study are interconnected and aimed at addressing the previously mentioned challenge.

– Firstly, a risk assessment tool with diverse time horizons is proposed to identify potential risks in the electrical network, enabling the implementation of detection and early warning systems for short-term (days) and long-term (years) risk mitigation strategies.
– Secondly, the development and application of technology are emphasized to enhance the monitoring and control capacity of the network, transforming it into both an energy supply structure and a data interaction hub for environmental risk information dissemination and proactive response.
– Thirdly, optimization of existing infrastructure and reduction of investments in new network infrastructure are targeted through the development of advanced control and management systems.

- Fourthly, digitalization and the utilization of IoT sensors, coupled with aerial robots or drones, are advocated for measuring environmental variables and validating alerts, thereby minimizing personal risk and response time. Additionally, AI-powered algorithms for efficient risk management and 3D visualization systems for network control identification are proposed.
- Finally, the study aims to demonstrate and validate these developments through prototype implementation in diverse pilot areas, highlighting scalability and replicability for broad national and international distribution network impact.

1.2   Project Innovations

The project introduces several innovations aimed at maximizing and ensuring the achievement of the previously established objectives. These innovations are outlined as follows:

- **Innovation 1 - Climate Risk Detection Platform:** The project proposes the development of a platform dedicated to detecting climate risks, vulnerabilities, load optimization, and providing recommendations or reconfigurations for decision-making. This platform will leverage machine learning techniques to enhance its capabilities.
- **Innovation 2 - IoT-Based Monitoring Network:** Another key innovation involves the establishment of an Internet of Things (IoT)-based monitoring network comprising gateways, sensors, weather stations, thermal cameras, and tele-surveillance cameras. These components will be strategically deployed to gather real-time data, which will then be integrated into a unified risk platform for comprehensive analysis.
- **Innovation 3 - Fleet of Intelligent Aerial Robots:** The project proposes the deployment of a fleet of intelligent aerial robots designed to autonomously validate warnings. This innovative approach aims to minimize risks for operators while simultaneously reducing response time in emergency situations. The integration of aerial robots into the system enhances the project's capacity for swift and efficient risk assessment and management.

2   Proposed Solution

This section outlines three key components designed to bolster the resilience of electrical grids. The first is the GridWatch Electrical Resilience Platform, a creation of IREC, which amalgamates climate data with the electrical transportation and distribution system. This platform centralizes all relevant information for the visualization of electrical system interactions, integrating external diagnostic tools and employing mathematical algorithms and AI for fault location and resolution. It incorporates various tools such as local weather stations, online weather systems, fire sensors, infrared cameras, and a fleet of drones. The second component focuses on the Automatic Detection of Operation Temperature Anomalies using Thermal Imaging, emphasizing the monitoring of power transformer temperatures through thermal imaging technology. It introduces a system architecture deployed by the University of Granada and ATIS with 20 thermal cameras, 9 industrial PCs, and a continuous anomaly detection system based on segmentation and an adaptive prediction model. The third component, developed by members of the University of Seville, addresses the limitations of current drone applications in electrical grid inspection and introduces a multi-drone system, combining multi-rotors and fixed-wing VTOLs for efficient power line inspection. The overall goal of these components is to augment the resilience and efficiency of electrical grids through advanced monitoring, fault detection, and inspection facilitated by a blend of technological tools, algorithms, and drone systems.

2.1   Electrical Resilience Platform: GridWatch

The GridWatch electrical resilience platform, developed by IREC, has been developed to unite climate information with the electrical transportation and distribution system. Figure 1 describes the principal elements of the GridWatch platform and the external interaction with the other elements involved in the project. This platform mainly fulfils three objectives:

1. Concentrate all the information in a single place where the interactions of the electrical system can be visualised.
2. Integrate external diagnostic and review tools to view and verify incidents.
3. Use different mathematical algorithms or artificial intelligence to locate electrical faults and how to solve them.

Mapstore2 [2], an open-source tool for data visualisation, has been used for the platform visualisation system. Geoserver [3], a geospatial information publishing tool, has also been used to render all the information on the platform.

Different tools have been integrated into the platform to have maximum information and thus be able to make the best decisions. The most notable systems integrated with the platform are detailed below:

- Local weather stations. A dozen stations have been installed in the vicinity of the pilot using Lora communications and mobile communications to send information to servers that, in turn, use the MQTT protocol to communicate measurements.
- Online weather system. Different sources, such as AEMET and Copernicus, have been used to obtain information on the climatological state.
- Fire sensors. Sensors capable of detecting forest fires have been integrated. These sensors send the information through MQTT.
- infrared cameras in transformation centres. These send possible anomaly detection alerts on the platform to be visualised there.
- The platform has been integrated with a fleet of drones. In this case, the platform can send the coordinates to be reviewed by the drones and receive the results of this inspection.

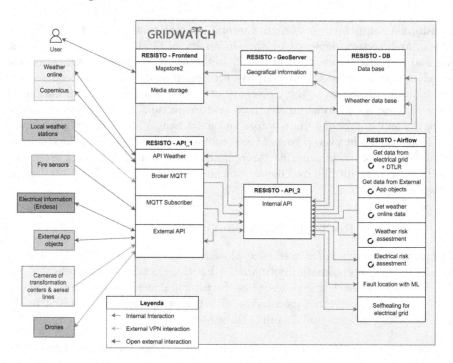

Fig. 1. GridWatch platform components and external interactions.

- Integration with the electrical system. The platform has integrated the available information from the electrical network, and for cases in which there is no observability, a Power Flow system has been implemented to determine the state of the network using the mathematical model modelled during this project.

On the other hand, the platform integrates different algorithms to increase the resilience of the network:

- Algorithm of effects on the electrical network. This algorithm calculates the possible interference of weather events with overhead power lines, such as temperature, wind, or fire risks.
- Recalculates the capacity of the lines. The DTLR algorithm is capable of recalculating the maximum capacity of the lines with the weather conditions; in this way, with more information on the status of these lines, better decisions can be made to redirect electricity or find critical points.
- Fault location system in the electrical system [4]. This algorithm developed at IREC uses machine learning methods to locate the location of the electrical fault based on the state of the last network cycles before the fault and the time of the fault. This method reduces the time to locate electrical faults since these systems are previously trained.

– Network reconfiguration system [5]. The platform also has an algorithm that, once the failure occurs, proposes new network configurations to keep the maximum number of clients connected. This algorithm uses a heuristic method to find mathematical solutions; in this case, it uses a genetic algorithm to determine the best solution in a short time.

2.2   Automatic Detection of Operation Temperature Anomalies Using Thermal Imaging

The oversight of electricity networks requires meticulous attention to potential overloads [6,7], given their significant impact on power transformers, responsible for approximately 12% of total failures [8]. Transformer malfunctions, in particular, present a significant hazard, capable of igniting fires with potentially severe economic and personal consequences due to the urban positioning of transformers [9]. To mitigate these failures, routine maintenance of installations is essential, including regular measurements. These measurements, among others [10], involve monitoring operational temperatures [11]. Consequently, measuring both transformer and ambient temperatures is a fundamental component of standard protocols for power transformer monitoring [12,13]. These parameters are pivotal variables requiring accurate and uninterrupted measurement and can also serve as predictors for other variables, such as reactive power or current intensity [14].

Temperature measurement of power transformers conventionally relies on integrated sensors, albeit susceptible to potential issues, limiting predictive capabilities for malfunctions [15]. In contrast, thermal imaging, a well-established technology offers advantages including independence from transformers, scalability, and diverse application effectiveness [16–19]. It operates without direct physical contact, minimizing susceptibility to transformer failures such as temperature peaks or fluctuations that may harm sensors. This technology not only monitors transformer temperature comprehensively but also individual components or adjacent equipment independently. Recent proposals suggest its use for correcting and monitoring temperature-related issues in electrical substations and power transformers [20–22]. Early failure prevention in the electrical grid and risk reduction are closely tied to artificial intelligence methods enabling the identification and notification of potential failures. The widespread impact of artificial intelligence, particularly big data and machine learning, extends across various societal domains [23,24], including autonomous transportation [25], neuroscience [26–28], healthcare [29,30] or automatic text translation [31]. Notably, the management of electrical grids has been significantly influenced by artificial intelligence advancements, empowering grids to make informed decisions in response to shifts in energy demand, renewable energy production, and extreme weather events. Furthermore, the escalating volume of data enables the application of machine learning for detecting and preventing anomalous behavior of the electrical network.

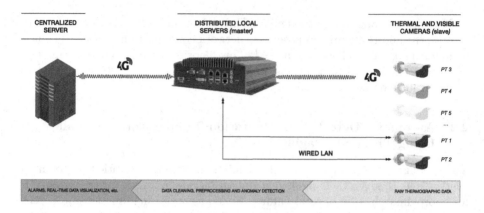

Fig. 2. Thermographic data acquisition architecture.

System Architecture. The proposed thermography data acquisition and processing system consists of 20 thermal cameras and 9 industrial PCs for control, as depicted in Fig. 2. Industrial PCs establish connections with cameras either via physical Ethernet cables when co-located or through 4G communication when at different sites. To ensure security, radio-link connections are VPN-secured, although their use was dismissed due to inadequate coverage in some locations.

Thermal image capture is initiated by industrial PCs, with acquisition frequency determined by connection type (one image per minute for physical links, one every 5 min for radio links). Upon receipt, industrial PCs handle storage and processing tasks. Additionally, industrial PCs are equipped with 4G connectivity for tasks such as monitoring, control, and data extraction, with external access facilitated through the SSH protocol, all secured by VPN for enhanced security.

Thermal Anomalies Detection System. The proposed thermal anomaly detection solution operates continuously on distributed servers independently of the thermal image acquisition system. Upon receiving a captured thermal image, the server processes it to check if the registered temperatures of transformer regions fall within optimal margins predicted by an adaptive model; if not, a thermal anomaly alarm is triggered. The system's flowchart is illustrated in Fig. 3, and a detailed description of each module follows.

– The thermographic data processing involves segmentation and temperature extraction submodules. Segmentation occurs through automated algorithms and manually-defined masks. Nine regions of interest (ROIs) were manually defined Fig. 4, including primary and secondary windings terminals, high and low voltage bushings, transformer body, and background temperature. Individual masks are crafted for each camera scene, allowing the computation of the mean temperature of the top 5% of pixels within each ROI. Automatic segmentation is computed employing Otsu [32] and Maximally Stable Extremal Regions Algorithm (MSER) [33] algorithms, to store the size of each

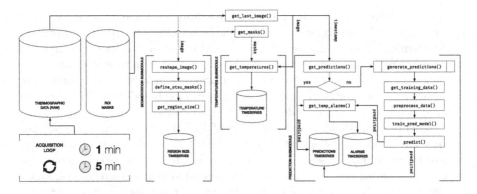

Fig. 3. Thermal anomalies detection system diagram.

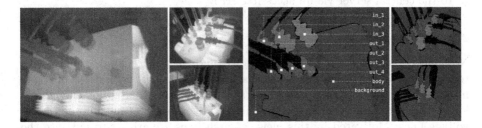

Fig. 4. Raw thermal data and manually-defined regions of interest.

ROI and identify deviations indicating potential anomalies such as vegetation growth or intruders.

– The prediction model and alarms submodule plays a critical role in evaluating thermal data extracted by the segmentation and temperature extraction submodules. Following image capture and processing, this submodule assesses if the extracted temperatures meet expected margins for each region. If anomalies are detected, specific region alarms are generated and relayed to the central server for operator response. These margins are dynamic, contingent upon factors such as time of day, ambient temperature, season, weather conditions, and transformer workload. Notably, the temperature data captured by the cameras exhibits stationarity over time, resulting in daily "duck curves" representing the transformer's load profile across 24 h. Leveraging this stationarity, future predictions are adaptively calculated based on historical observations. The proposed adaptive prediction model undergoes recurrent updates based on newly available temperature data, a characteristic known as online learning, which is particularly advantageous in dynamic environments with rapidly changing training data. However, determining the retraining frequency is crucial to balance prediction accuracy with computational efficiency and the risk of overfitting. In the proposed solution, the adaptive prediction model is retrained every 720 min (12 h), aligning with the frequency of thermal image acquisition. This approach ensures that the model remains responsive to the transformer's evolving temperature conditions while avoiding excessive computational costs. By incorporating the latest 24 h of temperature data into the training process, the model adapts to the current temperature dynamics, enabling accurate predictions for the subsequent 12-h time window. Thus, the model's adaptability enhances its performance in forecasting temperature variations. The prediction and alarm generation submodule verifies then the difference between the recorded temperature and the estimated value against a predefined threshold (set at a margin of 15 °C) for each region of interest. This threshold can be adjusted to fine-tune the sensitivity of the anomaly detection system. Subsequently, a temporary table is generated, encompassing the recorded temperature data, the predicted temperature values, and a control bit associated with each ROI indicating the presence or absence of a thermal anomaly alarm. This information is then extracted and transmitted to the central server via an accessible API.

2.3 Fleet of Drones

Nowadays, multi-rotors, with small range and endurance, and usually with remote pilots in the visual line of sight, are applied for local inspections of transmission towers [34,35] or grid segments [36]. However, this is not enough for long-endurance inspection of the electrical grid composed of medium and high-voltage lines. Motivated by this, new research lines are arising to mitigate the limitations of these robots [37]. There are also long range and endurance UAVs, usually large and heavy, which are used in military application, surveillance, maritime applications, environmental surveillance, and others. In addition, small fixed-wing systems, usually flying below 150 m, are also applied for surveillance and mapping of relatively large areas. However, they have constraints related to the accuracy due to the limitations of the on-board sensing systems. In the last years, new systems with vertical take-off and landing and flight as fixed wing have been developed. Different types of systems exist, including those with different propellers to fly as fixed wing and vertical take-off and landing (VTOL), as well as systems that can change the orientation of the propellers after take-off to fly as fixed wing and later changing again to the initial configuration for landing. However, these platforms are currently not efficient to perform the hovering required for detailed very close view and aerial manipulation for maintenance operation.

The inspection of large infrastructures such as electrical grid systems can be performed more efficiently with multiple UAVs [38]. The advantages when comparing with the use of a single UAV are: decreasing the total time for the whole inspection; minimizing delays for event detection; application of teaming techniques involving multiple specialized platforms for example to obtain closed view in local inspection and have long-range inspection; and improved reliability by avoiding dependencies of a single UAV.

The drones chosen for the power lines inspection are heterogeneous since the system includes multi-rotors and the fixed-wing VTOLs. This configuration of the team covers long range operation along the power lines, but also a detailed and close inspection of the transmission towers, including their grounding system in the base. However, as the flight time of the aerial robots is nowadays limited, compared to the large size of the power lines, the system also includes battery recharging stations where the UAVs autonomously land and take-off to extend their range and perform continuous operation.

A classification of different possible architectures for multi-drone systems can be found in [39], and the scheme that can fit better for the application addressed in this project is an architecture for intentional cooperation. An example of this type of architecture applied to a multi-drone team in field tests can be found in [40] and we have adopted that approach in RESISTO. The architecture is endowed with different modules that solve the usual problems that arise during the execution of multipurpose missions, such as task allocation, conflict resolution, task decomposition, and sensor data fusion. The approach had to satisfy two main requirements: robustness for operation in power line inspection scenarios and easy integration of different autonomous vehicles. An overview of the architecture of the multi-drone system is shown in Fig. 5 with the drones and their payloads on top, the main software modules on-board the drones are in the middle and the Ground Control Station (GCS) and the mission planner are at the bottom. The software development is mainly based on the Robot Operating System (ROS) [41] which stands as the established standard for developing robot applications, extending its utility to the domain of autonomous vehicles such as drones. Interacting directly with the autopilot at the lowest level, we have developed several ROS nodes that makes possible to control drones with autopilots supporting the MAVLink protocol, and or DJI autopilots. In addition, SMACH [42] is the ROS library applied for monitoring the mission inside the drones and the GCS.

The mission planner module autonomously computes the flight plans for all the drones. The tasks and all their associated parameters for each drone are defined in a file in YAML format. This YAML file plays a pivotal role in configuring precise flight paths and parameters for each UAV (such as the gimbal and heading angle, camera triggers for videos or pictures, speed, etc.) ensuring an efficient inspection.

To facilitate comprehensive mission management and supervision, an user-friendly graphical interface using React in JavaScript was developed for the GCS. This interface is essential for efficiently handling mission tasks, including loading, editing, commanding and monitoring.

Regarding the ROS nodes running within the on-board computer of the drone, the primary one is the vehicle node, which handles the drone's state and movement collecting data from the on-board sensors, and allows the interaction with the GCS thanks to the ROS communication options. Its functions are acting as a server to the client that will be at the GCS broadcasting telemetry data and providing basic control commands services.

The node that takes advantage of this vehicle node is the mission node, which will be an abstraction layer with higher level functionalities related to the mission. The whole mission process from its upload to its end is governed by a

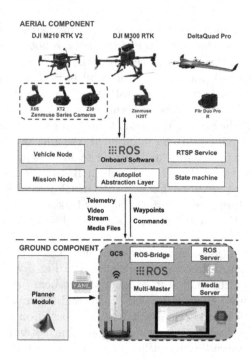

Fig. 5. Multi-drone system architecture with the ground segment composed by the Ground Control Station (GCS) and the mission planner module at the bottom, the main software modules on-board the drones in the middle and the drones and their payloads on top.

state machine, which monitors the connection with the GCS, correct upload and command actions and the running process gathering information and making this information transparent regardless of the autopilot and useful to visualize it with the Graphical User Interface.

The communication link between the Ground and Aerial components relies on the ROS multimaster-fkie [43] tool. This package enables the presence of a ROS-Master node on each CPU, facilitating the sharing of services and topics across a common network. Notably, the ROS nodes operating on the vehicles remain independent of the Ground Component once the mission starts, ensuring their continuous operation even if the connection to the GCS is lost.

Finally, a node to stream the video from the on-board cameras has been developed to operate through different streaming paradigms. The drones chosen for our application are the DeltaQuad Pro as the VTOL fixed-wing and the DJI Matrice Series drones as the multicopter part (DJI Matrice 210 V2 RTK and DJI Matrice 300 RTK). All the drones are equipped with both visual and thermal cameras on-board.

3 Discussion

To align with the overarching goals of the project, specific objectives have been delineated, focusing on the development of technology, supported by both hardware and software, essential for fulfilling the aforementioned general objectives. The scientific and technological objectives are outlined below:

- **Increase Network Observability:** RESISTO endeavors to revolutionize the design and monitoring of the electrical grid by enhancing its observability. This will be achieved through the installation of crucial sensors for predicting and detecting network faults, alongside the development of methodologies and software tools aimed at bolstering the capabilities of network control centers.
- **Increase Situational Awareness:** The project aims to establish an infrastructure integrating comprehensive information about the study area. This includes the implementation of a network comprising sensors, autonomous aerial robots, and devices such as thermal cameras in distribution centers, facilitating tele-surveillance of overhead lines. Through this infrastructure, full IoT coverage will be achieved, enabling thorough monitoring and augmenting knowledge about the network's status.
- **Increased Resilience:** Another primary objective of RESISTO is to enhance the resilience of the electrical network by detecting vulnerabilities and risks associated with extreme events in the long term. Corrective measures will be applied against identified vulnerabilities and risks, including fires and extreme winds. Continuous monitoring and short-term risk prediction will be conducted through integrated sensors, cameras, and software, enabling electrical control centers to anticipate disruptive events and activate emergency protocols promptly.
- **Facilitate Operation and Maintenance (O&M) Tasks:** Installation of sensors, thermal cameras, and remote surveillance systems will facilitate the development of algorithms for early detection of network failures. These algorithms will streamline O&M tasks by enabling early anomaly detection in substations, lines, and distribution centers. Data obtained will support preventive maintenance of critical components such as transformers, mitigating risks of overheating and malfunction. Additionally, optimization of network operation during emergency situations will be facilitated.
- **Adoption of Standardized Community Technologies:** RESISTO will adopt ICT standards developed by the European Union to enhance the existing European value chain, thereby promoting the adoption of standardized community technologies.
- **Promote Conversion of Electrical Grid Sensor Network:** The project aims to leverage the potential of the implemented infrastructure to predict and monitor network risks. Furthermore, it will serve as a 'first responder' to competent authorities, offering valuable information for detecting risks affecting both nature and society.
- **Increase Operational Capacity:** Through the project framework and installed technology, resources will be made available to network managers,

significantly enhancing event detection in the electrical network. This heightened speed of action will lead to reduced affected areas, necessitating fewer resources for impact mitigation and ultimately increasing the operational capacity of competent agencies.

4   Conclusions

The RESISTO project emerges as an innovative technological initiative and research transfer endeavor within Europe. In this article, the fundamental components of RESISTO are presented. First, the GridWatch electrical resilience platform serves as a comprehensive solution uniting climate data with the electrical transportation and distribution system. It aims to concentrate information for visualizing electrical system interactions, integrating external diagnostic tools, and utilizing artificial intelligence to detect and address electrical faults efficiently. The platform incorporates various tools and systems, including local weather stations, online weather sources, fire sensors, infrared cameras in transformation centers, and drones, to maximize information availability and facilitate informed decision-making. Particularly in this project, the GridWatch platform is integrated with a distributed network of 20 thermal cameras and servers for detecting thermal anomalies in power lines and electrical transformers, deployed in The Doñana National Park (Spain). This distributed network of cameras and servers features a machine learning-based system responsible for the recording, storage, analysis, and detection of thermal anomalies in different electrical installations. To accomplish this, it utilizes an adaptive algorithm that continuously learns from newly available temperature data and predicts the expected thermal behavior of the transformer accordingly. Upon detecting a thermal anomaly, it promptly notifies the GridWatch platform. Finally, in order to validate these thermal anomaly alarms, we have a fleet of drones consisting of DeltaQuad Pro for VTOL fixed-wing operations and DJI Matrice Series drones for multicopter operations equipped with thermal cameras. Additionally, a node has been developed to stream video from onboard cameras, enhancing real-time situational awareness during missions.

Acknowledgments. This work was supported by Spanish project RESISTO (2021/C005/00144188) funded by FEDER (Fondo Europeo de Desarrollo Regional) from Ministerio de Asuntos Económicos y Transformación Digital.

References

1. Intergovernmental Panel on Climate Change (IPCC): Climate Change 2021 – The Physical Science Basis: Working Group I Contribution to the Sixth Assessment Report of the Intergovernmental Panel on Climate Change. Cambridge University Press, Cambridge (2021)
2. GeoSolutions: MapStore 2 documentation (2023). Accessed 28 Feb 2024
3. GeoServer: Geoserver (2024). Accessed 28 Feb 2024

4. Stefanidou-Voziki, P., Cardoner-Valbuena, D., Villafafila-Robles, R., Dominguez-Garcia, J.L.: Data analysis and management for optimal application of an advanced ml-based fault location algorithm for low voltage grids. Int. J. Electr. Power Energy Syst. **142**, 108303 (2022)

5. Paradell, P., et al.: Increasing resilience of power systems using intentional islanding; a comparison of binary genetic algorithm and deep learning based method. In: 2021 IEEE International Conference on Cyber Security and Resilience (CSR), pp. 491–496 (2021)

6. Vitolina, S.: Development of lifetime data management algorithm for power transformers. In: Proceedings of the International Conference on Intelligent Systems, Modelling and Simulation, ISMS, September 2015, pp. 452–457 (2015)

7. Müllerová, E., Hrůza, J., Velek, J., Ullman, I., Stříska, F.: Life cycle management of power transformers: results and discussion of case studies. IEEE Trans. Dielectr. Electr. Insul. **22**(4), 2379–2389 (2015)

8. Yazdani-Asrami, M., Taghipour-Gorjikolaie, M., Razavi, S.M., Gholamian, S.A.: A novel intelligent protection system for power transformers considering possible electrical faults, inrush current, CT saturation and over-excitation. Int. J. Electr. Power Energy Syst. **64**, 1129–1140 (2015)

9. Dolata, B., Coenen, S.: Online condition monitoring becomes standard configuration of transformers-practical application for optimized operation, maintenance and to avoid failures. In: E-ARWtr2016 Transformers, Advanced Research Workshop on Transformers, La Toja Island, Spain, vol. 2 (2016)

10. Bakar, N., Abu-Siada, A., Islam, S.: A review of dissolved gas analysis measurement and interpretation techniques. IEEE Electr. Insul. Mag. **30**(3), 39–49 (2014)

11. Kunicki, M., Borucki, S., Zmarzły, D., Frymus, J.: Data acquisition system for on-line temperature monitoring in power transformers. Meas. J. Int. Meas. Confed. **161**, 107909 (2020)

12. Peimankar, A., Weddell, S.J., Jalal, T., Lapthorn, A.C.: Evolutionary multi-objective fault diagnosis of power transformers. Swarm Evol. Comput. **36**, 62–75 (2017)

13. Velasquez-Contreras, J.L., Sanz-Bobi, M.A., Arellano, S.G.: General asset management model in the context of an electric utility: application to power transformers. Electr. Power Syst. Res. **81**(11), 2015–2037 (2011)

14. Ramírez, J., et al.: Power transformer forecasting in smart grids using narx neural networks. In: Valenzuela, O., Rojas, F., Herrera, L.J., Pomares, H., Rojas, I. (eds.) ITISE 2019. CS, pp. 401–414. Springer, Cham (2020). https://doi.org/10.1007/978-3-030-56219-9_26

15. de Melo, A.S., Calil, W.V., Salazar, P.D.P., Liboni, L.H.B., Costa, E.C.M., Flauzino, R.A.: Applied methodology for temperature numerical evaluation on high current leads in power transformers. Int. J. Electr. Power Energy Syst. **131**, 107014 (2021)

16. Sirca, G.F., Adeli, H.: Infrared thermography for detecting defects in concrete structures. J. Civ. Eng. Manage. **24**(7), 508–515 (2018)

17. Linjun, L., Dai, F., Zaniewski, J.P.: Automatic roller path tracking and mapping for pavement compaction using infrared thermography. Comput. Aided Civ. Infrastruct. Eng. **36**(11), 1416–1434 (2021)

18. Bagavathiappan, S., Saravanan, T., George, N.P., Philip, J., Jayakumar, T., Raj, B.: Condition monitoring of exhaust system blowers using infrared thermography. Insight-Non-Destr. Test. Condition Monit. **50**(9), 512–515 (2008)

19. Itami, K., Sugie, T., Vayakis, G., Walker, C.: Multiplexing thermography for international thermonuclear experimental reactor divertor targets. Rev. Sci. Instrum. **75**(10 II), 4124–4128 (2004)
20. Zarco-Periñán, P.J., Martínez-Ramos, J.L., Zarco-Soto, F.J.: A novel method to correct temperature problems revealed by infrared thermography in electrical substations. Infrared Phys. Technol. **113**, 103623 (2021)
21. Segovia, F.: Connected system for monitoring electrical power transformers using thermal imaging. Integr. Comput. Aided Eng. **30**(4), 353–368 (2023)
22. Ramirez, J.: Prediction of transformer temperature for energy distribution smart grids using recursive neural networks. In: ITISE 2019, Proceedings of Papers, Volume 1, September 2019, pp. 167–177 (2019)
23. Górriz, J.M., et al.: Artificial intelligence within the interplay between natural and artificial computation: advances in data science, trends and applications. Neurocomputing **410**, 237–270 (2020)
24. Górriz, J.M., et al.: Computational approaches to explainable artificial intelligence: advances in theory, applications and trends. Inf. Fus. **100**, 101945 (2023)
25. Ma, Y., Wang, Z., Yang, H., Yang, L.: Artificial intelligence applications in the development of autonomous vehicles: a survey. IEEE/CAA J. Automatica Sinica **7**(2), 315–329 (2020)
26. López-García, D., Peñalver, J.M.G., Górriz, J.M., Ruz, M.: MVPAlab: a machine learning decoding toolbox for multidimensional electroencephalography data. Comput. Meth. Prog. Biomed. **214**, 106549 (2022)
27. López-García, D., González-Peñalver, J.M., Górriz, J.M., Ruz, M.: Representational similarity analysis: a preliminary step to fMRI-EEG data fusion in MVPAlab. In: Vicente, J.M.F., Álvarez-Sánchez, J.R., de la Paz López, F., Adeli, H. (eds.) Artificial Intelligence in Neuroscience: Affective Analysis and Health Applications, pp. 84–94. Springer, Cham (2022). https://doi.org/10.1007/978-3-031-06242-1_9
28. Jafari, M., et al.: Emotion recognition in EEG signals using deep learning methods: a review. Comput. Biol. Med. **165**, 107450 (2023)
29. López-García, D., Ruz, M., Ramírez, J., Górriz, J.M.: Automatic detection of sleep disorders: multi-class automatic classification algorithms based on support vector machines. In: International Conference on Time Series and Forecasting, ITISE 2018, vol. 3, pp. 1270–1280 (2018)
30. Jafari, M., et al.: Empowering precision medicine: AI-driven schizophrenia diagnosis via EEG signals: a comprehensive review from 2002–2023. Appl. Intell. **54**, 35–79 (2024). https://doi.org/10.1007/s10489-023-05155-6
31. Mohamed, Y.A., Kannan, A., Bashir, M., Mohamed, A.H., Adiel, M.A.E., Elsadig, M.A.: The impact of artificial intelligence on language translation: a review. IEEE Access **12**, 25553–25579 (2024)
32. Otsu, N.: A threshold selection method from gray-level histograms. IEEE Trans. Syst. Man Cybern. **9**(1), 62–66 (1996)
33. Matas, J., Chum, O., Urban, M., Pajdla, T.: Robust wide-baseline stereo from maximally stable extremal regions. Image Vis. Comput. **22**(10 SPEC. ISS.), 761–767 (2004)
34. He, T., Zeng, Y., Zhuangli, H.: Research of multi-rotor UAVs detailed autonomous inspection technology of transmission lines based on route planning. IEEE Access **7**, 114955–114965 (2019)
35. Baik, H., Valenzuela, J.: Unmanned aircraft system path planning for visually inspecting electric transmission towers. J. Intell. Robot. Syst. **95**(3), 1097–1111 (2019)

36. Iversen, N., Kramberger, A., Schofield, O.B., Ebeid, E.: Pneumatic-mechanical systems in UAVs: autonomous power line sensor unit deployment. In: 2021 IEEE International Conference on Robotics and Automation (ICRA), pp. 548–554. IEEE (2021)

37. Iversen, N., Schofield, O.B., Cousin, L., Ayoub, N., Bögel, G.V., Ebeid, E.: Design, integration and implementation of an intelligent and self-recharging drone system for autonomous power line inspection. In: 2021 IEEE/RSJ International Conference on Intelligent Robots and Systems (IROS), pp. 4168–4175. IEEE (2021)

38. Deng, C., Wang, S., Huang, Z., Tan, Z., Liu, J.: Unmanned aerial vehicles for power line inspection: a cooperative way in platforms and communications. J. Commun. **9**(9), 687–692 (2014)

39. Maza, I., Ollero, A., Casado, E., Scarlatti, D.: Classification of multi-UAV architectures. In: Valavanis, K.P., Vachtsevanos, G.J. (eds.) Handbook of Unmanned Aerial Vehicles, pp. 953–975. Springer, Dordrecht (2015). https://doi.org/10.1007/978-90-481-9707-1_119

40. Maza, I., Caballero, F., Capitan, J., Martinez de Dios, J.R., Ollero, A.: A distributed architecture for a robotic platform with aerial sensor transportation and self-deployment capabilities. J. Field Robot. **28**(3), 303–328 (2011)

41. Quigley, M., et al.: ROS: an open-source Robot Operating System. In: ICRA Workshop on Open Source Software (2009)

42. SMACH - a task-level architecture for rapidly creating complex robot behavior in ROS (2024). http://wiki.ros.org/smach. Accessed 05 Feb 2024

43. Multimaster fkie - The metapackage to combine the nodes required to establish and manage a multimaster network (2024). https://hackmd.io/@octobotics/rknm7a6ys. Accessed 05 Feb 2024

Multi-UAV System for Power-Line Failure Detection Within the RESISTO Project

Alvaro Poma$^{(\boxtimes)}$, Francisco Javier Roman-Escorza, Miguel Gil,
Alvaro Caballero, Ivan Maza, and Anibal Ollero

GRVC Robotics Lab, University of Seville, Seville, Spain
{apoma,fraromesc,mgil8,alvarocaballero,imaza,aollero}@us.es

Abstract. This paper presents our approach to the power-lines fault detection application with a team of multiple Unmanned Aerial Vehicles (UAVs). Our solution required proper integration of several commercial UAVs customizing their hardware and building a software architecture based on open-source tools under the ROS (Robotic Operating System) framework to enhance adaptability, specialization, and overall mission effectiveness. Besides, a planner coordinates mission tasks and optimizes flight paths, while an user-friendly Graphical User Interface (GUI) provides real-time and intuitive visualization and interaction, enhancing overall system usability and effectiveness in power-line inspection applications for fault detection. Finally, the paper includes experimental results in the power-lines located in the Doñana National Park (Spain), within the RESISTO project, which validate the overall approach and embedded mission planning method for real-world applications.

Keywords: Unmanned Aerial Vehicles · Smart grids · Artificial intelligence · Thermal imaging · Robotic Operating System

1 Introduction

Under the leadership of e-Distribución Redes Digitales, the RESISTO project represents a pioneering endeavor in Europe, characterized by its groundbreaking technological innovations and its commitment to transferring research outcomes into practical applications. Its main goal is to bolster the power grid of the Doñana National Park, located in Andalusia, in the south of Spain, by combining artificial intelligence with a diverse suite of state-of-the-art technologies. These encompass thermal surveillance cameras, weather stations, fire sensors, and an autonomous drone fleet. It is based on the GridWatch Electrical Resilience Platform[1], a software application by the Catalonia Institut for Energy Research - IREC, which amalgamates climate data with the electrical transportation and distribution system. This platform centralizes all relevant information for the visualization of electrical system interactions, integrating external diagnostic

---

[1] https://www.irec.cat/wp-content/uploads/2021/03/cataleg-IREC_202104-min.pdf.

© The Author(s), under exclusive license to Springer Nature Switzerland AG 2024
J. M. Ferrández Vicente et al. (Eds.): IWINAC 2024, LNCS 14675, pp. 262–272, 2024.
https://doi.org/10.1007/978-3-031-61137-7_24

tools and employing mathematical algorithms and AI for fault location and resolution. It incorporates various tools such as local weather stations, online weather systems, fire sensors, infrared cameras, and a fleet of drones.

Once an incident is located by GridWatch, the fleet of drones helps with the recovery part executing a mission to confirm or dismiss an incident giving real-time information. In addition, this UAVs fleet could be used for operational and maintenance tasks, especially in remote or hard-to-access areas.

In this article we describe and discuss drones integration in the RESISTO Project. The UAVs are capable of carrying out two types of power-line inspections as it is depicted in Fig. 1. The first case aims to detect hotspots or other issues along a critical span of a power-line. In the second case, the objective is to conduct an orbital flight surrounding a transmission tower to identify structural risks or failures, such as corrosion, cracks, or loose bolts, as well as related issues like vegetation encroachment or equipment malfunctions. As well as surrounding a transmission tower, another threats could be covered in, for example a fire detected along the power grid.

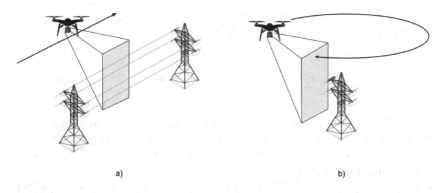

a)   b)

Fig. 1. Inspection Schema, a) Inspection of Power Line, b) Inspection of Electric Tower.

In order to compute an effective inspection plan, several critical factors must be carefully considered. Firstly, one must assess the elevation profile of the targeted area, alongside the heights of any towers present. Additionally, the limited autonomy of the UAV must be factored in, ensuring that flight paths align with operational capabilities. Moreover, collision avoidance measures need to be integrated seamlessly into the plan, prioritizing the safety of both the UAV and surrounding infrastructure.

The main contribution of this paper is a multi-UAV system designed for power-line inspection, showcasing a significant advancement in the integration of heterogeneous UAVs with varying capabilities for the RESISTO project. Leveraging open-source tools and state-of-the-art technologies, the system seamlessly integrates a multi-UAV team, a planner, and a Graphical User Interface (GUI).

2   System Description

To facilitate the integration of UAVs into the RESISTO project, a centralized architecture was employed. This architecture features a central node, functioning as a Ground Control Station (GCS) computer, responsible for the management and control of all UAVs through the implementation of the Robotic Operating System (ROS) [1]. The GCS enables control through a Web Application accessed via a web browser, facilitating communication with third-party applications such as GridWatch through an API. The system architecture is presented in Fig. 2.

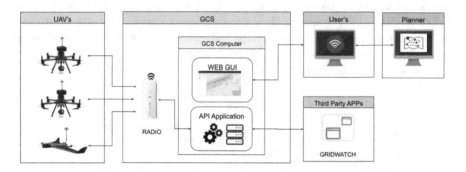

Fig. 2. General Overview of UAV system in fist step of Resistor project.

Each UAV is equipped with an onboard computer that communicates with the flight control unit (Autopilot). The onboard computer captures telemetry data and video footage, transmitting this information to the GCS while also receiving commands from it.

During the operation, GridWatch initiates a request to the GCS, specifying the towers or segments that require inspection. The user receives this information and provides it to the planner, which then generates a mission. This mission is sent back to the GCS for inspection. The calculated mission details are subsequently transmitted to each UAV using ROS. After the completion of the mission, the GCS downloads all photos captured during the operation. After that, it preprocesses these images to identify and detect potential issues before forwarding both the images and the analysis results to GridWatch.

2.1   Planner Description

As it was mentioned above, two distinct types of inspections are considered: the inspection of a specific point, involving the orbiting of a given transmission tower and its constituent elements, and segment inspections. Each necessitates a unique algorithm to adequately address its respective requirements.

Firstly, the inspection of a specific transmission tower demands the base coordinates, the coordinates of the point to inspect, inspection distance from the point to the UAV, and gimbal angle. With this information, the planner generates an orbit around the tower to inspect, satisfying the inspection distance and gimbal angle. During the mission, the UAV should take off from the base, fly through the nearest point of the orbit, follow the points on the orbit until the last one, while taking photos or videos of the point from those points. Once the last point of the orbit is reached, the UAV has to return home.

In contrast, for segments inspection, utilizing a multi-UAV team for the inspection of power lines results in shorter missions compared to employing a single UAV, which can result in longer mission times. Moreover, integrating multi-UAVs in the mission requires attending to the different capabilities of the UAVs in terms of battery capacity or flight speed, and the possibility of inspecting complex typologies may result in a harder problem to obtain an efficient mission.

A graph-based representation can express the problem of segment inspection as a directed weighted multigraph $\mathcal{I} = (\mathcal{N}, \mathcal{R}, \mathcal{C}, \mathcal{U})$. Here, $\mathcal{N}$ is the union of the pylons ($\mathcal{P}$) and the bases of the UAVs used ($\mathcal{B} = \{B_1, B_2, ..., B_\delta\}$). $\mathcal{R}$ represents all the possible paths between the nodes, while $\mathcal{L}$ is a subset of this that represents the power lines connecting the towers. The cost required to arrive from one node to another ($\mathcal{C}$) could be measured in terms of the time required ($\mathcal{T}$) or the battery capacity ($\mathcal{E}$) consumed on the path. Being a heterogeneous UAVs team, these sets are different for each UAV. Thus, the times and battery capacity required for a path depend on the weather conditions, making the problem asymmetric. The last set $\mathcal{U}$ represents all the UAVs involved in the mission.

To optimize the total mission time, the graph-based problem can be approached as a variation of the Vehicle Routing Problem (VRP), and its precise resolution can be achieved through Mixed-Integer Linear Programming (MILP) as it done at [2]. For this, $z_{i,j|k} \in \mathcal{Z}$ is defined as a binary variable representing if the path $r_{i,j|k} \in \mathcal{R}$ is traveled ($z_{i,j|k} = 1$) or not ($z_{i,j|k} = 0$). When utilizing a multi-UAV team to complete the mission, the optimization of the mission time consists of minimizing the time of the UAV that requires the most time, posing a min-max problem. Another approach to this min-max problem, integrated into the proposed planner, is to minimize simultaneously two sums: the total time required by all UAVs and the differences in the times of each UAV to balance the mission times. Thus, the variable $x_{u,v}$ is defined as the difference in the times required by the UAVs u and v in the set $\mathcal{U}$.

The MILP formulation to resolve these problems is as follows:

$$\min_{z_{i,j|k},x_{u,v}} \sum_{\{i,j\}\in\mathcal{N},i\neq j,k\in\mathcal{U}} c_{i,j|k}z_{i,j|k} + \sum_{\{r,q\}\in\mathcal{U},u<v} x_{u,v} \tag{1}$$

s.t.

$$\sum_{j\in\mathcal{P}} z_{0_k,j|k} \geq 1 \qquad \forall k \in \mathcal{U} \tag{2}$$

$$\sum_{i\in\mathcal{P}} z_{i,0_k|k} \geq 1 \qquad \forall k \in \mathcal{U} \tag{3}$$

$$\sum_{j\in\mathcal{N},j\neq i} \left(z_{i,j|k} - z_{j,i|k}\right) = 0 \quad \forall i \in \mathcal{N}, \forall k \in \mathcal{U} \tag{4}$$

$$\sum_{k\in\mathcal{U}} \left(z_{i,j|k} + z_{j,i|k}\right) \geq 1 \quad \forall\{i,j\}/r_{i,j|k} \in \mathcal{L}, i < j \tag{5}$$

$$\sum_{\{i,j\}\in\mathcal{N},i\neq j} \left(c_{i,j|r}z_{i,j|r} - c_{i,j|v}z_{i,j|v}\right) - x_{u,v} \leq 0$$
$$\forall\{u,v\} \in \mathcal{U}, u < v \tag{6}$$

$$\sum_{\{i,j\}\in\mathcal{N},i\neq j} \left(c_{i,j|v}z_{i,j|v} - c_{i,j|u}z_{i,j|u}\right) - x_{u,v} \leq 0$$
$$\forall\{u,v\} \in \mathcal{U}, u < v \tag{7}$$

$$\sum_{i\in\mathcal{S},j\notin\mathcal{S},k\in\mathcal{U}} \left(z_{i,j|k} + z_{j,i|k}\right) \geq 2\,h(\mathcal{S}) \qquad \forall\mathcal{S} \subset \mathcal{P} \tag{8}$$

where the objective functions (Eq. 1) embody the previously discussed min-max approach. Constraints (Eq. 2) and (Eq. 3) ensure that each UAV initiates the mission from its designated base and returns there upon completion. Furthermore, these constraints allow the UAVs to return to the bases, which serve as recharge stations, as many times as required to recharge their batteries.

Additional constraints (Eq. 4) ensure the synchronization of UAV departures and arrivals at nodes, while also maintaining a balanced frequency of UAV entries and exits at each node.

The main objective of the planning (inspecting the segments of the power grid) is defined by the constraints in Eq. 5, which ascertain that a UAV flies over all the segments, regardless of direction. Constraints 6 and 7 define the variable $x_{u,v}$, which represents the difference in mission times, where the variable $c_{i,j|v}$ represents the time that UAV u needs to fly from node i to node j.

The final constraints, represented by Eq. 8, serve to eliminate all subtours, ensuring that each UAV follows a unique tour that satisfies all preceding constraints. However, due to the potentially extensive number of subsets, these constraints are typically deferred from the initial stages of the optimization process. Instead, they are progressively integrated as the optimization progresses and when necessary, to rectify any violations [3].

To expedite the quest for the optimal solution, additional battery constraints can be introduced:

$$\sum_{\{i,j\}\in N, i\neq j} e_{i,j|k} z_{i,j|k} \leq \sum_{j\in P} z^k_{0,j|k} \quad \forall k \in U \tag{9}$$

These constraints ensure that the total battery consumption during each UAV inspection (left-hand side of the inequality) does not exceed or equal the number of times the UAV departs from its base (right-hand side of the inequality). This consideration is made under the assumption that the UAVs always commence their missions with fully charged batteries. In this constraint, $e_{i,j|k}$ denotes the percentage of battery consumption that UAV k experiences when flying from node i to node j.

2.2   Software Implementation

Several components were developed, including the GCS, the planner, and integration programs for UAVs. The planner application, implemented in MATLAB, plays a crucial role by enabling the selection and parameterization of missions. A comprehensive description of all its features was presented in 2.1.

The GCS, on the other hand, adopts a client-server architecture. Comprising a Web User Interface built with REACTjs, it offers a user-friendly platform for monitoring and commanding multiple UAVs. This is achieved through the submission of requests to the API application, enhancing the efficiency of the overall system Fig. 3.

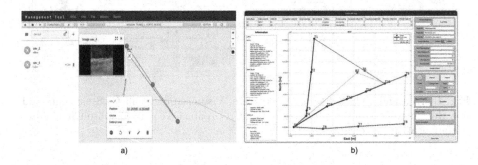

Fig. 3. Software interfaces, a) GCS main page Interface, b) Planning Interface.

The API Application is the core of the GCS that allows to serving as the central communication hub for the multi-UAV system. It manages the relay of messages from UAVs, handles ROS subscriptions and services, maintains persistent robot information, and processes client requests. In addition, it facilitates the process of downloading images from the UAVs for further processing and sends the results to GridWatch.

The Media server Mediamtx [4] allows to host the videostream of all the UAVs and RosBridge [5] allows to connect the GCS API application to ROS through the use of WebSocket. The communication link between the ground and aerial segments is established through the ROS multimaster-fkie [6] tool. This tool allows for the presence of a ROS-Master node on each CPU, enabling the sharing of services and topics over a shared network. In this manner, it is possible to read the topics that are running on other computers, and to access the topics and services of all the UAVs.

Regarding each UAV, different software and nodes of ROS are running on the onboard computer, so the UAV can communicate with the GCS using Python and C++ in Ubuntu 20 under ROS Noetic like it is shown in Fig. 4. Depending on the UAV branch, distinct derived backends are employed to control the UAV with ROS. For instance, DeltaQuad drones utilizes MAVROS, while DJI UAVs employ ROS OSDK. To send a waypoint mission to a UAV, the onboard backend creates an abstraction interface between the GCS and the derived autopilot's backend.

To send video streaming from the UAVs to MediaServer, we use the ROS-RTSP package [7] developed by Circus Monkey, which allows the transmission of video from a ROS topic or a camera connected to the onboard computer, establishing a RTSP server for real-time video publication with H.264 compression.

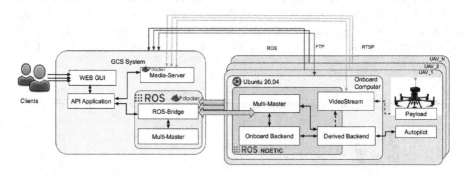

Fig. 4. UAV and GCS Software architecture. Visualization of all GCS elements and how they interact with the software running UAVs onboard computers through different communication protocols.

The entire system was implemented in simulation, mirroring real-world scenarios, thanks to the use of ROS. This enables the execution of software deliverables through the simulation of the autopilot. In the case of the DeltaQuad, software simulation was achieved using the PX4 Software in the Loop (SITL) with Gazebo. For the DJI, a Hardware in the Loop (HITL) approach was adopted, utilizing the UAV's own hardware for simulation purposes.

2.3   Hardware Implementation

For the integration of the drones with the GCS, each UAV is equipped with small single-board computers (SBCs). The SBCs chosen are the Jetson Orin Nano and the Raspberry Pi 4. To establish communication between the drone's autopilot and the SBCs, it is necessary to employ a UART to USB conversion mechanism, typically facilitated by an FTDI (Future Technology Devices International) chip. This conversion allows the autopilot to transmit telemetry data to the onboard computers via USB connection. In the particular case of the DJI, we needed an expansion module to make this connection possible.

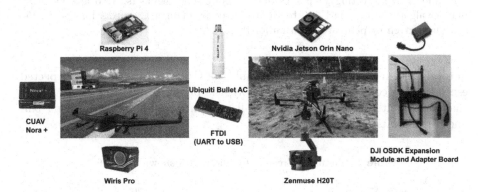

Fig. 5. Drones used with main hardware components highlighted. On the left side the DeltaQuad Pro with the Wiris Pro Camera, Pixhawk Autopilot and its SBC Raspberry Pi. On the right side, the DJI M300 RTK is shown with its expansion module that enables the UART connection and the power supply for the onboard computer and the Zenmuse H20T. Between them we have the Ubiquiti onboard and the FTDI chip because they are present in each of them.

Finally, Fig. 5 shows the hardware equipment of the UAVs for the autonomous inspection. The autonomous inspection system relies on WiFi communication between drones and ground stations. Ubiquiti Rocket Prism 5AC Gen 2 devices serve as ground stations, while Ubiquiti Bullet AC antennas are used for drone access points. With a range of up to 4 km, these devices enable effective data and command transmission for missions in various environments.

3   Validation

3.1   Planning Approach Simulation

The proposed planning algorithm described in this paper was extensively validated in simulation. The routes shown in Figs. 6a, 6b and 6c correspond to a mission where the UAVs had to inspect 11 pylons and 10 power-line segments. Some relevant information is presented in Table 1, showing notable reductions

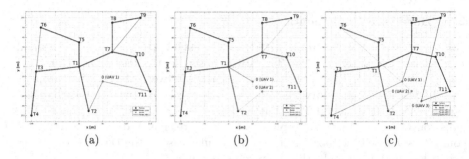

Fig. 6. Analysis of the impact of UAV quantity on planner algorithm performance in the context of inspecting 11 pylons and 10 power-line segments. a) Route given by planner algorithm for one UAV, b) Routes given by planner algorithm for two UAVs, c) Routes given by planner algorithm for three UAVs.

in total mission time with increased number of UAVs, accompanied by expected escalations in computation time. Notably, the planning process yielded results that significantly diminished the overall mission duration while ensuring balanced mission times for all UAVs.

Table 1. Simulation results for the routes shown in Fig. 6.

Case	UAVs	Routes	t^{comp} [s]	t^{insp} [s]
1	1	$\{0, 2, 1, 3, 4, 6, 5, 1, 7, 9, 8, 7, 10, 11, 0\}$	0.10	**235.05**
2	2	$\{0, 1, 3, 4, 6, 5, 1, 0\}$	0.74	122.85
		$\{0, 11, 10, 7, 9, 8, 7, 1, 2, 0\}$		**130.51**
3	3	$\{0, 4, 3, 1, 7, 0\}$	9.43	97.21
		$\{0, 6, 5, 1, 2, 0\}$		**98.03**
		$\{0, 9, 8, 7, 10, 11, 0\}$		97.17

3.2   Test Flights

The use case begins with fixed cameras and sensors detecting potential failures on the grid network. This information is forwarded by GridWatch and received in our GCS. Once we have an area to inspect, a process based on the one described in Sect. 2 is followed to provide a response and telemetry to GridWatch. Then, the role of the drones is to go to the area and take pictures and/or videos of the possible faults for confirmation. Figure 7 depicts the flight plans in order to confirm or dismiss the alarm.

Fig. 7. DJI M300 inspecting electrical infrastructure commanded from GridWatch. a) GCS capture of the mission to inspect a particular transmission tower. b) Raw image of the transmission tower objective. c) Processed thermal image of Electric tower mission with maximum temperature point shown.

4 Conclusions and Future Works

We have integrated commercial drone technology (DeltaQuad Pro, DJI M300) with ROS and open-source tools, as well as a GUI to govern them with a planner module for efficient missions computation. Testing both in simulation and real flight campaigns has shown the applicability of the system to different use cases related to power-lines inspection. As a result, this comprehensive approach has demonstrated the versatility of the system, paving the way for further advancements in the field of multi-UAV systems for power-line inspection. The implementation is available on GitHub under the MIT License: https://github.com/alvcaballero/multiUAV_system. Future plans involve integrating the planner into the GCS for workflow automation and user authentication.

Acknowledgments. This work was supported by the R+D+i project TED2021-131716B-C22, funded by MCIN/AEI/10.13039/501100011033 and by the European Union NextGenerationEU/PRTR. This work was also supported by Spanish project RESISTO (2021/C005/00144188) funded by FEDER (Fondo Europeo de Desarrollo Regional) from Ministerio de Asuntos Económicos y Transformación Digital.

References

1. Quigley, M., et al.: ROS: an open-source Robot Operating System. In: ICRA Workshop on Open Source Software (2009)
2. Nekovar, F., Faigl, J., Saska, M.: Multi-tour set traveling salesman problem in planning power transmission line inspection. IEEE Robot. Autom. Lett. **6**(4), 6196–6203 (2021)
3. Laporte, G.: What you should know about the vehicle routing problem. Nav. Res. Logist. **54**(8), 811–819 (2007)
4. Mediamtx - ready to use and zero dependency real-time media server. https://github.com/bluenviron/mediamtx. Accessed 7 Jan 2023

5. Jonathan Mace. Rosbridge suit. http://wiki.ros.org/rosbridge_suite. Accessed 15 June 2023

6. Alexander Tiderko, Multimaster fkie - ROS package for multimaster communications. http://wiki.ros.org/multimaster_fkie. Accessed 15 Jan 2023

7. ROS RTSP - ROS package for real-time video transmission. https://github.com/CircusMonkey/ros_rtsp. Accessed 15 Jan 2023

Smart Renewable Energies: Advancing AI Algorithms in the Renewable Energy Industry

Machine Learning Health Estimation for Lithium-Ion Batteries Under Varied Conditions

Gabriel M. C. Leite[1,2(✉)], Jorge Pérez-Aracil[1], Carolina Gil Marcelino[3],
Gabriel García-Gutiérrez[4], Milan Prodanovic[4], Enrique García-Quismondo[4],
Sergio Pinilla[4], Jesús Palma[4], Silvia Jiménez-Fernández[1],
and Sancho Salcedo-Sanz[1]

[1] Universidad de Alcalá (UAH), Alcalá de Henares, Spain
[2] Systems and Computing Department (PESC-COPPE), Federal University of Rio
de Janeiro (UFRJ), Rio de Janeiro, Brazil
gabriel.matos@uah.es
[3] Institute of Computing (IC), Federal University of Rio de Janeiro (UFRJ), Rio de
Janeiro, Brazil
[4] Instituto IMDEA Energía, Madrid, Spain

Abstract. To mitigate intermittency from renewable energy sources
and present a sustainable alternative to fossil-fuel-based transportation,
battery energy storage systems (BESSs) have drawn attention from both
academia and industry in the last years. Despite different alternatives,
Lithium-ion batteries (LIBs) have become the dominant technology for
BESSs and electric vehicles. Therefore, knowledge of lithium-ion battery aging and lifetime estimation is a fundamental aspect for ensuring
secure and reliable operations of different systems. This paper presents
an analysis of five machine learning models, namely linear regression,
k-nearest Neighbors (kNN), random forest (RF), support vector regression (SVR), multi-layer perceptron (MLP), in estimating the state of
health (SOH) of LIB cells under different conditions. A total of 12 battery cells, cycled under three different temperatures (15 °C, 25 °C, 35 °C)
and two discharge C-Rates (1C and 2C), were utilized for validation using
mean absolute error (MAE) and R square (R^2) coefficient as performance
indicators. Results indicated that both kNN and linear regression models achieved the lowest MAE values, with the linear regression model
obtaining the highest R^2 value. On the contrary, the MLP model showed
the worse results among all models tested. A statistical analysis corrob-
orated the results, indicating that the less complex learning models are
suitable for estimating the non-linear SOH of LIBs.

Keywords: Supervised machine learning · Lithium-ion battery · State
estimation · Regression model · Battery model

1 Introduction

Towards mitigating the effect of climate change, the European Union (EU) has
defined the challenging goal of becoming the first climate-neutral continent in the

J. M. Ferrández Vicente et al. (Eds.): IWINAC 2024, LNCS 14675, pp. 275–282, 2024.
https://doi.org/10.1007/978-3-031-61137-7_25

world by 2050 [4]. As a result, renewable energy sources (RES) have emerged as a crucial alternative for low-carbon energy generation [1,14]. However, the unpredictability and intermittency of RESs require advanced technologies and strategies to manage the mismatch between the renewable power supply and the end-use demand [7]. Energy storage systems (ESSs) are clear candidate solutions to mitigate these issues at the technical level [16]. Several storage technologies are employed in ESSs, such as pumped hydro storage [21] and battery energy storage systems (BESS) [3]. Besides the benefits of intermittency reduction and voltage stabilization in microgrids [5,10], Battery-based systems have recently drawn attention for their potential in transport electrification [11] [12]. Among the different available battery technologies, Lithium-ion batteries (LIBs) have become the dominant technology for BESSs and electric vehicles. LIB technologies, such as Lithium Nickel Manganese Cobalt Oxide - $LiNi_xMn_yCo_{1-x-y}O_2$ (NMC), Lithium Iron Phosphate - Li_xFePO_4 (LFP), and Nickel Cobalt Aluminum - $LiNi_xCo_yAl_zO_2$ (NCA), offer a high energy density and longer lifespan compared to lead acid batteries [2].

Despite the advantages and long life span of LIBs, performance deterioration still occurs. Thus, monitoring the state of health (SOH) of a battery plays a key role in ensuring a secure and reliable operation. The SOH indicates how much energy/power a battery can supply at the current health level, compared to its fresh state. However, unlike terminal voltage and current, a battery's SOH cannot be directly measured. In addition, the cycle aging process of a LIB is highly affected by external factors, namely current rates (C-Rate), external temperature, battery operating range, and depth of discharge (DoD), to name a few. Therefore, researchers attempt to estimate SOH using either experimental measurements, electrochemical models or data-driven methods [8]. Estimations based on experimental measurements not only take months to years to produce acceptable estimates but also are easily affected by measurement errors. Although estimations based on electrochemical models are not affected by the external environment, the estimates are limited by the model's computational complexity. In contrast, data-driven methods do not rely on either any mechanism modeling or prior knowledge.

In this work, we present an analysis of different supervised learning models for SOH estimation in NMC batteries using the discharge capacity as a health indicator. Accordingly, five supervised learning models are evaluated in estimating the discharge capacity at each cycle of 12 battery cells, considering 100% of DoD, 0.5C for charging, three different temperatures (15 °C, 25 °C, 35 °C), and two discharge C-Rates (1C and 2C). The remainder of this paper is organized as follows: Sect. 2 describes the methodology employed in the experimentation, and Sect. 3 presents both the acquired results and a discussion. Finally, Sect. 4 concludes and presents the final remarks about SOH estimation on NMC lithium-ion batteries.

2   Methods

This Section introduces the lithium-ion battery data set. Moreover, the experimental design description is detailed along with the data processing. The LIB dataset used in this research is available at the data repository of the Sandia National Laboratory (SNL) [15]. This dataset has been made available recently in 2020 and consists of several LFP, NCA, and NMC battery cells cycled with constant current - constant voltage (CCCV) charge and constant current (CC) discharge. Moreover, cells were tested under different temperatures, current rates, and DoDs. Among the different battery chemistries, this study focuses on the NMC cells due to their extensive use in electric vehicles [12,22]. Moreover, SOH has been studied for the parameters, temperature (15 °C, 25 °C, 35 °C), current rate (0.5C charge - 1C discharge (1C), 0.5C charge - 2C discharge (2C)), and DOD (100%).

Regarding the battery's technical details, all battery cells are from LG Chem (Part #18650HG2) manufacturer with a 3 Ah capacity, nominal voltage of 3.6 V, and charge and discharge cutoff voltages of 4.2 and 2.0, respectively. Finally, a total of 12 battery cells were employed, in which two cells per configuration are available. The data information is detailed in Table 1.

Table 1. Data set information encompassing the experimental configuration of each battery cell.

Cycles	Temperature (C)	DoD (%)	Charge Rate (C)	Discharge Rate (C)	Mirrors
510, 510	15	0–100	0.5	1.0	a, b
386, 386	15	0–100	0.5	2.0	a, b
517, 779	25	0–100	0.5	1.0	a, b
655, 1310	25	0–100	0.5	2.0	a, b
780, 780	35	0–100	0.5	1.0	a, b
780, 768	35	0–100	0.5	2.0	a, b

2.1 Experimental Design and Data Processing

To evaluate the supervised learning model's generalization ability for each cell in different configurations, data for mirror "a" is used for model creation, which was separated into 80% for training and 20% for validation. Afterward, 100% of data for mirror "b" is used for testing the built models on entirely unseen cells. The prediction of the state of health (SOH) at each cycle can be viewed as a regression problem. The learning model predicts the cell's discharge capacity in Ah at each cycle index based on the input features. The input data matrix comprises the following features with the unit measure in parenthesis: Cycle Index, Minimum Charge Voltage (V), Maximum Charge Voltage (V), Minimum Discharge Voltage (V), Maximum Discharge Voltage (V), Maximum Charge Current (A), Minimum Discharge Current (A), Environment Temperature (C), Charge Time (s), Discharge Time (s), Charge Voltage value at 10% of SoC (V).

Subsequently, five different supervised learning models have been employed, namely Linear Regression, Support Vector Regression (SVR), Random Forest regressor (RF), k-nearest Neighbors regressor (kNN), and Multi-layer Perceptron (MLP) [18,20]. Regarding model parameters and configurations, kNN was utilized with both weighted contribution and $k = 5$, and SVR was employed with an RBF kernel. The MLP model contained 2 hidden layers with 16 neurons each. Moreover, RF was configured to use a maximum depth of five, 10 estimators, and a maximum of three features. As it is known that LIBs follow a non-linear degradation [17], a purely linear regression model would not be able to estimate this non-linear behavior. Thus, we have employed the linear regression model along with a non-linear transformation of data. This transformation is obtained by performing a degree-2 polynomial transformation of features. Except for the specified parameters, every other parameter value was the standard from Scikit-learn library [13]. Lastly, the performance of each model in estimating SOH is evaluated according to both the mean absolute error (MAE) and the R square coefficient (R^2) [19], presented in Equations (1) and (2).

$$MAE = \frac{1}{N} \sum_{i=1}^{N} |y_i - \hat{y}_i|, \tag{1}$$

$$R^2 = 1 - \frac{\sum_{i=1}^{N}(\hat{y}_i - y_i)^2}{\sum_{i=1}^{N}(\hat{y}_i - \bar{y})^2}. \tag{2}$$

Here, N represents the number of times estimating SOH, $\bar{y}$ represents the average of real value. The variables y_i and $\hat{y}_i$ denote the i-th actual and predicted values, respectively. Furthermore, outliers are removed from the data by comparing each cell's data to its smoothed version. The smoothed version is the result of performing a symmetric smoothing using the Exponentially Weighted Moving Average (EWMA) [6,9]. It is important to note that the data cleansing procedure

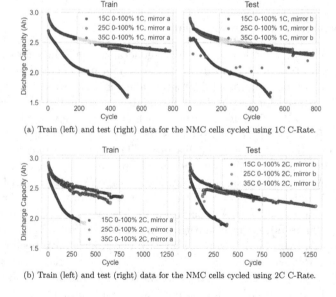

(a) Train (left) and test (right) data for the NMC cells cycled using 1C C-Rate.

(b) Train (left) and test (right) data for the NMC cells cycled using 2C C-Rate.

Fig. 1. Data set for the NMC cells.

is performed only on training data to avoid any type of data snooping. Figures 1a and 1b illustrate the train and test data for 1C and 2C C-Rates, respectively.

3   Results and Discussion

This Section presents the results obtained by each algorithm on estimating the SOH of each cell using the discharge capacity as a health indicator. As detailed in Table 1, the cycle life span of train cells varies between 386 and 780 cycles. On the other hand, cycle life span of test cells is between 386 and 1310 cycles. Thus, models are tested using different cells for predicting SOH for not only similar cycles but also in completely different cycles. As means of comparing the different algorithms, we have considered the average performance of each model over the cells test set, according to MAE and R^2 coefficient.

Figure 2a shows the MAE test results for the evaluated models. It can be noted that among the evaluated models, the linear regression and kNN obtained the lowest MAE values, 0.0218 and 0.0267, respectively. As the complexity of the model increases, so its MAE value increases, with the MLP model achieving the highest MAE value of 0.3584. This means that, for each cycle, the linear regression model would predict a discharge capacity that is either $0.0218/3.0 = 0.7\%$ below or 0.7% above the actual discharge capacity, in contrast to the 12% difference when using the MLP model. Besides the MAE indicator, the R^2 indicates how well the model predicts the test data, having 1.0 as the maximum value. Here, similarly to the MAE indicator, both linear regression and kNN models achieved the highest values, very close to the maximum. The negative R^2 value for the MLP model indicates that the model may have been poorly chosen to this problem.

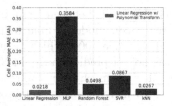

(a) MAE averaged over test cells per learning model. The green bar indicates the model with the lower average MAE value.

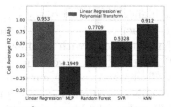

(b) R^2 averaged over test cells per learning model. The green bar indicates the model with the highest average R^2 value.

Fig. 2. Performance indicators for each learning model.

Despite the differences in the average values of each indicator, a statistical analysis is necessary to assess whether there are any statistical differences among algorithm results. Hence, a Kruskal-Wallis test is performed with the null hypothesis of mean MAE and R^2 equality, aiming to find possible differences between the algorithms considering both MAE and R^2. Using a significance value of 5%, a p-value below 0.05 is found indicating that there is a difference among the mean values. Thereafter, a Wilcoxon signed-rank test with the Holm-Bonferroni correction was applied to find out, by pairwise comparisons, which specific group's means are different. The posthoc test results indicated that: 1) Linear regression and kNN outperformed the other models but they are not statistically different concerning MAE values, and 2) the Linear regression model obtained a superior performance compared to the other models in terms of R^2 value.

To analyze the difference between linear regression and kNN performances, we have selected the battery cell at 25 °C. In this temperature, test data contain more cycles than train data, assessing the model's ability to estimate the discharge capacity for previously unseen cycles. Figure 3 shows that, despite the similarity between the train and test discharge capacity curve, kNN presents a higher error after cycle 600 for the cell discharged using 1C C-rate when compared to the linear regression estimates.

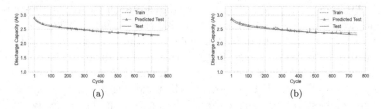

(a)   (b)

Fig. 3. (a) Linear regression model estimation on discharge capacity (Ah) and cycle index with 1C discharging for NMC cell at $25°C$. (b) kNN model estimation on discharge capacity (Ah) and cycle index with 1C discharging for NMC cell at $25°C$.

In the higher C-Rate case, there are more differences between train and test discharge capacity curves. Yet, the linear regression model is able to predict the discharge capacity with minimal error up to cycle 1000, which occurs 400 cycles after the last train cycle. In spite of the noisier prediction from kNN, the predicted discharge capacity curve does not deviate much from the test data. However, kNN's prediction errors commence to increase after cycle 750, 250 cycles earlier than the linear regression model does. This behavior contributes to lower the average R^2 value (Fig. 4).

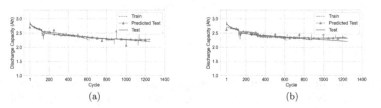

(a)   (b)

Fig. 4. (a) Linear regression model estimation on discharge capacity (Ah) and cycle index with 2C discharging for NMC cell at $25°C$. (b) kNN model estimation on discharge capacity (Ah) and cycle index with 2C discharging for NMC cell at $25°C$.

4   Conclusions

This paper presented a supervised-learning-based analysis for state of health (SOH) estimation in NMC lithium-ion batteries, using the discharge capacity as a health indicator. In this analysis, five different supervised learning models were evaluated in estimating the discharge capacity per cycle over 12 battery cells, which were cycled under different temperatures and current rate cycling conditions. The evaluated learning models were linear regression, k-nearest Neighbors (kNN), support vector regression (SVR), random forest (RF), and multilayer perceptron (MLP). In order to capture the non-linearity of the degradation behavior, the linear regression model was employed alongside a degree-2 polynomial transformation of the features. Furthermore, both mean absolute error (MAE) and R square coefficient (R^2) were employed to compare the performance attained by each model.

Among the evaluated models, the linear regression and kNN models achieved both the lowest average MAE and the highest R^2 values on the test data. A statistical analysis attested that, although these two models do not differ in terms of MAE, the linear regression model outperformed the kNN model concerning the R^2 indicator. Overall, the results presented in this study indicated that by employing a proper data transformation, less complex models are not only able to estimate the SOH of NMC batteries with minimal error under different conditions, but also outperform more complex models in a non-linear application. Finally, the findings of this study contribute to the viability of machine learning approaches towards increasing sustainability and the integration of renewable energy sources.

Acknowledgments. This research has been supported by projects PID2020-115454GB-C21 and TED2021-131777B-C22 of the Spanish Ministry of Science and Innovation (MICINN), and from CAPES (Grant number: 23038.006308/2021-70). The authors thank UAH and UFRJ for the infrastructure used to conduct this work.

References

1. Arantegui, R.L., Jäger-Waldau, A.: Photovoltaics and wind status in the European Union after the Paris Agreement. Renew. Sustain. Energy Rev. **81**, 2460–2471 (2018)
2. Calise, F., Cappiello, F.L., Cimmino, L., d'Accadia, M.D., Vicidomini, M.: Renewable smart energy network: A thermoeconomic comparison between conventional lithium-ion batteries and reversible solid oxide fuel cells. Renewable Energy (2023)
3. Chreim, B., Esseghir, M., Merghem-Boulahia, L.: Recent sizing, placement, and management techniques for individual and shared battery energy storage systems in residential areas: A review. Energy Rep. **11**, 250–260 (2024)
4. Fetting, C.: The european green deal. ESDN report **53** (2020)
5. Gomes, I.S.F., Perez, Y., Suomalainen, E.: Coupling small batteries and PV generation: a review. Renew. Sustain. Energy Rev. **126**, 109835 (2020)
6. Hunter, J.S.: The exponentially weighted moving average. J. Qual. Technol. **18**(4), 203–210 (1986)

7. Leite, G., Marcelino, C., Pedreira, C., Jiménez-Fernández, S., Salcedo-Sanz, S.: Evaluating the risk of uncertainty in smart grids with electric vehicles using an evolutionary swarm-intelligent algorithm. J. Clean. Prod. **401**, 136775 (2023)

8. Lipu, M.H., et al.: A review of state of health and remaining useful life estimation methods for lithium-ion battery in electric vehicles: Challenges and recommendations. J. Clean. Prod. **205**, 115–133 (2018)

9. Lucas, J.M., Saccucci, M.S.: Exponentially weighted moving average control schemes: properties and enhancements. Technometrics **32**(1), 1–12 (1990)

10. Ma, Q., Wei, W., Wu, L., Mei, S.: Life-aware operation of battery energy storage in frequency regulation. IEEE Transactions on Sustainable Energy (2023)

11. Marcelino, C.G., Leite, G.M.C., Jiménez-Fernández, S., Salcedo-Sanz, S.: An improved C-DEEPSO algorithm for optimal active-reactive power dispatch in microgrids with electric vehicles. IEEE Access **10**, 94298–94311 (2022)

12. Mohseni, P., Husev, O., Vinnikov, D., Strzelecki, R., Romero-Cadaval, E., Tokarski, I.: Battery technologies in electric vehicles: Improvements in electric battery packs. IEEE Industrial Electronics Magazine (2023)

13. Pedregosa, F., et al.: Scikit-learn: machine learning in Python. J. Mach. Learn. Res. **12**, 2825–2830 (2011)

14. Potrč, S., Čuček, L., Martin, M., Kravanja, Z.: Sustainable renewable energy supply networks optimization-the gradual transition to a renewable energy system within the European Union by 2050. Renew. Sustain. Energy Rev. **146**, 111186 (2021)

15. Preger, Y., et al.: Degradation of commercial lithium-ion cells as a function of chemistry and cycling conditions. J. Electrochem. Soc. **167**(12), 120532 (2020)

16. Rana, M.M., et al.: Applications of energy storage systems in power grids with and without renewable energy integration-a comprehensive review. J. Energy Storage **68**, 107811 (2023)

17. Schmalstieg, J., Käbitz, S., Ecker, M., Sauer, D.U.: A holistic aging model for li (nimnco) o2 based 18650 lithium-ion batteries. J. Power Sources **257**, 325–334 (2014)

18. Semeraro, C., et al.: Digital twin application in energy storage: trends and challenges. J. Energy Storage **58**, 106347 (2023)

19. Yang, B., et al.: Critical summary and perspectives on state-of-health of lithium-ion battery. Renew. Sustain. Energy Rev. **190**, 114077 (2024)

20. Yang, S., Zhang, C., Jiang, J., Zhang, W., Zhang, L., Wang, Y.: Review on state-of-health of lithium-ion batteries: Characterizations, estimations and applications. J. Clean. Prod. **314**, 128015 (2021)

21. Yang, W., Yang, J.: Advantage of variable-speed pumped storage plants for mitigating wind power variations: integrated modelling and performance assessment. Appl. Energy **237**, 720–732 (2019)

22. Zhao, G., Wang, X., Negnevitsky, M.: Connecting battery technologies for electric vehicles from battery materials to management. Iscience (2022)

Energy Flux Prediction Using an Ordinal Soft Labelling Strategy

Antonio M. Gómez-Orellana[1] , Víctor M. Vargas[1](✉) ,
Pedro A. Gutiérrez[1] , Jorge Pérez-Aracil[2] , Sancho Salcedo-Sanz[2] ,
César Hervás-Martínez[1] , and David Guijo-Rubio[2]

[1] Department of Computer Science and Numerical Analysis,
Universidad de Córdoba, Córdoba, Spain
{am.gomez,vvargas,pagutierrez,chervas}@uco.es
[2] Department of Signal Processing and Communications, Universidad de Alcalá,
Alcalá de Henares, Spain
{jorge.perezaracil,sancho.salcedo,david.guijo}@uah.es

Abstract. This paper addresses the problem of short-term energy flux prediction. For this purpose, we propose the use of an ordinal classification neural network model optimised using the triangular regularised categorical cross-entropy loss, termed MLP-T. This model is based on a soft labelling strategy, that replaces the crisp 0/1 labels on the loss computation with soft versions encoding the ordinal information. This soft label encoding leverages the inherent ordering between categories to reduce the cost of ordinal classification errors and improve model generalisation performance. Specifically, the soft labels for each target class are derived from triangular probability distributions. To assess the performance of MLP-T, six datasets built from buoy measurements and reanalysis data have been used. MLP-T has been compared to nominal and ordinal classification techniques in terms of four performance metrics. MLP-T achieved an outstanding performance across all datasets and performance metrics, securing the best mean results. Despite the imbalanced nature of the problem, which makes the ordinal classification task notably difficult, MLP-T achieved good results in all classes across all datasets, including the underrepresented classes. Remarkably, MLP-T was the only approach that correctly classified at least one instance of the minority class in all datasets. Furthermore, MLP-T secured the top rank in all cases, confirming its suitability for the problem addressed.

Keywords: Energy flux · Renewable energy · Ordinal classification · Unimodal distributions

1 Introduction

The prevalence of ordinal classification [9] problems is on the rise across various fields, including atmospheric events forecasting [8], time series classification [1],

J. M. Ferrández Vicente et al. (Eds.): IWINAC 2024, LNCS 14675, pp. 283–292, 2024.
https://doi.org/10.1007/978-3-031-61137-7_26

or industrial quality control [16], among others. Specifically, an ordinal classification problem involves determining the correct category for a given pattern from a discrete set of categories following a natural order relationship. While the literature typically addresses wave energy flux prediction through regression approaches [6], it can also be viewed from an ordinal perspective. This task involves classifying the amount of energy flux expected in the next hours within predefined intervals. These energy flux intervals, or categories, are essential for determining the appropriate adjustments of Wave Energy Converters (WECs) to transform wave energy into electricity and, hence, to anticipate the energy produced. When addressing energy flux ordinal prediction challenges, two significant factors come into play. Firstly, careful consideration should be given to misclassification costs, implying higher penalties for mispredictions that deviate further from the correct class. For example, misclassifying low energy flux as high may lead to an underutilisation of WEC capacity, resulting in missed energy production opportunities. Conversely, predicting a high energy flux as low might expose WECs to potential damage, incurring in higher maintenance costs. Secondly, exploiting the inherent order information from the problem improves the performance of predictive models. In consequence, it is essential to integrate these key factors into both the design and assessment phases of the model.

In the context of machine learning, a classification problem with J classes involves assigning the correct label $y_i \in \{C_1, C_2, ..., C_J\}$ to a given instance defined by an input vector $\mathbf{x}_i \in \mathcal{X} \subseteq \mathbb{R}^d$, where $d \in \mathbb{N}$ represents the number of input variables. In a nominal classification task, there is no predefined order among the classes, whereas in an ordinal classification problem, also known as ordinal regression, a specific order is established. This order between classes is defined as $C_1 \prec C_2 \prec ... \prec C_J$, where $\prec$ expresses the order relationship between the classes. However, unlike regression, the exact distances between pairs of categories in ordinal classification are unknown. Due to this inherent order relationship, the penalty for misclassification into non-adjacent classes is higher than that for misclassification into adjacent ones, with the magnitude of the penalty increasing as the distance between classes grows.

Ordinal classification is a challenging task, and numerous methodologies have recently been presented in the literature. In [13], the authors introduced an ordinal variant of the logistic regression approach, based on a set of thresholds that divide the space of continuous values into J segments (one for each class in the problem), which are fitted alongside the model. Two different approaches were proposed. The first one considered only the immediate thresholds of the target class C_j (i.e., thresholds $j - 1$ and j), whereas the second one considered all the thresholds.

On the other hand, a new research path based on soft labelling has recently emerged as a promising alternative to develop ordinal classification methodologies. Soft labelling approaches involve replacing the crisp 0/1 labels with alternatives (soft labels) that distribute the total probability among the different classes. The rationale behind this approach is to reduce the cost of classification errors and improve the generalisation performance of the model by exploiting the inherent order between categories. These soft labels are commonly obtained using an unimodal probability distribution, given that they provide a high probability for the target class and a low probability for the adjacent classes. The soft labels obtained using these distributions are integrated into the loss function in such a way that the error is modified for model optimisation, taking into consideration the ordinal information encoded within the soft labels. Prior studies have suggested diverse probability distributions for defining the soft labels. Liu *et al.* specifically advocated for the utilisation of Poisson, binomial, and exponential distributions [11]. Subsequently, in [15], the beta distribution was employed, demonstrating superior results compared to previous works. Lastly, [14] proposed a soft labelling approach based on triangular distributions, achieving excellent results and standing out as one of the simplest distributions.

Following this trend, in this study we propose the use of an ordinal soft labelling strategy, termed MLP-T and described in [14], to tackle the energy flux prediction. The main contributions of this work are summarised as follows: 1) implement an ordinal soft labelling strategy for the short-term prediction of energy flux, replacing the crisp 0/1 labels with soft versions encoding the ordinal information; 2) evaluate the performance of the proposal using six datasets obtained from buoys measurements and reanalysis data; and 3) compare the proposed approach with other nominal and ordinal classification techniques considering four different performance metrics.

The rest of the manuscript is structured as follows: in Sect. 2, we present details related to the datasets employed in this work along with the required preprocessing steps. The experimental design used to assess the methodology is outlined in Sect. 3. The obtained results are reported and discussed in Sect. 4. Finally, we draw conclusions and outline future directions in Section 5.

2   Data Description and Processing

2.1   Buoys Measurements and Reanalysis Data

We have considered data from two widely known sources of information: National Data Buoy Center (NDBC) [12] and National Center for Atmospheric Research (NCAR) [10]. Concerning NDBC data, six buoys anchored in the South West Coast of the USA are taken into account, as illustrated in Fig. 1. The energy flux (F_e) is obtained from two variables collected by the buoys, the Significant Wave Height (SWH) and the Average Wave Period (AWP), as $F_e = 0.49 \cdot \text{SWH}^2 \cdot \text{AWP}$, where F_e is represented in kilowatts per metre (kW/m), SWH is measured in metres and AWP is measured in seconds.

Regarding NCAR data, seven reanalysis variables are used: air temperature, omega vertical velocity, precipitable water content, pressure, relative humidity, and components South-North and West-East of wind speed. Since these variables are gridded as nodes of reanalysis available each 2.5° latitude-longitude, a sub-grid is used for each buoy considering the four closest nodes of reanalysis surrounding its location. Besides, an autoregressive model is employed, incorporating the last past value of the output variable at time instant t.

The energy flux obtained from the buoys measurements (collected every 1 h) and the reanalysis variables (sampled every 6 h) are combined using the SPAMDA software [7], calculating each reanalysis variable as the weighted average of the four nodes of reanalysis with respect to their distance from the buoy (i.e., the smaller the distance, the higher the weight). As a result of the data integration, each dataset consists of 5844 instances (4-times daily during the period 2017-2020), with each instance comprising eight input variables and one target variable. Since this study focuses on energy flux short-term prediction, the target variable (F_e) is expressed at the time instant $t + 6h$, whereas the input variables are expressed at the time instant t. Finally, the datasets partitioning has been carried out as follows: years 2017 to 2019 (4380 instances) compose the training dataset, while year 2020 (1464 instances) conforms the test dataset.

2.2   Obtaining Ordinal Labels

As this study addresses the energy flux prediction using an ordinal soft labelling strategy, the target variable is discretised by replacing the continuous value of each instance with an ordinal label or class ($\mathcal{C}$). For this purpose, a hierarchical clustering is applied to each buoy to group its instances into homogeneous clusters (labels) by energy flux values. Specifically, such hierarchical clustering process is applied using the target variable of the training dataset, with $k = 4$ being the number of clusters to generate (i.e. labels: 1, 2, 3 and 4). Table 1 shows the ranges of the F_e values derived from the hierarchical clustering applied to the training dataset of each buoy, as well as the distribution of instances per class. Note that, in order to discretise the output variable for the test sets, the minimum of $\mathcal{C}_1$ and the maximum of $\mathcal{C}_4$ are set to 0 and inf, respectively, to consider the full domain of the F_e.

Table 1. Ranges for each class ($\mathcal{C}_1, \ldots, \mathcal{C}_4$), along with their distribution of instances, derived from the training dataset of each buoy.

Buoy	Ranges[1]				Train distribution			
	$\mathcal{C}_1$	$\mathcal{C}_2$	$\mathcal{C}_3$	$\mathcal{C}_4$	$\mathcal{C}_1$	$\mathcal{C}_2$	$\mathcal{C}_3$	$\mathcal{C}_4$
46025	[0.37, 4.74]	(4.74, 10.21]	(10.21, 33.33]	(33.33, 100.73]	3279	769	309	23
46026	[0.81, 17.74]	(17.74, 39.98]	(39.98, 131.86]	(131.86, 267.58]	3225	871	272	12
46047	[1.26, 23.72]	(23.72, 44.33]	(44.33, 82.15]	(82.15, 322.51]	3433	576	296	75
46053	[0.18, 7.39]	(7.39, 20.15]	(20.15, 40.76]	(40.76, 110.36]	3532	715	98	35
46059	[1.84, 37.16]	(37.16, 83.36]	(83.36, 226.91]	(226.91, 886.75]	3451	646	249	34
46069	[0.95, 26.44]	(26.44, 53.62]	(53.62, 166.02]	(166.02, 387.86]	3594	570	205	11

[1]Energy flux values are expressed in kW/m.

Therefore, the problem addressed in this study can be expressed as follows:

$$\mathcal{D} = \left\{ \mathbf{X}, \mathbf{y} \right\} = \left\{ (\mathbf{x}_i, y_i) \, ; \ i = 1, 2, \ldots, N \right\}, \tag{1}$$

where $\mathcal{D}$ is the dataset used, N is the number of instances in the dataset, $\mathbf{X} = (\mathbf{x}_1, \mathbf{x}_2, ..., \mathbf{x}_N)$ is the input matrix, $\mathbf{x}_i^T = (x_{i1}, x_{i2}, ..., x_{i8})$ is the vector containing the eight input variables of the i-th instance, and $\mathbf{y} = (y_1, y_2, ..., y_N), y_i \in \{\mathcal{C}_1, \mathcal{C}_2, ..., \mathcal{C}_J\}$ are the ordinal labels.

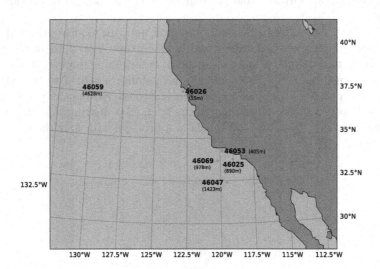

Fig. 1. Geographical location of the six buoys considered in the study. The water depth at the location of each buoy is indicated within brackets.

The datasets considered in this study present a high degree of diversity. The energy flux ranges obtained from hierarchical clustering for $\mathcal{C}_4$ vary from 100.73 kW/m to 886.75 kW/m (Table 1) as a function of water depth at the buoy mooring location (Fig. 1). In addition, the number of instances of the minority class ($\mathcal{C}_4$) ranges from 11 to 75, whereas that of the majority class ($\mathcal{C}_1$) ranges from 3225 to 3594. As a result, $\mathcal{C}_4$ presents very low Imbalance Ratios (the ratio of the number of instances in the minority class to that of the majority class, IR $\in [0, 1]$) ranging from $3.06e^{-3}$ to $2.18e^{-2}$, which highlight the imbalanced nature of the problem.

3   Experimental Settings

This section outlines the different methodologies used in this study. It encompasses both nominal classification approaches and ordinal classification methods. Furthermore, the section delineates the training and evaluation scheme employed for all these approaches.

3.1   Compared Methodologies

Five different approaches are applied, including two nominal methodologies (LR, MLP) and three ordinal approaches (LogisticIT, LogisticAT, MLP-T):

1. LR. Logistic regression.
2. MLP. A standard artificial neural network model with a softmax output and optimised using the categorical cross-entropy loss.
3. LogisticIT [13]. Ordinal logistic regression using immediate-thresholds.
4. LogisticAT [13]. Ordinal logistic regression employing all-thresholds approach.
5. MLP-T [14]. An ordinal classification neural network model optimized using the triangular regularised categorical cross-entropy loss. This methodology introduces two crucial parameters, η and α, determining the weight of the soft labels against the crisp labels and the probability assigned to the adjacent classes, respectively. Detailed explanations of these parameters can be found in [14]. Figure 2 shows an example of the triangular distributions that can be employed to determine the soft labels in a problem with four classes.

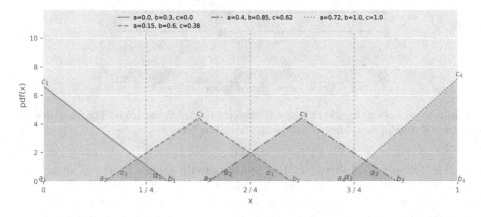

Fig. 2. Example of the triangular distributions used to generate the soft labels for an ordinal classification problem with four classes. Each distribution corresponds to one target class, and the soft labels are derived from the area under these distributions within each class interval. For each triangular distribution, the values of its three parameters (a, b, c) are shown. These values were obtained using $\alpha = 0.1$, that determines the error in adjacent classes.

3.2 Model Training

The training scheme employed for all approaches maintains consistency: a randomised search approach, guided by the Average Mean Absolute Error (AMAE) [2] metric, is applied using a 3-fold strategy over the training dataset. To fit the models, the parameter search algorithm conducts a maximum of 50 iterations of the 3-fold, exploring diverse parameters values drawn from the ranges outlined in Table 2.

Table 2. Range of values used for fitting the parameters of each technique.

Technique(s)	Parameter description	Range of values
LR, LogisticAT, LogisticIT	Regularisation	$\{10^{-3}, 10^{-2}, \ldots, 10^{3}\}$
MLP, MLP-T	Number of hidden neurons	$\{5, 8, 10, 15, 20, 50, 100\}$
	Initial learning rate	$\{10^{-4}, 10^{-3}, 10^{-2}, 10^{-1}\}$
	Momentum	$\{0.60, 0.62, 0.64, \ldots, 1.00\}$
	Number of iterations	$\{500, 1000, 1500, \ldots, 3000\}$
MLP-T	Unimodal η	$\{0.50, 0.85, 1.00\}$
	Triangular α	$\{0.01, 0.02, 0.03, \ldots, 0.2\}$

4   Results and Discussion

This section presents and discusses the results obtained from the experimental design described in Sect. 3. Table 3 shows the results for the Balanced Accuracy (BA) [3], Minimum Sensitivity (MS) [5], Average Mean Absolute Error (AMAE) [2] and Maximum Mean Absolute Error (MMAE) [4] metrics for each buoy. For stochastic methodologies, the Mean and the Standard Deviation (SD) obtained from the results of 30 independent runs are shown as $Mean_{SD}$. In addition, both the mean value of the metric and the mean rank of the methodology across the six buoys are shown in the last two columns.

From a descriptive standpoint of models performance, the MLP-T methodology achieves the best performance in 20 out of 24 cases (across the four metrics and six buoys) and secures the second-best performance in the remaining four buoys. Conversely, the LR methodology attains the top result in the four cases where the MLP-T technique does not, positioning itself as the runner-up. Furthermore, when considering mean values of metrics across all datasets, the MLP-T approach consistently outperforms others, securing the best result for all four metrics, while LR consistently secures the second-best performance. Notably, MLP, serving as the nominal alternative to the MLP-T approach, records the worst mean result in all cases. Lastly, analysing the mean rank across all datasets, again the MLP-T approach attains the top rank in all cases.

Additionally, all methodologies except MLP-T yield zero values in the MS metric for certain buoys, indicating that those models struggle to properly classify the minority classes of the problem. By contrast, the MLP-T methodology achieves commendable results in those buoys where other models fail to classify certain classes.

It is also worth mentioning that only two of the five considered methodologies have a random component: MLP and MLP-T. Furthermore, the MLP methodology yielded significantly worse results than its ordinal alternative MLP-T. While the former produced the least favorable outcomes in all cases, the ordinal alternative consistently achieved the best mean results and ranks. In consequence, conducting a statistical analysis considering the random methodologies is not

Table 3. Results for each of the metrics considered. The results for the stochastic methods include the mean and Standard Deviation (SD) for the 30 executions, MeanSD.

				BA				
Technique	46025	46026	46047	46053	46059	46069	Mean	Rank
LR	_0.494_	_0.726_	**0.640**	_0.639_	_0.610_	_0.551_	_0.610_{0.073}_	_1.833_
LogisticAT	0.476	0.639	0.560	0.555	0.604	0.494	0.555_{0.057}	3.333
LogisticIT	0.459	0.633	0.537	0.552	0.590	0.491	0.544_{0.058}	4.333
MLP	0.487_{0.012}	0.495_{0.010}	0.523_{0.025}	0.569_{0.031}	0.517_{0.017}	0.490_{0.015}	0.514_{0.028}	4.333
MLP-T	**0.723**_{0.083}	**0.768**_{0.044}	_0.636_{0.016}_	**0.700**_{0.057}	**0.695**_{0.043}	**0.584**_{0.099}	**0.684**_{0.060}	**1.167**

				MS				
Technique	46025	46026	46047	46053	46059	46069	Mean	Rank
LR	_0.000_	**0.636**	**0.456**	_0.391_	0.250	_0.000_	_0.289_{0.234}_	_2.500_
LogisticAT	_0.000_	0.409	0.347	0.217	_0.452_	_0.000_	0.238_{0.183}	3.250
LogisticIT	_0.000_	0.424	0.236	0.217	0.398	_0.000_	0.213_{0.168}	3.417
MLP	_0.000_{0.000}	0.000_{0.000}	0.122_{0.100}	0.189_{0.060}	0.017_{0.064}	_0.000_{0.000}	0.055_{0.074}	4.500
MLP-T	**0.451**_{0.185}	_0.613_{0.084}_	_0.448_{0.018}_	**0.521**_{0.049}	**0.496**_{0.115}	**0.101**_{0.192}	**0.438**_{0.160}	**1.333**

				AMAE				
Technique	46025	46026	46047	46053	46059	46069	Mean	Rank
LR	_0.524_	_0.282_	_0.415_	_0.361_	_0.402_	_0.460_	_0.407_{0.076}_	_2.000_
LogisticAT	0.551	0.368	0.519	0.467	0.423	0.525	0.476_{0.064}	3.333
LogisticIT	0.574	0.374	0.531	0.470	0.440	0.538	0.488_{0.067}	4.500
MLP	0.529_{0.011}	0.512_{0.010}	0.539_{0.028}	0.451_{0.032}	0.504_{0.019}	0.537_{0.057}	0.512_{0.030}	4.167
MLP-T	**0.289**_{0.084}	**0.242**_{0.044}	**0.395**_{0.016}	**0.301**_{0.056}	**0.315**_{0.043}	**0.428**_{0.097}	**0.328**_{0.064}	**1.000**

				MMAE				
Technique	46025	46026	46047	46053	46059	46069	Mean	Rank
LR	_1.000_	**0.394**	_0.647_	_0.609_	0.750	_1.000_	_0.733_{0.216}_	_2.583_
LogisticAT	_1.000_	0.621	0.765	0.870	_0.655_	_1.000_	0.818_{0.151}	3.417
LogisticIT	_1.000_	0.606	0.764	0.870	_0.655_	_1.000_	0.816_{0.155}	3.083
MLP	_1.000_{0.000}	1.000_{0.000}	1.051_{0.104}	0.886_{0.044}	0.983_{0.064}	1.033_{0.183}	0.992_{0.053}	4.750
MLP-T	**0.578**_{0.176}	_0.408_{0.079}_	**0.584**_{0.021}	**0.481**_{0.050}	**0.532**_{0.102}	**0.905**_{0.179}	**0.581**_{0.157}	**1.167**

deemed necessary. A simple descriptive analysis is enough to demonstrate the superiority of the MLP-T methodology.

From the perspective of datasets, the buoy 46026, with a water depth of 55 metres, performs the best of all buoys for the BA, AMAE and MMAE metrics in all methodologies except MLP. Furthermore, this buoy achieves the best results across all datasets for the MS metric in three methodologies (LR, LogisticIT and MLP-T). These results indicate that this buoy is one where nominal methodologies can generally classify all classes adequately, despite the ordinal nature of the problem. In contrast, nominal methodologies face challenges in accurately classifying energy flux in buoys with deeper water depth.

On the other hand, the buoy 46053, with a water depth of 405 metres, achieves the best performance in all metrics with the MLP-T approach, so it can be said that there is a certain interaction of the results obtained in all metrics between the methodology used and the buoy analysed.

Finally, the imbalanced nature of the datasets increases the challenge of achieving accurate ordinal classification of the energy flux. This is evident in the MS metric, which, in all methodologies except the MLP-T methodology, shows values of 0 for buoys 46025 and 46069.

5   Conclusions

In this paper we addressed the problem of energy flux prediction using an ordinal soft labelling strategy that replaces the crisp 0/1 labels with smooth versions encoding the ordinal information, derived from triangular probability distributions. The methodology used, termed MLP-T, is an ordinal classification neural network model optimised using the triangular regularised categorical cross-entropy loss. MLP-T was compared with other nominal and ordinal classification approaches in the short-term energy flux prediction problem using six datasets.

MLP-T achieved the best performance in 20 out of 24 comparisons (four metrics per each of the six datasets) and obtained the second-best performance in the remaining four cases. In addition, MLP-T secured the best mean results for all four metrics. Again, MLP-T obtained the top rank in all comparisons. This outstanding performance confirms the excellence of the MLP-T approach for the problem being studied. Despite the imbalanced nature of the datasets, which highly difficult the task of ordinal classification, MLP-T achieved good classification results for the minority class across the different datasets. In contrast, the nominal and other ordinal approaches examined struggled to classify at least one instance of the minority class in two of the six datasets.

As future research lines, we propose to broaden the study in three ways: 1) considering more buoys from other locations; 2) simultaneously predicting long-term prediction horizons could enhance the conclusions and offer a better ability to anticipate unexpected events; and 3) studying the performance of MLP-T for the short- and long-term prediction of other resources of renewable energy.

Acknowledgments. The present study has been supported by the "Agencia Estatal de Investigación (España)" (grant ref.: PID2020-115454GB-C22/AEI/10. 13039/501100011033) and the Spanish Ministry of Science and Innovation (grant refs.: PID2020-115454GB-C21 and TED2021-131777B-C22). Antonio Manuel Gómez-Orellana has been supported by "Consejería de Transformación Económica, Industria, Conocimiento y Universidades de la Junta de Andalucía" (grant ref.: PREDOC-00489). David Guijo-Rubio has been supported by the "Agencia Estatal de Investigación (España)" MCIU/AEI/10.13039/501100011033 and European Union NextGenerationEU/PRTR (grant ref.: JDC2022-048378-I).

Disclosure of Interests. The authors have no competing interests to declare that are relevant to the content of this article.

References

1. Ayllón-Gavilán, R., Guijo-Rubio, D., Gutiérrez, P.A., Bagnall, A., Hervás-Martínez, C.: Convolutional and deep learning based techniques for time series ordinal classification. arXiv preprint arXiv:2306.10084 (2023)
2. Baccianella, S., Esuli, A., Sebastiani, F.: Evaluation measures for ordinal regression. In: 9th International Conference on Intelligent Systems Design and Applications, pp. 283–287 (2009)

3. Brodersen, K.H., Ong, C.S., Stephan, K.E., Buhmann, J.M.: The balanced accuracy and its posterior distribution. In: 2010 20th International Conference on Pattern Recognition, pp. 3121–3124. IEEE (2010)
4. Cruz-Ramírez, M., Hervás-Martínez, C., Sánchez-Monedero, J., Gutiérrez, P.A.: Metrics to guide a multi-objective evolutionary algorithm for ordinal classification. Neurocomputing 135, 21–31 (2014)
5. Fernández, J.C., Martínez, F.J., Hervás, C., Gutiérrez, P.A.: Sensitivity versus accuracy in multiclass problems using memetic pareto evolutionary neural networks. IEEE Trans. Neural Netw. 21(5), 750–770 (2010)
6. Gómez-Orellana, A., Guijo-Rubio, D., Gutiérrez, P., Hervás-Martínez, C.: Simultaneous short-term significant wave height and energy flux prediction using zonal multi-task evolutionary artificial neural networks. Ren Energy 184, 975–989 (2022)
7. Gómez-Orellana, A.M., Fernández, J.C., Dorado-Moreno, M., Gutiérrez, P.A., Hervás-Martínez, C.: Building suitable datasets for soft computing and machine learning techniques from meteorological data integration: a case study for predicting significant wave height and energy flux. Energies 14(2), 468 (2021)
8. Guijo-Rubio, D., et al.: Ordinal regression algorithms for the analysis of convective situations over Madrid-Barajas airport. Atmos. Res. 236, 104798 (2020)
9. Gutiérrez, P.A., Perez-Ortiz, M., Sanchez-Monedero, J., Fernandez-Navarro, F., Hervas-Martinez, C.: Ordinal regression methods: survey and experimental study. IEEE Trans. Knowl. Data Eng. 28(1), 127–146 (2015)
10. Kistler, R., et al.: The NCEP-NCAR 50-year reanalysis. Bull. Am. Meteor. Soc. 82(2), 247–267 (2001)
11. Liu, X., et al.: Unimodal regularized neuron stick-breaking for ordinal classification. Neurocomputing 388(7), 34–44 (2020)
12. National Data Buoy Center: National Oceanic and Atmospheric Administration of the USA. http://www.ndbc.noaa.gov/ (2023). Accessed 13th Dec 2023
13. Rennie, J.D., Srebro, N.: Loss functions for preference levels: regression with discrete ordered labels. In: IJCAI Multidisciplinary Workshop on Advances in Preference Handling. vol. 1, pp. 1–6. AAAI Press, Menlo Park, CA (2005)
14. Vargas, V.M., Gutiérrez, P.A., Barbero-Gómez, J., Hervás-Martínez, C.: Soft labelling based on triangular distributions for ordinal classification. Inform. Fusion 93, 258–267 (2023)
15. Vargas, V.M., Gutiérrez, P.A., Hervás-Martínez, C.: Unimodal regularisation based on beta distribution for deep ordinal regression. Pat Recog 122, 1–10 (2022)
16. Vargas, V.M., Gutiérrez, P.A., Rosati, R., Romeo, L., Frontoni, E., Hervás-Martínez, C.: Deep learning based hierarchical classifier for weapon stock aesthetic quality control assessment. Comput. Ind. 144, 103786 (2023)

Medium- and Long-Term Wind Speed Prediction Using the Multi-task Learning Paradigm

Antonio M. Gómez-Orellana[1], Víctor M. Vargas[1],
David Guijo-Rubio[2]([✉]), Jorge Pérez-Aracil[2], Pedro A. Gutiérrez[1],
Sancho Salcedo-Sanz[2], and César Hervás-Martínez[1]

[1] Department of Computer Science and Numerical Analysis,
Universidad de Córdoba, Córdoba, Spain
{am.gomez,vvargas,pagutierrez,chervas}@uco.es
[2] Department of Signal Processing and Communications, Universidad de Alcalá,
Alcalá de Henares, Spain
{david.guijo,jorge.perezaracil,sancho.salcedo}@uah.es

Abstract. Renewable energies, particularly wind energy, have gain significant attention due to their clean and inexhaustible nature. Despite their commendable efficiency and minimal environmental impact, wind energy faces challenges such as stochasticity and intermittence. Machine learning methods offer a promising avenue for mitigating these challenges, particularly through wind speed prediction, which is crucial for optimising wind turbine performance. One important aspect to consider, regardless of the methodology employed and the approach used to tackle the wind speed prediction problem, is the prediction horizon. Most of the works in the literature have been designed to deal with a single prediction horizon. However, in this study, we propose a multi-task learning framework capable of simultaneously handling various prediction horizons. For this purpose, Artificial Neural Networks (ANNs) are considered, specifically a multilayer perceptron. Our study focuses on medium- and long-term prediction horizons (6 h, 12 h, and 24 h ahead), using wind speed data collected over ten years from a Spanish wind farm, along with ERA5 reanalysis variables that serve as input for the wind speed prediction. The results obtained indicate that the proposed multi-task model performing the three prediction horizons simultaneously can achieve comparable performance to corresponding single-task models while offering simplicity in terms of lower complexity, which includes the number of neurons and links, as well as computational resources.

Keywords: Wind speed · Renewable energy · Multi-task paradigm · Medium and long-term prediction

1 Introduction

Renewable energies have two main virtues: they are clean and they are inexhaustible. In the last decade, they have attracted significant attention from

J. M. Ferrández Vicente et al. (Eds.): IWINAC 2024, LNCS 14675, pp. 293–302, 2024.
https://doi.org/10.1007/978-3-031-61137-7_27

energy production authorities, nations, and energy companies. One renewable source that has stand out over the others is the wind energy with a huge global impact [15]. The main reason is its commendable efficiency, abundant resource availability, and the minimal pollution generated by wind farms. Moreover, wind energy emerges as one of the most promising renewable options in terms of integration into the electric power system [12], thanks to both its inherent natural and cost-effective attributes and to the continuous improvements in the technology used to convert the kinetic energy of wind into electrical energy. Another advantage of this renewable energy source is its capability to provide energy autonomously.

Nevertheless, wind energy has its drawbacks, notably stochasticity and intermittence [1], which result in either insufficient supply during peak hours or wasted energy during periods of low consumption. However, these challenges can be mitigated to some extent through the application of machine learning methods. In particular, the wind speed prediction plays a key role in determining the potential energy output of a wind turbine [3]. Each turbine is equipped with cut-in and cut-out speeds to mitigate both previous inconveniences: 1) the cut-in speed to ensure a maximum energy generation; and 2) the cut-out speed to avoid any damage to the turbines, and hence no supply for a long time. When these issues arise, the deployment of diesel-based energy for electricity generation becomes necessary. By anticipating them, significant enhancements in the optimal performance of wind turbines can be achieved. In this way, the development of accurate and reliable wind speed forecasting methods is imperative [6].

This field has been extensively explored from various perspectives. For instance: Gutiérrez et al. [5] compared several nominal and ordinal classifiers to estimate daily wind speed in wind farms using pressure measurements. They treated wind speed as a discrete variable, transforming wind speed prediction into a classification problem with four categories: *low, moderate, high,* and *very high,* which naturally followed an ordered relationship. Joseph et al. [10] introduced a novel bidirectional long short-term memory model for near real-time wind speed forecasting from a regression standpoint. Additionally, they devised a 3-stage feature extraction procedure, which involved auto- and cross-correlations combined with RReliefF filter algorithms and the Boruta-RF wrapper method. Finally, hybrid tasks combining regression and classification approaches have also been proposed. For example, Peláez et al. [14] presented a hierarchical approach for hourly wind speed prediction. This approach comprised two distinct levels: firstly, a data preprocessing phase utilising clustering methods to group similar patterns into clusters, followed by fitting a regression model for each cluster using only information from that cluster.

Regardless of the methodology employed and the approach used to tackle the problem, an important aspect to consider in wind speed forecasting is the prediction horizon [16]. This categorisation typically spans very short-term (a few seconds to 30 min ahead), short-term (30 min to 6 h ahead), medium-term (6 h to 1 day ahead), and long-term (more than 1 day) forecasts. Focusing on medium- and long-term prediction horizons, we propose the use of a multi-task methodology able to address wind speed forecasting tasks across various prediction horizons simultaneously.

The primary objective of this study is to demonstrate that a multi-task model, which handles multiple prediction horizons, can achieve comparable performance to several individual models, each dedicated to one prediction horizon. Furthermore, this multi-task approach provides advantages in terms of lower complexity, not only in terms of the number of models to be trained (one model for all tasks vs. one model per task) but also in terms of model architecture itself, which includes the number of neurons, links, and computational time associated.

Multi-task learning [17] is a machine learning paradigm aimed at leveraging information from multiple related tasks to enhance the generalisability of all tasks, and it has been applied to fields such as autonomous driving [8], robotic-assisted surgery [9], and renewable energy [4], to mention a few.

Typically, the continual learning paradigm [13], where tasks are learned sequentially, is employed in the community. Conversely, multi-task paradigm learns multiple tasks simultaneously, using shared resources, and requiring lower model complexity and inference time than the traditional approach of using independent models for each task.

Our approach involves an examination of the advantages provided by multi-task prediction models for wind speed forecasting. To this end, we consider three distinct medium- to long-term prediction horizons: 6 h, 12 h, and 24 h ahead. The proposed multi-task approach has been tested for wind speed prediction at a wind farm located in Spain. Specifically, wind speed observations spanning from 2003 to 2013, along with several ERA5 Reanalysis variables serving as inputs, have been considered to assess the performance of the proposed multi-task approach.

The remainder of the manuscript follows this structure: in Sect. 2, we provide an in-depth overview of the data utilised in this study. The experimental framework employed to evaluate the methodology is delineated in Sect. 4. Subsequently, the acquired findings are presented in Sect. 5. Lastly, conclusions are drawn, and avenues for future research are outlined, in Sect. 6.

2 Data Description

This section first describes the wind speed data collected by a wind farm in Spain. Then, the ERA5 Reanalysis variables considered are presented.

2.1 Wind Speed Data

Data from a medium-size wind farm located in Spain is considered (Fig. 1). Specifically, a time series of hourly wind speed data recorded from January 2003 to February 2013 is used as target variable.

Fig. 1. Geographical location of the wind farm highlighted by a circle.

2.2   Predictive Variables

Meteorological variables from the widely known ERA5 reanalysis [7] are used as input variables. ERA5 provides hourly data gridded as reanalysis nodes available each 0.25° latitude-longitude. Table 1 shows the selected reanalysis variables, which correspond to the reanalysis node closest to the wind farm location. As can be seen, the input variables include pressure, the West-East and South-North components of wind speed at different heights, temperature, and the proportion of the grid box covered by clouds.

Table 1. Reanalysis variables considered.

Variable	Description	Variable	Description
sp	Surface pressure	v100	100 m v-component of wind
msl	Mean sea level pressure	t2 m	2m temperature
u10	10m u-component of wind	d2 m	2 m dewpoint temperature
u10n	10m u-component of neutral wind	lcc	Low cloud cover
u100	100m u-component of wind	mcc	Medium cloud cover
v10	10m v-component of wind	hcc	High cloud cover
v10n	10m v-component of neutral wind	tcc	Total cloud cover

In addition to the reanalysis variables, an autoregressive (AR) component is also considered as input, using past values of the target variable at time instants $t - 1\,\mathrm{h}$ and $t - 2\,\mathrm{h}$.

3   Multi-task Artificial Neural Networks

ANNs [2] have demonstrated excellent performance compared to other techniques in addressing non-linear problems. Multilayer Perceptron (MLP) [2] can be considered the most widely used type of ANN, consisting of one input layer, at least one hidden layer and one output layer.

As aforementioned, the goal of this study is to simultaneously predict wind speed at $t + 6$h, $t + 12$h and $t + 24$h prediction horizons. Therefore, the problem is addressed considering the multi-task regression paradigm, defined as:

$$\mathcal{D} = \left\{ \mathbf{X}, \mathbf{Y}^{6h}, \mathbf{Y}^{12h}, \mathbf{Y}^{24h} \right\} = \left\{ \left(\mathbf{x}_i, y_i^{6h}, y_i^{12h}, y_i^{24h} \right); \; i = 1, 2, \ldots, N \right\}, \quad (1)$$

where $\mathcal{D}$ stands for the dataset used, N is the number of patterns in the dataset, $\mathbf{X} = (\mathbf{x}_1, \mathbf{x}_2, ..., \mathbf{x}_N)$ represents the input matrix, $\mathbf{x}_i^T = (x_{i1}, x_{i2}, \ldots, x_{i16})$ is the vector composed of the 16 input variables of the i-th pattern (the 14 variables of Table 1 plus the 2 AR values), and $\mathbf{Y}^{6h} = (y_1^{6h}, y_2^{6h}, \ldots, y_N^{6h})$, $\mathbf{Y}^{12h} = (y_1^{12h}, y_2^{12h}, \ldots, y_N^{12h})$ and $\mathbf{Y}^{24h} = (y_1^{24h}, y_2^{24h}, \ldots, y_N^{24h})$ are the target values of wind speed at $t + 6$h, $t + 12$h and $t + 24$h prediction horizons, respectively.

In consequence, a multi-task MLP regression model, termed MLP-MT, is considered to tackle the wind speed prediction. Specifically, the input layer of the model is composed of 16 neurons, while the output layer contains three linear neurons to simultaneously forecast the wind speed at the three prediction horizons. Hence, the output of the model for the i-th pattern is expressed as:

$$f(\mathbf{x}_i, \boldsymbol{\Theta}) = \left(f^{6h}(\mathbf{x}_i, \boldsymbol{\Theta}), f^{12h}(\mathbf{x}_i, \boldsymbol{\Theta}), f^{24h}(\mathbf{x}_i, \boldsymbol{\Theta}) \right), \quad (2)$$

where $\boldsymbol{\Theta} = (\mathbf{W}, \mathcal{B})$ contains the trainable parameters of the model, $\mathbf{W}^T = (\mathbf{w}_1, \mathbf{w}_2, \ldots, \mathbf{w}_m)$ denotes the weights connecting the inputs with the m hidden neurons, and $\mathcal{B} = (\boldsymbol{\beta}^{6h}, \boldsymbol{\beta}^{12h}, \boldsymbol{\beta}^{24h})$ contains the synaptic weights connecting the hidden neurons with the three outputs. $f^{6h}(\mathbf{x}_i, \boldsymbol{\Theta})$, $f^{12h}(\mathbf{x}_i, \boldsymbol{\Theta})$ and $f^{24h}(\mathbf{x}_i, \boldsymbol{\Theta})$ are the outputs at $t + 6$h, $t + 12$h and $t + 24$h prediction horizons, respectively, and are expressed as:

$$f^{6h}(\mathbf{x}_i, \boldsymbol{\Theta}) = f^{6h}(\mathbf{x}_i, \mathbf{W}, \boldsymbol{\beta}^{6h}) = \beta_0^{6h} + \sum_{j=1}^{m} \beta_j^{6h} B_j(\mathbf{x}_i, \mathbf{w}_j), \quad (3)$$

$$f^{12h}(\mathbf{x}_i, \boldsymbol{\Theta}) = f^{12h}(\mathbf{x}_i, \mathbf{W}, \boldsymbol{\beta}^{12h}) = \beta_0^{12h} + \sum_{j=1}^{m} \beta_j^{12h} B_j(\mathbf{x}_i, \mathbf{w}_j), \quad (4)$$

$$f^{24h}(\mathbf{x}_i, \boldsymbol{\Theta}) = f^{24h}(\mathbf{x}_i, \mathbf{W}, \boldsymbol{\beta}^{24h}) = \beta_0^{24h} + \sum_{j=1}^{m} \beta_j^{24h} B_j(\mathbf{x}_i, \mathbf{w}_j), \quad (5)$$

where $B_j(\mathbf{x}_i, \mathbf{w}_i)$ stands for the basis function for each hidden neuron, which, in this study, corresponds to the sigmoid function [11], formulated as follows:

$$B_j(\mathbf{x}_i, \mathbf{w}_j) = \frac{1}{1 + e^{-\left(w_{j0} + \sum_{k=1}^{d} w_{jk} x_{ik}\right)}}, \quad j = 1, ..., m, \quad 0 < B_j(\mathbf{x}_i, \mathbf{w}_j) < 1. \quad (6)$$

This basis function non-linearly transforms the vector $\mathbf{x}_i^T = (x_{i1}, x_{i2}, \ldots, x_{id})$ containing the input variables ($d = 16$). The vectors $\boldsymbol{\beta}^{6h^T} = (\beta_0^{6h}, \beta_1^{6h}, \ldots, \beta_m^{6h})$, $\boldsymbol{\beta}^{12h^T} = (\beta_0^{12h}, \beta_1^{12h}, \ldots, \beta_m^{12h})$ and $\boldsymbol{\beta}^{24h^T} = (\beta_0^{24h}, \beta_1^{24h}, \ldots, \beta_m^{24h})$ denote the synaptic weights connecting the hidden neurons with the three outputs, including β_0^{6h}, β_0^{12h} and β_0^{24h} as biases. In addition, $\mathbf{w}_i^T = (w_{0i}, w_{1i}, w_{2i}, \ldots, w_{mi})$ denotes the synaptic weights connecting the i-th input neuron with each of the m hidden neurons, with w_{0i} being the bias.

4   Experimental Settings

This section describes the experimental design carried out in this study to evaluate the proposed MLP-MT approach in medium- and long-term wind speed prediction. In addition, the training and evaluation scheme used is delineated.

The dataset has been divided into train and test datasets as follows: years 2003 to 2009 (56859 instances) are used for model training, whereas years 2010 to February 2013 (22756 instances) are used for model evaluation.

To compare the performance of the proposed MLP-MT approach, a single-task MLP model for each prediction horizon is considered. In this way, MLP-ST-6h, MLP-ST-12h, and MLP-ST-24h refer to the model addressing the wind speed prediction at $t + 6h$, $t + 12h$, and $t + 24h$, respectively.

Concerning model training, a randomised search strategy, guided by the Mean Squared Error (MSE) metric (Eq. (7)), is performed considering a 3-fold scheme over the train dataset. Specifically, the search strategy performs a maximum of 30 iterations of the 3-fold, exploring different sets of parameters values selected from the ranges summarised in Table 2.

Table 2. Range of parameters values considered for fitting the models compared.

Model	Description of the parameter	Range of values
	Number of hidden neurons	$\{10, 15, 20, 25, 30\}$
MLP-MT, MLP-ST-6h,	Initial learning rate	$\{10^{-5}, 10^{-4}, 10^{-3}\}$
MLP-ST-12h, MLP-ST-24h	L2 regularisation strength	$\{10^{-3}, 10^{-2}, \ldots, 10^2, 10^3\}$
	Number of iterations	$\{1000, 1500, 3000\}$

Regarding model evaluation, three performance metrics are used. One of the most widely used metrics in regression problems is the MSE, which is calculated as follows:

$$\mathrm{MSE}^t(\mathbf{x}, \boldsymbol{\Theta}) = \frac{1}{N} \sum_{i=1}^{N} \left(y_i^t - f^t(\mathbf{x}_i, \boldsymbol{\Theta})\right)^2, \tag{7}$$

where $t \in \{6h, 12h, 24h\}$ represents the prediction horizon being evaluated.

In this way, the Root Mean Square Error (RMSE) is defined as follows:

$$\mathrm{RMSE}^t(\mathbf{x}, \boldsymbol{\Theta}) = \sqrt{\mathrm{MSE}^t(\mathbf{x}, \boldsymbol{\Theta})}. \tag{8}$$

Finally, the Standard Error of Prediction (SEP) is also considered for comparing the performance of the models developed, which is formulated as follows:

$$\text{SEP}^t(\mathbf{x}, \boldsymbol{\Theta}) = \frac{100}{|\overline{y^t}|} \sqrt{\text{MSE}^t(\mathbf{x}, \boldsymbol{\Theta})}, \tag{9}$$

where $\overline{y^t}$ stands for the average of the target value of all instances in dataset. The SEP has the advantage of being dimensionless, since it represents a relative error expressed as a percentage.

5 Results and Discussion

This section presents the results of the proposed multi-task model, referred to as MLP-MT, using the experimental settings detailed in Sect. 4. Additionally, we include the results for the three single-task models (MLP-ST-6h, MLP-ST-12h, and MLP-ST-24h) to provide a comprehensive comparison. Each single task model is trained independently addressing a specific prediction horizon. Table 3 provides this comparison. The upper part of the table displays the results achieved for the proposed multi-task model, while the results for the single-task models are presented below. Notably, for comparison purposes, the multi-task model results are calculated independently for each prediction horizon, whereas the results for single-task models correspond to each individual output. In addition to the evaluation metrics described in Sect. 4, we compute the structural and computational complexities of the model architecture in terms of #Neurons, #Links and Time (in seconds). The results are presented as the Mean and Standard Deviation (STD) of 30 independent executions (Mean$_{STD}$). Note that the total complexities for the single-task models are computed as the sum of the means for each single-task model, ensuring a fair comparison against the multi-task model.

As can be seen in Table 3, the results achieved by the single-task models are better than those achieved by the multi-task approach. However, it is worthy of mentioning that these differences are generally negligible, occurring in most cases in the third decimal place, which indicates a similar performance. In addition, another potential of the multi-task model resides in the structural and computational simplicity. The multi-task model has a comparable #Neurons and #Links than any of the single-task models, requiring a similar computational time. However, the multi-task model performs three tasks simultaneously, whereas each single-task model is performing only one task at a time. When considering the total #Neurons, #Links and computational time, it is evident that the multi-task model is a much simpler and more cost-effective solution than using three independent simple-task models. Approximately, the #Neurons, #Links and computational time of the multi-task model is one-third of those associated with the three single-task models combined.

In the remainder of this section, the results derived from the experimental results are analysed from a statistical perspective. Due to the page limit

Table 3. Results for the 30 executions of each model are displayed, showing the Mean and Standard Deviation (STD) of 30 independent executions (Mean$_{STD}$). The total number of hidden neurons (#Neurons) and links (#Links) and the total computational time (in seconds) are also presented.

Method	Horizon	MSE	RMSE	SEP	#Neurons	#Links	Time (s)
MLP-MT	6 h	$12.038_{0.117}$	$3.470_{0.017}$	$44.061_{0.213}$			
	12 h	$17.014_{0.076}$	$4.125_{0.009}$	$52.380_{0.116}$	23_7	460_{138}	2589_{2128}
	24 h	$20.191_{0.093}$	$4.493_{0.010}$	$57.056_{0.131}$			
				Total	23_7	460_{138}	2589_{2128}
MLP-ST-6h	6 h	$11.873_{0.065}$	$3.446_{0.010}$	$43.759_{0.120}$	23_6	463_{120}	2202_{1825}
MLP-ST-12h	12 h	$17.012_{0.073}$	$4.125_{0.009}$	$52.377_{0.113}$	20_8	403_{153}	2761_{1973}
MLP-ST-24h	24 h	$20.171_{0.042}$	$4.491_{0.005}$	$57.028_{0.059}$	23_7	456_{133}	3084_{2252}
				Total	66_7	1322_{137}	8048_{4230}

restrictions, we only include statistical tests for the RMSE metric because the conclusions obtained for the MSE and SEP metrics are very similar.

Given our consideration of three single-task models (MLP-ST-6h, MLP-ST-12h, and MLP-ST-24h) alongside the multi-task model (MLP-MT), we obtain a total of six samples, each consisting of 30 values that correspond to the 30 independent executions performed. For each execution, identical random seeds are used across all models, enabling paired comparisons. Firstly, we conduct a non-parametric Kolmogorov-Smirnov test of normality for the aforementioned six samples. Notably, the p-values are all above the confidence coefficient $\alpha = 0.050$. Consequently, we ensure that the distributions of all samples follow a normal distribution.

Since the same random seeds are employed, the resulting samples can be considered dependent. Consequently, we conduct three paired t-tests to compare each single-task model with the corresponding prediction horizon output of the multi-task model. The outcomes are presented in Table 4, where the last column displays the p-values obtained for each comparison. These p-values indicate significant differences in the average RMSE results, favouring the MLP-ST-6h method, at a confidence level of $\alpha = 0.050$. However, the MLP-ST-12h and MLP-ST-24h models do not exhibit significant differences compared to the 12h and 24h outputs of the MLP-MT multi-task model.

Table 4. Paired t-test results comparing performance of the MLP-MT model with the single-task models considering the RMSE metric.

Compared methods	MPD	LVCI	UVCI	t-value	df	p-value (two-sided)
MLP-MT - MLP-ST-6h	0.0238	0.0168	0.0308	6.966	29	**<0.001**
MLP-MT - MLP-ST-12h	0.0002	−0.0039	0.0045	0.116	29	0.909
MLP-MT - MLP-ST-24h	0.0022	−0.0024	0.0068	0.982	29	0.334

MPD: Mean of Paired Differences, LVCI: Lower Value of the 95% Confidence Interval.
UVCI: Upper Value of the 95% Confidence Interval. df: degrees of freedom.

Based on the findings presented in this section, it can be concluded that the proposed MLP-MT multi-task model achieves comparable performance against the three single-task models. Specifically, only the single-task model for the 6h prediction horizon, MLP-ST-6h, achieved significantly better results than the 6h output of the MLP-MT model. Consequently, the multi-task model introduced in this study for addressing the medium- and long-term wind speed prediction problem exhibits excellent performance with much lower complexity compared to combining the three single-task models required to achieve equivalent conclusions.

6 Conclusions

In this study, we tackle the challenge of wind speed prediction by employing a multi-task model capable of forecasting wind speeds across three distinct prediction horizons (6h, 12h, and 24h). Referred to as MLP-MT, our approach utilises a MLP regression model with three outputs tailored to each prediction horizon. The primary objective is to replace the need for individual models dedicated to predicting wind speeds over specific time frames. To evaluate its effectiveness, we compare the performance of our multi-task model against three single-task MLP models, namely MLP-ST-6h, MLP-ST-12h, and MLP-ST-24h. These single-task models focus solely on predicting wind speeds for a specific time horizon.

To evaluate the performance of our proposal, we conduct experiments on a dataset built as follows: hourly wind speed data from a medium-sized wind farm located in Spain is used as target variable, and 14 ERA5 Reanalysis variables are considered as input variables, along with an AR model at time instants $t - 1h$ and $t - 2h$. We compare our multi-task approach with the single-task models using three metrics: MSE, RMSE, SEP. Our findings reveal that the single-task models achieve superior performance only in 6h prediction. Conversely, for the 12h and 24h horizons, both the multi-task model and the single-task models demonstrate comparable performance. In addition, although the multi-task approach simultaneously addresses three prediction horizons, it offers the advantage of reduced model complexity (a smaller number of neurons and links), leading to computational efficiency, which is the main contribution of this work.

In summary, our study suggests that the MLP-MT model presented herein represents a promising approach for addressing simultaneously medium- and long-term wind speed prediction across 6h, 12h, and 24h prediction horizons.

Acknowledgments. The present study has been supported by the "Agencia Estatal de Investigación (España)" (grant ref.: PID2020-115454GB-C22/AEI/10.13039/5011 00011033), and by the projects PID2020-115454GB-C21 and TED2021-131777B-C22 of the Spanish Ministry of Science and Innovation (MICINN). Antonio Manuel Gómez-Orellana has been supported by "Consejería de Transformación Económica, Industria, Conocimiento y Universidades de la Junta de Andalucía" (grant ref.: PREDOC-00489). David Guijo-Rubio has been supported by the "Agencia Estatal de Investigación (España)" MCIU/AEI/10.13039/501100011033 and European Union NextGenerationEU/PRTR (grant ref.: JDC2022-048378-I).

Disclosure of Interests. The authors have no competing interests to declare that are relevant to the content of this article.

References

1. Baïle, R., Muzy, J.F.: Leveraging data from nearby stations to improve short-term wind speed forecasts. Energy **263**, 125644 (2023)
2. Bishop, C.M., et al.: Neural networks for pattern recognition. Oxford University Press (1995)
3. Dorado-Moreno, M., et al.: Multiclass prediction of wind power ramp events combining reservoir computing and support vector machines. In: 17th Conference of the Spanish Association for Artificial Intelligence, pp. 300–309 (2016)
4. Guijo-Rubio, D., Gómez-Orellana, A.M., Gutiérrez, P.A., Hervás-Martínez, C.: Short-and long-term energy flux prediction using multi-task evolutionary artificial neural networks. Ocean Eng. **216**, 108089 (2020)
5. Gutiérrez, P.A., Salcedo-Sanz, S., Hervás-Martínez, C., Carro-Calvo, L., Sánchez-Monedero, J., Prieto, L.: Ordinal and nominal classification of wind speed from synoptic pressurepatterns. Eng. Appl. Artif. Intell. **26**(3), 1008–1015 (2013)
6. Hanifi, S., Liu, X., Lin, Z., Lotfian, S.: A critical review of wind power forecasting methods-past, present and future. Energies **13**(15), 3764 (2020)
7. Hersbach, H., et al.: Era5 hourly data on single levels from 1979 to present. Copernicus climate change service (c3s) climate data store (cds) **10**(10.24381) (2018)
8. Ishihara, K., Kanervisto, A., Miura, J., Hautamaki, V.: Multi-task learning with attention for end-to-end autonomous driving. In: Proceedings of the IEEE/CVF Conference on Computer Vision and Pattern Recognition, pp. 2902–2911 (2021)
9. Islam, M., Vibashan, V., Lim, C.M., Ren, H.: St-mtl: Spatio-temporal multitask learning model to predict scanpath while tracking instruments in robotic surgery. Med. Image Anal. **67**, 101837 (2021)
10. Joseph, L.P., Deo, R.C., Prasad, R., Salcedo-Sanz, S., Raj, N., Soar, J.: Near real-time wind speed forecast model with bidirectional LSTM networks. Renewable Energy **204**, 39–58 (2023)
11. Lippmann, R.P.: Pattern classification using neural networks. IEEE Commun. Mag. **27**(11), 47–50 (1989)
12. Msigwa, G., Ighalo, J.O., Yap, P.S.: Considerations on environmental, economic, and energy impacts of wind energy generation: projections towards sustainability initiatives. Sci. Total Environ. **849**, 157755 (2022)
13. Parisi, G.I., Kemker, R., Part, J.L., Kanan, C., Wermter, S.: Continual lifelong learning with neural networks: a review. Neural Netw. **113**, 54–71 (2019)
14. Peláez-Rodríguez, C., Pérez-Aracil, J., Fister, D., Prieto-Godino, L., Deo, R., Salcedo-Sanz, S.: A hierarchical classification/regression algorithm for improving extreme wind speed events prediction. Renew. Energy **201**, 157–178 (2022)
15. la Tour, M.A.D.: Photovoltaic and wind energy potential in Europe-a systematic review. Renew. Sustain. Energy Rev. **179**, 113189 (2023)
16. Wang, J., Song, Y., Liu, F., Hou, R.: Analysis and application of forecasting models in wind power integration: A review of multi-step-ahead wind speed forecasting models. Renew. Sustain. Energy Rev. **60**, 960–981 (2016)
17. Zhang, Y., Yang, Q.: A survey on multi-task learning. IEEE Trans. Knowl. Data Eng. **34**(12), 5586–5609 (2021)

Data Augmentation Techniques for Extreme Wind Prediction Improvement

Marta Vega-Bayo[1](✉), Antonio Manuel Gómez-Orellana[2](✉),
Víctor Manuel Vargas Yun[2](✉), David Guijo-Rubio[1](✉),
Laura Cornejo-Bueno[1](✉), Jorge Pérez-Aracil[1](✉),
and Sancho Salcedo-Sanz[1](✉)

[1] Department of Signal Processing and Communications, Universidad de Alcalá,
Alcalá de Henares, Spain
{marta.vega,david.guijo,laura.cornejo,jorge.perezaracil,
sancho.salcedo}@uah.es
[2] Department of Computer Science and Numerical Analysis,
Universidad de Córdoba, Córdoba, Spain
{am.gomez,vvargas}@uco.es

Abstract. Predicting extreme winds (i.e. winds speed equal to or greater than 25 m/s), is essential to predict wind power and accomplish safe and efficient management of wind farms. Although feasible, predicting extreme wind with supervised classifiers and deep learning models is particularly difficult because of the low frequency of these events, which leads to highly unbalanced training datasets. To tackle this challenge, in this paper different traditional data augmentation techniques, such as random oversampling, SMOTE, time series data warping and multidimensional data warping, are used to generate synthetic samples of extreme wind and its predictors, such as previous samples of wind speed and meteorological variables of the surroundings. Results show that using data augmentation techniques with the right oversampling ratio leads to improvement in extreme wind prediction with most machine learning and deep learning models tested. In this paper, advanced data augmentation techniques, such as Variational Autoencoders (VAE), are also applied and evaluated when inputs are time series.

Keywords: Extreme wind speed prediction · Data augmentation · Machine learning · Deep learning

1 Introduction

Wind power is one of the main sources of renewable and clean energy, contributing to the economy's decarbonization in developed countries. However, wind power is an energy source with high variability and intermittence, among other issues. In particular, extreme wind equal to or greater than 25 m/s may cause the shutdown of wind turbines, thus having a large impact on wind power production. For this reason, extreme wind prediction in wind farms is essential, both

J. M. Ferrández Vicente et al. (Eds.): IWINAC 2024, LNCS 14675, pp. 303–313, 2024.
https://doi.org/10.1007/978-3-031-61137-7_28

for the secure maintenance and operation of wind farms, and for wind power forecasting and efficient power management.

Previous works have proved the feasibility of wind speed prediction using machine learning algorithms, using meteorological information of the wind farm surroundings as predictor variables. Nevertheless, predicting extreme winds equal to or greater than 25 m/s is particularly challenging, given that it is an extremely rare event. First, samples of extreme winds are scarce, which makes it difficult to apply novel deep learning models, which are often data-intensive, and increase the risk of model overfitting. Second, datasets are extremely unbalanced for this prediction problem, which makes conventional supervised classification models focus on predicting samples of the majority class, usually with a poor performance on predicting samples of the minority class, such as extreme winds.

Data augmentation techniques are proposed in this paper to improve the prediction of extreme wind speeds with machine learning models. Data augmentation techniques increase the size and, desirably, the quality of datasets and have been applied to solve difficulties such as data scarcity, data unbalanced and overfitting. Traditional data augmentation techniques include data warping and oversampling techniques, such as SMOTE [1]. However, generative artificial intelligence, such as GANs or VAEs, has been proposed as a data augmentation technique with good results.

This work proposes to apply different data augmentation techniques to generate synthetic samples of extreme wind speed (equal to or greater than 25 m/s). Their performance and usefulness is to be evaluated through using those synthetic samples as part of the training dataset of machine learning models, used to predict extreme wind, and through the measurement of the improvement obtained thanks to data augmentation. Given that previous works suggest that the best data augmentation technique depends on the data at hand, in this work, data augmentation techniques are to be tested and evaluated with different types of data: time series and three-dimensional data with two dimensions representing location and one dimension representing time evolution.

2   Background on Data Augmentation Techniques

Data augmentation (DA) techniques are techniques which increase the size of a given dataset by adding either copies of existing samples, modifications of existing samples o new synthetic samples [3,4]. In the following subsections, different data augmentation techniques are described.

Data Warping Techniques

Data warping techniques generate synthetic samples by inflicting modifications on existing samples. Many different types of modifications can be inflicted. For instance, synthetic samples might be generated by adding random noise to existing samples. Additionally, when dealing with one-dimensional data, such as time series, synthetic samples might be generated by scaling the amplitude of the signal, by modifying its speed, or smoothly drifting parts of it, among many other possible modifications. Likewise, when dealing with two-dimensional data, such as images, modifications might consist of rotating, flipping or cropping and resizing parts of an image, etc. Finally, when dealing with multidimensional data, data warping might consist of filtering the data, for instance, with a low pass filter, a high pass filter or a white top hat filter, among other possibilities.

Oversampling Techniques

Oversampling techniques have been extensively applied to unbalanced classification and regression problems. Nevertheless, they can also be applied as data augmentation techniques. The simplest technique, random oversampling, adds new samples that are copies of randomly selected samples. SMOTE (Synthetic Minority Oversampling Technique) [1] is one of the most extensively used oversampling techniques. To generate synthetic samples, SMOTE first randomly selects one sample. Then, it randomly selects one of its K-Nearest Neighbours. Finally, SMOTE generates a new synthetic sample by selecting a random intermediate point between those two pre-selected points.

Generative Artificial Intelligence

Generative AI is an artificial intelligence model that can generate new synthetic samples once trained. The most representative techniques of generative AI are generative adversarial networks (GANs) and variational autoencoders (VAEs). Below, VAEs, which have been applied in this work, are described.

VAEs [5] are neural networks composed of an encoder and a decoder. The encoder transforms input data into probability distributions of points in the latent space Z, generally of a much lower dimension than the input data. By contrast, the decoder transforms points z into output data.

The training of VAEs is carried out like any other neural network training. However, the function loss used in the training process of VAEs comprises two terms. On the one hand, the reconstruction error (i.e. MSE) between input and output signals, thanks to which models aim to generate signals similar to those present in the input dataset. On the other hand, the KL loss (Kullback-Leibler Divergence) is also considered, which measures the divergence between the distributions generated in the latent space Z and the presumed $N(0,1)$, being this component of the loss function useful as a regularization technique, enabling models to generate diverse and truly novel samples.

Once trained, VAEs can be used to generate new synthetic samples. To do so, points in the latent space Z are first selected (i.e. randomly, by uniform sampling, by applying SMOTE to previously coded real samples, etc.) and then transformed with the decoder into output data. Note that the training process of VAEs does not guarantee that samples of different classes will be mapped into different regions of the latent space Z. To control the class of synthetic samples, different architectures have been proposed, such as Conditional-VAEs (CVAEs) [7] or class-informed VAEs (CI-VAEs) [6].

In CVAEs, encoders have as input not just the input sample but also the label attached to it. Decoders have as input not just the point z in the latent space but also the label attached to the training sample during the training process or the desired label during the later generation of synthetic samples. On the other hand, the structure of CI-VAEs takes as a starting point the structure of traditional VAEs. Then, a classifier (i.e. MLP) is added internally to predict the sample's label based on the sample's position once mapped in the latent space Z. This classifier is neither used nor available externally. Nevertheless, during the training process, its entropy is measured and used as a third component of the function loss. Thus, during the training process, if samples of different classes are mapped by the encoder in distinct regions of the latent space Z, the classifier's performance and the overall loss of the VAE decreases.

3   Experiments and Results

Extreme wind, with an intensity equal to or greater than $25\,\text{m/s}$, is proposed to be predicted using machine learning and deep learning models, having as predictive variables meteorological information of the wind farm surroundings at previous time instants. In particular, the prediction of extreme wind is posed here as a binary classification problem. As described below, two different sets of predictive variables are proposed and tested: one dataset is one-dimensional, and another dataset is three-dimensional. Additionally, those two datasets are proposed to be augmented by applying different data augmentation techniques. Details of the datasets, machine learning algorithms, data augmentation techniques and experiments are provided below.

Data Sets

Data available for the experiments are, on the one hand, a time series of hourly averaged wind speed intensity measured at a given location over the Iberian peninsula. Data are available from 1995-11-23 to 2013-02-17, although some values are missing. In this location, extreme winds are rare events, which comprise only 0.31% of the total amount of samples. In particular, once missing values are removed, there are 134303 samples, and only 422 are considered extreme winds. Additionally, predictive data available includes meteorological variables given by the ERA5 Reanalysis model [2], which gives hourly averaged data with a spatial resolution of $0.25 \times 0.25°$.

Considering the available data, two different datasets are proposed as predictive variables for the extreme wind prediction problem. Both datasets contain the time series of wind speed measured at the location of interest at $t = 0, \ldots, t = -4$. Additionally, the first dataset contains time series ($t = 0, ..., t = -4$) of several variables of ERA5 (v100, u100, wind speed at 100m, t2m, msl and d2m) at the north-west point of the ERA5 grid closest to the location of interest. Thus, the first dataset is one-dimensional, composed of a time series of meteorological variables.

The second dataset considered, in addition to the time series ($t = 0, ..., t = -4$) of wind speed at the location of interest, contains time series of u100, v100 and wind speed at 100m at a grid 2×2 around the location of interest, and time series of t2m, msl and d2m at a grid 8×8 around the location of interest. Thus, the second dataset is three-dimensional (location in two dimensions map and time).

Experimental Design and Data Processing

Each dataset (one-dimensional and three-dimensional) is split into train and test following the 80–20 rule, being the split stratified. The same partition is used with both datasets and in every execution of the experiments. The train partition of each dataset is used to train different models of machine learning or deep learning without applying oversampling and applying different data augmentation techniques to add new samples of the minority class (wind speed equal to or greater than 25 m/s) with two different oversampling ratios (0.2 and 0.0125). For each combination (dataset, AI model, DA technique and ratio), the experiment is executed 30 times to compute average results. Bellow, the AI models and DA techniques used are described.

Machine learning models and deep learning models

As previously explained, the prediction of extreme wind is posed as a binary classification problem. When using the one-dimensional dataset, which is composed of time series, the following models are trained and tested:

- Random Forest Classifier (RFC) with 100 estimators.
- Multilayer Perceptron (MLP) with two layers of 300 and 100 nodes.
- Long short-term memory (LSTM), alongside the time dimension, being the model composed of 100 units and a dense layer with 100 nodes.
- 1-Dimensional Convolutional Neural Network (1D-CNN), alongside the time dimension, being the model composed of two 1D convolutional layers of 64 filters and a dense layer with 100 nodes.

When using the three-dimensional dataset, which is composed of time series of data over a 8×8 grid of locations at most, in addition to the models described above, the following models are also trained and tested,

- 2-Dimensional Convolutional Neural Network (2D-CNN), alongside the two dimensions representing location, comprises two 2D convolutional layers of 64 filters and a dense layer with 100 nodes.
- 3-Dimensional Convolutional Neural Network (3D-CNN), being the model composed of two 3D convolutional layers of 64 filters and a dense layer with 100 nodes.

Data Augmentation Techniques

When considering the one-dimensional dataset, the following traditional DA techniques are applied and evaluated: Random oversampling, SMOTE, and data warping alongside the time dimension, consisting of either noise addition, convolution with a flattop window, drifting or time warping. On the other hand, when using the three-dimensional dataset, in addition to the DA techniques listed above, multidimensional data warping is also applied and evaluated. In particular, the multidimensional data warping consists in, either noise addition, Gaussian filtering, white or black top hat filtering, or 45º or −45º rotation of those variables which are provided over a 8×8 grid.

Additionally, with the one-dimensional dataset, advanced data augmentation techniques are applied and evaluated. In particular synthetic samples are generated with VAEs with different structures. In particular, VAE, CVAE and CI-VAE, being, always the latent space of 12 dimensions; the encoder composed of two one-dimensional convolutional layers of 128 and 64 filters, a dense layer of 100 nodes and a two dense layers of 12 nodes; and the decoder composed of a dense layer of 100 nodes, a dense layer of 5×64 nodes and three one-dimensional transposed convolutional layers of 64, 128 and 7 nodes. The structure of the CI-VAE also contains an internal classifier which is an MLP of one layer with 32 nodes and one output neuron.

Given that VAEs are composed of neural networks, different models are generated each time a VAE is trained, even with the same dataset. For this reason, a VAE selection process is applied: 32 VAEs are trained and evaluated, and the best one is selected, considering that the best VAE is the one which beats according to the following equation:

$$|0.5 - bCNN| + |0.5 - 1NN| \tag{1}$$

where:

- bCNN is the accuracy given by a 1D-CNN classifier trained to distinguish between real and synthetic samples of the minority class, when tested with real and synthetic samples that the model has not seen before.
- 1NN is the accuracy given by a 1-Nearest Neighbour classifier with k = 1 trained to distinguish between real and synthetic samples of the minority class, when tested with real samples that the model has not seen before.

Once the VAE-based model is selected, in order to generate new synthetic samples of the minority class, real samples are encoded with the encoder; then, SMOTE is applied in the latent space Z, thus generating synthetic samples in the latent space, z; and finally, those samples z are decoded with the decoder.

4   Results and Discussion

Results Without DA Techniques

Table 1 shows average results obtained when predicting whether wind speed at $t = 1$ is going to be equal or greater than 25 m/s, or not, using different classifiers (RFC, MLP, LSTM and convolutional neural networks) using different

Table 1. Average predictive performance without data augmentation.

DATASET USED	SCORE	RFC	MLP	LSTM	CNN1D	CNN2D	CNN3D	Mean
One-Dimensional Dataset	Accuracy	0.9971	0.9974	0.9974	0.9975	-	-	0.8713
	Precision	0.5233	0.5718	0.5760	0.5879	-	-	0.5829
	Recall	0.7393	0.6913	0.6917	0.7397	-	-	0.6834
	F1-Score	0.6121	0.6227	0.6246	0.6532	-	-	0.6251
Three-Dimensional Dataset	Accuracy	0.9974	0.9968	0.9974	0.9967	0.9973	0.9976	0.9972
	Precision	0.6064	0.5204	0.5916	0.5083	0.5624	0.6039	0.5655
	Recall	0.5714	0.4778	0.6139	0.6052	0.6579	0.6861	0.6021
	F1-Score	0.5831	0.4871	0.5983	0.5367	0.5989	0.6393	0.5739

sets of predictive variables (either time series, or 3D data with two dimensions representing the location and one dimension representing time evolution).

As shown in Table 1, the best average result is obtained with 1D-CNN using as predictors time series (one-dimensional dataset). In particular, an average f1-score of 0.6532 is obtained, which proves the feasibility of predicting extreme wind using deep learning models. Using f1-score instead of accuracy as a comparison metric, given the extremely unbalanced nature of the problem, Table 1 shows that results are much better with the one-dimensional dataset than with the three-dimensional dataset, the only exception being the 3D-CNN classifier, which leads to an average f1-score of 0.6393, thus outperforming some classifiers with the one-dimensional dataset.

Results Obtained with Traditional DA Techniques

Table 2 shows average results obtained applying different DA techniques over the minority class, with different oversampling ratios, to different classifiers, with different types of dataset as predictors. Table 2 also shows the improvement obtained due to the application of DA in comparison with the average results without DA (and shown in Table 1).

First, as shown in Table 2, when using the one-dimensional dataset, the smaller oversampling ratio (0.0125) always outperforms the bigger one (0.2). Nonetheless, when using the three-dimensional dataset, results are inconclusive. With RFC, LSTM, 2D-CNN and 3D-CNN, the use of the smaller ratio (0.0125) also generally outperforms the bigger one. But, with MLP and 1D-CNN, which coincidentally are the models with worse results with the three-dimensional dataset without DA, the use of the bigger ratio (0.2) leads to better results. This suggest the need to adapt the oversampling ratio to the problem at hand.

Second, Table 2 shows that, when using the one-dimensional dataset, the use of DA techniques with ratio 0.0125 leads to improvements with every classifier. Likewise, when using the three-dimensional dataset, the use of DA techniques with ratio 0.0125 almost always leads to improvements. This results prove the value of using DA techniques.

Third, if, with the 0.0125 ratio, results obtained with the one-dimensional dataset are compared to those obtained with the three-dimensional dataset, results are still worse with the three-dimensional dataset. Nevertheless, now, after the application of DA, results are close-by. With the one-dimensional

Table 2. Average predictive performance with data augmentation techniques.

DATASET USED	DA TECHNIQUE	RATIO	SCORE	RFC	MLP	LSTM	CNN1D	CNN2D	CNN3D	Mean
One-dimensional Dataset	Random oversampling	0.2	Accuracy	0.9973	0.9974	0.9974	0.9972	-	-	0.9973
			Precision	0.5655	0.5694	0.5798	0.5402	-	-	0.5637
			Recall	0.6560	0.7103	0.6944	0.7337	-	-	0.6986
			F1-Score	0.6048	0.6276	0.6272	0.6198	-	-	0.6199
			Improvement	-1.20%	0.79%	0.42%	-5.11%	-	-	-1.32%
One-dimensional Dataset	SMOTE	0.2	Accuracy	0.9968	0.9976	0.9976	0.9975	-	-	0.9974
			Precision	0.5013	0.6038	0.6135	0.5934	-	-	0.5780
			Recall	0.6869	0.6937	0.6782	0.7067	-	-	0.6914
			F1-Score	0.5767	0.6416	0.6405	0.6413	-	-	0.6250
			Improvement	-5.79%	3.04%	2.56%	-1.82%	-	-	-0.49%
One-dimensional Dataset	1D data warping	0.2	Accuracy	0.9975	0.9974	0.9975	0.9973	-	-	0.9974
			Precision	0.6194	0.5721	0.5981	0.5654	-	-	0.5887
			Recall	0.6417	0.6929	0.6706	0.6853	-	-	0.6726
			F1-Score	0.6204	0.6239	0.6283	0.6155	-	-	0.6220
			Improvement	1.35%	0.20%	0.59%	-5.77%	-	-	-0.97%
One-dimensional Dataset	Random oversampling	0.0125	Accuracy	0.9974	0.9975	0.9975	0.9976	-	-	0.9975
			Precision	0.5622	0.5941	0.5813	0.6031	-	-	0.5852
			Recall	0.7226	0.7087	0.7357	0.7329	-	-	0.7250
			F1-Score	0.6313	0.6435	0.6457	0.6589	-	-	0.6449
			Improvement	3.14%	3.34%	3.38%	0.88%	-	-	2.66%
One-dimensional Dataset	SMOTE	0.0125	Accuracy	0.9974	0.9976	0.9977	0.9977	-	-	0.9976
			Precision	0.5714	0.6059	0.6216	0.6187	-	-	0.6044
			Recall	0.7226	0.7151	0.7175	0.7262	-	-	0.7203
			F1-Score	0.6367	0.6509	0.6623	0.6656	-	-	0.6539
			Improvement	4.01%	4.53%	6.04%	1.90%	-	-	4.09%
One-dimensional Dataset	1D data warping	0.0125	Accuracy	0.9974	0.9976	0.9974	0.9977	-	-	0.9975
			Precision	0.5646	0.5981	0.5715	0.6194	-	-	0.5884
			Recall	0.7067	0.6937	0.7290	0.7095	-	-	0.7097
			F1-Score	0.6264	0.6395	0.6389	0.6603	-	-	0.6413
			Improvement	2.33%	2.70%	2.29%	1.08%	-	-	2.09%
Three-Dimensional Dataset	Random oversampling	0.2	Accuracy	0.9971	0.9974	0.9975	0.9978	0.9972	0.9973	0.9974
			Precision	0.5606	0.5870	0.5883	0.6549	0.5466	0.5734	0.5851
			Recall	0.5698	0.6563	0.6675	0.6500	0.6960	0.6569	0.6494
			F1-Score	0.5545	0.6154	0.6212	0.6478	0.6091	0.6075	0.6092
			Improvement	-4.91%	26.34%	3.83%	20.70%	1.69%	-4.96%	6.16%
Three-Dimensional Dataset	SMOTE	0.2	Accuracy	0.9973	0.9974	0.9976	0.9977	0.9974	0.9976	0.9975
			Precision	0.6072	0.5866	0.6181	0.6305	0.5819	0.6113	0.6059
			Recall	0.5599	0.6647	0.6734	0.6802	0.6746	0.6687	0.6536
			F1-Score	0.5618	0.6192	0.6390	0.6505	0.6174	0.6315	0.6199
			Improvement	-3.65%	27.13%	6.81%	21.19%	3.09%	-1.21%	8.02%
Three-Dimensional Dataset	1D data warping	0.2	Accuracy	0.9973	0.9973	0.9973	0.9977	0.9973	0.9971	0.9973
			Precision	0.5681	0.5706	0.5643	0.6345	0.5631	0.5413	0.5736
			Recall	0.6679	0.6405	0.6849	0.6667	0.6623	0.6647	0.6645
			F1-Score	0.6075	0.5997	0.6123	0.6489	0.6047	0.5926	0.6109
			Improvement	4.19%	23.12%	2.34%	20.89%	0.96%	-7.30%	6.45%
Three-Dimensional Dataset	Multidimensional data warping	0.2	Accuracy	0.9971	0.9973	0.9974	0.9971	0.9972	0.9975	0.9973
			Precision	0.5503	0.5814	0.5776	0.5526	0.5529	0.5942	0.5682
			Recall	0.6044	0.5044	0.6647	0.5578	0.6810	0.6535	0.6109
			F1-Score	0.5695	0.5363	0.6136	0.5495	0.6052	0.6185	0.5821
			Improvement	-2.33%	10.11%	2.56%	2.39%	1.04%	-3.24%	1.43%
Three-Dimensional Dataset	Random oversampling	0.0125	Accuracy	0.9977	0.9973	0.9976	0.9970	0.9974	0.9977	0.9975
			Precision	0.6657	0.5719	0.6179	0.5342	0.5776	0.6336	0.6001
			Recall	0.5647	0.6262	0.6627	0.6956	0.6956	0.6905	0.6559
			F1-Score	0.6065	0.5954	0.6344	0.5971	0.6249	0.6571	0.6192
			Improvement	4.01%	22.23%	6.03%	11.25%	4.34%	2.79%	7.90%
Three-Dimensional Dataset	SMOTE	0.0125	Accuracy	0.9977	0.9974	0.9977	0.9970	0.9976	0.9978	0.9975
			Precision	0.6552	0.5874	0.6366	0.5375	0.6151	0.6367	0.6114
			Recall	0.5889	0.5893	0.6357	0.6940	0.6516	0.6983	0.6430
			F1-Score	0.6133	0.5844	0.6337	0.5960	0.6267	0.6618	0.6193
			Improvement	5.18%	19.97%	5.91%	11.05%	4.63%	3.52%	7.91%
Three-Dimensional Dataset	1D data warping	0.0125	Accuracy	0.9979	0.9975	0.9975	0.9971	0.9975	0.9977	0.9975
			Precision	0.7100	0.6012	0.6051	0.5401	0.6006	0.6283	0.6142
			Recall	0.5607	0.5825	0.6631	0.6897	0.6631	0.6897	0.6415
			F1-Score	0.6201	0.5890	0.6287	0.6012	0.6225	0.6542	0.6193
			Improvement	6.35%	20.93%	5.09%	12.01%	3.92%	2.33%	7.91%
Three-Dimensional Dataset	Multidimensional data warping	0.0125	Accuracy	0.9971	0.9972	0.9975	0.9969	0.9974	0.9975	0.9973
			Precision	0.5461	0.5774	0.5990	0.5275	0.5845	0.5897	0.5707
			Recall	0.6060	0.4964	0.6563	0.5690	0.6536	0.6687	0.6083
			F1-Score	0.5698	0.5292	0.6223	0.5384	0.6108	0.6224	0.5821
			Improvement	-2.29%	8.65%	4.01%	0.31%	1.97%	-2.64%	1.43%

dataset, the best result is obtained with 1D-CNN+SMOTE(0.0125), which leads to an average f1-score of 0.6656. When using the three-dimensional dataset, the best result is obtained with 3D-CNN+SMOTE(0.0125), which leads to an average f1-score of 0.6618, which, despite not being superior, is close-by.

Coincidentally, improvements obtained due to the application of DA techniques are much bigger when the tree-dimensional dataset is being used than when the one-dimensional dataset is being used. With the one-dimensional dataset the best average result is obtained with 1D-CNN+SMOTE(0.0125), which has an improvement of 1.9%; whereas with the three-dimensional dataset the best average result is obtained with 3D-CNN+SMOTE(0.0125), which has an improvement of 3.52%. Likewise, with the one-dimensional dataset, the biggest improvement is 6.04% with LSTM-SMOTE(0.0125); whereas with the three-dimensional dataset, the biggest improvement is 27.13% with MLP+SMOTE(0.2).

Results Obtained with VAEs as DA Technique

Table 3 shows average results obtained predicting extreme wind speed with different classifiers using VAEs as DA technique with different oversampling ratios.

Table 3. Average predictive performance with VAEs.

DATASET USED	DA TECHNIQUE	RATIO	SCORE	RFC	MLP	LSTM	CNN1D	CNN2D	CNN3D	Mean
One-dimensional Dataset	VAE	0.2	Accuracy	0.9966	0.9974	0.9972	0.9972	-	-	0.9971
			Precision	0.4796	0.6044	0.5546	0.5452	-	-	0.5459
			Recall	0.7238	0.6024	0.6631	0.6758	-	-	0.6663
			F1-Score	0.5744	0.5960	0.6007	0.5982	-	-	0.5923
			Improvement	−6.17%	−4.28%	−3.82%	−8.42%	-	-	−5.70%
One-dimensional Dataset	CVAE	0.2	Accuracy	0.9971	0.9976	0.9973	0.9962	-	-	0.9971
			Precision	0.5284	0.6077	0.5649	0.4484	-	-	0.5373
			Recall	0.7087	0.6873	0.6960	0.6933	-	-	0.6963
			F1-Score	0.6027	0.6399	0.6185	0.5356	-	-	0.5992
			Improvement	−1.55%	2.76%	−0.97%	−18.01%	-	-	−4.61%
One-dimensional Dataset	VAE ci	0.2	Accuracy	0.9969	0.9976	0.9975	0.9973	-	-	0.9973
			Precision	0.5106	0.6163	0.6044	0.5557	-	-	0.5718
			Recall	0.7333	0.6619	0.6802	0.7214	-	-	0.6992
			F1-Score	0.6001	0.6323	0.6287	0.6227	-	-	0.6210
			Improvement	−1.96%	1.55%	0.66%	−4.67%	-	-	−1.14%
One-dimensional Dataset	VAE	0.0125	Accuracy	0.9974	0.9973	0.9975	0.9977	-	-	0.9975
			Precision	0.5758	0.5685	0.5765	0.6139	-	-	0.5837
			Recall	0.6929	0.6940	0.7321	0.7206	-	-	0.7099
			F1-Score	0.6273	0.6202	0.6434	0.6607	-	-	0.6379
			Improvement	2.47%	−0.40%	3.02%	1.15%	-	-	1.55%
One-dimensional Dataset	CVAE	0.0125	Accuracy	0.9976	0.9976	0.9977	0.9976	-	-	0.9976
			Precision	0.5956	0.5980	0.6218	0.5983	-	-	0.6034
			Recall	0.7052	0.7250	0.7421	0.7274	-	-	0.7249
			F1-Score	0.6436	0.6510	0.6730	0.6526	-	-	0.6550
			Improvement	5.14%	4.55%	7.75%	−0.10%	-	-	4.28%
One-dimensional Dataset	CI-VAE	0.0125	Accuracy	0.9974	0.9975	0.9976	0.9977	-	-	0.9976
			Precision	0.5656	0.5946	0.5968	0.6172	-	-	0.5935
			Recall	0.7310	0.7175	0.7452	0.7544	-	-	0.7370
			F1-Score	0.6364	0.6455	0.6594	0.6766	-	-	0.6545
			Improvement	3.97%	3.67%	5.57%	3.58%	-	-	4.19%

First, Table 3 shows that, with the oversampling ratio of 0.0125, almost every VAE-based model leads to improvements with almost every classifier. Secondly, Table 3 shows that, within VAE-based modes and oversampling ratio of 0.0125, for every classifier, the best VAE-based model is always one of the modified architectures designed to control the label of the synthetic sample: CI-VAE with the 1D-CNN classifier and CVAE with RFC, MLP and LSTM.

Finally, the joint analysis of Tables 2 and 3 shows that, with the one-dimensional dataset and oversampling ratio of 0.0125, for every classifier, the best DA technique is always one of the VAE-based models. Moreover, improvement is significant. For instance, with the 1D-CNN model, the best traditional DA technique, SMOTE, led to an improvement of 1.9%; whereas the best VAE-based technique, CI-VAE leads to an improvement of 3.58%.

5 Conclusions

Extreme wind prediction is essential to achieve efficient and secure operation of wind farms. In this work, we have proved the feasibility of predicting extreme wind using AI models (RFC, MLP, LSTM, and CNNs), using meteorological time series of the wind farm surroundings as predictors. Given the scarcity of extreme wind samples and the unbalanced nature of the problem, we have proposed to apply DA techniques to improve prediction.

Traditional DA techniques (random oversampling, SMOTE and time series and multidimensional data warping) have been applied and evaluated. Firstly, results show that the best oversampling ratio depends on the dataset and model. Secondly, results show that with the right oversampling ratio, applying most DA techniques leads to improvements with most AI models. Finally, we have shown that improvements thanks to DA are significantly greater in the complex three-dimensional dataset than in the one-dimensional dataset.

Acknowledgments. The present study has been supported by the "Agencia Estatal de Investigación (España)" (grant ref.: PID2020-115454GB-C22/AEI/10.13039/5011 00011033), and by the projects PID2020-115454GB-C21 and TED2021-131777B-C22 of the Spanish Ministry of Science and Innovation (MICINN). Antonio Manuel Gómez-Orellana has been supported by "Consejería de Transformación Económica, Industria, Conocimiento y Universidades de la Junta de Andalucía" (grant ref.: PREDOC-00489). David Guijo-Rubio has been supported by the "Agencia Estatal de Investigación (España)" MCIU/AEI/10.13039/501100011033 and European Union NextGenerationEU/PRTR (grant ref.: JDC2022-048378-I).

Disclosure of Interests. The authors declare that they have no known competing financial interests or personal relationships that could have appeared to influence the work reported in this paper.

References

1. Chawla, N.V., Bowyer, K.W., Hall, L.O., Kegelmeyer, W.P.: Smote: synthetic minority over-sampling technique. J. Artif. Intell. Res. **16**, 321–357 (2002)
2. Hersbach, H., et al.: The era5 global reanalysis. Q. J. R. Meteorol. Soc. **146**(730), 1999–2049 (2020)

3. Iglesias, G., Talavera, E., González-Prieto, A., Mozo, A., Gómez-Canaval, S.: Data augmentation techniques in time series domain: a survey and taxonomy. Neural Comput. Appl. **35**(14), 10123–10145 (2023), 3
4. Khosla, C., Saini, B.S.: Enhancing performance of deep learning models with different data augmentation techniques: a survey. In: 2020 International Conference on Intelligent Engineering and Management (ICIEM), pp. 79–85. IEEE, London, United Kingdom (Jun 2020), 1
5. Kingma, D.P., Welling, M., et al.: An introduction to variational autoencoders. Found. Trends Mach. Learn. **12**(4), 307–392 (2019)
6. Nabian, M., Eftekhari, Z., Wong, A.: CI-VAE: a class-informed deep variational autoencoder for enhanced class-specific data interpolation (2023). https:// openreview.net/forum?id=jdEXFqGjdh
7. Sohn, K., Lee, H., Yan, X.: Learning structured output representation using deep conditional generative models (2015)

Autoencoder Framework for General Forecasting

Dušan Fister[1]([✉])(ID), C. Peláez-Rodríguez[2](ID), L. Cornejo-Bueno[2](ID),
J. Pérez-Aracil[2](ID), and S. Salcedo-Sanz[2](ID)

[1] Faculty of Electrical Engineering and Computer Science, University of Maribor ,
Koroška Cesta 46, 2000 Maribor, Slovenia
dusan.fister@um.si

[2] Department of Signal Processing and Communications, Universidad de Alcalá,
28805 Alcalá de Henares, Spain
{cesar.pelaez,laura.cornejo,jorge.perezaracil,sancho.salcedo}@uah.es

Abstract. Artificial intelligence backed forecasting systems, especially various types of autoencoders, are frequently used for short-term and medium-term weather forecasting. Sometimes, however, theirs validation is limited to specific weather occurrences, such as heatwaves or coldwaves, which limits the time period and location of forecasting significantly. We emphasise thorough model validation that validates the autoencoder's performance throughout the whole year for the whole possible area that autoencoder is trained for. Basic experimenting shows some limitations for proposed autoencoder, as at least one of the two benchmarks, i.e., the climate, overperforms performance of proposed autoencoder on average basis with regard to the utilised two stage autoencoder structure and suggests that further modifications to generalise the utilised autoencoder are needed.

Keywords: autoencoders · temperature forecasting · validation and testing

1 Introduction

Temperature forecasts are a subclass of numerical weather prediction (NWP) problem. Classical NWP is done using understanding the underlying physics, such as projecting the movement of air masses, their convection, precipitation, etc. NWP utilising the physical (dynamical) models is a challenging and computer-intensive task. But the results of dynamic NWP often carry uncompromising quality, of up to 10 d ahead. On the other hand, the rise of machine learning (ML) and deep learning (DL) paradigms, offers an ingenious way to model the weather patterns through time and infer the most statistically likely scenario of what might happen in near future. As physics is self-taught in this scenario, the DL-NWP is more besieged than the classic way, which opens this field to a wide number of researchers.

J. M. Ferrández Vicente et al. (Eds.): IWINAC 2024, LNCS 14675, pp. 314–322, 2024.
https://doi.org/10.1007/978-3-031-61137-7_29

DL is a more and more rising field with many scholarly applications. In what follows, a short literature review is attached. Gong et al. [3] have shown experiments for a pleade of DL tools, which can be tailored to do the weather forecasting, such as convolutional neural network (CNN), convolutional LSTM (ConvL-STM), Stochastic Adversarial Video Prediction (SAVP), etc. Variuos architectures, such as autoencoders (AE), variational autoencoders (VAE), generative adversarial networks (GANs) and others, may be built from mentioned tools. Researchers got promising results for a localised, central Europe forecasting scenario. Donnelly et al. [1] on the other hand employed a global approach with a low resolution, but utilised only a single year for both training and testing (non-overlapping samples). Fister et al. [2] employed several machine learning algorithms but were focused only into predicting August temperatures (supposed to be the hottest month within a year) for two different locations. Melinc and Zaplotnik [6] proposed the VAE design for a data assimilation step during the data fusion between many sources. Here, the background-error covariance was measured within the latent space of the VAE. A state-of-the-art U-net, by Ronneberger et al. [7], devoted for advanced image segmentation especially among biomedical sciences, was often practised between climate researchers. In the recent history, it has been sucessfully applied to several different applications, such as identification, error management as well as forecasting. Hoeller et al. [5] utilised the U-net for detection (identification) of convective cold pools. Cold pools typically form and expand below thunderstorms and may be an indicator of their forthcoming. Gronquist et al. [4] utilised an U-net to identify and predict weather uncertainty. The challenge remains for how to model the uncertainty and error of the DL-NWP. One of the possible methods is as Integrative Forecasting System (IFS) from European Centre for Medium-Range Weather Forecasts (ECMWF) is practising, i.e. to run several simulations in parallel with slightly different initial conditions. For the large-scale DL-NWP models, this becomes computationally intensive, hence [4] proposed to model weather uncertainty on a small set of simulations. Finally, the U-nets were viable also to directly predict the variable of interest, such as precipitation, for example in Sadeghi et al. [8].

AEs, VAEs and U-nets are able to predict the regression or classification value of the variable of interest for the wide or even global area. Some case studies validate the models developed (1) locally by taking into account some of the geographical points, (2) some at the continental level, (3) some globally. We emphasize the importance of thorough model validation, which means that the model is validated for the whole definition area it is able to output, during a period of the whole year.

2   Methodology

A two stage autoencoder (AE+AE) framework, is taken as a methodology to be applied for a forecasting experiments. The implemented methodology is similar to the [2] as follows. The AE+AE framework consists of two separate AE stages. First stage AE does not do any forecasting. Instead, it only extracts the statistical anomalies. Statistical anomalies are calculated as a difference between the actual temperature at time t and AE-output temperature for time t. These statistical anomalies are then fed into the second stage AE, which does the forecasting with a lead forecasting time of either 1, 2, 3 or 4 weeks. Using it, one is able to get the forecasted temperature for a whole region, instead of a single location. First stage may be universal, while the second is different for each lead time. Figures 1 and 2 show such architecture graphically.

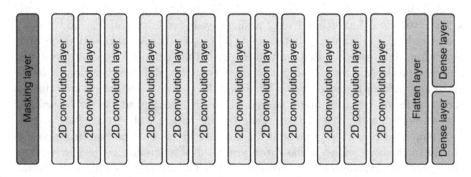

Fig. 1. An encoder part of the AE+AE, hearth of a temperature forecasts. Decoder on the other hand is implemented by a 3-layered 2D convolution transpose layers.

The AE+AE framework architecture was as follows. Inputs into the AE+AE should be normalised within 0 and 1. The first input layer of the AE+AE is the random masking layer. The masking layer masks input coordinates, hence effectively causing the constant learning gradient. Masking is done at pixel (coordinate) level, for each image dimension separately. A random uniform distribution from 0 to 1 is drawn and for occasions of $N(0,1) < 0.5$, a pixel is set to 0. Otherwise, pixel is left untouched. Next, a series of 2D convolution layers with aumenting number of filters follows. A series is concluded with the flatten and dense layers to derive the latent space. Latent space is next widened using the transposed convolution back to the original size image. However, only a single output dimension (t2m) is output. Table 1 depicts the experimental settings of the AE+AE framework.

3   Experiments and Results

The motivation of experiments is to forecast weekly mean t2m for each geographic location possible with varying 4 different forecasting lead times. Forecasting geographic coordinates are defined in Table 1. Forecasting lead times vary from $lt = 1$ to $lt = 4$. Forecasting is done using two different benchmarks, i.e., the climate and persistence methods, which are well known in the climate communion, and the proposed AE+AE framework. Forecasts are done for the whole testing sample, which consists samples of a 1 year. For each of the three methods, an error is calculated, by comparing the predicted forecasts and the ground truth. Upon these errors, statistical analysis is derived, by averaging the errors for all geographic locations and for the whole year of samples. Also, errors graphics are plotted and visualized to determine the areas of lowest and largest errors. This section is divided into four subsections, the data handling, experimental setup, results, and the discussion.

3.1 The Data

The region of interest selected to make forecasts is the Europe, North Africa, West Asia and North Atlantic (visualised later within experiments). Climate data are obtained from the ECMWF's ERA5 reanalysis web service, specialised for data assimilation globally[1]. Input (explanatory) variables are selected are 500 hPa geopotential height (z500), sea surface temperature (sst) and air temperature at the height of 2 m (t2m). Time frame from the beginning of the year 2000 to the end of the year 2019 is selected for the training. The year 2020 is selected as a testing sample. First 52 weeks of the each year of the analysis are incorporated.

The downloaded data comes at the 0.25° raster of geographic latitude and longitude, at the hourly data. Due to predicting a weekly mean t2m, the data are averaged by week to the 1° raster. Output (dependent) variable is t2m (which comes with the lead time). The data thus defines the architecture of the AE+AE framework, as seen in Fig. 2.

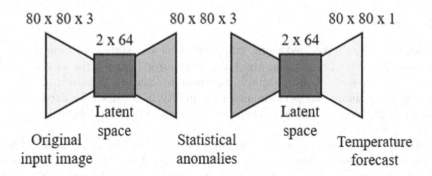

Fig. 2. Two stage AE+AE architecture with two latent spaces. Input variables=500 hPa geopotential height (z500), sea surface temperature (sst) and air temperature at 2 m height (t2m). Output variable = t2m.

3.2 Experimental Setup

Table 1 outlines the most fundamental settings of the DL-NWP algorithm utilised and climate experimental setup. As mentioned, climate forecasts using three distinctive methods are done for the whole region selected, with the goal of the proposed DL-NWP to overcome the two benchmark methods.

---

[1] https://cds.climate.copernicus.eu/#!/home.

Table 1. * = no. of samples valid for the first stage AE, for the second stage AE, the no. of training samples decreases linearly by increasing the lead time. Additionally, within the training sample, the 15 per cent of the samples are devoted to validation to do the early stopping. ** = no. of testing samples is limited to one year (52 weeks), if no lead time selected. However, with lead time larger than zero, the no. of samples decreases by amount of lead time, e.g., if lead time equal to 2, no. of testing samples equal to 50.

Property	Setting
Learning algorithm	Adam
Initial learning rate	0.001
Batch size	32
No. of training samples	1,040*
No. of testing samples	52**
Training sample dates	Jan. 2000 – Dec. 2019
Test sample dates	Jan. 2020 – Dec. 2020
Validation size	15%
Max. epochs	5,000
Input image dimension	$80 \times 80 \times 3$
Geographic latitude selected	from $0°$ to $80°$
Geographic longitude selected	from $-40°$ to $40°$

3.3   Results

Quality of results is verified using graphical plots and statistical indicators. A graphical plot sketches a mean absolute yearly error between the forecast and actual t2m, for each of the geographic coordinate. Statistical indicators on the other hand evaluate the performance and quality of results with error terms, also on yearly mean basis. Statistical results are outlined in Table 2, graphical results in Figs. 3–5.

Statistical analysis shows that the single best method according to the MAE, which is more reliable than the ME, is a climate method. AE+AE is not much behind. The interesting part is that by increasing the forecast lead time, the error does not rise significantly. In fact, it shows a trend of decreasing error. Statistical analysis well shows the magnitudes of mean errors but does not answer how the error is distributed, e.g., what areas contribute most to the error generation and which least. Graphical analysis on the other hand shows distributions of errors. These are divided into two images for each method, the mean yearly error (ME) and mean absolute yearly error (MAE). All the images are generated for the forecasting lead time of 4 weeks ($lt = 4$). The ME should be treated with caution due to the balancing effect throughout the year.

As seen from images of graphical analyses, the sea surfaces score the lowest errors. Typically, t2m's for sea surfaces often change with lower rates, i.e., slower, than the ground surfaces. Sea surfaces hence have larger momentums than

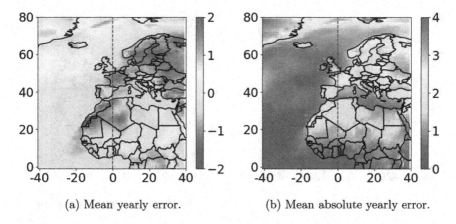

(a) Mean yearly error.   (b) Mean absolute yearly error.

Fig. 3. Climate predictions, 4 weeks. Labels represent geographic coordinates. Color-bars represent the intensity of the yearly error. Atlantic ocean and Equatorial Africa score very low mean absolute yearly errors. Eastern and Northern Europe on the other hand score higher levels of error, mainly negatives (as seen from left image) (Color figure online).

ground surfaces. Such scenario is tailored to the persistence method, although the graphic outlines poor persistence performance for higher latitudes. Contrary, for lower latitudes close to the equator, errors for persistence are close to zero. Ground surfaces on the other hand for latitudes higher than 20° are of close to the maximal error (4°). Climate errors are of lower magnitudes than the persistence for almost all area. The problem of climate method is that it is prone to the effect of global warming effect, as its forecast bases on the past, either recent or long ago. History of t2m's over past 20 years includes a negative offset that underpredicts the actual t2m on an average basis, which is seen as a constant low-scale error, especially over sea surfaces. Ground surfaces for Eastern

Table 2. Statistical analysis. The table is divided into four columns which represent the lead times from 1 to 4 weeks. One can note, that climate method scores the lowest MAE for all forecasting scenarios.

	1 week			2 weeks		
	AE+AE	climate	persistence	AE+AE	climate	persistence
MAE	1.506	1.308	1.344	1.494	1.297	1.718
ME	0.185	−.321	−.027	0.067	−.315	−.049
	3 weeks			4 weeks		
	AE+AE	climate	persistence	AE+AE	climate	persistence
MAE	1.506	1.294	2.048	1.480	1.279	2.404
ME	−.283	−.312	−.084	−.031	−.307	−.111

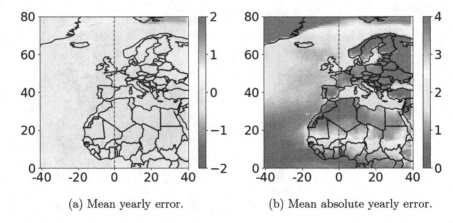

(a) Mean yearly error.   (b) Mean absolute yearly error.

Fig. 4. Persistence predictions, 4 weeks. Labels represent geographic coordinates. Colorbars represent the intensity of the yearly error. The mean yearly error shows a very abundant image, but only due to the twofold nature of the persistence methodology. As it follows history throughout the whole year, i.e., in winter when the temperature is falling, it scores negative error, and vice-versa in summer, it effectively balances itself automatically, hence scoring a very low mean error value. However, the mean absolute plot realises that especially the land, either Europe or Africa, are impossible to forecast well using persistence methodology (Color figure online).

Europe and South Grenlandia expose largest errors. As AE+AE framework is trained with the similar data climate method is utilising for its forecasts, the AE+AE shows similar performance than the climate. Still, the AE+AE scores larger mean errors which can be attributed to the uncertainty and error of the DL-NWP. Effectively, the AE+AE will perform similar to the climate.

3.4   Discussion

Literature outlines that AI methods, such as AE+AE, may enhance temperature forecasts during specific periods, e.g., such as heatwave periods. However, its performance may degrade for an overall, whole-year, forecast scenario. Therefore the performance of AE+AE may be better for a part of the output image and worse for other parts. The goal of this research was to test the AE+AE for a whole-year temperature forecasts for the whole region AE+AE was trained for. Instead of selecting a single location, our goal was to penalize all geographic coordinates available. Instead of taking a single week, or month, we took the whole year performance. Compared to two different benchmarks, i.e., climate and persistence, plots realised that climate method performed only a bit better than AE+AE regarding the overall performance for parts of Europe and Africa (land). For sea and oceans, AE+AE performed to a very similar degree. Persistence did well the ME but very bad MEA indicator. The reason for it lies in the fact of well balancing the positive and negative error throughout the year; hence, the ME is not an indicator with confidence (MEA on the other hand is). Statistical analysis showed that although AE+AE is a serious competitor, it was still unable to overcome both the climate and persistence methods. The climate method gained errors less than AE+AE.

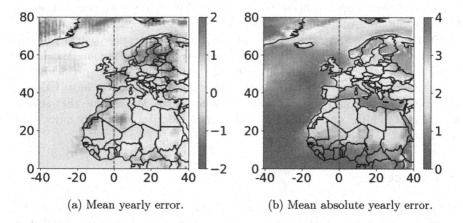

(a) Mean yearly error.   (b) Mean absolute yearly error.

Fig. 5. AE+AE predictions, 4 weeks. Labels represent geographic coordinates. Colorbars represent the intensity of the yearly error. Mean absolute yearly error is very similar to the climate absolute yearly error (Color figure online).

4   Conclusion

We have employed a simple analysis between two weather forecasting benchmarks, i.e. climate and persistence methods, and a deep learning numerical weather prediction method, the two staged autoencoder. The first stage autoencoder was implemented without prediction horizon. It was implemented only to derive anomalies between the actual state of the weather and the transformation as projected by statistical learning. Such obtained anomalies have been input into the second stage autoencoder, which came with a time horizon prediction.

Although our initial motivation was to employ a two stage autoencoder that would generally outperfom both benchmarks, this was not the case. Climate method was generally better than the proposed framework in all four cases. These experiments outline that overall forecasts for the whole region simultaneously are challenging. Therefore, its performance in future must be improved not only to be usable for a localised and short-term transient phenomena, but also for a more general scenario. Further potential for improvements we see in including the date or at least season information for processing. Whether the deep learning numerical weather prediction method would have the information on what part of the year is, different treatment of anomalies for summer and winter times could have been implemented. Additionally, this would enhance the process of understanding weather patterns throughout the year. Finally, of crucial importance is that we employ an analysis of explanatory variables to identify drivers or keys that importantly contribute to the formation of temperatures weeks ahead.

The employed deep learning numerical weather prediction method follows the climate method to a higher extent. Due to its process of learning, which is far from perfect, it consists of an error imposed for deviation from past years (which climate is also prone to) and as well as error which is imposed by imperfections in training. Hence, proposed deep learning method will in general perform poorer than the climate. Additional mechanisms are therefore necesarry to enhance it.

Still, as some empirical analyses show, for some geographic points for some limited seasons, the deep learning methods may easily overcome the classic benchmarks, especially, if the deep learning methods are learnt specifically, for instance, only for high summer. On the other hand, the average basis balances statistical learning and ruins affinity of the forecasts. We assume that several hierarchical models, or even better an attention module, could very much solve this issue.

References

1. Donnelly, J., Daneshkhah, A., Abolfathi, S.: Forecasting global climate drivers using gaussian processes and convolutional autoencoders. Eng. Appl. Artif. Intell. **128**, 107536 (2024)
2. Fister, D., Pérez-Aracil, J., Peláez-Rodríguez, C., Del Ser, J., Salcedo-Sanz, S.: Accurate long-term air temperature prediction with machine learning models and data reduction techniques. Appl. Soft Comput. **136**, 110118 (2023)
3. Gong, B., et al.: Temperature forecasting by deep learning methods. Geosci. Model Develop. **15**(23), 8931–8956 (2022)
4. Grönquist, P., et al.: Predicting weather uncertainty with deep convnets. arXiv preprint arXiv:1911.00630 (2019)
5. Hoeller, J., Fiévet, R., Engelbrecht, E., Haerter, J.O.: U-net segmentation for the detection of convective cold pools from cloud and rainfall fields. J. Geophys. Res.: Atmos. **129**(1), e2023JD040126 (2024)
6. Melinc, B., Zaplotnik, Ž.: Neural-network data assimilation using variational autoencoder. arXiv preprint arXiv:2308.16073 (2023)
7. Ronneberger, O., Fischer, P., Brox, T.: U-Net: convolutional networks for biomedical image segmentation. In: Navab, N., Hornegger, J., Wells, W.M., Frangi, A.F. (eds.) Medical Image Computing and Computer-Assisted Intervention – MICCAI 2015: 18th International Conference, Munich, Germany, October 5-9, 2015, Proceedings, Part III, pp. 234–241. Springer International Publishing, Cham (2015). https://doi.org/10.1007/978-3-319-24574-4_28
8. Sadeghi, M., Nguyen, P., Hsu, K., Sorooshian, S.: Improving near real-time precipitation estimation using a u-net convolutional neural network and geographical information. Environ. Modell. Softw. **134**, 104856 (2020)

Prediction of Extreme Wave Heights via a Fuzzy-Based Cascade Ensemble Model

C. Peláez-Rodríguez[1]([✉])[ID], L. Cornejo-Bueno[1][ID], Dušan Fister[2][ID],
J. Pérez-Aracil[1][ID], and S. Salcedo-Sanz[1][ID]

[1] Department of Signal Processing and Communications, Universidad de Alcalá,
28805 Alcalá de Henares, Spain
`cesar.pelaez@uah.es`
[2] University of Maribor, Koroška cesta 46, 2000 Maribor, Slovenia
`dusan.fister@um.si`

Abstract. This paper addresses the critical challenge of accurately forecasting extreme wave heights, a crucial aspect for offshore operations often underexplored in existing literature. Employing a fuzzy-based cascade ensemble of regression models, our approach involves successive partitioning of training data into fuzzy-soft clusters, enabling specific regression models to analyze distinct segments of the target domain. Integration of individual model predictions into a fuzzy-based ensemble, with pertinence values assigned based on previous layer predictions, enhances accuracy by prioritizing certain events. The simplicity of our approach, eliminating the need for data balancing techniques, and its efficacy in predicting extreme wave heights with remarkable results distinguish it from existing methods. Since the optimal data partitioning is specific to the problem, an optimization strategy using two evolutionary algorithms as DE and CRO is employed to determine specific parameters of the methodology, including the number of membership functions, shapes of membership functions, and learning rate. This optimization strategy further enhances its performance, making it a promising solution for wave forecasting challenges.

Keywords: Extreme wave height · Extreme forecasting · Fuzzy-based ensemble · Ensemble learning

1 Introduction

Sea surface wind waves constitute a stochastic phenomenon with the capacity to exert a profound impact on various domains of science, logistics, and technology. They have the potential to alter the trajectory and speed of ships, inducing hull resonance and the risk of fractures. Additionally, they can inflict substantial

This research has been partially supported by the project PID2020-115454GB-C21 of the Spanish Ministry of Science and Innovation (MICINN).

damage on ports, underwater engineering and structures safeguarding coastlines [9]. Moreover, the significant strides made in recent decades to exploit the abundant energy resource inherent in ocean waves [7] have sparked a growing interest in offshore renewable facilities. Therefore, comprehending wave conditions, especially forecasting significant wave height, is of paramount importance for offshore operations.

In this context, accurate wave forecasting poses a fundamental challenge that affects multiple facets of wave energy harvesting and marine related industry. Given the intermittent and stochastic nature of waves, precise wave forecasts are crucial for ensuring stable harvesting operations, optimizing wave farms and shipping routes, or assessing of extreme wave loads on marine structures such as wind turbines [21] or cross-bridges [19]. Generally, wave prediction models can be divided into data-driven or physical-driven frameworks. Numerous wave models, based on energy transfer equations, have been developed to describe the complicated nature of wave generation, propagation and decay [2]. These numerical models provide effective results in large-scale space and time ranges, but with the disadvantage of the high costs in terms of computing resources and time [10]. Alternatively, statistical approaches and artificial intelligence techniques are currently employed to forecast uncertain future times by analyzing potential relationships and dependencies within extensive time series datasets. Specifically, with the advancement of wave buoys providing real-time wave datasets and historical events over the long term, soft computing techniques, including Machine Learning (ML) and Deep Learning (DL), are gaining prominence in this field [1,8,9,16,22].

Specifically, extreme waves influence coastal engineering activities and have an immense geophysical implication. Therefore, their study, observation and prediction from few hours to few days in advance are decisive for planning of mitigation measures against natural coastal hazards, ship routing, design of coastal and offshore structures [6]. Precise prediction of extreme wave heights is still an evading problem, due to its extremely complex, non stationary, non linear, uncertain and hence not yet fully understood physical process of generation [4]. The prediction of these extreme events has represented and important field of research in recent years [4,14,15].

In this paper, we propose the application of a fuzzy-based ensemble methodology [12] for accurate prediction of extreme wave events. Specifically, the proposed algorithm for extremes prediction includes a fuzzy-based cascade ensemble of regression models, where different regressors are fitted with a particular portion of the training data, depending on the target variable value. The training data are partitioned into fuzzy-soft subsets, where each sample is assigned to a pertinence value for each subsets, in accordance with the corresponding membership function, dependent on the target variable value. The shapes of the membership functions play an essential role in the method's performance, along with other hyperparameters, which are optimised by means of a two evolutionary algorithms: Differential Evolution (DE) and Coral Reef Optimization with Substrate Layers (CRO-SL) [13]. Different ML regression methods, including two random neural network methods (ELM and RVFL), Linear Regression (LR) and Random Forest (RF) are considered. This methodology is validated by addressing a real forecasting problem utilizing four years of measured data from a station located on the southwest coast of the United States. The predictive variables encompass wave height measurements from nearby stations in preceding hours, along with Reanalysis variables providing information on various meteorological factors. Methods used for performance comparison include Machine Learning (ML) and Deep Learning (DL) approaches for time series forecasting.

2   Fuzzy-Based Cascade Ensemble Methodology

Figure 1 illustrates the architecture of the proposed framework. Initially, the training data undergoes partitioning, forming fuzzy-soft clusters based on the target variable value. Subsequently, each cluster is utilized to train a distinct regression model, focusing on a specific range of the training data. To calculate the forecast value of an incoming test sample, input data are independently fed to each regressor, resulting in a prediction value $(\hat{y}_{\mathcal{M}_i})$ for each model. These individual predictions are then input into a fuzzy-based ensemble, where the prior layer's prediction, along with the shapes of the membership functions, is used to determine the pertinence values of each prediction. The ensemble output is further weighted with the previous layer's forecast value, based on a hyperparameter known as the learning rate (ε). Given its layered structure, this framework is repeated sequentially. Additionally, the parameter m defines the number of groups in which each cluster is divided, so the total number of subgroups belonging to a layer n would be equal to m^n.

Fig. 1. Fuzzy-based cascade ensemble of regressors architecture.

2.1   Data Clustering

The developed method employs a cascade architecture that is organized into multiple layers, with the clustering process executed within each layer. The parameter m determines the number of groups into which each cluster from the previous layer (or the total set of training data in the initial layer) is divided. The clustering process is carried out based on the target value variables following the procedure below:

1. Data within a given subset are sorted according to the target value
2. m membership functions are defined, each associated with a new data subset
3. The bases of these membership functions divide the target domain (in percentiles) of a specific subset into m regions
4. New data clusters are then formed from each subset based on this domain division

The definition of membership function shapes plays a pivotal role, making it a critical parameter that influences the success or failure of the algorithm. To address this, two robust evolutionary optimization algorithms have been utilized to obtain the most optimal shapes for the membership functions (Sect. 2.3). In all instances, triangular membership functions, like the ones depicted in Fig. 2, are considered.

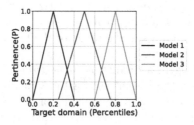

Fig. 2. Example of triangular membership functions.

2.2   Prediction

The presented framework initiates with the prediction of an initial regression model ($\mathcal{M}_0$) trained using all the training data without performing any clustering (Eq. (1)), corresponding to Layer 0. Subsequently, the output of a specific layer is computed as the average of the predictions of each model, weighted by its pertinence value. This calculation is represented by Eqs. (2), and (3) for the first, and n layers, respectively. In these equations, i encompasses all the regression models ($\mathcal{M}i$) belonging to a layer, $\hat{y}\mathcal{M}_i$ denotes the output of $\mathcal{M}_i$, p_i denotes the pertinence value of the evaluated sample for $\mathcal{M}_i$, p_i^* represents the pertinence value of the parent model of $\mathcal{M}_i$, and m signifies the number of clusters formed in each division.

In addition, a learning rate (ε) is introduced with the aim of preserving the generality of the prediction. Consequently, for each layer, the output from the previous layer is considered by a factor of $1 - \varepsilon$.

$$\hat{y}_0 = \hat{y}_{\mathcal{M}_0} \tag{1}$$

$$\hat{y}_1 = \frac{(\hat{y}_{\mathcal{M}_1} \cdot p_1 + \hat{y}_{\mathcal{M}_2} \cdot p_2 + \hat{y}_{\mathcal{M}_3} \cdot p_3)}{p_1 + p_2 + p_3} \cdot \varepsilon + \hat{y}_0 \cdot (1 - \varepsilon) \tag{2}$$

$$\hat{y}_n = \frac{\sum_{i=1}^{m^n}(\hat{y}_{\mathcal{M}_i} \cdot p_i \cdot p_i^*)}{\sum_{i=1}^{m^n} p_i \cdot p_i^*} \cdot \varepsilon + \hat{y}_{n-1} \cdot (1 - \varepsilon) \tag{3}$$

2.3 Hyperparameter Tuning via Evolutionary Optimization

Given the sensitivity of factors influencing the predicted value, such as the number of membership functions (m), their shapes, and the learning rate (ε), evolutionary computation is employed to find an optimal set of values for these parameters. Isosceles triangular functions, ranging from 0 to 1, are employed as membership functions. The evolutionary algorithm optimizes the position, base width of these functions, and the learning rate. For this purpose, the full training data (or 70% of the total data) have been divided into a specific training and a specific validation sets (i.e., 75% and 25%, respectively), and the error encountered in the prediction of these validation data has been used as the fitness function of the optimization algorithm. Cases with 2, 3 and 4 membership functions have been tested, and thus for each case, the number of variables to optimize are 3, 5 and 7, respectively (the first model membership function always starts in 0, and the last model membership function finishes in 1).

Since no constraints enforce the overlapping of membership functions, there is a possibility that a target variable domain value has an associated pertinence value of 0 for all models. To avoid errors due to division by 0, a term of $0.001 \cdot \hat{y}_0$ is added in Eq. (3) when computing the predicted value in layer n. This ensures that even if all membership values are 0 for a specific sample, the prediction for that point will be influenced by the initial model. The updated prediction equation is expressed in Eq. (4).

$$\hat{y}_n = \frac{(\sum_{i=1}^{m^n}(\hat{y}_{\mathcal{M}_i} \cdot p_i \cdot p_i^*)) + 0.001\hat{y}_0}{(\sum_{i=1}^{m^n} p_i \cdot p_i^*) + 0.001} \cdot \varepsilon + \hat{y}_{n-1} \cdot (1 - \varepsilon) \tag{4}$$

In order to perform this hyperparameter optimization, two evolutionary algorithms have been considered: Differential Evolution (DE) [18] and Coral Reef Optimization with Substrate Layers (CRO-SL) [13].

2.4 Regression Methods

Four different ML regression models have been implemented to perform the regression task. These models include two random neural network methods (ELM [11], and RVFL [17]), Linear Regression (LR) [5] and Random Forest (RF) [3].

3 Data and Predictive Variables

This section describes the data available for this research, including the target wave height data and the predictors variables use to perform the prediction.

In first place, wave height data acquired from a station owned and maintained by National Data Buoy Center, located in the southwest coast of the United States (39.23N, 123.98W) is used as target variable (Station ID: 46014). This time series is depicted in Fig. 3. The acquired data corresponds to four years (2017–2020), with a temporal resolution of 6 h. The first 75% of the data (2017–2019) is used to train the ML models, and the remaining 25% of data (2020) is used for testing the methodology performance.

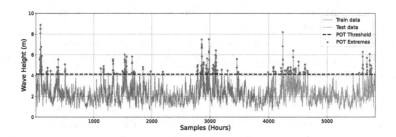

Fig. 3. Target time series.

Regarding the predictive variables, Table 1 list the meteorological variables used as input variables. These encompass 7 reanalysis variables derived from geographical nodes in close proximity to the station, along with 9 measured wave height values from nearby stations, including the station under consideration for prediction. Since a time prediction horizon of 24 h is considered to perform the prediction, a 24-hour delay between the target and predictors has been established.

Table 1. Predictive variables considered at each node from the ERA-5 reanalysis dataset.

Variable	Description	Procedence	Variable	Description	Procedence
air		Renalaysis	wvht25	Wave height	Station 46025
omega		Reanalysis	wvht26	Wave height	Station 46026
pr_wtr		Reanalysis	wvht42	Wave height	Station 46042
pres		Reanalysis	wvht47	Wave height	Station 46047
rhum		Reanalysis	wvht53	Wave height	Station 46053
uwnd		Reanalysis	wvht59	Wave height	Station 46059
cre vwnd		Reanalysis	wvht69	Wave height	Station 46069
wvht14	Wave height	Station 46014	wvht86	Wave height	Station 46086

4   Experiments and Results

4.1   Evaluation Metrics

In order to assess the performance of the extreme wave height prediction models, different evaluation metrics were used. First, a common metric for regression problems, Mean Absolute Error (MAE) has been considered:

$$\text{MAE} = \frac{1}{N} \sum_{i=1}^{n} |y_i - \hat{y}_i| \tag{5}$$

where $\hat{y}$ represents predicted values (provided by the proposed model) and y are the actual observed values. The subscript i is used to refer to a single sample $y_i = y[i]$.

Then, the prediction only of the extreme events is evaluated, since the accurate prediction of these points is precisely the scope of this work. For this purpose, it is first necessary to establish the threshold beyond a point is considered as an extreme event. Figure 3 illustrates the threshold defined to separate extreme data (outliers) from non-extreme data (non-outliers), set at the mean + 2 times the standard deviation of the wave height values [20]. In order to measure the performance of the regressors on these outlier data, a new indicator, named Extreme Events Mean Absolute Error (EEMAE), has been used, which corresponds to the MAE (Eq. (5)) calculation on these values.

4.2   Algorithms for Comparison

The performance of the fuzzy-based cascade ensemble have been assessed by employing different time series regression algorithms for comparison (benchmarks hereafter). Shallow ML methods on the original data and state-of-the-art deep learning methods were tested, including: Linear Regression (LR), Regression Trees (RT), Random Forest (RF), Lasso Regression, Support Vector Regression (SVR), Least Square Support Vector Regression (LSSVR), Multilayer Perceptron (MLP), ELM, RVFL, Recurrent Neural Networks (RNNs), Gated Recurrent Units (GRUs), Long Short-Term Memory (LSTM), 1-D Convolutional Neural Networks (1D-CNN), a combination of two of these methods (1D-CNN + LSTM), Residual Network (ResNet) and InceptionTime.

4.3   Results

In first place, the optimization algorithms (DE and CRO) were applied for three different values of m in regression model (LR, RF, ELM and RVFL). The fitness function in the optimization algorithms was set as the minimization of the sum of MAE and EEMAE, seeking for a model that performs consistently well in both extremes and non-extremes values. Figure 4 shows the performance according to this metric considering different parameter combinations. It can be observed that there are no significant differences discernible between the utilization of DE

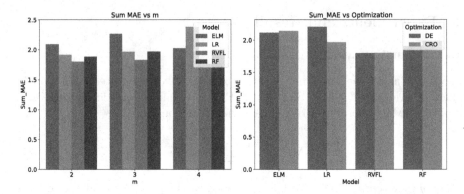

Fig. 4. Results obtained for the different parameter combinations considered in the proposed methodology (models, values of m and optimization algorithms).

or CRO as optimization algorithm. Regarding the ML models employed for the regression task, it is observed that the RVFL achieves the better results.

Finally, in Fig. 5, a comparison between the proposed fuzzy ensemble methodology and the set of ML and DL algorithms considered as benchmark is presented. In the proposed methodology, aach model is represented by its best-performing case (combination of m and optimization algorithm). Here, we observed that the fuzzy ensemble models provided much better results in terms of extreme prediction, exhibiting a notable decrease in the EEMAE metric. Furthermore, they demonstrate a highly competitive performance in the MAE metric.

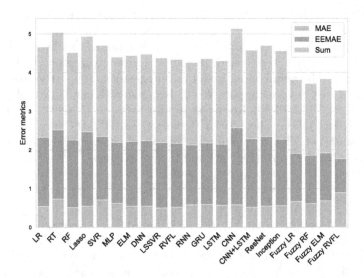

Fig. 5. Performance comparison between proposed methodology and benchmarks (ML and DL).

A comprehensive assessment of the overall performance of these methods, considering the Sum of MAE and EEMAE, reveals that the proposed methodology achieves a well-balanced outcome in both extreme and non-extreme events.

5 Conclusions

The anticipation of extreme wave heights stands as a paramount challenge in the realm of wave forecasting today. Accurately predicting the occurrence and severity of these extreme events holds substantial economic importance, acting as a preventive measure against potential damages to facilities.

This paper emerges to address the necessity for accurate wave height predictions, with a specific emphasis on the correct forecasting of extreme waves-an aspect that has been relatively underexplored in the current state of the art literature. For this, a fuzzy-based cascade ensemble of regression models is applied, the proposed layered framework involves a successive partition of the training data into fuzzy-soft clusters according to the target variable value, and further training a specific regression model within each designated cluster, so that each model can analyse a particular part of the target domain.

An inherent advantage of the proposed approach lies in its simplicity, as it eliminates the need for data balancing techniques. Instead, it relies on the ensemble of diverse regression models, each concentrating on a specific segment of the data spectrum. The effectiveness of this approach hinges on the precise partitioning of training data into subsets. To achieve this, since the optimal data partitioning is specific to the problem, an optimization strategy is employed to determine specific parameters of the methodology, including the number of membership functions, shapes of membership functions, and learning rate.

Remarkable results have been achieved, outperforming the state-of-the-art methods used as benchmark models. The proposed methodology excels in predicting extreme wave heights while maintaining high accuracy for non-extreme events, showcasing its efficacy in overcoming the limitations of existing methods.

References

1. Afzal, M.S., Kumar, L., Chugh, V., Kumar, Y., Zuhair, M.: Prediction of significant wave height using machine learning and its application to extreme wave analysis. J. Earth Syst. Sci. **132**(2), 51 (2023)
2. Booij, N., Holthuijsen, L., Ris, R.: The" swan" wave model for shallow water. In: Coastal Engineering 1996, pp. 668–676 (1996)
3. Breiman, L.: Random forests. Mach. Learn. **45**(1), 5–32 (2001)
4. Dixit, P., Londhe, S.: Prediction of extreme wave heights using neuro wavelet technique. Appl. Ocean Res. **58**, 241–252 (2016)
5. Draper, N.R., Smith, H.: Applied regression analysis, vol. 326. John Wiley & Sons (1998)
6. Dysthe, K., Krogstad, H.E., Müller, P.: Oceanic rogue waves. Annu. Rev. Fluid Mech. **40**, 287–310 (2008)

7. Falcao, A.F.d.O.: Wave energy utilization: a review of the technologies. Renew. Sustain. Energy Rev. **14**(3), 899–918 (2010)
8. Fan, S., Xiao, N., Dong, S.: A novel model to predict significant wave height based on long short-term memory network. Ocean Eng. **205**, 107298 (2020)
9. Feng, Z., Hu, P., Li, S., Mo, D.: Prediction of significant wave height in offshore china based on the machine learning method. J. Marine Sci. Eng. **10**(6), 836 (2022)
10. Güner, H.A.A., Yüksel, Y., Çevik, E.Ö.: Estimation of wave parameters based on nearshore wind-wave correlations. Ocean Eng. **63**, 52–62 (2013)
11. Huang, G.B., Zhu, Q.Y., Siew, C.K.: Extreme learning machine: Theory and applications. Neurocomputing **70**, 489–501 (12 2006). https://doi.org/10.1016/j.neucom.2005.12.126
12. Peláez-Rodríguez, C., Pérez-Aracil, J., Prieto-Godino, L., Ghimire, S., Deo, R., Salcedo-Sanz, S.: A fuzzy-based cascade ensemble model for improving extreme wind speeds prediction. J. Wind Eng. Ind. Aerodyn. **240**, 105507 (2023)
13. Pérez-Aracil, J., Camacho-Gómez, C., Lorente-Ramos, E., Marina, C.M., Cornejo-Bueno, L.M., Salcedo-Sanz, S.: New probabilistic, dynamic multi-method ensembles for optimization based on the cro-sl. Mathematics **11**(7), 1666 (2023)
14. Petrov, V., Soares, C.G., Gotovac, H.: Prediction of extreme significant wave heights using maximum entropy. Coast. Eng. **74**, 1–10 (2013)
15. Rueda, A., Camus, P., Méndez, F.J., Tomás, A., Luceño, A.: An extreme value model for maximum wave heights based on weather types. J. Geophys. Res.: Oceans **121**(2), 1262–1273 (2016)
16. Shamshirband, S., Mosavi, A., Rabczuk, T., Nabipour, N., Chau, K.w.: Prediction of significant wave height; comparison between nested grid numerical model, and machine learning models of artificial neural networks, extreme learning and support vector machines. Eng. Appl. Comput. Fluid Mech. **14**(1), 805–817 (2020)
17. Shi, Q., Katuwal, R., Suganthan, P.N., Tanveer, M.: Random vector functional link neural network based ensemble deep learning. Pattern Recogn. **117**, 107978 (2021)
18. Storn, R., Price, K.: Differential evolution-a simple and efficient heuristic for global optimization over continuous spaces. J. Global Optim. **11**(4), 341–359 (1997)
19. Ti, Z., Li, Y., Qin, S.: Numerical approach of interaction between wave and flexible bridge pier with arbitrary cross section based on boundary element method. J. Bridg. Eng. **25**(11), 04020095 (2020)
20. Viselli, A.M., Forristall, G.Z., Pearce, B.R., Dagher, H.J.: Estimation of extreme wave and wind design parameters for offshore wind turbines in the gulf of maine using a pot method. Ocean Eng. **104**, 649–658 (2015)
21. Zilong, T., Wei, D.X.: Layout optimization of offshore wind farm considering spatially inhomogeneous wave loads. Appl. Energy **306**, 117947 (2022)
22. Zilong, T., Yubing, S., Xiaowei, D.: Spatial-temporal wave height forecast using deep learning and public reanalysis dataset. Appl. Energy **326**, 120027 (2022)

Machine Learning as Applied to Shape Parameterization of Submerged Arch Structures

Waldemar Hugo LLamosas-Mayca[1]([⊠]), Eugenio Lorente-Ramos[2],
Jorge Pérez-Aracil[2], Alejandro M. Hernández-Díaz[1],
Manuel Damián García-Román[1], and Sancho Salcedo-Sanz[2]

[1] University of La Laguna, Avda. Ángel Guimerá Jorge 1,
38206 San Cristóbal de La Laguna, Santa Cruz de Tenerife, Spain
{wllamosa,ahernadi,mroman}@ull.edu.es
[2] University of Alcalá, Ctra. Madrid-Barcelona, km 33, 28805 Alcalá de Henares,
Madrid, Spain
{eugenio.lorente,jorge.perezaracil,sancho.salcedo}@uah.es

Abstract. Submerged structures are usually designed under arch-type forms. Such forms may be performed through different parametric functions, and their design procedure usually involves several variables in order to obtain an efficient, economical and safe installation. Past works have found that for intermediate depth ratios, the momentless (or funicular) shape of the submerged arch is a geometrical form between the parabola and the ellipse curve. Alternatively, some authors have proposed the shape parameterization of the submerged arch's centerline in order to approach an efficient design that takes into account not only the arch's mechanical behaviour, but other design aspects such as its enclosed airspace or the arch's serviceability. Such processes traditionally involve, regardless of an optimizer, the implementation of a finite element model and the corresponding parametric function. However, this may be greatly simplified through the use of machine learning. In this work, several regressors are trained in order to predict the fitness function that governs the multi-objective optimization of a submerged arch. To this aim, three different parametric functions are considered: conics, elliptics and Bézier curves, and a comparison of the regressor performance for each parametric shape function is presented.

Keywords: Submerged structures · Shape parameterization · Machine learning

1 Introduction

Arches are a type of structures able to support loads in which the internal resistance is provided mainly by its geometry [12]. In this sense the submerged arches were traditionally underwater installations designed pointing to funicular

J. M. Ferrández Vicente et al. (Eds.): IWINAC 2024, LNCS 14675, pp. 333–344, 2024.
https://doi.org/10.1007/978-3-031-61137-7_31

or momentless structures type. Some works in the last years proposed a linear combination of conic curves (in particular, ellipse and parabola) for defining the shape of submerged arches [5]. Additionally, they have used metaheuristic techniques in order to obtain the optimal shape to minimize the bending moments (close to funicular condition) and to maximize the serviceability design conditions (such as the enclosed airspace). In this work we propose a methodology to predict fitness values from a database that relates individuals who define the shape of a submerged arch and the fitness obtained for them. The arches' shapes have been defined by Conics Parabola-ellipse, Elliptic and Bézier curves parameterization.

2   Physical Approach to the Problem

For the analysis of a symmetrical submerged arch we have used the scheme and coordinate system shown in Fig. 1 where the distance between supports or span is $2B$, its height is H measured on the axis of symmetry and the distance between the water surface and the line of supports is D.

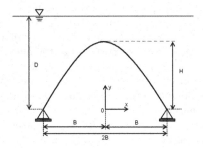

Fig. 1. Coordinate system and geometry of a submerged arch.

2.1   Funicular Equilibrium

The arches in which the resultant of internal forces is a single normal force for any cross section perpendicular to their axis, are commonly called funicular or momentless arches.

The funicular line of a submerged arch due the effect of the hydrostatic pressure acting on it and its self-weigth is defined by $y(x)$ [5] and is obtained by solving the boundary conditions problem shown in Eq. 1. This equation results from applying the equilibrium equations to the free body diagram shown in Fig. 2 and can be solved by methods of numerical integration such as Runge-Kutta [1].

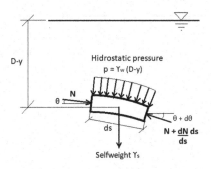

Fig. 2. Differential element forces equilibrium.

$$\frac{dN}{dx} = \frac{N\gamma_s}{\sigma_o}\frac{dy}{dx}$$

$$\frac{d^2y}{d^2x} = -\left[\frac{\gamma_w\left(D - y(x)\right)}{N} + \frac{\gamma_s}{\sigma_o}\left(1 + \left(\frac{dy}{dx}\right)^2\right)^{-1/2}\right]\left(1 + \left(\frac{dy}{dx}\right)^2\right)^{3/2} \quad (1)$$

$$\left.\frac{dy}{dx}\right|_{x=0} = 0$$

$$y(0) = H; \quad N(0) = \sigma_o h$$

2.2   Arches Shape Parameterization

In this work we have analyzed arches whose shape are defined by the following parameterizations:

Parabola Ellipse Curves. This parameterization consists of the linear combination of the conics parabola and ellipse, as shown in Eq. 2 [5]. Each individual is defined by the parameters B, H, H', t, shown in Fig. 3, and h. In this definition, B is the x-coordinate of the arch' support, H is the height of the arch, H' and B' are the lengths of the semi-minor axis and the semi-major axis of the ellipse respectively, t is the parameter that defines the linear combination between both curves and h, which is the arch thickness at the apex.

Thus, for a given set of values B, H, H' and t, each curve is completely defined in terms of its radial coordinate r_{pe} and its angular coordinate φ.

$$r_{pe}\left(t, \varphi, B, H, H'\right) = (1 - t).r_p + t.r_e\left(\varphi\right) \quad (2)$$

Elliptic Curves. This parameterization consists of using Elliptic curves to define the arch geometry. In this parameterization, each individual is defined by p, q, H, λ, shown in Eq. (6), and h, where p, q and λ are dimensionless

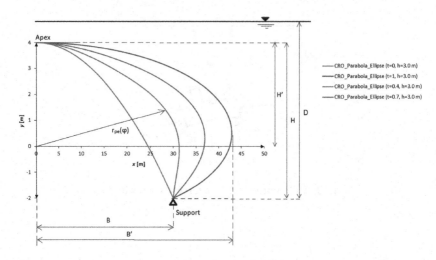

Fig. 3. Parabola Ellipse parameterization.

parameters, H is the height of the arch and h, which is the thickness at the apex of the arch. Let K be a (commutative) field. An elliptic curve E is an algebraic plane curve defined by a Weierstrass equation [4,9]

$$E : \quad y^2 + a_1 xy + a_3 y = x^3 + a_2 x^2 + a_4 x + a_6 \tag{3}$$

where $a_1, a_2, a_3, a_4, a_6 \in K$, with discriminant $\Delta \neq 0$.

The discriminant of the Weierstrass Eq. (3) is:

$$\Delta = -b_2^2 b_8 - 8b_4^3 - 27b_6^2 + 9b_2 b_4 b_6 \tag{4}$$

where:
$$b_2 = a_1^2 + 4a_2$$
$$b_4 = 2a_2 + a_1 a_3$$
$$b_6 = a_3^2 + 4a_6$$
$$b_8 = a_1^2 a_6 + 4a_2 a_6 - a_1 a_3 a_4 + a_2 a_3^2 - a_4^2$$

For practical purposes, the discriminant of the canonical expression may be simplified to:

$$\Delta = -4p^3 - 27q^2 \tag{5}$$

Some examples of elliptic curves are shown in Fig. 4.

For our purpose, it is convenient to rotate the curve a quarter turn clockwise and to operate with the expression resulting in this affine transformation. In this order, we make the substitutions $x \rightarrow -y$, $y \rightarrow x$, and the *canonical* expression of the elliptic curve is obtained Eq. (6):

$$x^2 = -(\lambda y)^3 - p\lambda y + q,$$
$$p, q, \lambda \in K. \tag{6}$$

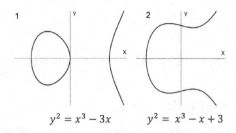

$$y^2 = x^3 - 3x \qquad y^2 = x^3 - x + 3$$

Fig. 4. Graphical examples of elliptic curves. 1: elliptic curve with two components (closed oval and pseudo-line); 2: elliptic curve with only one component (pseudoline)

Bézier Curves. This parameterization consists of using Bézier curves to define the arch geometry. In this parameterization, each individual is defined by the coordinates of the control points $P1 = (0,0)$, $P2 = (p2x, p2y)$, $P3 = (p3x, p3y)$, $P4 = (p4x, p4y = p3y$, $P5 = P2$, $P6 = (2B, 0)$, shown in Fig. 5, and h which is the thickness at the apex of the arch.

Bézier curves are polynomial curves expressed using Bernstein's polynomials that express them in a way analogous to Newton's binomial and expressed using the Casteljau algorithm [3].

The equations to represent a Bézier curve can be written as follows:

$$x(t) = \sum_{i=0}^{n} b_i B_i^n(t) \tag{7}$$
$$t \in [0, 1]$$

where the Bernstein polynomials are:

$$B_i^n(t) = \binom{n}{i} (1-t)^{n-i} t^i, where, \quad \binom{n}{i} = \frac{n!}{(n-i)!i!} \tag{8}$$

3   Methodology

From a database generated by evaluating an objective function, calculating the "fitness" value of various submerged arches defined by the parameteri zations mentioned above, a machine learning algorithm has been trained to predict the value of "fitness" from the individual who defines the arch.

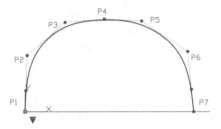

Fig. 5. Bezier parameterization control points

3.1   Finite Element Modelling

The arch's geometry configuration has been defined according to the parameterizations described above and its structural response (maximum absolute values of bending stress, compressive stress and vertical displacement), subjected to the corresponding hydrostatic load and its self-weight, which have been calculated using the finite element software ANSYS [11]. To this aim, a symmetric plane simply supported arch has been modeled using BEAM188 elements, with a Young's modulus $E = 27664, 49 \cdot 10^3 \, kN/m^2$. The area of the arch's enclosed airspace is also determined, and the functional to be optimized (minimized in this case) is calculated using the following expression:

$$f = p_m \cdot \max(|M_s|) + p_a \cdot \frac{1}{A_s} \tag{9}$$

in which p_m and p_a are, respectively, the weights for the bending stress and the enclosed area (in this work, $p_m = 0.7$ and $p_a = 0.3$ for all the cases evaluated), $\max(|M_s|)$ represents the maximum absolute bending moment value along the beam, and A_s is the area under the arch's centreline. Moreover, a restrictive condition is imposed to find the optimal arch shape as follows:

$$\max(d_y) < B/150 \tag{10}$$

in which d_y represents the deflection of the curved beam along the guideline of the arch.

3.2   Surrogate Models

Surrogate models are mathematical models that approximate the behaviour of a system that is usually too computationally expensive to solve exactly. This model allows us to perform a higher number of simulations in less time, even if they have a lower level of accuracy.

In this case, we will make use of surrogate models to accelerate the optimization of the arch's geometry through a light-weight model that will replace the fitness function. This way, we are able to perform more function calls in less time, helping the optimization process.

This surrogate model will be implemented as a regression model that will be trained using input parameters that define the geometry of the submerged arches and setting as the target the fitness of said arch. We will compare each of the parameterizations in order to decide which one yields a better surrogate model.

To implement this surrogate model we will consider the following machine learning models.

Linear Regression. Linear regression model is a statistical method that tries to approximate the data with a linear function, it can be defined with the following equation:

$$\hat{y}(\mathbf{x}; \beta) = \beta_0 + \sum_{i=1}^{M-1} \beta_i x_i \qquad (11)$$

Using linear regression, we obtain a function $\hat{y}(\mathbf{x})$ that represents a M dimensional hyperplane that is fitted to our dataset. Depending on how this fitting is performed we can have different types of linear models.

Classic Linear Regression. To obtain the optimal set of parameters for a classic linear regression model, we obtain the vector β that minimizes the Mean Squared Error (MSE) Eq. 12 between the target variable and the output of the model:

$$MSE = \frac{1}{N} \sum_{i=1}^{N} (y_i - \hat{y}(\mathbf{x}, \beta)_i)^2 \qquad (12)$$

Ridge (L2 Regularization). The optimal parameters when applying L2 regularization will be those that minimize the function E_{Ridge} Eq. 13 which consists of the MSE added to a regularization term that depends on the square of the parameters.

$$E_{Ridge} = MSE + \alpha \sum_{i=0}^{M-1} \beta_i^2 \qquad (13)$$

Ensemble Methods. In this work we are going to make use of two well known ensemble methods:

Random Forest. The Random Forest algorithm combines a set of weak models based on decision trees in order to construct a strong classifier [2]. Each weak model is trained using a random set of input variables $\mathbf{x}_i$ that will produce a prediction function $h_i(\mathbf{x}_i)$. The response of all the weak models will be combined with the Eq. 14, where M is the number of estimators used.

$$f(\mathbf{x}) = \frac{1}{M} \sum_{i=0}^{M} h_i(\mathbf{x}_i) \qquad (14)$$

Each weak classifier will be trained as a regular decision tree.

Support Vector Machines (SVM). Support Vector Machines (SVM) are ML models used for classification problems [8], as well as regression tasks [10] that have been successfully applied to a variety of different problems as explained in [7]. They consist of the construction of an hyperplane that is adjusted to the training data using a tolerance margin C. To train this model, we find the parameter ω that optimizes Eq. 15.

$$\omega^* = \frac{1}{2} \arg\min_{\omega} \omega^\intercal \omega + C + \sum_{i=1}^{N} (\xi_i + \xi_i^*) \tag{15}$$

It is very common for this type of model to implement the kernel trick, which consists of transforming the space of the features with the function $\Phi(x)$ by substituting dot products with the kernel function Eq. 16.

$$K(x, y) = \langle \Phi(x), \Phi(y) \rangle \tag{16}$$

In this work we will consider the following kernels.

Linear Kernel

$$\text{Linear Kernel:} \quad K_{linear}(x, y) = x^\intercal y$$

Polynomial Kernel

$$\text{Polynomial Kernel:} \quad K_{poly}(x, y) = (x^\intercal y + c)^d$$

Gaussian Kernel

$$\text{Gaussian Kernel:} \quad K_{gaussian}(x, y) = e^{||x-y||^2/2\sigma^2} = e^{\gamma ||x-y||^2}$$

Multi-layer Perceptron (MLP). MLPs are one of the most used ML models for classification and regression problems. It consists of a number of input nodes or neurons, that are processed by hidden layers and are passed to the output layer. Each hidden layer l consists of a set of neurons, each obtaining their value $a_{l,i}$ from the application of an activation function $\sigma(x)$ over a linear combination of the values of the previous layer added to a bias b Eq. 17.

$$a_{l,i} = \sigma(W_{l,i} \cdot a_{l-1} + b_{l,i}) \tag{17}$$

To train this model, we fit the weights $W_{l,i}$ and biases $b_{l,i}$ so that the error of the network's output is as small as possible. The most used algorithm to perform this optimization is Stochastic Gradient Descent (SGD), which is explained in detail in [6].

4   Results

In this Section we will discuss the implementation of the models to develop the surrogate model in order to find the best way to approximate the fitness function for an arch.

4.1 Training of Models

We trained each of the ML models with samples from each of the parameterizations of the arches. We have 2000 samples for each model, each containing the parameters that define the geometry of a different arch, along with its fitness, calculated as shown in Eq. (9). To perform the training of the models, we will split each dataset into two sets, a training set and a testing set. Each model will be trained with the training set and evaluated with the testing set.

The data is preprocessed by standardizing the values, obtaining the new dataset z by subtracting from each feature c of each data point i their average value $\bar{x}_c$ and dividing by their standard deviation σ_{x_c} as shown in Eq. 18. This standardization is applied to the input variables as well as the target variables to avoid issues with the training of gradient based algorithms.

$$z_{c,i} = \frac{x_{c,i} - \bar{x}_c}{\sigma_{x_c}} \tag{18}$$

We will make use of three metrics to evaluate each of the models: the R2 score Eq. 19, the Root of the Mean Squared Error (RMSE) Eq. 20 and the Mean Absolute Error (MAE) Eq. 21. The R2 score will be a number smaller than or equal to 1, where a perfect model will have a score of 1, obtaining lower values as the modeling differs from the real data. The MAE and RMSE scores will be positive values; the lower they are, the less error our model makes when approximating the original function.

$$R^2(\mathbf{y}, \hat{\mathbf{y}}) = 1 - \frac{\sum_{i=1}^{N}(y_i - \hat{y}_i)^2}{\sum_{i=1}^{N}(y_i - \bar{y})^2} \tag{19}$$

Table 1. Comparison of the performance of each model using the data of the Bézier Curves parameterization. The rows are ordered by the R2 score in validation, the first model is the one the fits the data with a lower error.

Model	R2 Train	R2 Validation	RMSE Train	RMSE Validation	MAE Train	MAE Validation
MLP	0.957	0.937	2.967×10^6	3.591×10^6	1.809×10^6	2.045×10^6
RandomForest	0.964	0.730	2.717×10^6	7.434×10^6	1.210×10^6	3.314×10^6
SVR (Gaussian kernel)	0.730	0.693	7.434×10^6	7.927×10^6	3.890×10^6	4.199×10^6
SVR (Polynomial kernel)	0.541	0.512	9.693×10^6	9.995×10^6	5.077×10^6	5.233×10^6
Linear Regression	0.162	0.158	1.310×10^7	1.313×10^7	8.653×10^6	8.666×10^6
Ridge	0.160	0.157	1.312×10^7	1.311×10^7	8.605×10^6	8.616×10^6
SVR (Linear kernel)	-0.110	-0.110	1.507×10^7	1.508×10^7	6.835×10^6	6.843×10^6

$$RMSE(\mathbf{y}, \hat{\mathbf{y}}) = \sqrt{\frac{1}{N} \sum_{i=1}^{N} (y_i - \hat{y}_i)^2} \qquad (20)$$

$$MAE(\mathbf{y}, \hat{\mathbf{y}}) = \frac{1}{N} \sum_{i=1}^{N} |y_i - \hat{y}_i| \qquad (21)$$

To compare the performance of each algorithm, we perform 5 repetitions of cross validation with 5 splits and 10 repetitions using the training data set. We take the average score obtained in the training splits and the validation splits

Table 2. Comparison of the performance of each model using the data of the Elliptic Curves parameterization. The rows are ordered by the R2 score in validation, the first model is the one the fits the data with a lower error.

Model	R2 Train	R2 Validation	RMSE Train	RMSE Validation	MAE Train	MAE Validation
Random Forest	0.960	0.728	3.417×10^5	8.912×10^5	5.744×10^4	1.494×10^5
MLP	0.693	0.356	9.468×10^5	1.371×10^6	3.201×10^5	3.661×10^5
Ridge	0.335	0.223	1.393×10^6	1.506×10^6	4.818×10^5	4.887×10^5
Linear Regression	0.359	0.216	1.368×10^6	1.513×10^6	5.330×10^5	5.429×10^5
SVR (Gaussian kernel)	0.148	0.090	1.577×10^6	1.630×10^6	3.573×10^5	3.644×10^5
SVR (Linear kernel)	-0.025	-0.027	1.730×10^6	1.737×10^6	2.661×10^5	2.660×10^5
SVR (Polynomial kernel)	0.305	-0.056	1.425×10^6	1.756×10^6	3.372×10^5	3.669×10^5

Table 3. Comparison of the performance of each model using the data of the Parabola Ellipse Curves parameterization. The rows are ordered by the R2 score in validation, the first model is the one the fits the data with a lower error.

Model	R2 Train	R2 Validation	RMSE Train	RMSE Validation	MAE Train	MAE Validation
MLP	0.724	0.314	1.714×10^6	2.702×10^6	4.669×10^5	5.450×10^5
SVR (Gaussian kernel)	0.036	0.095	3.203×10^6	3.103×10^6	5.085×10^5	5.152×10^5
SVR (Polynomial kernel)	0.013	0.043	3.241×10^6	3.191×10^6	5.456×10^5	5.479×10^5
Ridge	0.030	-0.017	3.212×10^6	3.289×10^6	7.727×10^5	7.748×10^5
Linear Regression	0.030	-0.019	3.212×10^6	3.293×10^6	7.767×10^5	7.789×10^5
SVR (Linear kernel)	-0.011	-0.023	3.280×10^6	2.299×10^6	3.745×10^5	3.746×10^5
Random Forest	0.919	-4.529	9.283×10^5	7.670×10^6	1.025×10^5	3.298×10^5

and show them in their respective tables to compare the models. We performed this comparison for the arches parameterized by Bézier curves (Table 1), Elliptic curves (Table 2) and Parabola Ellipse curves (Table 3).

From each parameterization, we pick the model with the best R2 Validation score and evaluate them with the test dataset. We then compare the RMSE and MAE scores of the final models to compare their performance, as shown in Table 4. Note that we don't use the R2 score to compare between different datasets since it is dependent on the average value of the target variable, which is not guaranteed to be the same across datasets.

Table 4. Score of the selected models for each parameterization.

Parameterization	Best Model	RMSE Test	MAE Test
Bezier curves	MLP	3.591×10^6	2.045×10^6
Elliptic curves	Random Forest	5.511×10^5	1.154×10^5
Parabola Ellipse curves	MLP	2.871×10^6	3.987×10^5

5   Conclusions

After examining each of the parameterizations discussed, we have found that the best approximation to the fitness function consists in modeling it with elliptic curves, using a Random Forest model to approximate the calculations, followed by a parameterization made with Bézier curves using a regular Neural Network to approximate the fitness function.

The results obtained show us a methodology that will allow us to determine the optimal submerged arch geometry without having to carry out complex structural calculations of finite elements, which represents a significant saving in computer calculation time. A future line of research is to apply this methodology to other types of civil engineering structures.

References

1. Ascher, U.M., Petzold, L.R.: Computer methods for ordinary differential equations and differential-algebraic equations, vol. 61. Siam (1998)
2. Breiman, L.: Random forests. Mach. Learn. **45**, 5–32 (2001)
3. Farin, G., Hoschek, J., Kim, M.-S., Kim, M.-S.: Handbook of Computer Aided Geometric Design. Elsevier Science I& Technology, Amsterdam (2002)
4. Fulton, W.: Algebraic curves. An Introduction to Algebraic Geom **54** (2008)
5. Hernández-Díaz, A.M., Bueno-Crespo, A., Pérez-Aracil, J., Cecilia, J.M.: Multi-objective optimal design of submerged arches using extreme learning machine and evolutionary algorithms. Appl. Soft Comput. **71**, 826–834 (2018)
6. Rumelhart, D.E., Hinton, G.E., Williams, R.J.: Learning representations by back-propagating errors. Nature **323**(6088), 533–536 (1986)

7. Salcedo-Sanz, S., Rojo-Álvarez, J.L., Martínez-Ramón, M., Camps-Valls, G.: Support vector machines in engineering: an overview. Wiley Interdiscip. Rev.: Data Mining Knowl. Disc. **4**(3), 234–267 (2014)
8. Schölkopf, B., Smola, A.J.: Learning with kernels: support vector machines, regularization, optimization, and beyond. MIT press (2002)
9. Silverman, J.H.: The Arithmetic of Elliptic Curves. Springer New York, New York, NY (2009)
10. Smola, A.J., Schölkopf, B.: A tutorial on support vector regression. Stat. Comput. **14**, 199–222 (2004)
11. Stolarski, T., Nakasone, Y., Yoshimoto, S.: Engineering analysis with ANSYS software. Butterworth-Heinemann (2018)
12. Tadjbakhsh, I.: Stability and optimum design of arch-type structures. Int. J. Solids Struct. **17**(6), 565–574 (1981)

Bioinspired Applications

Towards the Conformation of Constructive Political Discussion Groups. A Computational Approach

Pedro Pinacho-Davidson[1]([✉]), Valentina Hernández[1], Ricardo Contreras[2],
Pedro Salcedo[1], María Angélica Pinninghoff[1], and Karina Fuentes-Riffo[1]

[1] Universidad de Concepción, Concepción, Chile
ppinacho@udec.cl
[2] Universidad Adolfo Ibañez, Peñalolén, Chile
https://www.udec.cl/, https://www.uai.cl/

Abstract. This research developed a new optimization model for creating constructive political discussion groups, focusing on political representativeness, lexical compatibility, and gender representation. The study introduced heuristic and metaheuristic algorithms to solve this optimization problem, effectively generating balanced and representative groups. These contributions are significant in computational political science, enhancing democratic and inclusive political discourse.

Keywords: group conformation · political discussion · combinatorial optimization

1 Introduction

Political participation is vital for Sustainable Development Goal (SDG) 16, underpinning democratic validity and governance efficacy [4,7]. Latin American social upheavals illustrate the urgency of engagement, essential for equitable societies and the goals of SDG 16, which advocates for inclusive, just, and effective societal structures [1]. Discussions on regulatory statutes and public policies often lead to conflicts without consensus, especially when participants have differing ideologies. However, when ideologies align, two issues arise: lack of intellectual challenge leading to unrefined ideas, and feedback that reinforces rather than critiques original thoughts, impeding intellectual growth and critical thinking [3]. This study aims to develop a system for constructive political discourse among diverse viewpoints, considering political representation, subject expertise, and gender diversity. It introduces an optimization model to characterize individuals for effective group discussions, along with algorithms for the model and their performance evaluation. This work seeks to enhance political discussions, promoting understanding and reconciliation in contemporary democratic processes. Current methods for characterizing individuals for collaborative purposes focus on education and

---

[1] Promote peaceful and inclusive societies for sustainable development, provide access to justice for all and build effective, accountable and inclusive institutions at all levels https://sdgs.un.org/goals/goal16.

J. M. Ferrández Vicente et al. (Eds.): IWINAC 2024, LNCS 14675, pp. 347–357, 2024.
https://doi.org/10.1007/978-3-031-61137-7_32

diverse attributes. For example, in online courses, student engagement, measured by their platform interactions, is used for group formation using k-means [13]. Another approach, "Lexical Availability" (LA), assesses an individual's known lexicon to form groups with similar lexical knowledge, using hierarchical clustering based on Levenshtein distance [11]. This concept evolved into a combinatorial problem aimed at minimizing lexical distance differences within groups [12]. Additionally, Bacterial Algorithms have been employed for grouping based on similar Individual Differences in Lexical Availability (LAIs), comparing their efficacy with genetic algorithms [5, 8, 10]. In a workplace context, an algorithm was initially used to form groups based on workers' skills for complex tasks. However, due to high time costs rendering it is impractical for more than 20 workers, a heuristic approach was adopted to decrease execution time significantly [9]. The process of grouping students for specific tasks was redefined to align with a problem solvable by a known exact algorithm [6]. Additionally, group creation for tasks with varying difficulties involved characterizing students by personality, gender, and competencies, and tasks by required skills. To form these groups, both exact and metaheuristic methods were proposed, with the latter proving more time-efficient for larger student numbers. The solution quality varied based on the skills' relevance to the task [2].

2 Characterization of People

The formation of groups is based on the characterization of the individuals involved. We propose the characterization of each person across three dimensions: **political thinking**, which determines their stance on various sociopolitical issues, **gender**, which identifies the gender they subscribe to, and **collaboration skills**, which help ascertain an individual's aptitude for debating and contributing arguments among their peers, thereby establishing their lexical level on relevant concepts.

2.1 Political Thinking

This dimension has four axes to explain a person's political stance, each axis represented by a number ranging from 0 to 1 where these two numbers represent the extreme thoughts of each axis. These are as follows:

1. **Economy**: Ranges from *"Equality"* (0) favoring wealth distribution, social programs, and socialism, to *"Market"* (1) supporting economic growth, low taxes, privatization, and laissez-faire capitalism.
2. **Diplomacy**: Extends from *"Nation"* (0), indicating patriotism, nationalism, and aggressive foreign policy, to *"Globalization"* (1), denoting cosmopolitanism, globalism, and support for peaceful policies and world government.
3. **State**: Spans from *"Freedom"* (0), emphasizing civil liberties, democracy, and minimal state intervention, to *"Authoritarianism"* (1), advocating strong state control, government surveillance, and censorship.

4. **Society**: Ranges from "*Tradition*" (0), valuing traditional morals and often religious views, to "*Progress*" (1), focusing on social change, rationality, environmental action, and scientific advancement.

This characterization draws from 8Values [1], offering a 70-question test to assess 8 values (extremes of four axes) with answers ranging from Strongly Agree to Strongly Disagree. The resulting percentages provide a detailed understanding of an individual's position on each axis, facilitating effective characterization.

2.2 Collaboration Skills

The collaborative dimension is designed to represent the ability of individuals to communicate with each other based on their lexical knowledge, paralleling the approach taken in [12]. For this purpose, the same four axes as those found in the political dimension will be employed: **Economy, Diplomacy, State, and Society**. Likewise, these axes have values that range from 0 to 1, representing a *Personal Lexical Availability Index* (LAIp) for each of the axes. The LAIp is calculated via the following procedure:

1. A lexical availability test is administered to all participants. This test presents the participant with a topic, such as "Economy", and the participant is then given 2 min to respond with all the words they know about this topic. This test is conducted for each of the four political thought axes.
2. The Lexical Availability Index (LAI) is calculated using the data from the entire population. Essentially, the LAI will yield a list of all the words used (one list per axis) in order of decreasing significance. This implies that the initial words were used more frequently, and the final words were used less often by the participants. Its formula is as follows:

$$LAI = \sum_{i=1}^{r} \lambda^{(i-1)} \frac{f_i}{N}, \tag{1}$$

where r is the total number of different words, f_i is the frequency of mentions of word i, λ is a weighting factor for each position, giving more importance to the first term (being the most frequent) and decaying as positions advance (typically, $\lambda = 0.9$ is chosen), and finally, N is the number of participants.
3. Lastly, with this information, it is possible to calculate the LAIp. This value will tell us how much vocabulary the person handles compared to the general population. In other words, the closer the value is to 1, the greater the person's understanding, and they command a wide vocabulary on that topic. Conversely, a value closer to 0 signifies that the person possesses a low lexicon and understands very little about the topic. This index is calculated with the following formula:

$$LAIp = \sum_{i=1} \left(\frac{LAI_i}{rp} \right), \tag{2}$$

where LAI_i is the lexical availability index of word i, and rp is the number of responses from person p.

2.3   Gender

This dimension is used to organize groups using a gender equity criterion. For this purpose, three types of genders are considered: Female, Male, and Non-Binary.

3   Developed Model

$$\text{Minimize} : \alpha \sum_{g}^{L} PoI + \beta \sum_{g}^{L} GeI + \gamma \sum_{g}^{L} GrI \tag{3}$$

$$\text{subject to} : \sum_{i=1}^{n} x_{ij} \leq m, \forall j \in [1, l] \tag{4}$$

$$\sum_{j=1}^{l} x_{ij} = 1, \forall i \in [1, n] \tag{5}$$

$$x_{ij} \in 0, 1 \tag{6}$$

where α, β, and γ represent the weighting factors for the political, gender, and collaborative dimensions, respectively, and x_{ij} is a variable that determines if subject i belongs to group j.

Each term of the sum in the objective function is then defined as follows:

– **Political Imbalance** (PoI)

$$\sum_{e}^{\#AxesP} |X_T^e - \bar{X}_j^e| \tag{7}$$

where:
  • $\bar{X}_j^e = \frac{\sum_{i=1}^{N} x_{ij} * D_{i,e}}{\sum_{i=1}^{N} x_{ij}}$
  • $\bar{X}_j^e$: Target average of group j on axis e.
  • X_T^e : Total average of all participants on axis e.
  • $D_{i,e}$: Data corresponding to individual i on axis e.

– **Gender Imbalance** (GeI)

$$\sum_{g \in Genders} |P_T^g - P_j^g| \tag{8}$$

where:
  • P_T^g: Total average or target percentage of gender g.
  • P_j^g: Percentage of gender g for group j.

– **Group Incompatibility** (GrI)

$$\sum_{e}^{\#AxesP} \sqrt{\frac{\sum_{i=1}^{N} x_{ij} * (LAIp_i^e - L\bar{A}Ip_j^e)^2}{m_j}} \tag{9}$$

where:
  • $LAIp_i^e$: Personal LAI of individual i on axis e.
  • $L\bar{A}Ipj^e$: Average personal LAI for group j on axis e.
  • m_j : Size of group j.

4   Algorithmic Approach

This section outlines a series of algorithms developed incrementally, beginning with a basic greedy heuristic and its randomized variant, foundational for trajectory-based metaheuristics. We introduce a Greedy Randomized Adaptive Search Procedure (GRASP) and an Iterated Greedy (IG) algorithm, alongside a brute force algorithm for exact comparisons, facilitating an effective approach to the problem's complexity.

4.1   Greedy Algorithm

The first heuristic is quite simple and involves adding individuals to each available group while attempting to minimize the value of the objective function. The algorithm can be reviewed in Algorithm 1.

Algorithm 1: Greedy Algorithm

Data: Dataset, M, L
Result: Grouped individuals
$X \longleftarrow$ Initialize solution with no groups assigned;
i $\longleftarrow$ 0 ;
while $i <$ *number of participants* **do**
    bestGroup $\longleftarrow$ 0 ;
    bestVO $\longleftarrow$ 0 ;
    for j *in UnreadyGroups* **do**
        if *GroupEmpty(j)* **then**
            UpdateGroup(X, i, j) ;
            break ;
        end
        vo $\longleftarrow$ GroupObjectiveFunction(Group(j), i) ;
        if $vo < bestVO$ **then**
            bestVO $\longleftarrow$ vo ;
            bestGroup $\longleftarrow$ j ;
        end
    end
    UpdateGroup(X, i, bestGroup) ;
    i $\longleftarrow$ i+1 ;
end

Where N is the number of participants, L is the number of groups, and M is the maximum number of individuals that can be assigned to a group.

The algorithm begins by selecting the first L participants and assigning them in order to groups from 1 to L, thus initially each group has a single participant. After this, each of the participants k from the remaining participant set is evaluated in each of the L groups. Based on this evaluation, the group that minimizes the objective function with the addition of k is chosen, and k is placed in this group. If a group reaches its maximum capacity (M), it is closed and is no longer considered for accepting more individuals. In this way, successive assignments of individuals only consider the available groups.

4.2   GRASP

A randomized greedy algorithm, guided by parameter R, extends the deterministic greedy approach (Algorithm 2). It selects from the top K candidate groups for solution construction. With probability R, a participant joins a random group from these K groups; with $1 - R$, they join the best group for minimizing the objective function. This GRASP repeats for a set number of iterations, yielding the best solution at the end.

4.3   IG

The Iterated Greedy (IG) algorithm, building on the Greedy and GRASP algorithms, involves partially destroying a GRASP-generated solution and reconstructing it. This process (Algorithm 3) handles N participants, with L groups each hosting up to M individuals. Utilizing GRASP's framework, it employs randomness percentage R and a top K group list. After assigning all individuals, the last D groups are dismantled, and the ungrouped individuals (*FreeIndividuals*) are reassigned. This cycle repeats for *Iterations*, culminating in the best solution found.

Additionally, for a precise benchmark, we implemented an exhaustive search algorithm (brute force) that explores all assignment options, ensuring the delivery of the optimal solution by thoroughly examining the entire search space.

Algorithm 2: GRASP

Data: Dataset, M, L, R, K, *Iterations*
Result: Grouped individuals
X ⟵ Initialize solution with no groups assigned;
it ⟵ 0 ;
while *it ¡ Iterations* **do**
  i ⟵ 0 ;
  BestGroups ⟵ {∅} ;
  while *i ¡ number of participants* **do**
    bestGroup ⟵ 0 ;
    bestVO ⟵ 0 ;
    for *j in UnreadyGroups* **do**
      if *GroupEmpty(j)* **then**
        UpdateGroup(X, i, j) ;
        break ;
      end
      vo ⟵ GroupObjectiveFunction(Group(j), i) ;
      UpdateList(BestGroups, K) ;
    end
    UpdateGroup(X, i, BestGroups, R) ;
    i ⟵ i+1 ;
  end
  it ⟵ it + 1 ;
end

Algorithm 3: Iterated Greedy Algorithm

Data: Dataset, M, L, R, K, D, *Iterations*
Result: Grouped individuals
X ⟵ Initialize solution with no groups assigned;
it ⟵ 0 ;
BestAssignment ⟵ Initialize solution to zero ;
while *it ¡ Iterations* **do**
  i ⟵ 0 ;
  X ⟵ GRASP(Dataset, M, L, R, K, *Iterations*) ;
  FreeIndividuals ⟵ DestroyGroups(X, D) ;
  X ⟵ GRASP(FreeIndividuals, M, L, R, K, *Iterations*) ;
  if *BestAssignment ¡ X* **then**
    BestAssignment ⟵ X ;
  end
  it ⟵ it + 1 ;
end

5   DataSets for Evaluation

To evaluate the algorithms, we created two data sets: an artificial set split into two subsets with different data distributions, and a second set derived from real-world data, enabling a comprehensive analysis across varied scenarios.

5.1   Artificial Datasets

The artificial datasets consist of two subsets, each with 1000 entries (people) characterized by nine attributes across three dimensions: politics (four axes), gender (one axis), and collaboration (four axes). Dataset 1, using normal distributions, and Dataset 2, employing varied distributions, were designed to test the model under different scenarios. Dataset 2 includes balanced (normal distribution), left-leaning (beta distribution, $\alpha = 2$, $\beta = 5$), polarized (beta distribution, $\alpha = 0.5$, $\beta = 0.5$), and another left-leaning distribution (beta distribution, $\alpha = 3$, $\beta = 1.5$). Each attribute axis in the datasets is generated from one of these distributions.

5.2   Real Dataset

Real-world dataset was assembled in collaboration with first-year computer engineering students from the University of Concepción. This dataset consists of data from 24 students who participated in lexical availability tests via a dedicated online platform[2]. The tests were focused on key concepts utilized for individual characterization: Economy, Diplomacy, State, and Society.

Additionally, each participating individual completed the *8values* political classification questionnaire[3]. This tool provided a deeper understanding of the students' political leanings, enhancing the complexity and usefulness of the dataset.

6   Experiments and Results

In our exploratory experiments, we assessed the solution quality and execution times of four algorithms on the synthetic dataset, limiting their execution time uniformly, except for the brute force algorithm. The objective function parameters were consistently set as $\alpha = \beta = \gamma = 1$.

6.1   Empirical Verification of Problem Complexity

We conducted two tests to evaluate the problem's complexity. The first test measured the execution time of the exhaustive search algorithm with increasing numbers of individuals (N). Subsequently, we compared the performance of our

---

[2] http://www.lexicones.com/grupos-politicos/encuesta.php.
[3] https://8values.github.io/.

algorithms in scenarios where the brute force method was feasible, enabling us to analyze their scalability and efficiency. This approach provided empirical insights into the balance between computational intensity and solution accuracy.

Figure 1 illustrates the brute-force algorithm's exponentially growing time consumption for problem configurations with 4 to 12 individuals. Significantly, for a configuration of 12 individuals, the completion time exceeds 4000 s, emphasizing the method's substantial and impractical computational demands at larger scales. Table 1 presents the performance of all algorithms on smaller problems where the number of individuals (N) is equal to or less than 12. Given the scale of these instances, the brute-force algorithm unsurprisingly emerges as the most effective solution. Despite excluding the brute force algorithm from the analysis, the Iterated Greedy (IG) algorithm demonstrates clear superiority over the other developed algorithms.

6.2   Experiments with Artificial Dataset

Tests were conducted using a set of fixed parameter configurations (all permutations). This take as reference the following domains for each parameter $R = \{0.05, 0.1, 0.2, 0.5, 0.8\}$, $K = \{1, 5, 10, 20\}$ and $D = \{1, 5, 10, 20\}$. The reported results correspond to those obtained with the optimal configuration.

Three test scenarios were developed using two datasets (Dataset 1 and 2), each involving 50 groups with a maximum of 20 members for the 1000 individuals in the datasets, and each experiment was replicated 20 times to calculate an average. $E1$ use Dataset 1 to mimic the distribution of individuals within each

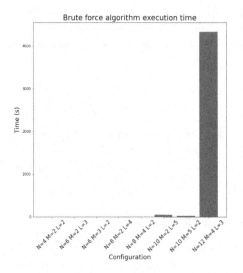

Table 1. A Comparative results for all algorithms in the available range of the brute-force algorithm

N	L	M	Br. force	Greedy	GRASP	IG
4	2	2	0.835	1.547	1.204	0.862
6	3	2	1.061	2.049	1.940	1.646
6	2	3	0.612	1.248	1.174	0.870
8	4	2	1.158	2.907	2.716	2.430
8	2	4	0.469	1.380	1.308	1.077
10	5	2	1.303	3.638	3.515	3.189
10	2	5	0.426	1.407	1.338	1.156
12	3	4	0.679	2.199	2.103	1.809

Fig. 1. Time Consumption for Brute Force algorithm with different configuracions of problem instances

Table 2. Best objective values achieved by the three developed algorithms across the predefined scenarios.

Algorithm	$E1$	$E2$	$E3$
Greedy	32.80	17.69	19.72
GRASP	32.744	17.16	19.37
IG	**31.63**	**16.44**	**18.31**

group. $E2$ employ Dataset 2, with the same aim as $E1$, reflecting the group's individual distribution. In $E3$, the target value is adjusted to contrast with population means, heightening the tension between variables during objective function evaluation. Table 2 presents the outcomes of the objective function across all experiments using the three algorithms, with IG consistently delivering the best results.

6.3   Political Discussion Experiment

With the help of first-year computer engineering students, we compiled a dataset with realistic distributions. To observe the behavior of groups formed by computational algorithms, a social experiment was conducted using the Iterated Greedy (IG) method, due to its consistent superiority in previous tests. Figure 2 shows group distributions, depicting political axes' target averages (segmented lines), gender ratio, and collaborative axes' standard deviations between member of each group. The alignment of political means with population averages reflects an accurate political spectrum representation, while low standard deviations in LAI highlight lexical homogeneity, particularly in concepts like Diplomacy.

To gauge the real quality of groups formed by our algorithm and to capitalize on the context of Chile's upcoming constitutional vote (September 2022), we conducted a social experiment involving algorithm-generated groups in a debate. Participants discussed the new constitutional draft, focusing on Housing and Plurinationality. After the 30-minute debates, participants repeated their lexical availability tests and completed surveys to assess their perceptions of the experiment. The summarized feedback from the post-activity survey revealed:

1. Participants experienced well-being, comfort, respect, and relaxation in group dynamics.
2. Most found the discussion atmosphere cordial.
3. While ideas shared similarities, they weren't identical, allowing for idea juxtaposition.
4. The experience was rated positively, mainly attributed to constructive dialogue.

This article underscores a beneficial side effect: participants' enhanced understanding of key concepts like Economy, Diplomacy, Society, and State, fostering civic education. This educational gain is evidenced in Table 3, comparing

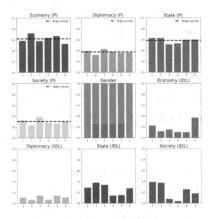

Fig. 2. Characterization of created discussion groups

Table 3. A Comparative results for all algorithms in the available range of the brute-force algorithm

Subj	LAIp before	LAIp after	Diff
Ind-1	0.432	0.500	+0.069
Ind-2	0.373	0.414	+0.041
Ind-3	0.940	1.088	+0.148
Ind-4	0.615	0.757	+0.143
Ind-5	0.923	0.747	−0.176
Ind-6	1.044	0.965	−0.079
Ind-7	0.836	0.905	+0.069
Ind-8	0.790	1.026	+0.236
Ind-9	0.734	0.950	+0.216
Ind-10	0.792	0.518	−0.274
Ind-11	0.699	0.805	+0.106
Ind-12	0.918	1.054	+0.136
Ind-13	0.734	0.922	+0.187

each individual's Personal Lexical Availability Index (LAIp) before and after the debate. Notably, the 'difference' column reveals a general increase in this index post-debate.

7   Conclusions

This study presents a new model for forming political discussion groups based on political, collaborative, and gender criteria. Experiments reveal the problem's complexity, with brute-force methods being impractical for groups larger than 12 individuals. Addressing this, the study employed heuristics and metaheuristics, leading to an effective Iterated Greedy (IG) solution. Additionally, a social experiment yielded positive participant feedback and notable civic learning, underscoring the model's practical efficacy.

Future directions for this study include exploring alternative characterizations of political thought beyond means over normal distributions, such as different distributions or discretized thought sets mirroring the political spectrum. Additionally, the research could expand to formulating the top T groups, rather than including all individuals in a group, aligning with organizer-defined target distributions. This approach could facilitate small-scale debates or focus group activities, building on the study's foundational work for further exploration.

References

1. GitHub - 8values/8values.github.io: The 8values political quiz — github.com. https://github.com/8values/8values.github.io. Accessed 20 July 2023
2. Andrejczuk, E., Bistaffa, F., Blum, C., Rodríguez-Aguilar, J.A., Sierra, C.: Synergistic team composition: a computational approach to foster diversity in teams. Knowl. Based Syst. **182**, 104799 (2019)
3. Campos-Domínguez, E.: Twitter y la comunicación política. Profesional de la Información **26**(5), 785–794 (2017)
4. Dahl, R.A.: Political equality, then and now. Tocqueville Rev. **27**(2), 461–475 (2006)
5. Górriz, J.M., et al.: Computational approaches to explainable artificial intelligence: advances in theory, applications and trends. Inf. Fusion **100**, 101945 (2023)
6. Manyà, F., Negrete, S., Roig, C., Soler, J.R.: Solving the team composition problem in a classroom. Fundamenta Informaticae, **174**(1), 83–101 (2020)
7. United Nations. Transforming our world: The 2030 agenda for sustainable development. https://sustainabledevelopment.un.org/post2015/transformingourworld (2015) Accessed 06 June 2023
8. Pinninghoff J., M.A., Contreras A., R., Salcedo L., P., Contreras A., R.: Genetic algorithms as a tool for structuring collaborative groups. Natural Comput. **16**(2), 231–239 (2016). https://doi.org/10.1007/s11047-016-9574-1
9. Rahman, H., Roy, S.B., Thirumuruganathan, S., Amer-Yahia, S., Das, G.: Optimized group formation for solving collaborative tasks. VLDB J. **28**(1), 1–23 (2018). https://doi.org/10.1007/s00778-018-0516-7
10. Ricardo Contreras, A., Valentina Hernández, P., Pinacho-Davidson, P., Angélica Pinninghoff J., M.: A bacteria-based metaheuristic as a tool for group formation. In: Ferrández Vicente, J.M., Álvarez-Sánchez, J.R., de la Paz López, F., Adeli, H. (eds.) Bio-inspired Systems and Applications: from Robotics to Ambient Intelligence: 9th International Work-Conference on the Interplay Between Natural and Artificial Computation, IWINAC 2022, Puerto de la Cruz, Tenerife, Spain, May 31 – June 3, 2022, Proceedings, Part II, pp. 443–451. Springer International Publishing, Cham (2022). https://doi.org/10.1007/978-3-031-06527-9_44
11. Rojas, D.F., Zambrano, C.D.C., Salcedo, P.A.:Metodología de análisis de disponibilidad léxica en alumnos de pedagogía a través de la comparación jerárquica de lexicones. *Formación universitaria*, **10**(4), 03–14 (2017)
12. Rojas, D.F., Zambrano Matamala, C., Salcedo Lagos, P.: Método para la formación de grupos colaborativos mediante disponibilidad léxica. *REDIE: Revista Electrónica de Investigación Educativa*, (21), 17 (2019)
13. Sanz-Martínez, L., Er, E., Martínez-Monés, A., Dimitriadis, Y., Bote-Lorenzo, M.L.: Creating collaborative groups in a MOOC: a homogeneous engagement grouping approach. Behav. Inf. Technol. **38**(11), 1107–1121 (2019)

Topic Detection in COVID-19 Mortality Time Series

Manuel Graña[✉], Goizalde Badiola-Zabala, and Guillermo Cano-Escalera

Computational Intelligence Group, University of the Basque Country, UPV/EHU,
San Sebastian, Spain
manuel.grana@ehu.es

Abstract. The mortality of COVID-19 has been analyzed from a predictive point of view, building models that failed to predict the medium and long term evolution of the time series. Looked in a retrospective way, it is possible to appreciate that the mortality impact of the pandemic was very different across countries. In this paper we deal with the discovery of representative patterns, i.e. topics in latent Dirichlet analysis (LDA), that may explain the observed mortality time series. The choice of the number of topics is a balance between the minimization of perplexity, and the avoidance of overfitting. We find that countries can be clustered according to the coefficients of the decomposition of their time series into topics, and that this decomposition has a geopolitical correspondence, i.e. countries with the same dominant topic representation belong to the same geographical and/or political domain.

1 Introduction

Out of the hundreds of thousands of papers published somehow related with COVID-19 pandemic, those dealing with Machine Learning and like predictive approaches were mostly dealing with predicting the individual patient risks for severe disease [4]. Most epidemiological works, have focused on the prediction of the number cases applying epidemiological models [8], classical statistical tools as well as Machine Learning [6] and Deep Learning tools [1].

Why focus on mortality time series? While number of cases reported maybe heavily influenced by the testing pressure, the political decisions about who is to be tested more frequently, and the quality of the testing materials, procedures, and even personnel qualifications, the deaths attributed to COVID-19 have less confusing factors and appear to be a more rigorous account of the pandemic impact on the society. The only confusing factor seems to be whether the death was due to COVID-19 or COVID-19 was detected while the person was about to die from other causes. This confusion was a key issue during the Omicron wave [5].

In this paper we do not try to make any kind of extrapolation of the data, such as the prediction of the actual death toll of the pandemic by means of regression methods [3]. In fact, we do not question the published data, taking

J. M. Ferrández Vicente et al. (Eds.): IWINAC 2024, LNCS 14675, pp. 358–367, 2024.
https://doi.org/10.1007/978-3-031-61137-7_33

it at face value. In other words, we think that across the world all governments are clever enough to count deaths. Instead, we look for patterns of the mortality across countries that give an indirect picture of the diversity of circumstances and responses to the pandemic. To this end, we apply latent Dirichlet analysis (LDA) in order to extract latent templates of mortality time series. The decomposition (or explanation) of each country COVID-19 mortality time series into these templates should allow to find clusters of similar countries and to appreciate the dissimilarity among the countries belonging to different clusters.

The underlying hypothesis of the pandemic response is that there is a single well isolated and identified pathogen as the cause and that there is only one feasible strategy to cope with it, namely vaccination and social control measures. In other words, because the pathogen is unique the treatment should be the same for everybody. However, any casual inspection finds quite diverse results in terms of mortality time series patterns under a rather uniform set of measures taken by governments across the world that appear to contradict this hypothesis. Our ongoing work discovers underlying patterns of mortality and their spatial distributions of their expression that would allow to look for underlying causes for the diversity focusing on the actual policies implemented in the countries.

2 Materials and Methods

The code and data are published in zenodo[1] as well as figures and future versions of this work as long as it is evolving.

2.1 Our World in Data

"Our world in data" (OWID) is a web site devoted to the publication of relevant data for the pressing geopolitical and economic questions. It is hosted by the University of Oxford and has been extensively funded by Bill and Melinda Gates Fundation, thus it is not suspicious of being on the side of the conspiracy theorists. OWID has been publishing relevant data for the follow up of COVID-19 pandemic[2], aggregating it from several sources. Mortality time series were taken from the John Hopkins COVID-19 site until march 2023, when it stoped updating data after the WHO published the end of the pandemic and most countries stopped reporting. For this work, we have taken the dataset as published on the first days of 2023, which we thinks covers the pandemic evolution. We consider the seven day rolling average time series, to avoid artifacts due to reporting irregularities, such as zero deaths in weekends.

2.2 Latent Dirichlet Analysis

Latent Dirichlet Allocation (LDA) [2] is a technique originally proposed for population genetics analysis [9] which has extensively been used for natural

---

[1] https://zenodo.org/doi/10.5281/zenodo.10403170.

[2] https://ourworldindata.org/explorers/coronavirus-data-explorer.

language processing. LDA aims to discover the latent topics $T = \{t_i\}_{i=1}^{K}$ underlying a set of documents $D = \{d_i\}_{i=1}^{M}$ and to explain the documents in terms of these topics. The documents are characterized by a vectorial representation $d_i = [c_{j,i}]_{j=1}^{V}$ where each vector entry is is a counter of the number of appearances in the document of the corresponding word in a vocabulary $V = \{w_i\}_{i=1}^{V}$. Thus the dimension of the vector representation is the size of the vocabulary. Each topic is defined by the vector of probabilities of appearances of the vocabulary words in the topic $t_i = [\varphi_{j,i}]_{j=1}^{V}$ $s.t.$ $\sum_j \varphi_{j,i} = 1$. The explanation of the documents in terms of topics $E = \{e_i\}_{i=1}^{M}$ is given by the probability of appearance of the topic in the document $e_i = [\theta_{j,i}]_{j=1}^{K}$ $s.t.$ $\sum_j \theta_{j,i} = 1$, i.e. by a mixture of topics. The model assumes that topic mixtures and the topics follow a Dirichlet distribution of parameters α and β, respectively. Given the set of topics T, LDA assumes a generative process, where first a topic mixture is sampled from Dirichlet distribution $e \sim Dirichlet(\alpha)$, then each word in the document is generated in a two step process: firstly a topic $z \in T$ is selected following the discrete distribution given by e, secondly, a word $w \in V$ from the vocabulary is selected according to the discrete distribution given by t_z. The induction of the latent topics can be done by several approaches. In this work, we have used the collapsed Gibbs sampling [7] which is the default matlab solver.

In order to determine an good number of topics (we avoid the term 'optimal' because we only partly used a cost function minimum in the decision) we have carried out a grid search on the number of topics between 3 and 40 topics looking for the minimum perplexity of the model explaining the training data. We did not split into training and validation because of the small sample size (the number of countries). Besides, we consider the ratio between the sample size and the number of topics, discarding perplexity minima for high values of this ratio, which we interpret as a predictor of overfitting.

In our work, documents are equated to the mortality time series of each country, words correspond to date, and the word counts are the number of death reported each day. Therefore, the topics correspond to the distribution of death probabilities along the time span considered, which is a value proportional to the mortality rate per day. Topics provide the qualitative shapes of prototypical mortality time series explaining the actual observed mortality time series. Interpretations of topics and their relation to the causes of mortality are outside the scope of the paper.

2.3 tSNE

We apply t-distributed Stochastic Neighbor Embedding (t-SNE) [10] in order to visualize in 2D the high dimensional topic mixtures explaining each country time series. This visualization allows to assess qualitatively the aggregation of country time series into clusters. In short, t-SNE models the conditional probabilities of two data samples being neighbors in the original space and the projection space, which in our case is 2D. Then it tries to find the best localizations of the points in 2D by minimizing a Kullback-Leibler divergence by gradient descent.

The formulation of this divergence is built up assuming that the distribution of distances among vector features in the original space is Gaussian, while in the visualization space it is a t-Student.

3 Results

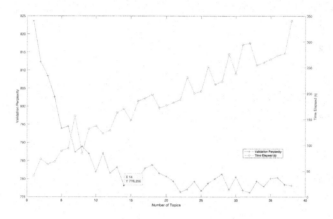

Fig. 1. The search for the number of topics with minimal perplexity

Figure 1 shows the result of our search for an optimal number of topics minimizing perplexity of the modeling of the dataset. We found some local minima over 20 topics, but we consider that the ratio of the number of topics to the sample size is too high, leading to overfitting, so we selected K = 14 as a good number of topics. Figure 2 plots the topics induced by LDA from the data. Each plot is a probability distribution, hence the values are very low, but we are interested in the shapes of the time series, specifically the occurrence of waves of maximal probability of death. Figure 3 shows the correlation among the topics plotted previously. High correlation means that topics may be redundant. It can be appreciated that most topics are uncorrelated, which can be interpreted as a good basis for representation of country mortality time series. Figure 4 shows the decomposition of countries time series into topics plotting the mixture probabilities. This figure has the limitation that some topics have the same color due to software limitations. Many countries have a largely dominant topic, meaning that they follow closely the mortality in time template. Some countries have a more uniform distribution among a small number of topics. Figure 5 shows the 2D visualization of the sample achieved by t-SNE. It is apparent that there are some very well differentiated clusters of countries that share similar mixtures of topics. Figure 6 encodes each country according to its more probable topic. It can be appreciated that there are some regions of the world where countries share similar codes. It is prominent that western Europe and North America seem to belong to the same cluster. Easter European countries shape another region, while Russia and some of its neighbors shape another. From this figure, it is clear that similar policies enforced by countries sharing a political view and some geographical features shaped the mortality results of the pandemic.

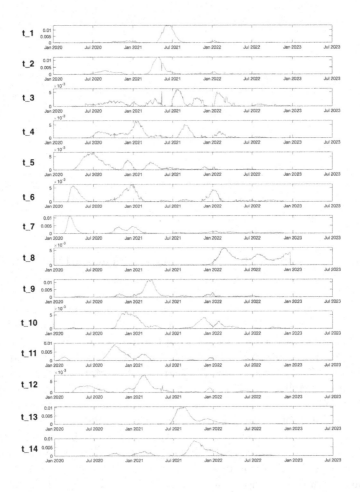

Fig. 2. The 14 topics uncovered by LDA

4   Discussion

From the point of view of the diversity of country mortality patterns, Fig. 2 provides some key insights. Topics #6 and #7 have big waves in spring 2020,

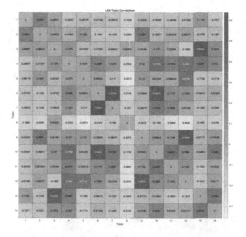

Fig. 3. Correlations among topics

corresponding to western European countries (with the exception of Portugal) and North America. Topic #6 has an Omicron wave, and the shapes of these topics at the beginning of the vaccination campaign have small differences. Topic #5 and #12, on the other hand, have first wave in the middle of the year 2020, summer in the northern hemisphere, winter in the southern hemisphere. In fact these topics are presented in South America and Africa, suggesting a seasonal effect in the virus, which later disappeared. Omicron wave was almost synchronous across the globe, regardless of hemisphere. Topic #8 shows a very late presentation of mortality, after entire populations were vaccinated. This topic was dominant in New Zealand, which enforced a strict zero covid policy. China is an special case in our study, because our data stops in the first days of 2023, before the explosion of cases and deaths that happened in the first months of the year after the Chinese government relaxed the zero covid policies.

Figure 6 provides a spatial interpretation key. Some countries, such as western Europe countries minus Portugal have very similar mortality time series patterns after enforcing rather similar policies. USA and Canada have similar response patterns to western Europe, though the absolute and relative count of deaths are rather different between Canada and USA. Apparently, the modulation of the final count of deaths over the time series templates is dependent of additional factors, which may be climatic or other underlying cultural, genetic or ethnic. For instance, the USA suffers an epidemic of obesity [11] and diabetes mellitus [12] which may be responsible for the extraordinary death toll of the pandemic. The case of Portugal is to be highlighted because it shows the differential impact of policies with its only neighboring country, specially during the first wave of spring 2020.

If examine the clusters of countries in Fig. 5 we find that some topics show some concentrated clusters with sparse outliers far from the them. Topic #1, for

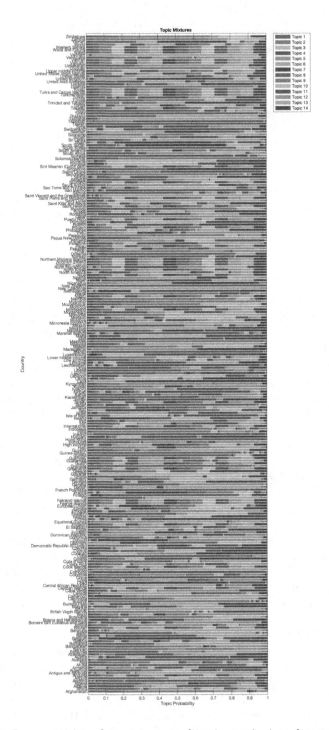

Fig. 4. Decomposition of countries mortality time series into detected topics

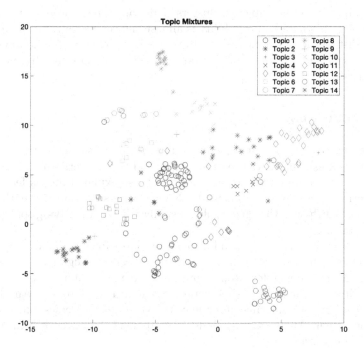

Fig. 5. Clusters of countries visualized by the tSNE 2D embedding of the countries decomposition into topics. Topic identification corresponds to the topic with maximal probability for a country.

Map of topics per country

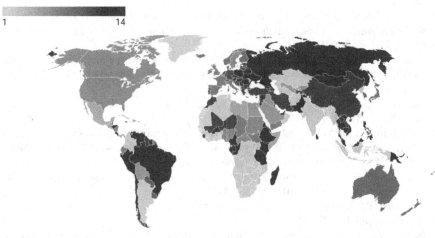

Fig. 6. Geographical location of topics

instance, appears in two separate clusters. This can correspond to countries with 'pure' topic #1, where its probability is almost one versus countries with a more uniform distribution of topics where topic #1 is 'by chance' the dominant one. This is an explanation for the appearance of this topic in quite diverse regions of the world.

5   Conclusions

We have carried out a latent topic detection that unveils some patterns of mortality time series explaining the observed mortality time series as a linear composition of such templates. Consideration of these explanations as feature vectors describing each country allows to detect clusters of countries with similar time series that have either geographical similarities or underlying sociopolitical affinities, or both.

Future works may consider additional measures for the determination of a good number of topics, such as avoiding the occurrence of highly correlated pairs of topics. More independent topics may lead to more parsimonious improved decompositions of mortality time series into mixtures of topics. Another line of work consists of exploring other feature extraction processes, such as Principal Component Analysis, Independent Component Analysis, or Non Negative Matrix Factorization.

References

1. Abbasimehr, H., Paki, R.: Prediction of COVID-19 confirmed cases combining deep learning methods and Bayesian optimization. Chaos, Solitons Fractals **142**, 110511 (2021)
2. Blei, D., Ng, A., Jordan, M.: Latent dirichlet allocation. In: Dietterich, T., Becker, S., Ghahramani, Z. (eds.) Advances in Neural Information Processing Systems, vol. 14, MIT Press (2001)
3. Collaborators COVID-19 excess mortality. Estimating excess mortality due to the COVID-19 pandemic: a systematic analysis of COVID-19-related mortality, 2020-21. Lancet 399(10334), 1513–1536 (2022)
4. Gallo Marin, B., et al.: Predictors of COVID-19 severity: a literature review. Rev. Med. Virol. **31**(1), 1–10 (2021)
5. Goldstein, E.: Mortality associated with omicron and influenza infections in France before and during the COVID-19 pandemic. Epidemiol. Infect. **151**, e148 (2023)
6. Górriz, J.M., Álvarez-Illán, I., Álvarez-Marquina, A., et al.: Computational approaches to explainable artificial intelligence: advances in theory, applications and trends. Inf. Fusion **100**, 101945 (2023)
7. Griffiths, T.L., Steyvers, M.: Finding scientific topics. Proc. Natl. Acad. Sci. U S A, **101**(Suppl 1) 5228–5235 (2004)
8. Iranzo, V., Pérez-González, S.: Epidemiological models and COVID-19: a comparative view. Hist. Philos. Life Sci. **43**(3), 104 (2021)
9. Pritchard, J.K., Stephens, M., Donnelly, P.: Inference of population structure using multilocus genotype data. Genetics **155**(2), 945–959 (2000)

10. Van Der Maaten, L., Hinton, G.: Visualizing data using t-SNE. J. Mach. Learn. Res. **9**, 2579–2625 (2008)

11. Suzanne,M.W., Louis, J.A.: Causes of obesity. Abdom Imaging **37**(5), 730–732 (2012)

12. Zimmet, P., Alberti, K.G., Magliano, D.J., Bennett, P.H.: Diabetes mellitus statistics on prevalence and mortality: facts and fallacies. Nat. Rev. Endocrinol. **12**(10), 616–622 (2016)

Multicenter Prospective Blind External Validation of a Machine Learning Model for Predicting Heart Failure Decompensation: A 3-Hospital Validation Study

Jon Kerexeta[1,2,3](✉) ⓘ, Esperança Lladó Pascual[4], Cristina Martin[1,2],
Nicola Goodfellow[5], Karina Anahi Ojanguren Carreira[4], Marco Manso[6],
Barbara Guerra[6], Stanke Ladislav[7], Vohralík Tomáš[8], Esteban Fabello[9],
Tatiana Silva[9], Michael Scott[5], Glenda Fleming[5], Andoni Beristain[1,2,3]ⓘ,
and Manuel Graña[3]ⓘ

[1] Vicomtech Foundation, Basque Research and Technology Alliance (BRTA),
20009 San Sebastián, Spain
jkerexeta@vicomtech.org
[2] e-Health Department, Biodonostia Health Research Institute,
Paseo Dr Begiristain s/n, 20014 San Sebastián, Spain
[3] Computational Intelligence Group, Computer Science Faculty,
University of the Basque Country, UPV/EHU, 20018 San Sebastián, Spain
[4] Clinica Humana, Balearic Islands, Spain
[5] Medicines Optimisation Innovation Centre, Bush Road, Antrim, Northern Ireland
[6] EDGENEERING Lda, 1600-001 Lisbon, Portugal
[7] Czech National e-Health Center, University Hospital Olomouc, Zdravotníků 248/7,
779 00 Olomouc, Czech Republic
[8] IT Department, University Hospital Olomouc, Zdravotníků 248/7,
779 00 Olomouc, Czech Republic
[9] Tree Technology S.A., Oviedo, Spain

Abstract. This paper presents the results of a multicenter prospective blind external validation study aimed at validating a machine learning model, HFPred, for predicting heart failure decompensation. The model, initially developed using self-reported daily questionnaires and health monitoring data, was trained on a cohort of 242 patients from Basurto Hospital, Bilbao. The validation study spanned three European cohorts, each with distinct objectives and patient demographics, providing a comprehensive assessment of the model's applicability. While the model accurately identified instances of decompensation, it also generated false alarms, primarily attributed to measurement errors and uncontrolled external factors. Despite these challenges, patient compliance was commendable, underscoring the potential benefits of the model. Future improvements include incorporating personalized alert thresholds and conducting non-blind pilot studies for enhanced predictive capabilities.

J. M. Ferrández Vicente et al. (Eds.): IWINAC 2024, LNCS 14675, pp. 368–377, 2024.
https://doi.org/10.1007/978-3-031-61137-7_34

Keywords: Heart Failure · Cardiac Decompensation · Machine Learning · Validation · Monitoring

1   Introduction

Since its beginning, the advancements in Information and Communication Technology (ICT) [1] have created numerous opportunities for telemedicine applications and innovative e-Health services [2]. This growth in these areas is pushing the development of advanced healthcare systems that provide continuous support not only to healthcare professionals and informal caregivers (like family members, siblings or close people) but also to the patients themselves.

As a result, telemedicine systems designed to monitor patients on the move and guide them in their daily routines are emerging. However, the full potential of mobile health data, which could be beneficial for both clinical professionals and patients, is often not fully exploited. For example, clinical data, when used in predictive models to identify high-risk patients, is sometimes not put into practice in real-life settings to assist healthcare professionals and patients. This valuable information is often not applied in real-life healthcare settings due to the scarcity of devices capable of supporting the implementation of such models and the skepticism of physicians towards these software solutions. Nevertheless, reported research results indicate that artificial intelligence, combined with predictive models and telemonitoring systems, has the potential to enhance the management of numerous diseases, including heart failure and diabetes [3].

In this context, we carried out a study [4] in which a predictive model based on self-reported questionnaires and health monitoring was developed to detect decompensation in patients with heart failure. The model utilized a daily questionnaire consisting of 8 questions, along with daily physiological data such as weight, blood oxygen saturation, blood pressure, and heart rate. Baseline data was also incorporated. A machine learning model was trained using this data to predict whether a patient would experience cardiac decompensation within the next 7 d. The cohort used for training and validation included 242 patients from Basurto Hospital in Bilbao, spanning 4 years of follow-up.

This paper presents follow-up validation of this predictive model in 3 European cohorts from health care centers involved in the project. This external multi-site validation provides additional confidence on the proposed model.

2   Material and Method

2.1   Predictive Model

The predictive model validated in this study, HFPred, was previously introduced in 2018 [4]. The cohort used to train the model consisted of 242 patients with diagnosed heart failure over four years (from 2014 to 2018) recruited at the hospital of Basurto, Bilbao (Spain). The models uses 5 daily physiological variables

Table 1. Variables monitored daily

Variable/question	Units/Answer
Physiological data	
Systolic blood pressure	mmHg
Diastolic blood pressure	mmHg
Oxygen saturation	%
Heart rate	bpm
Body weight	kg
Questionnaires	
1) Regarding episodes of swelling (oedema), in the last 3 d, your legs/feet or any other part of your body are better, worse or the same?	B/W/S
2) Compared to the last 3 d, today, do you feel better, worse or the same?	B/W/S B/W/S
3) In the last 3 d, did you take any unprescribed medication?	Yes/No
4) Can you walk or do activities like previous days? Say "No" if now you feel breathless or have more difficulty to breathe	Yes/No
5) Did you have a choking feeling or shortness of breath when you lay in bed?	Yes/No
6) Did you notice that you started coughing or have phlegm?	Yes/No
7) Does your medication suit you well? Say "No" if you relate your medication to any non-desired effect, such as feeling dizzy or blood pressure drop	Yes/No Yes/No
8) Are you following the diet and exercise recommendations provided by your doctor and nurse?	Yes/No

and an 8-question questionnaire filled daily by the patients. These variables (presented in Table 1) are crucial indicators of the patient's current condition and serve as the primary predictors of decompensation.

In addition, confusing factors such as age, smoking habits and recent decompensation within the past month, were also taken into account. The predictive model also takes into consideration additional data, such as the personalized thresholds for each daily variable. The personalized thresholds determine the point at which a variable is considered to be in an unfavorable value range for the patient. For example, if a patient's oxygen saturation level falls below 90, they are usually considered at risk. However, some patients may normally have levels below 90 without being decompensated or at risk. Thus, personalized thresholds are utilized to tailor the assessment to each individual patient.

Ultimately, a patient was classified as having experienced decompensation if they were hospitalized or visited the emergency department due to heart failure, or if they received diuretic treatment at home (considering the date of medication change if they had a consistent dosage).

New variables were derived from the given variables, which were adjusted to be independent of time to be able to train classic machine learning models.

These new variables included the duration of alert activation, and smoothed weight gain calculated by the moving average method [5].

The machine learning models used to train the data included Naïve Bayes [6], Decision Tree, Random Forest, Support Vector Machine, Neural Network, and Stochastic Gradient Descent. Among these models, NB performed the best according to AUC [7] values in the different testing sets. Therefore, the NB model was chosen for testing in these pilots. It is worth mentioning that we have since improved the model using another approach [8], but unfortunately, it was not ready in time for these pilots.

2.2 SHAPES - Medicines Control and Optimization

The European SHAPES [9] project conducted various pilots to enhance the elderly's quality of life. The project brought together different components from the different partners with the aim of achieving close monitoring and improving of the patient's well-being. HFPred was tested as part of a workpackage whose objective was to address the issues related to the adherence to medicines and treatments of older individuals who are living at home with chronic age-related illnesses and have either permanent or temporary reduced functions or capabilities. Different patient experimental pilots were conducted with different objectives. Three of them used the HFPred model, so in this article we will focus on these three.

The HFPred [4] model was utilized to assess in real-time the risk of decompensation. This risk assessment was not used for immediate intervention; instead, it was stored for post-hoc validation. This process is referred to as blind validation in the literature. The reason behind this is that machine learning model European TRL (Technology Readiness Levels [10]) did not permit clinicians to intervene based on the risk estimation by a machine learning model.

2.3 Pilot Sites

Each pilot had a different main objective, resulting in variations in the use of software (such as apps or websites), hardware, and patient typology. These pilots were carried out in a total of 3 different countries: the United Kingdom (UK), Spain, and the Czech Republic. All of them have been designed for a 3 month follow-up of patients.

Pilot 1: UK. The purpose of this pilot is to assist older patients with multiple health conditions. The focus of this particular scenario was on individuals aged 60 and above, who resided at home and did not have any cognitive impairments when enrolled in the study. These patients had multiple comorbidities such as heart failure, diabetes, and hypertension. Additionally, they were users of Android smartphones and had internet access.

Northern Health and Social Care Trust (NHSCT) conducted this pilot in the UK. Four patients took part in the study for a duration of 12 weeks.

In this pilot, we have utilized all baseline data and daily physiological monitoring data, no use was made of the questionnaires related to heart failure and the personalized thresholds. Therefore, risks are estimated without performing the daily well-being questionnaire and with the default variable's thresholds.

Pilot 2: Spain. This pilot focuses on predicting decompensation in heart failure patients who receive care at home. Specifically, the target individuals for this study were aged 60 and above, residing in their own homes, and experiencing stage 2 or 3 heart failure. The intended patients of this prediction tool were either the older adults themselves or any caregiver who either lived with them or visited them at least five times a week.

Clínica Humana clinic conducted this pilot study in Mallorca, Spain. From November 2022 to January 2023 (inclusive) with a group of 9 patients during the 12-week intervention period.

In this pilot study, we have utilized all baseline data, daily physiological monitoring data, and daily questionnaires. However, the personalized thresholds for individual patients have not been implemented.

Pilot 3: Czech Republic. The purpose of this pilot was to perform advanced telemonitoring of heart failure patients in their own homes. The specific target group consisted of 25 patients over the age of 60, who had been diagnosed with chronic heart failure, are in an advanced stage and may have had other medical conditions. This user group had limited knowledge and skills in using technology, so the digital solution aimed to offer a user-friendly experience that made it easy to use the provided system, including the application and the accompanying medical devices for monitoring various biomedical signals and parameters. The monitoring process took place in the patients' home environment.

The pilot site was conducted from 2023-02-14 to 2023-04-30 (both inclusive) with 24 patients.

In this pilot study, we have utilized all baseline data, daily physiological monitoring data, and daily questionnaires. However, the personalized thresholds for individual patients have not been implemented.

3   Results

Out of the three pilots, two instances of cardiac decompensation have occurred (one of them resulted in a fatality). These occurrences were both accurately identified and happened to the same individual. Conversely, we observed multiple false alarms, varying in frequency depending on the pilot.

3.1   Pilot 1: UK

None of the four patients in the cohort experienced a decompensation event, so it has not yet being possible to evaluate the model's ability to accurately predict decompensation in this specific group. Similarly, the model has not identified any false alarms as the maximum risk observed was only 0.49. Thus, the model in this pilot did not predict any cardiac decompensations while no cardiac decompensations were experienced by the participants.

Besides achieving low-risk outcomes, there was also a significant level of involvement in data monitoring and measurement, which is typically desirable in this monitoring process. All participants consistently reported their data on over 50% of the days, and two of them diligently reported their data every single day throughout the intervention period.

3.2 Pilot 2: Spain

The HFPred model correctly triggered a high risk alert for the patient who experienced two instances of cardiac decompensation. However, despite achieving a 100% accuracy, it has become evident that the number of false alerts has exceeded our initial expectations. The patient follow-up data can be found in Table 2.

Table 2. Summary of the 7 patients reports in pilot 2

Patients	Pilot duration	Reported days	Zero risk %	Low risk %	Middle risk %	High risk %	Mean risk %
1	91	76	77.63	80.26	9.21	10.53	0.15
2	91	77	37.66	75.32	11.69	12.99	0.22
3	63	54	24.07	25.93	46.3	27.78	0.45
4	62	32	50	78.12	12.5	9.38	0.18
5	77	35	34.29	62.86	28.57	8.57	0.27
6	92	80	58.75	67.5	26.25	6.25	0.18
7	90	72	6.94	6.94	4.17	88.89	0.83

We have excluded data from two out of the original nine participants due to poor pilot adherence (less than 7 days out of the 3 month monitored). The summary of aggregate risk data for the remaining seven patients is displayed in Table 2. Among these patients, it was observed that patient number 7 was estimated as high-risk for 88.9% of the pilot duration when monitored by the model. This is because his blood oxygen saturation is significantly lower than normal despite him being in good health. On the other hand, patient 1 was almost always (77.63%) assigned a risk score of 0.

In general, it is remarkable that the model successfully identifies the two instances of cardiac decompensation. Nevertheless, it exhibited more false alerts in this subsequent assessment compared to the original training cohort. There are various reasons for this, one being the inability to consistently reproduce results with all potential factors (personalized thresholds). Furthermore, anomalies have been discovered in the data, such as instances where a patient's weight suddenly increased by 10 kilos in a day and then decreased the next day (likely due exchanging measurement with another person being weighed with the same measuring device). In such cases, the model falsely indicated a risk when there was actually none.

It can be concluded that the HFPred accurately predicted the medical decompensations when they were true positive but it gave many false positives due to the fact that external factors were not controlled in the pilot. These factors may trigger some of the vital signs and cause a false high risk prediction (high blood pressure due to nervousness, low oxygen saturation due to incorrect lecture by the oximeter or some participants may have basal vital signs which are "out of range"). Therefore, these potential factors should be controlled and medical supervision should always be required to double check the prediction.

3.3   Pilot 3: Czech Republic

There were no cardiac decompensations during the pilot in these patients, so it is not possible to demonstrate that the model was able to predict decompensations in this cohort. However, there have been false positives as can be seen in Table 3.

Of the 24 patients monitored, there was one patient (15 in Table 3) who only reported data on two days. Among the rest, we have had a follow-up of at least 3 weeks, and nine have had a follow-up of nine months.

In this pilot we also see that the model provided more false alerts than desired. The patients that suffered the most false alerts were number 4 (28.12%) and number 12 (20.73%), the latter being one of the most frequently monitored. On the other hand, we have examples such as patients 18, 20 and 22, who, being patients who have reported the most days, do not have any high risk.

Patient number 7, has not had any reported day with 0 risk, as low oxygen saturation was a normal occurrence for this patient (similar to the case of patient number 7 in the Spain pilot). Furthermore, this patient frequently exceeded the normal thresholds for systolic blood pressure, indicating the need of threshold adjustment.

Table 3. Summary of the 24 patients reports

Patients	Pilot duration	Reported days	Zero risk (%)	Low risk (%)	Middle risk (%)	High risk (%)	Mean risk (%)
1	36	15	80	86.67	6.66	6.67	0.12
2	23	23	95.65	100	0	0	0.01
3	37	37	27.03	67.57	29.73	2.7	0.22
4	37	32	18.75	18.75	53.13	28.12	0.49
5	50	49	51.02	81.63	10.21	8.16	0.13
6	37	35	22.86	57.14	40	2.86	0.29
7	37	34	0	64.71	26.47	8.82	0.3
8	37	37	48.65	75.68	8.1	16.22	0.23
9	36	35	22.86	71.43	20	8.57	0.22
10	37	37	35.14	83.78	13.52	2.7	0.13
11	37	30	56.67	93.33	3.34	3.33	0.09
12	91	82	36.59	50	29.27	20.73	0.33
13	51	51	60.78	100	0	0	0.07
14	66	64	43.75	81.25	17.19	1.56	0.17
15	40	2	100	100	0	0	0
16	91	42	50	97.62	2.38	0	0.04
17	74	74	4.05	79.73	14.86	5.41	0.21
18	92	86	32.56	91.86	8.14	0	0.11
19	85	81	28.4	85.19	11.11	3.7	0.17
20	97	93	66.67	96.77	3.23	0	0.05
21	92	88	22.73	88.64	7.95	3.41	0.19
22	82	73	89.04	100	0	0	0.02
23	78	73	30.14	76.71	10.96	12.33	0.22
24	77	47	51.06	80.85	14.89	4.26	0.15

4 Discussion

The diverse pilot sites in UK, Spain, and the Czech Republic allowed us to assess the model's generalized validity in the context of different healthcare systems and patient demographics. Each pilot had distinct objectives, patient characteristics, and monitoring durations, providing a comprehensive evaluation of the model's applicability.

In the UK pilot, the absence of decompensation events among the monitored patients limited our ability to conclusively evaluate the model's predictive accuracy. Nevertheless, since there have been no false alerts, we could consider this aspect as satisfactory.

Conversely, the Spanish pilot showed the model's ability to accurately identify instances of cardiac decompensation. Despite achieving 100% accuracy in detecting decompensation events, the presence of false alarms raised concerns.

The variability in risk estimates among patients, as evidenced by Table 2, underscores the need for further refinement and individualization of the model.

The occurrence of these false alarms prompted a closer examination of the factors contributing to these alerts. It is important to note that many of these cases were caused by measurement errors, such as when someone else's data was recorded mistakenly or when impossible medical values were recorded. In a real-world clinical setting, healthcare professionals would likely identify these anomalies and ask the patient to remeasure their vital parameters after reviewing the alerts. However, due to the blinded nature of this follow-up, the clinicians have not been able to correct the measurement errors, and we only discovered them during the analysis. The same issue occurred with a patient who consistently had low blood oxygen saturation, highlighting the challenges of setting personalized thresholds for each parameter in this predictive model. Although the model could handle this situation, we had two problems here: firstly, that personalized modification was not implemented for the pilot, and secondly, that the clinicians would not be able to modify these personalized thresholds due to the blinded pilot.

Another patient in the Spanish pilot site, exhibited elevated risks when experiencing high blood pressures. This occurred as a result of the patient's anxiety while using the devices or encountering any issues. In such instances, the clinicians called him (due to the out-of-range variable), and once the patient calmed down, the readings were normal. Nonetheless, the risk had already been assessed.

Hence, we expect a significant decrease in these erroneous alerts during real follow-up. Nevertheless, it is important to acknowledge that the diverse backgrounds of the individuals tested might contribute to this outcome.

During the pilot conducted in the Czech Republic, the model has demonstrated a tendency to generate high alerts more frequently than desired. It is important to consider that the patients involved in this pilot are in the advanced stage of chronic heart failure, which naturally results in a deteriorated overall health condition. Furthermore, we have observed the necessity to modify the thresholds of the variables in this pilot due to the presence of patients with advanced disease who exhibit lower than normal oxygen saturation levels, even when they are in good health. If the pilot had not been conducted in a blinded manner, it would have been beneficial to identify unusual parameters for the purpose of contacting the patient or adjusting the thresholds, if it was implemented. Moreover, the program has seen strong adherence, leading to the belief that the model has reaped significant benefits.

5   Conclusions

Overall, we can conclude that the application of the HFPred prediction model has yielded satisfactory results in the three external pilot studies. Furthermore, besides its ability to forecast patient deterioration, we have observed commendable patient compliance, which invariably enhances patient well-being.

As future work, there are several aspects that require attention. Firstly, it is imperative to incorporate personalized alert thresholds into the system. Secondly, conducting a non-blind pilot study would be beneficial. Lastly, we should consider implementing newly developed models to further enhance the prediction capabilities.

Ethics Committees

Pilot 1: UK. Ethical approval was granted by Health and Social Care Research Ethics Committee (REC) B (REC reference: 21-NI-0169) and the Health Research Authority (IRAS ID: 284743). All participants provided written informed consent prior to participation in this study.

Pilot 2: Spain. The Research Ethics Committee of the Balearic Islands ensures as of 23/02/2022 that this pilot (CEI code IB 4770/22 PI and protocol code UC-PT3-001-CH) complies with the standards of Good Clinical Practice (CPMP/ICH/E6 R2) and with the legislation in force that regulates its operation.

Pilot 3: Czech Republic. The pilot study carried out by the Czech National eHealth Center was approved by the Ethics committee of the University Hospital and the Faculty of Medicine and Dentistry under Ref. No.: 51/21 (date of approval 08/03/2021).

References

1. Gorriz, J.M., et al.: Computational approaches to explainable artificial intelligence: advances in theory, applications and trends. Inf. Fusion **100**, 101945 (2023)
2. Hamdi, O., Chalouf, M.A., Ouattara, D., Krief, F.: eHealth: survey on research projects, comparative study of telemonitoring architectures and main issues. J. Netw. Comput. Appl. **46**, 100–112 (2014)
3. Chaudhry, S.I., et al.: Telemonitoring in patients with heart failure. N. Engl. J. Med. **363**(24), 2301–2309 (2010)
4. Larburu, N., Artetxe, A., Escolar, V., Lozano, A., Kerexeta, J.: Artificial intelligence to prevent mobile heart failure patients decompensation in real time: monitoring-based predictive model. Mob. Inf. Syst. **2018**, 1–11 (2018)
5. Hyndman, R. J.: Moving Averages (2011)
6. Bayes, T.: Naive bayes classifier. Article Sources Contributors, 1–9 (1968)
7. Handelman, G.S., et al.: Peering into the black box of artificial intelligence: evaluation metrics of machine learning methods. Am. J. Roentgenol. **212**(1), 38–43 (2019)
8. Kerexeta, J.: Prediction and analysis of heart failure decompensation events based on telemonitored data and artificial intelligence methods. J. Cardiovasc. Dev. Dis. **10**(2), 48 (2023)
9. Spargo, M., et al.: Shaping the future of digitally enabled health and care. Pharmacy **9**(1), 17 (2021)
10. Salinas-Perez, J.A., et al.: Patterns of mental healthcare provision in rural areas: a demonstration study in Australia and Europe. Front. Psych. **14**, 993197 (2023)

Fidex: An Algorithm for the Explainability of Ensembles and SVMs

Guido Bologna$^{(\boxtimes)}$ ⓘ, Jean-Marc Boutay, Quentin Leblanc, and Damian Boquete

University of Applied Sciences and Arts of Western Switzerland, Rue de la Prairie 4, 1202 Geneva, Switzerland
Guido.Bologna@hesge.ch

Abstract. A natural way to explain neural network responses is by propositional rules. Currently, the state of the art on XAI methods presents local and global algorithms, with local techniques aiming to explain single samples in their neighbourhood. We present here Fidex, a new local algorithm, which we apply to ensembles of neural networks, ensembles of decision trees and support vector machines. The key idea behind Fidex is the precise identification of discriminating hyperplanes. Its computational complexity for a neural network is linear with respect to the product of: the dimensionality of the classification problem; the number of training samples; the maximal number of antecedents per rule; and a constant related to a particular activation function approximating a sigmoid function. Based on Fidex, we formulated a global algorithm named FidexGlo. Essentially, FidexGlo uses Fidex to generate a number of rules equal to the number of samples. Then, a heuristic is deployed to remove as many rules as possible. FidexGlo was applied to four benchmark classification problems, providing competitive results with our previous global rule extraction technique. Fidex and FidexGlo are available at https://github.com/HES-XPLAIN/dimlpfidex.

Keywords: Model Explainability · Ensembles · Rule Extraction

1 Introduction

Before the advent of deep learning, the explainability of black-box models such as neural networks (NNs) or support vector machines (SVMs), was most of the time tackled by the extraction of propositional rules. A taxonomy characterizing rule extraction techniques into three main categories has long been valid [2]. Rule extraction strategies for SVMs that are functionally identical to multi-layer perceptrons (MLPs) were proposed in [7]. More recently, Guidotti et al. presented a review of black-box models with its "explanators", which encompasses deep models [9]. In addition, Adadi and Berrada proposed a description of explainable artificial intelligence (XAI), including neural networks [1].

Because deep models are more complicated than MLPs and SVMs, a key element of explainability approaches concentrates on the immediate region surrounding a sample [11]. This approach is defined as local. A global technique, on

J. M. Ferrández Vicente et al. (Eds.): IWINAC 2024, LNCS 14675, pp. 378–388, 2024.
https://doi.org/10.1007/978-3-031-61137-7_35

the other hand, takes into account all the data that define a problem. Furthermore, many other techniques used in image classification visualize areas that are mainly relevant for the outcome [14].

Decision trees (DTs) are widely used in Machine Learning. They represent transparent models because symbolic rules are easily extracted. However, when they are combined in an ensemble, rule extraction becomes harder [12]. We introduce Fidex, a new local approach to rule extraction that can be applied to NN ensembles, DT ensembles, and SVMs. The key idea behind Fidex is the precise characterisation of discriminating hyperplanes. Its computational complexity for a single neural network is linear with respect to the product of: the dimensionality of the classification problem; the number of training samples; the maximal number of rule antecedents per rule; and a constant related to a particular activation function approximating a sigmoid function.

Based on Fidex, we have formulated a global algorithm called FidexGlo. Essentially, FidexGlo depends on Fidex to generate a number of rules equal to the number of samples. Then, a heuristic is deployed to remove as many rules as possible. We applied FidexGlo to four benchmark classification problems. The results show that FidexGlo is competitive with our previous global rule extraction algorithm [3], and that its computational complexity is more advantageous. The various models employed in this study, the Fidex and FidexGlo algorithms, the experiments, and the conclusion are presented in the following parts.

2   Models and Algorithms

In this section we present the models used in this work, which are DIMLP ensembles, Quantized Support Vector Machines, and ensembles of DTs. Subsequently we describe our local/global rule extraction algorithms.

2.1   DIMLPs

The Discretized Interpretable Multi Layer Perceptron is a particular feed-forward neural network architecture from which propositional rules are extracted by determining discriminatory hyperplanes. For a general MLP model, let us denote $x^{(0)}$ as a vector for the input layer. For layer $l + 1$ ($l \geq 0$), the activation values $x^{(l+1)}$ of the neurons are

$$x^{(l+1)} = F(W^{(l)}x^{(l)} + b^{(l)}). \tag{1}$$

$W^{(l)}$ is a matrix of weight parameters between two successive layers l and $l + 1$; $b^{(l)}$ is a vector also called the bias and F is an activation function. Usually, F is a sigmoid $\sigma(x)$:

$$\sigma(x) = \frac{1}{1 + \exp(-x)}. \tag{2}$$

In a DIMLP, $W^{(0)}$ is a diagonal matrix. Moreover, the activation function applied to $x^{(1)}$ is a staircase function $S(x)$. Here, $S(x)$ approximates with Θ stairs a sigmoid function:

$$S(x) = \sigma(\alpha_{min}), \text{ if } x \leq \alpha_{min}; \tag{3}$$

α_{min} represents the abscissa of the first stair. By default $\alpha_{min} = -5$.

$$S(x) = \sigma(\alpha_{max}), \text{ if } x \geq \alpha_{max}; \tag{4}$$

α_{max} represents the abscissa of the last stair. By default $\alpha_{max} = 5$. Between α_{min} and α_{max}, $S(x)$ is:

$$S(x) = \sigma(\alpha_{min} + \left[\Theta \cdot \frac{x - \alpha_{min}}{\alpha_{max} - \alpha_{min}}\right] (\frac{\alpha_{max} - \alpha_{min}}{\Theta})); \tag{5}$$

with [ ] designating the integer-part function. For $l \geq 2$, DIMLP and MLP are the same model.

The discriminating axis-parallel hyperplanes are precisely identified thanks to the staircase activation function and to the $W^{(0)}$ diagonal matrix. Let us take an example with a step activation function, which is a simple special case. The step function is

$$t(x) = \begin{cases} 1 \text{ if } x > 0; \\ 0 \text{ otherwise.} \end{cases} \tag{6}$$

Figure 1 represents a DIMLP with an input neuron a hidden neuron and an output neuron. Below the network are samples belonging to two classes: circles and squares. Due to the step activation function of the hidden neuron we have a potential discriminant hyperplane in $-b/w$, which is equal to two. If the value of w' is zero, circles and the triangles cannot be distinguished, as the signal entering y will always be negative. With w' equal to 10 and b' equal to -5, if h is 0, the signal entering y is negative; else if h is equal to one the signal entering y is positive. We therefore have a hyperplane that allows us to define two propositional rules:

- if $x > 2$ then class is triangle;
- if $x \leq 2$ then class is circle.

With the staircase activation function, the maximum number of discriminating hyperplanes per input variable corresponds to the number of stairs Θ in Eq. 5. Our previous rule extraction algorithm (ORE) [3] was based on the construction of a DT with a hyperplane at each node. Each path from the root to a leaf represented a propositional rule. Finally, a greedy algorithm progressively removed rule antecedents and rules [3]. Its computational complexity is $O(d^4 \cdot \Theta^4 \cdot s^2)$ [3].

The position of the hyperplanes hp_i for each input variable x_i is

$$hp_i = \frac{1}{w_i} \cdot (\ (\alpha_{min} - b_i) + \frac{k}{\Theta} \cdot (\alpha_{max} - \alpha_{min}) \ ); \tag{7}$$

with $k = 0, \ldots, \Theta$.

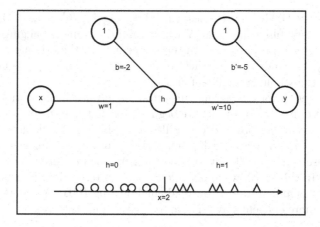

Fig. 1. Example of a DIMLP network which discriminates between two classes of data: circles and triangles at the bottom. Since the activation function of h is a step function, a hyperplane is found at $x = 2$, which corresponds to the ratio $-b/w$. The presence or absence of this hyperplane depends on the values of w' and b'.

2.2 QSVM

A Quantified Support Vector Machine (QSVM) is a DIMLP network with two hidden layers [5]. Neurons in the first hidden layer carry out a normalization of the input variables. The activation function of the neurons in the second hidden layer is related to the SVM kernel. For instance, with a dot kernel the corresponding activation function is the identity, while with a Gaussian kernel the activation function is Gaussian. The number of neurons in this layer is equal to the number of support vectors, with the incoming weight connections corresponding to the components of the support vectors.

Weights between the input layer and the first hidden are frozen during training. Specifically these weights are:

– weights: $w_i = K/\gamma_i$, with γ_i as the standard deviation of input variable x_i on the training set and K a constant equal to one;
– bias: $b_i = -K \cdot \mu_i/\gamma_i$, with μ_i as the average of input variable x_i on the training set.

After the normalization, the staircase activation function (Eq. 5) is applied. During training, weights above the first hidden layer are modified according to the SVM training algorithm [13].

2.3 Ensembles

The accuracy of multiple integrated models is frequently greater than that of a single model. Two important representative learning algorithms for ensembles are bagging [6] and boosting [8]. They have been applied to both DTs and NNs. In this work, we use DIMLP ensembles trained by bagging [6]. Specifically, bagging is rooted on resampling methods. With s training samples, bagging selects for each classifier s samples drawn with replacement from the original training set. Consequently, the individual models differ slightly, which is advantageous as compared to the whole ensemble of classifiers.

Many strategies for extracting rules from single neural networks have been proposed, but only a few authors have begun to extract rules from neural network ensembles. To generate propositional rules from single networks and ensembles, we introduced DIMLP networks [3]. In previous work, we performed rule extraction from ensembles of DTs by transforming them into ensembles of DIMLP networks [4]. In this work, we apply rule extraction to random forests (RFs) and shallow tree ensembles trained by gradient boosting (GB). We perform it in a different and more efficient way relative to our previous rule extraction technique (see Sect. 2.4).

2.4   The Fidex Algorithm

Fidelity refers to how well the extracted rules mimic the behaviour of a model. This is a measure of the accuracy with which the rules represent the decision-making process of a neural network, for example. Specifically, with s samples in a training set and s' samples for which the classifications of the rules match the classifications of the model, the fidelity is s'/s.

The Fidex local rule extraction algorithm strongly uses fidelity. We assume that we have d input variables $x_1 \ldots x_d$. Furthermore, let us denote L_{xi} the list of hyperplanes for input variable x_i; L_{xi} is calculated according to Eq. (7). The purpose of Fidex is to determine a propositional rule R with respect to sample S. The fidelity of R to be reached in ρ steps is ϕ, and is calculated with all the samples of the training set. The Fidex algorithm is the following:

1. Given sample S and rule $R = \emptyset$;
2. for $n = 1 \ldots \rho$ do
3.   for all input variables x_i randomly selected and for all L_{xi} do
4.   find the hyperplane h^* allowing the highest increase of fidelity;
5.   end for
6.   if the increment of fidelity is strictly positive then $R = R \cup h^*$;
7.   if fidelity reaches value ϕ then exit;
8. end for

Fidex computational complexity depends mainly on its loops and corresponds to $O(\rho \cdot d \cdot \Theta \cdot s)$; with s the number of training samples. Note that the s factor appears as for each new rule antecedent Fidex has to determine whether a sample is covered by R or not. Finally, Θ is due to the number of hyperplanes in each list of possible hperplanes L_{xi}.

The execution of Fidex is managed by four parameters:

- ρ: maximal number of Fidex steps (which is strongly related to the number of rule antecedents);

- ϕ: fidelity of the rule;
- p: dropout of input variables;
- q: dropout of hyperplanes.

Parameter ρ is the maximum number of iterations and is related to the maximum number of rule antecedents; its default value is equal to 10. The default value of ϕ, which corresponds to the fidelity that has to be reached is 100%. Note that Fidex could end before attaining ϕ. In that case, Fidex can simply be executed again with the same values of the parameters since it is non-deterministic, or with different values.

The execution time of Fidex can be accelerated by considering two dropout parameters: p and q. Essentially, p determines at each step the proportion of input variables that will not be taken into account. The excluded variables are selected randomly. Parameter q is similar, but with respect to excluded hyperplanes in L_{xi}. Default values for p and q are equal to 0. If variables x_i are selected with always the same order, for instance from 1 to d (see step 3) and without dropout, Fidex is deterministic.

2.5 The FidexGlo Algorithm

FidexGlo is a global rule extraction algorithm[1] that generates a ruleset for a training set of size s. It corresponds to a covering technique that calls Fidex s times. It therefore first generates s rules and then uses a heuristic to select a subset of the rule base that covers all s samples. A simple heuristic would be to select the rules randomly and stop when all the training samples are covered. Another heuristic consists of ranking the rules in descending order according to the number of samples covered, then selecting the rules in descending order until all the samples are covered. As we are using the latter heuristic, the computational complexity is $O(\rho \cdot d \cdot \Theta \cdot s^2)$. The essential reason is that Fidex is called s times.

Rule extraction can be performed with an ensemble of DIMLPs, since it can be viewed as a unique DIMLP with an additional hidden layer (the one that averages all single network responses). Hence, the list of the hyperplanes for a DIMLP ensemble is the union of all the lists related to each single network (cf. Eq. 7). Hence, with ν networks in an ensemble, the computational complexity is $O(\nu \cdot \rho \cdot d \cdot \Theta \cdot s^2)$. Finally, with DT ensembles, the list of hyperplanes is compiled from the rules extracted from all the trees.

3 Experiments

3.1 Preliminaries

We applied several models to four classification problems retrieved from the Machine Learning Repository at the University of California, Irvine[2] [10]. We performed cross-validation experiments; Table 1 describes the datasets.

---

[1] Available at https://github.com/HES-XPLAIN/dimlpfidex.
[2] https://archive.ics.uci.edu/ml/index.php.

Table 1. Datasets used in the experiments. From left to right, columns designate: dataset name; number of samples; number of input features; and number of classes.

Dataset	Samples	Inputs	Classes
Breast Cancer	683	9	2
Heart Disease	270	13	2
Ionosphere	351	34	2
Spam	4601	57	2

Training datasets were normalized by Gaussian normalization. The following models were used with the four classification problems:

- RF: Random forests with FidexGlo;
- RF-ORE: Random forests with our old rule extraction algorithm [4];
- GB: Gradient boosting with FidexGlo;
- GB-ORE: Gradient boosting with our old rule extraction algorithm [4];
- QSVM-L: QSVM with linear kernel and with FidexGlo;
- QSVM-G: QSVM with Gaussian kernel and with FidexGlo;
- DIMLP-BT: DIMLP ensembles trained by bagging with FidexGlo;
- DIMLP-BT-ORE: DIMLP ensembles trained by bagging with our old rule extraction algorithm.

For RFs, GBs and SVMs we used default parameters defined in the Scikit Python Library. Specifically, for GBs the maximal depth of the trees is equal to three, while for RFs depth is not limited. All DIMLP ensembles were trained by back-propagation with default learning parameters [4] and only a hidden layer with the number of neurons equal to number of inputs. By default, a DIMLP ensemble includes 25 networks, whereas for RFs and GBs the number of trees is 100.

The Tables of the results include in the columns:

- Average predictive accuracy of the model (ratio of the number of correctly classified testing samples to the total number of testing samples);
- Average fidelity on the testing samples;
- Average predictive accuracy of the rules;
- Average predictive accuracy of the rules when rules and model agree;
- Average number of extracted rules;
- Average number of rule antecedents.

3.2   Results

Table 2 depicts the results obtained by the different models. On average, Fidex-Glo generated more rules than our old rule extraction algorithm, but with fewer rule antecedents. This trend is also observed in the other classification problems. Moreover, the average fidelity obtained with FidexGlo is always higher than that provided by our former rule extraction algorithm. For the "Breast Cancer" dataset, the highest predictive accuracy of the rules was obtained by QSVM-L (97.2%), which is equal to the predictive accuracy of RFs. DIMLP-BT with FidexGlo and QSVM-G provided the highest fidelity with 99.6%.

Table 2. Average results obtained on the "Breast Cancer" dataset by ten repetitions of 10-fold cross validation trials. Standard deviations are given between brackets.

Model	Tst. Acc	Fid	Rul. Acc. (1)	Rul. Acc. (2)	#Rul	Avg. #Ant
RF	97.1 (0.2)	99.1 (0.3)	96.9 (0.3)	97.4 (0.2)	30.0 (0.8)	2.6 (0.0)
RF-ORE [4]	**97.2** (0.2)	98.4 (0.5)	96.6 (0.5)	**97.7** (0.2)	24.2 (0.5)	3.4 (0.0)
GB	97.0 (0.3)	99.2 (0.4)	97.0 (0.3)	97.4 (0.4)	29.5 (0.6)	2.6 (0.0)
GB-ORE [4]	96.9 (0.4)	98.8 (0.3)	96.2 (0.5)	97.1 (0.5)	22.6 (0.6)	3.3 (0.0)
QSVM-L	97.1 (0.1)	99.5 (0.2)	**97.2** (0.2)	97.4 (0.1)	15.2 (0.4)	**2.2** (0.0)
QSVM-G	97.1 (0.2)	**99.6** (0.2)	97.0 (0.2)	97.4 (0.4)	15.0 (0.5)	2.3 (0.0)
DIMLP-BT	97.1 (0.1)	**99.6** (0.2)	97.0 (0.3)	97.2 (0.2)	15.5 (0.5)	**2.2** (0.0)
DIMLP-BT-ORE	97.1 (0.1)	98.7 (0.3)	96.4 (0.4)	97.3 (0.2)	**12.3** (0.5)	2.7 (0.1)

As shown in Table 3, on the classification problem "Heart Disease", the highest average predictive accuracy of the rules was again obtained by QSVM-L (83.9%). DIMLP-BT ensembles reached the highest average predictive accuracy (86.1%), and the highest average predictive accuracy of the rules when ensembles and rules agree (86.4%). Finally, the highest average fidelity was provided by GB, at 96.4%.

Table 3. Average results obtained on the "Heart Disease" dataset.

Model	Tst. Acc	Fid	Rul. Acc. (1)	Rul. Acc. (2)	#Rul	Avg. #Ant
RF	82.3 (0.8)	95.5 (0.8)	80.8 (1.3)	83.1 (0.8)	52.9 (0.9)	2.9 (0.0)
RF-ORE [4]	82.7 (1.6)	93.2 (1.7)	81.4 (1.6)	84.4 (1.1)	39.7 (1.1)	4.1 (0.0)
GB	81.3 (0.8)	**96.4** (1.0)	80.6 (1.4)	82.1 (1.1)	46.7 (1.1)	2.9 (0.0)
GB-ORE [4]	79.9 (1.9)	94.1 (1.5)	79.7 (1.9)	81.7 (2.1)	34.8 (0.7)	3.8 (0.0)
QSVM-L	83.9 (0.7)	96.3 (1.0)	**83.9** (0.7)	84.7 (0.8)	27.5 (0.8)	**2.6** (0.0)
QSVM-G	82.3 (0.7)	96.0 (1.1)	81.3 (1.0)	83.1 (1.0)	32.3 (0.8)	2.7 (0.0)
DIMLP-BT	**86.1** (1.0)	95.3 (1.2)	83.3 (1.5)	**86.4** (0.9)	28.7 (0.7)	**2.6** (0.0)
DIMLP-BT-ORE	**86.1** (1.0)	94.6 (0.7)	82.3 (1.1)	86.2 (0.9)	**20.9** (0.8)	3.3 (0.0)

With the "Ionosphere" dataset the results presented in Table 4 highlight that the highest average predictive accuracy was obtained by QSVM-G (94.5%). Once again, GB provided the highest average predictive accuracy of the rules (94.2%), as well as the highest average fidelity (98.9%).

Table 4. Average results obtained on the "Ionosphere" dataset.

Model	Tst. Acc	Fid	Rul. Acc. (1)	Rul. Acc. (2)	#Rul	Avg. #Ant
RF	93.3 (0.3)	98.4 (0.6)	93.8 (0.7)	94.2 (0.5)	31.3 (0.9)	2.5 (0.0)
RF-ORE [4]	93.2 (0.4)	95.3 (1.0)	91.5 (1.3)	94.4 (0.6)	33.2 (1.2)	4.0 (0.1)
GB	93.9 (0.4)	**98.9** (0.5)	**94.2** (0.5)	94.6 (0.4)	29.3 (0.8)	2.5 (0.0)
GB-ORE [4]	92.8 (1.0)	96.5 (1.0)	91.0 (1.1)	93.4 (0.9)	29.5 (1.2)	3.5 (0.2)
QSVM-L	86.5 (0.7)	95.5 (1.0)	88.3 (0.7)	89.2 (0.9)	27.6 (1.0)	2.5 (0.0)
QSVM-G	**94.5** (0.6)	97.6 (0.6)	93.5 (0.4)	**95.1** (0.4)	26.2 (0.6)	2.5 (0.0)
DIMLP-BT	93.1 (0.4)	98.0 (0.6)	94.1 (0.4)	94.5 (0.4)	23.0 (1.1)	**2.3** (0.0)
DIMLP-BT-ORE	93.1 (0.4)	96.2 (0.9)	92.5 (0.7)	94.5 (0.4)	**19.3** (0.5)	2.9 (0.1)

Table 5 depicts the results for the "Spam" classification problem. Random forests and the rulesets they generated provided the highest average predictive accuracies (95.4% and 95.2%, respectively). Again, GB reached the highest average fidelity (98.9%). With RF, FidexGlo generated the highest average number of rules. This trend is also observed in the previous classification problems. This could be explained by the fact that with an unlimited tree depth, the number of rules tends to be very high.

Table 5. Average results obtained on the "Spam" dataset.

Model	Tst. Acc	Fid	Rul. Acc. (1)	Rul. Acc. (2)	#Rul	Avg. #Ant
RF	**95.4** (0.1)	98.7 (0.1)	**95.2** (0.2)	**95.9** (0.1)	410.9 (3.9)	2.7 (0.0)
GB	94.6 (0.1)	**99.3** (0.1)	94.5 (0.1)	94.9 (0.1)	230.2 (4.1)	2.9 (0.0)
QSVM-L	93.6 (0.1)	99.2 (0.1)	93.5 (0.1)	93.9 (0.1)	227.5 (2.5)	2.9 (0.0)
QSVM-G	94.4 (0.1)	99.1 (0.1)	94.3 (0.1)	94.8 (0.1)	247.7 (3.5)	3.0 (0.0)
DIMLP-BT	94.7 (0.1)	99.0 (0.1)	94.6 (0.1)	95.1 (0.1)	288.7 (2.1)	**2.5** (0.0)
DIMLP-BT-ORE	94.7 (0.1)	98.8 (0.2)	94.6 (0.2)	95.2 (0.2)	**90.3** (1.3)	5.5 (0.1)

4   Conclusion

To explain the classifications of the black box-models, we have introduced a new local algorithm and a new global algorithm named Fidex and FidexGlo, respectively. The key idea behind them is to determine the discriminant hyperplanes while maximising the fidelity of the underlying model. We applied them to SVMs, ensembles of DTs, and ensembles of NNs. On four classification problems, FidexGlo performed very well compared to our former global rule extraction technique, which has been compared to many other rule extraction techniques (in previous research). Our next step will be to apply Fidex to deep models such as convolutional NNs.

Acknowledgments. This work was in part conducted in the context of the Horizon Europe project PRE-ACT (Prediction of Radiotherapy side effects using explainable AI for patient communication and treatment modification), and it has received funding through the European Commission Horizon Europe Program (Grant Agreement number: 101057746). In addition, this work was supported by the Swiss State Secretariat for Education, Research and Innovation (SERI) under contract number 2200058. Finally, this work was in part carried out with funding from the University of Applied Sciences and Arts of Western Switzerland (HES-SO) and the Engineering and Architecture domain.

Disclosure of Interests. The authors have no competing interests to declare that are relevant to the content of this article.

References

1. Adadi, A., Berrada, M.: Peeking inside the black-box: a survey on explainable artificial intelligence (xai). IEEE Access **6**, 52138–52160 (2018). https://doi.org/10.1109/ACCESS.2018.2870052
2. Andrews, R., Diederich, J., Tickle, A.B.: Survey and critique of techniques for extracting rules from trained artificial neural networks. Knowl.-Based Syst. **8**(6), 373–389 (1995). https://doi.org/10.1016/0950-7051(96)81920-4
3. Bologna, G.: Is it worth generating rules from neural network ensembles? J. Appl. Log. **2**(3), 325–348 (2004). https://doi.org/10.1016/j.jal.2004.03.004
4. Bologna, G.: A rule extraction technique applied to ensembles of neural networks, random forests, and gradient-boosted trees. Algorithms **14**(12), 339 (2021). https://doi.org/10.3390/a14120339
5. Bologna, G., Hayashi, Y.: QSVM: a support vector machine for rule extraction. In: Rojas, I., Joya, G., Catala, A. (eds.) Advances in Computational Intelligence: 13th International Work-Conference on Artificial Neural Networks, IWANN 2015, Palma de Mallorca, Spain, June 10-12, 2015. Proceedings, Part II, pp. 276–289. Springer International Publishing, Cham (2015). https://doi.org/10.1007/978-3-319-19222-2_23
6. Breiman, L.: Bagging predictors. Machine Learn. **24**(2), 123–140 (1996)
7. Diederich, J.: Rule extraction from support vector machines, vol. 80. Springer Science & Business Media (2008). https://doi.org/10.1007/978-3-540-75390-2_1
8. Freund, Y., Schapire, R.E.: A decision-theoretic generalization of on-line learning and an application to boosting. J. Comput. Syst. Sci. **55**(1), 119–139 (1997). https://doi.org/10.1006/jcss.1997.1504
9. Guidotti, R., Monreale, A., Ruggieri, S., Turini, F., Giannotti, F., Pedreschi, D.: A survey of methods for explaining black box models. ACM Comput. Surv. (CSUR) **51**(5), 1–42 (2018). https://doi.org/10.1145/3236009
10. Lichman, M.: UCI machine learning repository, university of California, Irvine, school of information and computer sciences (2013). http://archive.ics.uci.edu/ml
11. Ribeiro, M.T., Singh, S., Guestrin, C.: Why should i trust you?: explaining the predictions of any classifier. In: Proceedings of the 22nd ACM SIGKDD International Conference on Knowledge Discovery and Data Mining, pp. 1135–1144. ACM (2016)

12. Van Assche, A., Blockeel, H.: Seeing the forest through the trees: learning a comprehensible model from an ensemble. In: Kok, J.N., Koronacki, J., Mantaras, R.L., Matwin, S., Mladenič, D., Skowron, A. (eds.) ECML 2007. LNCS (LNAI), vol. 4701, pp. 418–429. Springer, Heidelberg (2007). https://doi.org/10.1007/978-3-540-74958-5_39
13. Vapnik, V.N.: An overview of statistical learning theory. IEEE transactions on neural networks **10**(5), 988–999 (1999). https://doi.org/10.1109/72.788640
14. Zhang, Q.s., Zhu, S.C.: Visual interpretability for deep learning: a survey. Front. Inform. Technol. Electron. Eng. **19**(1), 27–39 (2018). https://doi.org/10.48550/arXiv.1802.00614

Mitigating Class Imbalance in Time Series with Enhanced Diffusion Models

Ryan Sijstermans, Chang Sun[ID], and Enrique Hortal[(✉)][ID]

Department of Advanced Computing Sciences, Maastricht University, Maastricht,
The Netherlands
enrique.hortal@maastrichtuniversity.nl

Abstract. This study introduces a novel approach to mitigate class
imbalance in time series data using enhanced diffusion models by integrating oversampling techniques and classifier-free guidance to generate
high-quality synthetic time series data. Our results indicate significant
improvements not only concerning data quality but also in handling
class imbalances, showcasing the potential of the proposed approach
in improving the performance of machine learning models in scenarios
where data annotation distribution is skewed. The efficacy of our approach was demonstrated using the UniMiB SHAR dataset with a focus
on enhancing the automatic fall detection for patients. This research
opens new avenues for data augmentation addressing critical challenges
in training algorithms with balanced data representation. Such advancements hold significant implications for a variety of real-world contexts,
especially within the healthcare sector.

Keywords: Diffusion models · Data augmentation · Imbalanced
dataset

1 Introduction

Deep learning models have demonstrated significant potential in diverse disciplines, yet their performance is heavily influenced by the quality and quantity of
the available training data [1]. Acquiring vast, diverse, and high-quality datasets
poses a challenge in numerous real-world scenarios, particularly in the healthcare domain, where data collection is costly and fraught with privacy issues.
Furthermore, data scarcity is compounded by imbalance issues, where one or
more classes are underrepresented. For instance, in rare disease research, the
outstanding challenge is the rarity of conditions and data scarcity which hinders
accurate diagnoses and effective treatments. Such data scarcity and imbalance
lead to models that inherently favour the majority classes, thereby undermining
the model's capacity to accurately classify the minority ones [10]. This is a critical concern especially when the primary goal of these models is to detect the
minority class.

One approach to address this challenge is to generate synthetic data to augment the minority class(es) in the imbalanced dataset. Generative Adversarial

J. M. Ferrández Vicente et al. (Eds.): IWINAC 2024, LNCS 14675, pp. 389–399, 2024.
https://doi.org/10.1007/978-3-031-61137-7_36

Networks (GANs) have been extensively employed for this purpose for various data modalities, including tabular data [16], images [4], and time series data [19]. Nonetheless, the issue of mode collapse in GANs has been highlighted, indicating that GAN's generators often struggle with producing a diverse range of data, alongside their complex and unstable training processes [15].

Recently, another promising generative approach, Diffusion Models, has quickly gained popularity due to its capability to outperform GANs in generating images of greater realism and diversity [17] while also enhancing distribution coverage and requiring simpler training procedures [5]. Contrary to the GAN's adversarial training mechanism, diffusion models initially introduce noise into the data, subsequently learning to reconstruct the original input from this perturbed data. Through this process, they learn the underlying data distribution, enabling the generation of new instances from random noise.

The application of diffusion models to time series data is still under development. While several studies have explored its use for time-series forecasting and imputation [2], efforts in time-series generation are mainly restricted to two works: SSSD-ECG [3], which employs structured state-space layers to address time-dependence, and TSGM [12], utilizing an auto-regressive approach. However, these models are primarily designed to enhance the quality of generated data without explicitly addressing data augmentation potential.

Furthermore, recent research suggests that diffusion models for image generation encounter challenges when dealing with imbalanced data distributions [14]. The imbalance leads to a predisposition towards the characteristics of dominant classes, limiting the models' ability to capture detailed features and variations of underrepresented classes, and resulting in decreasing fidelity and diversity. Although some strategies have been proposed to alleviate this issue [14], research in this area remains scarce. Particularly, the exploration of this issue within the context of time-series data is yet to be undertaken. This study aims to utilize diffusion models for the generation of synthetic time series data to facilitate data augmentation, especially in scenarios characterized by limited and imbalanced datasets.

2   Material and Methods

2.1   Data

The models proposed in this study are validated using the multi-class time-series UniMiB Smartphone-based Human Activity Recognition (SHAR) dataset [13]. This dataset comprises 11,771 samples collected from 30 subjects of ages ranging from 18 to 60 years. Each instance includes 151 timesteps over 3 s, with three-dimensional acceleration data sampled at 50 Hz. The dataset categorizes these instances into 17 classes: 9 "activities of daily living" (ADL) and 8 fall types. Due to the uneven performance of different activities by the subjects, the dataset exhibits class imbalance—ranging from 1,985 instances in the majority class to approximately 200 in four minority classes. Additionally, it is important to note that this dataset is also significantly skewed across subjects, making data augmentation even more challenging.

2.2   Diffusion Model

Diffusion models [8] represent a category of generative models designed to synthesize data instances from noise through an iterative denoising process. These models operate by incrementally introducing Gaussian noise into the training data, subsequently training to reverse this noising process to reconstruct the original dataset. This reversal technique, once learned, is employed on random Gaussian noise to generate new data instances.

While originally developed for unconditional generation, diffusion models can be modified for conditional generation by integrating the class label into the reverse diffusion process. This adaptation enables the generation of class-specific data, enhancing the model's effectiveness and applicability in situations requiring data synthesis to reflect the categorical characteristics [3].

Concerning diffusion models focused on time-series data, we explore SSSD-ECG [3], a Structured State-Space Diffusion model specially designed for creating ECG signals. Unlike common models that rely on convolutional methods for reconstructing data [8] or use dilated convolutions for audio tasks [11], SSSD-ECG employs S4 layers [7]. These layers excel at capturing long-term patterns in data, making them well-suited for analyzing ECG sequences.

2.3   Modifications for Imbalanced Data Handling

Given the challenges encountered by diffusion models in generating high-fidelity and diverse images for minority classes [14], we hypothesized that these constraints could also benefit the generation of time series data. We apply the SSSD-ECG time-series diffusion model (hereinafter "SSSD" model) to the imbalanced UniMiB SHAR dataset, investigating various adjustments aimed at enhancing synthetic time series creation for minority classes. Our approach incorporates strategies from both the fields of class imbalance in classification and existing diffusion model development. Despite the differences between classification and generation tasks, techniques developed for mitigating class imbalance in classification may offer benefits for generation challenges. To tackle the class imbalance issue, we explore a data-level strategy—oversampling— and investigate the application of classifier-free guidance to elevate overall data quality. Below, each modification is elaborated, detailing the rationale and implementation specifics of these strategies.

Baseline. To establish a benchmark for evaluation, our experimental setup began with the "Base" model, utilizing the unaltered SSSD model trained using data from all categories. The optimization of hyperparameters was concentrated on the number of residual layers, the dimensional configuration of the S4 layers' state space, learning rate, and batch size. The remaining parameters are consistent with those outlined in the SSSD study [3], except for adjustments required due to the distinctive features of the dataset, like variations in input dimensions and quantity of classes. Optimal settings were identified by their influence on validation loss.

Oversampling. To tackle class imbalance, data-level techniques modify the training data distribution to reduce imbalance effects [10]. The two primary methods are *random oversampling*, adding copies of minority class instances, and *random undersampling*, removing instances from the majority class. Given our study's focus on enhancing minority class generation where data is scarce, we opt for oversampling due to its potential for improving model learning across all classes, despite the risk of overfitting it may introduce.

For our first imbalance correction strategy, we implement random oversampling by duplicating instances from minority classes until each class aligns with that of the largest class (class 4), increasing the training dataset from 9,056 to 26,758 instances, ensuring uniform class representation. This approach, referred to as "Oversampled" model, prepares the SSSD model to learn from a more balanced dataset, albeit with increased computational demands.

Classifier-Free Guidance. In addition to modifying the training process of the SSSD model to address the data imbalance challenge, we investigate the use of classifier-free guidance (CFG) to improve the conditional sampling process for creating synthetic data. CFG, combines the concept of classifier guidance with the random removal of the class label y with a fixed probability during training, improving the conditional generation. By applying a guidance weight w, we can steer generated instances closer to the target class distribution, enhancing fidelity at the potential cost of diversity [9].

In data augmentation, the quality and variety of the generated data are just as crucial as its accuracy and representativeness. Therefore, we not only experimented with a range of positive w values but also investigated the impact of negative w values ($-0.5 \leq w < 0$). We hypothesize that a slightly negative w could promote diversity by relaxing the strict adherence to the target class distribution by blending conditional and unconditional predictions. In the context of imbalanced datasets, where learning minority class distributions is challenging, combining CFG with imbalance-handling techniques is expected to improve model performance in learning these distributions.

2.4   Data Quality Evaluation

To evaluate the impact of the proposed modifications to the SSSD model and test the quality of the generated data, we compare synthetically generated data across different models with authentic data. In this study, high-quality synthetic data is characterized by its fidelity (closely resembling real data), diversity (spanning the real data's variability), and utility (retaining informational value for training subsequent downstream models) [19]. To comprehensively assess the synthetic data across these dimensions, we explore various assessment techniques from the time-series generation field, utilizing metrics and classifier outcomes. Unlike image generation, which predominantly relies on metrics such as Inception Score (IS) and Fréchet Inception Distance (FID), evaluating synthetic time series lacks a universally accepted metric [18]. For quality evaluation, we use a set of metrics commonly applied in synthetic time-series analysis, summarized below and illustrated in Fig 1).

Maximum Mean Discrepancy (MMD) [6] is a statistical tool measuring the alignment between two distributions via mean embeddings in kernel space, with lower MMD indicating closer similarity. It employs the radial basis function (RBF) kernel, choosing bandwidth (σ) through median heuristic from real data. To address bias in imbalanced datasets, MMD scores are calculated per class and aggregated via macro average, ensuring equitable representation of class-specific distributional similarities.

Kolmogorov-Smirnov Statistic (KS) measures distribution differences by comparing empirical cumulative distribution functions. A lower score indicates greater overall distribution similarity. KS statistics are averaged per class and aggregated using a macro average to mitigate majority class bias. It complements MMD and is computed using the SDMetrics[1].

Discriminative Score [19] assesses the similarity between real and synthetic data by training a discriminator. A two-layer LSTM is trained on a combined training set comprising real and synthetic data, with instances labelled as "real" or "synthetic". The discriminator's accuracy is then evaluated on the combined test sets, and the discriminative score is defined as $|accuracy - 0.5|$. A low score signifies that the synthetic data is difficult to distinguish from real data.

Predictive Score [19] measures the synthetic data's ability to replicate real data's conditional temporal distributions. A two-layer LSTM predicts future

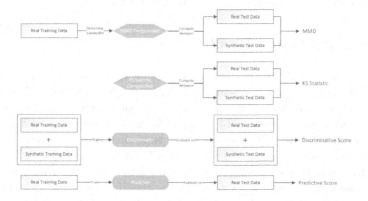

Fig. 1. A overview of data splitting in training and evaluation process for *data quality evaluation*.

---

[1] Synthetic Data Metrics: https://docs.sdv.dev/sdmetrics/.

time vectors from past timesteps, specifically predicting timesteps 1 to 151 from 0 to 150 across all features. The score is the Mean Absolute Error (MAE) against the real data's ground truth. Diverging from TimeGAN's approach, which predicts the last feature from previous ones, we predict all features due to our dataset's lack of strong feature correlations, focusing on assessing the replication of temporal dynamics.

2.5 Data Augmentation Evaluation

Moreover, we explore the potential of synthetic data to enhance classifier performance through data augmentation. We assess the utility of synthetic data generated by different models and investigate the effectiveness of the SSSD model, when integrated with various imbalance-handling strategies, in boosting classifier accuracy involving imbalanced data. We explore two methods of augmenting the real data - "training" augmentation and "balance" augmentation as resolving class imbalance is not always desirable as it alters the underlying data distribution. Consequently, the "training" augmentation method involves enriching the real dataset with synthetic data created based on the real training set's labels, effectively doubling the dataset size. This approach not only increases the number of learning instances per class but also preserves the initial class distribution skewness. A classifier is then trained on this augmented training dataset and subsequently evaluated on the real test dataset.

Then, we explored the "balance" augmentation approach where synthetically generated data is used to balance all classes following the strategies described in Sect. 2.3. For this method, the number of instances for each class is increased to match the number of instances in the largest class. We train a classifier on the real training data combined with the synthetic "balance" data, after which the classifier is evaluated on the real test data. These models are compared with an approach trained exclusively on real training data and tested on the real test set, denoted as "Train on Real, Test on Real" or TRTR.

3   Experiments and Results

Firstly, the UniMiB SHAR dataset was randomly split into training, validation and test sets following an 80-10-10 split, ensuring that each subject's data was uniquely assigned to one of the splits. This division allows for the testing of models on previously unseen subject data, facilitating objective and unbiased performance evaluation. It is worth noticing that, due to the disparate data distributions across subjects, we observed noticeable differences between the evaluation on the validation set during training and the final evaluation on the test set. For this reason, we present the results for the classifier-based metrics evaluated on both the validation and test sets to give a more comprehensive overview of the models' performance. Furthermore, data normalization was applied, scaling values between -1 and 1, to optimize for use in the diffusion model.

Before training the SSSD models with imbalance handling, various hyper-parameter experiments were performed based on the base SSSD model. Considering practical constraints, we halved the number of residual layers from 36, as proposed in the original SSSD study [3], to 18, as comparable performances where observed with a significant reduction in training time. Additionally, the state space dimensionality of the S4 layers was increased from 64 to 128 as it enhanced the model's expressiveness, resulting in significantly lower loss metrics. Through testing various batch sizes (4,8,16,32,64,128) and learning rates (1e-5,5e-5,1e-4,5e-4,1e-3), we identified optimal settings at values 4 and 5e-4 respectively. Except for adjustments for dataset-specific parameters like input channels, we maintained other hyperparameters as per the original specification. These optimized hyperparameters were subsequently applied to the SSSD models designed for imbalance handling.

To determine the optimal classifier-free guidance (CFG) weight w, we trained SSSD models with 10% label dropout and generated synthetic validation data for w values in the range $[0, 0.1, 0.2, \ldots, 2, 3, 4]$, evaluating them against MMD, KS statistic, Discriminative score, and Predictive score metrics. For the Discriminative and Predictive scores, we utilized a moving average with a window size of 3 to smooth out fluctuations and highlight trends. From this analysis, we selected $w = 0.9$ for the Base model and $w = 1.5$ for the Oversampled model. We also explored the effect of negative CFG weights ($w \in [-0.5, \ldots, -0.1]$) on the Oversampled model (as this model had the highest risk of overfitting and could therefore benefit the most from more diversity) to potentially enhance diversity at the expense of fidelity, eventually focusing further on $w = -0.2$.

3.1 Data Quality Evaluation

For each version of the SSSD models, both with and without CFG, we produced synthetic training and validation data guided by actual training and validation labels (depicted as sets 1 and 3 in Fig. 2). Subsequently, these synthetic datasets were assessed using set 4 as the evaluation set. The MMD and KS statistics were utilized to measure the synthetic data against the real test dataset, while Discriminative and Predictive scores involved training models on combined synthetic and real training datasets, followed by evaluation on both synthetic and real test datasets. Moreover, to provide an additional comparative baseline, these metrics were also calculated for the real dataset, with MMD and KS comparing real test to validation datasets, and the Predictive score derived from real training tested against the real test dataset. Given the nature of the Discriminative score, its calculation was exclusive to comparisons between real and synthetic datasets. Each metric underwent five iterations of calculation, with averages reported in Table 1, offering insights into the synthetic data's relative quality versus the real data.

Our findings provide a comprehensive assessment of the synthetic data quality, showcasing the potential of SSSD models in enhancing data augmentation techniques. The iterative approach to metric evaluation, including multiple computations for accuracy, underscores the robustness of our methodology in gen-

Table 1. Evaluation of data quality. The best score for each metric is in bold. For the CFG models, scores that improved over the model without CFG are italicized. The performance of the real data is provided for context.

Data	MMD	KS	Discriminative	Predictive
Real	0.044	0.140	-	0.209
Base	0.069	0.191	0.038	0.219
Oversampled	**0.067**	**0.177**	0.098	0.216
Base CFG 0.9	0.079	0.211	*0.026*	0.222
Oversampled CFG 1.5	0.080	0.209	*0.079*	*0.214*
Oversampled CFG -0.2	0.087	0.207	0.154	0.223

erating high-quality synthetic datasets. However, it reveals that the benefits of applying CFG modifications are not uniformly observed. Further exploration is required to understand the constraints of these modifications.

3.2   Data Augmentation Evaluation

We also investigate the effectiveness of synthetic data in classification tasks by training classifiers on two augmented datasets, "training" and "balanced" (as shown in sets 1 and 2 in Fig. 2), followed by evaluation against a separate real test set. These results are compared with those when using solely the original dataset (labelled TRTR). To highlight augmentation's impact on minority classes, we report the F1 score for each class individually, displayed in Table 2, with scores from training label augmentation on the left and balance label augmentation on the right. In scenarios involving classifier-free guidance (CFG), synthetic validation sets were created under various CFG weights to identify the ideal CFG configuration. Upon identification, this optimal weight was employed to generate synthetic datasets for both direct model performance assessment and augmentation of the real dataset to boost subsequent model training efficacy. This dataset generation strategy is outlined in Fig. 2.

Contrary to the quality metrics discussed in Sect. 3.1, CFG's benefits for augmentation effectiveness, particularly for minority classes, are evident. The F1 scores exhibit significant improvements for models utilizing classifier-free guidance (CFG), especially under optimal CFG weights, indicating that synthetic data not only aids in model training but also substantially favours class balance. The process of conditional data generation, leveraging real data labels to direct synthetic data creation, plays a pivotal role in improving classification task performance. It is noteworthy, however, that while the "balanced" configuration yields marginal improvements in certain instances, these enhancements are not consistently superior to those observed with the "training" counterparts. This suggests a need for further exploration into alternative balancing strategies.

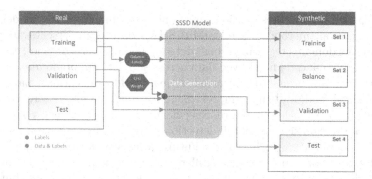

Fig. 2. Conditional data generation process for *data augmentation evaluation*. Labels from real data are given as conditional input to the SSSD models.

Table 2. F1 Scores for the data augmentation evaluation. C=colours indicate an increase (green) or decrease (red) in score compared to the TRTR performance, colour intensity indicates de degree of the change. OS stands for Oversampled. For the CFG models, the used w value is mentioned after their name.

Class	TRTR	Training					Balanced				
		Base	OS	Base CFG 0.9	OS CFG 1.5	OS CFG -0.2	Base	OS	Base CFG 0.9	OS CFG 1.5	OS CFG -0.2
1	0.174	0.400	0.533	**0.655**	0.606	0.429	0.438	0.444	0.545	**0.727**	0.833
2	0.667	0.656	0.607	0.000	**0.679**	0.702	0.588	0.509	0.667	**0.772**	0.711
3	0.996	0.996	**1.000**	0.996	**1.000**	0.992	0.994	0.996	0.979	**0.998**	0.992
4	0.971	0.973	0.986	0.953	0.989	0.986	0.952	0.965	0.963	**0.995**	0.949
5	**0.902**	0.897	0.845	0.873	**0.902**	0.902	0.817	**0.907**	0.820	0.902	0.788
6	**0.953**	0.947	**0.953**	0.934	**0.953**	0.953	0.947	**0.953**	0.953	0.953	0.947
7	0.836	0.849	0.841	0.794	0.875	0.867	0.815	0.825	0.854	**0.880**	0.827
8	0.766	0.471	0.776	0.655	**0.885**	0.894	0.375	0.545	**0.783**	0.632	0.619
9	0.745	0.875	0.783	0.000	0.870	0.898	0.732	0.762	0.773	**0.885**	0.939
10	0.604	0.446	0.317	0.508	0.506	0.476	0.494	0.400	0.615	0.597	0.529
11	0.161	0.391	0.301	0.312	0.340	0.345	0.246	0.328	0.188	0.418	0.442
12	0.426	0.436	0.622	0.267	0.599	0.628	**0.738**	0.705	0.528	0.578	0.514
13	0.633	0.619	0.738	0.800	**0.837**	0.647	0.620	0.667	0.791	0.690	0.713
14	0.493	0.386	0.384	0.355	0.494	0.531	0.389	0.418	0.366	0.533	0.212
15	0.541	0.489	**0.673**	0.517	0.645	0.531	0.636	**0.761**	0.589	0.538	0.535
16	0.195	0.256	0.222	0.372	**0.480**	0.242	**0.448**	0.286	0.344	0.388	0.290
17	0.434	0.283	0.336	0.153	**0.540**	0.419	0.353	0.429	0.353	0.532	0.390
Mean	0.617	0.610	0.642	0.538	**0.718**	0.673	0.622	0.641	0.654	**0.707**	0.661

4 Conclusions

In this work, the primary objective was to address the problem of data augmentation concerning class imbalance in time series data. To that end, we explore techniques from literature for both diffusion models and for dealing with class imbalance in classification. Our research successfully addresses this challenge through innovative modification of diffusion models. The proposed methodology not only enhances the quality of synthetic data generation but also ensures a

more balanced data representation for training machine learning models. The
application of our method to the UniMiB SHAR dataset underscores its potential in various domains requiring robust data augmentation techniques, especially
when class-imbalanced and skewed data across subjects are predominant. These
characteristics are frequently observed in real-world applications, particularly
in the medical field, and thus, improvements in this area are closely associated
with advancements in patient care. Specifically, in this case, they relate to the
accuracy and responsiveness of fall detection systems, which are vital for elderly
care and rehabilitation technologies. Future work will focus on exploring the
applicability of our approach across different datasets and refining the model to
accommodate a broader range of imbalance scenarios, further contributing to
ensuring data representation is balanced and reflective of diverse scenarios.

References

1. Al-Jarrah, O.Y., Yoo, P.D., Muhaidat, S., Karagiannidis, G.K., Taha, K.: Efficient machine learning for big data: a review. Big Data Res. **2**(3), 87–93 (2015)
2. Alcaraz, J.M.L., Strodthoff, N.: Diffusion-based time series imputation and fore-casting with structured state space models. arXiv preprint arXiv:2208.09399 (2022)
3. Alcaraz, J.M.L., Strodthoff, N.: Diffusion-based conditional ECG generation with structured state space models. arXiv preprint arXiv:2301.08227 (2023)
4. Antoniou, A., Storkey, A., Edwards, H.: Data augmentation generative adversarial networks. arXiv preprint arXiv:1711.04340 (2017)
5. Dhariwal, P., Nichol, A.: Diffusion models beat GANs on image synthesis. Adv. Neural. Inf. Process. Syst. **34**, 8780–8794 (2021)
6. Gretton, A., Borgwardt, K.M., Rasch, M.J., Schölkopf, B., Smola, A.: A kernel two-sample test. J. Mach. Learn. Res. **13**(1), 723–773 (2012)
7. Gu, A., Goel, K., Ré, C.: Efficiently modeling long sequences with structured state spaces. arXiv preprint arXiv:2111.00396 (2021)
8. Ho, J., Jain, A., Abbeel, P.: Denoising diffusion probabilistic models. Adv. Neural. Inf. Process. Syst. **33**, 6840–6851 (2020)
9. Ho, J., Salimans, T.: Classifier-free diffusion guidance. arXiv preprint arXiv:2207.12598 (2022)
10. Johnson, J.M., Khoshgoftaar, T.M.: Survey on deep learning with class imbalance. J. Big Data **6**(1), 1–54 (2019)
11. Kong, Z., Ping, W., Huang, J., Zhao, K., Catanzaro, B.: DiffWave: a versatile diffusion model for audio synthesis. arXiv preprint arXiv:2009.09761 (2020)
12. Lim, H., Kim, M., Park, S., Park, N.: Regular time-series generation using SGM. arXiv preprint arXiv:2301.08518 (2023)
13. Micucci, D., Mobilio, M., Napoletano, P.: UniMiB SHAR: a dataset for human activity recognition using acceleration data from smartphones. Appl. Sci. **7**(10), 1101 (2017)
14. Qin, Y., Zheng, H., Yao, J., Zhou, M., Zhang, Y.: Class-balancing diffusion models. arXiv preprint arXiv:2305.00562 (2023)
15. Saxena, D., Cao, J.: Generative adversarial networks (GANs) challenges, solutions, and future directions. ACM Comput. Surv. (CSUR) **54**(3), 1–42 (2021)
16. Sun, C., van Soest, J., Dumontier, M.: Generating synthetic personal health data using conditional generative adversarial networks combining with differential pri-vacy. J. Biomed. Inform. **143**, 104404 (2023)

17. Tashiro, Y., Song, J., Song, Y., Ermon, S.: Csdi: conditional score-based diffusion models for probabilistic time series imputation. Adv. Neural. Inf. Process. Syst. **34**, 24804–24816 (2021)
18. Yadav, P., Gaur, M., Fatima, N., Sarwar, S.: Qualitative and quantitative evaluation of multivariate time-series synthetic data generated using MTS-TGAN: a novel approach. Appl. Sci. **13**(7), 4136 (2023)
19. Yoon, J., Jarrett, D., Van der Schaar, M.: Time-series generative adversarial networks. In: Advances in Neural Information Processing Systems **32** (2019)

Measuring Spatial Behaviour and Cognition: A Method Based on Trajectories Analysis and Supported by Technology and Artificial Intelligence

Michela Ponticorvo[✉], Maria Luongo, Antonietta Argiuolo, and Onofrio Gigliotta

NAC Lab Orazio Miglino, Department of Humanistic Studies, University of Naples "Federico II", Naples, Italy
michela.ponticorvo@unina.it

Abstract. Spatial cognition is a fundamental cognitive process for adapting to the environment, and it has been extensively researched in humans, animals, and artificial agents using various methods, such as clinical and comparative studies. Spatial cognition and related skills can be deduced from behaviours, such as reaching for an object, returning to a familiar area after an extended run, or identifying the corner in an enclosure where food is hidden.

In this paper, we will propose a method based on trajectory analysis with index calculation and we will illustrate two examples of applying this method 1) to a neuro-psychological test and 2) analyzing the performance of agents in a behavioural task. The results suggest that this method can complement traditional measures of spatial cognition.

Keywords: Spatial cognition · spatial behaviour · psychometric test · behavioural task

1 Introduction

Many behaviors exhibit a spatial aspect, encompassing not only orientation and navigation but also tasks like recalling the parking side of our car, judging numerical comparisons, or evaluating the efficient arrangement of furniture in a room. The underlying cognitive process governing these behaviors is spatial cognition. Spatial cognition is the cognitive function enabling humans and animals to acquire and utilize knowledge about their environment, aiding in determining their location, acquiring resources, and navigating back to their nest or home [36]. Spatial cognition is a vast area of research including not only psychology but also geography, environmental research [19], and the exploration of related neural mechanisms [25]. Therefore, a diverse array of paradigms and related methodologies exists, including the study of spatial skills based on behavior in humans, animals, and artificial neuro-agents that allow us to model the underlying neural substrate of specific aspects of spatial cognition [14,15].

J. M. Ferrández Vicente et al. (Eds.): IWINAC 2024, LNCS 14675, pp. 400–409, 2024.
https://doi.org/10.1007/978-3-031-61137-7_37

The contexts for studying these behaviors are equally diverse: it can be conducted in laboratories, real-life and naturalistic situations, as well as in simulations or virtual reality, considering recent technological advancements. A common thread is the utilization of tasks assigned to participants-be they humans, animals, or artificial agents-and the measurement of performance often expressed in terms of correct choices, identification, or reaching. This aspect is crucial as it consolidates various elements (disambiguation, decision, movement, representation, strategy, etc.) into a single set of data.

In this paper, we propose to enhance traditional performance information by incorporating micro-level measurements that highlight different aspects of the overall strategy employed to accomplish the task. This approach aims to deepen and broaden the measurement process, creating richer connections between behavior and the construct of spatial cognition. Specifically, we will describe two examples of the application of this method: in the first case, we will illustrate how to calculate informative indexes on the braking tray task (BTT). For the second application, we will demonstrate how to extract positions from videos and recordings of trajectories associated with spatial tasks and then calculate informative indexes.

2 Measurement of Spatial Performance with the Baking Tray Task - BTT

2.1 The BTT

The Baking Tray Test, abbreviated as BTT, is an ecological test designed to evaluate deficits in visual-spatial skills by prompting participants to simulate a daily activity. In this test, participants are tasked with arranging a series of 16 disks on a 75 × 100 cm surface as evenly as possible, as if they were arranging biscuits on a baking sheet. The efficacy of the test lies in its ability to identify patients with neglect by counting the disks placed on the right versus the left. An imbalance indicates spatial processing issues in the left-right dimension.

Notably, there isn't a single correct answer for the BTT; instead, multiple strategies for disks arrangement exist [2, 8–10].

2.2 The E-BTT, Enhanced Version of BTT

An enhanced version called E-BTT has been developed by Cerrato and colleagues [1, 3, 4, 11], incorporating a hybrid digital and physical prototype. This version utilizes an interface with tangible tools or concrete objects that participants manipulate in their peripersonal space. The cubes, equipped with ArUco markers [21], can be detected by a camera, which then transfers information on cube positioning to software. Importantly, the enhanced version maintains the simplicity of administration and the ecological value of the original test while providing precise information such as test execution time and the spatial coordinates (X and Y) of the cube layout strategies (Fig. 1).

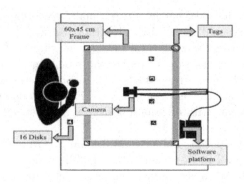

Fig. 1. E-BTT: software and hardware system to collect data on spatial skills

The traditional measure on BTT performance consists in the count of cubes in the two halves of space and subtracting the cubes placed on the right from those on the left. A difference greater than 2 cubes is considered a sign of hemineglect [6,34]. More recently, Facchin and colleagues [13] transformed the raw score of the BTT into a laterality bias calculating the ratio between cubes on the right minus cubes on the left on total cubes.

This approach expresses lateralization in terms of percentage and is more effective than the original right-left difference [13]. If a positive value is obtained, more cubes were arranged on the right; conversely, with a negative result, it indicates a more imbalanced configuration toward the left. Furthermore, the authors have established cutoffs: -12.5% for the left and 18.7% for the right.

With the E-BTT version is possible to calculate more and varied indexes: the first attempts were devoted to compare the number of cubes in the quadrants, to identify spatial clusters, the area with the convex polygon [8,10,11].

These attempts were focused on the position of the cubes without considering the positioning order; indeed the E-BTT involves having access to new types of data, no longer just frequencies, but spatial coordinates and their order. This clearly implies that traditional methods of data analysis (right-left difference, laterality bias) become obsolete or do not fully exploit the potential offered by the application of the E-BTT. Therefore, new methods were proposed to open to this aspect of data analysis that considers the whole performance. Palumbo and colleagues [26] treated the sequence of sixteen X coordinates as a single trajectory and applied a mixed model of data clustering (MGHD - Mixture of Generalized Hyperbolic Distributions) to identify homogeneous groups of behavior. The results revealed the emergence of three groups: the first composed of individuals starting from various positions and following no specific pattern; the second group comprised those who started on the right but moved to the left in a rhythmic motion; finally, the third group consisted of individuals starting from the left side.

We then proposed the analysis of Euclidean distances and new indices referred to laterality, but also to verticality and organization [3,4]. We will see an example of the application of these indexes to describe the whole performance.

2.3   Materials and Method

The sample consisted of 122 healthy participants (97 female, mean age = 21.33, SD = 3.84). Some of the data were used in studies on pseudoneglect [31,32] and reported in the studies by Argiuolo and colleagues [3,4]. The study was approved by the University of Naples "Federico II" Local Ethics Committee and was conducted in accordance with the Declaration of Helsinki. Informed consent was obtained by all participants. We computed a variety of indexes, whose extended description can be found in the cited studies, which provide insights into the spatial arrangement and quality of the disk placement during the measurement. The indexes are categorized into spatiality (indicating where the disks were placed), and quality, indicating how the disks were placed.

a. **Quality indexes**: Quality indexes pertain to the final sequence's quality and organization, drawing from the visual search literature on cancellation tasks. For the E-BTT task, the following quality indexes were selected: Quadrant analysis, Total Area, Total Time, Within Distance (WD), Number of Intersections, Intersections Rate, Longest Path, Global Speed, Best R (RX and RY), Standardized Angle, Between Distance from Optimal Sequences

b. **Laterality Indexes**: All indexes measured using the X coordinates are considered measures of laterality. These indexes provide insights into how much to the right or left a disk or the entire sequence is located. Specific laterality indexes include: First X, Right/Left Disks' Difference (R/L Difference), Laterality Bias (LB), Distance Lateral Gradient.

These indexes have different trends and are different between individuals, allowing to identify specific features and individual fingerprints.

2.4   Results

Figure 2 reports the plot and some indexes on laterality and organization for 2 participants.

The same index on laterality bias, that in this case is 0 for both participants, corresponds to very different strategies in the plot and at a very different level of organization.

These indexes were used in some studies to differentiate between healthy and impaired participants [10,11] and were also the starting point of AI application. In the study by Ponticorvo et al. [27], the goal was to reconstruct the cube position with unsupervised Artificial Intelligence method: in more detail, two different neural networks were compared. A sigmoid neural network with a single internal layer and an auto-encoder with three hidden levels. The auto-encoder resulted more effective in reconstructing the cube position, indicating that it was able to extract a regular spatial pattern.

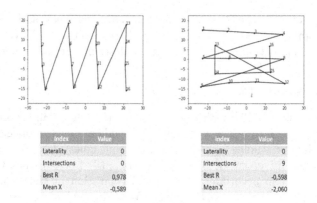

Fig. 2. Laterality indexes from E-BTT

Argiuolo and colleagues [5] used Support Vector Machine to discriminate between children and adults. Results showed that children did differ from adults in terms of laterality, verticality and quality. Children were less lateralized, on average, towards the left; they started spatial exploration from the bottom part of the frame, and they could be considered less organized than adults. In fact, children used much more space and did more intersections of the path than adults.

3   Measurement of Spatial Performance with the *Open field box* and the *Blue-wall task*

In spatial studies, two experimental conditions are widely used: *Open field box* and *Blue wall task*. These orientation tasks, often used in the study of spatial behavior, is conducted in a rectangular arena. In the human version of this experiment, the participant is placed in a rectangular room with walls uniformly painted white. In one corner, the experimenter places a very enticing object. During the training phase, the participant can see this reward, which the experimenter then hides. In the test phase, the reward is concealed. After a disorientation procedure designed to eliminate any sense of direction the subject may have retained due to inertia, the experimenter asks the subject to find this enticing object. At first glance, the participant cannot distinguish between the four corners, but in reality, they are not equivalent. Considering only the available information, i.e., the shape of the room, the subject can identify two corners: the first is the area where the reward is located, while the second is one that has the same geometric characteristics and is perceptually equivalent to the correct corner (the rotationally equivalent corner). If the subject considers the geometric configuration of the arena, they will choose the correct angle and its rotational equivalent with approximately equal frequency, making a systematic error. In the Blue wall task, the procedure is exactly the same, but the arena used is slightly different: one of the walls is colored. In this case, if the participants consider both the geometry and the local color information, they will seek the reward only in the correct corner. Otherwise, if they consider only the geometric information, they will also search in the rotationally equivalent corner. The correct solution to the task implies that the subject integrates information about the shape with other non-spatial information, such as the color of the wall.

3.1   The Blue-Wall Task in Humans, Animals and Artificial Agents

The Open field box has been used with many different species [12]: rats [24], chicks [35], pigeons [22], fish Xenotoca eiseni [33], rhesus monkeys [16] and humans [18]. The Blue wall has been used for many species too. They include rats [7,24], chicks [35], pigeons [22], fish Xenotoca eiseni [33], rhesus monkeys [16], and humans [17].

In a view of comparative studies where also artificial agents are welcome, we can report also that these tasks have been proposed to artificial agents [28–30].

3.2   From Correct Choices to Strategies, Trajectories and Indexes

Traditionally, in literature, the performance on these tasks is reported indicating the number of correct choices or the number of choices for each corner. This is undoubtedly a core measure but it does not shed light on how the task is solved (or not), which strategy is used, which are the features of the pathway leading to one corner. Focusing on this issue would help to clarify how the spatial representations determine the behaviour and, ultimately, to build better models on spatial cognition.

With simulated artificial agents, it is easy to collect the data on positions that will allow to draw the trajectories and to calculate indexes, as it has been shown in the previous section. We will now introduce a software that allows to extract the position from recordings to get precise information on agent's position be it an animal or a robot.

In natural large-scale environments, using tracking devices, such as GPS trackers, cameras, or sensors, to collect precise data on the movements and positions of individuals is now become quite affordable on the technical level. In addition to conventional applications in navigation and orientation, GPS has proven highly successful in studying the migratory behaviors of animals. This expanded usage has introduced new perspectives in comprehending the dynamics of wildlife, enabling scientists to precisely monitor the migratory paths, feeding habits, and nesting areas of various species [20]. The integration of tracking devices, accelerometers, and other technologies forms a potent tool for exploring and documenting the movement and behavior of individuals, making a significant contribution to our understanding of the ecology and biology of diverse species, both human and non-human [23,37].

3.3   Materials and Method

In order to gain a clearer insight into whether various types of spatial information influence distinct trajectories and strategies in solving spatial tasks, we conducted an analysis of video recordings on animals. The video recordings underwent processing using custom-developed software tailored to track the movement within the arena. The tracking process occurred following a 2-seconds calibration period at a rate of 60 frames per second. The result yielded a set of coordinates (X and Y) corresponding to a frame duration of 1/60 of a second, measured in centimeters. These coordinates were then used to calculate specific indices, to a more thorough understanding of how various types of spatial information influence the trajectories and their decision-making processes during spatial activities. The indices that were used are the following:

- Length: lenght of the trajectory, in centimeters, is the total distance of the explored space;
- Time, measured in seconds, of spatial performance;
- Speed: is calculated by dividing the Length by the total time;
- Along the edges: is the percentage of points that are along the edges of the arena;
- Center SX, Center, Center DX, Bottom Side DX, Top Side DX, Bottom Side SX, Top Side SX, Top Center, Bottom Center and Center: indicates the position of the points in the arena, based on its division into nine quadrants;
- Turning Points: the points of change of direction, highlighting the phases in which the animal modify their trajectory. The minimum angle between vectors that represents a significant change in direction is set at 36°.

3.4   Results

Figure 3 provides a detailed comparison between two trajectories, named "trajectory 261" and "trajectory 263," which share a common endpoint but show

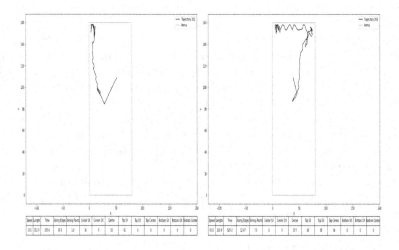

Fig. 3. The image illustrates two subplots showing distinct trajectories (in black) derived from position tracking. Both trajectories converge to the same exit point at coordinates (0, 160). Below each subplot, a table presents the values of the calculated indices associated with the respective trajectories.

different index values. Quantitative analysis reveals nuanced changes in indices, indicating a different strategy for solving the task.

4   Conclusions and Future Directions

Moving from the report of overall performance in terms of indexes to the extraction of indexes that help to understand the spatial organization can provide interesting insights in different domains. In clinical research irregular exploratory patterns can be identified among patients, contrasting with the more organized and regular patterns observed in neurologically healthy subjects.

In comparative psychology it can help to highlight the similarities and differences in behavior among different species. In this context, trajectory analysis can be a relevant subject of study, especially when examining the movements and paths taken by animals in various contexts. Trajectory analysis can help understand how individuals, including animals and artificial agents, navigate and orient themselves in space. This can be particularly relevant for understanding the cognitive processes underlying orientation, cognitive map formation, and movement planning. It can reveal specific behavioral patterns, such as preference for particular paths, resource-seeking, or response to environmental stimuli. These patterns can be indicative of cognitive, emotional, or motivational processes.

Starting from trajectory analysis, Artificial Intelligence (AI) can be used for data analysis by implementing AI algorithms to analyze vast amounts of trajectory data efficiently or for pattern recognition, to identify patterns, deviations, and trends in spatial behavior that may not be immediately apparent through traditional analysis.

References

1. Argiuolo, A., Ponticorvo, M.: Analysing E-BTT data: the E-TAN ANALYST prototype. In: 2022 IEEE International Conference on Metrology for Extended Reality, Artificial Intelligence and Neural Engineering (MetroXRAINE), pp. 367–371. IEEE (2022)
2. Argiuolo, A., Ponticorvo, M.: E-TAN platform and E-baking tray task potentialities: new ways to solve old problems. In: PSYCHOBIT (2020)
3. Argiuolo, A., Somma, F., Bartolomeo, P., Gigliotta, O., Ponticorvo, M.: Organization measures in the Enhanced Baking Tray Task. Front. Psychol. **13**, 1039064 (2022)
4. Argiuolo, A., Somma, F., Bartolomeo, P., Gigliotta, O., Ponticorvo, M.: Indexes for the E-baking tray task: a look on laterality, verticality and quality of exploration. Brain Sci. **12**(3), 401 (2022)
5. Argiuolo, A., Somma, F., Casella, M., Gigliotta, O., Ponticorvo, M.: Putting the pieces together: exploring the dimensionality of enhanced baking tray task indexes in school-aged children. In: 2023 IEEE International Conference on Metrology for Extended Reality, Artificial Intelligence and Neural Engineering (MetroXRAINE). IEEE (in press)

6. Bailey, M.J., Riddoch, M.J., Crome, P.: Test-retest stability of three tests for uni-lateral visual neglect in patients with stroke: Star Cancellation, Line Bisection, and the Baking Tray Task. Neuropsychol. Rehabil. **14**(4), 403–419 (2004)
7. Benhamou, S., Poucet, B.: Landmark use by navigating rats (Rattus norvegicus) contrasting geometric and featural information. J. Comp. Psychol. **112**(3), 317 (1998)
8. Cerrato, A., Ponticorvo, M., Gigliotta, O., Bartolomeo, P., Miglino, O.: The assessment of visuospatial abilities with tangible interfaces and machine learning. In: Ferrández Vicente, J.M., Álvarez-Sánchez, J.R., de la Paz López, F., Toledo Moreo, J., Adeli, H. (eds.) IWINAC 2019. LNCS, vol. 11486, pp. 78–87. Springer, Cham (2019). https://doi.org/10.1007/978-3-030-19591-5_9
9. Cerrato, A., Ponticorvo, M.: Enhancing neuropsychological testing with gamification and tangible interfaces: the baking tray task. In: Ferrández Vicente, J.M., Álvarez-Sánchez, J.R., de la Paz López, F., Toledo Moreo, J., Adeli, H. (eds.) IWINAC 2017. LNCS, vol. 10338, pp. 147–156. Springer, Cham (2017). https://doi.org/10.1007/978-3-319-59773-7_16
10. Cerrato, A., et al.: E-TAN, a technology-enhanced platform with tangible objects for the assessment of visual neglect: a multiple single-case study. Neuropsychol. Rehabil. **31**(7), 1130–1144 (2021)
11. Cerrato, A., Ponticorvo, M., Gigliotta, O., Bartolomeo, P., Miglino, O.: Btt-scan: uno strumento per la valutazione della negligenza spaziale unilaterale. Sistemi intelligenti **31**(2), 253–270 (2019)
12. Cheng, K., Huttenlocher, J., Newcombe, N.S.: 25 years of research on the use of geometry in spatial reorientation: a current theoretical perspective. Psychon. Bull. Rev. **20**, 1033–1054 (2013)
13. Facchin, A., Beschin, N., Pisano, A., Reverberi, C.: Normative data for distal line bisection and baking tray task. Neurol. Sci. **37**, 1531–1536 (2016)
14. Gigliotta, O., Bartolomeo, P., Miglino, O.: Approaching neuropsychological tasks through adaptive neurorobots. Connection Sci. **27**(2), 153–163 (2015). https://doi.org/10.1080/09540091.2014.968094
15. Gigliotta, O., Malkinson, T.S., Miglino, O., Bartolomeo, P.: Pseudoneglect in visual search: behavioral evidence and connectional constraints in simulated neural circuitry. eNeuro **4**(6) (2017). https://doi.org/10.1523/ENEURO.0154-17.2017
16. Gouteux, S., Thinus-Blanc, C., Vauclair, J.: Rhesus monkeys use geometric and nongeometric information during a reorientation task. J. Exp. Psychol. Gen. **130**(3), 505 (2001)
17. Gouteux, S., Spelke, E.S.: Children's use of geometry and landmarks to reorient in an open space. Cognition **81**(2), 119–148 (2001)
18. Hermer, L., Spelke, E.: Modularity and development: the case of spatial reorientation. Cognition **61**(3), 195–232 (1996)
19. Hirtle, S.C.: Geographical Design: Spatial Cognition and Geographical Information Science. Springer, Cham (2022). https://doi.org/10.1007/978-3-031-02194-7
20. Hromada, S.J., et al.: Using movement to inform conservation corridor design for Mojave desert tortoise. Mov. Ecol. **8**(1), 1–18 (2020)
21. Kedilioglu, O., Bocco, T.M., Landesberger, M., Rizzo, A., Franke, J.: ArUcoE: enhanced ArUco marker. In: 2021 21st International Conference on Control, Automation and Systems (ICCAS), pp. 878–881. IEEE (2021)
22. Kelly, D.M., Spetch, M.L., Heth, C.D.: Pigeons'(Columba livia) encoding of geometric and featural properties of a spatial environment. J. Comp. Psychol. **112**(3), 259 (1998)

23. Luongo, M., Simeoli, R., Marocco, D., Ponticorvo, M.: The design of a game-based software for children with autism spectrum disorder. In: 2022 IEEE International Conference on Metrology for Extended Reality, Artificial Intelligence and Neural Engineering (MetroXRAINE), pp. 318–322. IEEE (2022)

24. Margules, J., Gallistel, C.R.: Heading in the rat: determination by environmental shape. Animal Learn. Beh. **16**(4), 404–410 (1988)

25. Morrow, L., Ratcliff, G.: Neuropsychology of spatial cognition: evidence from cerebral lesions. In: Spatial Cognition, pp. 5–32. Psychology Press (2022)

26. Palumbo, F., Cerrato, A., Ponticorvo, M., Gigliotta, O., Bartolomeo, P., Miglino, O.: Clustering of behavioral spatial trajectories in Neuropsychological Assessment. In: Smart Statitistcs for Smart Applications, pp. 463–470. Pearson (2019)

27. Ponticorvo, M., Coccorese, M., Gigliotta, O., Bartolomeo, P., Marocco, D.: Artificial intelligence applied to spatial cognition assessment. In: International Work-Conference on the Interplay Between Natural and Artificial Computation, pp. 407–415. Springer, Cham (2022). https://doi.org/10.1007/978-3-031-06242-1_40

28. Ponticorvo, M., Miglino, O.: Encoding geometric and non-geometric information: a study with evolved agents. Anim. Cogn. **13**, 157–174 (2010)

29. Ponticorvo, M., Walker, R., Miglino, O.: Evolutionary robotics as a tool to investigate spatial cognition in artificial and natural systems. In: Artificial Cognition Systems, pp. 210–237. IGI Global (2007)

30. Ponticorvo, M., Miglino, O.: Is language necessary to merge geometric and non-geometric spatial cues? The case of the "BLUE-WALL TASK". In: Modeling Language, Cognition And Action, pp. 209–213 (2005)

31. Somma, F., et al.: Further to the left: Stress-induced increase of spatial pseudoneglect during the COVID-19 lockdown. Front. Psychol. **12**, 573846 (2021)

32. Somma F., et al.: Valutazione dello pseudoneglect mediante strumenti tangibili e digitali. Sistemi Intelligenti **32**, 533–549 (2020). https://doi.org/10.1422/99075

33. Sovrano, V.A., Bisazza, A., Vallortigara, G.: Modularity as a fish (Xenotoca eiseni) views it: conjoining geometric and nongeometric information for spatial reorientation. J. Exp. Psychol. Anim. Behav. Process. **29**(3), 199 (2003)

34. Tham, K.: The baking tray task: a test of spatial neglect. Neuropsychol. Rehabil. **6**(1), 19–26 (1996)

35. Vallortigara, G., Zanforlin, M., Pasti, G.: Geometric modules in animals' spatial representations: a test with chicks (Gallus gallus domesticus). J. Comp. Psychol. **104**(3), 248 (1990)

36. Waller, D.E., Nadel, L.E.: Handbook of spatial cognition (pp. x-309). American Psychological Association (2013)

37. Williams, H.J., et al.: Optimising the use of bio-loggers for movement ecology research. J. Anim. Ecol. **89**, 186–206 (2019)

Clustering COVID-19 Mortality Time Series

Murat Razi and Manuel Graña[✉]

Computational Intelligence Group, University of the Basque Country, UPV/EHU,
San Sebastian, Spain
`manuel.grana@ehu.eus`

Abstract. The undisputed assumption during the COVID-19 pandemic, was that the isolated pathogen SARS-COV-2 was spreading worldwide with the same mortal effects. However, examining the mortality records it is possible to appreciate substantial differences between countries in their response to the pandemic. This paper looks for clusters of countries that may shate some features explaining the diversity of the response. First, the paper extracts latent mortality patterns by Principal Component Anaylsis (PCA), Independent Component Analysis (ICA), and Non-negative Matrix Factorization (NNMF). Clustering is then carried out over the coefficients of the respective transformations of the countries mortality time series. The choice of the number of latent patterns has been guided by the explained variance in PCA and the avoidance of overfitting taking into account the ratio of representatives to the size of the dataset. Additionally, direct clustering of the mortality time series has been carried out by K means. This paper discusses some common findings that point to cultural and socio-economic factors underlying the response.

1 Introduction

Out of the hundreds of thousands of papers published somehow related with COVID-19 pandemic, those dealing with Machine Learning and like predictive approaches were mostly dealing with predicting the individual patient risks for severe disease [5]. Most epidemiological works, have focused on the prediction of the number cases applying epidemiological models [6], classical statistical tools as well as Machine Learning and Deep Learning tools [7,12].

This paper focus on the retrospective study of mortality time series per country as they provide a more definitive account of the evolution of the pandemic. Coding a decease as COVID-19 has a single confusor which is if the death was due to COVID-19 or it has been incidentally diagnosed but it was not the main cause of death [3]. Nevertheless, the differences in coding criteria may influence the final death toll attributed to the pandemic. In this regard, some studies do consider that many countries in Africa and Asia did not counted properly the death, so they extrapolate a regression model predicting a much higher number of deaths in those countries [8], in this light the catastrophic results in USA do not stand out below the performance of poor countries. Contrary to this view,

© The Author(s), under exclusive license to Springer Nature Switzerland AG 2024
J. M. Ferrández Vicente et al. (Eds.): IWINAC 2024, LNCS 14675, pp. 410–419, 2024.
https://doi.org/10.1007/978-3-031-61137-7_38

we take the reported deaths at face value and we try to find clusters of mortality patterns in time that can be associated with underlying conditions in the management of the pandemic response.

To this end, we apply Principal Component Anaylsis (PCA), Independent Component Analysis (ICA), Non-negative Matrix Factorization (NNMF) in order to find latent components of the mortality time series per country that provide a basis for a reduced dimensionality representation of the time series, which may even be considered as some kind of "explanation", and it is often used in Machine Learning for feature extraction prior to classification. We carry out clustering of the countries over the features provided by PCA, ICA, and NNMF. Moreover, we carry out the clustering on the raw data by means of K-Means Clustering (KMC) keeping the cluster representatives as templates of mortality time series.

The underlying hypothesis of the pandemic response is that there is a single well isolated and identified pathogen as the cause and that there is only one feasible strategy to cope with it, namely vaccination and social control measures. In other words, because the pathogen is unique the treatment should be the same for everybody and the expected mortality results should be uniform. However, the clustering study reported in this paper shows that mortality results can be very disimilar between clusters. Such dissimilarity can not be attributed to the pathogen, thus it should be attributed to other conditions, such as geographical localization, enforced policies, and the general health status of the country's population. Detailed analysis of such conditions is beyond the scope of the paper.

2   Materials and Methods

The code and data are published in zenodo[1] as well as figures and future versions of this work as long as it is evolving.

2.1   Our World in Data

"Our world in data" (OWID) is a web site devoted to the publication of relevant data for the pressing geopolitical and economic questions. It is hosted by the University of Oxford and has been extensively funded by Bill and Melinda Gates Foundation, thus it is not suspicious of being on the side of the conspiracy theorists. OWID has been publishing relevant data for the follow up of COVID-19 pandemic[2], aggregating it from several sources. We have used "new_deaths_smoothed_per_million" data for all analysis. Mortality time series were taken from the John Hopkins University COVID-19 site (also extensively funded by Bill and Melinda Gates Foundation) until march 2023, when it stopped updating data after the WHO published the end of the pandemic and most countries stopped reporting. For this work, we have taken the dataset as

---

[1] https://zenodo.org/doi/10.5281/zenodo.10403170.
[2] https://ourworldindata.org/explorers/coronavirus-data-explorer.

published on the first days of 2023, which we thinks covers the pandemic evolution. We consider the seven day rolling average time series, to avoid artifacts due to reporting irregularities, such as zero deaths in weekends.

2.2 Mathematical Methods

PCA. Principal Component Analysis (PCA) [1] is a widely used statistical method in data analysis and dimensionality reduction. In the context of a scientific paper, PCA is often employed to extract essential features or patterns from complex datasets, facilitating a more concise representation of the information contained within the data. The primary objective of PCA is to transform the original variables of a dataset into a new set of uncorrelated variables, called principal components. These components are linear combinations of the original variables and are ordered by the amount of variance they capture. The first principal component accounts for the maximum variance in the data, followed by subsequent components in decreasing order of variance. PCA involves finding the eigenvectors and eigenvalues of the covariance matrix

$$C = \frac{1}{n-1} \sum_{k=1}^{n} \left(X_k - \bar{X}\right)\left(X_k - \bar{X}\right).$$

The eigenvectors represent the directions of maximum variance in the data, and the corresponding eigenvalues indicate the magnitude of variance along these directions. The eigenvalue equation is given by $Cv = \lambda v$ where C is the covariance matrix, v is an eigenvector, and λ is the corresponding eigenvalue that corresponds to the variance explained by this eigenvector. The eigenvectors are sorted based on their corresponding eigenvalues in descending order. The eigenvector with the highest eigenvalue corresponds to the first principal component, the second-highest to the second principal component, and so on. The resulting principal components provide a new basis for representing the data, emphasizing the directions of maximum variance and allowing for dimensionality reduction while retaining essential information.

ICA. Independent Component Analysis (ICA) [2] is a powerful statistical technique used for blind source separation and the extraction of independent signals from observed mixtures. In the context of this study, ICA was employed to untangle complex relationships within the dataset, revealing hidden patterns and uncovering independent sources of variability. ICA assumes a linear mixing model, where the observed data X is a linear combination of independent source signals S through a mixing matrix A: i.e. $X = A.S$. The goal of ICA is to estimate the inverse of the mixing matrix (A^{-1}) or its pseudoinverse (A^{+}) to recover the independent source signals (S) from the observed data (X): $S = A^{-1}.X$. ICA relies on statistical measures of independence to guide the estimation of the mixing matrix. Common measures include negentropy, mutual information, and higher-order statistics. One popular algorithm for implementing ICA is FastICA.

It is an iterative optimization algorithm that maximizes non-Gaussianity, a surrogate measure for independence. The algorithm iteratively refines estimates of the independent components until convergence.

NNMF. Non-Negative Matrix Factorization (NMF) [3] is a mathematical technique used for decomposing a non-negative matrix V of size $m \times n$ into the product of two lower-dimensional matrices, both non-negative, W and H such that $V \approx WH$. NMF minimizes the reconstruction error between the original matrix V and the approximated matrix WH. The objective function often used is the Frobenius norm: $min_{W,H} \| V - WH \|_F^2$. The optimization process involves iteratively updating W and H to minimize the objective function. Multiplicative Update Rules are commonly used for iterative updates, given by:
$$W_{ij} \leftarrow \frac{(VH^T)_{ij}}{(WHH^T)_{ij}} \text{ and } H_{ij} \leftarrow \frac{(W^TV)_{ij}}{(W^TWH)_{ij}}.$$
This method is particularly useful for data analysis, feature extraction, and topic modeling, where the non-negativity constraint ensures the interpretability of the factors. Matrix W represents the basis vectors or features, and matrix H represents the coefficients for combining these features to reconstruct the original data.

K-Means Clustering. K-means clustering [4] is a classical unsupervised machine learning algorithm employed for data analysis and pattern recognition. The algorithm operates by partitioning a dataset into K distinct clusters, where each cluster represents a group of data points that share similar characteristics. The process involves iteratively assigning data points to clusters based on proximity and updating cluster centroids until convergence.

2.3 Spectral Clustering

Spectral clustering [11] is a machine learning technique used for partitioning a dataset into meaningful and homogeneous clusters. It is particularly effective when dealing with datasets that exhibit complex structures, such as non-convex shapes or irregular patterns. The process starts with the construction of the similarity graph among the data samples. Then, second eigenvector of the Laplacian of the graph provides the optimal graph cut. In its original formulation, spectral clustering finds the partition of the similarity graph into two clusters, multi-cluster induction is done by recursive splitting of the graph. In this paper, spectral clustering is used on coefficients of PCA, ICA and NNMF to cluster countries into different latent topics which is yielded by each analysis. K-means is not clustered again with spectral clustering.

3 Results

Figure 1 plots the latent components of countries COVID-19 mortality time series induced by PCA, ICA, and NNMF and the cluster representatives found by

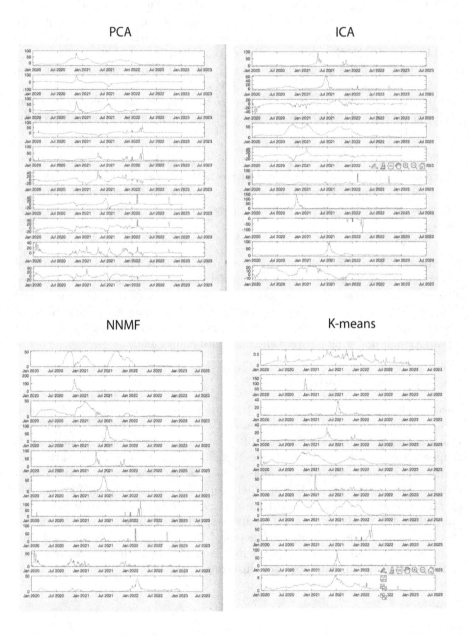

Fig. 1. The latent representatives of COVID-19 mortality time series uncovered by PCA, ICA, NNMF and K-Means.

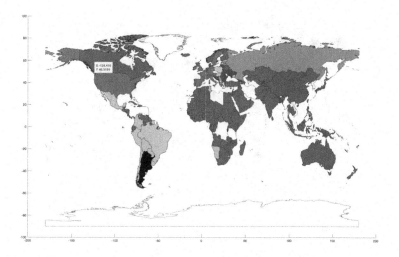

Fig. 2. Clustering of countries achieved by K-means into 10 clusters

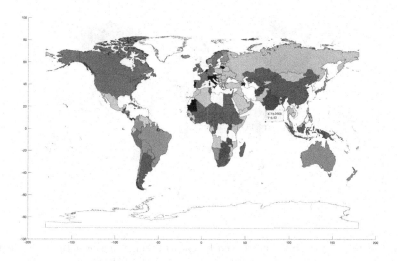

Fig. 3. Clustering of countries achieved by spectral clustering over the coefficients of PCA transformation considering 10 first eigenvectors and 10 clusters.

K-means clustering from the data downloaded from OWID site. The number of latent components was first selected in the PCA approach accounting fo 90% of the total variance. Moreover, the ratio of the number of latent components to the sample greater than 1:20 seem to be conducting to overfitting. Then, the same number was applied to the other approaches for comparison.

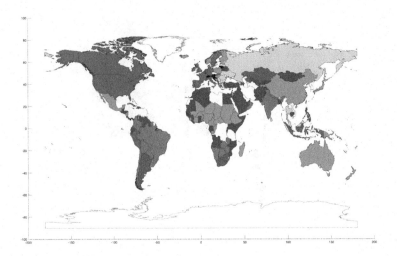

Fig. 4. Clustering of countries achieved by spectral clustering over the coefficients of ICA transformation considering 10 components and 10 clusters.

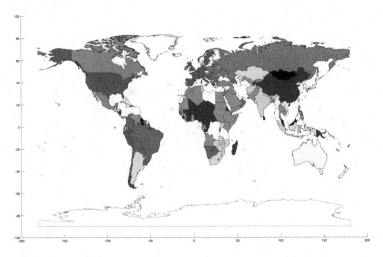

Fig. 5. Clustering of countries achieved by spectral clustering over the coefficients of NNMF transformation considering 10 components and 10 clusters.

Figures 2, 3, 4, and 5 provide the graphical representation of the country clusters found by K-means, and the spectral clustering over the PCA, ICA, and NNMF respectively. The color coding of the clusters is not preserved between figures, therefore only qualitative appreciations can be extracted from the visualizations.

4   Discussion

Regarding the templates of time series that are shown in Fig. 1, only the NNMF patterns give the impression of realistic time series showing features, like the strong peak in spring 2020 that was characteristic of some countries, that can be found in the actual COVID-19 mortality time series. The K-means representatives are, by definition, averages of the mortality patterns of countries in the cluster, therefore representative features are blurred by this averaging process. Regarding PCA and ICA, the latent mortality templates minimize some cost function like the reconstruction error or the statistical independence of latent templates, thus their likelihood as actual templates is not good. For instances, some templates include negative values that are impossible (with the exception of some lousy reporting countries, like Spain). These observations may have some relevance when commenting on the clustering results.

A salient observation is that some western Europe countries (Spain, France, Belgium, Germany, United Kingdom) appear in the same cluster with USA in all approaches, suggesting a strong underlying similarity in pandemic management, and mortality results. Portugal and Italy join this cluster of countries in the K-means and ICA approaches. It is almost self-evident that these countries did apply very similar policies and that their demographics are similar. For instance, they have a very aged population. Older people were the most at risk by this pathogen.

The K-means clustering in Fig. 2 is heavily influenced by the magnitude of the data samples. This may explain a large cluster (red color) of countries whose main commonality is that the impact of the pandemic was low relative to population size. Another significant cluster is the USA plus the western Europe countries, Portugal included, which suffered an extraordinary death toll. Another cluster of importance includes Mexico and most areas of South America, with the notable exclusion of Argentina. Argentina and South Africa are clustered in the remaining approaches, maybe due to geographical similarities.

The PCA based clustering in Fig. 3 seems to be influenced by the latitude of the countries, so Canada is included in the USA cluster, which also surprisingly includes Peru. However, Australia and New Zealand cluster with Japan, Norway, Finland, and Iceland. There are big clusters of central Africa countries and China, South America countries, and Russia with its neighbors. Notably, Portugal, Italy, Netherlands, Switzerland, Austria and some Balcan states form another cluster. On the other hand, neighboring India and Pakistan do not belong to the same cluster. Pakistan join some muslim countries, though it is rather unclear the role of religion in the pandemic response.

The ICA based clustering in Fig. 4 is quite similar to the PCA based, if we account for some changes in color assigned to the clusters. Here Portugal, Italy and Netherlands join the USA cluster. The interesting particularity of Portugal is that its response appears out of sync with other European countries, notably with its neighbor Spain in the spring of 2020.

Finally, the NNMF clustering in Fig. 5 confirms the USA plus western Europe cluster with the exclusion of Portugal, Ireland, Netherlands and Switzerland, whose patterns are out of sync at some periods of the pandemic, and the inclusion of Peru. On the other hand, Canada and Mexico, which are neighbors of USA form another cluster with Portugal, Ireland, Switzerland, Austria, Netherlands, Israel and Turkey. Other clusters also confirmed with some changes which can be due to the specifics of the NNMF transformation and the aspect of its representatives.

5 Conclusions

We have carried out a clustering of COVID-19 mortality time series per country that finds well defined clusters showing geographical localization as well as some intra-cluster common patterns of response to the pandemic. It is apparent that such well defined differences in pandemic mortality results can not be attributed to the pathogen, which has been declared to be uniformly identified across the globe, thus they must be attributed to pandemic management policies and other conditions. Overall, our results pose more questions than answers are provided. Future works may carry out a more extensive clustering analysis to assess whether the reported clusters are due to computational chance. Also, detailed causal analysis relative to other variables can be carried out in order to find the most dominant pandemic management features that could be related to the diversity of pandemic mortality results.

References

1. Jolliffe, I.T.: Principal Component Analysis, Springer, 2nd Edition (2002)
2. Comon, P.: Independent component analysis, a new concept? Signal Process. **36**(3), 287–314 (1994)
3. Lee, D.D., Seung, H.S.: Algorithms for non-negative matrix factorization. In: Advances in Neural Information Processing Systems 13 (NIPS 2000) (2000)
4. MacQueen, J.B.: A method of classifying plants based on relative growth rate. In: Proceedings of the Fifth Berkeley Symposium on Mathematical Statistics and Probability, Vol. 1 (1967)
5. Gallo Marin, B., et al.: Predictors of Covid-19 severity: a literature review. Rev. Med. Virol. **31**(1), 1–10 (Jan 2021)
6. Iranzo, V., Pérez-González, S.: Epidemiological models and Covid-19: a comparative view. Hist. Philos. Life Sci. **43**(3), 104 (2021)
7. Abbasimehr, H., Paki, R.: Prediction of Covid-19 confirmed cases combining deep learning methods and Bayesian optimization. Chaos, Solitons Fractals **142**, 110511 (2021)
8. Collaborators COVID-19 Excess Mortality. Estimating excess mortality due to the Covid-19 pandemic: a systematic analysis of Covid-19-related mortality, 2020–21. Lancet **399**(10334), 1513–1536 (Apr 2022)
9. Goldstein, E.: Mortality associated with omicron and influenza infections in France before and during the Covid-19 pandemic. Epidemiol. Infect. **151**, e148 (2023)
10. Van Der Maaten, L., Hinton, G.: Visualizing data using t-SNE. J. Mach. Learn. Res. **9**, 2579–2625 (2008)

11. Ng, A.Y., Jordan, M.I., Weiss, Y.: On spectral clustering: analysis and an algorithm. In: Advances in Neural Information Processing Systems (NIPS) (2002)
12. Gorriz, J.M., et al.: Computational approaches to explainable artificial intelligence: advances in theory, applications and trends. Inform. Fusion **100**, 101945 (2023)

Matrix Representation of Virus Machines

Antonio Ramírez-de-Arellano[1,2(✉)] [iD], Francis George C. Cabarle[1,2,3] [iD],
David Orellana-Martín[1,2] [iD], Mario J. Pérez-Jiménez[1,2] [iD],
and Henry N. Adorna[3] [iD]

[1] Research Group on Natural Computing, Department of Computer Science
and Artificial Intelligence, Universidad de Sevilla, Avda. Reina Mercedes s/n,
41012 Seville, Spain
{aramirezdearellano,fcabarle,dorellana,marper}@us.es
[2] SCORE Lab, I3US, Universidad de Sevilla, 41012 Seville, Spain
[3] Department of Computer Science, University of the Philippines Diliman,
1101 Quezon City, Philippines
{fccabarle,hnadorna}@up.edu.ph

Abstract. Virus machines are unconventional and bio-inspired models of computation based on the transmission of viruses among hosts. Virus machines are known to be computationally complete (they are algorithms), able to solve computationally hard problems. In this work we present a novel matrix representation for virus machines. Discrete structures such as vectors and matrices are useful in many technical domains, both in theory and practice. The hosts, number of viruses, and the instructions to control virus transmission are represented as vectors and matrices. In this way the computations of virus machines can be described by linear algebra operations. We also use our matrix representation to show invariants, helpful in formal verifications, of such machines.

Keywords: Virus machine · Matrix representation · Natural computing

1 Introduction

Nowadays, overtaking conventional computers is one of the main goals of computer science, not only by hardware improvements, but also by theoretical aspects. The field of *Unconventional Computing* constructs computing paradigms different from the conventional Turing Machines or machines with the well-known Von Neumann architecture, providing novel perspectives with respect to previous points of view in computer science. Within this field, *Natural Computing* takes inspiration from what occurs in nature to design these novel computing paradigms [16].

Viruses [18] have shocked humanity on numerous occasions. Some pandemics such as influenza, smallpox, or more recently COVID19 have shown us what this simple but powerful biological structure can do.

© The Author(s), under exclusive license to Springer Nature Switzerland AG 2024
J. M. Ferrández Vicente et al. (Eds.): IWINAC 2024, LNCS 14675, pp. 420–429, 2024.
https://doi.org/10.1007/978-3-031-61137-7_39

In 2015, the authors of [9] presented a new computing paradigm called *Virus Machines* with takes inspiration from the biological viruses to construct non-deterministic computing models. Very briefly, virus machines have a network of *instructions* that control how viruses are *transmitted* in a separate network of virus *hosts*. Since its relaunch at the previous IWINAC Conference in [5], where the authors presented some arithmetic calculations with these devices, several related works have been presented. In [6], the authors defined two virus machines that compute pairing functions, which result crucial in pairing-based cryptography, generating and recognizing modes of virus machines were formally defined in [15], opening a new field in computational complexity theory through these devices. Recently, virus machines were used to attack cryptosystems in [14].

In this work we present a matrix representation of virus machines. Due to this representation, the reasoning with virus machines can be done with operations in linear algebra. Representation with discrete structures such as matrices and vectors have proven useful in various domains of science to help solve theoretical and real-world problems. Another unonventional and bio-inspired model with an extensive work on their matrix representations are spiking neural P systems [2,19], with their further semantics and variants [4,8,12]. Such representations are helpful in the automatic design, or simulations of such systems, for instance in massively parallel processors [1,4,11], their formal verification [10].

The idea for the matrix representation is to represent the hosts, instructions, number of viruses and other elements of a virus machine using vectors and matrices. At any instant t the state or *configuration* of the machine is given by a *configuration vector* describing the number of viruses in each host. An *instruction vector* describes which instructions to activate or not. A *virus transmission matrix* describes the effect of applying an instruction to the hosts in the machine. Given these discrete structures and others provided later, the evolution or *computation* of a virus machine is described by linear algebra operations on such structures. Using the matrix representation, an interesting property of the machine known as an *invariant* is represented. Invariants can help, among other things, with the formal verification of solutions.

The present work is organized as follows. In Sect. 2 we briefly provide the basic definitions of virus machines, including an example. Section 3 provides our results: the vectors, matrices, and equations to represent virus machines, their computations, and invariants. Lastly, Sect. 4 provides conclusions and directions for investigations.

2   Virus Machines

In [9], Virus Machines were introduced as a universal model of computation, in the sense that they can calculate every set computable by a Turing machine. While the formal definition can be followed in the founding work, we remark on the syntax here, while the semantics will be explained with an explicit example.

First, let us formally define the **syntax** of virus machines.

Definition 1. *Let a virus machine Π of degree (p,q) with $p,q \geq 0$ defined as:*

$$\Pi = (\Gamma, H, I, D_H, D_H, G_C, n_1, \ldots, n_p, i_1, h_{out})$$

where:

- $\Gamma = \{v\}$ *is the singleton alphabet.*
- $H = \{h_1, \ldots, h_p\}$ *is the ordered set of hosts, h_{out} can be either in H or not (for this work, we will suppose always $h_{out} \notin H$, $I = \{i_1, \ldots, i_q\}$ the ordered set of instructions.*
- $D_H = (H \cup \{h_{out}\}, E_H, w_H)$ *is the weighted and directed (WD) host graph, where the edges are called channels and $w_H : H \times H \cup \{h_{out}\} \to \mathbb{N}$.*
- $D_I = (I, E_I, w_I)$ *is the WD instruction graph and $w_I : I \times I \to \{1, 2\}$.*
- $G_C = (E_H \cup I, E_I)$ *is a unweighted bipartite graph called channel-instruction graph, where the partition associated is $\{E_H \cup I\}$.*
- $n_1, \ldots, n_p \in \mathbb{N}$ *are the initial number of viruses in each host $h_1, \ldots, h_p$, respectively.*

2.1 Explicit Example

Following Definition 1, informally a VM Π is a heterogeneous graph: a graph D_H of nodes known as *hosts* and connected by directed and weighted edges known as *channels*; a graph D_I of nodes known as *instructions* and connected by directed and weighted edges; an unweighted and undirected graph G_C connecting at most one host to exactly one channel. For easy reference (see Fig. 1): we represent hosts, instructions, the number of viruses as rounded rectangles, ovals, and natural numbers, respectively; channels between hosts and links between instructions are weighted arcs, while links between instructions and channels are broken lines.

Here, we describe in an informal way how Π from Fig. 1 *computes* (specifically, *generates*) the set of natural numbers $\mathbb{N}$. By convention, the computation starts by activating the instruction i_1 at step 1 (or instant 1). The *instantaneous description* of Π at step 0 is $ID_0 = (1, 0, i_1, 0)$, which means that hosts h_1 and h_2, have 1 and 0 viruses, respectively, instruction i_1 is first activated and the environment does not contain viruses. Note that i_1 has an edge in the channel (h_1, h_2) between hosts h_1 and h_2: Since h_1 has one virus, activating i_1 means opening the channel (h_1, h_2) so that one virus is removed from h_1 and two viruses are sent to h_2 since the weight of (h_1, h_2) is 2. We note that all channels are closed unless an activated instruction opens it.

In Step 1, only instruction i_2 is activated since i_1 has exactly one arc left. Activating i_2 means opening channel (h_2, h_1). The instantaneous description ID_1 at step 2 is $(0, 2, i_2, 0)$. Opening (h_2, h_1) means removing one virus from h_2 and sending one virus back to h_1. Now i_2 has a *nondeterministic choice* due to two unweighted arcs from itself: to activate i_1 or i_3.

First let us consider if i_2 is activated at step 2 so we have $ID_2 = (1, 1, i_2, 0)$. The reader can check that, following the above description from previous steps,

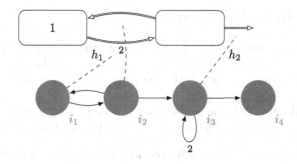

Fig. 1. A virus machine Π of degree $(2,4)$ generating the natural number set.

at step 3 we have $ID_3 = (0, 3, i_2, 0)$. At step 3, a similar nondeterministic choice to step 1 is made by i_2. Next we consider if i_3 is activated instead of i_1.

At step 4, we have $ID_4 = (1, 2, i_3, 0)$. A self-arc of i_3 has weight 2 which means this arc has *higher priority* than the unweighted arc (i_3, i_4). In this way for step 4 and step 5, we keep activating i_3. The result of these steps of activation is h_2 releasing 2 viruses to the environment, that is, at step 5 we have $ID_5 = (0, 0, i_3, 2)$. Hence in this nondeterministic branch of the computation we say the *output* is 2. The reader can check, in order to generate other elements of the set $\mathbb{N}$, to keep activating i_1 instead of i_3 after i_2. We take the *union* of all possible nondeterministic numbers computed in this way to generate the set $\mathbb{N}$.

Remark 1. It is important to note that the out-degree of each instruction is at most 2. Without loss of generality, those instructions from which highest weight path is unique and the out-degree is 2, they are represented by a weight 2, in any other circumstance, the weight of the arcs is 1.

2.2 Brief Definitions

In this subsection, there are some brief additional definitions.

Definition 2. *A VM with input of degree (p, q, r), with $p, q \geq 1$, and $1 \leq r \leq p$ is a tuple: $\Pi = (\Gamma, H, H_r, I_C, I_H, D_H, D_C, G_C, n_1, \ldots, n_p, i_1, h_{out})$, such that: $H_r \subseteq H$ is an ordered set of input hosts; Π without H_r is a VM of degree (p, q).*

The semantics associated is, for a given VM Π of degree (p, q, r), for each input $(\alpha_1, \ldots, \alpha_r) \in \mathbb{N}$, it is written as $\Pi + (\alpha_1, \ldots, \alpha_r)$, and the initial configuration is the same as a VM of degree (p, q), but adding to the input hosts the corresponding α_j. For more information, we refer to [15].

Definition 3. *It is said that a VM with input Π of degree (p, q, r) computes a partial function $f : \mathbb{N}^r - \rightarrow \mathbb{N}$, if for each tuple $x = (\alpha_1, \ldots, \alpha_r) \in \mathbb{N}$:*

- *if $f(x) = y$, then all the computations of $\Pi + x$ halt and return y;*
- *if $f(x)$ is not defined, then all the computations of $\Pi + x$ are non-halting.*

3 Matrix Representation

Regarding the semantics of a VM, for any step or instant $t \geq 0$, the *instantaneous description* of Π is $ID_t = (a_{1,t}, a_{2,t}, \ldots, a_{p,t}, u_t, a_{0,t})$, where each $a_{i,t}$ is the number of viruses in the host h_i, the instruction u_t is next activated, and the environment contains $a_{0,t}$ viruses.

For the following definitions, consider a VM Π of degree (p, q), with the notation fixed above and in Definition 1, at any instant t of its computation.

Definition 4. *We define the* **configuration vector** *as the vector*

$$\overrightarrow{c}_t = \langle a_{1,t}, a_{2,t}, \ldots, a_{0,t} \rangle,$$

and the **instruction vector** *as the vector*

$$\overrightarrow{i}_t = \langle r_{1,t}, r_{2,t}, \ldots, r_{q,t} \rangle,$$

where $r_{m,t} = 1$ *if* $u_t = i_m \in I$, *otherwise* $r_{m,t} = 0$, *for* $1 \leq m \leq p$. *That is, if the activated instruction is* $i_j \in I$, *then the component* $r_{j,t}$ *is the only non-zero element of* $\overrightarrow{i}_t$.

In particular, vector $\overrightarrow{c}_0 = \langle n_1, n_2, \ldots, n_p \; 0 \rangle$, *and* $\overrightarrow{i}_0 = \langle 1, 0, \ldots, 0 \rangle$, *is the* **initial configuration vector** *and* **initial instruction vector**, *respectively.*

Definition 5. *A* **virus transmission matrix** *of* Π *is defined as*

$$M_\Pi = [m_{k,j}]_{q \times p+1},$$

where

$$m_{k,j} = \begin{cases} -1, & \text{if instruction } i_k \text{ activates to remove a virus from host } h_j, \\ w, & \text{if } h_j \text{ (or the environment) receives } w \text{ viruses when } i_k \text{ activates,} \\ 0, & \text{otherwise.} \end{cases}$$

As an example for Definition 4 and Definition 5, we apply them to the deterministic Π_{sub} in Fig. 2. Π_{sub} is a VM with input of degree $(3, 4, 2)$, computing the subtraction function $f(a, b) = a \overset{\bullet}{-} b$, that is, $a - b$ if $a \geq b$ and 0 otherwise. Following the example in Sect. 2.1, the operation of Π_{sub} can be easily checked, so we omit its details and refer instead to [5]. We have $\overrightarrow{c}_0 = \langle a, b, 0, 0 \rangle$ and $\overrightarrow{i}_0 = \langle 1, 0, 0, 0 \rangle$, that is, hosts h_1 and h_2 have a and b viruses each, respectively, h_3 and the environment are empty, and instruction i_1 is first activated. The virus transmission matrix $M_{\Pi_{sub}}$ of Π_{sub} is given by Eq. 1.

$$M_{\Pi_{sub}} = \begin{pmatrix} 0 & -1 & 1 & 0 \\ -1 & 0 & 1 & 0 \\ -1 & 0 & 0 & 1 \\ 0 & 0 & 0 & 0 \end{pmatrix} \tag{1}$$

Recall that $M_{\Pi_{sub}}$ relates the effects of the instructions (the rows) to the hosts (the columns). For instance, row 1 of $M_{\Pi_{sub}}$ shows on the one hand that

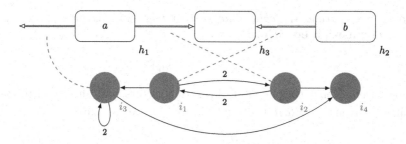

Fig. 2. The VM Π_{sub}.

i_1 has no effect (hence, the 0 elements) on column 1 (for h_1) and column 4 (for the environment). On the other hand, i_1 removes 1 and adds 1 virus each to h_2 and h_3, respectively. Similarly, row 2 shows that i_2 removes and adds 1 virus to h_1 and h_3, respectively, but has no effect on h_2 and the environment. Next, we provide definitions to continue representing the computations of a VM.

Definition 6. *The **instruction control matrices** are matrices defined as*

$$M_{I,1} = [a_{k,j}]_{q,q}, \ \ and \ M_{I,2} = [b_{k,j}]_{q,q},$$

where

$$a_{k,j} = \begin{cases} 1, & if \ (i_k, i_j) \in E_I \ and \ w_I((i_k, i_j)) = 1, \\ 0, & otherwise. \end{cases}$$

$$b_{k,j} = \begin{cases} 1, & if \ (i_k, i_j) \in E_I \ and \ w_I((i_k, i_j)) = 2, \\ 0, & otherwise. \end{cases}$$

To obtain the **configuration transition equation** and the **instruction transition equation,** we need to compute some partial results. Depending on the existence or not of a virus in the origin host, the next configuration is changed or not, respectively.

Define the following *partial configuration* vectors

$$\overrightarrow{c}_t' = u_t \cdot M_\Pi, \ \overrightarrow{c}_t'' = \overrightarrow{c}_t + \overrightarrow{c}_t', \ \overrightarrow{c}_t''' = \overrightarrow{c}_t'' I_{p+1 \times p+2} \tag{2}$$

where $I_{p+1 \times p+2}$ is the identity matrix with $p+1$ rows and $p+2$ columns, since there is one column more than rows, the last column is filled with zeros. The idea behind each vector is: $\overrightarrow{c}_t'$ is the vector to be subtracted from $\overrightarrow{c}_t$ if there was a virus in the origin host. $\overrightarrow{c}_t''$ is the result of the subtraction between $\overrightarrow{c}_t$ and $\overrightarrow{c}_t'$. If there exists a -1, then it means that there were no viruses present in the origin host. We extend the vector $\overrightarrow{c}_t''$ with one more zero in the vector $\overrightarrow{c}_t'''$ for the following technical detail: Let $m_t = min(\overrightarrow{c}_t''')$ the **control coefficient at instant t**, then m_t is 0 if there was at least one virus in the origin host and -1 otherwise. To obtain the next configuration vector we have the following result.

Theorem 1. *Let Π be a VM with q instructions and p hosts, M_Π is the virus transmission matrix, $\overrightarrow{c}_t$ and $\overrightarrow{i}_t$ are the configuration and instruction vectors at* *instant t, respectively. We obtain the next configuration vector $\overrightarrow{c}_{t+1}$ using the following* **transition equation***:*

$$\overrightarrow{c}_{t+1} = \overrightarrow{c}_t + (1 + m_t)\overrightarrow{c}'_t.$$

We apply Definition 6, the partial configuration vectors, and Theorem 1 to $M_{\Pi_{sub}}$ as follows. Given $\overrightarrow{c}_0 = \langle a, b, 0, 0\rangle$ and $\overrightarrow{i}_0 = \langle 1, 0, 0, 0\rangle$ we have

$$\overrightarrow{c}'_0 = \overrightarrow{i}_0 \cdot M_{\Pi_{sub}} = \langle 0, -1, 1, 0\rangle, \overrightarrow{c}''_0 = \overrightarrow{c}_0 + \overrightarrow{c}'_0 = \langle a, (b-1), 1, 0\rangle,$$

with $\overrightarrow{c}'''_0 = \overrightarrow{c}''_0 \cdot I_{4\times 5} = \langle a, (b-1), 1, 0, 0\rangle$. We also have $m_0 = min(a, (b-1), 1, 0, 0)$ so that if $b > 0$ we have $m_0 = 0$. The *next configuration* of $M_{\Pi_{sub}}$ is

$$\overrightarrow{c}_1 = \overrightarrow{c}_0 = (1 + m_0) \cdot \overrightarrow{c}'_0 = \langle a, b, 0, 0\rangle + \overrightarrow{c}'_0 = \langle a, (b-1), 1, 0\rangle.$$

Next, we provide definitions to obtain the equation for the next instruction, taking into account the value of m_t defined above.
Let the *partial instruction* vectors and *control sum* be

$$\overrightarrow{i}_{t,1} = \overrightarrow{i}_t \cdot M_{I,1}, \overrightarrow{i}_{t,2} = \overrightarrow{i}_t \cdot M_{I,2}, \overrightarrow{i}'_t = \overrightarrow{i}_{t,1} + 2\overrightarrow{i}_{t,2}, s_t = i'_t \cdot 1_{q\times 1} \quad (3)$$

s_t is the **control sum at instant** t, being $1_{q\times 1}$ a column vector with q ones. s_t is a scalar number that has 4 possible values:

$$s_t = \begin{cases} 0, & \text{if the current instruction has no next instructions,} \\ 1, & \text{if the current instruction has one next instruction,} \\ 2, & \text{if the current instruction has two next instructions,} \\ & \quad \text{both of them with an arc of weight 1,} \\ 3, & \text{if the current instruction has two next instructions, one with an arc} \\ & \quad \text{of weight 1 and one with an arc of weight 2,} \end{cases}$$

$$(4)$$

If we *restrict the system to be deterministic* (that is, $s_t \neq 2$), then we can define the next instruction i_{t+1} as follows:

$$\overrightarrow{i}_{t+1} = \frac{(1-s_t)(2-s_t)(3-s_t)}{6}\overrightarrow{i}_{t,1} + \frac{(-s_t)(2-s_t)(3-s_t)}{-2}\overrightarrow{i}_{t,1} +$$
$$+ \frac{(-s_t)(1-s_t)(2-s_t)}{-6}(m_t \cdot \overrightarrow{i}_{t,1} + (1+m_t)\overrightarrow{i}_{t,2}) \quad (5)$$

Simplifying the terms for $\overrightarrow{i}_{t+1}$ we have the following result to obtain the next activated instruction.

Theorem 2. *Let Π be a VM of degree (p, q), M_Π the virus transmission matrix, $M_{I,1}$ and $M_{I,2}$, the instructions control matrices, $\overrightarrow{c}_t$ and $\overrightarrow{i}_t$ are the configuration and instruction vectors at instant t, respectively. We obtain the next configuration vector $\overrightarrow{i}_{t+1}$ using the following* **instruction control equation***:*

$$\overrightarrow{i}_{t+1} = \frac{2 - s_t}{6}(((m_t 2)s_t^2 + (5 - m_t)s_t + 3)\overrightarrow{i}_{t,1} + s_t(1 - s_t)(1 + m_t)\overrightarrow{i}_{t,2}), \quad (6)$$

where $\overrightarrow{i}_{t,j} = M_{I,j}\overrightarrow{i}_t$, for $j \in \{1,2\}$, m_t and s_t are the control coefficient and the control sum at instant t, respectively.

Remark 2. Theorem 2 is true if and only if Π is deterministic. An idea to make Eq. 5 well defined for all values of s_t is to add a term $0_{1 \times q}$.

Applying the partial instruction vectors, s_t, and Theorem 2 to $M_{\Pi_{sub}}$ we have $s_0 = 3$ from Eq. 4 since the weights of the arcs of i_1 has a sum of 3. Since $s_0 = 3$ this means that only the rightmost term of Eq. 5 is nonzero and we have $\overrightarrow{i}_1 = 1 \cdot \overrightarrow{i}_{0,2} = \langle 0, 1, 0, 0\rangle$. Thus, the *next instruction* to be activated is i_2.

After showing how an explicit transition works, let us present another interesting scope; in [5] the authors formally verified this device by searching invariant formulas which highlight relevant loops of the device. For this example, the following invariant holds,

$$\phi(k) \equiv ID_k = \left(a - \left\lfloor\frac{k}{2}\right\rfloor, b - \left\lceil\frac{k}{2}\right\rceil, k, i_{1+mod(k,2)}, 0\right), 0 \le k \le min\{2(a+1)-1, 2b)\}.$$

The idea that represents this invariant is that every two steps, we decrease by one the values a and b until one of them is zero. This invariant can also be represented by the configuration vectors in Definition 4 as:

$$\overrightarrow{c}_k = \left\langle a - \left\lfloor\frac{k}{2}\right\rfloor, b - \left\lceil\frac{k}{2}\right\rceil, k, i_{1+mod(k,2)}, 0\right\rangle, \overrightarrow{i}_k = \langle mod(k,2), mod(k+1,2), 0, 0\rangle,$$

for $0 \le k \le min\{2(a+1) - 1, 2b)\}$. So we could now rewrite the invariants in $\phi(k) = (\overrightarrow{c}_k, \overrightarrow{i}_k)$. Let us suppose that $a \ge b$, then the invariant is true for $\phi(2b)$. Thus in the instantaneous description ID_{2b}, instruction i_3 will be the next instruction. Then, from that point on, the following invariant holds:

$$\phi'(k) \equiv ID_{2b+k} = (a - b - k, 0, 2b, i_3, k), \text{ for } 0 \le k \le a - b,$$

whose configuration vectors are $\overrightarrow{c}_{2b+k2} = \langle a - b - k, 0, 2b, k\rangle$, and $\overrightarrow{i}_{2b+k} = \langle 0, 0, 1, 0\rangle$, rewriting the invariant as $\phi'(k) = (\overrightarrow{c}_{2b+k2}, \overrightarrow{i}_{2b+k})$.

After the $a - b$ steps, the $a - b$ viruses are sent to the environment. Since no more viruses are available in the host h_1, the next instruction is i_4, which leads to a halting instantaneous description $ID_{2b+a-b+2}$ represented as vectors $\overrightarrow{c}_{2b+a-b+2} = \langle 0, 0, 2b, a - b\rangle$, and $\overrightarrow{i}_{2b+a-b+2} = \langle 0, 0, 0, 0\rangle$.

4 Conclusion

In this work, a novel matrix representation of any deterministic VM is presented and formally defined. In addition, an explicit example is shown to clarify the computations and invariants using the representation. The matrix representation gives steps towards further formal verifications [2,10], the automatic design or implementations of VMs on massively parallel processors such as GPUs [8,11]. Such implementations give steps towards several practical applications of VMs.

Some shortcomings from the present work include: VMs are by definition non-deterministic, only determinism is covered in the present work. Some ideas to implement non-determinism can include the use of stochastic features for VMs, or the use of breadth-first-like trees [1,8], with further ideas and challenges similar to those mentioned in [3,17]. The sequential behaviour of VMs seems to be another limitation in time cost. Variants and extensions should be studied to enhance the time efficiency of the basic VM. Thus, extensions of our matrix representation must be properly defined. We also note that vectors and matrices in this work are *sparse*, that is, there are more zero than nonzero elements. In this way the representation and algorithms must be revised for improved implementations [4]. VMs can be further explored through their matrix representations, in relation to models such as SN P systems, Petri nets, and their variants [7,13].

Acknowledgements. The research described in this work was supported by the Zhejiang Lab BioBit Program (Grant No. 2022BCF05). F.G.C. Cabarle is supported by *QUAL21 008 USE* project (PAIDI 2020 and FEDER 2014–2020 funds).

References

1. Aboy, B.C.D., et al.: Optimizations in CuSNP Simulator for spiking neural P systems on CUDA GPUs. In: 2019 International Conference on High Performance Computing and Simulation (HPCS), pp. 535–542. IEEE (2019)
2. Adorna, H.N.: Matrix representations of spiking neural P systems: Revisited, pp. 227–247. arXiv preprint arXiv:2211.15156 (2022)
3. Martínez-del Amor, M.Á.: A vision for the next generation of P system simulators. Bull. Int. Membr. Comput. Soc. **12**, 83–88 (2021)
4. Martínez-del Amor, M.Á., Orellana-Martín, D., Pérez-Hurtado, I., Cabarle, F.G.C., Adorna, H.N.: Simulation of spiking neural P systems with sparse matrix-vector operations. Processes **9**(4), 690 (2021)
5. Ramírez-de Arellano, A., Orellana-Martín, D., Pérez-Jiménez, M.J.: Basic arithmetic calculations through virus-based machines. In: Ferrández Vicente, J.M., Álvarez-Sánchez, J.R., de la Paz López, F., Adeli, H. (eds.) Bio-inspired Systems and Applications: from Robotics to Ambient Intelligence, pp. 403–412. Springer International Publishing, Cham (2022)
6. Ramírez-de Arellano, A., Orellana-Martín, D., Pérez-Jiménez, M.J.: Using virus machines to compute pairing functions. Int. J. Neural Syst. **33**(05), 2350023 (2023). https://doi.org/10.1142/s0129065723500235
7. Cabarle, F.G.C., Adorna, H.N.: On Structures and Behaviors of Spiking Neural P Systems and Petri Nets. In: Csuhaj-Varjú, E., Gheorghe, M., Rozenberg, G., Salomaa, A., Vaszil, G. (eds.) CMC 2012. LNCS, vol. 7762, pp. 145–160. Springer, Heidelberg (2013). https://doi.org/10.1007/978-3-642-36751-9_11
8. Carandang, J.P., Cabarle, F.G.C., Adorna, H.N., Hernandez, N.H.S., Martínez-del Amor, M.Á.: Handling non-determinism in spiking neural P systems: Algorithms Simul. Fundam. Inf. **164**(2-3), 139–155 (2019)
9. Chen, X., Pérez-Jiménez, M.J., Valencia-Cabrera, L., Wang, B., Zeng, X.: Computing with viruses. Theoret. Comput. Sci. **623**, 146–159 (2016). https://doi.org/10.1016/j.tcs.2015.12.006

10. Gheorghe, M., Lefticaru, R., Konur, S., Niculescu, I.M., Adorna, H.N.: Spiking neural P systems: matrix representation and formal verification. J. Membr. Comput. **3**(2), 133–148 (2021)
11. Gungon, R.V., et al.: GPU implementation of evolving spiking neural P systems. Neurocomputing **503**, 140–161 (2022)
12. Jimenez, Z.B., Cabarle, F.G.C., de la Cruz, R.T.A., Buño, K.C., Adorna, H.N., Hernandez, N.H.S., Zeng, X.: Matrix representation and simulation algorithm of spiking neural P systems with structural plasticity. J. Membr. Comput. **1**, 145–160 (2019)
13. Leporati, A., Mauri, G., Zandron, C.: Spiking neural P systems: main ideas and results. Nat. Comput. **21**(4), 629–649 (2022)
14. Pérez-Jiménez, M.J., Ramírez-de-Arellano, A., Orellana-Martín, D.: Attacking cryptosystems by means of virus machines. Sci. Rep.**13**(1), 21831 (2023). https://doi.org/10.1038/s41598-023-49297-6
15. Ramírez-de-Arellano, A., Orellana-Martín, D., Pérez-Jiménez, M.J.: Generating, computing and recognizing with virus machines. Theoret. Comput. Sci. **972**, 114077 (2023). https://doi.org/10.1016/j.tcs.2023.114077
16. Rozenberg, G., Bäck, T., Kok, J.N.: Handbook of natural computing, vol. 4. Springer Berlin, Heidelberg, Heidelberg (2012). https://doi.org/10.1007/978-3-540-92910-9
17. Valencia-Cabrera, L., Pérez-Hurtado, I., Martínez-del Amor, M.Á.: Simulation challenges in membrane computing. J. Membr. Comput. **2**(4), 392–402 (2020)
18. Willey, J., Sherwood, L., Woolverton, C., Prescott, L.M.: Prescott's Principles of Microbiology. McGraw-Hill, Woolverton, Boston (2011)
19. Zeng, X., Adorna, H., Martínez-del-Amor, M., Pan, L., Pérez-Jiménez, M.J.: Matrix Representation of Spiking Neural P Systems. In: Gheorghe, M., Hinze, T., Păun, G., Rozenberg, G., Salomaa, A. (eds.) CMC 2010. LNCS, vol. 6501, pp. 377–391. Springer, Heidelberg (2010). https://doi.org/10.1007/978-3-642-18123-8_29

Networks of Splicing Processors with Various Topologies

Victor Mitrana[1,2]($\boxtimes$), Mihaela Păun[2,3], and José Angel Sanchez Martín[4]

[1] ETSISI, Polytechnic University of Madrid, Calle Alan Turing s/n, 28031 Madrid, Spain
victor.mitrana@upm.es
[2] National Institute of Research and Development for Biological Sciences, 296 Independentei Bd. District 6, 060031 Bucharest, Romania
mihaela.paun@incdsb.ro
[3] Faculty of Administration and Business, University of Bucharest, Bucharest, Romania
[4] ETSII, University Rey Juan Carlos, Madrid, Spain
joseangel.sanchez@urjc.es

Abstract. We consider networks whose nodes host splicing processors, that is processors that are able to simulate the DNA recombination by splicing. Several topologies for the underlying graph of these networks are investigated. More precisely, we show that each network of splicing processors with some underlying graph can be directly converted into an equivalent network having an underlying graph of a different topology. Several common topologies are considered: full-mesh, star, grid, and wheel (ring-star). We also investigate the time and size complexity of each of these simulations.

Keywords: DNA computing · Splicing · Splicing processor · Network of splicing processors · Underlying graph topology · Simulation

1 Introduction

DNA recombination is a laboratory technique that uses various enzymes to manipulate DNA sequences. The goal is to combine DNA molecules from various species or to generate genes having desired functions. The new DNA is often called recombinant DNA.

Roughly speaking, the technique consists in the following steps:

This study was supported by PNRR/2022/C9/MCID/I8 project 760096. This work was partially supported by Spanish Ministerio de Asuntos Económicos y Transformación Digital, Program UNICO under project B5GEMINI-AIUC (TSI-063000-2021-79). It was also performed through the Core Program within the National Research, Development and Innovation Plan 2022-2027, carried out with the support of MRID, project no. 23020101(SIA-PRO), contract no 7N/2022, and project no. 23020301(SAFE-MAPS), contract no 7N/2022.

J. M. Ferrández Vicente et al. (Eds.): IWINAC 2024, LNCS 14675, pp. 430–440, 2024.
https://doi.org/10.1007/978-3-031-61137-7_40

1. Cut the DNA at specific sites, by means of restriction enzymes, and separate the two resulting sequences with sticky ends.
2. A DNA sequence that matches with the sticky ends of a sequence obtained above is prepared and combined with that sequence.
3. Ligase enzymes are used to repair the hydrogen bonds between the nucleotides.

This procedure is illustrated in Fig. 1(a) [4], and has been formalized as an operation on strings in [5]. The general idea of the formal definition, as it was proposed in [14], may be explained as follows: a splicing rule is defined by a quadruple of strings written in the form of two pairs of strings. Each pair specifies the subsequences where each of the two strings is to be cut. As one can see, a formal splicing rule abstracts a restriction enzyme and the four strings indicate the sites where the enzyme cuts, see Fig. 1(b).

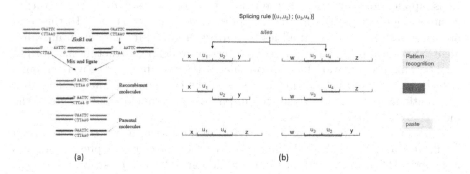

(a)   (b)

Fig. 1. (a) DNA recombination by splicing; (b) Formal operation of splicing.

This formal operation has been intensively investigated for more than three decades in a series of works: computational models based on splicing [3,7,13], problem solvers [8], various applications, software simulations, etc., see [6,15,16] for three surveys.

A highly parallel and distributed computational model, called network of splicing processors (NSP for short), was introduced in [10]. Informally, an NSP consists of a finite set of splicing processors which are placed in the node of an undirected graph. A splicing processor, that is an abstract concept, is defined as a sextuple with the following parameters: a finite set of splicing rules, as explained above, a finite set of axioms, that are strings, four sets of symbols that define two filters, the input and the output filter, by some syntactic random context conditions. We now informally describe a computation in a network of splicing processors on some input string. Two different types of computational steps are defined: splicing step and communication step. Each computation starts by a splicing step and then the two steps alternate with each other. In a splicing step, all processors are working in parallel, each one of them applying all the splicing rules it contains and can be applied to the strings present at that moment in the processor. It is worth noting an important assumption: a sufficient number of identical copies of every string that appears in the node are available for splicing, such that all the splicing rules that can be applied are actually applied to different copies. In a communication step, each processor is simultaneously a sender and a receiver: it sends throughout the network all its strings that can pass its output filter, and receives from all its neighbors all the strings sent out from their nodes, provided that they can pass its input filter. Obviously, as soon as a string arrives in a node, our assumption is again fulfilled. This is inspired by the common biological lab maneuver of DNA amplification. The condition for halting a computation is that the set of strings present in a predefined processor, called *Halt*, is nonempty. Several variants of NSP with underlying graphs of various topologies have been considered so far with different purposes: solving problems [11,12], simulations [2,9], arbitrary computations [1], etc. However, this wide variety of underlying graphs could lead to difficulties in possible implementations, applications, etc. This is the reason to have, if possible, networks with a common topology as: full mesh, star, grid, wheel (ring-star), etc. To this aim, an investigation of the possibilities to convert an arbitrary NSP into an equivalent NSP with an underlying graph of such a predefined structure has started in [17]. This investigation has not considered the possibility of conversion only, but also the computational time and size of the conversions. The present work is a continuation of the work started in [17] which completes the picture of the most common topology conversions.

The paper is organized as follows. In the next section, we give the formal definitions and notations following [17]. We then present the previous results accompanied by some hints of the constructions. By lack of space, we do not give all the details of our constructions.

2   Formal Preliminaries

The number of elements of a finite set X is denoted by $card(X)$. The set of all strings over an alphabet V is denoted by V^*, while $alpha(x)$, for $x \in V^*$, is the smallest subset of V such that $x \in (alph(x))^*$ holds.

We recall the formal definition of splicing, as illustrated in Fig. 1(b), following [14]. A *splicing rule* over an alphabet V is a quadruple of strings $[(u_1, u_2); (u_3, u_4)]$ such that $u_i \in V^*$, for $i = 1, 2, 3, 4$. For a rule $r = [(u_1, u_2); (u_3, u_4)]$, as above, and two strings α, β over V, we say that the strings γ, δ are produced by applying r to the pair (α, γ), if $\alpha = x_1 u_2 y, \beta = w u_3 u_4 z$ and $\gamma = x u_1 u_4 z, \delta = w u_3 u_2 y$ hold. This is denoted by $(\alpha \bowtie_r \beta) = \{\gamma\} \cup \{\delta\}$. Note that we have preferred to write $\{\gamma\} \cup \{\delta\}$ instead of $\{\gamma, \delta\}$ because γ and δ might be equal. For a set of strings X over V and a set of splicing rules R we define

$$\sigma_R(X) = \{\gamma \in V^* \mid \exists \alpha, \beta \in L, \exists r \in R \text{ such that } \gamma \in (\alpha \bowtie_r \beta)\}.$$

We define two boolean functions having as arguments strings over an alphabet V, and two disjoint subsets P, F of V, as follows:

$$\varphi^{(s)}(z; P, F) \equiv P \subseteq alph(z) \wedge F \cap alph(z) = \emptyset.$$
$$\varphi^{(w)}(z; P, F) \equiv alph(z) \cap P \neq \emptyset \wedge F \cap alph(z) = \emptyset.$$

The symbols of P are called *permitting symbols* while those of F are called *forbidding symbols*. Both functions require that z does not contain any forbidding symbol. The former function requires that z contains all permitting symbols, while the later function requires that z contains at least one permitting symbol. These functions are extended to a set of strings $X \subseteq V^*$ by

$$\varphi^{\beta}(X, P, F) = \{x \in L \mid \varphi^{\beta}(x; P, F)\}, \text{ with } \beta \in \{(s), (w)\}.$$

We now recall the definitions of splicing processors and networks of splicing processors following [17]. A *splicing processor* over an alphabet V is a 6-tuple (S, A, PI, FI, PO, FO), where:

♦ S is a finite set of splicing rules over V.

♦ A is a finite set of *auxiliary strings* over V. These auxiliary strings are to be used, together with the existing strings, in the splicing steps of the processors. Auxiliary strings are available at any splicing step.

♦ $PI, FI \subseteq V$ are the sets of permitting and forbidding symbols, respectively, which form the *input* filter of the processor.

♦ $PO, FO \subseteq V$ are the sets of permitting and forbidding symbols, respectively, which form the *output* filter of the processor.

The set of splicing processors over V is denoted by SP_V. A *network of splicing processors* is a 9-tuple $\Gamma = (V, U, \langle, \rangle, G, \mathcal{N}, \alpha, \underline{In}, \underline{Halt})$, where:

■ V and U are the input and network alphabet, respectively, $V \subseteq U$, and $\langle, \rangle \in U \setminus V$ are two special symbols.

■ $G = (X_G, E_G)$ is an undirected graph without loops with the set o nodes X_G and the set of edges E_G. Each edge is given in the for of a binary set. G is called the *underlying graph* of the network.

■ $\mathcal{N} : X_G \longrightarrow SP_U$ is a mapping, which associates with each node $x \in X_G$ the splicing processor $\mathcal{N}(x) = (S_x, A_x, PI_x, FI_x, PO_x, FO_x)$.

■ $\alpha : X_G \longrightarrow \{(s), (w)\}$ defines the type of the filters of a node.

■ $\underline{In}, \underline{Halt} \in X_G$ are the *input* and the *halting* node of Γ, respectively.

Given an NSP Γ as above, we define the size of Γ, denoted by $size(\Gamma)$, as the order of G. A *configuration* of an NSP Γ is a mapping $C : X_G \to 2^{U^*}$, which associates a set of strings with every node of the graph. As we shall see later, each string that appears in the set of strings associated with a node appears in a sufficiently large number of copies, such that a multiset of strings, each string having an arbitrary large multiplicity, is actually associated to a node by the mapping C. However, we shall simply consider here the support of these multisets. It is worth mentioning that the auxiliary strings are not included in these sets unless they were obtained during the computation. For an NSP Γ and a string $w \in V^*$, the initial configuration of Γ on w is defined by $C_0^{(w)}(\underline{In}) = \{\langle w \rangle\}$ and $C_0^{(w)}(x) = \emptyset$ for all other $x \in X_G$. We define a computation of an NSP Γ on the input string w as a sequence of configurations, starting with the initial one, where the configurations are alternatively changed by splicing steps and communication steps. A configuration C is changed by a splicing step resulting a configuration C', if for each node x, $C'(x)$ is obtained by applying all the splicing rules in the set S_x that can be applied to the strings in $C(x) \cup A_x$. Formally, we write this as $C \Rightarrow C'$ if

$$C'(x) = \sigma_{S_x}(C(x) \cup A_x), \text{ hold for all } x \in X_G.$$

A configuration C is changed by a communication step resulting a configuration C' by a communication step if the following actions take place simultaneously for all nodes of the network:

(i) all the strings that can pass the output filter of each node are sent out of that node;
(ii) all the strings that left their nodes enter all the nodes connected to the sender ones, provided that they can pass the input filter of the receiving nodes.

Note that, according to this definition, those strings that are sent out of a node and cannot pass the input filter of any node are lost.

Formally, we write $C' \models C$ iff for all $x \in X_G$

$$C'(x) = (C(x) - \varphi^{\alpha(x)}(C(x), PO_x, FO_x)) \cup$$
$$\bigcup_{\{x,y\} \in E_G} (\varphi^{\alpha(y)}(C(y), PO_y, FO_y) \cap \varphi^{\alpha(x)}(C(x), PI_x, FI_x))$$

holds. For an intuitive representation of a communication step in an NSP, Fig. 2 shows the flow between two nodes.

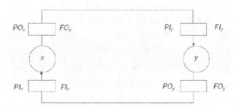

Fig. 2. Communication between two connected splicing processors.

For an NSP Γ, a computation on an input string w is defined as a sequence of configurations $C_0^{(w)}, C_1^{(w)}, C_2^{(w)}, ...$, where $C_0^{(w)}$ is the initial configuration of Γ on w, $C_{2i}^{(w)} \Rightarrow C_{2i+1}^{(w)}$ and $C_{2i+1}^{(w)} \models C_{2i+2}^{(w)}$, for all $i \geq 0$. A computation on an input string w *halts* if there exists $k \geq 1$ such that $C_k^{(w)}(\underline{Halt})$ is non-empty, or no further new configuration can be computed. Such a computation is called an *deciding computation*. As the halting node is used just for ending the computation, we shall consider that $S_{\underline{Halt}} = A_{\underline{Halt}} = \emptyset$. Furthermore, because as soon as a string enters $\underline{Halt}$, the computation halts and no string goes out, we may also consider that $PO_{\underline{Halt}} = FO_{\underline{Halt}} = \emptyset$.

Given an NSP Γ with the input alphabet V, we define the following computational complexity measure. The *time complexity* of the finite computation $C_0^{(x)}, C_1^{(x)}, C_2^{(x)}, \ldots C_m^{(x)}$ of Γ on $x \in V^*$ is denoted by $Time_\Gamma(x)$ and equals m. The time complexity of Γ is the partial function from $\mathbf{N}$ to $\mathbf{N}$,

$$Time_\Gamma(n) = \max\{Time_\Gamma(x) \mid x \in L(\Gamma), |x| = n\}.$$

3   Simulations Between Topologies

In what follows we say that an NSP is a full mesh, star, grid, and wheel NSP if its underlying graph is a complete, star, grid, and wheel graph, respectively. In this section we shall investigate the following problems:

P1. Given an arbitrary NSP, Γ, is it possible to construct algorithmically a full mesh, star, grid, and wheel NSP, Γ', such that w is decided by Γ if and only if w is decided by Γ'? If this is the case we say that Γ and Γ' are equivalent.

P2 If the answer to problem P1 is affirmative, then the following two problems are to be investigated:

P2.1. Which is the relation between $size(\Gamma)$ and $size(\Gamma')$?

P2.2. Which is the relation between $Time_\Gamma(n)$ and $Time_{\Gamma'}(n)$?

Theorem 1. [17] **Full mesh topology**

P1. *Given an arbitrary NSP, Γ, one can construct an equivalent full mesh NSP Γ' such that the followings hold:*

P2.1. $size(\Gamma') = size(\Gamma) + 2$.

P2.2. $Time_{\Gamma'}(n) \in \mathcal{O}(Time_\Gamma(n))$.

Sketch of the Proof

We consider the arbitrary NSP $\Gamma = (V, U, <, >, G, \mathcal{N}, \beta, \underline{In}, \underline{Halt})$ whose underlying graph is $G = (X_G, E_G)$ and $X_G = \{\underline{In}, x_1, \ldots, x_{n-2}, \underline{Halt}\}$ for some $n \geq 2$. We construct the NSP $\Gamma' = (V', U', <, >, G', \mathcal{N}', \beta', \underline{In'}, \underline{Halt'})$, where the underlying graph of Γ' si shown in Fig. 3.

The rough idea is that a new symbol is added to the end of the input string in $\underline{In}$. As we shall see later, the role of this symbol is to point out to a splicing processor, and will be called pointer. It will be changed, after each simulation of a splicing step, in x_{comp}. Each processor y^s in Γ' is obtained by modifying the processor y of Γ with three goals:

(i) the new node, y^s does not permit the entrance of a string, unless it contains the added symbol pointing to y^s;

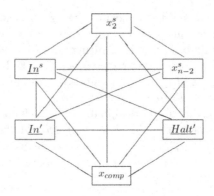

Fig. 3. The complete underlying graph of Γ'.

(ii) the node y^s simulates any splicing step in y;
(iii) the node y^s changes pointer value such that all the new strings can enter only x_{comp}.

The pointer symbol is updated in x_{comp}, in accordance with the edges of G, and the process resumes.

It is easy to note that $size(\Gamma') = size(\Gamma) + 2$. Furthermore, each (splicing, communication) step in Γ is simulated by two consecutive (splicing, communication) steps in Γ', the first one for simulating the actual splicing in y, and preparing the communication with x_{comp}, and the second one for updating the value of the pointer. It follows that $Time_{\Gamma'}(n) = 2Time_{\Gamma}(n)$ holds for every input string of length n.   □

Theorem 2. Star topology
P1. *Given an arbitrary NSP, Γ, one :can construct an equivalent star NSP Γ' such that the followings hold:*
P2.1. $size(\Gamma') = size(\Gamma) + 2$.
P2.2. $Time_{\Gamma'}(n) \in \mathcal{O}(Time_{\Gamma}(n))$.

It is immediate that the working mode of the NSP constructed in the proof of the previous theorem follows exactly the star topology shown in Fig. 4.

Theorem 3. [17] Grid topology
P1. *Given an arbitrary NSP, Γ, one can construct an equivalent grid NSP Γ' such that the followings hold:*
P2.1. $size(\Gamma') = 3size(\Gamma) + 3$.
P2.2. $Time_{\Gamma'}(n) \in \mathcal{O}(Time_{\Gamma}(n))$.

Sketch of the Proof
Let $\Gamma = (V, U, <, >, G, \mathcal{N}, \beta, \underline{In}, \underline{Halt})$ be a NSP with the underlying graph $G = (X_G, E_G)$ and $X_G = \{x_1, x_2, \ldots, x_n\}$ for some $n \geq 2$. By simplicity reasons,

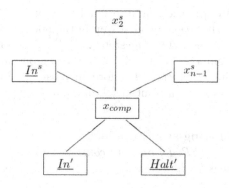

Fig. 4. The star underlying graph of Γ'.

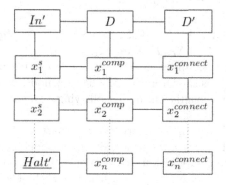

Fig. 5. The grid underlying graph of Γ'.

the input node is x_1, while the halting node is x_n. The underlying graph of Γ' is shown in Fig. 5.

We give now some informal explanations about the nodes of Γ'. As in the previous proofs, a pointer is added in $\underline{In'}$ to the end of the current string. All these string enters x_1^s and the simulation of a computation in Γ starts. Informally, the computation may be described as follows. Let us consider a splicing step in some node x_i of Γ, which transforms a string z into z'. Further on, z' is sent to some node x_j. We analyze the case $j > i$, the case $j < i$ could be treated analogously. These two steps (splicing and communication) described above are simulated in Γ' by a series of splicing and communication steps such that the string zt_i is transformed into $z't_i$ in x_i^s, then sent, via an itinerary that starts with the node x_i^{comp}, continues with the nodes $x_i^{connect}, x_{i+1}^{connect}, \ldots, x_j^{connect}$, and finishes with the nodes x_j^{comp} and x_j^s. It follows that an input string is accepted by Γ if and only if it is accepted by Γ'.

The construction shown in Fig. 5, proves that $size(\Gamma') = 3size(\Gamma) + 3$.

We now briefly analyze the computational time of Γ'. Following the above explanation, we infer that each splicing step in the node x_i of Γ is simulated as follows: one step in x_i^s, followed by one step in x_i^{comp}, and then at most n splicing steps in the nodes from $x_i^{connect}$ to $x_j^{connect}$. Finally, one more step is done in x_j^{comp} before the string enters x_j^s. Therefore, at most $n+3$ splicing steps in Γ' suffice. Since the size of Γ is constant, it follows that $Time_{\Gamma'}(n) \in \mathcal{O}(Time_\Gamma(n))$ holds. $\qquad\qquad\qquad\qquad\qquad\qquad\qquad\qquad\qquad\qquad\qquad\qquad\qquad\qquad$ $\square$

Theorem 4. Wheel (ring-star) topology
P1. *Given an arbitrary NSP, Γ, one can construct an equivalent wheel NSP Γ' such that the followings hold;*

P.2.1. $size(\Gamma') \leq 16size(\Gamma) - 8 + \sum_{k=1}^{n-1} card(PO_{x_k}) + \sum_{k=1}^{n} card(PI_{x_k})$.

P.2.2. $Time_{\Gamma'}(n) \leq 2size(\Gamma')(Time_\Gamma(n))$.

Sketch of the Proof Let $\Gamma = (V, U, <, >, G, \mathcal{N}, \beta, \underline{In}, \underline{Halt})$ be a NSP with the underlying graph $G = (X_G, E_G)$ and $X_G = \{x_1, x_2, \ldots, x_n\}$ for some $n \geq 2$. By simplicity reasons, the input node is x_1, while the halting node is x_n. The underlying graph of Γ' is shown in Fig. 6. The grey nodes represent straight line sub-networks between the adjacent nodes following an analogous sequence to the one established for x_i in Fig. 6.

A string w in Γ has an associated counterpart in Γ' of the form $w' = X_{k_z}^l w' X_k^r$ where $k \mid 1 \leq k \leq n$ identifies its target node and z is a synchronization label. During the computation of Γ, a node x may combine two generated strings to yield a new one. Nevertheless, while in Γ these strings arrive at that node simultaneously during the same communication step, the arrival of their counterparts to $x' \in \Gamma'$ can differ greatly because of the topological differences. We achieve synchronization of these strings through z as described below:

- After the simulation of a splicing step in $x_i \in \Gamma$, the synchronization label z of the strings yielded by $x_i' \in \Gamma'$ is updated to the maximum number of splicing steps required to enter the target node $x_j' \in \Gamma'$. We denote this value as ψ.
- During the computation of Γ', z is reduced by 1 for each splicing step performed. Since some of these steps don't involve $X_{k_z}^l$, they are accounted for in the closest splicing step involving z.
- Lastly, we introduce two nodes restricting entry to x_i': $x_i{}^f$ and $x_i{}^{f2}$. In each splicing step, strings residing in these nodes have their label z reduced by 1, keeping them synchronized with the ones flowing through the network. Note that because of the initial value ψ, any string targeting x_i' will ultimately enter one of these nodes with the same z as any of the other strings already inside these nodes and, consequently, they will be sent to x_i' at the same time.

Because of the need for string synchronization, a computational step in Γ will always require $\psi + 1$ steps in Γ'. This variable is bounded by either the number

Fig. 6. Wheel graph network Γ'.

of steps required by a string w' to travel from x_i' to x_j' ($i \neq j$) or the steps performed to return blocked strings to the node x_k', $1 \leq k \leq n$, and $\beta(x_k) = (s)$, whose associated $PO \neq \emptyset$ filters have the greatest cardinality. Nevertheless, for simplicity ψ may be set to be double the number of nodes in Γ'. □

4   Conclusion

We have discussed several direct simulations of arbitrary NSP by NSP having a common topology: full mesh, star, grid and wheel (ring-star). Each of these simulations is time efficient, namely the time function remains in the same complexity class. We also have evaluated the relationship between the size of the given NSP and the size of the constructed NSP. We hope that these simulations could be useful for possible implementations of NSP. Along these lines, it would be of a great interest to investigate the possibility of designing networks having a constant subnetwork that does not depend on the given NSP.

References

1. Bordihn, H., Mitrana, V., Păun, A., Păun, M.: Networks of polarized splicing processors. In: Martín-Vide, C., Neruda, R., Vega-Rodríguez, M.A. (eds.) Theory and Practice of Natural Computing, pp. 165–177. Springer International Publishing, Cham (2017). https://doi.org/10.1007/978-3-319-71069-3_13
2. Bordihn, H., Mitrana, V., Negru, M.C., Păun, A., Păun, M.: Small networks of polarized splicing processors are universal. Nat. Comp. **17**, 799–809 (2018)
3. Castellanos, J., Mitrana, V., Santos, E.: Splicing systems: accepting versus generating. In: Löwe, B., Normann, D., Soskov, I., Soskova, A. (eds.) Models of Computation in Context, pp. 41–50. Springer Berlin Heidelberg, Berlin, Heidelberg (2011). https://doi.org/10.1007/978-3-642-21875-0_5
4. Hardison, R.C.: Working With Molecular Genetics, Biology LibreTexts (2023)
5. Head, T.: Formal language theory and DNA: an analysis of the generative capacity of specific recombinant behaviours. Bull. Math. Biol. **49**, 737–759 (1987)
6. Head, T., Păun, G., Pixton, D.: Language theory and molecular genetics: generative mechanisms suggested by DNA recombination. In: Rozenberg, G., Salomaa, A. (eds.) Handbook of Formal Languages: Volume 2. Linear Modeling: Background and Application, pp. 295–360. Springer Berlin Heidelberg, Berlin, Heidelberg (2013). https://doi.org/10.1007/978-3-662-07675-0_7
7. Head, T.: How the structure of DNA molecules provides tools for computation. In: Biology, Computation and Linguistics. Frontiers in Artificial Intelligence and Applications vol. 228, 3–8. IOS Press. (2011)
8. Loos, R., Martín-Vide, C., Mitrana, V.: Solving SAT and HPP with accepting splicing systems. In: Runarsson, T.P., Beyer, H.-G., Burke, E., Merelo-Guervós, J.J., Whitley, L.D., Yao, X. (eds.) Parallel Problem Solving from Nature - PPSN IX: 9th International Conference, Reykjavik, Iceland, September 9-13, 2006, Proceedings, pp. 771–777. Springer Berlin Heidelberg, Berlin, Heidelberg (2006). https://doi.org/10.1007/11844297_78
9. Loos, R., Manea, F., Mitrana, V.: On small, reduced, and fast universal accepting networks of splicing processors. Theoret, Comput. Sci. **410** 406–416 (2009)
10. Manea, F., Martín-Vide, C., Mitrana, V.: Accepting networks of splicing processors. In: Cooper, S.B., Löwe, B., Torenvliet, L. (eds.) New Computational Paradigms, pp. 300–309. Springer Berlin Heidelberg, Berlin, Heidelberg (2005). https://doi.org/10.1007/11494645_38
11. Manea, F., Martín-Vide, C., Mitrana, V.: All NP-problems can be solved in polynomial time by accepting networks of splicing processors of constant size. In: Mao, C., Yokomori, T. (eds.) DNA Computing, pp. 47–57. Springer Berlin Heidelberg, Berlin, Heidelberg (2006). https://doi.org/10.1007/11925903_4
12. Manea, F., Martín-Vide, C., Mitrana, V.: Accepting networks of splicing processors: complexity results. Theoret. Comput. Sci. **371**, 72–82 (2007)
13. Mitrana, V., Petre, I., Rogojin, V.: Accepting splicing systems. Theoret. Comput. Sci. **411**, 2414–2422 (2010)
14. Păun, G.: On the splicing operation. Discret. Appl. Math. **70**, 57–79 (1996)
15. Păun, G., Rozenberg, G., Salomaa, A.: DNA computing: New Computing Paradigms. Springer, Berlin, Heidelberg (1998)
16. Rozenberg, G., Bäck, T., Kok, J.N. (eds.): Handbook of Natural Computing. Springer, Heidelberg (2012)
17. Sánchez Martin, J.A., Mitrana, V., Păun, M.: Networks of splicing processors: simulations between topologies. J. Membr. Comput. **5**(2), 108–115 (2023)

Brainstorming on Dataset Reduction from an Heuristic Bioinspired Green Computing Approach

Ana Paula Aravena-Cifuentes, Lucia Porlan-Ferrando,
J. David Nuñez-Gonzalez[✉], and Manuel Graña

Computational Intelligence Group, University of Basque Country UPV/EHU (Spain),
Eibar, Spain
{josedavid.nunez,manuel.grana}@ehu.eus

Abstract. Artificial intelligence has become essential in our daily lives, and over time we have become more dependent on it. As this tool becomes more precise, energy consumption increases, and this has become a concern for sustainability. Green learning is proposed as a solution to address these concerns. In this work, we propose to perform PV power generation prediction by applying training data size reduction using a machine learning approach performed with evolutionary techniques. In this way, the processing time of the classifier is accelerated without reaching a significant loss on the effectiveness of the classifier. The data reduction performed achieves a reduction of 17.13%, and the effectiveness is reduced by 1.47%. With respect to the initial problem, reducing the training time reduces the carbon footprint produced by energy consumption.

1 Introduction

Photovoltaic solar energy is a renewable, inexhaustible and non-polluting energy source obtained through the conversion of sunlight into electrical energy using photoelectric technology[1]. Their advantages include the fact that they do not add to environmental pollution, can safely store energy in batteries, and are easy to implement and install both commercially and residentially. In addition, their production also leaves a smaller carbon footprint on the environment compared to other energy sources [1]. This is why the last decades have seen an increase in the use of renewable energy sources that allow us to produce electricity in a sustainable way, such as solar photovoltaic energy [2].

Solar energy is highly variable, as it is produced by transforming solar radiation into electricity. Solar photovoltaic (PV) power generation depends on numerous factors, as changing as weather conditions can affect the intensity, duration and direction of solar radiation. These factors affect the prediction of solar generation, which is currently based on statistical and predictive models

---

[1] https://www.iberdrola.com/sostenibilidad/que-es-energia-fotovoltaica.

© The Author(s), under exclusive license to Springer Nature Switzerland AG 2024
J. M. Ferrández Vicente et al. (Eds.): IWINAC 2024, LNCS 14675, pp. 441–450, 2024.
https://doi.org/10.1007/978-3-031-61137-7_41

and Artificial Intelligence techniques[2]. These predictions allow us to adapt to the needs and coordinate production with electricity demand, minimizing the use of fossil fuels. Short-term forecasting is going to be fundamental for the effective integration of solar energy sources, being a very useful tool for grid reliability and stability [3]

To carry out these predictions, use has been made of artificial intelligence, which in the last decade has seen rapid advances in artificial intelligence (AI) and machine learning (ML) technology. In large part, the impressive advances have been based on the ability to build ever larger data sets that enable the design of increasingly complex neural networks [4]. Regarding Deep Learning technology one of the concerns that is not being given importance is its high carbon footprint. This is because the training of these networks is complex and deals with huge datasets, this makes it negatively affect sustainability goals [5].

One of the solutions that has been found is the reduction of training data without reducing the efficiency of the prediction model. This will decrease the execution time and carbon footprint incurred by machine learning systems. A very common practice to speed up instance-based classifiers is to reduce the size of their training set, i.e., replace it with a reduced set, in the hope that its accuracy will not worsen [6]. Data reduction can be carried out in multiple ways: feature selection and extraction, discretization, instance selection and generation, among others [7]. Our proposed method consists of reducing the training classifier by trying to maintain the mean and standard deviation values of the data, although it is also worth mentioning that the aim of this work is not to improve results, but to propose ideas between natural and artificial computation.

2   Related Works

2.1   Green Computing

Several scientific works have been devoted to the study of the use of technologies in a more sustainable way, due to the fact that the use of technologies and artificial intelligence are increasingly present in our daily lives. This section summarizes the research carried out in recent years and the results obtained.

Loïc et al. [8] propose a methodological framework to estimate the carbon footprint in any computational task in a standardized and reliable way and metrics are defined to contextualize greenhouse gas (GHG) emissions. To perform this estimation the authors used particle physics, weather forecasting models and natural language processing (NLP) algorithms. Their method considers different sources of energy use, such as processors and memory, computing facility overhead and geographic location, while balancing accuracy and practicality.

A. Sheryl et al. [9] enunciate a research in which they propose a technique in security-enhancing energy management based on a heuristic green computing technique and an optimized routing protocol. For this, they calculate the energy

---

[2] https://www.iic.uam.es/soluciones/energia/prediccion-generacion-energia-renovable/prediccion-generacion-energia-solar/.

requirements using a first-order radio model, which indicates how much energy is required to receive a packet of m bits. With all these collected energy data they comment that it is possible to construct some energy saving standards using the MIB model for energy management.

Ankita et al. [10] formulate a technique to implement green computing in the Internet of Things (IoT). IoT has to cope with massive connectivity of devices, thus in green computing, HD emerges as a mechanism to increase the uninterrupted lifetime of sensor-enabled IoT network. However, in conventional HD techniques, sensors consume a lot of energy, so this paper proposes a T-SWIPT technique that improves the energy efficiency of sensor-enabled IoT networks.

2.2 Dimensionality Reduction

The algorithms used in Machine Learning are capable of extracting important information from data sets with many features. However, each feature that is added increases the complexity of the execution. One of the solutions to this problem is dimensionality reduction, which consists of employing a set of techniques to remove excessive and unneeded features from the models.

Zihao et al. [11] present a comparison of dimensionality reduction techniques for multivariate spatiotemporal flow fields. The techniques compared are four: Principal Component Analysis (PCA), Independent Component Analysis (ICA), and two nonlinear techniques: Isometric Mapping (ISOMAP) and Locally Linear Embedding (LLE). The main results of this comparison are that ISOMAP and LLE models have lower reconstruction error, ICA has inaccurate data preservation and PCA is the most efficient method.

In the paper by Radhesyam et al. [12] the main contribution is the comparative study and evaluation of methods to reduce the classification level of remote hyperspectral images. The methods used are classified into three blocks: supervised, semi-supervised and unsupervised, in case of supervised and semi-supervised methods require labeled training samples. Which is very difficult to obtain, therefore, unsupervised methods are preferred.

Xiaoou [13] presents a reduced case study to provide a simplified circuit to protect an integrated power system with a renewable energy concept. An engineering simplification method is developed for interface safety zone modeling to measure the safety margin, safety distance, and overall interface distribution capacity.

2.3 Data Reduction

Data reduction is a powerful optimization technique that reduces data to its simplest form to free up storage capacity. There are many ways to reduce data, but the idea is very simple. The goal is to maximize capacity by compressing as much data as possible into physical storage.

Varin et al. [14] propose a new method that can reduce the training set size, this method is an improvement of a famous graph-based algorithm called

Optimum-Path Forest. The main concept to reduce the training set size is to use a segmented least squares algorithm (SLSA) to estimate the tree shape. This method could reduce the size by 7 to 21 % compared to the OPF algorithm, while the classification accuracy decreased insignificantly by only 0.2–0.5 %.

Lozano et al. [15] formulates in his thesis the construction of the training set from given data and, especially, in the condensation of this set; however, several classification techniques are also compared. He divides the condensing techniques into two blocks, the non-adaptive and the adaptive ones, in the first block there are techniques such as the Nearest Centroid Neighbour Rule, MaxNCN and Reconsistent. On the other hand, the second block includes NCN-based Adaptive Condensating Algorithms and Gaussian-based Adaptive Condensing Algorithms. After the study it was concluded that the techniques with the best results were MaxNCN, Hart and Reconsistent.

Stefanos et al. [6] enunciate k-NN classifier acceleration efforts and two new prototype generation algorithms for multi-label datasets. The first proposed algorithm is a variation of reduction by homogeneous clustering (RHC), and the second is a variation of RSP3, which is also a single-label, parameter-free prototype generation algorithm.

3   Experimentation and Results

In this section, we detail the experimentation carried out to evaluate the performance of the proposed reduction strategy. The approach presented in the benchmark study [2], which emphasizes the importance of customizing the predictive models for each specific location and of considering both the accuracy of the predictions and the environmental impact of the computational resources used in the process, serves as a basis and comparison of the new results obtained.

3.1   Data

This study utilises Location data from Pasion et al. [16], which includes information from twelve Department of Defense (DoD) solar installations located in various regions of the United States of America (USA) between 2017 and 2018.

The data is stored in a unique CSV file with 21,046 instances and 17 attributes. The attributes include solar power generation, as well as geographical, temporal, and meteorological features, with a sampling time ranging from 15 min to hours.

During data preprocessing, we assigned a numeric value to each unique value present in the 'Season' attribute column. For this case study, we only used data from the Travis location, which was identified as the best performing location in the previous study. Therefore, we filtered the database to include only data associated with this location.

Time, latitude, altitude, month, humidity, ambient temperature, wind speed, visibility, barometric pressure, cloud cover and season were the variables used for modelling.

3.2   Methodology

Inspired by the approach presented in previous research to tackle the problem of forecasting photovoltaic power generation, the methodology used in this study was developed. The goal was to reduce the amount of data required to train the regression model while considering change in the distribution of the data, accuracy of the prediction and the environmental impact of the computational resources used in the process.

First, the results obtained in Aravena-Cifuentes et al. [2] are reproduced. The base model is recreated, using Random Forest as a regressor and implementing five fold cross-validation, allowing us to go through several subsets of the main dataset in a systematic way, testing the model in different scenarios and proofing its robustness.

A data reduction function (Algorithm 1) is then developed, which randomly selects one instance per column from the original dataset, including both features and the target variable. These instances are removed from the original dataset. Then, the chosen instances are merged into one, which is concatenated onto the rest of the original dataset. Reduction is achieved by replacing the value of each column with randomly selecting one of the instances, without repetition, resulting in a twelve to one reduction.

Algorithm 1. Evolutionary Strategy

Require: Input data *data*
Ensure: Reduced dataset *combined_data* and combined index *combined_index*
   n_instances ← number of rows in *data*
   n_columns ← number of columns in *data*
   selected_values ← empty list
   indices ← list of indices of *data*
   instance_indices ← randomly select *n_columns* indices from *indices* without replacement
   for *i* in range(*n_columns*) **do**
       column_name ← name of column *i* in *data*
       instance_index ← i^{th} element of *instance_indices*
       selected_value ← value at row *instance_index* and column *i* in *data*
       append *selected_value* to *selected_values*
   end for
   reduced_data ← DataFrame containing *selected_values*
   rename the first row index of *reduced_data* to *instance_indices*[0]
   combined_data ← concatenate *reduced_data* with *data*[rows not indexed by *instance_indices*]
   combined_index ← list of indices of *combined_data*
   return *combined_data, combined_index*

The Random Forest regression models are evaluated using an iteration loop controlled by a fitness function (Algorithm 2) that quantitatively assesses the similarity between the original and the current training data based on their descriptive statistics. It checks if the differences in means, medians, and standard deviations are all within the specified percentage threshold (10%, 15%,17%,18%,19%,20%), allowing for a customizable threshold for acceptable differences.

Algorithm 2. Fitness Function

Require: Two dataframes $df1$ and $df2$, and a percentage threshold $percentage$
Ensure: Returns True if the descriptive statistics of $df1$ and $df2$ are similar within the specified threshold, otherwise returns False
    $stats\_df1 \leftarrow$ calculateStatistics($df1$)   ▷ Calculate summary statistics for $df1$
    $stats\_df2 \leftarrow$ calculateStatistics($df2$)   ▷ Calculate summary statistics for $df2$
    $mean\_similar \leftarrow$ compareMean($stats\_df1.mean, stats\_df2.mean, percentage$)
    $median\_similar \leftarrow$ compareMedian($stats\_df1.median, stats\_df2.median, percentage$)
    $std\_similar \leftarrow$ compareStd($stats\_df1.std, stats\_df2.std, percentage$)
    if $mean\_similar$ **and** $median\_similar$ **and** $std\_similar$ **then**
        return True
    else
        return False
    end if

During each iteration, the 5-fold cross-validation technique is applied, and the data reduction function is incorporated. Generation zero uses the complete train set, while the following generations gradually reduce its size by applying the data reducing function.

Two versions of this experiment are under evaluation, which will be referred to as Method 1 and Method 2. The first uses the entire training set for reduction, while the latter only uses the cases between June and September. This is because the dataset spans from 09/06/2017 to 03/10/2018, and there is more data available during those months.

Finally, objective evaluation metrics such as mean square error (MSE), mean absolute error (MAE), and coefficient of determination 1 (R^2) are calculated to assess the performance of the models at each fold, seed, and generation.

The coefficient of determination R^2 is calculated using Eq. 1.

$$R^2 = 1 - \frac{SS_{\text{res}}}{SS_{\text{tot}}} \tag{1}$$

where

SS_{res}: Sum of squared differences between predicted and actual values
SS_{tot}: Total sum of squared differences between actual values and their means.

Additionally, the mean absolute error (MAE) and the mean square error (MSE) are calculated using Eq. 2 and 3, respectively.

$$\text{MAE} = \frac{1}{n} \sum_{i=1}^{n} |y_{\text{pred}} - y_{\text{true}}| \tag{2}$$

where n is the number of instances.

$$\text{MSE} = \frac{1}{n} \sum_{i=1}^{n} (y_{\text{pred}} - y_{\text{true}})^2 \qquad (3)$$

where n is the number of instances.

3.3   Results

This section presents the achievements obtained through the implementation of data reduction techniques for predicting solar power generation. The results show the evolution of the model's performance throughout the optimisation process.

Figures 1, 2 and 3 compare the performance of Method 1 and Method 2 in terms of R-squared (R^2).

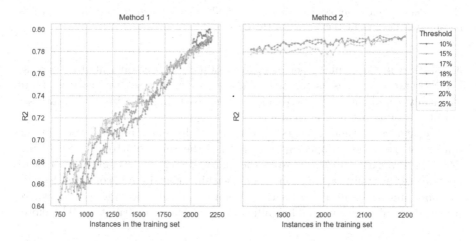

Fig. 1. Performance comparison between Method 1 and Method 2: The median of the seeds provided for each generation is shown in the graph.

The original training dataset consisted of 2197 instances; however, a reduction to 2000 instances (a 10% reduction) in both methods, while considering all thresholds, did not result in significant changes in the metrics measured. This is detailed in Fig. 3.

The optimal results for each method were achieved with a threshold value of 18% for Method 1 and 20% for Method 2. Out of these results, Method 2 achieves the largest reduction in the database, eliminating 17.13% of the total, with only a 1.5% difference in the value of R^2.

Method 1, on the other hand, achieves an 8.3% reduction with only a 0.78% decrease in the coefficient of determination.

Method 1 demonstrated that an increase in the threshold of the fitness function led to the production of more generations, which in turn reduced the number

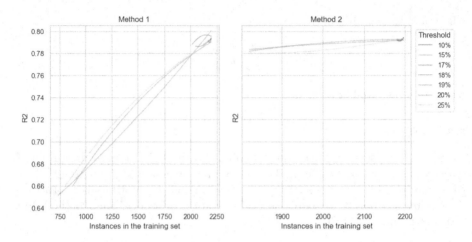

Fig. 2. Performance comparison between Method 1 and Method 2: A quadratic approximation was used to fit the trends in the data.

of instances in the training set data. Additionally, it demonstrated a decrease in performance metrics as the size of the training data set was reduced more drastically, highlighting the trade-off between reducing the size of the data set and maintaining predictive accuracy.

In contrast, Method 2 showed a different behaviour. The reduction in the number of instances stopped after increasing the threshold to 19%, 20%, and 25%. . This was expected because Method 2's reducing function only operates on a portion of the training data, constrained within a certain range of dates, leaving the remaining training data intact. Therefore, it quickly reaches a point where further data elimination would significantly impact the distribution. Therefore,

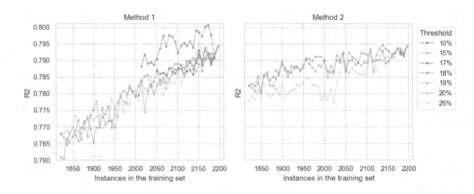

Fig. 3. Performance comparison between Method 1 and Method 2: Close-up considering the minimum instances achieved with Method 2.

despite the increase in the acceptance threshold, Method 2 reaches a reduction limit (Fig. 3).

4   Discussion and Future Work

As demonstrated in the previous section, it can be seen how, by decreasing the training set, the results obtained using the original set can be preserved. The difference in performance between Method 1 and 2 suggest that indiscriminate reduction of the training set, as is done in Method 1, may not necessarily compromise model accuracy and predictive power to a certain extend.

The results in this work emphasise the importance of data reduction strategies and suggest new opportunities for research and refinement.

Further research is required to optimise data reduction techniques. Future work could explore alternative algorithms and approaches, such as clustering or stratified sampling, to select the instances to be eliminated. In addition, other techniques to create artificial entities like GANs, SMOTE and BOSME [17] can also be studied, and/or transfer proposed contribution to other domains. [18]

Furthermore, the analysis can be expanded to incorporate additional locations and datasets to evaluate the generalisability and scalability of the proposed strategies.

On the other hand, an assessment of their environmental impact, including energy consumption and computational resources, would be useful to determine the sustainability of different data reduction strategies.

Acknowledgment. Authors received research funds from the Basque Government as of the Grupo de Inteligencia Computacional, Universidad del Pais Vasco, UPV/EHU, from 2007 until 2025. The current code for the grant is IT1689-22. Additionally, authors participate in Elkartek projects KK-2022/00051 and KK-2021/00070. The Spanish MCIN has also granted the authors a research project under code PID2020-116346GB-I00

References

1. Zazoum, B.: Solar photovoltaic power prediction using different machine learning methods. Energy Rep. **8**, 2–19 (2022)
2. Aravena-Cifuentes, A. P., Nuñez-Gonzalez, J. D., Elola, A., Ivanova, M.: Development of AI-Based Tools for Power Generation Prediction. Computation **11**(11), 232 (2023)
3. Almonacid, F., Pérez-Higueras, P.J., Fernández, E.F., Hontoria, L.: A methodology based on dynamic artificial neural network for short-term forecasting of the power output of a PV generator. Energy Convers. Manag. **85**, 389–398 (2014)
4. Jay Kuo, C.-C., Madni, A.M.: Green learning: introduction, examples and outlook. J. Vis. Commun. Image Represent. **90** (2023)
5. Schwartz, R., Dodge, J., Smith, N.A., Etzioni, O.: Green AI. Commun. ACM **63**(12), 54–63 (2020)
6. Ougiaroglou, S., Filippakis, P., Fotiadou, G., Evangelidis, G.: Data reduction via multi-label prototype generation. Neurocomputing **526**, 1–8 (2023)

7. Ramírez Gallego, S.: Reducción de datos apligada a Big Data. Doctoral thesis (2014)
8. Lannelongue, L., Grealey, J., Inouye, M.: Green algorithms: quantifying the carbon footprint of computation. Adv. Sci. 8(12) (2021)
9. Sheryl Oliver, A., Ravi, B., Manikandan, R., Sharma, A., Kim, B.-G.: Heuristic green computing based energy management with security enhancement using hybrid greedy secure optimal routing protocol. Energy Rep. 9, 2494–2505 (2023)
10. Jaiswal, A., Kumar, S., Kaiwartya, O., Prasad, M., Kumar, N., Song, H., Green computing in IoT: time slotted simultaneous wireless information and power transfer. Comput. Commun. 168, 155–169 (2021)
11. Wnag, Z., Zhang, G., Xing, X., Xu, X., Sun, T.: Comparison of dimensionality reduction techniques for multi-variable spatiotemporal flow fields. Ocean Eng. 291 (2024)
12. Vaddi, R., Phaneendra Kumar, B.L.N., Manoharan, P., Agilan deeswari, L., Sangeetha, V.: Strategies for dimensionality reduction in hyperspectral remote sensing: a comprehensive overview. Egyptian J. Remote Sensing Space Sci. 27, 82–92 (2024)
13. Liu, X.: Research on dimension reduction for visualitation of simplified security region of integrated energy system considering renewable energy access. Inter. J. Elect. Power Energy Syst. 156 (2024)
14. Chouvatut, V., Jindaluang, W., Boonchieng, E.: Training set size reduction in large dataset problems. IEEE (2015)
15. Albalate, L., Teresa, M.: Data Reduction Techniques in Classification Processes. Doctoral thesis (2007)
16. Williams, J., Wagner, T.P., et al.: Location Data. Mendeley Data V2 (2019). https://doi.org/10.17632/hfhwmn8w24.2
17. Rosario, D., Nuñez-Gonzalez, J.D.: Bayesian network-based over-sampling method (BOSME) with application to indirect cost-sensitive learning. Sci. Rep. 12, 1-18 (2022) Nature Portfolio
18. Gorriz, J.M., et al.: Computational approaches to explainable artificial intelligence: advances in theory, applications and trends. Inform. Fusion 100, 101945 (2023)

Diagnosis of Cervical Cancer Using a Deep Learning Explainable Fusion Model

Andrés Bueno-Crespo[1], Raquel Martínez-España[2],
Juan Morales-García[1]([✉]), Ana Ortíz-González[3], Baldomero Imbernón[1],
José Martínez-Más[4], Daniel Rosique-Egea[1], and Mauricio A. Álvarez[5]

[1] Escuela Politécnica Superior, Universidad Católica de Murcia, Murcia, Spain
{abueno,jmorales8,bimbernon}@ucam.edu, drosique6@alu.ucam.edu
[2] Information and Communications Engineering Department, University of Murcia, Murcia, Spain
raquel.m.e@um.es
[3] Pathology Department, University Hospital Complex of Cartagena, Cartagena, Spain
ana.ortiz5@carm.es
[4] Obstetrics and Gynecology Department, CIAGO Gynecological Center, Murcia, Spain
jmartinez14@ucam.edu
[5] Computer Science Department, University of Manchester, Manchester, UK
mauricio.alvarezlopez@manchester.ac.uk

Abstract. Cervical cancer continues to be a significant global health issue, ranking as the fourth most prevalent cancer affecting women. Enhancing population screening programs by refining the examination of cervical samples conducted by skilled pathologists offers a compelling alternative for early detection of this disease. Deep Learning facilitates the development of automatic classification models to aid experts in this task. However, it is increasingly important to bring explainability to the model in order to understand how the network learns to identify pathology. In this paper, the explainability created by a heatmap, using the Gradient-weighted Class Activation Mapping (Grad-CAM) technique, is merged with the original image by studying the different intensities for the overlap by means of a hybrid architecture composed by a Convolutional Neural Network and explainability techniques. Through this blending, a new image of the cell is created for training where the heatmap provides the original image of the cell with information about the location of the region of interest. Finally, it is observed that a 10% intensity provided by the heatmap is the most efficient value for this fusion, reaching accuracy values of 94% in a model that indicates whether or not a revision by the pathologist is necessary.

Keywords: Cervical Cancer · Explainable Model · Deep Learning (DL) · Grad-CAM · Convolutional Neural Network (CNN)

J. M. Ferrández Vicente et al. (Eds.): IWINAC 2024, LNCS 14675, pp. 451–460, 2024.
https://doi.org/10.1007/978-3-031-61137-7_42

1   Introduction

Cervical cancer remains a major health concern worldwide and stands as the fourth most common cancer among women according to recent estimates [13]. During 2020, this cancer affected 604.000 new individuals, and its mortality reached more than 340.000 deaths. It represents 6.5% of tumors affecting the female population of all ages and has a global cancer mortality of 7.7% according to data collected by GLOBOCAN in 2020. It is the leading cause of cancer death in women in several African countries and it is estimated that 85-90% of deaths from cervical cancer occur in underdeveloped countries, which have a mortality rate 18 times higher than in developed countries [13]. Regular medical screenings and the Human Papillomavirus vaccine have the potential to reduce both its incidence and mortality in high-income countries. Despite medical advancements, cervical cancer survival rates decrease substantially if not diagnosed in its early stages [8].

Screening strategies seek to detect those healthy individuals at risk of developing a disease, in order to provide initial treatments that result in lower morbidity and mortality. There are several tests that allow early detection of cervical cancer, such as HPV detection by PCR, vaginal cytology and colposcopy [9]. As a drawback of this PCR technique, detection of HPV infection is more expensive and less specific than cytology, so cervical cytology by Pap smears remains the most widespread screening method today.

To obtain a cervicovaginal cytology, the cervix is examined and the cells of the cervical mucosa are collected by brushing the vaginal fundus, exocervix and endocervix. This brushing is passed to a cell preservative liquid that acts as a fixative, and then it is processed in order to distribute the cells on a transparent slide that are stained with the Papanicolau technique, which will allow the cells to be visible with different dyes. The Bethesda System analyzes all the elements that can be found in the Papanicolaou cytology and establishes morphological and diagnostic categories. This system uses the terminology "squamous intraepithelial lesion (SIL)", which refers to the changes in the nucleus and cytoplasm that the squamous cell of the cervix acquires in the presence of HPV infection; which can be low grade (L-SIL) and high grade (H-SIL). In L-SIL, changes observed suggest HPV infection that has not been integrated into the host DNA, whereas in H-SIL the changes observed indicate that viral DNA has been integrated into the host cell. The risk of progression to cancer of L-SIL is low with lesions mostly spontaneously remitting, whereas H-SIL has a high risk of progression to cervical cancer. The Bethesda System uses the term ASCUS (atypical squamous cells of undetermined significance) for uncertain cases with suspicious but not certain findings of dysplasia. These 4 classes can be summarised into 2 classes, reviewable and non-reviewable. The H-SIL, L-SIL and ASC-US classes are situations that require further diagnostic tests to analyse the extent of the disease, hence they are categorised as reviewable cells. On the other hand, benign cells are categorised as non-reviewable. The Pap smear plays, while functional in detecting abnormalities, it demands a detailed inspection to identify lesions. This procedure requires skilled professionals, rendering it a time-consuming and labor-intensive task. Moreover, in the field of cytopathology there is a great inter- and intra-observer variability, as it is a skill with a certain subjective component influenced by factors such as observer fatigue, sample quality and laboratory artifacts in cytology processing, among others.

Deep learning techniques can help in the classification of these cells, obtaining a higher accuracy rate than a pathologist [6,14]. However, in addition to the great computational and classification capacity of these techniques, there is the disadvantage of poor explainability. These techniques are considered black boxes, where explaining the result explicitly is complicated. To counteract this disadvantage, it is possible to merge Deep Learning techniques with Explainable Artificial Intelligence methods. Numerous studies have focused on improving the explainability of Deep Learning models in the medical field, as highlighted in recent surveys [3,15].

Therefore, in this study we focus on proposing a hybrid architecture where, on the one hand, such an architecture is able to explain the results provided by the classification of medical images. On the other hand, the explanability provides relevant information that improves the classification results of these images. Specifically, we focus on the imaging of cervical cells categorised as H-SIL, L-SIL, AS-CUS and benign, grouping these images into reviewable and non-reviewable classes. In the term of explainable artificial intelligence methods, we use the heatmap method, specifically the Gradient-weighted Class Activation Mapping method (Grad-CAM), to generate heatmaps that indicate the most relevant parts of the images that are able to detail and specify the classification of the image. The Gradient-weighted Class Activation Mapping method has been selected after analysis of other methods such as LIME (local interpretable model-agnostic explanations) or occlusion sensitivity maps.

Thus, the findings of this study are as follows: a) Create a hybrid architecture capable of improving image classification using explainability methods for artificial intelligence; b) Apply the proposed architecture to a real sorting problem and explain the sorting of cervical cells.

The rest of the paper is organised as follows. Section 2 shows a brief review of some work on the use of Explainable Artificial Intelligence. Section 3 describes the proposal to merge Deep Learning techniques with Explainable Artificial Intelligence method to achieve an explanation of the classification of the cells. Section 4 the results obtained are shown and analysed. Finally, Sect. 5 presents the main conclusions, and discusses future works.

2 Related Work

Deep learning techniques are very accurate and obtain good classification and regression results in any application. However, they are black box techniques, where figuring out the reason for the results is often a costly job. Thus, in recent years, techniques are being developed to provide explainability to the results of techniques classified as black box techniques, [10]. These explainability techniques are included in the so-called explainable artificial intelligence systems

(XIA). These systems explain the relationship of the decision-making process, highlight weaknesses in the process, and provide insight into how the system will behave in the future. In the medical field, it is essential to know the explanation of the decisions made, hence the importance of obtaining an explanation of the results after the application of a black box technique [1].

Literature shows different methods of explainable AI applied to medical scenarios. The authors of [5] propose a model for classification of ovarian images with pathologies by means of a convolutional autoencoder neural network (CNN-CAE). In addition to this technique they also apply the gradient-weighted class activation mapping (Grad-CAM) technique to qualitatively visualize and verify the results of the CNN-CAE model. In [12], the Grad-CAM technique is also used for identifying the presence of metastases from digital histopathology images of lymph nodes. The results indicate the ability of the technique to detect in the image the tumor. The authors of [7] propose a hybrid architecture using CNN to create a heatmap and then connect the output of the heatmap to a neural network that classifies the original image along with the heatmap. For this purpose the last module of the architecture receives as input a 4-channel RGBS image, combines the original RGB image with the corresponding heatmap and provides as output the corresponding class, obtaining satisfactory results.

This brief literary summary proves that explicable IA techniques work and help not only to find the reasons for classifications and/or diagnoses, but also help to improve those diagnoses. This supports the use of these techniques for the classification of cervical images to make a diagnosis and to be able to accelerate and explain which are the most relevant regions that reveal the disease.

3 Proposed Model

3.1 Model Architecture

The creation of an explainable model allows for greater explainability of the classification decision made by the model. The aim is to obtain a more accurate model by starting from explainability and merging it with the original image, since explainability allows more information to be added to the image. Based on these premises, Fig. 1 shows the architecture proposed in this study. This architecture presents two stages, on the one hand a CNN model that allows to extract the heatmap that is superimposed on the original image depending on a weighting percentage determining by α parameter. This new image serves as input for another new CNN that makes up the second stage, where classification into four diagnostic modalities is performed. These initial classifications are converged to a binary classification into non-reviewable and reviewable to give the final output of the model. The reason for this final convergence is due to the large imbalance in the L-SIL and ASC-US classes. This means that it is not possible to perform a 4-class classification with high accuracy. In addition to the imbalance, there is little differentiation between the heatmaps of L-SIL and ASC-US cells.

This hybrid architecture allows initially using the Gradient-weighted Class Activation Mapping (Grad-CAM) method [11] integrated with a convolutional neural network (CNN), specifically with an Xception type network [2], to obtain a heatmap of each of the cells. Subsequently, this heatmap is merged with an overlight *Alpha* (α) with the original image. This fused image is taken as input to another Xception CNN to obtain a cell type classification.

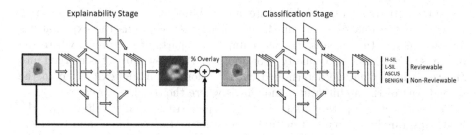

Fig. 1. Architecture of the proposed model composed of two Xception networks (explainability + classification).

The following metrics are used in the evaluation of the model Accuracy, Precision, Recall and F1 Score [4].

3.2 Dataset

The dataset used for this project was generously provided by the Pathologic Anatomy Service of the Complejo Hospitalario Universitario Santa Lucía-Santa María del Rosell located in Cartagena, Murcia (Spain). It comprises 1863 cell images, each meticulously labeled by cervical cancer experts into one of four distinct classes according to the Bethesda System. The class distribution is as follows: 389 H-SIL cells, 293 ASC-US cells, 182 L-SIL cells and 879 Benign cells. These 4 classes are summarised into two classes of reviewable and non-reviewable, with the reviewable ones grouped as H-SIL, L-SIL and ASC-US and the non-reviewable ones as benign. Thus we have 864 revisable cells and 879 non-revisable cells. In this dataset, 30 images of each subtype are used as a test and the rest are used for inter-ranging. Thus we have from the revisable classes a total of 90 test images and from the revisable class 30 images. This leaves a total of 849 non-reviewable images and 774 reviewable images for training.

It is important to note that these real dataset of cervix images is made up of cells that do not have any kind of pre-processing. The images are introduced to the proposed models without any pre-processing, so cells may be folded, blurred or even overlapped. Although this is the reality of the problem, it must be taken into account that it poses a greater challenge in the design and creation of classification models.

4   Results and Discussion

The proposed hybrid architecture has been evaluated using the datasets presented in Sect. 3.2. Thus, in these experiments, the adjustment of the parameter α that determines the degree of blending between the original image and the heatmap has been carried out. The idea is to find a balance between the contribution of information from the heatmap and the non-loss of information from the original image.

In the first stage of the architecture, a new dataset consisting of the heatmap for each of the images is obtained. This head map contains the explanations for each image, that means, the most important parts of the image where the image is to be classified as one type or another. This new dataset is merged into an over-light percentage determined by α. Fusion and model exit occur in the second part of the architecture, and this is where the α value is relevant.

We conducted experiments by testing various transparency values α for the heatmaps, ranging from 0 to 1, with 0.0 representing the real image and 1.0 solely the heatmap, encompassing all intermediate combinations. In the top part of the Fig. 2, all combinations can be observed by varying α parameter.

The lower part of Fig. 2 shows the expanded cells for $\alpha = 0.1$ and for $\alpha = 0.3$. This expansion is to depict in detail the heatmap with the image fusion for the values $\alpha = 0.1$ and $\alpha = 0.3$. In this image it can be seen how at $\alpha = 0.3$ the heatmap dilutes relevant shapes from the original image. For benign cells the heatmap at $\alpha = 0.1$ focuses on the cellular cytoplasm and not so much on the nucleus, since the nucleous/cytoplasm ratio is low, being this one of the typical characteristics of these kind of cells. For the L-SIL cell, one of the keys to its identification is that the nucleus is disproportionate to the cytoplasm, at $\alpha = 0.1$ this is reflected, however, at $\alpha = 0.3$, the heatmap also highlights the perinuclear halo around, that clinically reflects HPV active replication inside the cell, and takes it as the nucleus as well. This perinuclear halo with $\alpha = 0.1$ is perfectly distinguishable from the nucleus, while with a higher value it is diluted by the heatmap. Similar cases occur with ASC-US and H-SIL cells. For ASC-US cells, they have a disproportion between nucleus and cytoplasm, with a higher nucleus/cytoplasm ratio, with a lower cytoplasm density. When applying in these cells $\alpha = 0.1$, the heatmap is centered on the nucleus and not so much on the cytoplasm. Whereas at higher values of α the heatmap merges the nucleus with the cytoplasm and the relevant information that highlights ASC-US is lost. For H-SIL cells, even more fusion is affected, since this cell type is characterized by a larger nucleus and little or no cytoplasm around it, with the highest nucleus/cytoplasm ratio. When using the value of $\alpha = 0.1$ the heatmap is smoothly centered, in the reduced cytoplasm. The higher the value of α, the more the heatmap is centered on nuclei, removing the relevance of cytoplasm, which again determines a relevant loss of information from the original image.

Once all combinations between the real image and the heatmap with different α values have been obtained, a neural network Xception has been run 10 times separately to determine the best α. From these 10 executions, the mean of all of them is shown along with their standard deviation in Fig. 3. These figures show

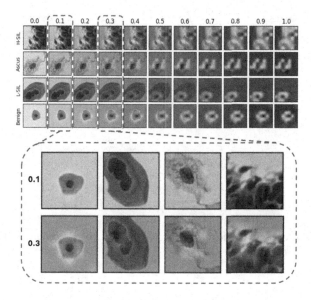

Fig. 2. Fusion between the original image and the heatmap. The influence of the heatmap on the original image is indicated, where 0.0 indicates the original image and 1.0 the heatmap. Also, a zoom is performed on α values 0.1 and 0.3 to observe in more detail the influence of the heatmap.

for each α value the mean value of the 10 runs marked with a dot in the figure and the deviation obtained is marked with a line. Each of the figures indicates the values obtained for each of the metrics described. It is interesting to note that there is a point where all the metrics drop considerably, making it clear that the heatmap does not provide as much information because the loss of information from the original image is much greater. Analysing in detail, we found that the optimal transparency value was $\alpha = 0.1$.

Table 1. Confusion Matrix from Training Using Image Combined with heatmap with 2 classes where $\alpha = 0.0$ corresponds to training the model with the original images and $\alpha = 0.1$ is the best α model for fusion. ACC is accuracy metric.

		Predicted $\alpha = 0.0$ - ACC=88%		Predicted $\alpha = 0.1$ - ACC=94%	
		Non-reviewable	Reviewable	Non-reviewable	Reviewable
Real	Non-reviewable	28	2	28	2
	Reviewable	12	78	5	85

The best model $\alpha = 0.1$ obtains a classification with an accuracy of 94%±2%, precision of 91%±3%, recall of 93%±2% and a f1-score of 92%±2%. This metrics can be seen in Fig. 3 and in Table 1. In this table, the confusion matrix shows

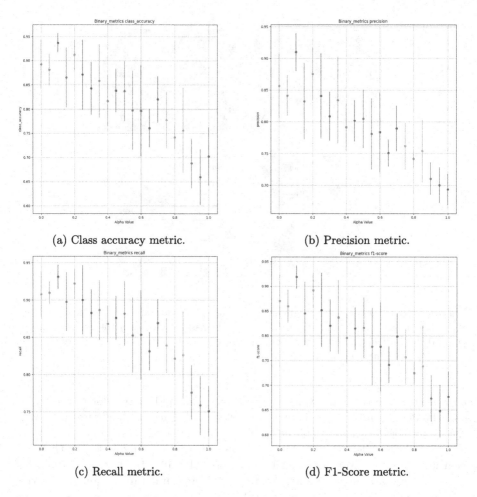

(a) Class accuracy metric.

(b) Precision metric.

(c) Recall metric.

(d) F1-Score metric.

Fig. 3. Metrics for each alpha value, indicating their mean and standard deviation. It is observed that the best results are obtained with an alpha value of 0.1, which indicates a 10% influence of the heatmap on the original image.

a comparison between the best model $\alpha = 0.1$ and the model with the original image $\alpha = 0.0$, which obtains an accuracy of 88%. As it can be seen in Fig. 3, this result obtained by fusion with the heatmap improves all the metrics with respect to the single training with the original images (represented in Fig. 2 as $\alpha = 0.0$). In this matrix confusion, it can be observed that the total number of correctly classified instances amounts to 113, with only 7 misclassified instances.

These results are satisfactory, since they imply that the model, in addition to obtaining an explanation of the most relevant parts of a cell to be classified, also obtains a binary classification that is superior to that of the pathologist, whose classification error is around 10%. Metrics for each alpha value are shown in detail in the Fig. 3 where their mean and standard deviation over 10 executions for each alpha can be observed for classification between reviewable and non-reviewable by the pathologist.

5   Conclusions and Future Work

In this study we have proposed a hybrid architecture to take advantage of the classification capability of CNNs together with the possibility of obtaining explainability of the results of these techniques. We have proposed a model that uses two Xception networks in two approaches, with the output of the first approach being the input to the second. The initial objective has been to create a heatmap with the Gradient-weighted Class Activation Mapping technique for each of the images and then merge it with the original image in order to combine as much information as possible and achieve a higher classification. The proposed architecture has been evaluated with a real dataset of cervix cells, which have no pre-processing, so cells may be folded, blurred or even overlapped, as they appear under the microscope. In addition, the transparency rate α that is applied in the fusion of the heatmaps and the original image has also been analysed. In this case, a sweep has been carried out by the α parameter, concluding that the best value is $\alpha = 0.1$. This value achieves an average accuracy of 94% with a standard deviation of 2% for a binary classification into reviewable and non-reviewable cells. These results are satisfactory, as so far we had a percentage of 88% maximum for the study using only original image without heatmap.

The training based on heatmaps obtained from explainability methods does not provide optimal results. However, by combining these maps with the original images, results closer to the originals are obtained, which opens up the possibility of conducting more thorough studies to improve model accuracy. By fusing the original image with the heatmap, the most important features for diagnosis are highlighted in the original image, allowing the CNN to focus more on these areas and potentially improve its accuracy. Also, this fusion can attenuate noise or irrelevant parts of the image, which helps the CNN to focus on the most relevant information, whereby the network learns to prioritise certain regions of the image over others allowing for better generalisation by highlighting relevant features and reducing noise.

Throughout the development of this project, several future avenues have been identified that can be explored to enhance and expand the results obtained. Between these avenues are remarkable, the obtaining a new dataset with balanced classes. After obtaining this datasets, the possibility of extending the architecture to a 4-class classification will be explored . In addition, other explainability methods can be studied in depth to compare and test whether they are more effective than the one studied here.

Funding. The present work was funded by PMAFI-21/21 project from the Support for Research Help Program of the Catholic University of Murcia, and the research stay mobility program "José Castillejo" CAS22/00482 of Andrés Bueno-Crespo funded by Ministerio de Ciencia, Innovación y Universidades.

References

1. Buhrmester, V., Münch, D., Arens, M.: Analysis of explainers of black box deep neural networks for computer vision: a survey. Mach. Learn. Knowl. Extract. **3**(4), 966–989 (2021)
2. Chollet, F.: Xception: Deep learning with depthwise separable convolutions. In: Proceedings of the IEEE Conference on Computer Vision and Pattern Recognition, pp. 1251–1258 (2017)
3. Hakkoum, H., Abnane, I., Idri, A.: Interpretability in the medical field: a systematic mapping and review study. Appl. Soft Comput. **117**, 108391 (2022). https://doi.org/10.1016/j.asoc.2021.108391, (Accessed 5 Sep 2023)
4. Huilgol, P.: Precision and recall essential metrics for machine learning. https://www.analyticsvidhya.com/blog/2020/09/precision-recall-machine-learning/ (Sep 2020), (Accessed 28 Feb 2024)
5. Jung, Y., Kim, T., Han, M.R., Kim, S., Kim, G., Lee, S., Choi, Y.J.: Ovarian tumor diagnosis using deep convolutional neural networks and a denoising convolutional autoencoder. Sci. Rep. **12**(1), 1–10 (2022), (Accessed 4 Sep 2023)
6. Martinez-Mas, J., et al.: Classifying papanicolaou cervical smears through a cell merger approach by deep learning technique. Expert Syst. Appl. **160**, 113707 (2020)
7. Murabito, F., Spampinato, C., Palazzo, S., Giordano, D., Pogorelov, K., Riegler, M.: Top-down saliency detection driven by visual classification. Comput. Vis. Image Underst. **172**, 67–76 (2018)
8. National Cancer Institute: Cervical cancer prognosis and survival rates (Apr 2023). https://www.cancer.gov/types/cervical/survival, (Accessed 06 Sep 2023)
9. National Cancer Institute: Cervical Cancer Screening — cancer.gov (Apr 2023).(Accessed 06 Sep 2023)
10. Rai, A.: Explainable ai: from black box to glass box. J. Acad. Mark. Sci. **48**, 137–141 (2020)
11. Selvaraju, R.R., Cogswell, M., Das, A., Vedantam, R., Parikh, D., Batra, D.: Gradcam: Visual explanations from deep networks via gradient-based localization. In: Proceedings of the IEEE International Conference on Computer Vision, pp. 618–626 (2017)
12. Suara, S., Jha, A., Sinha, P., Sekh, A.A.: Is grad-cam explainable in medical images? (2023)
13. Sung, H., Ferlay, J., Siegel, R.L., Laversanne, M., Soerjomataram, I., Jemal, A., Bray, F.: Global cancer statistics 2020: GLOBOCAN estimates of incidence and mortality worldwide for 36 cancers in 185 countries. CA: Cancer J. Clinicians **71**(3), 209–249 (2021).https://doi.org/10.3322/caac.21660, [Accessed 06-09-2023]
14. Taha, B., Dias, J., Werghi, N.: Classification of cervical-cancer using pap-smear images: a convolutional neural network approach. In: Valdés Hernández, M., González-Castro, V. (eds.) MIUA 2017. CCIS, vol. 723, pp. 261–272. Springer, Cham (2017). https://doi.org/10.1007/978-3-319-60964-5_23
15. Teng, Q., Liu, Z., Song, Y., Han, K., Lu, Y.: A survey on the interpretability of deep learning in medical diagnosis. Multimed Syst. **28**(6), 2335–2355 (2022)

Blockchain Framework Tailored
for Agricultural IoTs

Salaheddine Kably[1,2]([✉]), Nabih Alaoui[2], Mounir Arioua[1], Khalid Chougdali[1],
Samira Khoulji[3], and María Dolores Gómez-López[4]

[1] Engineering Sciences Laboratory, National School of Applied Sciences of Kenitra, Ibn Tofail
University, Kenitra, Morocco
salaheddine.kably@gmail.com
[2] Ecole Supérieure d'Informatique et du Numérique, TICLab Université Internationale de Rabat
Sala El Jadida, Rabat, Morocco
[3] Innovative Systems Engineering Laboratory, National School of Applied Sciences of Tetuan,
Abdelmalek Essaadi University, Tetouan, Morocco
[4] Agronomic Engineering Department, Technical University of Cartagena, Cartagena, Spain

Abstract. The proposed Multi-Zone Blockchain Framework for Agriculture IoT
significantly enhances agricultural IoT applications by integrating advanced,
secure blockchain technologies. It incorporates the Enhanced Blowfish Algorithm (EBA) for robust authentication and leverages a Bayesian-Direct Acyclic
Graph (B-DAG) for superior network optimization, ensuring data integrity while
maximizing resource efficiency. The framework's Gateway layer utilizes Recurrent Neural Networks (RNNs) to analyze sensor data streams for patterns or
anomalies before sending information to the cloud for deep data analysis based
on Google's BERT, enabling precise monitoring of environmental conditions
to inform agricultural decision-making. This approach not only optimizes crop
yield and resource management but also introduces efficient waste management practices, demonstrating a transformative step towards smarter, more secure
agricultural methodologies.

1 Introduction

In recent years, the agricultural sector has witnessed a paradigm shift driven by the
convergence of advanced technologies, such as the Internet of Things (IoT), artificial
intelligence (AI), and blockchain. These technologies hold immense potential to revolutionize traditional farming practices, enhance supply chain management, and address
pressing challenges in food security and sustainability [1]. Agricultural IoT systems,
characterized by interconnected sensors, actuators, and devices, enable real-time monitoring and management of farm operations, optimizing resource use and improving
crop yields [2, 3]. However, the widespread adoption of IoT in agriculture has introduced new challenges, including data security vulnerabilities, network inefficiencies,
and inadequate waste management practices [4, 5].

To address these challenges, recent research efforts have focused on integrating
blockchain technology into agricultural IoT frameworks [6, 7]. Blockchain, as a decentralized and tamper-proof ledger, offers enhanced security, transparency, and traceability,

© The Author(s), under exclusive license to Springer Nature Switzerland AG 2024
J. M. Ferrández Vicente et al. (Eds.): IWINAC 2024, LNCS 14675, pp. 461–473, 2024.
https://doi.org/10.1007/978-3-031-61137-7_43

making it an ideal solution for safeguarding agricultural data and transactions [8]. Furthermore, the incorporation of advanced AI techniques, such as Recurrent Neural Networks (RNNs) and Google's BERT, in the proposed framework's cloud layer enhances its analytical capabilities. RNNs, known for their ability to process sequential data, play a crucial role in analyzing sensor data streams, identifying patterns, and detecting anomalies in real-time [9]. Additionally, Google's BERT, a pre-trained natural language processing model, enables deep data analysis by extracting contextual information from textual data, thus facilitating more informed decision-making in agriculture [10, 11].

Despite the potential benefits of integrating blockchain and AI technologies into agricultural IoT frameworks, several challenges persist [12]. One significant challenge is ensuring the security and integrity of agricultural data transmitted and stored within the framework. With the increasing complexity and interconnectedness of IoT devices, agricultural systems become vulnerable to cyber-attacks, data breaches, and unauthorized access [13]. Maintaining data confidentiality, integrity, and availability is essential to prevent potential disruptions in agricultural operations and protect sensitive information [13]. Another challenge is optimizing network efficiency and scalability to accommodate the growing volume of data generated by IoT devices in agriculture [14]. Current network architectures may struggle to handle the large-scale data transmission and processing requirements of agricultural IoT systems, leading to bottlenecks, latency issues, and suboptimal performance Improving network optimization and scalability is crucial to ensure timely data delivery, seamless communication between devices, and efficient resource allocation in agricultural settings [8]. Furthermore, the lack of standardized protocols and interoperability among different IoT devices and platforms poses a significant challenge to the seamless integration of blockchain and AI technologies in agricultural IoT frameworks [15]. Diverse devices, protocols, and data formats may hinder data sharing, interoperability, and collaboration among stakeholders across the agricultural supply chain [16]. Developing standardized protocols and open-source frameworks is essential to promote interoperability, facilitate data exchange, and foster innovation in agricultural IoT applications [17].

2 Related Works

Authors in [14] presents a comprehensive study on the integration of Internet of Things (IoT) technologies and blockchain for enhancing traceability in agricultural practices, with a specific focus on hemp production. This multidisciplinary research combines technical innovation with agricultural science to address the challenges of traceability, authenticity, and quality assurance in the hemp industry. The study proposes a novel framework that utilizes IoT devices for real-time data collection at various stages of hemp production and employs blockchain technology to ensure the integrity, security, and transparency of the data collected. The research methodology includes the deployment of IoT sensors in hemp cultivation areas to monitor environmental conditions and plant growth, capturing data points such as temperature, humidity, soil moisture, and nutrient levels. This data is then recorded on a blockchain, creating an immutable record of the production process. The blockchain framework is designed to provide stakeholders, including farmers, regulators, and consumers, with access to verifiable and tamper-proof information regarding the origin, cultivation practices, and quality of hemp products. The study highlights the importance of user-centered design in the development of digital agricultural services, emphasizing the need for interfaces and systems that are accessible and useful for all participants in the supply chain. Through a real-world pilot project, the research demonstrates the practical application of the proposed framework and assesses its impact on the efficiency and transparency of hemp production. The findings suggest that integrating IoT and blockchain technologies can significantly enhance traceability and quality control in agriculture, offering a scalable model that could be adapted for other crops and production systems [18]. The study also identifies challenges and limitations, including the need for standardization in data collection and the high initial costs of technology deployment. However, the potential benefits, such as improved product quality, enhanced consumer trust, and compliance with regulatory requirements, are deemed to outweigh these challenges.

Authors in [19] propose a "Futuristic Approach in Agriculture and Food Supply Chain" explores the integration of Internet of Things (IoT) and blockchain technology in smart agriculture and the food supply chain. It addresses the challenges of increasing agricultural productivity sustainably amidst growing global food demands. The authors propose an innovative model that combines IoT's data collection and monitoring capabilities with blockchain's security and transparency to enhance efficiency, traceability, and reliability across the agricultural supply chain. This model is designed to overcome the limitations of current centralized systems by providing a distributed, efficient, and secure system for crop production and supply chain management. Through simulations, the proposed IoT-based agricultural protocol demonstrates significant improvements in network stability, energy consumption, and overall system efficiency compared to traditional methods [20]. The findings suggest that integrating IoT and blockchain technologies can significantly contribute to sustainable agriculture and food security by enabling more efficient resource use, reducing waste, and ensuring the authenticity and safety of food products.

Authors in [21], explores the integration of Internet of Things (IoT) and blockchain technologies in agriculture, presenting a comprehensive model to enhance agricultural practices and food supply chain management. It addresses the pressing need for sustainable food production, offering solutions to improve efficiency, traceability, and security from farm to table. By combining IoT's real-time monitoring capabilities with blockchain's secure, decentralized ledger, the proposed framework aims to optimize resource use, reduce waste, and ensure product authenticity. This innovative approach promises significant advancements in agricultural productivity and supply chain transparency, paving the way for more resilient and sustainable food systems.

Authors in [3] proposes a novel blockchain architecture aimed at enhancing the integrity and security of agricultural data. It introduces a model that integrates blockchain with smart contracts to automate processes and limit the risk of data manipulation, thereby ensuring safe storage for agricultural data. The architecture connects traditional farm systems with blockchain technology, utilizing sensors for environmental data collection. This approach promises to streamline the agricultural supply chain by automating transactions and decision-making processes through smart contracts based on collected data, leading to a more efficient and secure agricultural system. The study demonstrates a shift towards leveraging blockchain and smart contracts to address challenges in agriculture supply chain management, highlighting the potential for significant improvements in productivity, security, and transparency. The table presented below synthesizes the range of challenges identified and the advancements suggested across the reviewed literature (Table 1):

Table 1. Comparison of Features in Related Studies

Feature	[14]	[19]	[3]
Technology Focus	IoT and Blockchain	IoT and Blockchain	IoT and Blockchain
Application Domain	Agriculture and Food Supply Chain	Agriculture and Food Supply Chain	Agriculture and Food Supply Chain
Primary Challenges Addressed	- Security - Efficiency - Traceability	- Data - Management - Privacy - Interoperability	-Data Integrity - Security - Automation
Proposed Solutions	- Decentralized data management - Enhanced traceability and security	- Secure data exchange - Improved traceability	- Blockchain architecture - Smart contracts for process automation
Potential Impact	- Sustainable agriculture - Reduced waste	- Enhanced consumer trust - Compliance with food safety standards	- Streamlined transactions - Improved decision-making processes

3   Problem Definition

Agricultural practices, pivotal for global sustainability and food security, are currently facing a myriad of challenges. Traditional farming is being tested by its ability to scale and adapt to the growing demands for increased food production while maintaining environmental integrity. The integration of IoT in agriculture introduced the potential for smart farming, but this advancement has not been without its problems, particularly regarding data security, network efficiency, and comprehensive resource management.

Data integrity is critical in IoT agricultural systems, which heavily rely on sensor data for essential decision-making. Any compromise in data accuracy or security can have significant repercussions, leading to resource mismanagement and economic loss. The susceptibility of centralized systems to cyber threats necessitates a secure and resilient approach to data management.

The management of IoT networks in agriculture is equally challenging. These networks must handle large volumes of data efficiently; however, current systems often struggle with this task. The result can be inefficiencies and delays that negatively impact the timely and precise actions required for optimal agricultural output.

Resource management in agriculture isn't limited to the efficient use of water and nutrients but also encompasses effective waste management. The prevalent agricultural model frequently results in resource overuse and considerable waste, a situation made worse by ineffective supply chain mechanisms.

4 Solution Design

The proposed Multi-Zone Blockchain Framework seeks to address these issues head-on. It proposes a secure and scalable blockchain technology integration that promises to revolutionize agricultural IoT applications. The Enhanced Blowfish Algorithm (EBA) within the framework ensures robust authentication, essential for maintaining data security. Concurrently, a Bayesian-Direct Acyclic Graph (B-DAG) is employed for superior network optimization, as proved in the comparison below between a regular or linear Blockchain and our enhanced multizone blockchain with DAG optimization crucial for handling the data influx from various sensors efficiently (Table 2).

Table 2. Linear & Multizone -Blockchain comparison

Axes	Linear Blockchain	Multizone-Blockchain
Consensus	PoW or POS	PoAh
Transaction speed	Depends on hash speed (minutes, hours or days)	3 to 5 ms
Mining Time	Slow mining	Fast mining
Transaction validation	Hash verification	Hash verification
Chaining	Single and slow chaining	Fast chaining
Block-chain growth	exponential growth	Linear growth

The framework's Gateway layer utilizes Recurrent Neural Networks (RNNs) to analyze sensor data streams for patterns or anomalies. This step is crucial before forwarding the information to the cloud for deeper analysis. Google's BERT is then applied in the cloud layer, enabling detailed and precise monitoring of environmental conditions. Such a deep data analysis capability allows for informed decision-making in agriculture, vital for optimizing crop yields and managing resources effectively.

Resource efficiency and waste management are also critical. The conventional agricultural framework often results in the overutilization of inputs such as water, fertilizers, and pesticides, leading to substantial waste and environmental degradation. These inefficiencies not only compromise the sustainability of agricultural practices but also the economic viability for farmers. Furthermore, the increasing complexity of supply chains in agriculture necessitates greater transparency and traceability. Current systems lack the robustness to ensure that all stakeholders have access to accurate and timely information. This lack of transparency can lead to issues such as food fraud, supply chain inefficiencies, and barriers to enforcing responsible sourcing standards.

Addressing these problems requires a novel approach that can integrate enhanced security, improve network management, and facilitate efficient resource and waste management. The proposed Multi-Zone Blockchain Framework for Agriculture IoT represents a solution engineered to tackle these issues head-on. By incorporating advanced blockchain technologies and robust algorithms for authentication and network optimization, it offers a strategic advantage over traditional systems. The Enhanced Blowfish Algorithm (EBA) provides a high level of security, ensuring robust authentication across the network, while the Bayesian-Direct Acyclic Graph (B-DAG) enhances network optimization, enabling efficient data processing and management. The integration of Recurrent Neural Networks (RNNs) for analyzing sensor data ensures that patterns and anomalies are identified swiftly, enhancing the decision-making process for agricultural practices. Moreover, the application of Google's BERT in the cloud layer enables deep data analysis, which is crucial for monitoring complex environmental conditions. This data-driven insight assists in making precise agricultural decisions, optimizing crop yield, and managing resources effectively. Importantly, the framework's capability extends to improving waste management practices, which is vital for reducing the environmental footprint of farming operations.

The inclusion of efficient waste management practices in the framework is particularly transformative. It addresses the need for sustainable agriculture by minimizing waste throughout the supply chain, from production to distribution. This efficiency not only contributes to environmental conservation but also improves the overall profitability and sustainability of agricultural operations.

4.1 Multi-zones Blockchain Design

4.1.1 Authentication

The authentication process at the perception level involves verifying the legitimacy of IoT devices. This authentication relies on metrics such as Device ID, physically unclonable function (PUF), media access control address (MAC) address, and node location. Nodes initially register themselves with the Trusted Authority (TA), submitting their credentials for storage in the blockchain to ensure privacy. The TA employs the Enhanced Blowfish Algorithm (EBA) to generate secret keys for IoT nodes. A Random ID is periodically updated by the TA for each IoT node. Additionally, the proposed method utilizes four sub-keys generated by the Blowfish algorithm, stored in a 32-bit array (b[j]) known as B-array. These sub-keys vary based on input keys.

$$b[j] = b[j] XOR(j + 1) - th\,32 - bits\,input\,key \tag{1}$$

The enhancement made in the conventional blowfish algorithm is generating chaos based key generation (sub keys) $(CK_1, CK_2, CK_3, and\ CK_4)$ in which the generated key is completely chanciness in order and does not duplicate after number of cycles which can be formulate as,

$$Z_m + 1 = \forall Z_m(1 - Z_m) \tag{2}$$

where ∀ is variable that governs the chanciness of the keys, and Z_m denotes the confidence values that lie among (0, 1). The chaotic based key generation satisfies and evaluated in chaos theory which attains chaos features such as kindliness and chanciness.

```
Enhanced Blowfish Algorithm ()
Input: Chaotic positive values and variable parameters
Output: Chaotic sub keys CK₁, CK₂, CK₃, and CK₄
Begin
    Set and load the ∀, α, β
    Generate Chaotic sub keys using (3)-(6)
    Store sub keys in b[j] using (1)
    Generate rᵗ using authenticate metrics
    Update rᵗ periodically
End
```

4.1.2 Network Construction

Once the authentication of IoT devices is completed the edge node constructs the network graph of the IoT devices in order to effectively manage the traffic produced by those devices. The IoT nodes in the network are constructed into B-DAG in which connectivity between the nodes is computed by the Bayesian probability. The construction of B-DAG is based on the factors such as *number of transmissions, link stability, intimacy, location, and distance between the nodes.* The probabilistic way for labeling the relationship among variable is determine by Bayesian networks. In B-DAG model, the IoT nodes are signified as variables, edges between nodes are signified as relationship between them, parent nodes are roots, and children nodes are outcomes. The Conditional Probabilities (CDP) of the child nodes are stored distributivity in parent node. The B-DAG network is expressed as,

$$B - DAG\big[(Q, \partial)\big] \tag{3}$$

where Q represents the network structure of Bayesian in DAG which can be represented as $Q = (V^{er}, E^{dg})$ while $V^{er} = \{V_1^{er}, V_2^{er}, \ldots, V_n^{er}\}$ is the Bayesian network IoT nodes, E^{dg} is the edges among the nodes. ∂ is the network parameter of Bayesian which signifies the CDP for all nodes under the ailment of their parents.

If the E^{dg} among the IoT nodes is not present then B-DAG use factorization which can be formulated as,

$$pr(N/Q, \partial) = \prod_{i=1}^{c} pr\Big(N_i / \prod N_i, \partial_{N_i}\Big) \tag{4}$$

where $pr(N/Q, \partial)$ is the global distribution of N nodes which is distributed locally for $N_i - th$ node with ∂_{N_i} which is ailment under their parent $\prod N_i$. All the traffic generated by the IoT devices is sent to the edge nodes for effective computation. Figure 1 represents the B-DAG based network constructions in which vertices and edges of the parent and child nodes are represented.

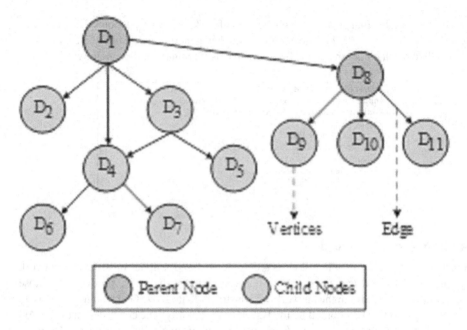

Fig. 1. B-DAG based network construction

4.1.3 Predictive Analysis Based on RNN

Once the network is constructed, all the emitted information pass through the application of neural networks which plays a crucial role in enhancing various aspects of agricultural data processing. This process involves three key steps.

Firstly, the training phase entails adjusting the weights of network connections based on the comparison between network output and training data, while evaluating network error. This step is essential for fine-tuning the network to accurately represent the underlying patterns in agricultural data.

Secondly, the verification step ensures the reliability of the trained network. During this phase, the values of connection weights remain constant, and the network's output is compared to the output generated during the training phase. This validation process ensures that the network maintains its accuracy and consistency in real-world scenarios.

Lastly, the generalization step evaluates the network's performance on unseen data, which simulates real-world agricultural scenarios that were not part of the training data. A network with good generalization capabilities can effectively process diverse agricultural data and adapt to new conditions, thus improving its utility and applicability in agricultural decision-making processes.

Compared to traditional feedforward neural networks, Recurrent Neural Networks (RNNs) offer distinct advantages due to their feedback connections, which introduce dynamic behavior. In agricultural applications, RNNs enable the processing of sequential data streams, where the output of neurons depends not only on the current input but also on the network's previous states. This dynamic nature of RNNs enhances their ability to capture temporal dependencies and patterns in agricultural data, making them well-suited for tasks such as crop yield prediction, weather forecasting, and pest detection.

4.1.4 Cloud Management Using BERT

Once the agricultural data has been processed through the predictive analysis phase utilizing RNNs, the resulting information is passed to the cloud layer for further analysis. Here, BERT is employed to extract contextual information and insights from textual data sources, such as weather reports, market trends, and expert recommendations.

By leveraging BERT's advanced language understanding capabilities, our framework can derive valuable insights from unstructured textual data, complementing the quantitative analysis performed by RNNs. This holistic approach enables more comprehensive decision-making in agriculture, incorporating both numerical and textual information to inform strategic agricultural practices.

Furthermore, the utilization of BERT in the cloud management phase enhances the scalability and flexibility of our framework. BERT's pre-trained model architecture allows for efficient processing of large volumes of textual data, enabling rapid analysis and decision-making in real-time. Additionally, the cloud-based deployment of BERT ensures accessibility and availability across agricultural stakeholders, facilitating collaborative decision-making and knowledge sharing. The Table 3 outlines the procedural details for each stage of the integration process between RNN and BERT.

Table 3. Parameters list used for the simulation purpose

Algorithm Step	Step Description
1. Preprocessing	Preprocess the sequential data X and textual data S as necessary, including tokenization, normalization, and scaling
2. RNN Analysis	- Input the preprocessed sequential data X into the trained RNN model. - Compute the hidden states and outputs of the RNN model based on the sequential input - Obtain insights and predictions from the RNN model regarding agricultural patterns, trends, and anomalies
3. BERT Analysis	- Input the preprocessed textual data S into the pre-trained BERT model - Utilize BERT's language understanding capabilities to extract contextual information and insights from the textual data - Obtain insights and predictions from BERT regarding contextual factors influencing agricultural decision-making
4. Integration	- Combine the outputs from the RNN analysis and BERT analysis to generate integrated insights - Apply appropriate aggregation or fusion techniques (e.g., concatenation, averaging, attention mechanism) to merge the insights from both models - Consider the relative importance of insights from RNN and BERT based on the specific agricultural application

(continued)

Table 3. (*continued*)

Algorithm Step	Step Description
5. Post-processing	- Perform any necessary post-processing steps on the integrated insights, such as filtering, smoothing, or feature engineering - Validate the integrated insights against domain-specific knowledge or rules to ensure their relevance and accuracy
6. Output	- Generate reports, visualizations, or alerts summarizing the integrated insights from both RNN and BERT analyses - Provide actionable recommendations for agricultural decision-making based on the integrated insights

4.2 Simulation Environment

Our proposed Multizone DAG Blockchain simulated in Network Simulator NS-3. In particular, it provides proper support for IoT protocols and operations. Therefore, we chose ns-3 as the simulation tool (Table 4).

Table 4. Parameters list used for the simulation purpose

Parameter		Value
Simulator version		3.26
OS		Ubuntu 14.04
RAM		4GB
Number of IoT nodes		50
Number of Fog nodes		10
Number of BGW		1
Number of cloud servers		3
Communication standard		Wi-Fi
Initial energy of IoT nodes		5j to 10 j
Packet generation rate		10 packets/sec
Packet size		512 bytes
Number of packets		100
Packet interval		0.1s
Number of zones		5
CubeHash parameters	R_{Ini}	100
	R_{fin}	100
	r	36

(continued)

Table 4. (*continued*)

Parameter		Value
Four-Q-Curve parameters	Key size	512 bytes
	Number of rounds	10
RNN	Hidden layers	10
	Activation function	sigmoid
	Learning rate	0.2
BERT	Initial population	100
	ran	0.2
	Maximum iteration	100
Simulation time		100 s

To facilitate agricultural operations, we simulate the sensors below to serve as environmental IoT sensors. Our simulation analysis will further explore the practical application of these sensors commonly utilized in agricultural settings (Table 5).

Table 5. Sensor deployed for simulation purpose

IoT sensor	Characteristic
Temperature Sensor	Measures ambient temperature and humidity levels in the environment
	Wireless (Bluetooth, LORA)
	Widely used in agriculture for monitoring microclimates and optimizing crop growth
Soil Moisture Sensor	Provides real-t ime data on soil moisture levels and temperature
	Wireless (LORA, Zigbee)
	Essential for irrigation management and ensuring optimal soil conditions
Weather Station	Collects data on rainfall, wind speed, and atmospheric pressure
	Wireless (Wi-Fi, LORA)
	Helps in weather forecasting and adapting farming practices to environmental changes

5   Conclusion

Our Multi-Zone Blockchain for Agriculture framework integrates various components to revolutionize agricultural data analysis. Through robust authentication mechanisms leveraging the Enhanced Blowfish Algorithm (EBA) and the periodic update of Random IDs by the Trusted Authority (TA), the framework ensures the legitimacy, privacy, and data integrity of IoT devices within the blockchain. Additionally, by constructing a Bayesian-Direct Acyclic Graph (B-DAG) network, the framework optimizes traffic management among IoT devices, considering factors such as connectivity, link stability, and location. This probabilistic modeling of relationships within the B-DAG network enables adaptive and dynamic network management tailored to agricultural IoT environments. Moreover, the integration of Recurrent Neural Networks (RNN) and Google's BERT enhances the framework's analytical capabilities, providing comprehensive insights into agricultural patterns and trends. By combining the predictive capabilities of RNNs with the contextual understanding provided by BERT, the framework enables informed decision-making in agriculture, facilitating sustainable and efficient farming practices. Moving forward, our next step will involve comparing the performance of our framework with existing agricultural IoT solutions, aiming to demonstrate its superiority in terms of data analysis capabilities and decision-making support. Furthermore, we will explore avenues for further optimization and enhancement to advance the field of agricultural IoT and contribute to the development of more intelligent and sustainable farming practices.

References

1. Kably, S., Arioua, M., Alaoui, N.: Lightweight blockchain network architecture for IoT devices. In: The 3rd International Symposium on Advanced Electrical and Communication Technologies (ISAECT2020) (2020). 978-0-7381
2. Zhao, Y., Li, Q., Yi, W., Xiong, H.; Agricultural IoT data storage optimization and information security method based on blockchain. Agric. 13(2) (2023). https://doi.org/10.3390/agricultu re13020274
3. El Mane, A., Chihab, Y., Tatane, K., Korchiyne, R.: Agriculture supply chain management based on blockchain architecture and smart contracts. Appl. Comput. Intell. Soft Comput. 2022 (2022). https://doi.org/10.1155/2022/8011525
4. Dlimi, Z., Ezzati, A., Ben Alla, S.: A lightweight blockchain for IoT in smart city (IoT-SmartChain). Comput. Mater. Contin. 69(2), 2687–2703 (2021). https://doi.org/10.32604/ cmc.2021.018942
5. Hasan, M.Z., Hanapi, Z.M., Hussain, M.Z., Hussin, M., Sarwar, N., Akhlaqi, M.Y.: Deep insight into IoT-enabled agriculture and network protocols. Wirel. Commun. Mob. Comput. 2022 (2022). https://doi.org/10.1155/2022/5617903
6. Novo, O.: Blockchain meets IoT: an architecture for scalable access management in IoT. IEEE Internet Things J. 5(2), 1184–1195 (2018). https://doi.org/10.1109/JIOT.2018.2812239
7. Ehsan, I., et al.: A conceptual model for blockchain-based agriculture food supply chain system. Sci. Program. 2022 (2022). https://doi.org/10.1155/2022/7358354
8. Kably, S., Arioua, M., Alaoui, N.: Lightweight direct acyclic graph blockchain for enhancing resource-constrained IoT environment. Comput. Mater. Contin. 71(2), 5271–5291 (2022). https://doi.org/10.32604/cmc.2022.020833

9. Kably, S., Benbarrad, T., Alaoui, N., Arioua, M.: Multi-zone-wise blockchain based intrusion detection and prevention system for IoT environment. Comput. Mater. Contin. **74**(1), 253–278 (2023). https://doi.org/10.32604/cmc.2023.032220

10. Falayi, A., Wang, Q., Liao, W., Yu, W.: Survey of distributed and decentralized IoT securities: approaches using deep learning and blockchain technology. Futur. Internet **15**(5) (2023). https://doi.org/10.3390/fi15050178

11. Qureshi, T., Saeed, M., Ahsan, K., Malik, A.A., Muhammad, E.S., Touheed, N.: Smart agriculture for sustainable food security using internet of things (IoT). Wirel. Commun. Mob. Comput. **2022** (2022). https://doi.org/10.1155/2022/9608394

12. Cecilia Eberendu, A., Ifeanyi Chinebu, T.: Can blockchain be a solution to IoT technical and security issues. Int. J. Netw. Secur. Appl. **13**(6), 123–132 (2021). https://doi.org/10.5121/ijnsa.2021.13609

13. Kotey, S.D., et al.: Blockchain interoperability: the state of heterogenous blockchain-to-blockchain communication. IET Commun. (January), 1–24 (2023). https://doi.org/10.1049/cmu2.12594

14. Ferrández-Pastor, F.J., Mora-Pascual, J., Díaz-Lajara, D.: Agricultural traceability model based on IoT and blockchain: application in industrial hemp production. J. Ind. Inf. Integr. **29**(July), 100381 (2022). https://doi.org/10.1016/j.jii.2022.100381

15. Zakariae, D., Abdellah, E., Saïd, B.A.: A lightweight blockchain framework for IoT integration in smart cities. Turk. J. Comput. Math. Educ. **12**(5), 889–894 (2021). https://doi.org/10.17762/turcomat.v12i5.1731

16. Xu, R., Nikouei, S.Y., Chen, Y., Blasch, E., Aved, A.: BlendMAS: a blockchain-enabled decentralized microservices architecture for smart public safety. In: Proceedings - 2019 2nd IEEE International Conference on Blockchain, Blockchain 2019, pp. 564–571 (2019). https://doi.org/10.1109/Blockchain.2019.00082

17. De Smet, R., Vandervelden, T., Steenhaut, K., Braeken, A.: Lightweight PUF based authentication scheme for fog architecture. Wirel. Netw. **27**(2), 947–959 (2021). https://doi.org/10.1007/s11276-020-02491-0

18. Dorri, A., Kanhere, S.S., Jurdak, R., Gauravaram, P.: LSB: A Lightweight scalable blockchain for IoT security and anonymity. J. Parallel Distrib. Comput. **134**, 180–197 (2019). https://doi.org/10.1016/j.jpdc.2019.08.005

19. Awan, S., et al.: IoT with blockchain: a futuristic approach in agriculture and food supply chain. Wirel. Commun. Mob. Comput. **2021** (2021). https://doi.org/10.1155/2021/5580179

20. Al Ridhawi, I., Kotb, Y., Aloqaily, M., Jararweh, Y., Baker, T.: A profitable and energy-efficient cooperative fog solution for IoT services. IEEE Trans. Ind. Inform. **16**(5), 3578–3586 (2020). https://doi.org/10.1109/TII.2019.2922699

21. Nigam, S., Sugandh, U., Khari, M.: The integration of blockchain and IoT edge devices for smart agriculture: challenges and use cases. Adv. Comput.Comput. **127**, 507–537 (2022). https://doi.org/10.1016/BS.ADCOM.2022.02.015

Enhancing Plant Disease Detection in Agriculture Through YOLOv6 Integration with Convolutional Block Attention Module

Abdelilah Haijoub[1]([✉]), Anas Hatim[2], Mounir Arioua[1], Ahmed Eloualkadi[3], and María Dolores Gómez-López[4]

[1] Engineering Sciences Laboratory, National School of Applied Sciences of Kenitra, Ibn Tofail University, Kenitra, Morocco
haijoub.abdel@gmail.com
[2] Laboratory of Information Technology and Modeling, National School of Applied Sciences of Marrakech, Cadi Ayyad University, Marrakech, Morocco
[3] Innovative Systems Engineering Laboratory, National School of Applied Sciences of Tetouan, Abdelmalek Essaadi University, Tetouan, Morocco
[4] Agronomomic Engineering Department, Technical University of Cartagena, Cartagena, Spain
lola.gomez@upct.es

Abstract. Plant diseases pose a significant threat to global agriculture, resulting in substantial crop losses each year. To address the pressing need for rapid and accurate disease identification, this study explores the efficacy of an enhanced YOLOv6 model incorporating the Convolutional Block Attention Module (CBAM) for detecting plant diseases, utilizing an open-source dataset. Encompassing a diverse range of healthy and infected plant leaves across various disease categories and crop types, our research aims to enhance disease identification in agriculture. Our evaluation of various YOLO models revealed that the augmented YOLOv6 integrated with CBAM outperforms traditional and other YOLO variants in plant disease identification. This model achieves exceptional accuracy, highlighting the importance of attention mechanisms in boosting the diagnostic accuracy of deep learning models. Such an enhancement is pivotal for developing real-time detection tools, empowering farmers to quickly identify and tackle crop diseases, thereby potentially reducing agricultural losses. This breakthrough demonstrates the augmented YOLOv6 model with CBAM as the most effective approach among the YOLO series for plant disease detection, underscoring its significance in advancing agricultural diagnostics and management. The conducted experiments validate the advantages of integrating YOLOv6 with attention mechanisms such as CBAM in the context of agricultural disease detection. This represents a significant stride towards the development of more accurate, rapid, and reliable diagnostic tools, enhancing crop management and protection strategies.

Keywords: Plant Disease Identification · CNN · CBAM · YOLOv6

© The Author(s), under exclusive license to Springer Nature Switzerland AG 2024
J. M. Ferrández Vicente et al. (Eds.): IWINAC 2024, LNCS 14675, pp. 474–484, 2024.
https://doi.org/10.1007/978-3-031-61137-7_44

1   Introduction

Plant diseases are a major concern in the field of agriculture, posing a significant threat to global food production. Each year, these diseases lead to substantial crop losses, impacting the livelihoods of farmers and the availability of food resources. Rapid and accurate disease identification is essential for effective disease management and prevention, as it allows for timely intervention and reduces the spread of infections.

In recent years, deep learning and computer vision techniques have shown great promise in revolutionizing the way we detect and diagnose plant diseases. Efforts to combat plant diseases using machine learning and computer vision techniques have gained considerable attention in recent years. Researchers have explored various methods to develop accurate and efficient disease detection models. One popular approach has been the use of convolution neural networks and object detection models to identify diseased plant leaves from images. Central to these technological advancements, image processing has emerged as a key technique, highlighted by the contributions of authors [1] to [5]. These studies explored various techniques to obtain information from images of plant leaves, using methods such as color, texture, and shape analysis to identify signs of disease. For instance, Husin et al. [1] investigated the feasibility of detecting chili diseases through the inspection of leaf characteristics, while Barbedo et al. [2] suggested a method based on color transformations and color histograms to identify multiple plant diseases. The integration of machine learningbased methods, notably SVM, KNN, and BPNN, has marked a significant evolution in the precision of disease detection. [6] to [10] have demonstrated how these models can be trained to effectively recognize plant diseases from features extracted from images. For example, Al Bashish et al. [6] developed a framework for identifying and classifying diseases of leaves and stems using K-Means for segmentation, followed by classification through a neural network, achieving remarkable precision.

Convolutional Neural Networks have introduced a technological breakthrough by enabling deep analysis of images for accurate disease detection. The contributions of authors [11] to [16] illustrated the effectiveness of CNNs in learning discriminative features of diseases from complex visual data. Chen et al. [11], for instance, explored the use of meta-learning for disease detection in situations with a limited number of examples, while Ashwinkumar et al. [12] proposed a model based on MobileNet optimized for leaf disease classification. The introduction of YOLO models for object detection has opened new paths for real-time crop surveillance. [17] to [24] adapted YOLO to identify areas affected by diseases on leaves, demonstrating these models' ability to provide rapid and accurate diagnostics. For example, Mathew et al. [17] and Wang et al. [18] have shown how YOLOv3 and YOLOv5 can be used to effectively detect diseases in apple and tomato leaves, offering a promising solution for largescale disease management. Our current contribution continues these efforts by exploring the application of YOLOv6 enhanced with CBAM for even more precise plant disease detection. By combining the speed and efficiency of YOLO with the selective attention capabilities of CBAM, we aim to overcome the limitations of previous approaches and offer a robust solution for early disease detection, thus contributing to crop protection and reducing agricultural losses.

The remainder of the paper is structured as follows: Sect. 2 provides a comprehensive description of the methodology, including discussions on YOLO, YOLOv6, and CBAM. Section 3 elaborates on the experimental setup and results, covering hardware and software configuration, dataset description, and analysis of results. Lastly, the paper is concluded in the final section.

2 Methods

Joseph Redmon and Ali Farhadi created the real-time object detection technology known as YOLO (You Only Look Once), which has seen several advancements from its first release in 2015 to YOLOv7 [27] in 2022. Each iteration has brought significant improvements in network architecture, efficiency, and detection accuracy. YOLOv1 [25] laid the groundwork with a unique approach using a single convolutional neural network, while subsequent versions, YOLOv2 [26] through YOLOv7 [27], have continued to refine object detection by introducing new network architectures, enhanced convolution techniques, and streamlined versions for improved performance on resource-constrained devices.

In addressing plant disease detection, traditional methods often encounter challenges, such as high false positive rates caused by external variables like variations in light and the diverse appearance of the foliage. To overcome these limitations, our approach departs from the standard YOLOv5-based object detection techniques, opting for the enhanced YOLOv6 [28] model. To mitigate the impact of external interferences, we have incorporated the Convolutional Block Attention Module (CBAM) [29], which enhances the model's ability to focus on significant features for accurate disease identification.

2.1 YOLOv6 Architecture

YOLOv6 builds upon the foundational principles of the YOLO architecture, prioritizing both efficiency and precision in object detection. Its design comprises several key components:

Convolutional Backbone: At its core, YOLOv6 employs the CSPDarknet53 as its convolutional backbone. This design integrates Cross-Stage Partial (CSP) networks with Darknet53, optimizing for a balanced representation of features that contributes to both speed and accuracy enhancements.

Neck: To adeptly handle objects of varying scales, YOLOv6 incorporates a multiscale feature integration neck. This pyramid-shaped structure facilitates the merging of spatial features across different levels, ensuring robust detection across a spectrum of object sizes.

Head: Recognizing the diverse requirements of object detection tasks, YOLOv6 is offered in multiple variants. Ranging from YOLOv6-small to YOLOv6-xlarge, these models provide a spectrum of options tailored to specific performance and efficiency needs.

2.2   CBAM

CBAM, or Convolutional Block Attention Module, represents a strategic enhancement to neural network architectures, focusing on the refinement of feature selection. The module comprises two pivotal elements:

Channel Attention Module: This component scrutinizes the feature maps across channels, allocating attention weights based on the relative importance of each channel. The outcome is a reweighted feature map that emphasizes the most significant channels.

Spatial Attention Module: Complementing the channel-focused attention, this module assesses the spatial dimensions of the feature map. By assigning spatial attention weights, it highlights areas of the image that are essential for accurate detection.

2.3   Integration of CBAM into YOLOv6

The integration of CBAM into the YOLOv6 architecture marks a significant leap forward in plant disease detection technology. By enabling selective focus on pertinent features within complex images, this combined approach mitigates the challenges posed by varying lighting conditions and the diversity of plant appearances. Specifically, the CBAM module is incorporated at the head layers of YOLOv6, enhancing the model's precision without compromising its inherent speed.

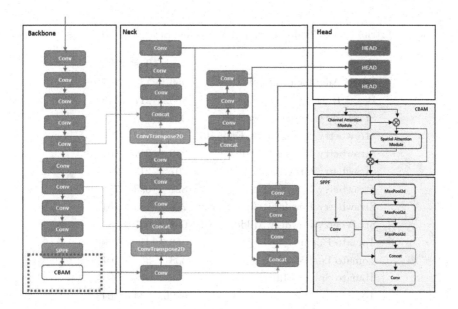

Fig. 1. Proposed Enhanced YOLOv6 Architecture with CBAM Integration.

This synergistic incorporation of YOLOv6 and CBAM offers a potent solution for the accurate detection of plant diseases, addressing critical needs in crop monitoring and protection by minimizing false positives and maximizing detection accuracy.

3 Experimental Setup and Results

3.1 Hardware and Software Configuration

Our study utilized a high-performance computing setup to evaluate different YOLO models under the same conditions. This setup included a workstation powered by an Nvidia Quadro RTX 5000 GPU, complemented by 32GB of RAM and an Intel Xeon processor with a 3.60GHz clock speed across 8 cores. Running on Ubuntu 18.04 LTS and leveraging CUDA 11.7.0, this system was optimized for GPU acceleration, enabling efficient training and testing of YOLO models. Image processing was managed through OpenCV, and PyTorch was used for its flexibility and compatibility with CUDA to implement the models.

3.2 Dataset

The dataset for detecting diseases in Beans, Strawberries, and Tomatoes comprises 5494 pre-processed images, annotated for YOLO PyTorch. It spans categories like 'Angular Leafspot,' 'Leaf Mold,' and 'Bean Rust,' streamlining automated disease detection.

Table 1. Distribution of Train, Test, and Validation Set Image Numbers by Class

Class	Train	Test	Valid
Beans Angular LeafSpot	956	131	277
Beans Rust	1652	217	463
Strawberry Angular LeafSpot	226	295	193
Strawberry Anthracnose Fruit Rot	166	132	85
Strawberry Blossom Blight	258	211	161
Strawberry Gray Mold	207	213	200
Strawberry Leaf Spot	821	698	779
Strawberry Powdery Mildew Fruit	278	134	151
Strawberry Powdery Mildew Leaf	669	607	584
Tomato Blight	352	41	100
Tomato Leaf Mold	353	35	101
Tomato Spider Mites	358	31	99
Total	6006	2344	3043

3.3   Metrics for Object Detection

Object detection models are evaluated using key metrics such as Mean Average Precision (mAP), which averages precision across classes at various IoU thresholds; Precision, measuring the accuracy of detections; Recall, indicating the percentage of correctly identified positives; Intersection-over-Union (IoU), assessing bounding box accuracy by their overlap ratio; and mAP@50-95, an aggregate measure of mAP calculated at IoU thresholds from 0.50 to 0.95 in increments of 0.05, offering a comprehensive evaluation of model performance across different levels of detection difficulty.

3.4   Analysis of Results

This section outlines the outcomes from training and evaluating various iterations of the Yolo object detection framework. Each model underwent training utilizing the identical dataset and conditions, with all training images set to a resolution of 640x 640 pixels. The assessment of these models was performed using a set of new, previously unseen images to ensure a robust test of their capabilities beyond the training data. The precise details of the training configurations employed are thoroughly recorded in Table 2. Through this methodology, our goal is to shed light on the comparative effectiveness and adaptability of each model variant when confronted with novel imagery.

Table 2. Training Configuration Parameters for YOLO Models

Parameter	Value
Batch size	16
Momentum	0.73375
Learning rate	0.00269
Number of iterations	250 epochs
Fixed image size	640×640
Weight decay	0.00015

The models were evaluated using a variety of metrics, including precision, recall, mAP@0.5 IoU, AP@0.5 IoU 95, GFLOPS, number of parameters, and training duration. The findings are detailed in Table 3.

In our study, we focused on evaluating the impact of incorporating CBAM into YOLOv6. This integration led to a notable precision increase to 0.906 from the original YOLOv6's precision of 0.9, while also maintaining robust performance metrics such as mAP@0.5 and MAP@0.5-95. Importantly, YOLOv6+CBAM demonstrated a significant improvement over YOLOv7 in terms of MAP@0.5-95, showcasing its superior detection capabilities in more challenging conditions.

Table 3. Comparative Analysis of YOLO Models

Model	Precision	Recall	mAP@0.5	MAP@0.5–95	Training (h)	GFLOPS	Parameters
YOLOv6	0.9	0.854	0.897	0.732	1.904	11.9	4,229,618
YOLOv7	0.868	0.867	0.895	0.694	7.65	105.3	37,255,890
YOLOv6+CBAM	0.906	0.845	0.9	0.736	1.7	12	4,483,111

The performance enhancements achieved by YOLOv6+CBAM were realized without an increase in computational cost, evidenced by comparable GFLOPS and parameter counts to the original YOLOv6. Moreover, the training time for YOLOv6+CBAM was slightly reduced, indicating an optimization in the model training process alongside its enhanced efficiency.

The YOLOv6+CBAM model stands out in the object detection field, achieving exceptional precision at 0.906, outperforming other models listed in Table 4. This precision is vital for applications requiring high accuracy. Despite a competitive recall rate of 0.845, there's room for improvement to ensure comprehensive object detection. The model also demonstrates a strong mAP@0.5, showcasing its effectiveness in various scenarios, though it slightly lags behind the highest rates.

Table 4. State-of-the-Art Performance Comparison

Model	Precision	Recall	mAP@0.5	GFLOPS
Nanodet-plus [31]	0.887	0.929	0.892	8.4
Improved YOLOv5 [30]	0.888	0.97	0.931	8.3
Ours	0.906	0.845	0.9	12

The integration of the CBAM into YOLOv6, while enhancing feature discernment, raises the model's computational demand, as indicated by its GFLOPS. This highlights YOLOv6+CBAM as a precision-focused model, ideal for critical accuracy applications, with future enhancements aimed at improving recall and computational efficiency.

Our method demonstrated the effectiveness of incorporating attention mechanisms, such as CBAM, to enhance detection performance, as highlighted in Table 4. This approach underscores the critical balance needed between computational efficiency and detection accuracy, emphasizing the importance of advanced feature discernment for improved object detection.

Fig. 2. Detection of Plant Diseases on Tomato and Strawberry Leaves Using YOLOV6+CBAM Object Recognition Model.

4   Conclusions

Our research introduces a significant advancement in plant disease detection by integrating the Convolutional Block Attention Module with YOLOv6, achieving a notable precision of 90.6%. This integration highlights the importance of attention mechanisms in enhancing object detection models' accuracy, especially in the complex domain of agriculture. The YOLOv6+CBAM model demonstrates a commendable balance between computational efficiency and detection accuracy, addressing key challenges in agricultural diagnostics such as variable environmental conditions and diverse symptom presentation. While the model demands higher computational resources, the improvement in diagnostic precision presents a valuable trade-off. Future efforts will aim at optimizing the model further to improve recall and reduce computational load, broadening its applicability in real-world agricultural settings. Our findings, showcased in the State-of-the-Art Performance Comparison, mark a step forward in using advanced machine learning to combat plant diseases, potentially reducing crop losses and enhancing food security globally.

References

1. Husin, Z.B., Shakaff, A.Y., Aziz, A.H., Farook, R.B.: Feasibility Study on plant chili disease detection using image processing techniques. In: Third International Conference on Intelligent Systems Modelling and Simulation 2012, pp. 291-296. IEEE (2012)
2. Barbedo, J.G., Koenigkan, L.V., Santos, T.T.: Identifying multiple plant diseases using digital image processing. Biosys. Eng. **147**, 104–116 (2016)
3. Khirade, S.D., Patil, A.B.: Plant disease detection using image processing. In: International Conference on Computing Communication Control and Automation, pp. 768-771. IEEE (2015)
4. Zhang, S.W., Shang, Y.J., Wang, L.: Plant disease recognition based on plant leaf image. J. Anim. Plant Sci. **25**(3), 42–45 (2015)
5. Pydipati, R., Burks, T.F., Lee, W.S.: Identification of citrus disease using color texture features and discriminant analysis. Comput. Electron. Agric. **52**, 49–59 (2006)
6. Al Bashish, D., Braik, M., Bani-Ahmad, S.: A framework for detection and classification of plant leaf and stem diseases. In: International Conference on Signal and Image Processing, pp. 113-118. IEEE (2010)
7. Arivazhagan, S. Newlin Shebiah, R. Ananthi,S. Vishnu Varthini S.: Detection of unhealthy region of plant leaves and classification of plant leaf diseases using texture features. CIGR J. **15**(1) 211-217 (2013)
8. Pujari, J.D., Yakkundimath, R., Byadgi, A.S.: Image processing based detection of fungal diseases in plants. Procedia Comput. Sci. **46**, 1802–1808 (2015)
9. Prasad, S., Peddoju, S.K., Ghosh, D.: Multi-resolution mobile vision system for plant leaf disease diagnosis. SIViP **10**, 379–388 (2015)
10. Pujari, D.J., Yakkundimath, R., Byadgi, A.S.: SVM and Ann based classification of plant diseases using feature reduction technique. Int. J. Interact. Multimedia Artif. Intell. **3**(6) 6-14 (2016)
11. Chen, L., Cui, X., Li, W.: Meta-learning for few-shot plant disease detection. Foods **10**(10), 2441 (2021)

12. Ashwinkumar, S., Rajagopal, S., Manimaran, V., Jegajothi, B.: Automated plant leaf disease detection and classification using optimal mobilenet based convolutional neural networks. Mater. Today Proc. **51**, 480–487 (2022)

13. Malathy, S., Karthiga, R.R., Swetha, K., Preethi, G.: Disease detection in fruits using image processing. In: 6th International Conference on Inventive Computation Technologies (ICICT) 2021, pp. 747-752. IEEE (2021)

14. Jadhav, S.B., Udupi, V.R., Patil, S.B.: Identification of plant diseases using convolutional neural networks. Int. J. Inf. Technol. **13**(6), 2461–2470 (2020)

15. Agarwal, M., Singh, A., Arjaria, S., Sinha, A., Gupta, S.: Tomato leaf disease detection using convolution neural network. Procedia Comput. Sci. **167**, 293–301 (2020)

16. Abbas, A., Jain, S., Gour, M., Vankudothu, S.: Tomato plant disease detection using transfer learning with C-GAN synthetic images. Comput. Electron. Agric. **187**, 106279 (2021)

17. Mathew, M.P., Yamuna Mahesh, T.: Determining the region of apple leaf affected by disease using Yolo V3. In: 2021 International Conference on Communication, Control and Information Sciences (ICCISc) 2021, p. 1-4. IEEE (2021)

18. Wang, H., Shang, S., Wang, D., He, X., Feng, K., Zhu, H.: Plant disease detection and classification method based on the optimized lightweight YOLOv5 model. Agriculture **12**(7), 931 (2022)

19. Li, D., Ahmed, F., Wu, N., Sethi, A.I.: Yolo-JD: a deep learning network for jute diseases and pests detection from images. Plants **11**(7), 937 (2022)

20. Tian, Y., Yang, G., Wang, Z., Wang, H., Li, E., Liang, Z.: Apple detection during different growth stages in orchards using the improved Yolo-V3 model. Comput. Electron. Agric. **157**, 417–426 (2019)

21. Li, X., et al.: Fast and accurate green pepper detection in complex backgrounds via an improved Yolov4-tiny model. Comput. Electron. Agric. **191**, 106503 (2021)

22. Li, J., Qiao, Y., Liu, S., Zhang, J., Yang, Z., Wang, M.: An improved yolov5-based vegetable disease detection method. Comput. Electron. Agric. **202**, 107345 (2022)

23. Gong, X., Zhang, S.: An analysis of plant diseases identification based on deep learning methods. Plant Pathol. J. **39**(4), 319–334 (2023)

24. Mathew, M.P., Mahesh, T.Y.: Leaf-based disease detection in bell pepper plant using Yolo V5. SIViP **16**, 841–847 (2021)

25. Redmon, J., Divvala, S., Girshick, R., Farhadi, A.: You only look once: unified, real-time object detection. In : IEEE Conference on Computer Vision and Pattern Recognition (CVPR), pp. 779-788. IEEE (2016)

26. Redmon, J., Farhadi, A.: Yolo9000: better, faster, stronger. In: IEEE Conference on Computer Vision and Pattern Recognition (CVPR), pp. 7263-7271. IEEE (2017)

27. Wang, C.-Y., Bochkovskiy, A., Liao, H.-Y.M.: Yolov7: trainable bag-of-freebies sets new state-of-the-art for real-time object detectors. In: IEEE/CVF Conference on Computer Vision and Pattern Recognition (CVPR), pp. 7464-7475. IEEE (2023)

28. Chuyi, L.: YOLOv6: a single-stage object detection framework for industrial applications. arXiv preprint. arXiv preprint arXiv:2209.02976 (2022)

29. Woo, S., Park, J., Lee, J.-Y., Kweon, I.S.: CBAM: convolutional block attention module. In: Ferrari, V., Hebert, M., Sminchisescu, C., Weiss, Y. (eds.) ECCV 2018. LNCS, vol. 11211, pp. 3–19. Springer, Cham (2018). https://doi.org/10.1007/978-3-030-01234-2_1
30. Li, Zhang, J., Yang, Z.,J., Qiao, Y., Liu, S., Wang, M.: An improved y olov5-based vegetable disease detection method. Comput. Electron. Agric. **202**, 107345 (2022)
31. LNCS Homepage. https://github.com/RangiLyu/nanodet. (Accessed 07 Feb 2024)

The Implementation of Artificial Intelligence Based Body Tracking for the Assessment of Orientation and Mobility Skills in Visual Impaired Individuals

Roberto Morollón Ruiz[1]([✉]) [iD], Joel Alejandro Cueva Garcés[1] [iD], Leili Soo[1] [iD], and Eduardo Fernández[1,2,3,4] [iD]

[1] Miguel Hernandez University, Elche, Spain
{rmorollon,lsoo,e.fernandez}@umh.es, joel.cueva@alu.umh.es
[2] CIBER-BBN, Madrid, Spain
[3] John Moran Eye Center, University of Utah, Salt Lake City, USA
[4] Radboud University, Nijmegen, Netherlands
https://cortivis.org/

Abstract. Visually impaired individuals face immense challenges during navigation. A comprehensive understanding of orientation and mobility (O&M) skills would shed light on the difficulties they face and expand the scope of therapeutic interventions. Here, we aim to complement the existing metrics of performance measurement in O&M assessments by presenting the methodological implementation of body tracking using artificial intelligence (AI) tools. We video-recorded a participant navigating a line marked on the floor within an indoor environment designed to replicate real-world conditions. Utilizing the YOLOv8 neural network for human detection and tracking, we transformed raw data to determine participant locations. To assess the efficacy of our body-tracking system, we examined deviations from the designated route. We found minimal disparities and a strong positive correlation between the marked path and the tracked route. Hence, our YOLOv8-based body-tracking system accurately captures participant locations. Furthermore, we provided two practical applications of the body tracking data: first, the real-time estimation of participant speed throughout the task, and second, the precise measurement of the total path length covered. Here, we presented a body tracking implementation which can capture the precise locations of participants in complex environments. This data analysis offers insights into the dynamic interactions between individuals with vision impairments and their surroundings, complementing existing measures of Orientation and Mobility (O&M) performance with additional outcome metrics.

Keywords: Visual impairment · Orientation and Mobility (O&M) · Navigation · Artificial Intelligence · Object detection · Body tracking · You Only Look Once (YOLO) · Accessibility · Assistive technologies

J. M. Ferrández Vicente et al. (Eds.): IWINAC 2024, LNCS 14675, pp. 485–494, 2024.
https://doi.org/10.1007/978-3-031-61137-7_45

1   Introduction

Vision impairment affects over 2.2 billion people across the world [5,11]. As vision is pivotal for daily functioning, its loss profoundly impacts individuals' quality of life [6,30]. Vision problems significantly hinder individuals' ability to navigate unaided, leading to a loss of independence [1]. Therefore, measuring O&M in visual impairment is crucial for gaining knowledge of individuals' navigational abilities and identifying areas where support is needed to enhance mobility and spatial awareness [3]. Additionally, monitoring O&M performance over time enables practitioners to track progress, evaluate the effectiveness of rehabilitation programs to individual needs, essential for promoting individuals' autonomy, safety and well-being [27].

The navigational skills of visually impaired individuals have been studied for decades [26]. Previous research has evaluated these skills using metrics such as time, speed, collisions and aid usage [7]. However, these outcome measures do not fully capture the complexity of the challenges faced within the environment. To address this gap, we implemented an artificial intelligence (AI) based body tracking method for assessing visually impaired individuals during orientation and mobility (O&M). This approach aims to uncover patterns and insights that could inform more personalised and effective rehabilitation strategies. In addition to validating the performance of the proposed body-tracking implementation, we show how the data can be used to calculate the deviations from the proposed route, the speed of the participant in any given moment of time and the path length.

Body tracking is a process of capturing and analysing human movement. It is used across diverse scientific and technological fields, including healthcare, rehabilitation and human-computer interfaces. Despite its wide utility, body tracking technologies have limitations related to accuracy, computational complexity and usability [13]. Body tracking is achieved using various technologies, including depth sensors [14], inertial measurement units (IMUs) [19] electromyography (EMG) [8] and computer vision algorithms [21]. Markerless motion capture techniques using computer vision algorithms, have emerged as a prominent approach, enabling the tracking of human body movements without physical markers [16]. They rely on feature detection, image segmentation, and joint landmarks to estimate trajectories over time. However, it is crucial to recognize that markerless motion capture methods may face challenges such as occlusion and accuracy issues, which can impact their reliability in real-world applications [9].

The integration of AI has revolutionised body tracking and object detection processes. AI-based techniques using machine learning and deep learning, have significantly enhanced the accuracy of body tracking algorithms. Object recognition, a key component of computer vision, is used to identify and distinguish objects from images and videos. However, while AI-based methods offer promising results, they are not without limitations. Factors such as model complexity, training data quality and computational resources can influence the performance and scalability of AI algorithms [4,15,18,25]. In terms of AI-based object detection, various methods have been developed. These include You Only Look Once

(YOLO) [20,24], Histogram Oriented Gradient (HOG) [29], Region-based Convolutional Neural Network (R-CNN) [23], Single Shot Detector (SDD) [28], Spatial Pyramid Pooling (SPP-Net) [32], CenterNet and EfficientNet. These methods differ in terms of speed, accuracy and computational requirements, allowing practitioners to choose the most suitable approach based on their specific needs and constraints [2,12].

For our study, we chose to utilise YOLO due to its real-time object detection capabilities and streamlined inference process. While YOLO excels in detecting large objects with well-defined features in a resource-efficient manner, it may encounter challenges with small, complex shapes, occluded regions or overlapping objects. Additionally, the performance of YOLO can be influenced by factors such as image resolution, with higher resolutions leading to more accurate but computationally intensive results. By addressing these considerations, we aim to provide a balanced evaluation of the capabilities and limitations of YOLO in our study. In particular, we run a demo experiment where the task of the participant was to follow a marked line on the floor. We use this line to validate the location of the participant as estimated by the AI body-tracking.

2   Methods

2.1   The Testing Environment

The experimental setup forms a critical foundation for exploring O&M challenges faced by visually impaired individuals. We are using an indoor laboratory environment, StreetLab, which is designed to simulate the real-world for the study of vision, hearing and O&M. With dimensions of 100 m^2, this controlled setting comprises diverse spatial configurations, incorporating elements such as intersections and obstacles, to mirror the intricacies of urban navigation. A key facet of the experimental setup is the integration of a 4-camera recording system strategically positioned to achieve complete coverage of the experimental area. This system operates to provide a multi-perspective view of the participants' movements. All the processes were performed in a MSI Katana model laptop with i7 intel core CPU, 32GB RAM, 1T of SSD and a RTX 3060, on a Windows 11 OS. We used Reolink software for recording the videos.

2.2   Behavioural Task

To test the system, the participant completed a total of 10 trials consisting of five routes completed back and forth (see Fig. 1). Four routes were in C-shape (15 m) and one in O-shape (20 m). A volunteer was asked to perform the routes by strictly following a line drawn on the floor, starting after hearing the word "Go". The volunteer was instructed to walk along the line at a steady pace, ensuring that their movements adhered closely to the designated path. We observed and confirmed the volunteer's ability to accurately follow the designated route drawn in the floor while maintaining consistency in movement patterns.

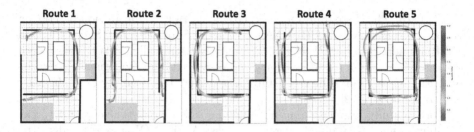

Fig. 1. The five predefined routes marked on the floor in the StreetLab environment completed by one participant to validate the performance of the AI body-tracking system.

2.3 Pre-processing of Videos

The recordings of the task from different cameras were synchronized and segmented using Shotcut software. First, the raw video footage captured by the four cameras (see Fig. 2A) were synchronised to ensure temporal alignment across the cameras. For this, we used the audio timestamps ("Go"). Once the videos were synchronised, we segmented them into individual trials (see Fig. 2B). The videos were saved in mp4 format, with a resolution of 1280 × 720p and 60fps. Thereafter, we used matrix transformation to calibrate the images captured from different camera perspectives into a overhead perspective. We first obtained the four corners of the room as reference points. We applied a geometrical matrix transformation, including rotation, scaling and shearing (see Fig. 2C). After this, the images from the cameras were combined, selecting the observed areas and discarding the occluded areas, aligning the results on a common 2D plane, obtaining a single cohesive representation from the calibrated images(see Fig. 2D).

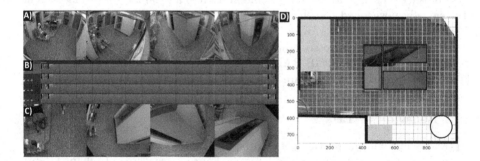

Fig. 2. A) Four images from the point of view of the cameras and the four reference points. B) Synchronization of the videos and trial extraction. C) Geometrical images transformed. D) Combination of the images to obtain the overhead view and the 2D grid of the map.

2.4 Body Tracking

After pre-processing the videos, we implemented a pre-trained Yolov8n [10,20] object detection neural network to identify human figures in each video frame. We extracted the medial lower coordinate, representing the closest point of the person to the floor. A matrix transformation using the reference points was applied to adjust the position of the person on each image. A DBSCAN clustering algorithm [17] is used to obtain the tracking across different frames and cameras. After extracting the raw data, a graphic user interface was developed to observe the data, to average the overlapped data, interpolate the missing data and to apply a polynomial fit with 20 freedom degrees [31]. This data process addresses frame dropout, smoothness of the data and normalisation over time. The final data were superimposed on the StreetLab map, providing a stereographic recognition system of the participants' position and movements on a reconstructed overhead perspective, in the X and Y spatial dimensions over time.

2.5 Analysis

In order to validate the performance of the body-tracking, we analysed the distance and the determination coefficient R^2 between the estimated location of the participant and the pre-defined route indicated on the floor. A t-test was applied to know significant differences. We also calculated two different outcome measures easily extracted: the velocity in any given moment of time and the path length of the participant. We compared the average speed (length of the line divided execution time) and the average of the momentary velocity (mean of summation of the distances between consecutive points divided time intervals). We also compare the difference between the proposed route (line on the floor) and the performed route (summation of distances between points). Descriptive statistics, means and standard deviations, were calculated for all variables.

3 Results

Implementing the body-tracking system, we were able to know the exact location of the participant within the environment at any given moment of time. First of all, we validate the accuracy of the body-tracking data by comparing the participant's location to the pre-defined route and then we calculated examples of outcome measures that can be extracted from the body-tracking data, momentary velocity and the path length.

3.1 Validation: Deviation from the Route

To validate the body tracking method, we assessed the deviations between the body-tracking estimations and the pre-defined routes. We found minor differences between the pre-defined route and the body-tracked location (M = .37, SD = 8.51) in cms. The average determination coefficient of correlation among the pre-defined routes and performed routes is .909 R^2 (see Fig. 3A).

3.2   Example Outcome Measure Validation

Speed. We compared the traditional speed (m/s) (M = 1.36, SD = .1136) (see Fig. 3B) with the average of instantaneous speed (M = 1.37, SD = .1144)(see Fig. 3C). The t-statistic calculated for the comparison was F(10) = 0.3198, p-value = .752. There is no significant difference between traditional speed measurements and average momentary velocity (see Fig. 3D).

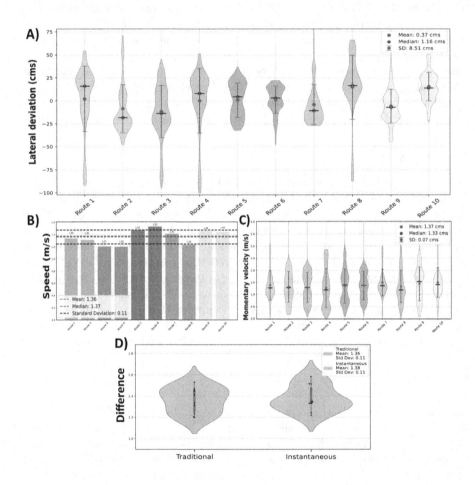

Fig. 3. A) The average deviation is .375 ± 8.51 cm. R^2 = .909. B) Traditional speed average 1.36 ± .136 m/s. C) Instantaneous speeds average is 1.37 ± .114 m/s. D) T-test F(10) = -.319, p-value = .752, there are not significant differences.

Path Length. To validate the path length measure, we compared the length of the line marked on the floor against the length of the path derived from the body tracking of the participant. We found that the AI body-tracking based path was 85.11 ± 96.96cms longer than the line route.

Table 1. Results of Distance route and Path Length.

Route	Distance route (cm)	Path length (cm)	Difference (cm)
Route 1	1500	1493.28	6.71
Route 2	1500	1541.42	41.42
Route 9	1500	1658.05	158.05
Route 8	1500	1681.89	181.89
Route 7	1500	1374.34	125.65
Route 6	1500	1523.18	23.18
Route 5	1500	1601.12	101.12
Route 4	1500	1664.39	164.39
Route 3	2000	2112.36	112.36
Route 10	2000	2201.10	201.10
Mean ± SD			85.11 ± 96.96

4   Discussion

We developed an AI-based body tracking system for complementing traditional O&M assessments that measure additional outcome metrics such deviation, momentary velocity and path length. We introduced the step-by-step implementation and accuracy validation against a predefined route followed by the participant. Validation revealed minimal differences between the marked route and the location of the participant estimated by our body-tracking, showing accurate tracking. Additionally, we validated the path length and the momentary velocity of the participant comparing them against the length of the marked line and the average speed of the participant, respectively.

Current O&M tasks relies on average measures like completion speed and obstacle contacts [7], insufficient for capturing the dynamic nature of navigation [22]. These average metrics rely on subjective observer-based measures and overlook variability in navigational behavior. There is a need for objective methods that provide detailed insights into navigation strategies and environmental interactions. The developed body-tracking system allows precision of participant position, analysis of movement patterns, trajectories, and spatial distribution to discern distinct strategies reflecting cognitive processes. For example, individuals with visual impairments may navigate closer to walls for tactile feedback. Quantifying these patterns enables assessment of consistency and accuracy, identification of errors or challenges, tracking of movement patterns over time, and evaluation of intervention effectiveness in promoting adaptive behaviors and navigational proficiency.

Integration of our AI-based body tracking system offers continuous real-time measurement of participant position and speed, allowing for comparisons to reference trajectories and extraction of momentary velocity and path length, unlike traditional assessments relying on average speed measures. It enhances the understanding of navigational behaviors and identifies subtle changes over time, pinpointing specific challenges for tailored interventions and rehabilitation optimization. Measuring path length is crucial for assessing navigational efficiency, providing insights into spatial awareness, orientation abilities, and decision-making processes. Shorter paths may indicate efficient routes, while longer paths may suggest inefficiencies, informing tailored mobility training programs and enhancing understanding of navigational behaviors for individuals with visual impairments.

Based on the video recordings and AI-based body-tracking, it is possible to analyse more than only the path length, deviations and momentary velocity. For example, further extension of our paradigm would be to implement the identification and localization of moving and stationary elements in the area, to better understand how the individuals navigate within an environment, uncovering trends in participants' navigational behaviour lost in the average metrics. This deeper level of analysis can inform the development of more personalised and effective interventions to support individuals with visual impairments in improving their mobility skills.

Future research should enhance the accuracy and accessibility of body tracking technology for real-world applications, developing portable, user-friendly systems, available for the visually impaired people, address technical complexity, resource requirements, and biases in AI. Despite these hurdles, our body tracking method offers scalability and versatility, suitable for diverse O&M tasks and environments. Its adaptability across different conditions, whether indoors or outdoors, controlled settings or real-world scenarios, enhances its applicability and generalizability. While our work demonstrates the effectiveness of AI body tracking in controlled laboratory environments, further exploration is needed in diverse settings and populations, including practical scenarios, outdoor environments, and dynamic activities.

5   Conclusion

In summary, we have presented an AI-based body-tracking method for evaluating O&M performance among visually impaired individuals. We validated the accuracy of the body-tracking against a pre-defined marked route on the floor. Additionally, we provided and validated two example uses of the body-tracking, momentary velocity and path length calculation. Future studies could explore real-world applications, consider diverse populations, address technical limitations, and prioritise user-centric design. By advancing AI algorithms and fostering interdisciplinary collaborations, we can create more inclusive and empowering navigation assessment tools for individuals with visual impairments, ultimately enhancing their independence and quality of life.

Acknowledgements. This research was funded in part by grants DTS19/00175 and PDC2022-133952–100 from the Spanish "Ministerio de Ciencia, Innovación y Universidades" and by the European Union's Horizon 2020 Research and Innovation Programme under Grant Agreement No. 899287 (NeuraViPeR).

References

1. Altunay, B., Yalcin, G., Saraç, M.U.: Orientation and mobility problems of adults with visual impairment and suggestions for solutions. Eğitimde Nitel Araştırmalar Dergisi **28**, 300–330 (2021)
2. AlZaabi, A., Abi Talib, M., Nassif, A.B., Sajwani, A., Einea, O.: A systematic literature review on machine learning in object detection security. In: 2020 IEEE 5th International Conference on Computing Communication and Automation (ICCCA), pp. 136–139. IEEE (2020)
3. Ayton, L.N., et al.: Harmonization of outcomes and vision endpoints in vision restoration trials: recommendations from the international hover taskforce. Trans. Vis Sci. Technol. **9**(8), 25–25 (2020)
4. Azzeh, M., Nassif, A.B.: Fuzzy model tree for early effort estimation. In: 2013 12th International Conference on Machine Learning and Applications. vol. 2, pp. 117–121. IEEE (2013)
5. Bourne, R., et al.: Trends in prevalence of blindness and distance and near vision impairment over 30 years: an analysis for the global burden of disease study. Lancet Glob. Health **9**(2), e130–e143 (2021)
6. Chadha, R.K., Subramanian, A.: The effect of visual impairment on quality of life of children aged 3–16 years. Br. J. Ophthalmol. **95**(5), 642–645 (2011)
7. Chang, K.y.J., Dillon, L.L., Deverell, L., Boon, M.Y., Keay, L.: Orientation and mobility outcome measures. Clin. Exp. Optom. **103**(4), 434–448 (2020)
8. Chen, K.B., Ponto, K., Tredinnick, R.D., Radwin, R.G.: Virtual exertions: evoking the sense of exerting forces in virtual reality using gestures and muscle activity. Hum. Factors **57**(4), 658–673 (2015)
9. Clemente, C., Chambel, G., Silva, D.C., Montes, A.M., Pinto, J.F., Silva, H.P.D.: Feasibility of 3d body tracking from monocular 2D video feeds in musculoskeletal telerehabilitation. Sensors **24**(1), 206 (2023)
10. Devi, S.K., Subalalitha, C.: Deep learning based audio assistive system for visually impaired people. Comput. Mater. Continua **71**(1), 1205–1219 (2022)
11. Flaxman, S.R., et al.: Global causes of blindness and distance vision impairment 1990–2020: a systematic review and meta-analysis. Lancet Glob. Health **5**(12), e1221–e1234 (2017)
12. Freund, Y., Schapire, R.E.: Experiments with a new boosting algorithm. In: Proceedings of the Thirteenth International Conference on International Conference on Machine Learning (ICML'96), pp. 148–156. Morgan Kaufmann Publishers Inc. (1996)
13. Garcia, S., Petrini, K., Rubin, G.S., Da Cruz, L., Nardini, M.: Visual and non-visual navigation in blind patients with a retinal prosthesis. PLOS ONE **10**(7), e0134369 (2015)
14. Gedik, O.S., Alatan, A.A.: 3-D rigid body tracking using vision and depth sensors. IEEE Trans. Cybern. **43**(5), 1395–1405 (2013)
15. Goswami, P.K., Goswami, G.: A comprehensive review on real time object detection using deep learing model. In: 2022 11th International Conference on System Modeling and Advancement in Research Trends (SMART), pp. 1499–1502. IEEE (2022)
16. Hesse, N., Baumgartner, S., Gut, A., van Hedel, H.J.: Concurrent validity of a custom method for markerless 3D full-body motion tracking of children and young adults based on a single RGB-D camera. IEEE Trans. Neural Syst. Rehabil. Eng. **31**, 1943–1951 (2023)

17. Hou, J., Gao, H., Li, X.: Dsets-dbscan: a parameter-free clustering algorithm. IEEE Trans. Image Process. **25**(7), 3182–3193 (2016)
18. Howard, J.: Artificial intelligence: implications for the future of work. Am. J. Ind. Med. **62**(11), 917–926 (2019)
19. Jatesiktat, P., Anopas, D., Ang, W.T.: Personalized markerless upper-body tracking with a depth camera and wrist-worn inertial measurement units. In: 2018 40th Annual International Conference of the IEEE Engineering in Medicine and Biology Society (EMBC), pp. 1–6. IEEE (2018)
20. Jocher, G., Chaurasia, A., Qiu, J.: Yolo by ultralytics. URL: https://github.com/ultralytics/ultralytics (2023)
21. Lee, S.H., Yoo, J., Park, M., Kim, J., Kwon, S.: Robust extrinsic calibration of multiple RGB-D cameras with body tracking and feature matching. Sensors **21**(3), 1013 (2021)
22. Lewis, L., Sharples, S., Chandler, E., Worsfold, J.: Hearing the way: requirements and preferences for technology-supported navigation aids. Appl. Ergon. **48**, 56–69 (2015)
23. Li, G., Hui, X., Lin, F., Zhao, Y.: Developing and evaluating poultry preening behavior detectors via mask region-based convolutional neural network. Animals **10**(10), 1762 (2020)
24. Lowe, D.G.: Distinctive image features from scale-invariant keypoints. Int. J. Comput. Vision **60**, 91–110 (2004)
25. Nassif, A.B., Shahin, I., Attili, I., Azzeh, M., Shaalan, K.: Speech recognition using deep neural networks: a systematic review. IEEE access **7**, 19143–19165 (2019)
26. Psathas, G.: Mobility, orientation, and navigation: conceptual and theoretical considerations. J. Visual Impairment Blindness **70**(9), 385–391 (1976)
27. Seki, Y., Sato, T.: A training system of orientation and mobility for blind people using acoustic virtual reality. IEEE Trans. Neural Syst. Rehabil. Eng. **19**(1), 95–104 (2010)
28. Shi, W., Bao, S., Tan, D.: FFESSD: An accurate and efficient single-shot detector for target detection. Appl. Sci. **9**(20), 4276 (2019)
29. Tao, Y., Zongyang, Z., Jun, Z., Xinghua, C., Fuqiang, Z.: Low-altitude small-sized object detection using lightweight feature-enhanced convolutional neural network. J. Syst. Eng. Electron. **32**(4), 841–853 (2021)
30. Wang, C., Chan, C.L.W., Chi, I.: Overview of quality of life research in older people with visual impairment. Advances in Aging Research (2014)
31. Wang, F., et al.: Object-based reliable visual navigation for mobile robot. Sensors (Basel) **22**(6), 2387 (2022). https://doi.org/10.3390/s22062387
32. Zhang, X., Zhang, Y., Hu, M., Ju, X.: Insulator defect detection based on yolo and SPP-Net. In: 2020 International Conference on Big Data and Artificial Intelligence and Software Engineering (ICBASE), pp. 403–407. IEEE (Oct 2020)

Application of Graph Fourier Transform in the Diagnosis of Left Bundle Branch Block from Electrocardiographic Signals

Beatriz del Cisne Macas Ordóñez[1,2,4(✉)] (iD),
Diego Vinicio Orellana Villavicencio[3] (iD), Marco Augusto Suing Ochoa[3] (iD),
and María Paula Bonomini[2,4,5] (iD)

[1] Facultad de Ingeniería, Instituto de Ingeniería Biomédica, Universidad de Buenos Aires, Buenos Aires, Argentina
bmacas.ext@fi.uba.ar
[2] Instituto Argentino de Matemática "Alberto P. Calderón" (IAM), CONICET, Buenos Aires, Argentina
[3] Facultad de Energía, las Industrias y los Recursos Naturales No Renovables, Universidad Nacional de Loja, Loja, Ecuador
[4] Departamento de Electrónica, Tecnología de Computadoras y Proyectos, Universidad Politécnica de Cartagena, Cartagena, Spain
[5] Grupo Inteligencia Artificial - Universidad Tecnológica Nacional (UTN), Facultad Regional Haedo, Haedo, Bs. As., Buenos Aires, Argentina

Abstract. In recent years, there has been a growing interest in left bundle branch block (LBBB) due to its role as an indicator for evaluating the benefits of cardiac resynchronization therapy (CRT). Considering that LBBB arises from spatial electrical heterogeneity, we hypothesized that graph theory could effectively represent this variability. In our study, we used Fourier graph transform to analyze and filter frequencies in the transformed space, aiming to classify associated signals. Our results showed an accuracy of 97.87%, indicating a promising application of graphs in diagnosing LBBB. These findings are encouraging and point towards further exploration of the potential of graph theory to enhance LBBB diagnosis.

Keywords: LBBB Diagnosis · Graph Signal Processing (GSP) · Graph fourier transform

1 Introduction

In recent years, left bundle branch block (LBBB) has been a topic of interest, as early detection has been found to be a key indicator for assessing the benefits of Cardiac Resynchronization Therapy (CRT) [1]. Since LBBB arises from spatial electrical heterogeneity, the hypothesis that graph theory could provide an effective representation of this variability has been proposed as a promising tool, offering a visual and structured representation of these complex electrical interconnections in the cardiac muscle. Patient selection for CRT involves specific

J. M. Ferrández Vicente et al. (Eds.): IWINAC 2024, LNCS 14675, pp. 495–503, 2024.
https://doi.org/10.1007/978-3-031-61137-7_46

diagnostic criteria, such as QRS duration ≥ 140 ms (men) or ≥ 130 ms (women), QS- or rS-configurations of the QRS complex in leads V1 and V2, and mid-QRS notching or slurring in ≥ 2 of leads V1, V2, V5, V6, I and aVL [2]. However, even with these criteria in place, around 30-40% of patients do not experience positive outcomes from CRT, despite our best efforts [11].

Invasive diagnostic methods, such as electrophysiological study, and non-invasive techniques like echocardiography, are expensive, pose risks, and demand highly specialized personnel. Consequently, there is an imperative to explore novel features to enhance accuracy in assessment and optimize therapeutic management. Recently, processing based on spectral graph theory has emerged as a promising alternative across various application domains [3].

The graph Fourier transform (GFT), analogous to the Fourier transform (FT), decomposes the Laplacian matrix of a graph into eigenvalues and eigenvectors. The eigenvalues represent frequencies, while the eigenvectors serve as the Fourier basis functions, allowing signals to be represented in both the vertex domain and the spectral domain of the graphs [4]. Consequently, graphs facilitate the representation of complex relationships between data and the extraction of features in a different way than is traditionally done.

However, current research on the application of graph theory to automatic LBBB detection is limited. This study aims to leverage this methodology to improve the classification accuracy of LBBB, strict LBBB and healthy subjects using ECG signals. We will evaluate the performance of our method and compare it with previous algorithms using statistical analysis of signal sets [5]. In summary, this work focuses on exploring the potential of graph theory to improve LBBB detection and classification, which could have a significant impact on the diagnosis and treatment of LBBB.

2   Methodology

Figure 1 provides an in-depth explanation of the methodology employed in this work.

ECG Database. Two data sets were used. The first data set included 299 normal electrocardiographic recordings from a 12-lead database developed by Chapman University, Shaoxing People's Hospital and Ningbo First Hospital. These expertly labeled recordings with a sampling rate of 500 Hz represent a homogeneous control group devoid of cardiac pathology. The second dataset incorporated a cohort of heart failure patients from the MADIT-CRT clinical trial, accessible through the THEW project at the University of Rochester. This cohort consists of 330 patients with strict left bundle branch block (sLBBB) and 193 with non-strict left bundle branch block (LBBB). In summary, the analyzed database includes three ECG categories: healthy subjects (299), sLBBB (330) and non-strict LBBB (193), all with 12 leads.

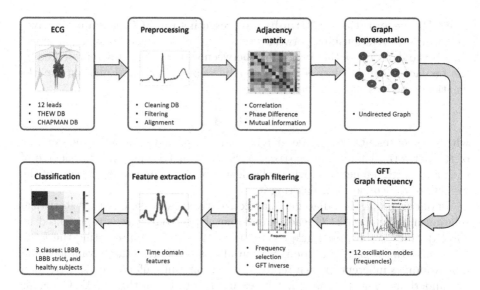

Fig. 1. Schematic description of the methodology used. The process includes creating a graph from the ECG time series, then filtering the vertices of the graph, and finally classifying the LBBB.

Database Preprocessing. In this phase, we first performed a manual check to identify and remove erroneous, incomplete, and duplicate records from the database. To mitigate artifacts arising from both the electrical network and muscle electrical activity, we apply zero-phase bandpass filtering within the frequency range of 0.05 to 35 Hz. ECG recordings typically last approximately 10 s and span 4 to 6 beats. To obtain a representative beat from each subject, we employ a beat averaging procedure. We then extract an analysis window spanning 200 milliseconds before and after the R-wave peak. This additional step not only reduces the volume of data to be processed, but also facilitates the alignment of beats in different subjects, thus improving the consistency of subsequent analyses.

Adjacency Matrix. Formally, a graph $G = (V, E)$ is an ordered pair where V is a set of vertices and E is a set of edges [6]. Vertices (also called nodes) represent individual entities, while edges represent the relationships between these entities. In our context, the vertices correspond to the 12 ECG measurement electrodes. However, establishing relationships between vertices is not a simple process due to the absence of directly measurable variables. Therefore, mathematical or statistical methodologies are necessary to infer possible correlations between electrodes. To evaluate the advantages and limitations of different approaches to construct the graph from ECG time series, we examined three mathematical tools: Pearson's correlation coefficient, the cross-correlation function, and the phase difference.

ECG Representation as Graphs. Representing the ECG as graphs involves capturing the relationships between vertices in an adjacency matrix. In graph theory, the structure of the connections between vertices is usually represented by the Laplacian matrix, derived from the adjacency matrix [6]. Equation 1 mathematically defines the Laplacian matrix.

$$L = D - A \tag{1}$$

where, D represents the degree matrix, and A represents the adjacency matrix of the network. The degree matrix is a diagonal matrix denoting the degree of each node within a network, where the degree of a node indicates the sum of the weights of the connections entering it.

In our scenario, the adjacency matrix is derived from the observed statistical relationships between ECG leads. Consequently, the database is represented by three distinct graphs, each graph consists of 12 vertices, representing the ECG leads, and 132 edges. This configuration allows to analyze the advantages and disadvantages inherent in each representation, offering different perspectives on the underlying data that may not be easily discernible in the raw ECG signals alone.

Graph Fourier Transform. The graph Fourier transform (GFT) is a mathematical tool that decomposes the Laplacian matrix of a graph into eigenvalues and eigenvectors. Analogous to the classical Fourier transform, the eigenvalues represent frequencies and the eigenvectors form what is known as the Fourier basis of graphs [7]. Equation 2 describes the mathematical formulation of the GFT.

$$GF\left[f\right]\left(\lambda_l\right) = \hat{f}\left(\lambda_l\right) = \langle f, \mu_l \rangle = \sum_{i=1}^{N} f(i)\mu_l^*(i) \tag{2}$$

where:

- The signal f maps a real number $f(i)$ to each vertex of the graph.
- λ_l and μ_l correspond to the eigenvalues and eigenvectors of the Laplacian matrix sorted in ascending order.
- μ_l^* corresponds to μ_l^T.

Graph Filtering. Graph denoising can be conceptualized similarly to classical signal processing techniques, such as the Fourier transform applied to time series data. In this analogy, a common method is to compute the Fourier transform of the signal, preserving the informative frequency bands in the frequency domain and attenuating or removing frequencies considered uninformative. An inverse Fourier transform is then performed to return to the time domain, resulting in filtered data [8].

In the field of graph theory, since L is a real symmetric matrix, its eigenvectors form an orthogonal basis. Therefore, there exists an inverse graph fourier transform (iGFT), and it is written as:

$$\text{iGFT}\left[\hat{f}\right](i) = f(i) = \sum_{l=0}^{N-1} \hat{f}(\lambda_l)\mu_l(i) \tag{3}$$

Consequently, to perform signal filtering on graphs, first the GFT is performed, then the magnitudes of each frequency (or oscillation mode) are adapted, and finally the iGFT is applied to return to the time domain. With this approach, the filtering does not consider only present and past values of a vertex (ECG lead), but the activity of all vertices is included in the processing.

Feature Extraction and ECG Classification. The feature space was generated by extracting the amplitude of the ECG signal, which had been filtered using Graph Theory tools. With a sampling rate of 500 Hz and an analysis window of 200 ms, each lead produced 100 samples. Consequently, the feature matrix had dimensions of $1,200 \times 822$, with 822 observations and 1,200 features. To mitigate dimensionality, principal component analysis (PCA) was applied, resulting in 26 features accounting for 95% of the variance in the data.

To classify the three types of records (healthy ECG, LBBB, and sLBBB), five classifiers widely used in biosignal processing were employed: cubic support vector machine (cSVM), cosine k-Nearest Neighbors (cKNN) and quadratic discriminant analysis (QDA), quadratic support vector machine (qSVM), Ensemble Subspace k-Nearest Neighbors (esKNN). In order to increase the reliability of the results presented here, a randomized class-balancing process was performed, resulting in an 26×297 matrix, where 26 represented the number of features and 297 the number of observations. This dataset was randomly divided into a training set (70%) and a test set (30%). The training and testing processes were repeated N times ($N = 1000$) to statistically validate the reliability of the results.

3   Results

The GFT matrix, derived from each subject, comprised 12 spectral components. To assess whether specific individual projections of the GFT contain a substantial amount of useful information for discriminating between different cardiac conditions (healthy, sLBBB, LBBB), a signal reconstruction (iGFT) was performed by sequentially isolating individual projections. For example, in Fig. 2, the initial three bars outline the results of the iGFT with three methods of obtaining the adjacency matrix (Pearson Correlation, Cross-correlation function, and phase difference), but considering only the first projection and excluding the others.

The twelve projections depicted in Fig. 2 represent the frequencies in ascending order. The first projection shows the lowest frequency, representing minimal amplitude variation between leads. In contrast, the twelfth projection shows a high frequency, indicating significant differences in signal amplitudes between adjacent leads.

The data presented in Fig. 2 indicate that there is no dominant spectral component. Although the initial spectral component includes a higher proportion of discriminatory information (77.84%), it is not sufficient to achieve optimal classification. The remaining projections (2-11) yield classification rates around 60%. Given that the task involves classification into 3 classes (with a chance level of 33%), these individual projections improve classification performance by approximately 30% above chance level. Therefore, it can be inferred that these projections contain relevant information for classification.

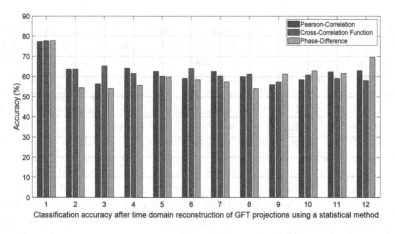

Classification accuracy after time domain reconstruction of GFT projections using a statistical method

Fig. 2. Classification accuracy after time domain reconstruction of GFT projections using a statistical method

Subsequently, based on the classification results of individual spectral components, an exhaustive search was conducted to identify the most effective combination of components to achieve optimal classification. Once the combination of individual components reconstructed in the time domain was executed, this method resulted in an average classification accuracy of 97.87% with a standard deviation of 1.3; a promising result that is better to traditional BRIHH classification methods.

The most difficult conditions to classify are sLBBB and LBBB, since their morphologies are aberrant, as evidenced by observing their signals in the time domain. However, the results obtained are better than traditional methods using QRS width. The true positive rate (TPR) achieved for sLBBB is approximately 82.8% and the true positive rate achieved for LBBB is approximately 87.9%. The ROC curves shown in Fig. 2 highlight the best performance of the classifiers used, where Phase Difference stands out with the highest accuracy. This method allowed an average accuracy of 97.87% to be achieved, demonstrating its effectiveness in the classification of LBBB. Regarding the cluster dispersion illustrated in Fig. 2, the feature matrix was reduced to three dimensions for visualization purposes.

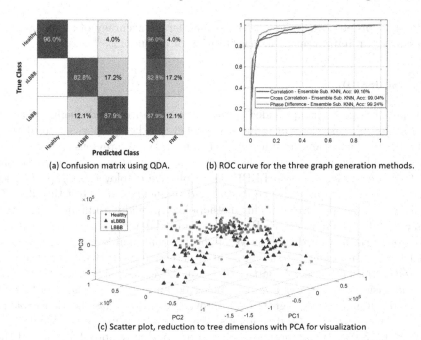

(a) Confusion matrix using QDA.   (b) ROC curve for the three graph generation methods.

(c) Scatter plot, reduction to tree dimensions with PCA for visualization

Fig. 3. Classifier Performance: PCA, Confusion Matrix, and ROC Analysis

Table 1. Classification results using Graph Signal Filtering

	Pearson Correlation		Cross Correlation		Phase Diff		ECG-SVM	Class improvement	
	Avg	Max	Avg	Max	Avg	Max		Avg	Max
QDA	96.39%±2.6	100%	96.42%±2.4	100%	97.22%±1.9	100%	88, 20%	8.98%	11.80%
cKNN	97.04%±1.0	100%	98.77%±1.2	100%	98.94%±1.0	100%		10.84%	11.80%
cSVM	97.86%±1.3	100%	97.07%±1.6	100%	97.88%±1.2	100%		9.68%	11.80%
qSVM	97.50%±1.5	100%	96.28%±2.3	100%	97.86%±1.3	100%		9.66%	11.80%
esKNN	98.99%±1.1	100%	99.23%±1.0	100%	99.15%±0.9	100%		11.03%	11.80%

To evaluate the amount of information useful for classifying ECG types from the previously filtered signal using graph theory, we trained and tested five classifiers widely used in the field of biosignal processing. The results of this analysis are presented in Table 1. It is noteworthy that all models tested achieved accuracies above 96%, which represents an improvement of approximately 8% over the value achieved using data extracted directly from the ECG. This result suggests that filtering using GFT allows us to discard information irrelevant to our task, thus improving the performance of the classifiers. Another relevant aspect is that all the methods explored to create the graph from the time series outperformed the raw ECG data. However, the phase difference method showed a slight improvement, indicating that factors such as inter-lead synchronization are important in the study of LBBB and deserve further analysis. In conclusion, the method proposed here demonstrates an average accuracy of about 99±1%, representing an improvement in classification of about 11%.

4 Discussion

Artificial intelligence has provided several tools for automated diagnose of several illnesses [9]. Our study introduces a novel graph theory approach for detecting LBBB in electrocardiographic (ECG) signals. While previous literature has utilized graphs with ECG, they have primarily focused on other applications [10]. Our specific focus lies in LBBB detection. We employ the Graph Fourier Transform (GFT) to analyze the spatial and frequency characteristics of ECG signals associated with LBBB. This methodology provides a unique perspective to enhance the accuracy in LBBB detection and classification.

In comparison with the initiative of the International Society for Computerized Electrocardiology for the automated detection of LBBB, where the best reported precision by the 7 participants was 82%, with a sensitivity of 69% and a precision of 87%, our approach achieved an average precision of 97.87% [2]. His result indicates a significant improvement in our classification capability. Furthermore, our method compares favorably with a previous work [5] that relies on more traditional methods, focused on specific temporal features of the QRS complex for the detection of the three groups: healthy individuals, LBBB, and sLBBB, and achieved an accuracy of 97.87%. This finding suggests that the attained accuracy is consistent with other approaches for detecting LBBB using machine learning techniques and signal processing. The obtained results demonstrate a classification accuracy of 97.87%, indicating that the proposed approach holds promise in enhancing LBBB detection. Nevertheless, it is important to note that this study relies on data from a limited patient cohort, and further validation through independent clinical studies is necessary to confirm its efficacy in clinical practice.

In summary, the study presents a novel approach to enhance LBBB detection using GSP tools. While the results are promising, further research and clinical validation are needed to fully assess its effectiveness and applicability in real clinical settings. Nonetheless, this work lays the groundwork for future investigations into the use of graph techniques for biological signal analysis, potentially making a significant impact on the diagnosis and treatment of cardiovascular diseases.

5 Conclusion

The use of GSP via the Graph Fourier Transform has proven to be a potentially valuable alternative for identifying and classifying Left Bundle LBBB, achieving an average classification accuracy of 88.42%. This methodology has shown consistency with methods based on QRS complex width, enabling a clear distinction between LBBB, strict LBBB, and healthy subjects. This research has focused primarily on spectral filtering within the graph domain. However, an alternative approach worth exploring is the investigation of the effectiveness of features extracted directly from the graph (e.g. clustering coefficient) for LBBB detection.

References

1. Ortega, D.F., Barja, L.D., Logarzo, E., Mangani, N., Paolucci, A., Bonomini, M.P.: Non-selective His bundle pacing with a biphasic waveform: enhancing septal resynchronization. Europace **20**(5), 816–822 (2018). https://doi.org/10.1093/europace/eux098. (PMID: 28520951)
2. Zusterzeel, R., et al.: The 43rd international society for computerized electrocardiology ECG initiative for the automated detection of strict left bundle branch block. J. Electrocardiol. **51**(6S), S25–S30 (2018). https://doi.org/10.1016/j.jelectrocard.2018.08.001. Epub 2018 Aug 1 PMID: 30082088
3. Wang, J., Calhoun, V., Stephen, J.M., Wilson, T.W., Wang, Y.: Integration of network topological features and graph Fourier transform for fMRI data analysis. In: Proceedings of the 2018 IEEE 15th International Symposium on Biomedical Imaging (ISBI 2018), Washington, DC, USA, 4-7 April, pp. 92-96 (2018)
4. Shuman, D.I., Ricaud, B., Vandergheynst, P.: Vertex-frequency analysis on graphs. Comput. Harmon. Anal. **40**, 260–291 (2016)
5. Macas, B., Garrigòs, J., Martìnez, J.J., Ferràndez, J.M., Bonomini, M.: An explainable machine learning system for left bundle branch block detection and classification. Integrat. Comput.-Aided Eng. **31**(1), 43–58 (2023)
6. Marcus, D.A.: Graph theory: A problem oriented approach. Washington D.C, Mathematical Association of America (2008)
7. Ricaud, B., Borgnat, P., Tremblay, N., Gonçalves, P., Vandergheynst, P.: Fourier could be a data scientist: from graph fourier transform to signal processing on graphs. Comptes Rendus Physique **20** (2019) https://doi.org/10.1016/j.crhy.2019.08.003
8. Dong, X., Thanou, D., Toni, L., Bronstein, M., Frossard, P.: Graph signal processing for machine learning: a review and new perspectives. IEEE Signal Process. Mag. **37**(6), 117–127 (2020)
9. Górriz, J., et al.: Computational approaches to explainable artificial intelligence: Advances in theory, applications and trends. Inform. Fusion **100**, 101945 (2023)
10. Liu, S., Shao, J., Kong, T., Malekian, R.: ECG arrhythmia classification using high order spectrum and 2D graph fourier transform. Appl. Sci. **10**(14), 4741 (2020). https://doi.org/10.3390/app10144741
11. Ortega, D., Logarzo, E., Barja, L., Paolucci, A., Mangani, N., Mazzetti. E., Bonomini M.P.: Novel implant technique for septal pacing. a noninvasive approach to nonselective his bundle pacing. J. Electrocard**63**, 35-40 (2020)

Strict Left Bundle Branch Block Diagnose Through Explainable Artificial Intelligence

Beatriz del Cisne Macas Ordóñez[1,2,3]($\boxtimes$) (ID), Javier Garrigos[3] (ID),
Jose Javier Martinez[3] (ID), José Manuel Ferrández[3] (ID), Suraj Karki[4],
and María Paula Bonomini[2,3] (ID)

[1] Facultad de Ingeniería, Instituto de Ingeniería Biomédica, Universidad de Buenos
Aires, Buenos Aires, Argentina
bmacas.ext@fi.uba.ar
[2] Instituto Argentino de Matemática "Alberto P. Calderón" (IAM), CONICET,
Buenos Aires, Argentina
[3] Departamento de Electrónica, Tecnología de Computadoras y Proyectos,
Universidad Politécnica de Cartagena, Cartagena, Spain
[4] Nepal Engineering College, Pokhara University, Lekhnath, Nepal

Abstract. This study explores the use of SHapley Additive exPlanations (SHAP) values, a machine learning technique, to validate and refine electrocardiographic criteria for strict Left Bundle Branch Block (LBBB). The research utilizes a 1D convolutional neural network (CNN) model to analyze a database of heart failure patients, including those with strict LBBB, non-strict LBBB, no LBBB, and a healthy control group. The model's performance was evaluated using five classification schemes, with an accuracy exceeding 81% in all cases. The study found that lead V3 emerged as one of the most valuable leads in the classification task across all proposed combinations, a surprising result given its lack of prominence in clinical LBBB diagnosis. This finding suggests that the link between V3 and LBBB, unexplored until now, warrants further investigation. The study concludes that the integration of SHAP values with traditional electrocardiographic analysis can enhance clinical decision-making and optimize patient care in the context of LBBB.

Keywords: LBBB diagnosis · CNN1D · Shap values

1 Introduction

Left bundle branch block (LBBB) is a common electrocardiographic finding associated with a variety of cardiac conditions. However, the distinction between strict and non-strict LBBB criteria remains challenging, impacting clinical decision-making and patient outcomes, in particular regarding cardiac resynchronization therapy outcomes [1,5]. Electrocardiographic criteria have traditionally been relied upon for diagnosis, yet their accuracy and consistency remain subjects of debate. To address this issue, novel approaches leveraging advanced

J. M. Ferrández Vicente et al. (Eds.): IWINAC 2024, LNCS 14675, pp. 504–510, 2024.
https://doi.org/10.1007/978-3-031-61137-7_47

machine learning explainatory techniques, such as SHAP (SHapley Additive exPlanations) values, have emerged as promising tools for elucidating the underlying mechanisms of diagnostic criteria [2].

Shap values offer a systematic framework for quantifying the contribution of each electrocardiographic feature to the classification of LBBB. By providing insights into the relative importance of individual features, SHAP values can enhance our understanding of the diagnostic process and facilitate the identification of robust criteria for distinguishing strict LBBB from other conditions [3]. This study aims to utilize Shap values to validate and refine electrocardiographic criteria for strict LBBB, thereby improving diagnostic accuracy and patient management strategies.

Through the integration of SHAP values with traditional electrocardiographic analysis, we seek to establish a more comprehensive and reliable approach to the diagnosis of LBBB. By elucidating the complex interplay between electrocardiographic features and diagnostic outcomes, this research has the potential to enhance clinical decision-making and optimize patient care in the context of LBBB.

2   Materials and Methods

Study Population. The LBBB database contains a subset (n=602) of heart failure patients included in the MADIT-CRT clinical trial, publicly available at the THEW project, from University of Rochester (Rochester, NY) [4]. From this subset, 330 patients have strict LBBB (sLBBB), 193 present not strict LBBB (LBBB) and 79 show no LBBB (noLBBB) at all.

Since the noLBBBB group is not a healthy group, we included a fourth group with 300 healthy patients. The healthy database is from a collaboration between Chapman University, Shaoxing People's Hospital (Shaoxing Hospital Zhejiang University School of Medicine), and Ningbo First Hospital.

The aim of this piece of paper was to utilize Shap values to confirm the electrocardiographic criteria for sLBBB. Therefore, a post-hoc explainability analysis was performed using SHAP values to assess whether the most valuable leads in the classification matched those of the clinical criteria.

CNN Architecture. A 1D convolutional neural network (CNN) model was implemented using the TensorFlow-Keras library. This model consists of a series of convolutional layers, followed by normalization and ReLU activation layers, and finally max-pooling layers to extract relevant features from the input data. The architecture of the model is summarized in Table 1. The model was compiled using the Adam optimizer with a learning rate of 0.001, and the categorical cross-entropy loss function. The total number of parameters in the model is 11736, of which 11624 are trainable and 112 are non-trainable.

Table 1. Summary of the neural network architecture.

Layer (type)	Output Shape	Param #
input_1 (InputLayer)	(None, 160, 12)	0
conv1d (Conv1D)	(None, 151, 32)	3872
batch_normalization (BatchNormalization)	(None, 151, 32)	128
re_lu (ReLU)	(None, 151, 32)	0
dropout (Dropout)	(None, 151, 32)	0
max_pooling1d (MaxPooling1D)	(None, 75, 32)	0
conv1d_1 (Conv1D)	(None, 66, 16)	5136
batch_normalization_1 (BatchNormalization)	(None, 66, 16)	64
re_lu_1 (ReLU)	(None, 66, 16)	0
dropout_1 (Dropout)	(None, 66, 16)	0
max_pooling1d_1 (MaxPooling1D)	(None, 33, 16)	0
conv1d_2 (Conv1D)	(None, 24, 8)	1288
batch_normalization_2 (BatchNormalization)	(None, 24, 8)	32
re_lu_2 (ReLU)	(None, 24, 8)	0
dropout_2 (Dropout)	(None, 24, 8)	0
max_pooling1d_2 (MaxPooling1D)	(None, 12, 8)	0
flatten (Flatten)	(None, 96)	0
dense (Dense)	(None, 12)	1164
dense_1 (Dense)	(None, 4)	52

3   Results

Model Performance. Five classification schemes were analyzed based on temporal series. Ternary (*healthy* vs *LBBB* vs *sLBBB*) and quaternary (*healthy* vs *LBBB* vs *sLBBB* vs *noLBBB*) classification experiments were accomplished on a 12-lead and 3-lead basis. In all cases, performances were over 81%. Notice that in all proposed combinations, V_3 came out as one of the most valuable leads in the classification task. This observation was particularly surprising, since V_3 is not a relevant lead in the clinical diagnose of LBBB.

Table 2 shows the performances of the test groups in a k-fold validation scheme (k = 5) for every case. In particular, Table 3 shows the classification report for the first row of Table 2. It is important to note that performances resulted outstanding over groups so close such as LBBB and sLBBB. Moreover, the addition of the noLBBB group added difficulty in the classification task, due to its extreme heterogeneous nature, since noLBBB patients is a collection of diseased patients with only one thing in common: they do not exhibit LBBB pathologies.

Table 2. Different classification schemes and lead importance

Leads	Accuracy	LBBB	sLBBB	noLBBB	Healthy	Importance
12-leads	0.9012	1	1	1	1	V_3, V_4, V_5, V_1, V_6
12-leads	0.8104	1	1	1	0	V_1, V_3, V_6, V_5, aV_r
12-leads	0.9172	1	1	0	1	V_6, V_5, V_2, V_3, V_1
12-leads	0.8265	1	1	0	0	V_3, V_1, V_6, V_2, III
$V_3 - V_1 - V_6$	0.9186	1	1	1	1	V_3, V_6, V_1

Table 3. Classification report for the case belonging to the first row of Table 2.

Class	Precision	Recall	F1-score	Support
0	0.9333	0.9333	0.9333	15
1	0.8182	0.7297	0.7714	37
2	0.9016	0.9167	0.9091	60
3	0.9524	1.0000	0.9756	60
Accuracy				0.9070
Macro avg	0.9014	0.8949	0.8974	172
Weighted avg	0.9042	0.9070	0.9048	172

Shap Analysis. Fig. 1 shows a summary plot related to Table 3; the experiment on 12-lead among all 4 classes. Notice that the five most important leads for classification resulted mostly precordial leads, among them, V_3, a transitional lead.

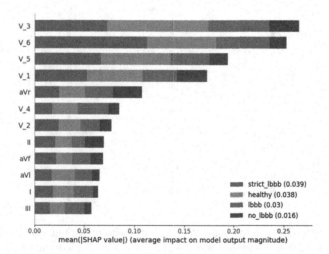

Fig. 1. Summary plot for 12-lead classification of *LBBB* vs *sLBBB* vs *noLBBB* vs *Healthy*

At this point, we insist on this fact: this result matches the clinical electrocardiographic criteria for sLBBB for 4 out of the 5 most important leads of Fig. 1: aV_r, V_1, V_5 and V_6, but V_3. More importantly, according to Table 2, V_3 appeared in all top-five leads for every classification scheme, all of them containing at least a LBBB group.

Figure 2, on the other hand, shows the Shap analysis of a paradigmatic patient, with $sLBBB$ as ground truth label. For the sake of clarity, only the 5 most important leads, derived from Fig. 1, were included. Waveforms excerpts relevant for classification were colored on a rainbow colormap, according to the Shap values on those samples. Note that V_5 and V_6 accounted for most of the descending flanks of the QRS complex in the LBBB and sLBBB classes.

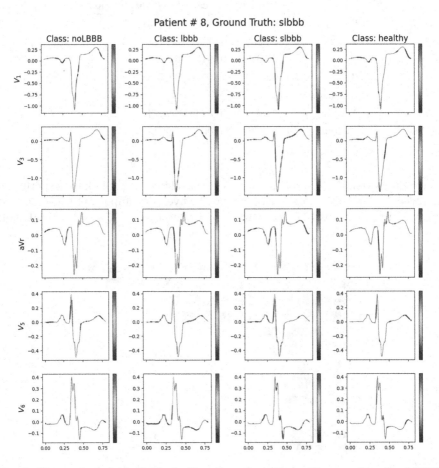

Fig. 2. Shap analysis for individuals. Paradigmatic patient with ground truth $sLBBB$. Shap values exceeding threshold are colored on a rainbow colormap. (Color figure online)

4   Discussion and Conclusions

In this work, we have explored Explainable Artifitial Inteligence (xAI) to confirm the strict LBBB electrocardiographic criteria. The criterium was mostly explained by Shap values, in terms of lead importance since leads V_1, V_5, V_6 and aV_r resulted 4 out of the 5 most important leads in 5 classification experiments [7]. Surprisingly, lead V_3 appeared in every proposed experiment as one of the most important leads for classification. As far as we know, this is not reported in the literature and deserves further investigation.

Regarding the performances obtained by the 1DCNN, metrics were comparable to those obtained in [3]. Furthermore, experiments including the fourth healthy class dramatically improved, probably due to an increased number of observations. In that piece of paper, Shap analysis was applied on a set of vectorcardiographic features, while in this work, features are actually samples of the waveforms, thus obtaining morphological information related to LBBB diagnose.

It is also worth mentioning a work by Peguero and Lo-Presti proposing a left ventricular hypertrophy (LVH) criteria [6]. Here, the lead V_4 substantially increase the LVH detection since it is the lead that better sees the mesocardium, the muscle with the lowest conduction velocity, associated to the final portions of the QRS complex. There, the authors claim that transitional leads (V_3 and V_4) reflect in a larger extent distal muscle in the cardiac contraction, where velocity is minimal, which in turn provokes greater slurs and notches in the ECG waveforms. Moreover, note that V_5 in this example is serving as the transitional lead, supporting the fact that transitions may play an important role in LBBB classification. With this inference in mind, it is sensitive to think of V_3 as a valuable lead for LBBB diagnose, giving credit in turn, to the findings of Fig. 1 and Table 2. Thus, we may conclude that the link between V_3 and LBBB, unexplored until now, deserves some further investigation.

References

1. Barba-Pichardo, R., Moriña-Vázquez, P., Fernández-Gómez, J., Venegas-Gamero, J., Herrera-Carranza, M.: Permanent his-bundle pacing: seeking physiological ventricular pacing. Europace **12**, 527–533 (2010)
2. Górriz, J., et al.: Computational approaches to explainable artificial intelligence: advances in theory, applications and trends. Inform. Fusion **100**, 101945 (2023)
3. Macas, B., J, G., JJ, M., JM, F., Bonomini, M.: An explainable machine learning system for left bundle branch block detection and classification. Integrated Comput.-Aided Eng. **31**(1), 43–58 (2023)
4. Moss, A.J., et al.: Cardiac-resynchronization therapy for the prevention of heart-failure events. N. Engl. J. Med. **361**(14), 1329–1338 (2009)
5. Ortega, D.F., Barja, L.D., Logarzo, E., Mangani, N., Paolucci, A., Bonomini, M.P.: Nonselective his bundle pacing with a biphasic waveform. enhancing septal resynchronization. Europace **20**, 816–822 (2018)

6. Peguero, J.G., Lo Presti, S., Perez, J.A., Issa, O., Brenes, J.C., Tolentino, A.: Electrocardiographic criteria for the diagnosis of left ventricular hypertrophy. J. Am. Coll. Cardiol. **69**(13), 1694–1703 (2017). https://doi.org/10.1016/j.jacc.2017.01.037
7. Strauss, David G.and Selvester, R., Wagner, G.: Defining left bundle branch block in the era of cardiac resynchronization therapy. Am. J. Cardiol. **107**, 927–934

Cardiac Impulse Propagation in Left Bundle Branch Block

Beatriz del Cisne Macas Ordóñez[1,2,3](✉)(iD), Fernando Ingallina[4],
Diego Vinicio Orellana Villavicencio[5](iD), and María Paula Bonomini[2,3](iD)

[1] Facultad de Ingeniería, Instituto de Ingeniería Biomédica, Universidad de Buenos
Aires, Buenos Aires, Argentina
bmacas.ext@fi.uba.ar
[2] Instituto Argentino de Matemática "Alberto P. Calderón" (IAM), CONICET,
Buenos Aires, Argentina
[3] Departamento de Electrónica, Tecnología de Computadoras y Proyectos,
Universidad Politécnica de Cartagena, Cartagena, Spain
[4] Instituto de Investigaciones Médicas Alfredo Lanari, Universidad de Buenos Aires,
Buenos Aires, Argentina
[5] Facultad de Energía, las Industrias y los Recursos Naturales No Renovables,
Universidad Nacional de Loja, Loja, Ecuador

Abstract. Recently, left bundle branch block (LBBB) diagnose has
gained interest due to its association with cardiac resynchronization
therapy (CRT) outcome. This work analyzes differences in the conduction velocity of the cardiac electrical impulse in the Healthy, LBBB, and
strict LBBB (sLBBB) groups. Two databases were employed: the first
contained healthy electrocardiographic (ECG) records obtained from the
Chapman University, Shaoxing People's Hospital, and Ningbo First Hospital databases, and the second was derived from the MADIT-CRT study,
including ECG records from subjects with heart failure. The results show
a significant decrease in propagation velocity in the LBBB and sLBBB
groups. Vectorcardiographic loops were obtained, clearly demonstrating
differences in duration and shape between the groups, indicating slower
depolarization in subjects with LBBB and sLBBB. These results suggest
that the study of cardiac electrical impulse propagation velocity could
potentially be useful for timely detection of LBBB.

Keywords: LBBB Diagnosis · Cardiac impulse propagation velocity ·
VCG

1 Introduction

Currently, left bundle branch block (LBBB) has been a subject of increasing
research since its ability to predict cardiac resynchronization therapy (CRT)
outcome. Patient selection for CRT involves specific diagnostic criteria, such as
QRS duration ≥140 ms (men) or ≥130 ms (women), QS- or rS-configurations of
the QRS complex in leads V1 and V2, and mid-QRS notching or slurring in ≥2
of leads V1, V2, V5, V6, I and aVL [2].

J. M. Ferrández Vicente et al. (Eds.): IWINAC 2024, LNCS 14675, pp. 511–517, 2024.
https://doi.org/10.1007/978-3-031-61137-7_48

An estimated rate of 30–40% of patients are considered non-responders because they do not show a favorable response to this treatment [8,9]. In view of this rate of non-responders, there is a need to develop new biomarkers to identify with greater precision the candidates to benefit from this therapy.

As reported in [10], LBBB is widely characterized by large spatial heterogeneity. This heterogeneity is caused by variations in the conduction velocity of the electrical heart impulse. Here, we compared conduction velocity between healthy, Left Bundle Branch Block (LBBB), and Strict Left Bundle Branch Block (sLBBB) patients, with the aim of obtaining more detailed information on the cardiac electrical behavior in each group. It is expected that the findings of this study will contribute to a better understanding of the underlying pathophysiology of LBBB and provide useful insights for enhancing the diagnosis of this condition.

2   Materials and Methods

2.1   Database

Two datasets were utilized in this study. The first dataset comprised 299 normal electrocardiogram recordings with a sampling rate of 500 Hz. This dataset was generated by Chapman University, Shaoxing People's Hospital, and Ningbo First Hospital. A cohort of heart failure patients from the MADIT-CRT clinical study was included in the second dataset. This group was made available via the University of Rochester's THEW project.

In this cohort 330 patients in this cohort have stringent left bundle branch block (sLBBB), while 193 patients have non-strict left bundle branch block (LBBB). To summarize, the examined database comprises three 12-lead ECG categories: LBBB (193), sLBBB (330), and healthy patients (299).

2.2   Signal Processing

Due to differences in sampling rate, both databases were resampled to 200 Hz. Afterwards, electrocardiogram (ECG) records were used as the basis for the generation of vectorcardiograms by means of kors transformation as shown in Table 1. This transformation poses the orthogonal leads, x,y,z, as linear combinations of the eight linearly independent ECG leads [1].

After obtaining the vectorcardiogram records, we applied a filter butterworth order 4 between 0.5-40 Hz. Subsequently, we performed R-peak detection, from which we calculated consecutive RR intervals for each vectorcardiogram (VCG) lead.

Moving forward, we utilized the lead with the least variability as our primary reference and extracted the segment corresponding to a cardiac cycle. Then, we aligned the QRS complexes using the Woody technique. The aligned segments were averaged to obtain an average beat for each patient.

Table 1. Coeficientes para la transformación de regresión de Kors.

Lead	V1	V2	V3	V4	V5	V6	I	II
x	–0.13	0.05	–0.01	0.14	0.06	0.54	0.38	-0.07
y	0.06	–0.02	–0.05	0.06	–0.17	0.13	—0.07	0.93
z	–0.43	–0.06	–0.14	–0.20	–0.11	0.31	0.11	–0.23

The three-dimensional coordinates x,y,z of the vectorcardiographic records were segmented into consecutive points, and the difference between those positions was computed. using: Where, x_{i+1} is the value of the next point, x_i represents the value of the current point, and Δx_i indicates the difference between these two neighboring points in the x coordinate.

From the differences obtained previously, the velocity in each sample was calculated using the Euclidean norm of the differences of successive points in the three coordinates (X, Y, Z), respectively.

The velocity was calculated using the following formula:

$$V_i = \sqrt{(\Delta x_i)^2 + (\Delta y_i)^2 + (\Delta z_i)^2}$$

where the differences in the coordenadas X, Y, and Z in the example i are Δx_i, Δy_i, and Δz_i, respectively.

Regarding the velocity attained during the sampling period, the maximum velocity value is found among all discrete points. Additional calculations are made in relation to the maximum velocity value and the times from the beginning and end of the QRS complex to the maximum velocity time.

3   Results

Fig. 1 shows the box plot between the Healthy, LBBB, sLBBB groups. The tuckey test resulting in an average difference of 0.0452 (p <0.05) between Healthy and LBBB, while in Healthy and sLBBB the mean difference was 0.0715 (p <0.05) and between LBBB and sLBBB it was 0.0263 (p <0.05). These results confirm the presence of a delay in the ventricular activation of the cardiac muscle in the LBBB and sLBBB groups.

Figure 2 shows the velocity signals over time, acquired through the VCG from each subject in the Healthy, LBBB and sLBBB groups. From these signals, the average velocity signal for each group was derived, identifying the maximum point of average velocity (Vmax) within the average signal. On the other hand, Fig. 2 illustrates shows how the mean heart rate in the Healthy group is reached later than in LBBB and sLBBB, suggesting synchronized heart rate.

Conversely, in the LBBB and sLBBB groups, the maximum heart rate is reached earlier than in the Healthy group, possibly due to a lack of synchronization in heart rate propagation. Additionally, it is shown that in the Healthy group, the cardiac cycle's propagation velocity is greater than in the other groups

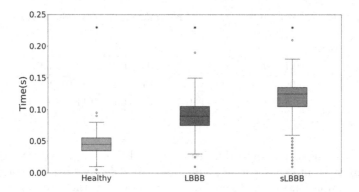

Fig. 1. Boxplot of the time duration between the peak velocity and the end of the QRS complex.

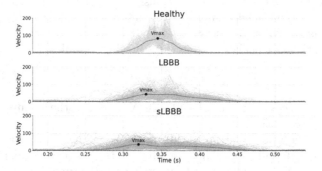

Fig. 2. Comparative analysis of average cardiac velocities among healthy, LBBB, and sLBBB groups.

and exhibits a consistent pattern, whereas in the LBBB group, the decrease in velocity may be due to a delay in left ventricle activation.

Finally, there is a decrease in velocity amplitude for the sLBBB group, which is less than for the other groups, resulting in a significant delay in the activation of the left ventricle.

In Fig. 3, a graphical representation of a representative loop for each group (Healthy, LBBB, and sLBBB) is depicted. The Healthy loop illustrates how the initial section associated with ventricular activation is longer, indicating rapid and efficient depolarization. In contrast, the loops of LBBB and sLBBB exhibit a narrower segment in this initial section, suggesting a slower rhythm of ventricular depolarization. Additionally, the presence of notches in the sLBBB loop indicates even slower conduction compared to Healthy and LBBB. This analysis underscores the significance of cardiac electrophysiological coordination for effective cardiac contraction and offers a detailed perspective on the physical distinctions between healthy individuals and those with LBBB and sLBBB. The results show a significant reduction in the propagation velocity of the cardiac impulse in the LBBB and sLBBB groups, reflecting dysfunction in the electrical coordination of the heart for these groups.

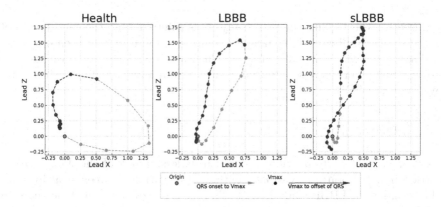

Fig. 3. Comparing Vectorcardiogram Loops in the Healthy, LBBB, and sLBBB Groups, Segmented by QRS Maximum Velocity.

4   Discussion

In this study, we analyzed the VCG data of three groups: healthy individuals and those with left bundle branch block (LBBB) and strict left bundle branch block (sLBBB), aiming to examine differences in the velocity of cardiac electrical impulse propagation. The LBBB and sLBBB groups exhibited significantly lower propagation velocities compared to the healthy group. Additionally, there was a notable variation in the shape and duration of the vectorcardiographic loops among the three groups. These results suggest that cardiac electrical coordination is necessary for effective contraction, thus indicating that the analysis of cardiac impulse propagation velocity could be very useful for the diagnosis of LBBB. These findings contrast with previous research studying the speed of propagation of the cardiac impulse and the presence of LBBB [7]. The accumulated evidence supports the idea that changes in electrical conduction can significantly contribute to the timely detection of LBBB [4].

Bacharova [6] offers an interesting perspective by pointing out that while traditionally most intraventricular conduction abnormalities have been attributed to issues with the His-Purkinje (HP) conduction system, her study emphasizes the role of ventricular myocardium in these anomalies. Factors such as left ventricular hypertrophy, ischemia, cardiomyopathy, and advanced aging can alter the ventricular activation sequence, which is reflected in the electrocardiogram as atypical patterns of QRS complexes, as seen in the case of LBBB.

The experimental findings of Jang [5] support our observations by reporting that the decrease in cardiac wave conduction velocity under pathological conditions such as LBBB may be related to structural changes in cardiac tissue, including the presence of fibrosis and disruption of normal electrical conduction. These results enhance our understanding of the underlying mechanisms of LBBB and support the utility of cardiac impulse propagation velocity as a diagnostic biomarker.

Based on the findings of this study, it is inferred that the integration of advanced clinical diagnostic techniques could contribute to, and even optimize, the diagnosis of candidates who may benefit from CRT. This is because research into new biomarkers has the potential to enhance our understanding of the pathophysiology of LBBB.

5   Conclusion

In summary, this study provides a detailed understanding of the differences in ventricular activation and cardiac rhythm propagation between healthy individuals and with LBBB and sLBBB. The results show a distinct decrease in ventricular activation in the LBBB and sLBBB groups, along with changes in heart rate and cardiac rhythm synchronization. These findings demonstrate the clinical use of a detailed analysis of electrocardiographic and vectorcardiographic señales, in addition to highlighting the significance of a coordinated cardiac electrical system for effective cardiac contraction.

Despite its inherent limitations, this study allows us to expand our understanding of cardiac physiology by focusing on the electrical impulse's propagation velocity. This opens the door to potential findings related to the cardiac muscle's despolarization and repolarization processes. Additionally, this study may lead to the discovery of new biomarkers for the detection of cardiac physiology anomalies, such as LBBB. En el futuro, estos biomarcadores podrían ser empleados para mejorar el pronóstico y la precisión diagnóstica de varias enfermedades cardíacas.

References

1. Edenbrandt, L., Pahlm, O.: Vectorcardiogram synthesized from a 12-lead ECG: superiority of the inverse Dower matrix. J. Electrocardiol. **21**, 361–367 (1988)
2. Zusterzeel, R., et al.: The 43rd International Society for Computerized Electrocardiology ECG initiative for the automated detection of strict left bundle branch block. J. Electrocardiol. **51**(6S), S25–S30 (2018). https://doi.org/10.1016/j.jelectrocard.2018.08.001. Epub 2018 Aug 1 PMID: 30082088
3. Mullens, W., Auricchio, A., Martens, P., Witte, K., Cowie, M.R., Delgado, V., et al.: Optimized implementation of cardiac resynchronization therapy: a call for action for referral and optimization of care. Europace **23**, 1324–1342 (2021)
4. Fernández, J.M.F., Spagnuolo, D.N., Politi, M.T., et al.: Vectorcardiography-derived index allows a robust quantification of ventricular electrical synchrony. Sci. Rep. **12**, 9961 (2022). https://doi.org/10.1038/s41598-022-14000-8
5. Jang, J., Whitaker, J., Leshem, E., Ngo, L., Neisus, U., Nakamori, S., et al.: Local conduction velocity in the presence of late gadolinium enhancement and myocardial wall thinning: a cardiac magnetic resonance study in a swine model of healed left

ventricular infarction. Circ. Arrhythm. Electrophysiol. **12**, e00717 (2019). https://doi.org/10.1161/CIRCEP.119.007175

6. Bacharova, L., Palam, Z., de Luna, B.: The primary alteration of ventricular myocardium conduction: the significant determinant of left bundle branch block pattern. Cardiol. Res. Pract. **2022**, 3438603 (2022). https://doi.org/10.1155/2022/3438603

7. Macas, B., Garrigos, J.J., Martinez, J.J., Ferrandez, J.M., Bonomini, M.P.: An explainable machine learning system for left bundle branch block detection and classification. Integrated Comput.-Aided Eng. **31**(1), 43–58 (2023)

8. Ortega, D.F., Barja, L.D., Logarzo, E., Mangani, N., Paolucci, A., Bonomini, M.P.: Non-selective His bundle pacing with a biphasic waveform: enhancing septal resynchronization. EP Europace **20**(5), 816–822 (2018)

9. Ortega, D., Logarzo, E., Barja, L., Paolucci, A., Mangani, N.E.M., Bonomini, M.P.: Novel implant technique for septal pacing. a noninvasive approach to nonselective his bundle pacing. J. Electrocardiol. **63**, 35-40

10. Bonomini, M.P., Ortega, D.F., Barja, L.D., Mangani, N., Arini, P.D.: Depolarization spatial variance as a cardiac dyssynchrony descriptor. Biomed. Signal Proces. Control **49**, 540–545

Wearable Device Dataset for Stress Detection

Andrea Hongn[1,3]([✉]) [iD], Lara Eleonora Prado[2] [iD], Facundo Bosch[2],
and María Paula Bonomini[3,4] [iD]

[1] Universidad de Buenos Aires, Facultad de Ingeniería, Instituto de Ingeniería
Biomédica (IIBM), Buenos Aires, Argentina
`ahongn.ext@fi.uba.com.ar`
[2] Departamento de Ciencias de la Vida, Instituto Tecnológico de Buenos Aires
(ITBA), Ciudad Autónoma de Buenos Aires, Buenos Aires, Argentina
[3] CONICET, Instituto Argentino de Matemática "Alberto P. Calderón" (IAM),
Buenos Aires, Argentina
[4] Departamento de Electrónica, Tecnología de Computadoras y Proyectos,
Universidad Politécnica de Cartagena, Cartagena, Spain

Abstract. Stressful situations produce physiological changes that are
difficult to measure. Among the acute stress body effects, increased blood
glucose level is of interest in diabetes research field. The emergence of
wearable device technology allows non-invasive monitoring of physiological variables that reflect these responses to stimuli. This work aims to
identify the presence of stress from a wearable device signals. The procedure to record multivariate portable physiological variables following
a protocol designed to induce stress conditions is presented as well as
a stress presence/absence classification to evaluate the performance of
these signals. Non-invasive physiological variables were collected from 35
people in stress-inducing conditions through the Empatica wristband.
Signals from electrodermal activity, heart rate, blood volume pulse and
interbeat interval were processed and the selected features fed a multi-
task Extreme Gradient Boosting algorithm(XGBoost). The model is then
evaluated using leave-one-out validation and achieved an accuracy of
84% for binary classification between acute stress state and acute stress
state free. The developed dataset becomes a valuable resource for stress
research and a first step in modeling glycemic changes during acute stress
to improve an artificial pancreas control algorithm.

Keywords: Acute Stress · Empatica E4 · Electrodermal Activity ·
Heart Rate Variability

1 Introduction

In daily life, individuals face diverse stressful situations, prompting varied emotional and physical responses. Emotional reactions are typically assessed using
self-report measures or behavioral observation. In contrast, physiological changes

© The Author(s), under exclusive license to Springer Nature Switzerland AG 2024
J. M. Ferrández Vicente et al. (Eds.): IWINAC 2024, LNCS 14675, pp. 518–527, 2024.
https://doi.org/10.1007/978-3-031-61137-7_49

can be registered through hormonal assays or physiological signals monitoring. Among the latter, wearable device technology facilitates real-time non-invasive acquisition of physiological data without the need for office visits [1].

During acute stress episodes, the body releases hormones such as glucocorticoids and catecholamines, which, among other effects, increase glucose levels. These fluctuations becomes a challenge for individuals with Type 1 Diabetes Mellitus (T1DM), where the partial or total lack of insulin production fails to regulate glycemic variations. Addressing this situation, the artificial pancreas emerges as a system aimed at automating insulin delivery, with three principal components: a continuous glucose monitor, an insulin pump, and a control algorithm. The effectiveness of this control algorithm depends on ability of handling disturbances [2,3], for example food intake, mental stress and physical activity. Therefore, the development of a model that relates glycemic changes with real-time physiological data through wearable devices during acute stress situation could improve control algorithm performance. Before modeling glycemic changes, it is fundamental to discern between stress and non-stress states non-invasively, purpose of this research.

This work presents the procedure to develop a database with non-invasive physiological records under stress and non-stress conditions. To support its value and validate its potential, a binary stress classification is performed.

2   Methods

Data collection process was accomplished in two stages. Initially, a cohort of 18 volunteers underwent the protocol. A few months later, another group of 18 volunteers participated, following an updated protocol with improvements based on initial experience. Anaerobic and aerobic physical activity data and voice recordings were collected too, but are not analyzed in the present work.

Enrollment in the study was facilitated via an online form and the exclusion criteria comprised individuals undergoing psychiatric treatment or taking medication that could potentially impact physiologic responses. Prior to conducting the tests, each participant signed an informed consent.

2.1   Signal Acquisition: E4 Device

To monitor physiological signals, the Empatica E4 wristband was used. It includes a Photoplethysmography (PPG) Sensor; a 3-axis Accelerometer; an Infrared Thermopile for peripheral skin temperature (SK) readings and an Electrodermal Activity (EDA) Sensor. Combining EDA and PPG sensors simultaneously, this device enables the measurement of sympathetic nervous system activity and heart rate.

The E4 was placed on the participant's non-dominant hand in order to introduce fewer motion artifacts when performing the tests.

2.2 Stress Induction

For the stress induction, a protocol based on previous studies [4,5] was designed to induce stress in participants. The tests involved were intended to elicit physiological and psychological responses associated with stress. These tests include speaking tasks, mental arithmetic challenges, cognitive tests under time pressure, and exposure to emotionally arousing stimuli. While the entire procedure was recorded for research purposes in order to have voice records, this recording also served to introduce additional stressors. Rest intervals were set between each test to allow for recovery, minimize cumulative fatigue, and enable the assessment of task efficiency.

Protocol Design. The original protocol started with a 3-minute baseline recording, to use as a reference. First stress test was an adaptation of the widely used Stroop Test [6,7], adapted from PsyToolkit [8,9]. Afterwards, a 5-minute-rest period was imposed, followed by a modified version of the Trier Mental Challenge Test [10], obtained through Millisecond Software, LLC. This test involved a series of mathematical tasks within a 5 s time limit while an annoying sound stimulus was played in the background. Participants were also instructed to vocalize their responses aloud, which further added to the cognitive load and performance demands of the task. Once again, a 5-minute-period came before the final block. In the latter, participants were asked to express their opinion about controversial topics and suddenly were instructed to defend the opposite opinion over the same subject. Finally, participants were tasked with counting backward from 1021 in decrements of 13, providing the answers aloud. Each of these tests had a time limit of 30 s.

Before and after every task and rest period, participants were required to verbally express their self-perception stress level on a scale ranging from 1 to 10. A summary of the protocol is shown in Fig. 1.

Fig. 1. Stress Induction Procedure

Protocol Improvements. The procedure was accomplished remotely via video call, without the need for participants to physically attend the institution. Additionally, after showing minimal effects on physiological variables and self-perceived stress compared to other tasks, the Stroop Test was removed from the protocol, and both the baseline and rest periods were extended to accommodate the relaxation process effectively. Also, during the non - stress stages, participants were exposed to a relaxing video. Lastly, the counting back test was separated from the opinion task by a rest period.   .

2.3 Signal Processing

Data Conditioning. Signals from PPG -*Heart Rate (HR), Blood Volume Pulse (BVP) and Inter Beat Intervals (IBI)*- and EDA sensors were chosen for analysis, due to significance as stress indicators [11]. Logs were downloaded as csv files from Empatica Connect app and "tags.csv" file, containing temporal tags of events stored as the time on which the E4 button is pressed during the procedure, was used to segment the signals in stressor and non-stressor blocks. The number of stress blocks was not the same for all subjects, due to changes in protocol(Stroop Task was removed from the second version). As a consequence the number of rest blocks are not the same as the stressing ones.

Data was conditioned for processing using popular Python libraries such as scipy, pandas, numpy, and matplotlib. EDA was low-filtered using a Butterworth order-5 filter with a 2 Hz cut off frequency. For BVP signal, a passband Butterworth order-5 filter of 0.5–10 Hz. No filter was used for HR and IBI signals.

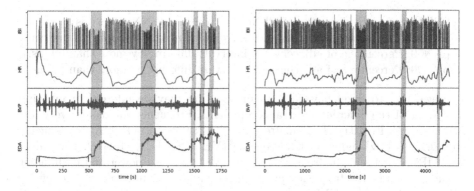

Fig. 2. E4 signals for first (left) and final protocol (right). Acute stress blocks are shaded

2.4 Feature Extraction

General statistical (mean and standard deviation) features were computed from all signals of each segment, and particular ones for EDA and IBI signals, detailed below. Feature extraction took into consideration the duration of the blocks and data samples were normalized to [−1,1].

Electrodermal Activity. This measure is related to affective and cognitive states, including mental or emotional sweating,regulated by the activation of the autonomic nervous system (ANS). Therefore, EDA could be used as an index of emotional or cognitive stimulation related to stress or mental health [12].

The filtered signal was decomposed in tonic (Skin Conductance Level) and phasic (Skin Conductance Response) components. To characterize EDA signal, features related to Skin Conductance Response(SCR) events were derived. From the phasic component, which corresponds to rapid changes in skin response, open-source Python Neurokit2 [13] functions were applied to identify the SCR peaks and onsets. This allowed to calculate the rise-time, recovery- time, amplitude (absolute value) and height of the peak (from the onset value). Additionally,the density of SCR events considering the length of the signal for each block was computed.

Heart Rate Variability. Heart Rate Variabilitiy (HRV) is considered a measure of neurocardiac function that reflects heart-brain interactions and ANS dynamics [14]. It can be investigated non-invasively using relatively basic signal processing techniques. There are several time-domain, frequency-domain and non-linear indices to characterize HRV. In the present work, time-domain and frequency-domain characteristics were [5,18] extracted processing IBI signal. Common time domain measures are:

- SDNN: Standard deviation of all Normal to Normal(NN) intervals.
- RMMSD: Root mean-square of successive differences of adjacent NN intervals.
- pNN50: Percentage of adjacent NN intervals differing by more than 50 ms.
- pNN20: Percentage of adjacent NN intervals differing by more than 20 ms.

Regarding to frequency domain, information may be inferred quantifying the power of the different spectral components. Frequency bands are: very low frequency (VLF; $\leq 0.04\,Hz$), low frequency (LF; $0.04-0.15\,Hz$), high frequency (HF; $0.15-0.4\,Hz$) and very high frequency (VHF; $\geq 0.4\,Hz$) [15] [16]. The widely used HRV metrics in the frequency domain are the total power and in different frequency bands, the frequency peaks in the bands, the normalized frequencies LFn and HFn, dividing LF and HF by the total power, and the ratio obtained by dividing the LF power by the HF power. Table 1 contains the 35 features chosen to represent all signals.

Feature Optimization and Classification. From 35 features extracted, a feature importance analysis in XGBoost was applied to reduce the number of them. The approach was to evaluate feature importance for all features and for each feature group depending on the nature of the signal. Data was imbalanced so feature importance analysis was repeated several times applying different balancing techniques, obtaining similar results. This way, a reduced group of the most important 21 features was obtained accounting for every group of physiological signals (EDA, IBI/HRV, HR, BVP). From this subset, random combinations

Table 1. Features extracted

E4 Signal	Type	Features
BVP(2)	Statistical	mean, std
HR(2)	Statistical	mean, std
IBI(20)	Statistical	$max,min,mean$,hr_mean_ibi
	HRV Time Domain	pnn20, pnn50, rmssd, sdnn
	HRV Frequency Domain	total_power, ratio, VLF_power, VLF_peak, LF_power, LF_peak, LH_n HF_power, HF_peak, HF_n VHF_power, VHF_peak
EDA(11)	Statistical	mean_raw_eda, std_raw_eda, mean_tonic_eda, std_tonic_eda, mean_phasic_eda, std_phasic_eda
	SCR Events	peaks_density, scr_mean_amp, scr_mean_height, scr_mean_risetime, scr_mean_recoverytime

of not highly correlated features were generated, always preserving at least one feature per physiological measure.

Sub sampled sets of selected features fed a XGBoost machine learning model with binary output:stress/no-stress. A proportion of 80:20 was destined for training and testing, respectively. The set providing best accuracy was selected. For model evaluation, leave-one-subject-out (LOOCV) scheme was applied. The performance of the model was assessed by the following metrics: Accuracy, Precision, Recall and F1-score.

3   Results

Stress Inducement. From 36 subjects, one register was discarded due to wrong wristband placement. The protocol designed for stress induction showed efficiency, it reflected on the participants auto perceived stress levels, shown in Fig. 3, and physiological changes. The arithmetic tasks were identified as the stressor tasks exhibiting the highest performance.

Feature Optimization. Figure 4 shows the features per each signal obtained after reducing its dimension (35 →21) by means of feature importance. To complete the feature selection procedure, a high correlation filter with a threshold equal to 0.4 was applied between features. Finally, subsets generated after this analysis contained combinations between 9 and 12 not correlated features.

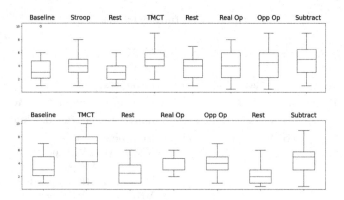

Fig. 3. Stress auto reported level for first (above) and final protocol version

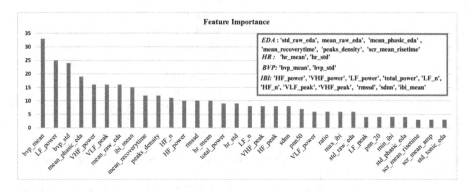

Fig. 4. Selected features for each signal type *(box)* from feature importance

Classification. A total of 242 segments were generated for 35 subjects with 35 features each. Out of these segments, 43,8% belongs to the non-stress class and 56,2% represents the stress condition. The unbalancing of data was mitigated by sub sampling the stress class to match the size of the non stress class.

Different sizes sets with selected features fed an XgBoost algorithm for a binary classification on stress/non-stress states, achieving an 84% accuracy for 11 and 10 features. LOOCV average classification metrics of best sets are shown in Table 2, showing the best performance for the set containing: bvp_mean, HF_n, mean_phasic_eda, bvp_std, hr_std, scr_mean_risetime, mean_recoverytime, ibi_mean, total_power, VHF_peak, VLF_peak.

Table 2. LOOCV Performance metrics for different set after feature optimization

no features	Accuracy	Precision	Recall	F1	Features detail
12	82%	84%	81%	78%	bvp_mean, mean_raw_eda, bvp_std, mean_phasic_eda, total_power, hr_mean, VLF_peak, peaks_density, hr_std, rmssd, HF_n, VHF_peak
11	84%	85%	84%	82%	bvp_mean, HF_n, mean_phasic_eda, bvp_std, hr_std, scr_mean_risetime, mean_recoverytime, ibi_mean, total_power, VHF_peak, VLF_peak
10	84%	82%	78%	78%	bvp_mean, VHF_power, bvp_std, hr_mean, hr_std, std_raw_eda, VHF_power, mean_phasic_eda, peaks_density, rmssd, LF_n
9	83%	84%	79%	78%	bvp_mean, mean_recoverytime, scr_mean_risetime, bvp_std, hr_std, mean_phasic_eda, ibi_mean, total_power, HF_n

4 Discussion and Conclusion

The designed protocol to induce stress achieved its intended objective, as evidenced by changes in physiological variables and self-reported stress levels. The improvement of extending rest times allowed better signal recovery for the upcoming stress task and getting better non stress states as depicted in Fig. 3. Although tags facilitate the segmentation process, it must be taken into account that there is an extended response in the reaction to the stressful stimulus.

The E4 device showed robustness as an accurate wearable device for stress detection, however BVP signal is particularly sensible to motion artifacts, being an issue to improve, specially when working on free-living conditions. This was not a problem for this work because the protocol was designed for minimum motion, based on previous research experience [5].

After processing EDA, BVP, HR and IBI signals, 35 features were extracted. Unlike other research, the IBI signals used were those provided by Empatica. After applying a feature importance analysis and high correlation filtering, the selected features were in concordance with another studies [18] [4], being EDA and HRV metrics on the top of importance, despite in this work BVP showed significance importance. A binary acute stress classification through XGBoost evaluated with LOOCV achieved a 84% accuracy, showing better performance than another ML algorithms used in another works [18] [5].

For future research, expanding the classification to rest, stress, and physical activity is expected, evaluating whether the selected characteristics also work for these states. For this, it would be promising to incorporate the analysis of skin temperature and accelerometer data. These signals are not widely used in similar researches yet, so its a new field to explore.

This work presents the development of validated multi-variable wearable physiological dataset from 35 subjects under acute stress conditions, valuable resource for researchers in the field of stress investigation. Furthermore, this experience encourages us to continue with the line of research to improve the control algorithm of the artificial pancreas. By repeating this same procedure in patients with T1DM, in addition to incorporating continuous glucose measurement and adding ambulatory recording of daily stress events, it seems possible to model the effects of stress on glycemia.

References

1. Crosswell, A.D., Lockwood, K.G.B.: Best practices for stress measurement: how to measure psychological stress in health research (2020)
2. Turksoy, K., et al.: Classification of physical activity: information to artificial pancreas control systems in real time. J. Diabetes Sci. Technol. **9**(6), 1200–1207 (2015)
3. Garelli, F., et al.: Non-hybrid glycemic control of type 1 diabetes ambulatory patients. Revista Iberoamericana de Automática e Informática Industrial **19**, 318–329 (2022)
4. Iqbal, T., et al.: Stress monitoring using wearable sensors: a pilot study and stress-predict dataset. Sensors (Basel, Switzerland) **22**(21), 8135 (2022)
5. Campanella, S., Altaleb, A., Belli, A., Pierleoni, P., Palma, L.: A method for stress detection using empatica E4 bracelet and machine-learning techniques. Sensors **23**, 3565 (2023)
6. Stroop, J.R.: Studies of interference in serial verbal reactions. J. Exp. Psychol. **18**, 643–662 (1935)
7. MacLeod, C.M.: Half a century of research on the stroop effect: an integrative review. Psychol. Bull. **109**, 163–203 (1991)
8. Stoet, G.: PsyToolkit - a software package for programming psychological experiments using Linux. Behav. Res. Methods **42**(4), 1096–1104 (2010)
9. Stoet, G.: PsyToolkit: a novel web-based method for running online questionnaires and reaction-time experiments. Teach. Psychol. **44**(1), 24–31 (2017)
10. Pruessner, H.: Kirschbaum: low self-esteem, induced failure and the adrenocortical stress response. Personality Individ. Differ. **27**(3), 477–489 (1999)
11. Iqbal, T., Elahi, A., Redon, P., Vazquez, P.: A Review of Biophysiological and Biochemical Indicators of Stress for Connected and Preventive Healthcare (2021)
12. Rahma, O., et al.: Electrodermal activity for measuring cognitive and emotional stress level. J. Med. Signals Sensors **12**(2), 155–162 (2022)
13. Makowski, D., et al.: NeuroKit2: a Python toolbox for neurophysiological signal processing. Behav. Res. Methods **53**(4), 1689–1696 (2021)
14. McCraty, R., Shaffer, F.: Heart rate variability: new perspectives on physiological mechanisms, assessment of self-regulatory capacity, and health risk. Global Adv. Health Med. **4**(1), 46–61 (2015)

15. Pham, T., Lau, Z.J., Chen, S.H.A., Makowski, D.: Heart rate variability in psychology: a review of hrv indices and an analysis tutorial. Sensors **21**(12), 3998 (2021)
16. Sornmo, L., Laguna, P.: Bioelectrical Signal Processing in Cardiac and Neurological Applications, 2nd edn. Elsevier Academic Press, Location (1999)
17. Pruessner, H.: Kirschbaum: low self-esteem, induced failure and the adrenocortical stress response. Personality Individ. Differ. **27**(3), 477–489 (1999)
18. Cosoli, G., Poli, A., Scalise, L., Spinsante, S.: Measurement of multimodal physiological signals for stimulation detection by wearable devices. Measurement **184**, 109966 (2021)

Author Index

J. M. Ferrández Vicente et al. (Eds.): IWINAC 2024, LNCS 14675, pp. 529–533, 2024.
https://doi.org/10.1007/978-3-031-61137-7

Printed in the United States
by Baker & Taylor Publisher Services